BORDERLINE AND NARCISSISTIC PATIENTS IN THERAPY

Borderline and Narcissistic Patients in Therapy

Edited by

Nonna Slavinska-Holy, Ph.D.

INTERNATIONAL UNIVERSITIES PRESS, INC.
Madison   Connecticut

616.8585 B728

Borderline and narcissistic
patients in therapy

Copyright © 1988, Nonna Slavinska-Holy

All rights reserved. No part of this book may be reproduced by any means, nor translated into a machine language, without the written permission of the publisher.

Library of Congress Cataloging in Publication Data

Borderline and narcissistic patients in therapy.

   Includes bibliographies and indexes.
   1. Borderline personality disorder. 2. Narcissism.
3. Psychotherapy. 4. Psychoanalysis. I. Slavinska-Holy,
Nonna. [DNLM: 1 Narcissism. 2. Personality Disorders—
therapy. 3. Psychoanalytic Therapy—methods.
WM 190 B7278]
RC569.5.B67P667 1988   616.85'8   87-33921
ISBN 0-8236-0572-8

Manufactured in the United States of America

*To all creative colleagues
who dedicate their work
to healing*

CONTENTS

Contributors   xi
Preface   xv
Acknowledgments   xxi
Introduction   xxiii

Part I. CONTEMPORARY CLINICAL PERSPECTIVES

1. Implications of DSM-III Diagnosis for Group Psychotherapy with Borderline and Narcissistic Patients
   HOWARD D. KIBEL, M.D.   3
2. Combined Individual and Group Treatment with Borderline and Narcissistic Patients
   NORMUND WONG, M.D.   17
3. Psychoanalytic Therapy of Developmental Arrests
   FRANK M. LACHMANN, PH.D.   47
4. Some Contributions of Self Psychology to the Treatment of Borderline and Schizophrenic Patients
   BARRY MAGID, M.D.   59
5. The Working-Through Process with a Hospitalized Borderline Adolescent and Her Family
   DEBORAH HAMM, M.D. and EDWARD R. SHAPIRO, M.D.   77
6. Expressive Group Therapy with Borderline Patients
   M.H. STONE, M.D. and R. WEISSMAN, M.S.W.   95
7. The Restoration of the Impaired Self in Group Psychoanalytic Treatment
   L.E. HEARST   123

8. Mirroring and Group Therapy
   MALCOLM PINES, F.R.C.P., F.R.C. PSYCH., D.P.M.   143
9. Group Level "Boundarying" Control as an Isomorphic Prosthesis for Narcissistic and Borderline Patients
   JAMES E. DURKIN, PH.D.   171
10. The Transference-Countertransference Neurosis in Psychoanalysis: The Intersubjective Context of Dream Formation
    RICHARD B. ULMAN, PH.D.   203
11. Projective Identification in the Psychoanalytic Therapy of a Borderline Patient
    NONNA SLAVINSKA-HOLY, PH.D.   221
12. The Difficult Patient: An Intersubjective Perspective
    BERNARD BRANDCHAFT, M.D. and ROBERT D. STOLOROW, PH.D.   243
13. Erotic Countertransference and Transformation: Borderline and Narcissistic Patients in Combined Treatment
    NONNA SLAVINSKA-HOLY, PH.D.   267
14. Treating Creative Diegophrenics in Psychoanalysis in Groups
    ALEXANDER A. WOLF, M.D. and IRWIN L. KUTASH, PH.D.   283
15. Liberating the Creative Self Through Active Combined Psychotherapy
    ARNOLD W. RACHMAN, PH.D., F.A.G.P.A.   309

Part II. AUXILIARY TREATMENT MODALITIES AND RESEARCH CONCERNS

16. Psychodramatic Techniques in Work with Borderline Patients
    JAMES M. SACKS, PH.D.   343
17. Dual Analytic Therapy with Spouse Cotherapists: Perspectives on the Borderline Marriage
    JOHN P. BRIGGS, M.D. and MURIEL A. BRIGGS, M.A.   359

18. The Pharmacological Therapeutic Community
    FERNANDO D. ASTIGUETA, M.D.   377
19. Residential Treatment in a Psychotherapeutic Community
    SERGE VERHAEST   399
20. A Study of Intrapsychic Structures and Processes in Three Groups of Patients: One Schizophrenic, One Borderline, and One Neurotic
    LAURICE W. GLOVER, M.S.S.W.   427
21. The Effect of Maternal Narcissism on the Attachment Relationship
    NANCY S. MOLITOR, PH.D.   461
22. Patterns of Socioaffective Development in Disturbed Mothers' Perceptions of, and Interactions with, Their Infants
    JULIE A. HOFHEIMER, PH.D. and MAURICE APPREY, M.A.C.P.   469
23. Implications of Object Relations Theory for Research on Group Psychotherapy of Borderline Patients
    LES R. GREENE, PH.D.   499

Name Index   521
Subject Index   527

CONTRIBUTORS

Maurice Apprey, M.A.C.P. Associate Professor of Behavioral Medicine, and Psychiatry: Assistant Dean of Student Affairs, School of Medicine, and Faculty of the Division of Psychoanalytic Studies, University of Virginia, Charlottesville, VA

Fernando D. Astigueta, M.D. Chief of Psychiatry, Social Rehabilitation Clinic, Post Graduate Center for Mental Health, New York, and Faculty, Department of Psychiatry, Beth Israel and Mount Sinai Hospitals, New York

Bernard Brandchaft, M.D. Training and Supervising Analyst, Los Angeles Psychoanalytic Institute, and Assistant Clinical Professor of Psychiatry, UCLA School of Medicine.

John P. Briggs, M.D. Private practice, Tarrytown, New York

Muriel A. Briggs, M.A. Private practice, Tarrytown, New York

James F. Durkin, Ph.D. Amherst, Massachusetts

Laurice W. Glover, M.S.S.W. Faculty, Senior Supervisor, Training Analyst, Psychoanalytic Institute of the Postgraduate Center for Mental Health; Assistant Clinical Professor, Department of Psychology, Albert Einstein College of Medicine, Yeshiva University, New York; Consultant for Group Process Department, Bronx Psychiatric Center; and private practice, New York

Les R. Greene, Ph.D. Associate Professor, Department of Psychiatry, Yale University School of Medicine, VA Medical Center, West Haven, CT.

Deborah Hamm, M.D. Instructor of Psychiatry, Columbia University, College of Physicians and Surgeons, and Assistant Attending Psychiatrist, Presbyterian Hospital of Columbia University, New York

L. E. Hearst. Training and Supervision Group Analyst, Institute of Group Analysis, London

Julie A. Hofheimer, Ph.D. Research Fellow and Developmental Psychologist, Frank Porter Graham Child Development Center, and Division of Neonatal Perinatal Medicine, University of North Carolina, Chapel Hill, NC

Howard A. Kibel, M.D. Coordinator of Group Psychotherapy, New York Hospital–Cornell Medical Center, Westchester Division, White Plains, NY; Associate Professor of Clinical Psychiatry, Cornell University Medical College; and President, American Group Psychotherapy Association

Irwin L. Kutash, Ph.D. Senior Supervisor, Training and Faculty, New York Center for Psychoanalytic Training; New Jersey Institute for Further Psychoanalysis; and Clinical Associate Professor, New Jersey College of Medicine and Dentistry, Newark, NJ

Frank M. Lachmann, Ph.D. Faculty, Senior Supervisor, Training Analyst, Postgraduate Center for Mental Health, New York.

Barry Magid, M.D. Associate Supervisor, Postgraduate Center for Mental Health, and Supervisor, Institute of Continuing Psychotherapy, New York

Nancy S. Molitor, Ph.D. Chicago, Illinois

Malcolm Pines, FRCP, FRC Psych., D.P.M. Director, The Tavistock Clinic, Adult Department, London

Arnold Rachman, Ph.D. Faculty, Supervisor, Training Group Analyst, Group Therapy Department, Postgraduate Center for Mental Health, and private practice, New York

James M. Sacks, Ph.D. Director, Psychodrama Center of New York, and private practice, New York

Edward R. Shapiro, M.D. Associate Clinical Professor of Psychiatry, Harvard Medical School, Boston; Director, Adolescent and Family Treatment and Study Center, McLean Hospital, Belmont, MA; and Faculty, Boston Psychoanalytic Institute

Nonna Slavinska-Holy, Ph.D. Supervisor, Faculty, Psychoanalytic Institute, and Senior Supervisor, Group Psychotherapy Department, both of the Postgraduate Center for Mental Health, and Supervisor, Group and Family Studies Division, Department of Psychiatry, Albert Einstein College of Medicine, Yeshiva University, New York

Robert D. Stolorow, Ph.D. Faculty, Southern California Psychoanalytic Institute, Los Angeles, CA

M. H. Stone, M.D. Clinical Professor of Psychiatry, Mount Sinai Medical School; Chief of Borderline Research, Beth Israel Medical Center; and Professor of Clinical Psychiatry, Cornell University Medical Center, New York

Richard B. Ulman, Ph.D. Associate Research Professor of Psychiatry, New York Medical College, and Training and Supervising Analyst, Training and Research Institute for Self Psychology, New York

Serge Verhaest, Associate Professor, Catholic University of Leuven, Belgium

R. Weissman, M.S.W. Department of Social Work, Westchester Division, New York Hospital–Cornell Medical Center, White Plains, NY

Alexander A. Wolf, M.D. Senior Supervisor, Faculty and Training Analyst, Postgraduate Center for Mental Health, New York

Normund Wong, M.D. Clinical Professor of Psychiatry, University of California at San Francisco; Director of Research and Director of Group Psychotherapy, Letterman Army Medical Center, San Francisco; and Faculty, San Francisco Psychoanalytic Institute

PREFACE

It was not without trepidation that we ventured into this project, being fully aware of the difficulties inherent in dealing with psychoanalytic concepts that have generated so much heated debate among theoreticians and practitioners. Yet, the psychopathologies referred to as borderline and narcissistic disorders are unquestionably still at the center of professional interest and attention. Since they continue to be the subject of wide-ranging clinical exploration despite, or because of, the existing imprecisions and difficulties, we felt the need to assemble and present some of this material. Furthermore, a newfound sense of gratification, derived from working successfully with these patients, which is in sharp contrast to the impotence reported by the profession not long ago, encouraged us to persist in our investigation of the progress that has been made in this area.

In contrast with the many publications on the subject that are limited by one person's perspective, this compilation offers a cross section of views held by leading practitioners who have distinguished themselves through their creative contributions. These represent the "creative ferment" and the force that moves the scientific process forward. In addition, this volume serves as a mirror for actual clinical endeavors in that its range encompasses treatment modalities extending from dyadic to group and auxiliary dimensions. We present a multidimensional perspective, both in scope and in depth, accompanied by inventive research and discussions. We believe this to be a broad and scholarly sample of the blossoming professional activity.

For the most part, these contributions represent a movement away from dualistic and instinctual positions toward holistic and integrative ones, in which the analyst's personality and the therapeutic relationship occupy a central focus for those concerned with the issues of healing. We wish to share these fascinating developments with our colleagues in the hope of deepening their respect for the humanity of both patient and analyst.

Despite the diverse titles of the chapters of this book, there is in fact a cohesion and interrelatedness in that they indeed represent the central areas of clinical concern. We move from descriptive–diagnostic and etiological considerations, through what constitutes restoration and facilitation of new growth, with emphasis upon areas of working through, to the assessment of the effectiveness of our interventions. We stress a view of the psychotherapist as a human being, working in a joint energic–affective field with the patient or group of patients, whether in private practice, at a day-treatment center, or with an inpatient institution.

In the first chapter in the volume, "Implications of DSM-III Diagnosis for Group Psychotherapy with Borderline and Narcissistic Patients," Howard Kibel examines the diagnostic process, the first step in evaluating patients for therapy. Kibel reviews the pioneering work of Kohut and Kernberg in the study of these personality disorders, in relation to the implications of *The Diagnostic and Statistical Manual* (DSM-III) descriptions of these conditions. Paying particular attention to group psychotherapy, Kibel investigates the treatment ramifications of DSM-III nosology.

Normund Wong's contribution discusses an approach to treating these same patients that involves combining individual and group therapy. He suggests that combined treatment, which emphasizes expression and reconstruction, may be the most effective way to help these patients.

In "Psychoanalytic Therapy of Developmental Arrests," Frank Lachmann discusses the psychopathology that reflects a defective sense of self. He presents two clinical vignettes that further explore and describe different cases of developmental arrest.

Barry Magid investigates the manifest picture of borderline and schizophrenic patients, as well as their covert, intrapsychic organization. He discusses the applicability and efficacy of self psychology theory in the treatment of severely disturbed patients. He draws on his experience in private practice, as well as in a state hospital day-treatment program, presenting three diverse case histories that demonstrate the broad possibilities for utilizing principles stemming from self psychology theory.

Deborah Hamm and Edward Shapiro expand the consideration of the intrapsychic in their discussion of the working-through process in treatment of a hospitalized adolescent and her family. The authors chart the young woman's improvement in the context of intensive individual and family therapies. The case study includes a discussion of theoretical and technical issues surrounding the working-through process.

The chapters by Michael Stone and Robin Weissman, Lisbeth Hearst, Malcolm Pines, and James Durkin all focus exclusively upon issues arising in the treatment of borderline and narcissistic patients in the group, a form of therapy that contemporary practitioners have begun to include increasingly alongside individual treatment. Stone and Weissman's chapter represents a comprehensive exploration of the many issues that arise in group treatment of borderline patients, and provides guidelines for the composition of such groups for expressive group therapy in a hospital setting. The specific advantages of both homogeneous and heterogeneous groups are discussed by Hearst in her investigation of the optimal setting for group treatment of borderline and narcissistic patients, and the population of patients who suffer from an impaired or mutilated self. Pines emphasizes the mirroring functions of the group, stressing how the group analytic situation can combine "caretaking" with more classical psychoanalytic approaches; while Durkin draws attention to the group's boundarying function, in an attempt to synthesize the psychodynamic and general systems theory approaches in group treatment of borderline and narcissistic patients.

As the feasibility of treating these difficult patients has improved, an awareness of, and a fascination with, still uncharted terrain has emerged. Some authors have turned their attention in the more humanistic direction of the therapist's personality and his or her attunement to the patient, asking such questions as what the relationship might be of the therapist's character and intrapsychic organization to the patient's intrapsychic and behavioral dimensions, and what the implications of this "mixed" terrain of analyst–patient in empathic interplay are for the success or failure of treatment. Several of the book's chapters investigate aspects of these questions.

In his contribution to the volume, Richard Ulman examines the reciprocal mutual influence of transference and countertransference and stresses the importance of the intersubjective experience of analysis in his presentation of a case of transference-countertransference neurosis.

Nonna Slavinska-Holy discusses projective identification in the case of one borderline patient, emphasizing the importance of projective identification as a means of access to the fragmentary borderline self. She stresses the need for the analyst to enter the patient's world of separate identities in order to become a recipient of the projections and allow the patient truly to relate to another person.

Bernard Brandchaft and Robert Stolorow feel that the therapist's ability to deepen his reflective self awareness when faced with "difficult" patients, can enable him to recognize and decenter from recurrent patterns in himself and can help him gain greater insight regarding his role as a therapist.

Slavinska-Holy views countertransference as an important therapeutic tool. In this chapter she describes her particular attention to erotic countertransference in her work with borderline and narcissistic patients—patients for whom sexuality is typically a chief focus—in order to show how an awareness and understanding of erotic countertransference can aid the healing process.

Another dimension of the new optimism surrounding treatment of borderline and narcissistic self disorders, which is in evidence in these chapters, is fostering creativity in these interesting patients. Alexander Wolf and Irwin Kutash's chapter details how creative diegophrenics can be treated through group psychoanalysis, outlining the components of creativity and illustrating the dynamics of diegophrenics. They describe how the ego functions of these patients can be enhanced in the process of freeing their creative potential.

Arnold Rachman's approach, as elaborated in his chapter, "Liberating the Creative Self through Active Combined Psychotherapy," advocates what he terms "Intensive Group Experiences," more active interactions that involve the dramatization of intrapsychic cnnflicts. He presents the case of a borderline patient who was enabled to recover himself through the combined treatment Rachman describes.

Part II of this volume, "Auxiliary Treatment Modalities and Research Concerns," further reflects the broadening perspectives of clinicians working with borderline and narcissistic patients. Included here are a sampling of new techniques developed, or approaches chosen, in response to the particular needs of these patients. Several examples of current research activity relevant to the treatment of these two psychopathologies are also presented to round out this survey of contemporary issues surrounding borderline and narcissistic patients in therapy.

The selective use of psychodrama in group therapy to facilitate self-expression and personal growth, is explored by James Sacks. According to Sacks, psychodrama can provide a safe and contained setting in which the borderline patient can develop toward a more authentic self.

In their chapter, John and Muriel Briggs discuss psychoanalytic treatment of couples by married cotherapists in private practice. Briggs and Briggs focus on the advantages and potential difficulties of husband-and-wife cotherapy teams. They bring their expertise to specific issues that arise in working with borderline patients in marital therapy.

The work of an innovative pharmacological community where severely disturbed patients are cared for on an outpatient basis through a variety of treatment modalities is depicted by Fernando Astigueta. He describes the patient population, the treatment objectives, the variety of therapy types used, and the history and general functioning of this unique therapeutic setting. In a complementary chapter, Serge Verhaest explains the therapeutic process in a long-term residential psychotherapeutic community for severely disturbed narcissistic and borderline patients. He also delineates the differences in treatment strategy and therapy evolution of these two groups of patients and provides clinical examples to illustrate these differences.

Laurice Glover's chapter, "A Study of Intrapsychic Structures in Three Groups of Patients: One Schizophrenic, One Borderline, and One Neurotic," provides a unique view of the similarities and differences of verbal responses in these patient populations. Verbal material from each group was gathered and analyzed for derivatives of intrapsychic structures and functioning. Glover's research suggests definitive points of contrast and convergence in the patient groups studied.

Nancy Molitor's chapter treats the important bond between infant and mother that is formed during the child's first year. She reviews research of the nature of this attachment relationship, focusing on the two maladaptive forms of attachment, resistant and avoidant. Molitor discusses how the infant–mother bond can be affected by maternal narcissism, and relates this personality organization and infant avoidance of the mother.

Julie Hofheimer and Maurice Apprey also contribute research on the interaction of disturbed mothers and their infants. They describe their study of five disturbed women through their infants' first year, exploring their intrapsychic and emotional experiences, as well as interactive dimensions.

Finally, Les Greene explores the advantages of object relations theory for group psychotherapy research on borderline patients. According to Greene, object relations' key formulations concerning the "reciprocal influence between intrapsychic organization and social relationships" offer an important opportunity for more sophisticated research ventures leading to new theoretical developments.

These last chapters demonstrate that despite the difficulties in doing research on these patients, encouraging efforts are being made to assess the effectiveness of treatment of these psychopathologies objectively and to unite theory and practice. The process of treatment continues to be complex, and at times elusive. The ethical issues of one imperfect human being attempting to "heal" another remain a constant concern. Theoretical foundations, especially in regard to group and other innovative treatment modalities, need refinement and clarification. Nonetheless, these techniques are invaluable when practiced with caution, openmindedness, and continual awareness by the creative and astute clinicians. We are witnessing new avenues for a deeper understanding of our patients, our therapeutic relations, and ourselves as clinicians. This book is an attempt to help enhance that understanding.

ACKNOWLEDGMENTS

I would like to make a few personal acknowledgments to those who helped in my conceptualization and assembly of this collection.

The late Harold Kelman of the Karen Horney group and the Postgraduate Center for Mental Health in New York City focused me on the importance of observing the therapist as well as the patient in the analytic interaction. David Shainberg inspired me with his wide-ranging mind and introduced me to three extraordinary persons: the Hindu visionary Jiddu Krishnamurti; theoretical physicist David Bohm; and psychologist–healer Colette Aboulker Muscat. Krishnamurti taught me a sense of what holism is truly about and David Bohm gave me a conceptual grasp of the remarkable relationship between mind and matter. Colette Muscat introduced me to new dimensions of imagery and their implications for mental and emotional health, and sustained me through some difficult times with her dedicated involvement. I am also grateful to Otto Kernberg for his perceptive supervision and for opening the door to a clearer theoretical horizon. No doubt many, if not all, of the contributors here would share in this acknowledgment.

The person who has had the most direct impact on this book is Malcolm Pines, former president of the International Association of Group Psychotherapy. This book is in fact an outgrowth of his invitation to publish some of my own clinical material and convene a panel on borderline and narcissistic personalities for the Seventh International Congress of Group Psychotherapy in Copenhagen, 1980.

Last, but certainly not least, I wish to thank all my colleagues who so generously contributed their insights and enabled this book to become a reality.

INTRODUCTION

Over the past few decades, the focus of psychoanalytic study has shifted from the oedipal level of psychopathology to an earlier, preoedipal one—from attention to structural conflict among the systems of ego, id, and superego to concern with a lack of integration within these systems. As a part of this shift, theoreticians have offered new conceptualizations of the etiology and treatment of various disorders, both in previously known and newly identified categories. The so-called borderline disorders and the disorders related to pathological narcissism are among the new categories identified by this work that have captured the imagination and attention of psychotherapists. Theoretical formulations, and their implications for treatment of these difficult patients with diverse complaints, have stirred much controversy, as well as ever-growing interest. It is not yet clear whether these two categories can be considered as separate and unique nosological entities, despite the many fruitful and fascinating contributions of many individuals in the profession. Controversy still prevails about these patients, who have baffled even the most skilled practitioners, and who had long been considered untreatable (or psychoanalytically inaccessible). At the same time, a new sense of optimism, stirred by indubitable evidence of therapeutic success, is growing, opening a fascinating new world to us.

This is a period of creative ferment, or creative confusion, depending on one's perspective; theories point in many different directions, some are exciting, some obscure. Yet, although these theoretical disputes will likely remain unresolved, many of us face the daily difficulty of integrating our own and others' insights in our treatment of these patients. This book is offered as an aid toward this daily endeavor.

While never losing sight of theoretical considerations, the contributors to this volume focus on the various treatment methodologies that they have developed to deal with the very broad range of pathology found in borderline–narcissistic self disorders. One of the most compelling aspects of the book is that it demonstrates how, in the forge of integrating theory and practice, theory has been tempered by these authors and bent into new creative shapes.

The question may arise as to why these two nosologies have been included as if they were one. In fact, despite differences cogently discussed elsewhere, fundamental similarities in the type of defensive mechanisms found in these patients seem to exist and call for similar treatment strategies. The similarity in the lack of authentic identity in these patients also calls for at least a juxtaposition of these two disorders.

In this time of exploration of the fit between the theoretical formulations and clinical data, it is important for us to observe the orientations of contemporary psychoanalytically trained clinicians, to discover what exactly is happening in the clinical setting—what is considered healing, and what the fundamental aspects of this healing are. Thus, this book will not undertake a review of the literature or focus on theoretical critique—theory is included only to the extent that it is relevant to understanding an individual clinician's contribution. It will not attempt to be a complete or exhaustive study of the clinical field, but rather will try to show where the special professional attention of leading clinicians lies, both in terms of their theoretical convictions, and treatment dimensions.

Part I
CONTEMPORARY CLINICAL PERSPECTIVES

Chapter 1
IMPLICATIONS OF DSM-III DIAGNOSIS FOR GROUP PSYCHOTHERAPY WITH BORDERLINE AND NARCISSISTIC PATIENTS

HOWARD D. KIBEL, M.D.

In recent years, despite increased interest in borderline and narcissistic conditions, confusion has persisted regarding the uses of these terms. By and large, this has followed from the variety of vantage points from which different clinicians have approached diagnosis. At one extreme are those who rely upon symptomatic and behavioral observations in order to make diagnosis; at the other extreme are those who aim to understand psychostructural roots. The advent of the American Psychiatric Association's *Diagnostic and Statistical Manual* (DSM-III) (1980) requires us to apply the terms *borderline* and *narcissistic* to specific personality disorders, with definite phenomenological criteria.

This burgeoning interest in the borderline and narcissistic conditions has resulted, in part, from an increased understanding of character pathology and a significant shift in the evolution of psychoanalytic theory toward early object relations. Kernberg (1975) and Kohut (1971), the pioneers in this field, have developed two separate and very different ego psychology systems. Those who have followed have borrowed from each, often producing a hybrid that is both confusing and misleading. Some writers have attributed every imaginable trait to borderline and narcissistic conditions, while others have been quite selective in their descriptions. Too many authors use the two diagnostic labels interchangeably, disregarding their very different meanings. Regrettably, it is common for nosology to be used casually in the service of discussion of other issues, such as psychodynamics, theory, and treatment. Imprecision with diagnosis obfuscates the usefulness of such contributions.

The term *borderline* has been used, in the literature, to refer to a state, pattern, character, syndrome, and personality organization (Gunderson and Singer, 1975). Clinical accounts have spanned a heterogeneous group of patients. Each of these descriptions reflects a subtle variation of labeling. Kernberg (1975) uses the term *borderline personality organization* aptly, to convey his psychostructural point of view. Using object relations theory, he has defined a specific developmental defect for these patients, namely, a lack in the integrative capacity of the ego, such that primitive defenses are employed to protect the central ego core built around positive introjections. For him, the diagnosis depends on the presence of characteristic ego pathology rather than the descriptive symptoms. Consequently, within this sphere of ego organization, a variety of pathological character types can be found (Kernberg, 1976). Yet, confusion occurs when one attempts to translate Kernberg's psychostructural formulations to a descriptive typology of personality.

Similarly, the term *narcissism* has been used in so many ways "to describe so many different aspects of self-interests and so many different levels of abstraction [that it] has led to considerable confusion in the psychoanalytic literature" (Pulver, 1970, p. 340). Kohut (1971) uses the term to refer to conditions in which the primary pathology lies in a precariously balanced and faulty self-esteem. He makes the diagnosis only *after* observing a particular spontaneously developing transference relationship during a trial analysis. Although his writings show clear articulations of psychoanalytic technique, they do not contain empirical diagnostic criteria. He specifically disavows "the traditional medical aim of achieving a diagnosis in which a disease entity is identified by clusters of recurring manifestations" (pp. 15–16). In giving short shrift to presenting symptoms, anamnesis, and the patient's history, he focuses on metapsychology and a specific therapeutic approach at the expense of phenomenology. Consequently, his term *narcissistic personality disorders* encompasses a spectrum, spanning several levels of ego development. In contrast, Kernberg views pathological narcissism as a specific defensive organization. Kohut's approach is incompatible with a descriptive one that defines narcissism in terms of overt grandiosity, self-centeredness, or interpersonal self-aggrandizement.

Modern ego psychology has made important advances in elucidating the vicissitudes and characterological expression of internal object relationships, which has increased our understanding of the borderline and narcissistic conditions. Unfortunately, these advances have occurred within the framework of two very different ego psychological systems (represented by Kernberg and Kohut) that are incompatible with each other. This incompatibility is not surprising because each system requires a high level of inference from clinical data. In contrast, descriptive psychiatry uses a relatively low order of inference to describe the characteristic features of disorders. DSM-III uses a purely descriptive approach. By virtue of its prominence within the mental health field and its application by statute in institutions, its terminology is highly influential. In DSM-III, the terms *borderline* and *narcissistic* are attached to specific personality syndromes, with definite phenomenological criteria required for diagnosis. The result is a superficial but precise definition of these disorders. This descriptive approach eschews in-depth psychology and its higher level of abstraction. Because DSM-III is designed to improve the reliability of diagnostic judgments, it purposely avoids such theorizing.

DSM-III and Descriptive Diagnosis

In DSM-III, the personality disorders are grouped into three clusters: (1) those characterized by odd or eccentric behavior (the paranoid, schizoid, and schizotypal disorders; (2) those characterized by dramatic, emotional, or erratic behavior (the histrionic, narcissistic, antisocial, and borderline disorders; and (3) those characterized by anxious or fearful behavior (the avoidant, dependent, compulsive, and passive–aggressive disorders. (This grouping was based only on intuition and impression. It has yet to be shown to be clinically valid.) Note that *behavior*, rather than underlying attitude or ego structure, defines the disorder; thus, *symptoms*, rather than any hypothesized intrinsic pathology, form the basis of nosology. DSM-III does not precisely define certain psychoanalytic categories, such as the "as-if," infantile, and inadequate personalities, which are considered borderline by Kernberg (1976) but in DSM-III might be classified as avoidant, dependent, passive–aggressive, and/or histrionic disorders. Patients whose chief complaints include depression of mood, ennui, and lack of zest, or hypochondriasis might be considered narcissistic by Kohut (1971) but not by DSM-III.

DSM-III defines "narcissistic personality disorder" as one in which there are *all* of the following: a grandiose sense of self-importance or uniqueness; preoccupation with fantasies of unlimited success; exhibitionistic needs for admiration; characteristic responses to threats to self-esteem; and typical disturbances in interpersonal relationships such as exploitiveness, lack of empathy, feelings of entitlement, and overidealization–devaluation reactions. These criteria are characteristic of both current and long-term functioning. This is the first major collaborative attempt to develop specific criteria for this diagnostic term. Akhtar and Thomson (1982) hailed this as a landmark in the evolution of a definition for the syndrome and stated that it deserves recognition and praise.

Kernberg's description of the narcissistic personality encompasses that found in DSM-III (Wong, 1980a). However, his definition, which is based upon the presence of an internal disturbance in self-regard, would also include patients whose overt behavior is quite different but conceals dominant narcissistic attitudes. He includes seemingly dependent individuals who are unable truly to depend upon anyone because of their deep distrust and deprecation of others, as well as those whose conscious feelings of insecurity and inferiority conceal unconscious fantasies of omnipotence and grandiosity. Many clinicians would agree with Kernberg's efforts to include covert as well as overt features in making the diagnosis. Certainly, the description in DSM-III would have been enriched by the inclusion of poorly concealed features, such as the presence of intense envy (and defenses against it), the corruptibility of value systems, and the coexistence of contradictory stances. These are regularly revealed in exploratory interviews or early in treatment.

The DSM-III criteria for narcissistic personality disorder characterize those narcissistic individuals who are moderately to extremely successful socially and/or vocationally. Their symptoms reflect relatively cohesive and somewhat stable aspects of self representations within the ego. From a structural point of view, this diagnosis would be applied only to those with a high-level narcissistic personality configuration. It would exclude many of the more disturbed narcissistic personalities that Kernberg describes, who function marginally and have lower level character pathology. For example, many inadequate personalities are outwardly deferent but inwardly envious and deprecating of others. Such an individual has the structural pathology of a grandiose self but the grandiosity is hidden because of externalization onto others (Volkan, 1980).

The borderline personality disorder in DSM-III is defined as a syndrome of instability (Frances, 1980), affecting interpersonal behavior, mood, and self-image. Unlike the narcissistic personality disorder, in the borderline no single feature is invariably present. There may be impulsivity with or without a history of physically self-damaging acts, a pattern of unstable and intense interpersonal relationships, affective instability, inability to modulate anger, or an identity disturbance with or without chronic feelings of emptiness. This definition approximates the widely used one of Gunderson and Singer (1975),[1] except that it does not allow for the presence of brief psychoticlike experiences and loose thinking in unstructured situations. Frequently, this disorder is accompanied by features of other disorders, so that in many cases more than one diagnosis is warranted. There have been some efforts to link the borderline personality disorder with the affective disorders (Akiskal, 1981). The variability of borderline symptoms leaves open the possi-

[1]These authors identified six features for diagnosing borderline patients during an initial interview: the presence of intense affect, usually depressive or hostile; a history of impulsive behavior; a certain social adaptiveness; brief psychotic experiences; loose thinking in unstructured situations; and relationships that vacillate between transient superficiality and intense dependency.

bility that future research will define phenomenological subtypes. In fact, preliminary evidence (Stone, 1981) already points in the direction of two variants within the DSM-III descriptive classification: one is marked by affective instability and the other is characterized by a disorganized life-style.

The DSM-III criteria for borderline personality disorder apply to many impulse-ridden individuals with poor ego controls and chaotic patterns of relationships. In contrast to those with a narcissistic personality disorder, borderline individuals would have unstable self-representations and lack a coherent sense of self. From a structural point of view, a borderline personality disorder indicates the presence of a true borderline personality organization (Kernberg, 1975), but it blends with many other personality disturbances at the same level of character pathology (e.g., the antisocial personality, drug and alcohol abusers, infantile or inadequate personalities).

DSM-III's descriptive nosology uses clear definitions for the terms *narcissistic* and *borderline* which are narrower and more circumscribed than those of Kohut and Kernberg. This standardization of nomenclature has heuristic value; it facilitates communication within the field and enhances diagnostic reliability. Yet, in other ways, it is too narrow. It does not include certain clinical variables that are essential to treatment considerations, such as ego structure, temperament, the vicissitudes of other character defenses, psychological mindedness, and motivation (Kibel, 1980). Each of these requires evaluation for treatment planning. For example, an individual with a narcissistic personality disorder who is charming and seductive will respond to group psychotherapy differently from one who is aloof. Thus, a descriptive diagnosis (or, for that matter, any singular diagnostic approach) describes only limited aspects of personality which bear directly upon treatment strategies and response. Given these confines of DSM-III, we can now suggest some implications that its descriptive nosology has for treatment.

Treatment Implications

Narcissistic Personality Disorder

Treatment of the narcissistic personality disorder is still in its formative stage. It is only in the last dozen years that this entity has been considered distinct from narcissistic pathology in general, which is found in many conditions. Yet, already there is a consensus that the psychotherapy of narcissistic personalities is arduous. In dyadic therapy, these patients are not easy to engage. Because of their excessive need to be admired and unusual degree of self-reference in interactions with others, they fail to consider the therapist as a separate, autonomous individual. They respond poorly to confrontation and interpretation. Because of their overall defensive style and underlying brittle self-esteem, they appear arrogant while remaining basically fragile. Because of their propensity to devalue treatment, on the one hand, and respond ragefully to imagined slights by the therapist, on the other, they induce powerful countertransferences. The therapist must approach these patients with equanimity and sensitivity.

Despite these difficulties, success has been claimed in treatment, particularly with individual psychoanalytic psychotherapy. Most authors advocate some sort of explorative, rather than supportive, approach. They declare that treatment can produce major characterological change, with near eradication of the defensive constellation that constitutes the disorder's descriptive diagnosis. However, modifications of traditional analytic technique are inevitably recommended. These vary considerably according to the particular author's notion of the etiology of the disorder. Kohut and others advocate the use of empathic understanding to soothe these patients' narcissistic wounds. They believe this is necessary to enable the defensive facade to wither, so that developmental anxieties can emerge, be appreciated, and be explored. Kernberg and his followers advocate persistent confrontation and interpretation of these patients' grandiose and abusive behaviors, which are viewed as inextricably intertwined with oral aggression.

The fact that success has been claimed with divergent approaches suggests the coexistence of contradictory stances in these patients. A successful explorative treatment probably uses both empathy and confrontation, in a balanced way, with recognition that these patients have both a fragile self-esteem and socially injurious character defenses. Interpretation, as a form of resonant understanding, may serve to nurture the therapeutic alliance while fostering reintegration. Unfortunately, more precise formulations of technique await more consistent use in the treatment literature of standard diagnostic nomenclature.

In the group psychotherapy literature, treatment recommendations are even more variable, but the prognostications are less optimistic. In therapy groups, these patients are prone to treat the group members as they have treated others throughout life. Their grandiose sense of self-importance tends to be stimulated by the interpersonal field. They demand excessive attention and find it difficult to share the therapist with others or share time appropriately. They want to use the group to gain admiration in order to fan their fantasies of brilliance and power. When thwarted in these efforts, their responses may be harsh, they may flee, or they may withdraw into a state of indifference.

Their exploitiveness, search for entitlement, and indifference to the suffering of others usually elicit intense, angry reactions from the other group members. To them, the group does not comprise unique individuals; it is an amalgam to be used for selfish ends. They are keenly attuned to their fellows' narcissistic idealization of the group leader (Stein, 1970). While initially they may follow suit, inevitably they became fiercely competitive with the leader for control. Since groups inherently heighten narcissistic concerns in all members, the quasi-public setting of a group causes these patients to experience therapeutic interventions as humiliating. Their usual effect upon others and their poor tolerance for confrontation make them either a focus for group resistance (Horner, 1975) or resistant themselves. For these reasons, group psychotherapy seems a poor choice for most patients with a narcissistic personality disorder (Slavson, 1955; Yalom, 1975). (In contrast, many patients with narcissistic traits or even more pervasive, but covert narcissism, may do well in group psychotherapy.)

Nevertheless, some patients with this disorder have been reported to do well in group therapy (Azima, 1983). Perhaps these are highly motivated, exceptional individuals who can temper their usual destructive interpersonal patterns during sessions. The use of conjoint or combined treatment may help narcissistic patients tolerate the group experience, particularly when individual treatment provides gratification of narcissism by means of an uninterpreted transference (Stein, 1964) or through especially supportive confrontation (Wong, 1980b). These patients are more likely to do well in a group that can "tolerate" them. Such a group must be cohesive, have a preponderance of well-integrated individuals, and have a long history of success working together through adversity. Consequently, for patients with a narcissistic personality disorder, evaluation of the prospective group will play a major role in determining compatibility for group psychotherapy.

Borderline Personality Disorder

Borderline patients have been studied longer than narcissistic patients; their treatment has been under examination for 30 years. Yet, there is still no consensus in the field because these patients show such wide variability in presentation. For example, there appears to be a remarkable contrast between borderline outpatients who voluntarily seek treatment and borderline inpatients, who may be referred by others and/or be in crisis (Gunderson and Singer, 1975). Yet, despite their differences, these patients are comparable. With standardized diagnostic instruments, these two groups show sufficient similarities in clinical features to indicate that they do, in fact, belong to the same diagnostic group (Koenigsberg, 1982). It is no wonder, then, that borderline patients have been treated with almost every conceivable modality, including pharmacotherapy (Klein, 1977), hospital treatment (Adler, 1973), family therapy (Rinsley, 1980), and individual and group psychotherapy. Variations on each modality have been recommended. For example, individual psychotherapeutic approaches have run the gamut from supportive, once-a-week or less, therapy (Zetzel, 1971), to an expressive psychoanalytic type.

Kernberg (1975) is an ardent advocate of the latter. He recommends a traditional analytic procedure with some modifications. He believes that significant characterological change can occur if the therapist persistently interprets the mechanism of splitting as it appears in the transference, and particularly confronts its negative aspects. He advises that, with unstable borderlines, tolerance for this method can be enhanced when someone other than the therapist (e.g., a social worker) structures the patient's daily existence. Recognizing that some of these patients regress considerably during the procedure, he recommends hospitalization when psychotic reactions develop that are broader in scope than the usual transference-limited ones.

Other clinicians (Friedman, 1975) recommend greater flexibility with psychoanalytic technique. Some borderline patients can indeed tolerate a basically expressive approach. Such patients usually have a naturally supportive structure in their life, maintain high degrees of reality testing, use projection and projective identification only in moderation, possess good basic capacities for relationships, have only mildly harsh superegos, and focus little on suicide or self-mutilation when under stress (Adler, 1980). For the more fragile borderlines, who cannot tolerate therapeutic regression, supportive approaches have proven quite successful.

Borderline patients may show primarily affective or interpersonal instability. This subdivision may prove useful for treatment planning. Certainly, those patients who are unpredictable, impulsive, extremely mercurial, or self-destructive require the kind of monitoring that only a supportive dyadic relationship can provide. However, many others, who suffer primarily from interpersonal disorganization, may benefit more from group psychotherapy; they may undergo greater change in a group even though their egos are fairly weak.

Patients with borderline personality disorder compulsively seek intense interpersonal encounters in order to create some semblance of internal coherency. Thus, groups are a natural medium of expression for them. Moreover, the social nature of therapeutic groups readily stimulates their symptoms. Either this process may increase these patients' anxiety so that therapy is not tolerated, or it may place clinical features in bold relief so as to make them uniquely available for treatment. As Horwitz (1977) noted, "paradoxically, the very qualities and defects which make the borderline patient a problematic group member are the same defects which are often best treated in a group setting" (p. 404). The challenge with these patients is to stimulate symptoms while providing therapeutic containment. A "holding environment," à la Winnicott (Kosseff, 1975; James, 1984), may be found within a cohesive group, where feelings of acceptance and belonging help to bolster self-esteem and gratify dependency needs. Concomitant supportive individual therapy may assist toward this end.

Compared to individual therapy, a group affords the more fragile borderlines the opportunity for social and emotional distance when needed; there is less pressure to participate, so patients may pace the intensity of their emotional involvement (Freedman and Sweet, 1954). Transference dilution helps to prevent unwarranted regressive reactions (Stein, 1963). By the same token, the social nature of the group provides opportunities for emotional (transference) gratification (Stein, 1970). A variety of multiple identifications (Sugar, 1971) can bolster patients' impoverished identities (Slavson, 1955). The reality orientation of a group produces a pull toward appropriate social responses and away from reactive psychosis. These built-in social modifiers of therapeutic intensity serve to self-regulate the treatment impact, thereby respecting these patients' fragile ego controls. Yet, at the same time, certain aspects of group psychotherapy work toward intensification of the experience. Specifically, the well-known phenomena of contagion, resonance, and inherent rivalry enhance the emotional responsiveness of group members. When a balance is achieved between the modifiers and enhancers of intensity, a controlled therapeutic regression may occur (Horwitz, 1980). Only then are these patients' disorganized patterns available for treatment. Achieving this balance is the art of therapy.

The relative suitability of group psychotherapy for patients with a borderline personality disorder will vary with the pattern of symptoms present. Thus, for one patient with a preponderance of interpersonal and self-image disturbances, group psychotherapy is the treatment of choice; for another with dysphoria, impulsivity, and significant suicidal potential, it is contraindicated. Additionally, the presence of accompanying features of other disorders will significantly affect treatment. Future research may define subtypes (Stone, 1981) and determine which ones respond best to group therapy. Currently, we must still depend largely upon clinical intuition in planning treatment.

Summary and Conclusion

There are problems inherent in any nosology of disorders of mental, emotional, or personality functioning. Yet, diagnosis is the first order of business when evaluating patients for treatment. To be useful, it ought to orient the clinician toward appropriate corrective measures. A diagnosis that is too broad floods the practitioner with a mass of data that is confusing and incapable of translation to clinical practice. Yet, one that is too narrow gives insufficient information for rational treatment planning. Likewise, when diagnosis is too superficial and broad, important differences between psychopathological states are blurred. Many attempts at in-depth diagnosis have resulted in a series of abstractions with idiosyncratic meaning. The challenge for nosologists is to develop a diagnostic methodology that is both reliable and practical. Current systems have not achieved this dual goal, but do reflect an improvement over past efforts. DSM-III has proven its diagnostic reliability but not its practical value for treatment planning.

Narcissistic and borderline personality disorders are defined in DSM-III according to specific phenomenological criteria, which has heuristic value for clinicians. The descriptive nosology of DSM-III personality disorders focuses on character defense, not character structure. This distinction may prove important to the selection of patients for treatment. Let us take group psychotherapy as an example.

Character defense refers to overt or covert behavior with a variety of conscious and unconscious aims. Character structure, on the other hand, refers to the very fiber of personality—the ego in general and the nature of internal object relations in particular. A therapy group is a unique modality for exposing and highlighting character defenses. Although internal object relations are reenacted within a group, their vicissitudes are many. Referring a patient to group because of a structural diagnosis can be erroneous, since character defenses are better predictors of group compatibility and therapeutic usefulness. Moreover, the language of psychostructure, which is derived from metapsychology, is too abstract for such practical application. In contrast, the language of descriptive psychiatry—of symptoms, defenses, motivation, frustration tolerance, insight, and so on—holds the promise of predicting treatment response. For this reason, using DSM-III's description of these disorders can be a starting point from which specificity of treatment can be evaluated.

References

Adler, G. (1973), Hospital treatment of borderline patients. *Amer. J. Psychiat.*, 130:32–36.
——— (1980), A treatment framework for adult patients with borderline and narcissistic personality disorders. *Bull. Menn. Clin.*, 44:171–180.
Akhtar, S., & Thomson, J. A. (1982), Overview: Narcissistic personality disorder. *Amer. J. Psychiat.*, 139:12–20.
Akiskal, H. S. (1981), Subaffective disorders: Dysthymic, cyclothymic, bipolar II disorders in the "borderline" realm. *Psychiat. Clin. N. Amer.*, 4:25–46.
American Psychiatric Association (1980), *Diagnostic and Statistical Manual of Mental Disorders* (DSM-III). Washington, DC: The American Psychiatric Association.
Azima, F. J. (1983), Group psychotherapy with personality disorders. In: *Comprehensive Group Psychotherapy*, 2nd ed., ed. H. I. Kaplan & B. J. Sadock. Baltimore, MD: Williams & Wilkins, pp. 262–268.
Frances, A. (1980), The DSM-III personality disorders section: A commentary. *Amer. J. Psychiat.*, 137:1050–1054.
Freedman, M. B., & Sweet, B. S. (1954), Some specific features of group psychotherapies and their implications for the selection of patients. *Internat. J. Group Psychother.*, 4:355–368.
Friedman, H. J. (1975), Psychotherapy of borderline patients: The influence of theory on technique. *Amer. J. Psychiat.*, 132:1048–1052.
Gunderson, J. G., & Singer, M. T. (1975), Defining borderline patients: an overview. *Amer. J. Psychiat.*, 132:1–10.
Horner, A. J. (1975), A characterological contraindication for group psychotherapy. *J. Amer. Acad. Psychoanal.*, 3:301–305.
Horwitz, L. (1977), Group psychotherapy of the borderline patient. In: *Borderline Personality Disorders*, ed. P. Hartocollis. New York: International Universities Press, pp. 399–422.
——— (1980), Group psychotherapy for borderline and narcissistic patients. *Bull. Menn. Clin.*, 44:181–200.
James, D. C. (1984), Bion's "containing" and Winnicott's "holding" in the context of the group matrix. *Internat. J. Group Psychother.*, 34:201–213.
Kernberg, O. (1975), *Borderline Conditions and Pathological Narcissism*. New York: Jason Aronson.
——— (1976), *Object Relations Theory and Clinical Psychoanalysis*. New York: Jason Aronson.
Kibel, H. D. (1980), The importance of a comprehensive clinical diagnosis for group psychotherapy of borderline and narcissistic patients. *Internat. J. Group Psychother.*, 30:427–440.
Klein, D. F. (1977), Psychopharmacological treatment and delineation of bor-

derline disorders. In: *Borderline Personality Disorders*, ed. P. Hartocollis. New York: International Universities Press, pp. 365–383.

Koenigsberg, H. W. (1982), A comparison of hospitalized and nonhospitalized borderline patients. *Amer. J. Psychiat.*, 139:1292–1297.

Kohut, H. (1971), *Analysis of the Self*. New York: International Universities Press.

Kosseff, J. W. (1975), The leader using object-relations theory. In: *The Leader in the Group*, ed. Z. A. Liff. New York: Jason Aronson, pp. 212–242.

Pulver, S. E. (1970), Narcissism: the term and the concept. *J. Amer. Psychoanal. Assn.*, 18:319–341.

Rinsley, D. B. (1980), Diagnosis and treatment of borderline and narcissistic children and adolescents. *Bull. Menn. Clin.*, 44:147–170.

Slavson, S. R. (1955), Criteria for selection and rejection of patients for various types of group psychotherapy. *Internat. J. Group Psychother.*, 5:3–30.

Stein, A. (1963), Indications for group psychotherapy and the selection of patients. *J. Hillside Hosp.*, 12:145–155.

——— (1964), The nature of transference in combined therapy. *Internat. J. Group Psychother.*, 14:413–424.

——— (1970), The nature and significance of interaction in group psychotherapy. *Internat. J. Group Psychother.*, 20:153–162.

Stone, M. H. (1981), Borderline syndromes: A consideration of subtypes and an overview, directions for research. *Psychiat. Clin. N. Amer.*, 4:3–24.

Sugar, M. (1971), Multitransference and divarications in group psychotherapy. *Internat. J. Group Psychother.*, 21:444–455.

Volkan, V. D. (1980), Narcissistic personality organization and "reparative" leadership. *Internat. J. Group Psychother.*, 30:131–152.

Wong, N. (1980a), Borderline and narcissistic disorders: A selective overview. *Bull. Menn. Clin.*, 44:101–126.

——— (1980b), Combined group and individual treatment of borderline and narcissistic patients. *Internat. J. Group Psychother.*, 30:389–404.

Yalom, I. D. (1975), *The Theory and Practice of Group Psychotherapy*, 2nd ed. New York: Basic Books.

Zetzel, E. R. (1971), A developmental approach to the borderline patient. *Amer. J. Psychiat.*, 127:867–871.

Chapter 2

COMBINED INDIVIDUAL AND GROUP TREATMENT WITH BORDERLINE AND NARCISSISTIC PATIENTS

NORMUND WONG, M.D.

The use of a combined individual and group approach for borderline and narcissistic patients appears to have arisen out of practical necessity, creative innovation, a desire to amalgamate the best features of individual and group treatment, and from sheer frustration when individual or group therapists felt that treatment had come to a standstill or was ineffective.

For the most part, this treatment modality was started by individual therapists who began to experiment with groups and to supplement individual sessions with group therapy when they discovered the unique advantages of the group. When a patient is in concurrent intermediate or long-term dyadic and group psychotherapy with the same therapist, we refer to the process as combined psychotherapy. If two or more therapists treat the patient concurrently but one therapist provides the individual treatment while the other one or two render group psychotherapy, we call the process conjoint therapy.

Conjoint versus Combined Treatment

Most advocates of combined group and individual therapy for borderline or narcissistic patients usually mean that individual therapy sessions are to be made available for the group patient on an intermittent basis with the same therapist. Opinions differ about the use of combined treatment on a regular and sustained basis. However, there is less disagreement over the issue of conjoint versus combined treatment. Two major advantages are evident with the combined approach: (1) more effective treatment of specific ego defects and (2) continuity of treatment focus.

A major defense mechanism employed by borderline patients is splitting, and having two or more therapists treating these patients separately in two different modalities tends to invite splitting even more. Under this arrangement, countertransference difficulties may arise not only between patients and their therapists but also between the therapists themselves. In particular, the boundaries of confidentiality may become fuzzy to the disadvantage of the patients. The issues of what properly can be conveyed by the individual therapist to the group therapist, and perhaps to peers in the group, and what is to be kept confidential in the group and away from the knowledge of the individual therapist are only a few of the items which may arise and promote resistance through the conjoint arrangement.

In order to deal with the problems engendered by splitting, as well as the other primitive ego defenses utilized by the borderline and narcissistic patient, the two or more therapists must conscientiously meet on a regular basis to discuss the patient's treatment. In practice, the lack of time and/or the presence of countertransference problems mediate against frequent meetings. Where splitting becomes a problem, one often sees the operation of primitive idealization as well. Because the individual therapist focuses sole attention on one patient, he becomes the idealized good, magical object while the group therapist is seen as the all bad, persecutory object who deprives the patient by sharing himself with other patients in the group. Sometimes the reverse is true.

In contrast, when the patient is treated in combined therapy with only one therapist, the chance for heightened resistance through the employment of these mechanisms is much diminished. Acting out through the use of the aforementioned defense mechanisms is kept within the group or reposited in the therapist where it can be observed and worked with. When projective identification is operating, such a one-sided emphasis is not as noticeable. The mechanisms of mutual denial and omnipotence also do not seem to be much affected by whether the borderline patient has one or several therapists treating him.

In the case of the seriously disturbed or regressed borderline patient who requires hospitalization, the use of different therapists doing individual and group therapy is frequently unavoidable. Such is usually not the case with outpatient groups. The borderline patient feels far more supported in a group setting knowing that the same therapist will be aware of events and can clarify the often fantastic and distorted perceptions stirred up in a group. If left untouched, these perceptions can cause patients to flee the group.

The emotional burden placed on the therapist resulting from the patient's continual devaluation and projective identification can also be considerably eased by the combined treatment method. His therapeutic task is lightened when the therapist is able to confront the borderline or narcissistic patient in an individual session with a particular piece of distorted reality and then in the group have group members again point out the distortion. Confrontation is more readily accepted and the borderline patient's sense of reality tends to be much improved. When there are separate therapists treating the patient with different modalities, the work on a particular item or area is often lost, or the therapeutic progress is much delayed. We are all too aware that often patients seek support for, and relief of, the anxiety engendered by their psychopathology rather than wishing to explore the basis of their illness, unless they are confronted repeatedly and consistently. It is far easier for patients to accept confrontation in the combined setting.

Special Advantages of Combined Treatment for Borderline and Narcissistic Patients

The application of individual or group therapy alone in the treatment of borderline and narcissistic disorders can prove quite unsatisfactory. The therapist who undertakes an individual approach with these patients frequently finds the task difficult, stressful, and unrewarding. In turn, the group therapist generally needs to see the borderline or narcissistic patient for one or more private sessions somewhere in the course of the group experience if therapy is to succeed. To many writers, conjoint therapy is more effective than either individual or group therapy alone. Combined therapy, however, may be the most effective therapy for the majority of borderline and narcissistic patients. As described in this chapter, combined treatment is an expressive and reconstructive, rather than a supportive approach. Let us now explore why and how it is effective with these patients.

Transference

When the therapist sees borderline or narcissistic patients in both the individual and group setting, the transference is better handled because there is opportunity for distancing, deflection, and dilution. These patients frequently experience a dyadic relationship as too stressful. Very primitive regressive reactions may occur in intensive individual therapy unless there is the opportunity for reality testing and support, which is found in a group setting. In a group, the terrified reactions of the borderline patient or the idealized transferences of the narcissistic patient toward the therapist have an opportunity to become modified through the eyes of peers, and the sense of reality and reality testing may be improved when perceptions of other patients are shared. The support gained from the group makes it less frightening for the patient to discuss his feelings about the therapist in individual therapy and also educates the patient about the significance of the transference.

Frequent denigration and primitive idealization can play havoc with the therapist who is unaccustomed to encountering the intense and often uncomfortable feelings aroused in work with these patients. Unlike the psychotic individual, who may also evoke primitive emotions in the therapist, the borderline patient is in much better contact with reality and his projections cannot be ignored or accepted with the technical neutrality often experienced by the therapists working with psychotic patients. The therapist's ability to regress and empathize, utilizing concordant identification (Racker, 1957), is severely taxed when he realizes that the borderline patient may leave a highly complex and successful task momentarily to come for therapy and then seemingly become disorganized, spewing forth very primitive emotions and regressed thinking, only to quickly reorganize and return to the former task once the session is over. The incongruity of such behavior in the face of denial from the borderline patient promotes a different mental frame of reference in the therapist, as contrasted to work with a psychotic patient or a better-integrated patient in analysis.

When combined therapy is employed, the therapist has far less "luggage" to encumber him in performing the arduous, demanding work with these patients, because peer members in the group lend considerable support to the therapist. The patients also benefit: The oral deprivation and aggression typical of the infantile and narcissistic character are readily confronted by the group, and the patient must learn to express and deal with these needs in a more adaptive way. Spotnitz (1957) has referred to the group experience as "first-rate training" for these patients.

Opportunities for Identification and Internalization

In the group setting, the borderline patient is exposed to a number of models with which to identify, while the predominantly narcissistic patient is afforded the opportunity to engage in pathognomonic but necessary transferences. It is crucial that opportunities be made available for identification and internalization. In a group, both healthy and pathological identifications may be made by patients with other members as well as the therapist. In any event, what occurs in the group may be observed by the therapist in vivo and dealt with either in the group or in the individual setting. Acting-in or acting-out behavior can be especially well controlled and worked with using the combined format.

Before identifications are stabilized in the group, and even during the life span of the group, borderline and narcissistic patients may project onto various members in tentative fashion different parts of their selves. In practice, the members may allow these partial identifications to occur or may reject them. If rejected, the borderline patient will select another individual and make that member an embodiment of one fragmented aspect of his or her self. Thus, the therapist engaged in combined therapy has an opportunity to observe firsthand the fragmentation of the borderline patient and the self-object transferences of the narcissistic individual. He sees how the patient struggles to keep separate or to integrate these different fragments or internal objects through the use of multiple identifications.

Use of the Therapist as Stabilizer

Where a patient shows outstanding narcissistic pathology, the combined approach is of great assistance in helping both therapist and patient understand the changes that are occurring. During these changes, the therapist can function as the stabilizer, integrator, and anchor upon whom the patient can depend. It is to be expected that there will be excessive swings as the patient struggles to evolve a whole and constant self. The therapist who can work with the patient individually and in the group setting has greater understanding and effectiveness in dealing with the evolving facets of the patient's emerging identity. Foremost is the need of the narcissistic patient to feel that he retains the therapist during the course of combined treatment as the archaic self-object until the patient is able to develop a stable, cohesive self. This is largely achieved via the individual setting.

Potential for Intensive and Reconstructive Therapy

Some group therapists feel that the narcissistic patient does not benefit from the group setting or that such a patient is good for the group. Yalom (1975) states that "the narcissistic patient generally has a stormier time of it in group therapy than in individual therapy" (p. 395). In his book (pp. 342–351), he describes in detail the relationship between Bill and Jan, emphasizing the narcissistic features of Bill's interactions with the group. He points out that the price paid by the group was enormous—that other members were neglected and many important issues were left untouched. Horner (1975) has found in her experience that the narcissistic personality disorder has not responded well to group treatment. She believes that "the group has been nonproductive for the patient at best, and destructive for both the patient and the group at worst" (p. 302). Other group therapists contend that, although group therapy may be effective in confronting a patient with the pathological aspects of his narcissism, the group does not provide the opportunity to allow the narcissistic patient a good enough one-to-one relationship with the therapist. Without such a relationship, the patient is unable to progress from the position of narcissistic fixation and entitlement. In addition, through his behavior, the narcissistic patient is likely to become the focus of negative transferences from other group members, to be scapegoated, and, eventually, to be extruded from the group.

Some therapists would place patients exhibiting excessive narcissistic manifestations in the same category as the paranoid, sociopathic, or acutely depressed patients, regarding them as unsuitable for the group on the basis that they are too disruptive, interfere with culture building, and prevent group cohesion. Group therapists who adhere to the group-as-a-whole approach often voice this opinion, recognizing that the narcissistic patient does not respond well to situations where he is afforded little opportunity for recognition of his uniqueness. In such cases, he may attempt to overidealize the leader but frequently becomes enraged and withdraws from the group.

The combined individual and group approach can overcome the aforementioned difficulties. In individual therapy, the transference reactions are allowed to develop without intrusion. Here the therapist can convey to the patient a sense of constancy, empathetic awareness, and security—the very feelings the narcissistic patient has lacked in his life. It is a rare group, indeed, which early in its life can give the patient the feeling of acceptance and stability and, later, the adaptability to satiate his immense oral needs. No doubt, in the beginning, the narcissistic patient is readily welcomed to drain off the primitive anxieties for the group. To the inexperienced group leader, the narcissistic patient is seen as the initiator of self-disclosure, catharsis, and universality. It is usually in the second stage of group formation described by Yalom (1975) that the group and the narcissistic patient come to grief. This stage is characterized by conflict, dominance, and rebellion. If the group leader does not properly understand and handle the narcissistic patient, he may bolt, the group may remain in chaos, or it may dissolve.

Nature of the Group

Homogeneous versus Heterogeneous Group Composition

It is readily observed that borderline patients come in many psychological sizes and shapes and manifest multiple varieties of characterologic features, personality attitudes, and behavioral dispositions. The degree and manifestations of narcissistic pathology will also vary among narcissistic personalities. And it is possible that different types of borderline and narcissistic patients require a different therapeutic approach. Nevertheless, I have found that groups composed of all borderline and narcissistic patients, classified according to *Diagnostic and Statistical Manual* (DSM-III) criteria, have not fared as well as a heterogeneous group with patients bearing different neurotic or characterological diagnoses. There are times when the immense oral demands, envy, rage, devaluation, and idealization typical of these patients exceed the tolerance of the group and the therapist. These pressures are compounded when the group membership is homogeneous. Discouragement, demoralization, and countertransference feelings are then more likely to occur.

Repression as well as higher level defense mechanisms tend to be lacking in borderline patients, while narcissistic patients may suffer from an inability to feel guilt and genuine empathy for others. There is little doubt that primitive feelings emerge with far greater rapidity in homogeneous groups of narcissistic or borderline patients; it has been my experience, however, that unless one deals with very high-level patients these groups show a rapid turnover rate with poor treatment results. In essence, there is a lack of altruism, interpersonal learning, therapeutic alliance, and hope, and an excess of universality, ventilation, and abreaction with little group cohesion.

Roth (1980) points out how a homogeneous group of borderline and narcissistic patients places an unusual strain on the therapist, interferes with the therapist's capacity for empathic regression, and pressures him "to become other than a psychotherapist" (p. 419). In a homogeneous group, there are few, if any, "healthy allies" (p. 419) to sustain and support the therapist. Furthermore, Roth concludes that with such a mixture it is not possible to conduct group therapy of the ordinary sort, as the narcissistic demands of the group tend to interfere with the leader's ability to reflect on the ongoing process.

A different opinion is expressed by Slavinska-Holy (1977), who feels that in combined treatment of borderline and narcissistic personality disorders a homogeneous closed group is preferred. She reasons that because these patients represent one psychopathological entity, "the therapeutic strategy and tactic is meaningful to all at the same time" (p. 3). By contrast, in a heterogeneous group that includes psychoneurotic individuals, a different treatment approach must be used because the patients are at different developmental levels. In a homogeneous closed group, borderline and narcissistic "individuals traverse together common ground as they move from one developmental stage to another, like a growing child" (p. 3). Contrary to the belief of other writers, Slavinska-Holy feels that these patients can offer to each other the necessary differences to facilitate group process and to promote a viable exchange that is conducive to growth.

Closed or Open-Ended Groups

Once the therapist and patient have agreed on the use of combined treatment, it is best to keep the group closed for the following reasons. One of the primary tasks of the therapist in the combined format is to provide reasonable but firm boundaries for the group and help bring about a consistent, good-enough holding environment which will permit regressive phenomena to emerge. Such a setting has been lacking in the lives of many borderline and narcissistic patients. If such an ambience can be established, one soon sees the full-blown presence of fantastic, primitive, opposing, and unintegrated self, object, and affect representation units. When this level of regression is reached, the group sessions can be intense and emotionally draining to all the participants. To heed the heightened emotions of the group and to maintain track of the oscillating object representations and self-representations called into play during a typical group session is analogous to riding a high-speed express train. Thus, it is rarely advisable to adopt an open-ended group format, as it is devastating to the newcomer to be exposed to the frenzy of a group of borderline and narcissistic patients operating at full speed, and unreasonable to expect the new member to catch the drift of the group. In fact, if the group is open ended from the start, there is little likelihood that it will progress to a working stage where the members can feel safe enough to reveal themselves. Only in those rare instances when the critical mass of the group dwindles to four is it advisable to bring before the group the possibility of introducing new members.

When to Introduce Combined Therapy

Some therapists may see their patients in individual treatment for a long time, place them in a group with themselves, and then withdraw the individual sessions. Other psychotherapists may begin treatment with borderline or narcissistic patients in a group but later see the patients only in individual treatment. Most practitioners of combined therapy, however, prefer a preparatory phase of individual therapy before adding group psychotherapy to the treatment plan. The duration and frequency of the individual therapy varies and appears to be guided by a variety of considerations. Papanek (1956), Schecter (1959), and Sager (1960) stress the need to establish a transference first and to work through some of its infantile aspects before placing the patient in combined treatment. According to Scheidlinger and Porter (1980), some clinicians wait until the transference manifestations are established in individual therapy and at least partially understood. The acute situation and symptoms for which the patient originally sought treatment should have subsided and the patient should be able to tolerate the anxiety and stresses of the group.

Wolberg (1960) carefully points out that the borderline

patient should not become a member of a therapeutic group until the patient's defenses of detachment have been penetrated and the fears of close relationships with other people are being overcome. The patient should have expressed a desire to join a group or have shown some effort to be a functioning part of a group (not necessarily a therapy group). Even though the patient is diagnosed as a borderline or narcissistic individual, there are additional considerations that determine the use of combined therapy. For example, Schecter (1959) feels that patients who tend to relate predominantly in a rather exclusive or "incestuous" manner or who show great difficulty communicating in pairing and sibling situations are candidates for combined treatment. Durkin (1964) and Tabachnick (1965) both believe that patients who are shown to have problems with "isolation" should be treated with combined therapy. According to these authors, such patients have a fear of interpersonal contacts, cannot communicate easily with others, and show a general inhibition of instinctual drive derivatives. Wilder (1974) recommended the use of combined treatment for those individuals who had been in analysis for a long time and were showing difficulty with the resolution of their transference neuroses. Combined treatment has also been used by many clinicians when they feel that patients are at a treatment impasse, manifest stubborn or long-standing resistances, have been unable to apply the insights gained either from group or individual therapy, or are close to termination in dyadic treatment and may benefit from a group experience. Combined therapy may be prescribed for those borderline and narcissistic patients who would gain from intensive psychotherapy but because of time and financial considerations cannot afford analysis. An attenuated version of combined treatment is practiced with psychiatric inpatients in many institutions, as described by Green (1953) and Beran (1961). Most clinicians who work with hospitalized borderline patients employ a combination of individual and group approaches. When patients are hospitalized for a lengthy period, such an approach may be very helpful in order to work through specific issues, manage distorted and dangerous fantasies, and reduce excessive anxiety.

Fried (1954, 1955) introduces combined therapy for passive–narcissistic patients with the rationale that they need to deal with reality. Such patients are able initially to gratify their dependency needs in the private sessions and they also have the opportunity to analyze the search for their unrealistic ego ideals. When combined therapy is employed, they are able to experience the devaluation of their unattainable ego ideals and to sustain the necessary disappointments with the aid of the group to enable them to form more of a self-identity. Aside from their diagnoses, Wolf (1974) feels that individuals amenable to combined treatment are those showing fairly intact egos who are the oldest or nearly the oldest siblings in a large family and were prematurely forced to assume surrogate parental roles; who experience sudden panic or severe depression; who are unable to verbalize basic problems; who are silent members, severe sadomasochists, or acting-out patients; or who are plateaued in treatment.

The decision as to when to place the patient in combined therapy also varies, depending on practical considerations such as the time available to the therapist and patient, and financial considerations. In private practice, it may take a long while before the clinician has a sufficient number of patients to employ the use of combined treatment. However, some therapists such as Hulse (1955) start all their patients in combined treatment from the very beginning and do not provide any preliminary individual sessions.

Once in combined treatment, patients may be seen in individual therapy for the same or a reduced number of visits or may be gradually withdrawn altogether from individual treatment. The number of individual sessions may range from a minimum of one visit every other week to as many as five meetings weekly. Most practitioners see their patients once or twice weekly in individual sessions and in one or two group sessions, each lasting 1½ hours. Papanek (1956) objects to too frequent group meetings. She recommends that groups be held not more than once a week and views additional meetings as superfluous and potentially harmful; there is the danger that group life may substitute for real life and that a gang culture hostile to the outside environment may develop. Aronson (1964) leaves the responsibility for the frequency of individual meetings with the patient, but with the understanding that the therapist may schedule an individual session when it seems indicated.

General Objectives of Individual Therapy in the Combined Approach

Before embarking on a course of combined treatment, the clinician should establish a diagnosis, understand the dynamics of the patient, establish a therapeutic alliance, and educate the patient to the process of therapy. These are usually accomplished in individual sessions. The duration of individual therapy may vary from a few weeks to a few years. Most practitioners of combined treatment tend to place their patients in individual therapy for one to two years before adding the group modality. However, some clinicians feel that if a patient remains in individual treatment too long before entering combined therapy, the patient may find it difficult to relinquish the fantasy of being special and, once in combined therapy, may show a variety of reactions ranging from excessive frustration to anxiety, rage, withdrawal, resentment, or undue dependency.

The objectives of individual therapy in combined treatment differ from group psychotherapy in several aspects. Regression to an earlier level of development occurs, and dreams, free association, and fantasies are encouraged and explored to a greater extent. More emphasis is placed on a detailed study of intrapsychic rather than interpersonal matters. Intense preoedipal and oedipal transferences are commonly encountered in individual psychotherapy, while in group therapy sibling transferences tend to predominate. Overall, the transference phenomena in individual treatment are usually more intense and regressed than in group therapy. More attention is paid to the working through of neurotic structures instead of underlying character defenses. Individual sessions may provide greater insight and depth of understanding.

Once group therapy is contemplated, the individual sessions serve additional functions. These include the development and maintenance of sufficient trust and confidence in the therapist to permit the patient to enter group therapy. Thus, one of the functions of individual therapy is to prepare the patient for a group experience by fostering a strong therapeutic alliance, or working relationship, which will enable the patient to withstand the anxiety and stresses of the group. When the patient is engaged in combined treatment, resistances and defenses brought out in a group can be examined and further worked through in the separate sessions.

In the group, the therapist and patient share another experience in common which will have an influence on their relationship in the dyadic situation and offer further material for study. In the group component of combined treatment, more of the therapist's personality is revealed and this data influences the transference in individual psychotherapy.

For patients with relatively weak ego structures, extra attention may have to be paid in individual sessions to supporting the patient and reducing the anxieties arising from the group experience. When the combined treatment format is employed, patients may request fewer or more individual sessions and the reasons for the request must be explored.

Similarly, material from the individual sessions will often be carried over to the group sessions. Those patients seen in group psychotherapy alone may manifest intense rivalry and envy toward those members in combined treatment, and there may be great anger toward the therapist, along with feelings of rejection.

General Objectives of Group Therapy in the Combined Approach

A few therapists favor the use of group therapy first and only later add individual sessions. They believe that individuals who are psychologically unsophisticated may learn how to think psychologically when placed in a group that is able to offer support, opportunities for universalization, altruism, ventilation, and catharsis. Scheidlinger and Porter (1980) point out that the group-first approach is useful if the transference in the dyadic relationship is viewed as too frightening to a patient. Also, individuals with previous psychoanalytic experience may be placed in a group before starting combined treatment.

Green (1953) and Beran (1961), who describe the treatment of inpatients, favor the use of group therapy first before starting combined therapy. Beran finds that withdrawn and suspicious persons cannot tolerate individual contacts in the beginning, but in a group their fears and suspiciousness are gradually lost when patients are offered an opportunity to give and take in a friendly group atmosphere.

In combined treatment, the group modality provides the advantages commonly ascribed to therapy groups in general. However, its objectives differ somewhat from the customary practice of group psychotherapy alone, for it is only half of the overall treatment. The impact of individual treatment and the presence of the same therapist in both settings are ever-present undercurrents in the group. In contrast to individual treatment, group therapy provides patients with opportunities to interact safely with others in a setting reflective of society at large, where they encounter mutual support, different learning situations, a chance to express and benefit from altruism, which in itself may be therapeutic, and opportunities for identification and catharsis. The group setting also promotes and encourages free expression of thoughts, behavior, and affects toward other patients and the therapist. In addition, the group provides multiple transference objects, a large number of stimuli in the treatment setting, feedback about the individual's behavior from a variety of perspectives, and an increase in personal awareness of the impact a person makes upon others. The emotional contagion often present in groups may help lift repressions in patients who in individual therapy alone cannot come to grips with their feelings. In the group, patients may feel more comfortable with aggressive feelings and receive help with acting-out behavior because of the reassurance and support offered by other members.

Group therapy also differs from individual treatment in that it works on a more conscious and less regressed level and tends to be more reality oriented and to focus less on fantasies. It also depends more on interaction among its members and activity than on free association. Its focus is more on the "here and now" than the "there and then." When combined with individual treatment, group therapy provides other additional functions. These include an outlet for and control of intense, unmanageable transference phenomena that otherwise could disrupt or even destroy treatment; the reduction and resolution of some resistances that are seemingly intractable in individual therapy; opportunities for risk taking to try out new behaviors that have been analyzed and worked through in individual treatment; and the management of excessive dependency needs, where the patient learns to share the therapist with others. By watching other members and their reactions to the therapist, through feedback from other group members, and through a reduction in the intensity of the transference, patients are afforded increased opportunities to strengthen and develop their observing ego. Confrontations and insights that may not have been effective in individual therapy may assume significance and validity when they are voices in the group setting. The group sessions can serve as a catalyst to promote progress in individual therapy.

Finally, the group sessions provide the therapist with a chance to see the social facets and interpersonal behaviors of the patient, which might otherwise be difficult to evaluate in individual treatment. The therapist can observe the adaptive mechanisms employed by the patient in a different setting and determine to what extent certain issues in individual treatment have been successfully worked through and applied in a group setting. Because most therapists feel that they must be more active and transparent in a group setting, combined treatment affords them a chance to see how adaptive and successful their behaviors are in the two arenas.

Specific Treatment Issues

In expressive or psychoanalytic combined therapy with borderline and narcissistic patients, the therapist strives to help the patient develop a solid identity where there is a stable integration of self-representations and object representations linked to appropriate affect units. The attainment of this goal is manifested through a reduction in the patient's inner turmoil and a sense of contentment with one's self. It is expressed externally through a socially appropriate and realistically adaptive behavior and the ability to love and to perform constructive work. Raw, primitive aggression in the guise of deviant behavior and bizarre fantasy life must be sublimated and channeled into constructive outlets. Overerotization of the self or object is modulated and reflected through a sound sense of self-esteem. Therapy aims to diminish use of earlier, primitive defense mechanisms such as denial, projection and projective identification, depersonalization, somatization, splitting, and primitive idealization, and to substitute in their place the more mature defenses and adaptive devices, such as sublimation, intellectualization, rationalization, and repression.

A developmental object-relations approach is advocated which stresses individuation–separation, striving for libidinal object constancy, and the transformation or maturation of the grandiose self, which eventually leads to the presence of mature self-esteem and an adult superego. In order for a mature superego to evolve, the patient must confront and resolve oedipal issues. However, the intent of this chapter is not to argue the merits of the various theories about borderline and narcissistic personalities which have been proposed by Modell (1968); Kohut (1971); Kernberg (1975); Mahler, Pine, and Bergman (1975); Masterson and Rinsley (1975); Rinsley (1978); Adler and Buie (1979) and others, but to share with the reader several trenchant treatment issues which arise in the combined treatment of these disorders.

Management of the Transference

Some of Kernberg's suggestions for individual expressive psychoanalytic therapy have been quite useful for the patient who is seen in combined treatment. Kernberg (1982) points out how conflict-laden object relationships in the context of regressed ego states rapidly emerge early in treatment. In a short time the transference reaction becomes full-blown and regressed, in contrast to the more gradual unfolding of internalized object relationships typically seen in the treatment of the neurotic individual. The affect oscillates rapidly from overidealization to gross paranoid distrust. Projections of self-representations and object representations are unstable and alternating. There is a quick cycling of positive and negative transference reactions. In the individual session, the therapist is well advised to heed his countertransference feelings and to use them in order to understand what is happening with the patient. The therapist should request clarification of the material, confront the patient's modulations, and interpret for the patient how the therapist understands the fluctuations and distortions. The negative transference must be especially addressed and interpreted or else the patient will experience a blurring of reality and may flee the treatment in panic. Interpretations should be made in the context of the here-and-now or relate to objects in the patient's immediate environment. Genetic reconstruction or interpretation should be attempted only after treatment is well underway and there is a firmly established therapeutic alliance. The patient's observing ego and reality testing must be in evidence. Positive transference manifestations need not be interpreted early in the therapy with borderline patients unless there is obvious splitting of all-good and all-bad objects and overidealization is seen as a resistance. The therapist must be aware that the patient's blind categorization into good and bad is an attempt to bring some order to inner chaos. Realistic limits must be imposed from the very onset of treatment to control acting out of the transference or else anxiety may increase in the patient, the treatment situation may be destroyed, and countertransference feelings may overwhelm the therapist.

With narcissistic patients at the start of therapy, I agree with Kohut that the pathognomonic transferences be allowed to evolve and develop in an unimpeded fashion. Ornstein (1982) states that the therapist's task is to listen, observe, and understand the patient's transferences. The therapist is to "articulate what is thus perceived in the context of the treatment setting. Articulation takes the form of understanding and explanation" (p. 510). Kohut (1971) feels that the spontaneous emerging or reawakening of pathognomonic selfobject transferences remobilizes the previously interrupted thrust in childhood to grow. In individual therapy, I endorse such a tactic, although I question the concept of a grandiose self whose normal development has been thwarted and whose growth can be resumed under the proper conditions. It is reasonable that the therapist should tolerate and attempt to understand the source of the patient's aggression. Yet it is difficult to explain the raw anger, hatred, and sadistic behavior solely as a response to previous narcissistic trauma. There is an exaggerated grandiosity which must be explained through additional factors. Interpretations about anger and grandiosity can be made by focusing first on people in the patient's immediate environment; eventually this material can be analyzed in the transference context, but only after a firm and stable working alliance has been established. Countertransference feelings, particularly feelings of fear, must be heeded by the therapist. As with the borderline patient, genetic interpretations are possible but they should only be presented when the treatment is well established.

In the group setting, a different tactic is recommended for the borderline and narcissistic patient. My comments apply to heterogeneous groups that include patients with neurotic and character disorders. In general, the therapist tends to be more active with borderline patients in the group. However, overactivity of the therapist often indicates the presence of countertransference feelings. In the group, other members can usually confront the borderline patient in a supportive manner to rectify the fantastic and distorted transference the patient has to the therapist. In the case of the narcissistic and borderline individual, the many strong reactions reflect the oral greed and envy at having to share the therapist.

Until the group becomes more cohesive and settles into a work orientation, the attachment of the borderline patient remains primarily to the therapist and not to the group as mother. The therapist needs to pay close heed to the rage and anger of the borderline patient, which represent the conflicting wish to have mother and yet separate from her via the group. The wish to remain attached usually dominates and the anger toward the therapist and the fear of engulfment are projected onto the other group members. An empathic, insightful interpretation from the leader usually stems the rage.

The narcissistic patient can form an idealizing transference to the leader or to the group, or can react negatively by denigrating the therapist or the members. Mirror transferences will usually surface. Where an idealizing transference is present, little needs to be done directly by the therapist, as the other members can afford an offsetting balance and can confront the narcissistic patient about the distortions without causing undue trauma. The therapist may gently and frequently point out the need of the narcissistic patient to idealize the group and/or the therapist and help the patient examine the past in order to understand the significance of the transference. This should be done when the idealizing transference becomes a resistance that impedes the progress of the group. More frequently it is the negative, hostile transference that commands the group's immediate attention. Here the patient is usually expressing anxiety, under pressure, and seeks soothing from the group and therapist. There is an incessant demand that all must hear out the patient regardless of the other problems before the group.

The recommendation of Stone and Whitman (1977) that the monopolizer be allowed to say more rather than less is appropriate in this situation. Often underlying the narcissistic patient's complaint of "the group is not good for me" or "the group doesn't understand me" is the fear that the group will not and cannot listen to the patient. Thus, the narcissistic patient mounts a premature, unwarranted offensive out of fear of potential rejection or attack. When the narcissistic patient is not assisted by the soothing responses of the group or therapist, the leader must firmly ask the patient to reflect quietly on the comments from the group and at a later time raise the issue again in the group and individual session. Otherwise, the patient may easily fall prey to becoming the group scapegoat.

Case Example

> An example of how the transference is managed in combined treatment is illustrated by the case of Sandra, a borderline patient displaying many narcissistic features. An attractive woman in her thirties, she joined the group in midcycle when two members left the group. Eager and enthusiastic, she idealized the group for the first few weeks but then rapidly became distrustful and denigrating of the group. An assertive and articulate individual, she managed to occupy much of the group's time spinning tale after tale of how she had been misunderstood and mistreated by her

hospital doctors and previous therapists. This group was different and would help her get well.

The great contrast she painted of her previous psychiatric experiences as totally bad, and the ideal and perfect picture she had of the therapy group and the therapist, repeatedly captured the attention of the group members, who puzzled at the extremes. She ignored the group's inquiries and felt attacked whenever such interventions were made. In elaborating her past to the group, she revealed how disappointed she was with her husband soon after their marriage for he failed to fulfill the expectations of the ideal man for whom she had so longed. Father had abandoned the patient and her mother for another woman when the patient was 5 years old. Consequently, for many years mother was filled with self-pity and anger over the abandonment and demanded that the patient be an appreciative and ever-present audience to hear how she had been mistreated.

It was apparent that Sandra assumed the role of her mother in the group, doing to the group what mother had done to her. The patient's annoyance and disinterest with Sandra caused her to become more anxious and soon she reported bizarre bodily preoccupations. She began to disparage the group and the leader. Because the therapist was well aware of the patient's background and dynamics from individual sessions and had a good working relationship, he was able to interpret to the patient with confirmation from the group members that Sandra was acting like her mother whenever she became overly anxious. One of Sandra's presenting symptoms had been episodes of depersonalization which occurred whenever she was overly stressed. To identify with mother meant that she repressed her own identity and thus she was safely detached and could not be attacked. Psychologically, it was mother, then, who was under siege and mother who retaliated by attacking the group. Indirectly, she had long wanted to strike back at mother and, by having the group attack her, she was fulfilling masochistically her own wishes for revenge.

The patient acknowledged that her shaky self-representation became submerged whenever she was overtaken by anxiety. Though not a true multiple personality, the patient became able to distinguish when mother was speaking and when she was allowing her self-identity to appear. The group was supportive in offering their comments about these identities as they appeared in group. It was apparent to Sandra and to the group that she had not successfully separated from mother. Her use of splitting when she was panic stricken was further confronted by the group and the therapist. The members wondered if she would feel rejected by them much as her parents had ignored her whenever she attempted to show her individuality. By having to listen to other members in the group, would she feel she was masochistically enduring the harangues of mother?

Preparation for these group confrontations and partial interpretations had been made by the therapist in the individual sessions. He then pointed out to the group that perhaps Sandra was angry and disappointed that she had to share the therapist with the other group members and this could be seen as a rejection, much as her father had deserted her in favor of someone else. Thus, the transference was interpreted first in terms of the patient's immediate response to the group, then in terms of her interactions with specific group members, and, eventually, in regard to her need for the idealizing and mirror transferences she was displaying to the leader and the group. Clarifying the patient's current material by making connections with her background, confronting her immediate behavior with the group members, and interpreting her reactions to the therapist was done gradually and consistently over the span of two years. In the beginning, however, it was necessary to confront the patient's immediate affects of overstimulation when she first joined the group and then to clarify the reasons for her anger and denigration of the group in order to keep her from becoming a group casualty.

The Group-as-a-Whole versus Individual-in-the-Group Approach

With borderline and narcissistic patients, it is suggested that the therapist treat the patient as an individual within a group rather than adhere to the group-as-a-whole construct. One should not ignore the use of appropriate and timely group interpretations. Apparent anxiety or other emotions which are experienced by most members of the group or a common shared belief or fantasy are best handled by a group-as-a-whole interpretation. If the group has a heterogeneous composition, the patients are usually at different developmental levels. Because a primary goal of therapy is to promote individuation of the patient, it follows that the group-as-a-whole approach may be inappropriate, especially where there are a significant number of borderline and narcissistic patients. Malan, Balfour, Hood, and Shooter (1976) have indicated that the strict analytic stance or Tavistock model is not useful for the category of patients we are discussing. Individuals who profit from the strictly analytic stance are those persons who exhibit exceptional insight or are highly motivated and have a special aptitude for any form of insight-oriented psychotherapy.

In the group, prolonged silences, lack of structure, indirect interpretations, and the frequent misperception of technical neutrality as a cold and arrogant attitude can play havoc with patients who have weak ego structures. A composite approach that acknowledges the curative factors of group therapy described by Yalom (1975), together with the principles in the group-centered approach advocated by Horwitz (1977b), offers a reasonable means to conduct group psychotherapy for borderline and narcissistic patients. Holistic interpretations are only made on an inductive basis and in a graded manner. The individual member's contribution is first dealt with and responded to in terms of that individual's characterological features. The therapist may then generalize from individual instances in the group and offer a comment of a group-wide nature.

The Changing Faces of the Narcissistic Patient

If one applies the DSM-III criteria, there is little difficulty in identifying a patient with a narcissistic personality disorder. Yet, individuals suffering from pathological narcissism in a less blatant form can be overlooked unless the therapist has a dynamic understanding of the concept. Using Kohut's perspective of the narcissistic character and technical approach, the therapist can provide an opportunity for the emergence of the grandiose self and foster the development of idealizing and mirror transferences if the patient possesses a narcissistic disorder. The appearance of these pathognomonic transferences confirms the presence of pathological narcissism. Viewed in this light, it may be said that many patients classified under the heading of "monopolizer," "doctor's assistant," and even "silent member" harbor narcissistic pathology. In combined therapy, and especially in the group setting, it is not unusual for the narcissistic personality to assume all these faces at some time during treatment. The monopolizer uses the opportunity to exhibit and to restore damaged self-esteem. A rebuff to such behavior from the therapist or by the group creates anxiety and increased resistance in the monopolizer. As the monopolizer's self-esteem is attacked, he experiences momentary depression, feelings of emptiness, and narcissistic trauma. Conversely, if the patient's grandiose, exhibitionistic demands strain reality or are not correctly handled, there is the propensity for overstimulation and the threat of fragmentation.

Failing to get an empathic response, the monopolizer may retreat and become a silent patient harboring primitive rage and respond only occasionally in a haughty and arrogant manner. Left unattended, such a patient may develop paranoid ideations and suspiciousness.

On the other hand, if there is a sufficiently empathic response, the patient's grandiosity may be transformed into an idealizing transference or become remobilized in the form of a mirror transference. The patient acting in the role of the doctor's assistant may show a mixture of these two pathognomonic transferences. The patient searches for the idealized external object from whom he wants support, approval, and the leadership that his own superego lacks. The patient may emulate or merge with the leader. The leader can be treated as an extension of the grandiose self. Further along in treatment, as the individual develops a more cohesive self, it is possible to point out the competitive strivings harbored by the patient toward the therapist or other members in the group. Lastly, the narcissistic patient may develop hypochondriacal complaints, drawing attention to himself not so much to exhibit as to indicate that there is a disturbance of the self shown through a disturbance in the body image. There is concern about the loss of body continuity, an estrangement between body and mind, and a pervasive state of tension. The patient is unable to verbalize the nature of the anxiety and at times attempts desperately to put into words and to rationalize the sense of disintegration of the self.

Case Example

The varying manifestations of the patient in combined treatment are illustrated through the case of Joe, an unmarried schoolteacher and part-time professional entertainer in his twenties. Joe was first seen by a urologist for unusual scrotal sensations and hypoanesthesia in the genital area. The urologist could find nothing wrong and referred him to a neurologist. No neurologic abnormalities were found and the patient was referred to psychiatric consultation. After six months in individual therapy, Joe was put in combined treatment. In the group, he acted the role of the entertainer and schoolteacher who not only could empathize with every member's problem but would provide numerous examples of his own. As the group members grew tired of his monologues and periodically interrupted him, he became increasingly irritable and resentful. He would find some reason not to show up for the next group meeting because of "a professional engagement out of town."

Upon his return to the group, he would be quiet and, when finally asked about his withdrawal, would pathetically describe the physical pain he was suffering which kept him from talking in the group. To be sure, his responses were consciously manipulative and he experienced a certain delight in making the group feel guilty for what he felt they had done to him. But he also continued to experience bizarre and distressing physical complaints during the first year of treatment and sought repeated consultations with medical specialists in the city. He had marked difficulty making any connection between the psychological problems and physical complaints.

As his symptoms subsided by the second year of treatment and he became more enamored of the group, he presented himself to friends as a successful result of therapy and would actively proselytize people for the group. During the second year of treatment, he assumed the role of the doctor's assistant. Although he did not understand the dynamics of his conflicts, he had shown a shift in growth from a brooding preoccupation of his body image to developing a more cohesive self, and was now engaged in a mirror transference with the therapist and the group.

The Group as a Transitional Object

Each group evolves its own norms and has its own personality, which determines to a great extent how successful and beneficial it will be for its members. To be sure, much depends on the knowledge and ever-evolving skills of the group therapist as well as on the composite personalities of the members of each group. Thus, we may encounter patients who have not done well with one group only to become adequate and even superior members in another. It is not unusual to find that long-standing borderline or narcissistic patients embark on an odyssey through therapy. In addition to individual treatment with several therapists, these patients may join one or more groups, especially if therapy is of a reconstructive nature.

Many practitioners who employ a combined treatment approach for narcissistic or borderline patients will engage them in individual treatment for a period far longer than the usual preparation time for group patients, carry out combined therapy, and then return them to individual treatment when the group terminates or if the patients are unsuccessful in the first group. In the event of the latter, the individual treatment is used profitably to explore the difficulties encountered by the patients in the group setting. Upon the resolution of the difficulties, these patients often return to another group and do well. A growing practice is to lengthen the intervals between individual sessions if the combined approach is used and to use the group as a transitional object to enable these patients to attain autonomy and to complete the separation–individuation process. A variation of this theme is to have patients enter a group prior to beginning individual therapy. However, with this approach, the patients may sustain narcissistic trauma without sufficient support, and unless skillfully handled, these patients may bolt the group and leave therapy completely.

Summary

Combined treatment of borderline and narcissistic patients offers two general advantages over conjoint and individual or group treatment alone. First, ego defects can be treated more effectively, and, second, compared to conjoint treatment, continuity of the treatment focus is maintained. Specific advantages of combined treatment include better management of the transference with more latitude for therapeutic distancing, deflection, and dilution required by these patients, increased opportunities for identification and internalization, the availability of the therapist to serve as a stabilizer and integrator, and greater potential to engage in intensive and reconstructive therapy.

Clinicians differ over the use of homogeneous or heterogeneous groups in regard to group composition for borderline and narcissistic patients. Homogeneous groups provide opportunities for members to traverse common ground, thus enhancing the group process and providing growth at an even pace. Heterogeneous groups permit the therapist and other group members greater tolerance and flexibility in dealing with these patients and allow for more peer support and less danger of developing destructive or nontherapeutic countertransference reactions. The use of closed-ended groups for borderline and narcissistic patients is recommended.

In combined therapy, patients are usually seen for individual psychotherapy and only later is group therapy added. The acute situation and symptoms for which patients originally sought treatment should have subsided and they should express a desire to join a group. Patients in either individual or group psychotherapy should be considered for combined treatment when treatment is at an impasse, there is heightened resistance or lack of adaptive insight, and when patients are close to termination in dyadic treatment and may benefit from a group experience. Practical considerations such as time and finances must also be taken into account.

An object relations developmental approach is recommended as the theoretical basis for the understanding and treatment of patients in combined treatment. Some treatment principles of Kernberg and Kohut are especially useful. Kernberg's suggestions on the management of the transference with borderline patients are of great value, while with higher-level narcissistic patients, Kohut's emphasis on allowing pathognomonic transferences to develop in an unimpeded fashion is highly recommended. In combined treatment, one should remember that it is usually the group that offers support and confrontation, while it is primarily the task of the therapist to provide individual and group interpretations. Numerous technical maneuvers are discussed, such as the management of the idealizing transference and the monopolizer in the group, and when to employ a group-as-a-whole versus the individual in the group approach. Finally, the many facades of the narcissistic patient and the concept of the group as a transitional object are described.

References

Adler, G., & Buie, D. H. (1979), The psychotherapeutic approach to aloneness in the borderline patient. In: *Advances in Psychotherapy of the Borderline Patient*, ed. J. LeBoit & A. Capponi. New York: Jason Aronson, pp. 433–448.

Aronson, M. L. (1964), Technical problems in combined therapy. *Internat. J. Group Psychother.*, 14:425–432.

Beran, M. (1961), Combined individual and group therapy within a hospital team set-up. *Internat. J. Group Psychother.*, 11:313–318.

Durkin, H. (1964), Discussion of symposium on combined individual and group psychotherapy. *Internat. J. Group Psychother.*, 14:444–449.

Fried, E. (1954), The effect of combined therapy on the productivity of patients. *Internat. J. Group Psychother.*, 4:42–55.

——— (1955), Combined group and individual therapy with passive narcissistic patients. *Internat. J. Group Psychother.*, 5:194–203.

Green, J. (1953), A treatment plan combining group and individual psychotherapeutic procedures in a state mental hospital. *Psychiat. Quart.*, 27:245–253.

Horner, A. J. (1975), A characterological contraindication for group psychotherapy. *J. Amer. Acad. Psychoanal.*, 3:301–305.

Horwitz, L. (1977a), Group psychotherapy of the borderline patient. In: *Borderline Personality Disorders*, ed. P. Hartocollis. New York: International Universities Press, pp. 399–422.

——— (1977b), A group-centered approach to group psychotherapy. *Internat. J. Group Psychother.*, 27:423–439.

Hulse, W. C. (1955), Transference. catharsis, insight and reality testing during concomitant individual and group psychotherapy. *Internat. J. Group Psychother.*, 5:45–53.

Kernberg, O. F. (1975), *Borderline Conditions and Pathological Narcissism*. New York: Jason Aronson.

——— (1982), The psychotherapeutic treatment of borderline personalities. In: *Psychiatry 1982 Annual Review*, ed. L. Grinspoon. Washington, DC: American Psychiatric Association Press, pp. 470–487.

Kohut, H. (1971), *The Analysis of the Self*. New York: International Universities Press.

Mahler, M. S., Pine, F., & Bergman, A. (1975), *The Psychological Birth of the Human Infant*. New York: Basic Books.

Malan, D. H., Balfour, F. H. G., Hood, V. G., & Shooter, A. (1976), Group psychotherapy: A long term follow-up study. *Arch. Gen. Psychiat.*, 3:1303–1315.

Masterson, J. F., & Rinsley, D. B. (1975), The borderline syndrome: The role

of the mother in the genesis and psychic structure of the borderline personality. *Internat. J. Psycho-Anal.*, 56:163–177.
Modell, A. H. (1968), *Object Love and Reality*. New York: International Universities Press.
Ornstein, P. H. (1982), On the psychoanalytic psychotherapy of primary self pathology. In: *Psychiatry 1982 Annual Review*, ed. L. Grinspoon. Washington, DC: American Psychiatric Association Press, pp. 498–510.
Papanek, H. (1956), Combined group and individual therapy in the light of Adlerian psychology. *Internat. J. Group Psychother.*, 6:136–146.
Racker, H. (1957), The meanings and use of countertransference. *Psychoanal. Quart.*, 26:303–357.
Rinsley, D. B. (1978), Borderline psychopathology: A review of aetiology, dynamics, and treatment. *Internat. Rev. Psycho-anal.*, 5/1:45–54.
Roth, B. E. (1980), Understanding the development of a homogeneous, identity-impaired group through countertransference phenomena. *Internat. J. Group Psychother.*, 30:405–426.
Sager, C. (1960), Concurrent individual and group analytic psychotherapy. *Amer. J. Orthopsychiat.*, 30:225–241.
Schecter, D. E. (1959), Integration of group therapy with individual psychoanalysis. *Psychiat.*, 22:267–276.
Scheidlinger, S., & Porter, K. (1980), Group therapy combined with individual psychotherapy. In: *Specialized Techniques in Individual Psychotherapy*, ed. T. B. Karasu & L. Bellak. New York: Brunner/Mazel, p. 426.
Slavinska-Holy, N. (1977), A schematic approach in psychoanalytic treatment of borderline and narcissistic patients in homogeneous groups. Paper presented at the Annual Meeting, American Group Psychotherapy Association, San Francisco. February.
Spotnitz, H. (1957), The borderline schizophrenic in group psychotherapy: the importance of individuation. *Internat. J. Group Psychother.*, 7:155–174.
Stone, W. N., & Whitman, R. M. (1977), Contributions of the psychology of the self to group process and group therapy. *Internat. J. Group Psychother.*, 24:343–359.
Sullivan, H. S. (1953), *The Interpersonal Theory of Psychiatry*, ed. H. S. Perry & M. L. Gawel. New York: W. W. Norton.
Tabachnick, N. (1965), Isolation, transference-splitting and combined therapy. *Compr. Psychiat.*, 6:336–346.
Wilder, J. (1974), Group analysis and the insights of the analyst. In: *The Challenge for Group Psychotherapy—Present and Future*, ed. S. De Schill. New York: International Universities Press.
Wolberg, A. (1960), The psychoanalytic treatment of the borderline patient in the individual and group setting. *Topic. Probl. Psychother.*, 2:174–197.
Wolf, A. (1974), Psychoanalysis in groups. In: *Challenge for Group Psychotherapy—Present and Future*, ed. S. De Schill. New York: International Universities Press.
Yalom, I. D. (1975), *The Theory and Practice of Group Psychotherapy*, 2nd ed. New York: Basic Books.

Chapter 3

PSYCHOANALYTIC THERAPY OF DEVELOPMENTAL ARRESTS

FRANK M. LACHMANN, Ph.D.

Developmental arrests refer to deficits in the formation of psychic structure; specifically, to psychopathology that reflects a defective sense of self. The psychoanalytic therapy of such pathology will be illustrated through the presentation of two clinical vignettes. In the first, the activation of merger fantasies in a selfobject transference are exemplified; in the second, the therapeutic acknowledgment of a developmental advance toward increased self-consolidation is described.

Before turning to the case material, I would like to comment on the distinction between pathology that appears to follow the traditional psychoanalytic model in which unconscious sexual and aggressive wishes are in conflict, and pathology that directly reflects a defective sense of self, an arrest in development.

A previous work (Stolorow and Lachmann, 1980) addressed the importance for psychoanalytic treatment of the distinction between psychopathology in which structural defects predominate and similar appearing psychopathology which reflects psychic conflict. Illustrated here was the crucial difference for framing therapeutic interventions that are a consequence of holding this distinction. In addressing psychic conflict, the analyst interprets that which the patient is attempting to ward off. In addressing developmental arrests, the analyst interprets

---

An earlier version of this chapter was presented at the symposium on Developments in the Theory and Therapy of Narcissistic and Borderline Personalities at the 1981 annual meeting of the American Orthopsychiatric Association in New York. An expanded version of this chapter appears in Silverman, Lachmann, and Milich (1982).

that which the patient is attempting to maintain or attain. Any patient's productions may at one point in the treatment be more accurately understood as reflecting deficits in structure formation and at another point in treatment be better understood as a subjectively experienced conflict. This distinction can be applied to the patient–therapist relationship (Stolorow and Lachmann, 1984/1985) in that transferences may reflect an attempt to establish and maintain a self–selfobject bond as well as embody an object relationship. These two transference currents have been described as comprising a figure and ground with one or the other occupying the figure against the background of the other.

For those patients whose predominant psychopathology is best characterized as reflecting developmental arrests, early developmental phases have not been traversed with sufficient success, which results in a precariously organized sense of self. Consequently, others, including the analyst, are not predominantly experienced as separate persons, but experienced predominantly as archaic selfobjects. Rather than being experienced as a "repository" for early conflicts, the analyst is "used" to restore a precarious sense of self (Stolorow and Lachmann, 1980).

In drawing the distinction between psychopathology and transferences that are based on structural conflict and/or developmental arrest, it is not suggested that each of these is manifested by a distinct kind of patient. These pathologies and transferences are not mutually exclusive. While there may be patients with whom the analyst can focus exclusively on either structural conflict or developmental arrests, there is a larger group whose treatment must focus on both issues. Often the psychoanalytic clinician must move back and forth from one focus to the other, sometimes even within the same session, depending upon what is subjectively salient for the patient.

Kohut (1984) has postulated that self pathology underlies all pathology. According to him sexual and aggressive wishes can eventuate in a variety of conflicts but such conflicts do not necessarily produce psychopathology. Only when self pathology underlies such conflicts is the outcome psychopathological conflict. Kohut thus conceptualizes self psychology as a superordinate theory. However, this conceptualization should not be misinterpreted to mean that the subjectively experienced conflicts of patients are to be bypassed. The analyst is obliged to address whatever is clinically salient in the patient's productions. Holding the position that self pathology is theoretically superordinate does not alter the requirement that the analyst respond to what is clinically salient, or at the moment experientially superordinate, for the patient. The present discussion will address only the level of clinical theory (Waelder, 1962), what is clinically salient for the patient, in describing the therapeutic interventions appropriate for structural conflicts and structural deficits.

The locus of the deficits have been described (Stolorow and Lachmann, 1980) as residing in the development of self and object representations, specifically in "the differentiation of subjective separation of self representations from representations of primary objects, principally the mother" and in the ability "to integrate or synthesize (self or object) representations with contrasting affective colorations" (pp. 3–4). This is a developmental task to which many factors contribute. Clearly though, the earliest phases of development can be viewed as crucial in furthering this structural development. Failure to experience one's mother as an adequately empathic, mirroring selfobject and failure to experience one's father as an idealized selfobject who accepts one's wish to merge with his valued qualities and strengths (Kohut, 1971, 1977) is at the base of a developmental arrest. Treatment requires that the analyst (1) accept the patient's need to use the analyst as a selfobject and not interfere with the establishment by the patient of a stable selfobject transference; (2) respond empathically and interpretively to inevitable ruptures in that transference so that its stability can be reestablished; and (3) explore the roots of the patient's structural vulnerabilities and restorative attempts.

The analyst's "empathic response" (Silverman, Lachmann, and Milich, 1982) comprises the expression of understanding, acceptance, and willingness to help, specifically focused on what is troubling the patient at the moment. Articulating this understanding to the patient is in itself therapeutic. It gives rise to an experience of satisfaction of symbioticlike needs in the patient. Through this response, which has been described by Winnicott (1965), Kohut (1971, 1977), Modell (1976), Stolorow and Lachmann (1980), and others, the patient is likely to experience the analyst as a requisite selfobject, without the analyst stepping outside the bounds of the analytic role. The following clinical vignette illustrates this point.

Case 1: Merger Fantasies in a Selfobject Transference

Helen,[1] a 31-year-old woman, entered psychoanalytic therapy because of difficulties in maintaining relationships with men. The patient's mother, in part because of her own psychopathology, and in part because of situational pressures, had been unable to provide her daughter with requisite responsiveness during long stretches of her infancy. Helen was the first-born child and within a very brief period of time three siblings followed. Soon after the birth of his children, her father developed a chronic illness, which added to Helen's difficulties in obtaining adequate mothering. In fact, as the oldest child, Helen had become a caretaker herself, in compliance with her mother's needs. By gradually developing a characterological self-sufficiency, she found ways to please her mother and to disavow her unfulfilled longings.

By the third year of her analysis, a good deal of time had been spent analyzing Helen's self-sufficiency. These efforts were successful in that, for the first time in her adult life, she began to experience the very yearnings that for so long had been disavowed. Evidence of their existence could be inferred from her complaints about her boyfriends. Understandably, these longings now found direct expression in the transference, with Helen voicing a desire to hold her analyst's hand. It soon became evident, however, that what was involved was more than a "wish." For what was at first a simple expression of desire soon turned into a desperate demand.

Helen announced that she would not continue treatment unless I allowed her to hold my hand while she lay on the couch. If I did not allow this, she would feel weak and vulnerable. For Helen, at that point in treatment, I was experienced as an idealized selfobject with whom she needed to merge in order to main-

---

[1]The case of Helen is described in greater detail in Silverman, Lachmann, and Milich (1982, pp. 205–212).

tain a sense of self-cohesion. Apparently, her previous characterological self-sufficiency, linked as it was to underlying grandiose fantasies, served to mask her "self-vulnerability." When her self-sufficiency gave way in analysis, longings to merge with an idealized selfobject as well as her vulnerability came forth.

Helen's awareness of her vulnerability intensified her need for the analyst as a selfobject, a need that became concretized in her demand that he hold her hand. At the time this demand was made, Helen could take no distance from it. She had, in effect, issued an ultimatum: "Do as I ask or I will have to find a new analyst—one who will permit me to merge, who will function as the idealized selfobject I need, and who will enable me to reestablish self-cohesion, rather than one who demonstrates his difference and separateness from me and thereby promotes my self-fragmentation." How might an analyst respond under these circumstances? Let us consider several possibilities.

First, one could remain silent, a frequent response during psychoanalytic treatment. With Helen, and in the situation described, silence would have been inappropriate. If the understanding of Helen's central motive was correct, such a response would have constituted a traumatic rupture of empathy. For, as the material had been formulated and understood, Helen's unusual demand was most importantly a response to the emergence of her precarious sense of self. Desperately she attempted to maintain a sense of cohesion by concretizing the functions she needed the analyst to provide for her (Atwood and Stolorow, 1984). To remain silent would have been to completely ignore the archaic longings that motivated Helen's behavior and Her sense of desperation. In fact, Helen's subsequent associations indicated that silence would have intensified the therapeutic stalemate, in that it would have repeated the unresponsive behavior of her mother, which had played an important role in creating the very problem that Helen needed to resolve in her treatment.

Other responses addressing other motives underlying her demand would have been equally inappropriate. For example, one supervisee, under comparable circumstances, commented to her patient, "You are making excessive demands on me, as you do on others. No wonder you are so often rebuffed and rejected by people." In a similar situation, another supervisee said, "Let us look at what you are trying to do to me by making this demand. You are trying to control me." Both of these interpretations were certainly plausible. They referred to motives that could be inferred from the patient's productions and they would even have been accepted, albeit painfully, by the patient. Yet these interventions would be off the mark both in their timing and with respect to their accuracy in recognizing salient themes. Both interventions would have addressed the behavioral consequences of the patient's developmentally arrested configuration, rather than her self pathology and the emergence of her vulnerability which deserved priority. Of course, both of those interventions can also be faulted because they have a pejorative ring to them. They may provoke a feeling of having been criticized, which, in turn, may suppress subsequent demanding behavior rather than opening it for further exploration and understanding. The patient becomes alerted to the emergence of such behavior and censors it before it gains expression. These suppressive attempts are often rationalized by therapists as "only voicing reality." Such interventions may even be successful at getting rid of certain behaviors, but the psychological state that produced the behaviors may still remain active and take its toll in other ways.

In response to Helen's "demand," the therapist might call her attention to the displacement of feelings from figures of her past onto the analyst: "You are reacting to me as if I were your mother (or father)." To be able to work with this interpretation, at that moment Helen must have available to her the capacity to take some distance from her immediate experience and contemplate its origins; but this is not always possible. The urgency of Helen's demand mirrored the hold that her psychological state had on her. The reality of her experience was such that, at least for the moment, self-reflection could not be counted on.

In this circumstance, an intervention is needed that provides the patient with some relief for her threatened sense of self. From an empathic vantage point, a response is required that conveys: (1) an understanding of the patient's precarious sense of self; (2) recognition of her need to feel connected to the analyst as an idealized selfobject; (3) acceptance of the demand without fulfilling it; (4) encouragement for further exploration.

In response to Helen's demand that I hold her hand, I commented to Helen that she was on the horns of a dilemma. If I did not give her my hand, she would feel rebuffed and hurt; if I did, I might be doing her a disservice. We would be enacting "something" that, at present, was not understood. In response to this intervention, Helen calmed down considerably and commented, "You know, I'm acting as though I've known you all my life."

With these words, Helen's capacity for self-reflection temporarily had been rescued from its domination by the urgency of her need to restore her damaged sense of self. Psychoanalytic exploration could then continue. Helen then reported for the first time in the analysis an incident which she placed at about the age of 2. She described a scene in which she screamed in her crib for her mother for so long that finally no sound could come out. Her mother never came.

How might we understand the preceding course of events? The analysis of Helen's self-sufficiency had revealed the vulnerability of her self-structure, and her disappointment at her mother's failure to respond to her when she screamed. Neither could her father, already ill at the time, provide for her the requisite source of strength. Holding the analyst's hand meant to her (in part) access to or merger with a source of strength, which would provide her with the sense of wholeness that she needed to function. The analyst would be there "at hand" in a way that her mother was not. Merging with the idealized analyst then would have enabled Helen to repair her sense of vulnerability. Putting her self-sufficiency under analytic scrutiny had exposed its defensive role and had also undercut her fantasy of merger. Helen's self-vulnerability was revived with its associated image of the disappointing mother. The demand that the analyst give her his hand can be understood as Helen's attempt to revive a oneness fantasy (Silverman, Lachmann, and Milich, 1982) in a concrete, drastic, and urgent form and to restore self-cohesion.

In response to the analyst's intervention, Helen felt less precarious. She was able to experience him again as an idealized selfobject. Her sense of self was bolstered, and the analysis continued with the emergence of her early memory of feeling abandoned by her mother.

In subsequent sessions, further material emerged that helped Helen work through the feelings stirred up by this memory. For instance, she said, "I was caught up in a gust of feeling. I couldn't help myself. I just now had a fantasy about getting up and walking around. I wanted to go to the window." This was an allusion to suicidal thoughts that had plagued Helen prior to entering treatment. The meaning of these thoughts, as discussed previously in her analysis, centered on how she would only feel separate from her mother if she, Helen, were dead. But now another meaning emerged: She would "disappear," thus abandoning her mother and reversing the roles in the early trauma.

Her wish for oneness with her mother was revived again in the transference. Helen continued: "I thought you would get apprehensive and then I cut the fantasy off." Questioned about her concern over the analyst's apprehension, Helen responded with a tone of disappointment: "You're not going to get apprehensive, you know better."

The analysis focused on Helen's dilemma of wanting to reinstate a feeling of merger, that she and her analyst shared a common characteristic, a feeling of apprehension, on the one hand but, on the other hand, her distressful recognition that they were different. Hence, she felt disappointed in that her wish could not be realized. I said to Helen, "That bothers you. While you are caught on the gust of feelings, I may not be." This was intended as an acknowledgement of a dawning phase-appropriate differentiation and self-consolidation. Nevertheless, Helen became visibly upset and said, "I don't like the whole idea. I don't like to admit it's so. I've always had a thing about feeling that I'm involved with something that nobody else is involved in." Helen later continued in pain and rage, ostensibly talking about her boyfriend, but clearly alluding to her analyst as well: "I give, give, give, and give, and all I get back is nonfeeling."

She began the next session by expressing her apprehension: "There's not one safe topic I can plunge into. I guess I'm becoming afraid of you. I was thinking, don't you ever get afraid? Are you ever afraid of your feelings or afraid of what I might say?" Though she was angry, the therapeutic relationship was not in jeopardy. I could address one aspect of what she was conveying: "You want to be sure I won't be scared so that you will be safe."

But Helen's remarks were expressing an additional meaning that now became clear: "I feel frightened and I expect it to frighten you, too. I want you to be afraid also. That means you are human. A part of me wants you to be close and that you and I should have similar emotions. But another part wants you to stand aside."

I responded to Helen: "You have wanted very much to feel that we are one, but you're now ready to also let me stand aside." She responded, "I guess that's good enough for now."

The analysis continued and Helen was helped to understand the history of the developmentally arrested configurations. The analyst facilitated this by accepting the role of an idealized selfobject, which made possible the unfolding of the patient's arrested development.

The vignette from the treatment of Helen has illustrated how the analysis of a character trait (i.e., self-sufficiency) as defensive and as self-maintaining promoted, ruptured, and then reinstated a selfobject transference, which in turn, led to the recovery of significant childhood memories and the firming and articulation of a budding sense of self-cohesion.

The clinician engaged in psychoanalytic treatment can assist a patient in establishing or maintaining a greater degree of self-cohesion in three ways. First, the use of the empathic vantage point focuses analytic attention on the nuances of the patient's subjective state, and in and of itself provides some measure of necessary satisfaction which strengthens the patient's self-cohesion. This, in turn, helps maintain a stable selfobject transference. In addition, by resisting the patient's overtures for more direct transferential enactments (hand-holding in Helen's case), the therapist lessens the possibility that the patient will become threatened by the loss of her sense of self.

Second, in the rare instance where a patient responds to even an empathic response with anxiety over a loss of sense of self, the analyst can explore with the patient both the nature of the anxiety and what it was in the treatment situation that triggered this anxiety.

Third, when a patient shows signs—often tentative and fraught with anxiety—of moving toward a more complex, enhanced, or mature self-organization, the analyst can affirm this effort, as the following case vignette illustrates.

Case 2: Therapeutic Acknowledgment of a Developmental Advance

Anita[2] established a selfobject transference of the idealizing type when she entered treatment at age 37 after two earlier analytic experiences. She sought help because of rapid and unpredictable fluctuations in both her self-esteem and in her evaluation of certain people in her life. She alternated between viewing herself in various devalued ways and as "unassailable," while her hus-

---

[2]The case of Anita is described in greater detail in Lachmann and Stolorow (1980) and Silverman, Lachmann, and Milich (1982).

band and certain friends were described alternately with contempt and with awe. When she viewed them with awe, she would describe feeling enthralled by their patience, wisdom, and capacity to make their own way in the world. So long as Anita viewed these people with reverence, she felt connected to them and valued herself. Quite clearly, they were selfobjects for her and their minute empathic failures severed her connection with them, or, put differently, made inoperative their vitally necessary self-esteem maintaining function for her.

During the third year of treatment, Anita showed signs of having established a firm, idealizing transference, whereby her developmental deficits had been sufficiently worked through so that the analysis now focused predominantly on her conflicted concerns. Her prior and pervasive states of deadness of depletion were no longer salient. In one session, Anita spoke of an acquaintance from her past who, by chance, was referred to "her" analyst. She became preoccupied with fantasies that "her" analyst would prefer the acquaintance to her. But, concurrently, she described the acquaintance in the most derogatory terms as a shallow person, who substituted sentimentality for feelings and talked endlessly about inconsequential things. Anita was convinced that this description was accurate and thus wondered how she could imagine that this woman could be preferred to her. Over the next several sessions the following interpretation presented here in summary form was offered to Anita: "When you start to question that I would prefer Mary (the acquaintance) to you, you are in effect saying that you feel that you have a place here and that you feel accepted by me. But to feel accepted seems to have a disorganizing effect on you. You avoid the disorganization by asserting your expectation of rejection."

Anita's response, again in summary form, was, "When you say something right, I have mixed feelings. I feel 'thank God' you understand, but I also envy your ability to connect with people." Further inquiry highlighted the novelty, to Anita, of her envy of the analyst. A developmental advance could now be affirmed, and I commented to Anita that she now felt a sense of parity with me. Anita added that she could even imagine leaving me without becoming disorganized.

Anita's envy was understood and underscored as a development from an archaic selfobject transference to a transference in which the analyst was also acknowledged as a separately organized person. Her words *thank God* may have reflected the remainder of the idealizing transference, in which awe and reverence were partially retained. However, the introduction of envy added a new dimension of differentiation, in that the analyst was now viewed as the possessor of a quality that she currently lacked but obviously imagined she would acquire.

The acknowledgment of the developmental advance illustrated in the treatment of Anita was understood as therapeutically crucial. In so acknowledging the advance, the idealizing selfobject transference was maintained and could become the basis for continuing structuralization and development. Or, put differently, not acknowledging this advance would have constituted an empathic failure, a rupture in the self-selfobject bond which had been so carefully established. Though such ruptures, when recognized, can then become therapeutically valuable, when unrecognized and when their effects remain undiscovered, they can revive the arrested configurations. In turn, self pathology, as manifested in the rapid fluctuations in self-esteem, may recur.

To help a patient achieve a greater sense of self-consolidation implies neither the renunciation of symbioticlike longings nor outgrowing ones needed for selfobjects. Symbioticlike longings and a sense of psychological separateness need not be incompatible. In fact, it is suggested that these are lifelong ever-present currents. A defining characteristic of the psychologically healthy person may well be comfort with both an ability to seek oneness or merger with idealized selfobjects and a sense of psychological separateness in ways that do not interfere with each other.

Conclusion

Empathic responses and affirmations of developmental advances for patients with developmental arrests in no way argues against the importance of understanding and interpreting psychic conflicts when these are experienced by these patients. A defining characteristic of effective psychoanalytic treatment is its recognition, understanding, and interpretation to the patient of both arrested and conflictual representational configurations.

References

Atwood, G., & Stolorow, R. (1984), *Structures of Subjectivity: Explorations in Psychoanalytic Phenomenology*. Hillsdale, NJ: The Analytic Press.
Kohut, H. (1971), *The Analysis of the Self*. New York: International Universities Press.
―――― (1977), *The Restoration of the Self*. New York: International Universities Press.
―――― (1984), *How Does Analysis Cure?* Chicago: University of Chicago Press.
Lachmann, F., & Stolorow, R. (1980), The developmental significance of affective states: implications for psychoanalytic treatment. In: *The Annual of Psychoanalysis*, Vol. 8, ed. The Chicago Institute for Psychoanalysis. New York: International Universities Press, pp. 215–229.
Modell, A. (1976), The holding environment and the therapeutic action of psychoanalysis. *J. Amer. Psychoanal. Assn.*, 24: 285–308.
Silverman, L., Lachmann, F., & Milich, R. (1982), *The Search for Oneness*. New York: International Universities Press.
Stolorow, R., & Lachmann, F. (1980), *The Psychoanalysis of Developmental Arrests: Theory and Treatment*. New York: International Universities Press.
―――― ―――― (1984/1985), Transference: The future of an illusion. In: *The Annual of Psychoanalysis*, Vol. 12/13, ed. The Chicago Institute of Psychoanalysis. New York: International Universities Press, pp. 16–38.
Waelder, R. (1962), Psychoanalysis, scientific method and philosophy. *J. Amer. Psychoanal. Assn.*, 10:617–637.
Winnicott, D. (1965), *The Maturational Process and the Facilitating Environment*. New York: International Universities Press.

Chapter 4

SOME CONTRIBUTIONS OF SELF PSYCHOLOGY TO THE TREATMENT OF BORDERLINE AND SCHIZOPHRENIC PATIENTS

Barry Magid, M.D.

This chapter will illustrate the extension of the concepts of self psychology to the treatment of severely ill patients not ordinarily considered analyzable. I will draw on work done both with patients seen in a private practice setting and others from a state hospital day treatment program to indicate the wide range of applicability of these ideas.

Self psychology (Kohut, 1977, 1984) has added a number of metapsychological concepts which lead to understandings of pathology and subsequent interventions quite different from those dictated by ego psychology or drive-based analytic models on the one hand, or behaviorally oriented models on the other.

The first of these is the placing of the self in a metapsychologically supraordinate position over the structural tripartite model of ego, superego, and id. The primary developmental task is the development of a cohesive self in an empathic environment which permits the child to participate fully in phase appropriate mirroring and idealizing relationships with the parents. Very early empathic failures lead to a chronically enfeebled self and a tendency to fragmentation. A gross inability to spontaneously reinstate developmentally arrested needs in the form of a mirror or idealizing transference differentiates the borderline and psychotic states from the narcissistic personality and behavior disorders. Empathic failures later in childhood, during a normal oedipal phase, cause the pathological oedipal complex which manifests in an otherwise reasonably coherent self as the seemingly drive- and conflict-centered symptoms of the neuroses. I have attempted to extrapolate from Kohut's formulations about the psychoanalytic treatment of narcissistic characters in the formation of the treatment principles which follow.

Of foremost importance is the promotion of self-cohesion by the enhancement of embryonic experiences of a developing self amid the more predominant experiences of fragmentation. It is crucial to note that this does not correspond to earlier concepts of strengthening the ego, particularly those that attempt to correct distortions in reality brought about by the patient's symptomatology or the transference. Self-cohesion, as Kohut has shown, is more readily promoted by interpretations which focus on, clarify, and acknowledge the subjective internal experience of the patient. While these latter attempts at "reality testing" may offer temporary corrections for the patient's misconceptions, they may also ultimately convey the analyst's inability to accept the patient's experience, and emerging self, as is, and therefore lead to increased self-hate and fragmentation, and not to increased ego strength as might be intended.

Treatment Principles: Self Cohesion and Empathic Acknowledgement

Focusing attention and directing our questions and interpretations to clarifying and acknowledging the patient's inner experience may in fact require the therapist, and the structure of the treatment setting itself, to tolerate, often for long periods, seemingly "crazy" behavior. Arrested needs for normal exhibitionistic mirroring and/or idealization, initially may be inseparable from delusional ideas and acting-out behaviors, which carry within them rudimentary, but still microstructure building, selfobject transferences. Interventions in the service of reality testing interrupt these behaviors and will be counterproductive insofar as they prevent the enhancement of a cohesive self experience. Improved self cohesion is seen as the sine qua non of improved ego functioning, not as resulting from it. Thus, the therapist does not focus on the pathology to correct the reality distortions, but rather focuses on whatever is the expression of health in the patient, whatever shows, even in a minor way, the momentary experience of "I know this," or "This is me."

Learning to recognize and value such moments may be a long and difficult process for a beginning therapist. Diane Shainberg (1983) has demonstrated the significant countertransferential, as well as didactic difficulties that arise when therapists attempt this basic alteration of their therapeutic stance. For many therapists, the focus on the correction of reality distortions is the essence of their professional self-image as objective observer and helper. Therapists under my supervision have often experienced intense anxiety and have shown great reluctance to relinquish this definition of their role.

Another consequence of this approach is that the content of the therapy need not seem to focus on dynamically "significant" material. For instance, a current events group that allows a severely disturbed patient to describe something he's seen on TV, even if mixed with a variety of delusional ideas, can significantly enhance his sense of self, in being able to say "I know this," being heard by others, and hearing their acknowledgement and appreciation of his knowing. In a small way, arrested needs for exhibitionistic display and responsive mirroring are being mobilized. Even though he is unable to mobilize the coherent transference of the analyzable patient, a moment like this may be said to embody a "microtransference" that both forms the nidus of more coherent relationships in the future, and offers structure building and fragmentation reducing opportunities in the present.

The Interpretation of Strong Affects

This leads us to consider further the role of exploring "significant" material, and the mobilization of strong affects. Many therapists in our day hospital treatment facility implicitly followed a model which encouraged patients to "express their feelings." Presumably based on concepts of repression and unconscious conflict, the patient in this model is seen as needing to channel previously unacknowledged libidinal and aggressive wishes into an appropriately sublimated verbal expression, there to be exposed to increased ego control, often with the temporary "auxiliary ego" support of the therapist or group. Other therapists followed a more explicitly cathartic approach, in which release of strong affect was a goal in itself (usually only within circumscribed limits, however, otherwise it could be considered acting out).

Self psychology offers a markedly different approach to affects. Anger, especially destructive rage, is always viewed as secondary to narcissistic injury. The therapeutic task is therefore first an interpretive reconstruction of the circumstances leading to the injury, including any unexpressed and, often with these patients, magical or delusional expectation which was frustrated, and second an acknowledgement of the validity of the injury, given the patient's subjective reality. Expression of anger is seen neither as an end in itself nor as a necessary component of primitive transference relationships. What has been considered the mobilization of a therapeutically necessary negative transference (Kernberg, 1975) is from the perspective of self psychology an often iatrogenically harmful diversion from the patient's real needs to form positive relationships.

Interpreting the patient's need to destroy, belittle, or render ineffective the analyst or the treatment misses the point of the underlying wish for a perfectly responsive empathic relationship which, from the patient's point of view, is constantly and unfairly being denied him, provoking his incohoate anger and leading to increasing fragmentation. The wish for a trustworthy, nonretaliatory selfobject connection may be most strongly repressed and defended against to avoid repeated narcissistic injury. The legitimacy of this guardedness must be acknowledged. This may even take the form of joining the patient in his resentment about how unfairly life has treated him, and specifically avoiding interpreting the reality distortions this entails. Negative transference manifestations may thus also be treated as necessary defensive positions that the patient must be permitted to maintain until resistances to a positive transference can be worked through.

Because these patients perceive their needs to have been

chronically misunderstood and neglected, within any given session there will inevitably appear frustrated, hostile comments about the world in general and the analyst in particular. Indeed, for borderline patients this chronic anger threatens to submerge all other feelings. When a particular frustrated underlying wish is accessible, it should be explored. However, often other trends may be apparent in the same material; that is, the tentative beginnings of other exhibitionistic or idealizing wishes not directly related to the manifested anger. (For instance, in the midst of a long, complaining, hypochondriacal rumination, a woman patient mentioned in passing that she had bought herself a new dress for the first time in a year.) These are both fresher and more fragile areas for the patient than their anger and we should address our inquiry gently in their direction when we recognize them. Although eventually we will also want to explore the sources of the anger, we must realize anger can be a nonproductive, stereotyped response for these patients, and that positive feelings—which put the patient in a subjectively more vulnerable position—may be resisted by this repetitive focus on their own anger.

Kohut (1977) pointed out that an enfeebled, fragmented self may defensively attempt to stimulate itself into a temporary state of increased aliveness through the expression of strong affect. While this may be a necessary defense for patients plagued with a chronic sense of deadness or emptiness, it contributes nothing to true structural change or development. A therapist may proceed practically indefinitely to encourage such patients to "let out their feelings" under the belief that he is uncovering more and more hitherto unconscious and repressed material, when, in fact, he is merely encouraging defensive self-stimulation, whose momentary excitement may be addicting to the therapist as well as the patient.

For patients with powerful anxious feelings as part of the chief complaint, some specific new approaches may be indicated. Many patients harbor idealistic or grandiose ideas of how their internal state should function. For them, any anxious feeling becomes evidence of their failure to live up to their expectations. The essential interpretive work may be first to uncover the grandiose ideas underlying such a patient's unconscious inability to tolerate himself as anyone other than a superman who should never suffer. Conversely, patients may privately harbor notions of a special internal damage indicated by the presence of the anxiety which corresponds inversely to their grandiose self-image. For example, one patient I will discuss had a recurrent fear that his anxiety resulted from being brain damaged by LSD. These patients make desperate attempts to suppress or escape their anxiety, the mere presence of which (beyond the discomfort of the feeling itself) is a severe narcissistic injury, and a vicious circle ensues. The experience of anxiety activates attempts at greater self-control, which when unsuccessful lead to increased self-reproach, impaired self-esteem, and diminished capacity to further tolerate the anxiety. The subjective anxious feeling thus mounts as the paradoxical manifestation of the desire to be under complete self-control, beyond all anxiety. It is necessary for such patients to learn to tolerate themselves as someone who feels anxiety, and not repeatedly have their self-images destroyed by its presence. It is the therapist's seemingly paradoxical task not to relieve the anxiety but to persuade or allow the patient to remain in it. Leaving the anxiety as is may be the only way to defuse the further generation of anxiety by escalating failures to subdue it.

Nonetheless when anxiety is not manageable by interpretative means, it may be so destructive to self-stability that it should be ameliorated with medication. This is particularly the case with borderline patients who suffer from recurrent panic states. In panic, the anxiety is no longer merely symptomatic of the chronic fragmentation, but, whatever the external trigger, becomes the source of even further fragmentation. The self and the defenses cannot contain it and there is no agency in the patient that can explore or understand interpretations of it.

I have found low doses of major tranquilizers (e.g., Trilafon 2–4 mg once or twice a day) often quite helpful to these patients. Occasionally I will recommend that a patient prone to such attacks take a small maintenance dose to help increase his threshold for handling anxiety. I may explain that they have the choice of using medication, either as needed, or prophylactically, to "help reduce the background noise," I might say, to allow the analysis to proceed more smoothly.

Relief of very severe anxiety by medication does not remove it from the arena of analyzability. Rather, it allows the anxiety to be experienced in a manageable way, precisely so that its origins may be analyzable, instead of it massively overwhelming the analytic capabilities of the patient.

Clinical Material

Three widely differing cases will be used to illustrate these ideas. The first is that of a reasonably well-functioning, though deeply unhappy graduate student in music whom I saw three times a week in my private practice. The second, a schizophrenic man, initially psychotic, but able to generally function in a stable, if limited fashion, whom I saw privately once a week; and the third, a mildly retarded unemployable adolescent treated under my supervision in the day treatment program of a state hospital, who had been hospitalized repeatedly for violent and psychotic behavior.

Case 1

The first patient, Mark, was a 30-year-old man who came to treatment ostensibly seeking medication for relief of severe anxiety attacks. He presented with many prominent borderline features. These included a history of chaotic homosexual relationships that had twice gotten him in trouble with the law. He suffered from pervasive chronic anxiety and periods of intense self-doubt and self-loathing. He harbored a long-standing, almost delusional, concern that his present suffering was the result of brain damage caused by an LSD trip many years previously. His manner with me was alternately angry, suspicious, demanding, and pleading. He was unable to arrive on time for any appointment and could not commit himself to seeing me regularly. He had ongoing consultations for the same symptoms with both a homeopathic physician and another analyst during the initial months of our relationship. My approach throughout this period was to empathize with his inability to trust me, as he had not been helped successfully in the past. I said I thought his internal confusion was so great that I didn't expect him to necessarily arrive on time or keep a regular treatment hour, but he had to do things in his own way and I would accommodate myself to him to the extent possible. This patient required, I believe, that I enact my acknowledgement of his intense distress by essentially "letting him win" certain significant arguments over whether he owed me fees for some missed sessions. Verbal acknowledgements and interpretations about the need for him to be sure I understood, to be sure he had made his point, which typically suffice with nonborderline analysands, were insufficient for him. "Winning" a few such arguments markedly increased his trust in me, and made him far more receptive to subsequent interpretations.

I never suggested he make any final choice between me and the other physicians. He reported that the homeopathic physician regularly urged him to give up on all therapy and trust himself to his drug treatment. Most of his early sessions he filled with descriptions of his anguish and anger. One interpretation I made finally proved decisive. He had been talking angrily about his homosexual lover and then about an older woman who lived in his building and with whom he had his first heterosexual experience immediately after breaking up with the male lover. He described how he wanted to go out to dinner on his 30th birthday with her and two other friends. He began to speak angrily of how they spoiled everything. I asked how it was spoiled. He momentarily stopped being angry and then described how he wanted to arrive at the restaurant, confirm his reservation with the maitre d', and be led grandly to his table. He did not speak of this scenario to anyone. The woman inadvertently arrived first and was already seated when he arrived. He was so enraged, he never spoke to her again or explained what happened. It was here I ventured to suggest how nice it would have been to have it all go the way he wanted, and what a shame it was that it had not. At this he became tearful and was able to talk about his wish to show off in front of his friends and his desire to be somebody important in the world. This interchange was crucial in that for the first time he allowed himself to expose vulnerably his desires for appreciation and his frustrated exhibitionism. His anger and subsequent increased sexual confusion could now be seen as a secondary reaction to his disappointment, which became a model for understanding a variety of disappointments and his reactions both in the present and in childhood. The inappropriate and grandiose expectations that everyone in the restaurant would magically know what he wanted were not interpreted. Subjectively they were the only valid form his arrested need for the mirroring of his grandiose self could take at this time. It was his frustrated exhibitionism that needed to be acknowledged, not the inappropriateness of its current vehicle.

He now was ready to commit himself to a more regular treatment with me. The "splitting" involved in his seeing multiple therapists was thus spontaneously resolved without interpretation when I was able to acknowledge his needs empathically. I do not think he had hostilely played one therapist off against the other or needed to diminish any of us or violate the rules of treatment. Rather, his fragmented self could only form fragmented, chaotic relationships. When a measure of self-cohesion was promoted by my empathically guided responsiveness, less fragmentation was manifested both in terms of symptoms and in relationships.

He was now able to exhibit, at first tentatively, then with more overt grandiosity, his fantasies about his special musical genius. In particular, he revealed a strong, secret identification with Mozart. It was important to him that I seemed to share his narcissistic glee about his fantasized uniqueness and not challenge him about its reality. Gradually we looked together at the injustices the world was perpetrating on his genius. The New Mozart was having to work at an accounting job to support himself. Much of our time had been filled with his chronic bitter denunciations of everyone at his office, but only now did it become clear that he routinely sabotaged his performance there—by lateness and sloppiness—as a way to prove to himself that he was unsuited for this mundane career. The worse he did in everyday life, the more he could convince himself he truly belonged only in an idealized realm of art and music. He wanted his specialness mirrored by me, but these embryonic positive transferential configurations were in constant danger of being swept aside by his chronic frustrated anger.

Throughout his treatment narcissistic injuries of one kind or another occurred in the face of his grandiose expectations. I disappointed him in many inadvertent ways: changing an hour, redecorating the office, ending sessions on time instead of giving him special (and unasked for) extra minutes. These events violated secret, unadmitted desires for an all-caring, clairvoyant, and omniscient analyst.

Early on, this wish was not admitted into conscious awareness, and his reactions to injury had an intensely borderline or even delusional quality. This might take the form of an angry insistence that he was indeed brain damaged, that I had incompetently misdiagnosed him, and that he should seek immediate medical, not psychiatric treatment. Giving up this quasi-delusional concern went hand in hand with acknowledging his desires for dependency on me. Once he was able to work through this transferential resistance, his reactions to narcissistic injuries were comparatively less severe, involving lateness for sessions and silent withdrawals, but no longer a breakdown in reality testing or sexual acting out (i.e., there was a shift from acting out to acting in as the positive transference was able to emerge). His promiscuous sexuality spontaneously receded over the course of the year as his transferential longings for me to care for him emerged. A continued empathic stance acknowledging the subjective validity of his sexualized longings helped him also tolerate his transferential feelings. To the extent that I was able to focus interpretatively on the disappointed grandiose wishes behind his fragmented, angry reactions, the more he could both admit them to himself and simultaneously attach them transferentially to me.

My interpretative stance remained unchanged throughout his treatment. What shifted was his need to introduce (and for me to accept) parameters of his own devising. Initially this included the right to see other therapists and doctors simultaneously, to occasionally "win" the right to miss appointments without penalty, and to have a handshake after each session. All these represent not modifications of analytic treatment in order to deal with the severely disturbed patient; rather they simply were individualized empathic responses to the manifestations of fragmentation that the patient experienced and created everywhere, and which he could not leave outside my office door simply because I might try to impose certain analytic "rules." In response to a consistent, empathic interpretive milieu, the patient's sense of himself gradually became less fragmented, and he could likewise engage in a more stable therapeutic relationship.

I think this patient represents someone who teetered on the borderline of analyzability, and illustrates the fluidity of the borderline–narcissistic continuum and its field dependence. In an even inadvertently unempathetic environment, he was prone to pronounced fragmentation and reactive rages. No doubt he would be diagnosed as borderline under such circumstances by many therapists. However, when responded to in a way he could feel as empathic, he was capable of significant reorganization and a stable idealizing transference eventually emerged. It is important to realize the extent to which the fit between therapist and patient can determine diagnosis and analyzability. I do not claim my greater empathic resources were the deciding factor here. This patient was certainly able to seize on any slight misstep, and might have broken off treatment the way he broke off with his woman lover. Indeed, he said he had seriously considered not returning after our first meeting because my office chairs were too far apart. I acknowledged how it might seem awfully far away and permitted him to make the adjustment he wanted—which was to move less than six inches closer. Like "winning" an argument over fees, the ability to actually move his chair, and not simply discuss its significance, was a necessary enactment for the solidification of the positive transference to proceed. I feel a theoretical orientation determined to focus on this patient's anger, manipulativeness, or need to form bad or hateful relationships could only lead to a stormier course of treatment.

Case 2

Martin, a 48-year-old man, was brought to my office by his brother in the midst of an acute psychotic episode. He was suffering from periods of intense anxiety, paranoid delusions about good and bad fields of energy flowing through his body, and grandiose identifications with Einstein and Krishnamurti. For many years he had lived at home with his mother, holding down a part-time manual labor job. His main social outlet was acting as coach to a local softball team, and part of his psychotic process involved feeling an overwhelming responsibility for the spiritual development of his teammates.

He had no previous psychiatric history, but I subsequently learned of what sounded like a similar episode 20 years earlier when he had been a graduate student in physics and suddenly left to spend the following decade working as a lumberjack and in the Forestry Service.

I was able to stabilize him on Thorazine, help enroll him briefly in a day treatment program as an alternative to hospitalization, and see him initially for once-, but soon twice-a-week therapy sessions. As a side effect of the medication he very quickly developed tardive dyskinesia, a potentially serious neurological disorder causing involuntary facial movements. As a result, all antipsychotic medication had to be prematurely discontinued. The reorganization he was able to achieve in therapy is thus not attributable to the effects of medication.

Both Martin and his brother had extensively studied the work of Krishnamurti for many years, and had come to me because they had heard I might be familiar and sympathetic with this philosophy. For Martin this quickly took the form of an intense idealization of me as embodying Krishnamurti's enlightened stance. This had the positive effect both of helping him make a firm commitment to treatment, and relieving him of some of the pressure to fill that role himself. As an idealized selfobject I was able to perform a stabilizing, soothing, and organizing function for him. To do so, I was not required to display any special spiritual powers, merely to be a consistent object who took seriously his need for a spiritual master, and who did not subvert that need by reality testing. Many of our sessions would consist of inquiring together how Krishnamurti might handle the situations which arose in Martin's everyday life, and this began to allow Martin to display some of his extensive reading and knowledge to me. I tried to press him to be as clear and specific as possible in his references, so as to use the topic to foster a sense of his own knowing, and not simply permit him to be reinvolved with a delusional self-image. His explaining to me what he knew became a primary tool of his reorganization. We eventually progressed through Eastern philosophy, forestry conservation, and Einstein's experiments with the photoelectric effect.

There was a continual issue about how to handle all the grandiose and delusional aspects that were contained in this material. On the one hand, the grandiosity was a positive and inevitable feature of the mirroring transference trying to emerge, which premature reality testing would abort. However, because this patient had not had successful opportunities for normal mirroring—and indeed was now structurally incapable of a sustained narcissistic transference—fragmentary and extreme forms of grandiosity were resorted to. When these identifications with saints and geniuses reached delusional proportions, however, they became brittle and unsustainable and the source of inevitable narcissistic injury. The patient then fled from painful contact into the solipsistic armor of a rigid delusional system.

Therefore I chose to direct my inquiry off target, respecting but not encouraging extreme grandiose confabulations. Arrested exhibitionistic needs could be encouraged in all the day-to-day activities that the patient had abandoned as unsatisfying. Our inquiry can reanimate these deadened aspects of everyday life with a new potential to be incorporated into the emergent transferential needs of the patient. Eventually Martin could introduce into the session detailed descriptions of how he painted his new apartment, with a proud enthusiasm hitherto reserved only for his religious preoccupations. Around the same time, he began to say how he no longer wanted to use the spiritual jargon of Krishnamurti, but wanted "to find his own words."

Thus, this patient's reconstitution did not primarily occur around improved reality testing nor through the expression of strong affects associated with conflict laden material. Rather, both of these were to follow the gradual decrease in self-fragmentation. Only after a year, when he was free from his severest anxiety attacks and back at work, could he profitably experience his own anger. Earlier, any attempt to explore angry feelings only overwhelmed his fragile self-cohesion and precipitated a return to the delusional somatic concerns he referred to as "an attack of the tubes." This consisted of the perception of his body as literally constructed of a series of metallic tubes, through which moved good and bad fields of energy. That he could explore this material at all was a sign of his recovery, not a precursor to it. Brief negative transference reactions to me were always disorganizing experiences for him, and were usually preceded by some empathic failure on my part, such as forgetting some detail he explained to me in a previous session.

Martin's treatment illustrates the potential for the successful emergence of positive narcissistic transference needs in a progressively stable manner even out of the disorganized, fragmented state of acute psychosis.

Case 3

I will now turn to a more difficult case both in terms of chronic pathology, and the problems of treatment in an institutional environment structured around reality testing and limit setting.

John was an 18-year-old mildly retarded young man whose treatment I supervised in a day hospital. He had been transferred from the inpatient unit to which he was brought by the police after incidents at home in which he had badly beaten his 3-year-old sister, threatened his mother, and made suicidal gestures.

He was obese, prematurely graying, with a blind and deviated eye, the result of an adolescent fight. The deformity gave him a quite unappealing and, to many, a dangerous appearance.

Although no gross thought disorder was noted, it was initially thought his reactions to his mother and sister were so extreme that underlying paranoid delusion material must have been present, and he was placed on antipsychotic medication. After a brief hospitalization, he was transferred to day hospital treatment where his impulsivity and acting out, rather than any overt psychotic process, were felt by most staff members to be the immediate problem.

Gradually it emerged that John was treated at home in an extremely ambiguous way by his mother. On the one hand he was a substitute father/husband, the father having deserted the family many years previously; and on the other he was a bad and failed child whose needs were passed over repeatedly by the mother in favor of his younger sister by a different father (who also was no longer in the home). Exploration of John's violence at home revealed it to be precipitated by a variety of subjectively perceived narcissistic injuries: for instance, when requests for cigarettes or food were ignored because his mother was busy with his sister. In addition, his attempts to be an independent adolescent were undercut as being either potentially criminal or dangerous to himself.

John had an evident need to attach himself to and idealize male staff whom he would follow around and often badger for attention. It was first of all my task to help staff recognize the appropriateness of his need and allow themselves to be used in this way rather than to immediately set limits to his demanding and to them, inappropriate behavior. When his need for attention was acknowledged as valid, and, to the extent possible in a given situation responded to, *then* it was possible for him to understand and self-impose further limits. Attempts to simply limit set (i.e., "I can't talk to you now, bring it up in group") would often lead to an angry withdrawal or outbursts directed at another patient or staff member. By allowing him an extra minute or two to verbalize an "inappropriate" question or request as a way of making contact, I acknowledged that he had a legitimate need. My response then was always, whether in an overt or tacit way, directed at an acknowledgement of his need or hurt and not toward correcting the inappropriateness in his still severely limited styles of expressing it.

Attempting to address the narcissistic hurt that precipitated abusing his young sister, often strained the empathic resources of the staff to their limit, with concern for the child often overwhelming any empathy for John's plight. One staff member completely refused to talk to him under any circumstances, so strongly did he feel for the sister. Indeed, only by setting a treatment goal of John moving out of the family house, and thereby acknowledging the staff's overwhelming concern for his sister, was I able to then make responding to John's own day-to-day needs seem legitimate to the staff as a whole.

No dramatic cure of John's symptoms was achieved. However, his behavior while in the day hospital was noticeably moderated and outburst-free during periods when his therapist was able to respond empathically. The instances where failures of empathy led to outbursts were understood more clearly, so that his behavior was now seen as responsive to outside forces, not simply the result of some congenital inability to control wild impulses. I think it is evidence that some new measure of self-cohesion was achieved that it became possible for him to indeed move out of his mother's house and into a structured residence.

John's bizarre appearance and retardation reduced the ordinary opportunity of an adolescent for phase appropriate exhibition. More and more extreme behaviors had to be resorted to because the ordinary ones were found to be unavailable. Thus, for staff it was necessary to recognize that often bizarre, seemingly inappropriate behaviors were being employed in the service of appropriate, but arrested developmental needs and that it was the need rather than the behavior that had to be responded to.

Interpretations that were most effective focused on acknowledging his subjective experience rather than correcting a distortion in reality. The expression of primitive rage reactions was seen following narcissistic injury both at home and with staff, and rather than being in any way cathartic or fostering the use of the therapist as a "bad object," such expressions led to increased splitting as a fragmentation product. Brandchaft and Stolorow (1984) have suggested, as was the case with Mark, that splitting is not a defense for handling aggression, but rather symptomatic of the fragmentation that results from severe narcissistic injury. Tolerance for grandiose, exhibitionistic, or demanding behaviors met hitherto arrested developmental needs and gradually led to increased self-control of affects as self-cohesion improved. Exploring day-to-day events where John could express normal adolescent concerns and expand feelings of mastery, rather than focusing on areas of particular conflict, gave rise to increasingly mature autonomous levels of functioning.

Summary

I have tried to outline specific principles of treatment for seriously disturbed patients that grow out of the theoretical framework of self psychology, which may be summarized as follows:

1. Interpretations focus on the empathic acknowledgement of the patient's subjective experience, instead of on the correction or interpretation of the patient's distortions of objective reality.
2. Release of strong affects is recognized and dealt with as a defensive means of stimulating a temporary aliveness in an enfeebled self.
3. Anger, in particular, is seen as arising from narcissistic injury.
4. Patients are helped to foster positive transferential relationships, their primary resistances being to giving in to a trusting, vulnerable position. Prolonged negative transferences are seen as either expressions of this resistance, or as iatrogenically induced by a nonempathic therapist rather than as arising out of any innate need to use the therapist as a "bad object."
5. In order to promote self-cohesion, the therapist focuses on experiences of the "emergent self," including moments of "I know/feel this" or "This is me," regardless of seemingly trivial or delusional content.

References

Brandchaft, B., & Stolorow, R. (1984), The borderline concept: Pathological character or iatrogenic myth? In: *Empathy II*, eds. J. Lichtenberg, M. Bornstein, & D. Silver. New York: Analytic Press.
Kernberg, O. (1975), *Borderline Conditions and Pathological Narcissism*. New York: Jason Aronson.

Kohut, H. (1977), *The Restoration of the Self*. New York: International Universities Press.
——— (1984), *How Does Analysis Cure?* Chicago: University of Chicago Press.
Shainberg, D. (1983), *Healing in Psychotherapy*. New York: Gordon and Breach.

Chapter 5

THE WORKING-THROUGH PROCESS WITH A HOSPITALIZED BORDERLINE ADOLESCENT AND HER FAMILY

DEBORAH HAMM, M.D.
EDWARD R. SHAPIRO, M.D.

One of the formidable problems we face as psychotherapists is that of explaining what facilitates the therapeutic changes we observe in our patients as we work with them. *Working through* is a term that has been liberally used to describe one aspect of the process of therapeutic change. Traditionally, working through refers to the gradual overcoming of the patient's resistance to remembering, and the replacement of repetitive acting out with ideas, affects, and memories (Laplanche and Pontalis, 1973). With expanded research in the area of infant development, the elaboration of object relations theory, the development of self psychology, and the increasing experience with analytically oriented treatment of patients with primitive character pathology, ideas about the necessary components for working through have been broadened to include aspects of the therapist's function. Included are such concepts as "containment," "holding" (Winnicott, 1960, 1969; Modell, 1976, 1978; Shapiro, 1982), "internalization," and "separation–individuation," all of which link parental functioning to therapeutic tasks.

In this chapter we will illustrate these concepts in a case study of therapeutic change in a hospitalized adolescent and her family. Over the course of a year's hospitalization, three specific areas of improvement in the adolescent were noted: (1) improved reality testing; (2) increased ego strength; and

(3) deepening identifications (particularly with the mother), all of which we believe contributed to a more solid individuation. Our intention is to show how the work of the family therapy significantly added to these changes.

The clinical data is taken from work with a borderline adolescent hospitalized on the Adolescent and Family Treatment Unit (AFTU), a 12-bed unlocked inpatient unit at McLean Hospital, Belmont, MA, which specializes in the treatment of borderline, schizoid, antisocial, and narcissistic adolescents and their families. The adolescent is hospitalized and the entire family is involved in a complex treatment program that includes intensive individual psychotherapy three times per week for the adolescent, weekly couple therapy for the parents, weekly family therapy for all family members, and a weekly multiple family meeting for all families. The individual therapist assumes administrative responsibility for the care of the patient on the unit and works in a close relationship to the couple therapist. The individual therapist and couple therapist jointly serve as family therapists.

The milieu is highly structured and designed to provide necessary ego support to the adolescents, with firm limit setting, and a carefully monitored privilege system. There are regular group meetings for the adolescents to study their relationships to each other and to authority. In addition there are frequent staff meetings in which both staff tensions and responses to tensions within the patient group are examined (Shapiro and Kolb, 1979).

We have chosen for discussion a family in which both the parents and the adolescent were involved in repetitive impulsive acting out. This behavior was linked to shared difficulties both with separation and with open acknowledgement of feelings of neediness. Over the course of a year's treatment, the adolescent and her family members showed considerable improvement in their abilities to recognize, openly acknowledge, and talk about their individual and collective difficulties. As family members began to explore and think about their relationships to each other, impulsive behavior markedly decreased, to be replaced by ideas, affects expressed in words, and increasingly coherent collaborative memories.

Theory

The concepts of "containment" and "holding" grew out of attempts to further delineate the therapeutic action of psychoanalysis and psychoanalytically oriented psychotherapy beyond the usual appreciation of the process of working through the transference and resistance (Winnicott, 1954; Bion, 1962; Modell, 1976, 1978). From the perspective of child development, "containment" refers to a mother's capacity lovingly to hold or to restrain her child when either is needed. The child in the midst of a temper tantrum is described as needing to be restrained so that he is reassured his anger will neither injure himself or others. In this respect, containment refers to non-anxious, firm limit setting. More generally, the concept pertains to the mother's capacity to stand protectively between her child and the outside world at a stage when the child has not yet internalized the mother's protective capabilities, and remains vulnerable to either excessive internal or external stress. This corresponds to the stage of development when object constancy has not been achieved and the child uses transitional objects to help negotiate a separation from mother (Winnicott, 1945).

Most theorists propose that the relevant developmental failures of the borderline patient occur during this time period, when the child is still unable to take care of his own needs adequately and requires the mother as an auxiliary ego (Winnicott, 1960; Kernberg, 1968; Modell, 1968; Shapiro, 1978). During this period, the child is still afraid that his anger will lead to the destruction or disappearance of the object and thus, abandonment. In such a setting, the mother's task is to "contain" the child's aggression toward her while maintaining a loving relationship in order to demonstrate to her child her "survival over time" (Winnicott, 1960). This task may not be managed well by anxious parents with their own separation conflicts or in relation to vulnerable children with excessive aggression.

Blos (1967) considers adolescence to be a second period of separation–individuation. For most adolescents, this requires reworking of earlier developmental tasks under the pressure of massive physiological change. It is during this period that florid borderline symptoms often appear, for the potential borderline adolescent is ill-equipped to meet this challenge as he or she has not adequately negotiated the first separation–individuation. Adolescents require similar kinds of containment and family support to individuate. For the borderline adolescent, this need is often frustrated by the family's inability to respond adequately.

Studies of families of borderline adolescents reveal evidence of a shared regression in the family as the patient enters adolescence (Zinner and E. Shapiro, 1975; E. Shapiro, Kolb, Shapiro, and Berkowitz, 1975). These family members have been described as sharing unconscious assumptions that are derived from earlier struggles around autonomy and dependence. Two major forms of these shared fantasies are delineated: the first, in which the borderline adolescent's autonomous moves are experienced by the family group as hateful devaluations, and the second, in which his manifestations of dependency are experienced as draining demands on meager resources (R. Shapiro and Zinner, 1971; Zinner and R. Shapiro, 1972; E. Shapiro et al., 1975; Zinner and E. Shapiro, 1975).

In our own work with these families, we regularly observe how family members disavow and project onto each other uncomfortable or unacceptable feelings, impulses, or aspects of their self-image which they consciously repudiate but with which they unconsciously identify and vicariously experience within family interactions (projective identification). These unintegrated affects, impulses, and images interfere with more realistic perceptions of each other and contribute to the frequency of unsatisfactory responses to misperceived needs.

A fundamental aspect of our work with these patients and their families is to help to recognize, articulate, contain, and feed back intolerable affects that are denied, projected, or acted out (E. Shapiro, 1982). This containing function both precedes and accompanies interpretive work. It includes a quality of empathic listening and responding in which particular attention is paid to establishing and sustaining a therapeutic alliance. It also applies to the therapist's ability to interpret his own experience of dystonic affects generated in him by the individual patient or by family members as a way of understanding conflicts or affects defended against in the family. The therapist's management and articulation of affects and ideas previously experienced by family members as intolerable, promote positive introjective identifications of the therapist that eventually facilitate change in the family interaction.

The growing capacity for individuals in such a family to acknowledge and reinternalize previously disavowed and projected affects or impulses promotes ego integration and flexibility. The subsequent reduction in the use of pathological projective defenses heightens reality testing and provides a new opportunity for deeper and more complex identifications among family members. Processes of identification persist throughout life and contribute to a deepening development of a sense of identity that corresponds with an increased acceptance of the limitations of others, an acceptance of separateness, and ego maturation (Modell, 1968). In our case study, ego maturation for the borderline adolescent was facilitated by: (1) working through pathological patterns of projective identification between mother and daughter that interfered with more realistic empathic identifications; (2) recognizing and determining the defensive meanings of unconscious shared family assumptions; (3) elucidating the covert meanings of impulsive family interactions; and (4) internalizing the holding function of the therapy through the process of identification with therapists and staff members.

Case Material

Vicki C. is an attractive 18-year-old girl who was admitted to the AFTU following two serious suicide attempts by overdose. She is the oldest of five children and the only girl in a religious Italian Catholic working-class family. Vicki's father holds a responsible position at his work that requires him to be called away from home frequently, and Vicki's mother also works full time away from the home. Mrs. C. suffers from chronic medical illness that does not currently interfere with her ability to work.

Prior to admission Vicki had become increasingly depressed and had started to drink heavily, to cut her wrists, and to indulge in promiscuous sexual behavior. At that time she was completing her senior year of high school, from which she managed to graduate despite prolonged absences from school when she would stay at home and sleep. Her parents claimed little knowledge of her truancy and alcohol abuse.

Vicki's first overdose followed the break-up of a long-standing relationship with her steady boyfriend. On the night of the break-up she drank heavily, swallowed a large number of aspirin, and fell asleep expecting to die. When she found herself alive and feeling ill the following morning, she told her mother what she had done. A few months later she overdosed with a larger number of pills, but immediately told her parents who then sought medical treatment.

Outstanding in Vicki's history was a marked impairment in her relationship with her mother. Vicki had become sexually involved with her boyfriend at approximately the same time that her mother had become involved in an allegedly nonsexual "relationship" with a man she met at work. Vicki was her mother's confidant and she would often intercept the man's phone calls to her mother. Vicki was also aware that this man had threatened suicide if her mother broke off her relationship with him and that at one point he had cut himself to manipulate her mother. Vicki was only vaguely aware that there were some parallels between these observations and her own behavior toward her mother. None of this information was shared with Mr. C., who remained apparently oblivious to the tense mother–daughter relationship.

Mr. C. eventually discovered his wife's liaison and threatened to divorce her. In response, Mrs. C.'s health began to deteriorate and she had a series of automobile accidents while intoxicated. Vicki began to worry about her mother's survival.

Both parents came from large extended families. Mr. C.'s parents divorced when he was quite young. Mrs. C. was the third of five children, and in her early adolescence she was sent away from her family to live with relatives. She acknowledged no difficulty with this separation and professed little curiosity as to why it had occurred.

In the course of family treatment, it became apparent that family members shared several unconscious fantasies. Two of these predominated and required extensive work in the therapy. The first was that the acknowledgment of feelings of neediness and dependence would lead to shame, humiliation, and ultimately rejection. This conflict was embedded in the shared developmental experience that dependency needs were treated as if they were draining demands on meager resources. Troubled relationships and individual pain were kept secret, preserving the illusion that they were "one, big, happy family." This shared family denial was an unsuccessful effort to defend against overwhelming affects. It also prevented them from thinking about their individual experiences and perceptions of each other. For example, when Mrs. C. abruptly left family therapy in the middle of a stormy session, there was no discussion of her departure by any family member and no curiosity as to why she had left. When her departure was noted by the therapists, the family was in unanimous agreement that she was "probably fine" and had left for some minor reason. In fact, she was feeling quite ill but could let no one know, since she had internalized the family's stance that "you have to take care of yourself."

The second predominating fantasy was that Vicki was the only "problem" in the family and that if she were "cured" all other difficulties would disappear. This fantasy was supported by a shared avoidance of Mrs. C.'s alcohol abuse, her chronic illness, and the fragility of Mr. and Mrs. C.'s marriage. Vicki remained in the untenable position of being both the family's "problem" and its potential "solution."

This delineation constituted a formidable resistance in the couple's work as both Mr. and Mrs. C. initially preferred to focus exclusively on their daughter's difficulties. This posture enabled them to avoid their own conflicts by projecting them onto Vicki. The defense prevented them from relating empathically to their daughter and contributed to the increasing alienation between all family members. As Vicki was increasingly pushed into the position of representing all neediness, aggression, and sexual impulses, her rebellion assumed more extreme and pathological proportions, and her reality testing began to falter.

Within the marriage, the complexity of each partner faded into complementary stereotypes. Mr. C. assumed the position of affect carrier, in which he often expressed exaggerated states of sadness, depression, anger, and love, while Mrs. C. remained in the role of the cool, aloof, controlling, and distant observer with minimal affective engagement. These rigidly defined roles served to protect Mr. C. from recognition of his own withdrawal and isolation and Mrs. C. from a recognition of her sadness, depression, and low self-esteem which was occasionally revealed in discrete dissociated episodes of self-destructive or suicidal behavior.

In her relationship with her mother Vicki took her father's

role by holding most of the feelings and having no effective way of managing them. This appeared to interfere with realistic mutual identifications between Mrs. C. and her daughter and contributed to their increasing alienation from each other. As Vicki's behavior indicated increasing need, Mrs. C. became more rejecting of her and more emotionally unavailable, which made Vicki feel even more helpless. (Psychological testing revealed Vicki's yearning for a fused relationship with a loving and nurturing woman with whom she simultaneously could not imagine achieving any real contact.)

Mrs. C. had no conscious access to any sadness or need she might have experienced in her own adolescence when she was sent away from her family. Her denial and her projection of these difficulties onto her daughter interfered with her ability to relate empathically to Vicki. Mrs. C. experienced her daughter as alien, finding it impossible to understand either Vicki's behavior or her intense affects.

The Treatment

During the initial phase of treatment, the hospital environment and treatment team served a holding function for the behavior of the patient and her family so that they could gradually begin to tolerate their feelings and to address the task of learning how they related to each other (E. Shapiro, 1982). This holding function was particularly important in the early period when family interaction was most chaotic and fragmented. This phase covered the first few months and was characterized by Vicki's repetitive testing of the therapist and the entire treatment by continued provocative behavior and temper tantrums. She would yell, scream, and throw things and would sometimes superficially cut her arms or legs. Vicki referred to these episodes as "taking a fit." This testing behavior was also directed at her parents, and it caused stress in their alliance and commitment to work actively in the program. It soon became clear that Vicki's dominant struggle was with her parents, and that she would not settle into addressing any therapeutic task until her parents clearly articulated and demonstrated their involvement with the staff.

In her individual therapy, Vicki initially attempted to maintain a limited relationship, avoiding introspection. Her conversation was superficial and devoid of affect. This "idle chatter" served to create the *illusion* of relatedness without any genuine affective connectedness. It preserved her belief that "work" was being done, for, after all, talking is the "work" of therapy. This gave her some comfort that she was being a "good girl" in complying with what she thought was requested of her.

Vicki's fantasy was that her therapist already knew everything about her. When she would run out of things to talk about, she would sit in silence, claiming that she did not know what to say or else had nothing to say. Often she would have difficulty sitting throughout her sessions.

After repeated interpretation and confrontation regarding her anxiety about intimacy and demonstration of the therapist's consistent interest in her, Vicki began tentatively to relate, in detached phrases, her experience of despair and loneliness. Only occasionally were her depressive descriptions accompanied by related sadness, and she began to notice that she was frequently "out of touch" with herself. She began to think about her fluctuating affective states and frequent mood swings. She expressed confusion as to why an incident that was distressful to her on one day would be completely forgotten on the following day. With help, she began to recognize her use of this form of temporal isolation and dissociation and she expressed curiosity and perplexity about it. In effect, she began to hold onto her experience over time, evidence of her growing ego strength. Her increased ability to tolerate her feelings and reflect on her experience was in part due to the supplementary ego functions of staff who contained her behavior and talked to her about it. It was also due to the continued value placed on her internal experience by a therapist who seriously considered the meaning of her words and who maintained a consistent interest in her and her family. This latter aspect was particularly important in that the therapist was present in family meetings and could use the shared experience to help Vicki recognize her attachment to, and dependency on, her mother as well as her guilt about her aggression and destructiveness toward her.

The emergence of heightened affective states and impulsive behavior continually punctuated Vicki's style of superficial relatedness. In the therapy there was an early and continued focus on helping Vicki and her family give meaning to what appeared to be random impulsive behavior, which could over time be traced to specific family dynamics.

For example, approximately three months into the therapy, Vicki cut herself on the arm after a phone call from a new boyfriend, who had told her of his attraction to another patient on the hall. She concealed what she had done from everyone for an entire week, during which time in her charming and lively manner, she betrayed no indication of her underlying stress.

The cutting incident was first understood as an angry reaction to intolerable feelings of rejection, designed both to punish her boyfriend and to elicit a caring response from him. She recalled the previous time she had cut herself while out with her old boyfriend. She had showed her wound to him, thinking that it would make him stay with her. She recalled another episode when she had started to jump in front of a truck, hoping he would rescue her.

In the family sessions, it became clear that there was an additional determinant of this cutting. The family had been pressuring Vicki to request a privilege to go out with them (which she had not done) with the idea that such a privilege would be a major step toward coming home. This request came at a time when the parents were beginning to address their marital problems more openly and were also beginning tentatively to address in the family therapy their anxieties about Mrs. C.'s illness, her alcohol use, and her previous "affair." The pressure on Vicki to get out of the hospital was a defensive effort to avoid this examination.

Vicki did not have the capacity to recognize or oppose her parents' pressure or to talk with her therapist about her need for the hospital and for emotional space from her family. Each time, when difficult problems emerged in the couple's therapy, there was a simultaneous pressure put upon Vicki by her parents and brothers to leave the program. Inevitably, in response to these pressures Vicki would act out or "take a fit," so that her behavior often served as a barometer for family resistance.

Not long after the cutting incident, Mr. C. told Vicki "in confidence" that he planned to leave her mother. Vicki's immediate response was to think about cutting herself again. This time, however, Vicki was beginning to be able to tolerate her feelings so that she could refrain from impulsive action while she thought about what her impulses meant. She also had increased trust in the nursing staff and could use them to help her manage her behavior. As she reviewed her impulse in therapy, she realized that cutting herself would give her a "reason" to tell her mother about her father's secret (she felt she could not hide a cut whereas she could hide her emotions), and that it would be a covert way to punish her father for confiding his marital problems to her. Holding onto her impulse led her to discover that she was in a position of mixed loyalty: either she betrayed her father by revealing his secret to her mother, or she held onto the secret, suffering the consequent guilt and fear of retaliatory abandonment by her mother. This bind was similar to the one she experienced earlier when her mother confided to her the secret about her affair.

Vicki was clear that her unwillingness to confront either parent with her dilemma resulted from an inner conviction that they would not listen to her. She felt that only a self-destructive action was capable of both catching their attention, and communicating her feelings about the bind in which she found herself. In part, her fear was based on experience in a family where words were often used to manipulate and not to convey meaning. Her defensive method of covert, coercive, and threatening behavior was not only characteristic of herself, but also characterized the couple's manner of interaction with each other. (For example, Mr. C. would occasionally "fix" the car so that Mrs. C., who frequently drove while intoxicated, could not leave the house in it. Mrs. C.'s frequent accidents also served as covert communication of her agitation and depression to her family.) The family therapy provided the context in which the validity of Vicki's fears could be explored and she could be joined by her family as they began increasingly to be able to recognize and articulate the covert meanings of their behavior.

In response to abandonment fears, Vicki regularly became intensely involved in relationships with other patients on the hall. When her parents began to talk more seriously about separating, Vicki became involved with a young patient who manipulated her with threats of suicide and information about himself that he demanded she keep confidential. With help in the family therapy, Vicki's mother was able to see the similarity in her daughter's behavior with her own past affair. This insight allowed Mrs. C. a more empathic understanding of her daughter's difficulties and contributed to a deeper reciprocal identification between mother and daughter. In addition, Vicki began to look at how she habitually became involved with boys who "needed" her to take care of them (like her mother). Vicki recognized her obsessive preoccupation with her mother's health. She began to realize how her position of protecting her mother was a response derived both from her love for her mother and from her fear of her own anger toward her.

The reluctance of family members to address Mrs. C.'s suicidal behavior openly was formidable. Vicki's brothers could not confront their need for, and anger at, a mother who was potentially rejecting of herself and them through suicide. Their difficulties were exacerbated by their experience of separation from Vicki, who had served as a nurturing figure to them. Mr. C. had less difficulty with his anger because of his numerous experiences of "rescuing" his wife, and his awareness of his frustration and anger about it. Only later did he become more aware of his projection of his own needs onto his wife.

The subject of Mrs. C.'s reckless driving actively emerged in the therapy when she was scheduled to take her driving exam on the same day that she had planned to take Vicki to an appointment outside the hospital. The fact that Mrs. C. would again be driving after a considerable time of not driving (which resulted from court intervention) was met with bland denial of any concern by family members. As there was little preparatory work around Vicki's pass on anyone's part, and no one was taking responsibility for thinking about Mrs. C.'s or Vicki's safety, the pass was denied by the therapist, who was acutely aware of her own anxiety about the potential danger. This anxiety was understood as a countertransference response determined in part by a containment of anxiety that family members felt about Mrs. C.'s safety but were unable to acknowledge or discuss. When the pass request was denied, Mr. C. responded with intense anger, yelling at the therapist, "You're going to have to trust her sometime." This response was interpreted as a projection of anxiety and anger at mother's recklessness, now displaced onto the therapist. The interpretation precipitated a discussion in which both Mr. C. and Vicki were able for the first time to tell Mrs. C. about their fear that she would drink and drive. The therapist's limit, one example of the holding function, allowed the anxieties in the family to surface.

Mrs. C. was surprised and moved by the extensiveness of the worry in her family and she began to talk about her depression and suicidal feelings. Her increased openness provided a basis in reality for Vicki's concerns about her, helped free Vicki from the isolated position of being the only needy and depressed member of the family, and allowed Vicki a more realistic identification with her mother. As Mrs. C. began to take more responsibility for her past and current behavior, Vicki became a more responsible daughter. It appeared that Vicki's identification with her mother deepened as it moved from an identification with mother's impulsivity to an identification with Mrs. C.'s increasing capacity to take responsibility for her own behavior.

In the family therapy, Mr. and Mrs. C. persistently drew Vicki into the middle of their marital conflict and Vicki regularly offered herself up as a mediator. In the individual therapy, Vicki had talked of her belief that she could actually save her parents' marriage and that she would feel the burden of full responsibility if they were to separate. This belief was founded upon an omnipotent fantasy, which defended against her feelings of helplessness, rage, and dependency. Vicki's acceptance of this mediating role was supported by her parents' conscious belief (and guilty projection) that she was the cause of much of the marital and family tension. This notion was that if Vicki's problems could be solved, their marital difficulties would dissipate. For Vicki, playing this role complied with unconscious parental wishes, and held other attractions for her as well. As each parent would alternately court her allegiance, she was invited into a wished for but conflicted dyadic relationship with one or the other of them, which alleviated her fear of being abandoned as she attempted to differentiate. The fact that Vicki's behavior actually did keep her parents "together" (i.e., intensely interactive with each other around her difficulties) reinforced her feelings of power, responsibility, and guilt.

The role held dangers for her in that it kept her tied into her parents' difficulties, leaving her little time or energy to address her own conflicts and independent needs. In addition, preserving the mediator role perpetuated her guilt and conflict about "winning" a desired dyadic relationship with one parent at the expense of the other (usually by betrayal).

During the later stages of Vicki's hospitalization, Mrs. C. disclosed to her family the fact that she and her husband had not had a sexual relationship for many years. Although this news was disturbing for her children to hear, they acknowledged some previous awareness of this fact. (Mrs. C. frequently slept alone in the living room.) Vicki used this disclosure to reassure herself that she was not the primary cause of her parents' difficulties, concluding, "If they haven't been sleeping together for all that time, it can't have that much to do with me." Following this discussion, Vicki spent much less time preoccupied with her parents and began to focus more exclusively on her own problems, beginning to deepen her transference relationship to her individual therapist. Around this same time, her parents decided to separate, and the family work shifted to exploring family relationships in the context of the planned separation.

As Mr. and Mrs. C. began to address their disappointment in their therapists and to review their fantasy that their marriage and family problems would magically be cured by the "hospital," they began to look more realistically at their mutual strengths and the bonds that they continued to share, such as the continued task of parenting their children. They tentatively started addressing their mutual dependency in sharing this task. Simultaneously, Vicki began to acknowledge her need for people and structure. As Vicki gradually relinquished her fantasy of "saving" her parents' marriage, she became more introspective. She began to appreciate the seriousness of her own difficulties, and she renewed her attempts to differentiate from her family.

At the time of discharge, the family work had terminated, and Mr. and Mrs. C. had separated with a commitment to continue couple's work to address the ongoing nature of their relationship. Vicki was preparing to enter a college where she had been accepted and she had plans to continue her individual psychotherapy. Both Vicki's and Mrs. C.'s self-destructive and suicidal behavior had been significantly diminished.

Discussion

For severely disturbed, hospitalized adolescents, the concomitant use of family therapy with individual treatment enables a more comprehensive view of the adolescent's difficulties and a richer framework for the working through process than individual therapy provides alone. It sets a context in which similarities between the behavior, conflicts, and experience of the adolescent and those of the parents and siblings can be noticed and explored. For the C. family, the treatment provided a context in which meaning and ideas could be attached to seemingly inexplicable behavior. Family therapy gives the therapists the advantage of being able to see "in action" where individual conflicts arise that promote misperceptions, so that these areas can be clarified. Interpretation of mutual projections facilitates a more empathic view of the adolescent's troubles and mitigates against the emotional abandonment that the borderline adolescent fears.

With successful family treatment, the borderline adolescent has an opportunity to have a new experience with parents without the contamination of aggressive projections, leading to more positive identifications and internalizations. In this case, the working through of the rigid projections characterizing Vicki's relationship with her mother facilitated more realistic mutual empathic identifications that promoted such internalization. As Mrs. C. became more aware of her own sadness, depression, and anger, she became more emotionally available to her daughter and more receptive to a deeper and more flexible exploration of their relationship. Vicki's recognition that she was not the only troubled member of her family was also validated. In addition, family therapy gave Vicki and her brothers the opportunity to explore the reality of their fears about their parents' troubled marriage. Previous to the treatment, they were left managing their escalating fears about parental divorce and family disruption alone.

Family therapy provides a space where the adolescent's fantasies about family members emerging in the individual therapy can be checked against the "reality" of the family (E. Shapiro, Zinner, R. Shapiro, and Berkowitz, 1977). Vicki's fantasy that she was responsible for the integrity of her parents' marriage could be checked against her parents' actions and covert communications. In this context a gradual elucidation and working through of the shared fantasy that marital problems stemmed from Vicki's disruptive behavior could be carried out. The notion of Vicki's destructive role persisted until the revelation of the long-standing failure of her parents' sexual relationship. With this information, and their increasing reality sense, family members were able to reconstruct their memories of parental difficulties and Vicki could more easily take responsibility for her angry and guilty wish that her parents *would* separate "to stop all the fighting."

The "containing" function of the individual therapy added to Vicki's progressive development of ego strength. The therapist's ability to tolerate the patient's affects empathically and help the patient identify and articulate these affects appeared to be an integral step in the patient's growing ability to become more introspective and link her affects with ideas. As the patient developed her capacity to experience, tolerate, and reflect upon her feelings, she correspondingly improved her ability to experience and sustain ambivalence. Her reality testing improved as the intensity of her affects and need for projection diminished.

Vicki used her individual therapy as a place to explore her independent feelings. The therapist helped bridge the patient's dependency on her family so that she could begin the process of negotiating differentiation from them. When sufficient differentiation had occurred within the family, Vicki could allow a deepening transference relationship in individual therapy without confusion and guilt about betraying family ties.

As Vicki's ego strength improved and as she developed more of a sense of continuity of her experience over time, she began to report more accurate discriminations of internally and externally derived experience. She became more receptive to exploring differences and similarities with family members which led to more complex identifications with them.

The working through of unconscious family assumptions and the projective identification characteristic of the marriage enabled Mr. and Mrs. C. to address their marital troubles more directly with each other. This relieved Vicki from some of the pressure she felt to stay involved between them and allowed her more space to address her independent needs.

Mr. and Mrs. C.s' decision to separate was a painful one for them and for their family. There were shared feelings of sadness expressed that had been long avoided. As Mr. and Mrs. C. began to talk about their continued dependence upon each other, Vicki found it less threatening to explore her own needs.

The initial chaos of unmanaged behavior, family disintegration, self-destructiveness, and confusion had been sufficiently contained and transformed so that new ideas and shared memories could be articulated. This allowed differentiation and growth in all family members.

References

Bion, W. R. (1962), *Learning from Experience*. London: William Heinemann.
Blos, P. (1967), The second individuation process of adolescence. *Psychoanalytic Study of the Child*, 12:162–186 New York: International Universities Press.
Kernberg, O. (1968), The treatment of patients with borderline personality organization. *Internat. J. Psycho-Anal.*, 49:600–619.
Laplanche, J., & Pontalis, J. B. (1973), *The Language of Psychoanalysis*, trans. Donald Nicholson-Smith. London: The Hogarth Press Ltd., p. 488.
Modell, A. (1968), *Object Love and Reality*. New York: International Universities Press.
────── (1976), "The holding environment" and the therapeutic action of psychoanalysis. *J. Amer. Psychoanal. Assn.*, 24:285–307.
────── (1978), The conceptualization of the therapeutic action of psychoanalysis, the action of the holding environment. *Bull. Menn. Clin.*, 42 6:493–504.
Shapiro, E. R. (1978), The psychodynamics and developmental psychology of the borderline patient: A review of the literature. *Amer. J. Psychiat.*, 135:1305–1315.
────── (1982), The holding environment and family therapy with acting out adolescents. *Internat. J. Psycho-Anal. Psychother.*, 9:209–226.
────── Kolb, J. E. (1979), Engaging the family of the hospitalized adolescent: the multiple family meeting. *Adol. Psychiat.*, 7:322–342.
────── ────── Shapiro, R., & Berkowitz, D. (1975), The influence of family

experience on borderline personality development. *Internat. Rev. Psycho-Anal.*, 2:399–411.
——— Zinner, J., Shapiro, R., & Berkowitz, D. (1977), The borderline ego and the working alliance: Indications for individual and family treatment in adolescence. *Internat. J. Psycho-Anal.*, 58:77–87.
Shapiro, R., & Zinner, J. (1971), Family organization and adolescent development. In: *Task and Organization,* ed. E. Miller. London: Tavistock Publications.
Winnicott, D. W. (1945), Primitive emotional development. In: *Collected Papers: Through Pediatrics to Psychoanalysis.* New York: Basic Books, 1975.
——— (1954), Metapsychological and clinical regression with the psycho-analytical set-up. In: *Collected Papers: Through Pediatrics to Psychoanalysis.* New York: Basic Books, 1975.
——— (1960), The theory of the parent–infant relationship. In: *The Maturational Processes and the Facilitating Environment.* New York: International Universities Press; 1965.
——— (1969), The use of an object and relating through identification. In: *Playing and Reality.* New York: Basic Books, 1971.
Zinner, J., & Shapiro, E. (1975), Splitting in families of borderline adolescents. In: *Borderline States in Psychiatry,* ed. J. Mack. New York: Grune & Stratton, pp. 103–122.
——— Shapiro, R. (1972), Projective identification as a mode of perception and behavior in families of adolescents. *Internat. J. Psycho-Anal.*, 53:523–530.

Chapter 6

EXPRESSIVE GROUP THERAPY WITH BORDERLINE PATIENTS

M. H. STONE, M.D.
R. WEISSMAN, M.S.W.

Group therapy can be a powerful instrument in the overall treatment of borderline patients. It is no easy matter, however, to create valid generalizations about the appropriateness of group techniques within the broad domain defined by the term *borderline*. The Kernberg criteria (1967, 1981) describe and demarcate a *level* of adaptive *function* (in between neurotic and psychotic), applicable to perhaps a seventh of the population. The "borderline personality disorder" of Gunderson and Singer (1975) and Gunderson and Kolb (1978) answers to a clinical syndrome, more narrowly defined than the Kernberg definition, yet still applicable to a sizable percentage of admissions to general psychiatric facilities. *The Diagnostic and Statistical Manual* (DSM-III) definition of "borderline personality" is narrower still, yet the diagnostic items are derived from a larger set (Spitzer, Endicott, and Gibbon, 1979), half of which are now set aside as belonging to the "schizotypal personality." Most patients currently being called *borderline* by Kernberg, Gunderson, and others (Benedetti, 1965; Grinker and Werble, 1977) show mixed features of schizotypal and "unstable" items (the latter now collected under the DSM-III "borderline personality" label, with the word *unstable* no longer appearing). The "unstable" items are predominantly affective in quality: intense, inappropriate anger; intolerance of being alone; af-

First published in *Contemporary Perspectives in Group Psychotherapy*, N. Slavinska-Holy, Ph.D., ed. London: Routledge & KeGan Paul. Reprinted by permission.

fective instability; impulsive and self-damaging acts, and so on. As most clinicians use the term *borderline* in contemporary parlance, affective (especially, depressive) features tend to overshadow schizotypal ones (Stone, 1980). This is particularly true in hospital settings, where the flamboyant self-injurious tendencies of certain borderline patients lead to suicide gestures, necessitating inpatient care. Borderline patients in office practice are as apt to be schizotypal as affective (Stone, 1980), whereas the former are rarely encountered in the hospital.

These distinctions are not without their implications for group therapy. Candor would compel us to admit that, while many borderline patients can benefit from one or another group technique, not all require such interventions for their ultimate social recovery. Some borderlines can scarcely improve unless they become involved in group therapy, whereas others have no special need for it. Between these extremes lie the majority, for whom group therapy is very much indicated at some *phase* of the treatment—but not at another. Some therapists who have become adept at various group techniques can treat certain borderline patients quite successfully using group as the only verbal treatment modality, while other therapists, lacking such skills, may achieve good results in the dyadic setting. Techniques permissible on an inpatient unit may be inappropriate with ambulatory borderlines.

We have thus far mentioned schizotypal and affective subtypes, but this by no means does justice to the multiplicity of diagnostic varieties within the borderline domain (Stone, 1981): organic and purely psychogenic types exist, and within the large affective group are many variants, including anorexia nervosa, cases of severe premenstrual tension, and hysteroid dysphoria (Klein, 1977). Indications for group therapy differ in accordance with all these diagnostic subtypes, but of equal importance, *personality type* must be taken into consideration. For certain personality types (any of which can coexist with a *borderline* diagnosis), group therapy has the highest priority among all potential treatment methods. For others, group therapy is either contraindicated, or can flourish only in highly specialized settings.

Indications for Group Therapy

Mere ability to withstand the pressures of group therapy does not constitute an indication for its use. By its very nature, group therapy tends to focus on social interaction rather than on psychodynamic issues, even if attention to the latter is marshaled at times by way of highlighting disturbances in the interpersonal field. To be sure, most borderlines (diagnosed according to any of the popular criteria) do exhibit such disturbances. They tend to be impulsive and to manifest exaggerated responses to the ordinary social stresses. In a hospital setting, the affectively ill borderlines will outnumber their schizotypal counterparts; in a group setting, there will usually be several who are abrasive (especially those who are symptomatically more *hypomanic* than depressed), along with others who are suspicious, withholding, openly hostile, contemptuous, or indiscreet. In an office setting, some of these traits will be encountered—alongside the very shy and avoidant. But it is well to keep in mind that, in comparison with psychotic patients, borderlines often show good socialization (especially those with affective rather than schizotypal symptoms); some experience so little difficulty in all but the most intimate social relationships that they stand in no urgent need of group therapy.

Borderline patients will be particularly apt to benefit from group therapy if they have developed an extreme self-consciousness and shyness in response to a pattern of interaction with caretakers who radically undermined their self-esteem. Such patients tend to assume that their fantasies, impulses, and ambitions are not only reprehensible but uniquely bad—as though no one else in the world had so tarnished a soul as theirs. The group setting soon makes it clear to them, through the verbalizations of its other members, that murderous, lustful, envious, or other fantasies the patient regarded as so dreadful and alienating are rather commonplace and acceptable.

Patients who have "secrets" and withhold from their therapists much information of an emotionally relevant nature are often helped, in the group setting, to reveal what they have so long and so unnecessarily guarded. Peer pressure may be more comfortable (in the sense of less humiliating) to respond to than pressure from a therapist. Or the other group members may, in the natural evolution of the group, reveal personal anecdotes similar in content to what the patient was too embarrassed to expose. Witnessing the relative innocuousness of someone else's comparable revelation may embolden the withholder to withhold no longer.

Shy and withholding persons tend not to be directly irritating to others, apart perhaps from the irritating consequences of withholding when continued within the context of a *group,* where the others are making more of an effort to be candid. But group therapy also has considerable potential for amelioration of truly irritating personality traits, some of which will not even be visible in the one-to-one situation; a borderline patient may be deferential to his therapist but nasty to everyone else.

The catalog of obnoxious traits one may observe in a borderline population, while lengthy and imposing, is not very different from what one may note as well among normal/neurotic people. But in the borderlines, these traits tend to be more frequent and more intense. Some involve *social insensitivity* and may take the form of tactlessness, rudeness, indiscretion, unsolicitousness, or an inability to empathize with the feelings of others. Various narcissistic traits may be seen, including indifference to the needs of others, outright contemptuousness, arrogance, or entitlement. Abrasiveness of one sort or another may be a prominent trait; in more extreme cases, behavior passes beyond abrasiveness to abusiveness and bellicosity. By definition, borderline patients are often unaware both of the existence of certain undesirable personality traits and of their expectable impact on others. This may be especially true if the patient's behavior is characterized, say, by relatively subtle forms of contemptuousness rather than by manifest hostility. Thus, a patient may have to be "educated" by other members of the group about the implications of his chronic late arrival at the meetings, or of his habitual dozing while the group is in progress, or of his monopoly of the conversation.

In some respects, discussion of indications for group therapy in relation to hospitalized borderlines becomes almost superfluous, since group treatment is always offered as an integral part of the weekly program. Nevertheless, it is worth remembering that there's a good reason why group therapy became institutionalized as a part of the integrated treatment approach with inpatient borderlines. It is precisely because borderlines manifest various split-off aspects of the personality only to one or a few other persons that the totality of the borderline's feeling-states can be recaptured only in a group, each of whose members necessarily evokes different reactions and emotions from the patient. No one person holds all the basic ingredients of the patient's total personality. But the *group* may hold all, or at least enough of the essential aspects to enable its members to "close the circle" on the patient. By this we refer to the ability of the group to portray back to the patient all his contradictory, conflicting emotional and behavioral tendencies. If the patient were, for example, hostile toward men, ingratiating toward women, servile toward authority, and egocentric to the point of caring little about the problems of other people, no one group member could be the recipient of all these attitudes. But the group as a whole would be, and thus could force the patient to become acquainted with the hitherto compartmentalized and disconnected segments of his personality. The typical borderline inpatient, who has made suicide gestures in the past, will often evoke pity in his attitude toward certain staff members or fellow patients. But the gestures may have been the sequelae of despair in interpersonal situations where the patient got to feel "rejected" over and over. And this "rejection" may have resulted from behavior calculated, however unwittingly, to alienate those with whom the borderline patient imagined himself trying to achieve intimacy.

In the one-to-one situation, depending on who the "other" is, the patient may be seen as pitiable, evoking sympathy, or as obnoxious, evoking alienation. If the therapist, working in the dyadic mode, happens to see the "nice" side of the patient and to experience him as pitiable, he will be perplexed as to why relationships have failed and why suicide gestures have been resorted to. But the *group* will almost surely contain a few persons to whom the patient relates in the more irritating way. There, it will become clear how, habitually alienating others, the patient keeps on feeling rejected and despondent. The two pieces of the puzzle, now brought within view of the therapist, also can be displayed to the patient. Groups designed to "close the circle" on different aspects of the borderline patient's split-off and compartmentalized psychic life usually contain between seven and ten group members, along with one or a pair of therapists. This is not the only format in which group therapy may be helpful to borderline patients, but it does serve to introduce us to the topic of group *composition*.

Composition of Groups

The makeup of groups helpful to borderline patients is more complex in relation to inpatients than to office patients. Partly this is a reflection of inpatients' suffering difficulties and handicaps in several important sectors of life, in contrast to their healthier ambulatory counterparts, whose problems may be limited to employer–employee situations and to intimate relationships.

Borderline patients in office practice who have problems, and personalities, amenable to group therapy are customarily treated in groups of six and ten patients. Beyond ten, there may be too little time for the patient to reveal himself adequately or to receive sufficient attention from the others in the group. With fewer than six patients there may be too little diversity of personality types among the patients: the *full* range of any given patient's problems may not come under focus for want of some particular personality type that might have been necessary as a catalyst for the exposure of one or another of those problems. A borderline patient who has a serious difficulty in relating to competitive males may have little opportunity to improve in this area in a small group that may contain no males or no one who is even noticeably competitive.

Groups with *ambulatory* borderline patients are often led by one therapist. The general level of psychopathology in such groups will not usually be of a sort where a therapist would feel overwhelmed without emotional support—and additional reality-testing capacities—of a cotherapist. The extent to which a cotherapist could be helpful in such groups is not easy to assess in any methodical way; the matter is often settled (to no one's detriment) by the personal preference of the therapist(s).

Under ideal circumstances, the members of the group will display a range of psychopathology (or, put another way, of adaptational level) that is fairly narrow. This is true in either office or hospital. If, in an ambulatory group, the members consist of a few very impulsive borderline patients, whose life histories contain many bizarre or repellent features, along with half-a-dozen high-functioning, socially conventional neurotic patients, the borderlines may come to feel like outcasts; or they may experience a kind of despair over the seemingly insurmountable gap stretching between their life potential and that of their better integrated group-mates.

For example, one office-based group in our experience was dysfunctional because of poor matching of adaptational levels: besides six stable neurotic persons, there were two of borderline function. One of the latter, though married, maintained a clandestine incestuous relationship with a sister. He indulged in a number of eccentric practices, such as keeping the fetus from one of his wife's miscarriages preserved in formaldehyde in a pickle jar on the living room mantelpiece. When his neurotic group-mates spoke, as they frequently did, of feeling "grossed out" by repugnant habits of this sort, the man grew defensive and hostile. Eventually he stormed out of the group in a paranoid rage and never returned. But prudence would have cautioned against his inclusion in the first place. The other borderline was a woman in her late twenties who was exceptionally impulsive and labile, given to frequent manipulative suicide gestures, episodes of drug abuse, and the like. The more she tried to emulate the healthier patients, the more dismally she failed. The more she failed, the more egregious, and the more dangerous, became her acts of self-vilification. Had she been among her functional peers, she would have not felt so humiliated. As it was, she, too, removed herself from the group (which then became comfortably homogeneous).

In the hospital setting, an opposite situation often prevails; the better-functioning borderlines come to regard group-mates who are chronically psychotic as pariahs whom the group cannot tolerate. Sometimes the psychotic patients feel hopeless, measuring their paltry levels of interpersonal and occupational success against the (often) better records of the borderlines (as the latter are apt to feel in the presence of still better-functioning neurotics). Therefore, if one were organizing a group of hospitalized patients with the hope of using what Kernberg has called an *expressive* (more analytically oriented), rather than supportive therapy, homogeneity of adaptive level should be striven for to the extent that conditions permit.

One may note, parenthetically, in inpatient groups composed mostly of borderlines but with one or two who are psychotic, the latter often serve as a bellwether in relation to prevailing group emotions. If the group is experiencing terror, for example (at impending loss of their therapists, at the near-suicide of one member, or at a vicious assault by another), the borderlines may suddenly fall silent, "selecting," instead, to have a psychotic patient, one who feels terror habitually and even more intensely than the others, serve as spokesperson for the group. As the group begins to feel more at ease, the "crazy" talk of the psychotic patient is no longer relevant and no longer tolerated. This shift is often heralded by the reassertion of dominance by one of the borderlines, who may even yell at his more ill group-mate to hush up.

Because inpatients are a captive audience to the staff of the unit in which they find themselves, attendance in group meetings is more easy to guarantee. There is a tendency to insist that all the patients attend, on the democratic principle that no one should be treated as an exception. Even the most well-meaning egalitarianism, of course, must be tempered by clinical judgment and fairness: some patients, at least temporarily, will be too disturbed by immersion in the group and should be excused. The group leader(s) will do well to explain the reason for this to the majority who remain, so that they realize that the exception represented humaneness and not arbitrariness or favoritism.

It is customary in hospital settings to have a large community meeting once a week, which all staff and patients must attend. These meetings, so useful in educating the staff quickly about the current problems of each patient and about the prevailing spirit of their group as a whole, usually have some of the attributes of group therapy. The community meeting can exercise great power. In the model society of the hospital unit, all the members of the "society" are present. It happens with a certain regularity that a pilferage has occurred, or else that someone has absconded with some object—a kitchen knife, a broken light bulb—with which he could hurt himself. Someone in that closed society knows who did it. Tremendous pressure can be brought to bear on the issue (and *should* be brought to bear if the danger is significant) by the staff. All weekend passes can be canceled—for the innocent as well as for the guilty. The more narcissistically inclined among the "innocent" will experience outrage. The more integrated will realize—and help the angry ones to realize—that everyone *is* his brother's keeper, whether he wants to be or not. Very few patients can "tough it out" under those circumstances. Whoever has taken someone else's belongings will usually confess; if not, and if the culprit is known to another patient, that patient, torn between loyalty to his fellow patient and loyalty to the group, will usually come down on the side of the group—which in this setting, also represents the side of maturity and health.

Among borderline inpatients, very few are without serious problems in getting along harmoniously with others—let alone with intimates. Many are demanding of attention, irascible if thwarted, and ill-disposed to do their share of chores of everyday living that may be assigned them as part of dormitory or hospital routine. They may be contemptuous of the ordinary rules and regulations of intramural life, whether these concern the hours for rising and for retiring, or more important issues having to do with the need to return on time from passes or with the prohibition against bringing alchohol or drugs into the hospital milieu. Because of these problems—having to do with the creation of a safe and serene atmosphere where treatment can flourish—groups are often instituted with the express task of helping patients to adapt better to these social needs and to develop civility. Eight or nine patients may be assigned to "daily living" or "dormitory" groups of this kind, led customarily by a member of the nursing staff. It is the nursing staff who are in the best position to get acquainted with the details of each patient's habitual ways of interacting with both fellow patients and staff members in the "closed society" of the hospital. Task-oriented groups centering on problems in daily living address themselves to matters of hygiene (which, if neglected, soon transcends the personal), neatness, concern for the rights of others, and so on.

Limitations of Group Therapy with Borderline Patients

We have alluded in passing to some of the kinds of problems encountered within the borderline domain which may stress the powers of group therapy to the breaking point or in other ways render participation useless. Though, for didactic purposes, we must try to categorize limitations that, for example, stem from the psychopathology of the patients, in practice, how much a limitation may be said to reside in the patient, as distinct from the leader(s) or the group as a whole, may not be easy to determine. The same borderline patient who might be able to "open up" and to benefit in a properly selected group may, as we noted earlier, become acutely uncomfortable and dysfunctional where the group composition is disadvantageous.

This caveat aside, we can still turn our attention to certain constellations of personality or symptom that militate against the success of almost any group. Borderline inpatients with mild antisocial tendencies may be susceptible to the shame engendered by group confrontation (over a minor theft, for instance). They are still within the limits of the more conventional forms of group therapy. But where antisocial tendencies are too firmly entrenched and dominate the personality, the group's efforts may fail.

For example, we had occasion to work with a 16-year-old boy remanded to a psychiatric facility in lieu of jail because of his having raped one woman and molested another. He came from a well-to-do family and had already suffered a number of unusual tragedies (including the suicide of a parent) of a sort that made it equally compelling to view him as a pitiable, if impulsive adolescent or as a ruthless psychopath. In view of his youth and initially personable facade, many staff members were disposed to give him the benefit of the doubt. He revealed nothing of himself in his one-to-one sessions, but it was hoped that the group could reach him. For several months he said not a word in the "expressive" group; the other patients were slow in confronting him about why he was in the hospital at all. They did not as yet know of his police record, yet they found him somehow intimidating. Over time it became clear that he was contemptuous of all the ward rules, not only breaking them at will but often upsetting (and occasionally attacking) other patients in the process. He had no remorse over his antisocial acts, nor even any awareness why others considered them wrong. It also became clear that the level of his antisocial behavior was quite beyond what any of the hospital groups could contain or work with. He was sent to a different institution, specializing in the treatment of delinquent youths. Groups of offenders, led either by a reformed person who once had similar tendencies or by a therapist who has, like Aichhorn (1925) and Schmideberg (1959), become adept at dealing with antisocial youngsters, may achieve good results just where conventional groups in conventional hospitals would fail.

Borderline patients with pronounced paranoid traits, even if ambulatory and capable of good involvement in one-to-one therapy, may become acutely uncomfortable in an expressive group and quit before giving themselves a chance to see that perseverance might make them more able to endure the disparaging remarks or "critical stares" of the other patients. A very skilled therapist may create an environment congenial to the remaining patients, but there will be a few such patients whose mistrustfulness beggars even the interventions of an "ideal" therapist, and group therapy must (at least temporarily) be abandoned.

Although narcissistic and paranoid traits are common among borderline patients, these seldom reach such dimensions as to render the patient no longer capable of benefiting from an expressive group therapy. But some patients are so abrasive and disruptive that they destroy any chances for therapeutic work being accomplished. They capture the spotlight and hold onto it for so long that the remaining members are rendered bit players in the life drama of the disruptive patient. For a few sessions the group will suffer this invasion with only minimal protest, but then it will feel drained. Unless the disruptiveness can be reversed by the group's confrontation and by the interventions of the leader(s), there will be a move toward expulsion.

We saw this process unfold in the hospital setting with an expressive group of about 10 borderline patients. One was a professional woman with grown children; she had been admitted because of suicide gestures when she felt herself failing at her job. Her behavior was consistently hostile. Sometimes she was sullen and silent, even when her behavior on the ward the day before was so outlandish as to make her the natural topic of conversation. Other times she was assaultive, pouring hot soup down another patient's back, hurling ashtrays, and the like. She would steal sharp objects with a view to hurting herself, but not own up to it despite the fact that everyone knew she was the culprit. Her behavior varied, except insofar as it was always outrageous. Over the course of eight months, nothing the group could do made any impression on this patient, who monopolized nearly every meeting, if not with her antics, with her silence. Though she was to remain another three months in the hospital, the group insisted at this point that she discontinue participating.

It is hard to estimate how many borderline patients lie outside the limits of conventional office and hospital groups; our experience would suggest a figure in the range of 1 in 20. Therapists must familiarize themselves with these limitations and develop clinical acumen regarding which borderline patients are amenable to their groups and which are not. Since the good of the group overrides the good of any one of its members, the "unworkable" patient should be excused as early as possible, so that the majority can derive the maximum benefit.

Therapeutic Considerations

Should the group leader allow patients he or she sees in one-to-one therapy to be included in the group as well, or would they be better off in a group led by someone who is not acquainted with them? This question often arises in connection with expressive groups for hospitalized borderlines. Arguments can and have been marshaled on both sides, but in our view either format is workable, except perhaps where, of eight or nine group patients, only one is concurrently receiving individual sessions from the leader. In that setting, certain transference and countertransference feelings become intensified, and at the same time harder to resolve. The patient may feel too "special"; the others may be keenly resentful (as though they were among the half-dozen adoptees of a family that had one "natural" child), and the therapist may bend over backwards not to show favoritism, which could be as detrimental as any favoritism.

The question also arises whether a cotherapist should be used routinely in helping to lead expressive group therapy with borderline inpatients. If so, should the therapist and cotherapist be of opposite sexes? Here again, advocates of either position can easily be found; impressive cases can be built up on either side of the argument. Usually this means that neither position has a clear-cut superiority, and much room exists for personal preference or institutional tradition. There are few disadvantages to the use of a cotherapist provided a reasonable degree of harmony exists between the two leaders. One distinct advantage concerns the seriousness of the inpatients' psychopathology: veiled and not-so-veiled threats of suicide are common; threats to elope from the hospital are also common. The atmosphere of the group will thus often take on a life-or-death quality. Careful decisions may have to be made, and access to the opinion of another professional may be valuable. The burden of dealing with suicidal patients (e.g., should they, having voiced certain threats, still be granted a weekend pass?) is shared.

The use of therapist and cotherapist can help alleviate the discomfort therapists are apt to experience as they enter the edge of the hurricane of intense emotion directed their way, episodically, by one or another group member or by the group as a whole. In this situation, quite typical of inpatient borderline groups, two heads probably are better than one in developing on-the-spot perspective about the reality—or about the irrationality—of the groups' invective, denunciation, panicky anxiety, or whatever. One experienced head, of course, may be quite as good as two inexperienced heads.

Transferentially, two therapists will eventually be reacted to by the group as mother and father, no matter which of the four combinations it is presented with (both male, both female, female leader with male cotherapist, or male leader with female cotherapist). It will be interesting to explore with the group what subtle differences are seized upon to label (where, say, there are two female therapists) one the "daddy" and the other the "mommy." However accurate the perceptions of the group, it still reveals a great deal about its members—their various and often primitive dependency needs, needs for limit-setting, approval, unconditional love, and so on. Given enough time to explore these reactions, the group should benefit as much from one combination of therapists as from another, provided only that the latter are of adequate and approximately equal skill.

To focus again on the expressive group, and here our remarks apply to ambulatory as much as to hospitalized borderlines, one may ask how "psychoanalytic" should the group be? Is it legitimate to dwell, for most of one session, on whichever patient seems most vocal or most upset that day? Is it useful to work with the dreams of one patient? Are techniques learned from the therapists' experience in Bion-type groups (such as those who have participated in group exercises sponsored by the A. K. Rice Institute) translatable directly into work with borderline groups?

In approaching these questions, it will be well to keep in mind certain critical differences between a borderline and a neurotic population. Neurotic people live from worry to worry. Borderline people live from crisis to crisis; many seem to indulge in what appears to be a chain-smoking of upheavals, where one catastrophe is lit on the end of the prior one. When half a dozen or more such persons are collected in one place to do group therapy, it is not to be expected that the atmosphere will often be conducive to the methodical and peaceful exploration of their common psychodynamics. More often it will be pertinent to the borderline group that the leaders and momentarily less uncomfortable patients help the most uncomfortable patient understand that the particular crisis in which he finds himself (e.g., romantic disappointment, death of a relative, therapist's vacation, job rejection) is not, as the patient feels convinced, the "end of the world."

In other words, the analytic orientation of the therapists will be employed more often in cutting through the displays of affect, the twists and turns of symbolic illusions, and so on, to the *real* underlying issue(s), than in making elegant connections between the current emotions and the childhood experiences of any given patient. A group, having been calm for weeks at a stretch, may suddenly and for no apparent reason become restless and charged with hostility, whether at each other or at the leader, when, just as suddenly, someone remembers that the leader had recently announced vacation plans. A new wave of denial may wash over the group, whose members now poohpooh the notion anyone could be upset over that, until finally the painful feelings about separation and loss can be acknowledged. This acknowledgment can be facilitated, however, by the gentle but insistent prodding of the leader—who makes the relevant interpretation and does not back down from his conviction, during the time the group is still scornfully rejecting his observation. It is in this fashion that the analytic method is applied to the theory of borderline groups.

Therapists who have had even a brief introduction to A.K. Rice techniques cannot help but be fascinated by the correspondences that seem to exist between the group taken as a whole and one individual human being. The group shows resistances, like any analysand; the group evolves through stages of dependency, repudiation of the leader(s), and sexual interests in each other reminiscent of the Freudian oral, anal, and genital stages of (individual) development. The group exhibits defenses (fight, flight, pairing) such as Bion (1959) spoke of, and manifests various ambitions (of "self-defense" against outsiders, or self-perpetuation, of achieving certain goals), just like individual persons. It can oscillate between mature application to appropriate therapeutic tasks and "neurotic" avoidance of any purposeful activity; it can show hilarity or panic, or it can lapse into incoherence or silence. All these phenomena are seen, in bolder relief and in greater intensity, in groups of borderlines. Yet the temptation to use A. K. Rice techniques, which stress long silences on the part of the scrupulously neutral "observer," who limits himself to occasional abstract and pithy remarks about the group-as-a-whole (e.g., "the group seems ill at ease with an observer who will not offer advice"), must, in the main, be avoided with borderlines. Many are rather concrete and not quick at catching the overtones of meaning implicit in such cool and general remarks. Prolonged silences tend to be painful and poorly tolerated in comparison with what one could anticipate with neurotics. And a word to the wise is not always sufficient with borderlines, whose primitive defenses (especially denial and withholding) often remain quite impregnable to quietly delivered intellectual comments, no matter how accurate they may be. The same brand of compassionate but unyielding confrontation that will be necessary, many times, to "get through" to a borderline patient in the one-to-one setting will be necessary in the group setting as well.

With borderline patients who are especially sensitive to possible humiliation, the group leader(s) may find it more effective to make certain confrontations; that is, relating to one group member as though the remark related to all the patients. If one patient has made a scathingly hostile comment, but, because of being markedly narcissistic or schizoid, is known not to withstand criticism at all well, a "general" confrontation, voiced in a neutral tone, about how the group seems "unusually edgy or angry right now" may get the point across to the primary author of that hostility without unduly bruising his feelings. The remark should be made in such a way that one's compassion is evident (as might not be the case if one cleaved to the cooler and more abstract technique Bion might have employed with a neurotic group). A partial or tentative interpretation may be added as well, so the confrontation is softened by being couched in an explanatory remark. This lets the patients (including the one for whom it was primarily intended) understand very clearly just why the confrontation was made. In this process, the "you're pretty angry today" gets changed in the therapist's mind to "the group seems pretty angry right now," but may finally emerge as, "Well, lately people have been rather calm and civil with each other—until I announced about my going away—and now I sense you've become quite angry with *one another*. Perhaps the anger is meant for *me,* but the group is a bit too intimidated to just let me have it."

With patients who are less vulnerable to humiliation, or in more drastic situations, blunter confrontations by the group leader may be quite appropriate. Patients with antisocial tendencies of any marked degree, for example, or who are "thick-skinned" for some reason, do not respond to our pussyfooting around critical issues. Often enough, it is the other group members, rather than the leader(s), who take responsibility for confrontation. The use of a bantering humor may be especially effective in "getting through" to the difficult patient. But the humor cannot be contrived, or, if it is sarcastic, be more hostile than compassionate. An example of spontaneous bantering interventions by the other group members is to be found in the following interchanges. They occurred after five minutes of tense silence. In a group of borderline inpatients, one was struggling with strong suicidal feelings. This patient (A.) started out in a very manipulative, tantalizing mode:

Pt. A.: I was thinking I might not be here next week.
Pt. B.: Why not?
Pt. A.: I might be dead.
Pt. C.: (blandly) That's scary.
Pt. B.: (banteringly) How will you do it? Please teach me! I wish *I* knew how to do it. If you figure out a foolproof way, let me know.
Pt. A.: (joking tone, smiling) Well, there's always the garage.
Pt. B.: Where do you put the hose? (for the carbon monoxide)
Pt. A.: (shrugging the shoulders) Let's ask an expert!
Pt. B.: We *can't* ask an *expert:* they're all *dead*!

Quite soon after this interchange, a dramatic shift in emotional tone took place in A., who now became, in a most genuine and affecting way, openly tearful about his feelings of hopelessness. The moment this occurred, the others in the group dropped their bantering manner and became patiently attentive, sympathetic, and reassuring. Since the hopelessness of their fellow group member reflected a response to a recent rejection in his interpersonal life, their remarks now centered on this theme, and on how each of them had also experienced, but had also surmounted, similar rejections. They reassured A. that he was not alone; the group's concern constituted a very realistic antidote to A.'s despondency and thus helped minimize the risk of self-destructive behavior.

It is of interest that, relative to A. and his forlornness, the other members of the group felt *giving*. Borderline patients tend to feel much more needy than expansive, often a product of harsh life circumstances combined with poor coping abilities. Always on the edge of the abyss, they can seldom afford to extend a helping hand to others. As one borderline patient, with characteristic concreteness, so tellingly phrased it, "if we *give* feedback to the others in the group, what do we get out of it for ourselves?!"—as though the giving of anything, even words of advice, could only lead to depletion.

Countertransference Issues

Because of the greater intensity of affect typical of borderline patients, when compared with their neurotic counterparts, and because of their tendency to be demanding (to the point of wanting to "actualize" transference wishes), and to be immersed more in negative (hostility, rage, envy, panic) than in positive feeling states, more emotion gets stirred up in their therapist as well. Countertransference problems are likely to arise more often and to be of greater intensity than would be expectable in reaction to neurotic patients. This is noticeable in group work as in individual therapy. Roth (1980) has stated the dilemma nicely: "A psychotherapy group composed entirely of identity-impaired persons has enormous potential to influence the therapist unconsciously through projective processes ... affect-laden demands and ... reproaches.... There is great pressure to become other than a psychotherapist" (p. 419).

The anger, frustration, and disappointment a group therapist may experience while conducting an expressive group with borderline patients may lead into "temptation"; specifically, the temptation to take certain hostile barbs too personally and answer back sarcastically or with impatience. Or, a therapist exasperated by the general silence or by the triviality of what is finally said, during the inevitable doldrums in which borderline groups periodically find themselves, may feel strongly tempted to dissolve the group altogether, in hopes of creating a "responsive" group more rewarding to the therapist's efforts. Roth (1980) has drawn attention to the *therapist's* need of "good-enough" patients (to enhance self-esteem through doing good work), in the same way Winnicott (1963) highlighted the patient's need of a "good-enough" mother.

In hospital-based work, we have sometimes become aware that a group therapist was the first to learn of a self-destructive threat on the part of a borderline patient (one whose behavior meantime engendered animosity in the therapist) who then "absent-mindedly" forgot to tell the nursing staff that weekend privileges ought to be canceled. Omissions of this sort can be minimized through the use of a cotherapist: two heads may indeed be better than one, in the sense that countertransference anger may be strong in one group leader but much less so in the other, who will still remember to relay crucial information to the staff. We have also seen inexperienced group therapists overreact, with a sense of guilt, to their patients' sadness at times of separation; for example, a guilt that prompted the therapist to "act out" in some way (reveal too much about his or her personal life, say) in an effort to placate the patients; or promise to make a party for them, ostensibly to mitigate their sense of loss but really with the hidden motive of deflecting anger.

Countertransference feelings are sometimes revealed in the way group leaders address their patients. It is generally a good policy to refer to outpatients by their title, as they would be known, say, at work: Mr., Mrs., Miss, Dr., and so on, followed by the last name. This is a formality which pays respect to the mature and adult aspects of our patients, even those who are dysfunctional, dependent, or psychotic. It establishes, and helps maintain, the professional boundary between therapist and patient. But in borderline groups, especially in hospitals, there will often be adolescents whom it would be something of an affectation to address in so formal a manner. Use of first names enhances emotional immediacy and impact. This advantage may be lost if the therapist is constantly stumbling over titles and last names. In outpatient groups, the therapist may want to maximize confidentiality, using *only* first names, so no group member will know the full identity of any other. Sometimes, of course, borderline patients in an office group will try to subvert the professional atmosphere of the sessions by getting "chummy" (in restaurants or at homes) after the group (Ormont, 1968).

Borderline patients are often very needy emotionally, and would feel alienated by too strict an adherence to a last-name policy within the group setting. We feel the best compromise consists of using the first names in addressing borderline group members when conducting the group, while using the title and last name (except for adolescents) when the therapist meets these same patients in other, non-group-oriented situations. In this way, the tendency toward overfamiliarity (or to infantilization) is reduced, while the full impact of our interventions within the group is preserved.

It is quite likely that, given exposure to a borderline group over any considerable length of time, the group leader will not only experience countertransference feelings, but will be buffeted by a whole sequence of such reactions, many of which are destined to be understood as mirroring the evolution of the group itself. Roth (1980) has alluded to such a phenomenon, and has written about it with commendable candor. He describes an initial "nightmare" stage, characterized by "extremely strong affects before, during, and after each group session" (p. 408). Since his reactions shifted from giddy enthusiasm to bleak despair, he was not being fanciful in speaking of a mania followed by depression. After this chaotic phase came one of "pairing and rebellion" (where the patients were encouraged, unwittingly, to band together against the leader), and a third of "forcing and interpretation." In the third phase, the therapist regained control and made helpful confrontations about the group's destructive wishes. Finally, a more mature phase was ushered in—similar to an "early group" of neurotic patients—where mutual care and concern emerged and were expressed.

One may see in this evolution something comparable to the early development of a borderline patient, in which primitive "oral" dependent and sadistic themes are demonstrated in the exaggerated forms of panic and destructiveness, followed by a stage of the "terrible twos," equally exaggerated (manifested, for example, by the assertion of separate "identity" via wholesale repudiation of the therapist). Only after the partial resolution of these primitive conflicts and attitudes does one begin to see something akin to healthy concern for other persons (experienced now in an integrated way, without the usual borderline need to keep good and bad impressions in separate mental compartments).

Borderline patients, singly or in groups, will tend to induce in their therapist the whole gamut of their own unrecognized and highly disturbing emotional states via their "projective identification" (Rosenfeld, 1965). *We* go through and, one hopes, eventually recognize what *they* went through and are going through *without* self-awareness. The better we can identify these countertransferential reflections of the borderlines' poorly defined inner states, the better we can translate these back to the patient(s), help them understand, and, ultimately, help them gain control over these states. One must keep in mind that the evolution of countertransference feelings Roth has described answers to an unavoidable, and, in a manner of speaking, normal counterpart of work with severely ill persons. The anger we feel at the patient who throws an ashtray at us, or who strikes another group member, is "countertransference"—in the sense of constituting a reaction to a patient. But it is a realistic feeling and different, qualitatively, from countertransference feelings generated because of our highly personal, neurotic reactions to, and misperceptions of, particular patients. Needless to say, borderline patients, and groups of borderline patients, may evoke strong neurotic–countertransference feelings as well. Group leaders need to become aware of both types of countertransference. Neurotic reactions (of animosity, discouragement, preference, love) evoked by a borderline patient that remind us of someone important in our own life, may, if they become too strong, have to be resolved through personal analysis. A good beginning place for the group leader's self-exploration, in this regard, is to notice which of the 8 or 10 patients is the favorite and which is most disliked. Such feelings are inevitable, as they would be in a large family. But the more unrealistic reasons there are for these polarized reactions, the more one is in the territory of neurotic countertransference, of a sort that, if unresolved, would intrude in some unwelcome way into the therapeutic work. Borderline patients in group therapy will be very quick to accuse us of favoring the "goody-two-shoes" or of being unfair to the group's scapegoat. This need pose no problem for the therapist, unless he indeed feels the kind of love or hate that, transcending the moment-to-moment vicissitudes of emotion expectable within the group, grows so intense as to destroy objectivity.

Evolution of the Borderline Group

In alluding to certain patterns of evolution in countertransference feelings in leaders of borderline groups, we are at once reminded of another set of patterns relating to the evolution of the group and its members. Several countervailing forces affect the patterns we actually observe in our work. The unresolved conflicts of the patients, individually and collectively, are all waiting, as it were, at the outset, to be dealt with in an order that mirrors the priorities (of intensity and acuteness) among these conflicts. In an emotional field where stranger-anxiety, envy, thwarted love feelings, contemptuousness of others, and feelings of entitlement are all important elements, one of these must necessarily take precedence over the others as group therapy begins. Usually this will be stranger-anxiety, as each group member voices his discomfort with the unfamiliar and as yet untrusted therapist(s). There is a "natural" order, one might say, similar in many respects to the sequential exploration of oral, anal, and genital themes in dyadic therapy. These correspond to the broad human themes of dependence, assertion, and love, and are quite analogous to the *flight* (to a safe person), *fight*, and *pairing* of which group therapists often speak. But group therapy is not conducted in the "state of nature"; it is carried out in particular places with particular constraints that may substantially affect the *order* in which relevant material is brought forward, or, if not the order, then at least the relative importance the group attaches to each theme.

On the inpatient unit of one psychiatric institute, for example, expressive groups of borderline patients had been organized and conducted for many years. Each of these was led by one, sometimes two psychiatric residents, who rotated through that service for one year. The patients were admitted mostly in the summer, and discharged the following spring, in lockstep with the residents' academic year. Those of us who observed these groups over the years could readily discern patterns that reflected the unvarying chronology of events within each academic rotation. During July and August, the therapists and patients were strangers to one another. Themes of mistrust, stranger-anxiety, and helplessness came to the surface, regardless of what other problems the patients might have had on their minds before entering the unit. Identity problems became more acute. Many borderline patients shored up their enfeebled sense of identity through absorption of the "other" [the as-if mechanism Deutsch spoke of (1942)]. But while each therapist (the new "important-other") remained an unknown quantity, many of the patients, unable as yet to feel whole through feeling emotionally at one with their therapists, felt lost.

By the fall, this anxiety had largely abated. If anything, it was supplanted by the excessive dependence characteristic of borderline persons. This was expressed in all-or-none terms either in the positive mode ("I need you desperately"; "I can't live without you or I will kill myself") or in the negative, through denial ("Who needs you?"; "I want to get rid of you"). Alliances began to occur around this time (four or five months into the work), such that certain patients in the group could be counted on to identify with the values of the therapist; for example, to the point of putting pressure on another patient to "fess up" to having stolen something. Two months earlier, the patients were all still united (for dear life) against the therapists, and would not even have revealed overhearing an intended suicide attempt. By late fall, the atmosphere in the groups was very much calmer; the patients were task-oriented and dwelled on issues of immediate general relevance (competitiveness for attention, envy of those who were recuperating faster, friendship, sexual feeling, and so on). It was as though the group would go on forever.

These halcyon days of comfort and accomplishment came crashing to a halt with the New Year, when it dawned on some of the patients that their therapists' tour of duty would end on June 30. Others reacted to the coming separation through panic or devaluation of their therapists, without as yet being able to acknowledge what they were reacting *to*. Episodes of acting out occurred. A rash of minor thefts broke out on the unit; a patient threw a brick at a passing car; a patient "couple" engaged openly in sex on the unit, in defiance of the hospital code, and so on. All these things happened "for no reason," according to the patients' vehement protestations, until someone made the linkage between this hostile impulsivity and the forthcoming loss of their by now cherished support figures. The spring was occupied with exploration within the group of loss in all its aspects: losses suffered years past as well as the one that was fast approaching. *Pairing* was more noticeable within the group: in part, because genuine friendships had time to develop over the preceding 9 or 10 months; in part, as a compulsive and defensive clinging-to-one-another, by way of minimizing the pain of losing their therapists. The few patients who remained on into the next academic year witnessed for themselves the same phenomena in the same cycle.

At another inpatient unit in a different hospital, borderline patients were also treated over extended periods (up to a year or so). But here the therapists were for the most part drawn from the permanent staff. Expressive groups were led by two cotherapists, who were able to work with their patients throughout the latter's stay, no matter how long that might be. Patients were added to a group at whatever random moment they happened to be admitted and left the group when ready to resume extramural life. Apart from the therapist's vacations, separations were rare (once in a while a therapist might leave to take a new post in a different city) and tended not to occur in unison. Hence the patients were not galvanized by an inflexible timetable that presented them, as if from a conveyor belt, successive problems concerning strangeness, familiarity, and premature loss. Instead, the groups behaved more like a family with many children where a few new children are added from time to time, and a few occasionally "grow up" and leave the fold. Issues of sibling rivalry occupied the center of the stage almost all the time. Those who were still quite ill felt intense envy toward those about ready to leave the hospital. The more disturbed patients, especially if they felt nowhere close to negotiating life in an orderly and adaptive fashion, would try to "excel" at being sick, and would, through suicide gestures, overstayed passes, elopements, or other impulsive acts, grab the group's attention away from the healthier patients.

Alberta Szalita once remarked, in a personal communication, that whereas the neurotic is concerned with who comes first in the family, the borderline person is concerned with annihilation: Who shall live and who shall die? In the group, this desperate and sharply polarized view might express itself as a collective wish on the part of the group to kill off the therapists and have the place to themselves. Or, each member might wish to kill off his six or seven rivals and have the therapist(s) all to himself. The themes of separation and loss, so central to borderline psychopathology, came up more by "accident" (e.g., when one of the group members suffered the death of a parent; when one of the staff members quit). These themes emerged with particular force when the unit chief left the hospital to assume a new post: the impending loss brought to the fore not only separation issues but also strong feelings related to authority (was it benign? or was it arbitrary and hostile?) and to the protection and caring those in authority were supposed to extend them.

Since as a rule office practice groups have no fixed duration and are led by therapist(s) who can remain with the group as long as the group remains together, the pattern here is more like the second inpatient pattern described; that is, the themes explored by an office group will emphasize sibling and authority conflicts, and touch on loss at random rather than at fixed times of the year.

Conclusion

Expressive group therapy with borderline patients involves interchanges and interrelationships of bewildering complexity. Not only is there an enormous array of *combinations* of people to which the therapist must pay attention, but the intensity of affect, as well as the urgency of the patients' demands, leave the therapist even less time to sort out the welter of stimuli, even less time to settle upon the most appropriate response, than would be the case in work with neurotic groups. The microdissection of "what went on" in one videotaped session could easily fill a book; not a book of scientific facts but of impressions, educated guesses, and intuitions. In a chapter such as this, we can do no more than provide some guidelines that may help improve the clinical skills or oil the empathic machinery of others working in this field. And we cannot offer straight guidelines, but only ones that are a bit wavy and irregular, owing to the peculiarities of our own personalities and the nonrepresentativeness of the patient samples who compose our "experience." No wonder there are disagreements even about fundamental issues, such as whether therapy proceeds better in homogeneous groups of *all* borderline patients or in heterogeneous groups (Wong, 1980). The therapist variable may be immensely important here. It may simply be that certain group leaders are, and remain, more comfortable with mixed groups, while others do better work where all the patients differ within only a narrow range of life experience, social class, and adaptational level. In our opinion, there is, in relation to controversial issues of this kind, not yet enough information available that would permit one to distinguish objective truth from personal, subjective truth with any great clarity.

We have expressed the view that, in general, it is more helpful to think of the comments of one group member as reflective of some important emotional trend latent in the group-as-a-whole rather than of that patient in isolation. Thus, if the first patient to speak in the group is bitter and angry, the therapist should consider him primarily as the spokesperson for the group's bitterness and anger and only secondarily as a complaining person situated, accidentally, in the midst of seven quiet and contented souls. Given the dramatic and eccentric nature of many responses from borderline patients, it is easy to lose sight of how resonant the vociferous and seemingly out-of-tune patient may be with the hidden feelings of his silent partners. But some therapists relate to their groups more as collections of individuals in juxtaposition, and, focusing on the experiences, fantasies, and dreams of individuals within the group, accomplish much useful work with this approach.

As we seek more convincing answers to the many questions about optimal techniques for expressive group therapy with borderlines, where are we to turn? Other sensitive and introspective therapists of the caliber of Roth (1980) may come forward and share their impressions about the shifting trends in countertransference reactions. Common patterns may emerge that would be most helpful in orienting others who concentrate on this clinical area. Beyond this, the time has come for us to devise more objectifiable measures of outcome relevant to group therapy, so that different techniques and different combinations of patient-types may be more meaningfully compared. This is a formidable task, but since all of us live more as group members than as individuals, it is well worth the effort.

References

Aichhorn, A. (1925), *Verwahrloste Jugend*. Vienna: Int. Psychoanal. Verlag.
Benedetti, G. (1965), *Psychopathologie und Psychotherapie der Grenzpsychose*. Proceedings of the Dikemark Seminar, Dikemark Sykhuset, Norway, April 29–May 1, pp. 1–29.
Bion, W. R. (1959), *Experience in Groups*. London: Tavistock Publications.
Deutsch, H. (1942), Some forms of emotional disturbance and their relationships to schizophrenia. *Psychoanal. Quart.*, 11:301–321.
Grinker, R. R., Sr., & Werble, B. (1977), *The Borderline Patient*. New York: Jason Aronson.
Gunderson, J. G., & Singer, M. T. (1975), Defining borderline patients: An overview. *Amer. J. Psychiat.*, 132:1–10.
―――― Kolb, J. E. (1978), Discriminating features of borderline patients. *Amer. J. Psychiat.*, 135:792–796.
Kernberg, O. F. (1967), Borderline personality organization. *J. Amer. Psychoanal. Assn.*, 15:641–685.
―――― (1981), Structural interviewing. In: *Borderline Disorders*, ed. M. H. Stone. Philadelphia: W.B. Saunders.
Klein, D. F. (1977), Psychopharmacological treatment and delineation of borderline disorders. In: *Borderline Personality Disorders: The Concept, the Syndrome, the Patient*, ed. P. Hartocollis. New York: International Universities Press, pp. 365–383.
Ormont, L. R. (1968), Group resistance and the therapeutic contract. *Internat. J. Group Psychother.*, 18:147–154.
Rosenfeld, H. A. (1965), *Psychotic States: Psychoanalytic Approach*. New York: International Universities Press.
Roth, B. E. (1980), Understanding the development of a homogeneous identity-impaired group through countertransference phenomena. *Internat. J. Group Psychother.*, 30:405–426.

Schmideberg, M. (1959), Psychiatric treatment of offenders. *Ment. Hygiene,* pp. 407–411.

Spitzer, R. L., Endicott, J., & Gibbon, M. (1979), Crossing the border into borderline personality and borderline schizophrenia. *Arch. Gen. Psychiat.,* 36:17–24.

Stone, M. H. (1980), *The Borderline Syndromes: Constitution, Adaptation and Personality.* New York: McGraw-Hill.

——— (1981), Borderline syndromes: A consideration of subtypes and an overview, directions for research. In: *Borderline Disorders,* ed. M. H. Stone. Philadelphia: W. B. Saunders.

Winnicott, D. W. (1963), The development of the capacity for concern. In: *Maturational Processes and the Facilitating Environment.* New York: International Universities Press, pp. 73–82, 1965.

Wong, N. (1980), Combined group and individual treatment of borderline and narcissistic patients: Heterogeneous versus homogeneous groups. *Internat. J. Group Psychother.,* 30:389–404.

Chapter 7
THE RESTORATION OF THE IMPAIRED SELF IN GROUP PSYCHOANALYTIC TREATMENT

L. E. Hearst

This chapter addresses the optimal group setting for borderline, narcissistic, and impaired self patients. The advantages of homogeneous (Roth, 1979) versus heterogeneous (predominately neurotic) groups (Feldberg, 1958; Pines, 1980) is discussed, along with approaches to combined individual and group treatment.

In Britain, where psychoanalytic psychotherapy is available under the National Health Service, we find many borderline and narcissistic patients being treated in the country's hospitals, day clinics, and outpatient clinics, while impaired self patients more often seek treatment in private practice. This reflects the different ego functioning of the three groups and their different socioeconomic stratifications: the severely narcissistically impaired and borderline patients often come from the so-called multiproblem families (Scheidlinger, 1982). The impaired self patients, who are often exceptionally capable and successful professionally, have satisfied the suffocating needs and emotional demands of their overinvolved parents at the expense of authenticity of experience; this results in the falsification and mutilation of the self. Their exceptional achievement in school, in higher education, and in their professions results in their reaching a higher socioeconomic level. Nevertheless, they are prone to depressive states, and overwhelming feelings of guilt

L. E. Hearst is an Associate at The Group-Analytic Practice, 88 Montagu Mansions, London, W1H 1LF, and a Training Analyst of the Institute of Group Analysis, London.

and shame. They are excessively sensitive and vulnerable, and are plagued by deep doubts about the value of living.

All three groups in individual psychoanalytic psychotherapy require a considerable modification of the analyst's professional posture and treatment technique (Winnicott, 1960; Kernberg, 1981). This is also the case when group psychotherapy is chosen as the preferred treatment modality. The therapist is required to modify not only his analytic stance, but the group setting, which must be created and maintained to fulfill its function as an accepting, holding, and containing organism capable of affording its members the facilitating environment they missed, to a greater or lesser extent, at the crucial maturational stages in infancy and childhood. The group analyst and the group will have to be as nearly indestructible and enduring as possible. There will have to be a withstanding of persistent, repeated destructive attacks on the therapist and the group setting he or she has created. Omnipotent controlling behavior, magic expectations, and prolonged negative transference experiences will have to be accepted and contained. A healthy "narcissistic group self" will have to be maintained, to be at the disposal of the undeveloped individual selves of the group members (Battegay, 1976).

Homogeneous versus Heterogeneous Groups

A small homogeneous analytic group, carefully placed in a suitable environment, is more likely to fulfill the required functions of these patients than the classical heterogeneous analytic group. For a long time, the group will concern itself with the holding functions of early childhood to the exclusion of the analytic, interpretive tasks of the classical group. It is this exclusive preoccupation with the remedial work which makes such a group unsuitable for more mature, neurotic patients. However, the group-specific therapeutic factors remain: through *socialization* the patients are brought out of their isolation into a social situation in which they can feel adequate. There is mutual and consistent support by virtue of the regular, predictable, and reliable meetings. What S. H. Foulkes calls the "condenser phenomenon" is at work in the homogeneous group, as it is in the heterogeneous one; the group amplifies and concentrates the components of the personal interactions, and exercises a loosening effect on deeply unconscious material. "That which the group members hold in common, through symbols, dreams and symptoms can be understood, because the shared symbol acts as a condenser" (Foulkes, 1964, p. 34). There is the all-important *mirror function* of the group, essential for the formation of the coherent self: the individual group member experiences himself in the reactions to him of the others. More specifically, he finds aspects of himself reflected in the other members of the group. The patient is able to confront split-off aspects of his social, psychological, and body images through the processes of identification and projective identification. The following case example will illustrate these phenomena.

Case Example: A Homogeneous Narcissistic Group

Such a group was conducted in the setting of a Child and Family Psychiatric Day Clinic. The group consisted of six young mothers, some with husbands and some without, who had been referred to the clinic because one of their children, usually the eldest daughter, had become unmanageable. The mothers experienced their daughters as wild, dangerous fiends, and demanded removal from the family into a children's home. The group formed with these mothers met once a week for a period of 90 minutes, and with interruptions of the usual holidays, continued for three years. In the early phases of the group's life, attendance was irregular and chaotic; group members were frequently absent without notifying the clinic or explaining their nonattendance in the following session. Appearance and disappearance were unpredictable. Group members would turn up at the clinic when no group session was taking place. When they did attend on the right day, some would come early, sometimes an hour or more before the appointed time, and sit noisily in the waiting room. At the end of the session, there would be a reluctance to leave the treatment room and the clinic itself. Some would linger in the corridors, leaning against doors.

In the session itself, these patients would have difficulty remaining in the chairs arranged in a circle. They would jump up, walk about, demand someone else's chair, or sit on the floor in front of the chair. Food would be passed around and noisily eaten. At times of great excitement, the food would be used as missiles and the room would be "messed up." Impulses would be acted out when they occurred. There was a dramatic inability to contain, defer, modify, and verbalize upsurging feelings. While motivation for treatment was high, due to great suffering and almost total inability to cope, participation in the group process within the setting provided was very difficult to achieve and maintain for any length of time. Yet, there was a flow of uncensored communication in the acting out. Its verbalization and consequent elevation to the social level took a long time to achieve, and its appearance and gradual perfection marked the beginnings of the middle life of this group.

From the group analyst's experiential viewpoint, the outstanding feature of this group was the constant oscillation between projections and projective identification. Feelings of inadequacy, weakness, lack of emotional boundaries, and fusion with the group were often replaced by the therapist's conviction that she was destroying the clinic's orderly functioning and attacking the well-being of her colleagues in the clinic. At other times, she would experience a sudden loss of energy and interest in the group's welfare, which was not to be explained simply as due to the great demands this group made on her; rather, it signaled a wish in the group "to have done with it all"—all the turmoil and pain and striving for change. The discharge into the therapist of dangerous impulses and unacceptable internal object constellations required her to receive and hold them in between sessions and over weeks at a time. Only then could she slowly feed them back in a modified, more mature and acceptable shape to the projector (Ogden, 1979). The holding and changing were the most stressful aspects of conducting the group, and were achieved, often far from perfectly, only with the help of clinic colleagues, and the attitude and outlook of the clinic itself. The discharge of these all-important holding and changing functions would probably be very difficult in the relative isolation of a private practice.

Another requirement of this group was the need to pay minute attention to the group room in which the sessions took place. It was important to maintain the room in a steady condition with regard to its furniture, decorative state, and the room temperature. The yearly timetable was carefully thought out and prepared at the beginning of the therapy year and adhered to in a manner which, in retrospect, seems almost superhuman. On the few occasions when the conductor was absent, a substitute therapist stepped in who was able to accept the rages and retaliatory behavior predominant in the group.

In group analytic terms, the middle phase of the group's life was characterized by an increasing ability to translate the highly individualistic, idiosyncratic expressions of unmanageable impulses and internal object relations into language, thus widening and deepening the zone of communication available to the group as a whole and to each member of the group (Foulkes, 1948). This brought about a new cohesion and sense of responsibility toward the group's life and made possible group analytic work which often approached that of a neurotic group. The process was achieved slowly, erratically, and with frequent setbacks, especially before and after breaks in the therapy, and at crises points in the lives of individual members, the clinic, or the outside world. Attendance became regular and group sessions acquired great importance for the members.

The group room had become a place where one was safer than one had been before in one's life. Each patient would seek out her own chair in the circle of identical chairs and respect those of the other patients. The small table in the middle of the circle, which at the initial stages of the group had often been attacked, now became almost sacrosanct and was defended in times of great agitation and individual outbursts of rages. Group members would bring valued objects from home, outings, or holidays, and place them on the table. Sometimes the conductor would be asked to "keep them safe till next time." It seemed unthinkable that the treatment room would be occupied by other groups also. When there was evidence of this, it was strenuously ignored. The table, the room, the fixed and carefully adhered to timetable throughout the year, and the repeatedly announced regular dates of holiday breaks, all these acquired a significance akin to Winnicott's transitional objects: they were supplied by the therapist/clinic/outside world and endowed by the group with their own meaning, which in turn was understood and respected by the outside world as represented by the therapist. They became an area of negotiation and renegotiation of representations of internal object relations. Thus the group life had become an "intermediate area of experience" between the inner and outer reality (Winnicott, 1953). There was thus an opportunity in the group to make up for the deficiencies of mothering in infancy.

It was noticeable that in this middle phase and in the final phase of the group's life, the group itself often took over the mothering functions (e.g., during the therapist's absence due to illness or in response to any unforeseen change). One such function was "remembering and repeating." One patient, staring into the middle of the circle onto the table, would ask, "How was it that time . . . ?" or "What happened then . . . ?" and one after the other of the group members would recount, with astonishing recall, what Mary had said or done "then," often weeks or months previously. It was reminiscent of the young child's request at bedtime to be told by Mother what he had done during the day, and insisting that every event be remembered and put in its place. Such a remembering and holding-together function was repeatedly asked for by one or the other of the group members and unfailingly supplied by someone in the group. It seemed as if the essential mothering functions which each patient individually had not received or been able to accept in her own infancy, and which she herself had then been unable to give to her own child, were now being effectively discharged and received in the group.

In the group analyst's own experience, there was a marked difference from the earlier stages of the group: the projections and projective identifications occurred less frequently. The main task, apart from holding the group analytic setting and guarding the group boundaries (Foulkes, 1975), was now one of a "total response" (Little, 1960, p. 29). The patients, now functioning on a much more mature level inside the group, continued to be unable to cope in the outside world with such agencies as housing authorities, schools, or the courts. It was important that it should be the group analyst, and not a social worker called in by the authorities or the clinic, who responded to the total needs of the group members and intervened, mediated, negotiated, and explained to the social agencies concerned. It is probably easier to discern in group analysis than it is in the dyad of individual psychotherapy whether such an intervention is collusive (due to the analyst's unresolved needs to be all-good and all-giving) or therapeutically indicated. The group itself will reflect the nature of the demand and its location in the total therapeutic situation. It will mirror the developmental level of the patient who requires such help and resonate to her need on various levels and in many individual ways. When the help is rendered, it is often verbally acknowledged and experienced as an interpretation. This was so with a patient who became almost speechless in the group, jumbling up words and unable to string them together to form a sentence. At that time, she was required to visit her child's school to discuss arrangements for a school vacation camp. The group's response was one of helplessness, consternation, and outbursts of rage and despair, followed by increased general anxieties and fears of getting lost on the way to the clinic. The group conductor verbalized these states, and offered to accompany the patient on her visit to the school and help with the vacation arrangements. Weeks later this patient said: "This was the first time that someone knew what I wanted and needed before I said it . . . before I knew it myself."

Karl Koenig speaks of "the steering object" (das steuernde Objekt) which emerges from the positive real and fantasized interaction between the child and the mother (Koenig, 1981). These interactions are internalized, that is, changed into internal object relations and internal regulation models. Such internalization is vitally important for all later negotiations with the outside world. It would seem that in "the speechless patient," this process had been missed to some degree. Life in the group required the reparative process of supplying "the steering object," time and again, thus making up for deficiencies at the appropriate stage of childhood.

Toward the end phase of the group, group members often discharged this function for one another, with the result that ego functioning increased dramatically. For most patients, it was easier to accept such help, as well as interpretations and insights, from their peers than from the mother–therapist. In this manner, mature parts of one patient were being "lent" to another. The observant ego, absent in one group member, was present in another or others. The group mobilized what health resided in it, probably in the service of the survival of the group-as-a-whole. This, in a manner, may be similar to that of the organism that mobilizes health-preserving and restoring processes in the face of potentially life-endangering malfunctioning or deficiencies.

This process is, of course, markedly more potent in the heterogeneous group, constituted as it is of patients who present the widest possible spectrum of personalities, character structures, and resistance patterns. Such a group can be conceptualized as "representing the norm from which each patient, individually, deviates" (Foulkes, 1948, p. 169). This norm is the "common sense" of the community of which the group is a small-scale model; thus the group is a carrier of values and identification models which are available for introjection. The observing ego can rest in one part of the group, while another part of the group is in a state of distorted perception due to a negative transference. At this stage, it is enough that the reality perception is present in the group, available, as it were in the body of the group, while it is temporarily absent in one or the other of the group members. Regressed functioning of one or some group members can be "carried" by another or others in the group, who at that time are functioning on a more mature level of responses and perception. In this manner, the group, with its group conductor, can offer the required response at the appropriate time. It also offers a "reservoir of (healthy) narcissism," which is at the disposal of the needy group member (Pines, 1972).

It can be seen that the heterogeneous analytic group has a vastly greater communal strength and a wider operational therapeutic field than the homogeneous analytic group. In spite of this great advantage, the narcissistically injured patients such as the ones described in the mothers' group will not be able to function sufficiently in such a group to make use of its potential; and the group analyst, whose concern is with both the patients' welfare and the maintenance in optimal condition of the central therapeutic agent, the group, will be cautious about including the narcissistic patient in the classical heterogeneous group.

Combined Treatment Approaches

The question arises whether treatment is best combined with individual therapy and whether the therapist is to be the same for both. One's attitude to combined treatment is determined by the underlying concept of the nature of group analytic therapy in general, the space it occupies (i.e., the "inside" and "outside" of the therapeutic situation), and the place of "boundary incidents" (Foulkes, 1975, p. 132). Most of the time, the small homogeneous analytic group as well designed to afford the greedy, needy narcissistic patient the necessary gratification: this is at times provided by the attention of the therapist, at others by those of one member of the group, and often by the group-as-a-whole. When the temporary demands get overpowering, the group tends to "resonate" with them. The communicational links are regressively activated on different developmental levels simultaneously and early ego and superego developmental stages are mobilized, as are the corresponding defenses (Foulkes, 1975). This enables the group to be in touch with the needs of each member.

In practice, the group itself often asks the therapist to give extra group sessions to one of its members, or it endorses such a need when voiced by the patient in the group. At the same time, the individual sessions given arouse intense jealousy and destructive envy, which then become the group content and are treated as such by verbalization, clarification, linking, and interpretation. In this manner, the individual sessions are treated within the context of the group analytic treatment instead of being split off from it. The individual treatment sessions become a "boundary incident," an occurrence on the boundary of the precisely defined therapeutic space of the group, which, nevertheless, belongs psychologically to the therapeutic situation. This concept denies the outside–inside polarity and brings into the group session all that takes place within the psychological context of the group.

Such extra-group individual sessions must always be brought into the group situation and become part of the group matrix, that is, of the operational field of interactions and relationships within the therapy group. In this sense, the individual sessions with the group member and the group therapist are an integral part of the group treatment; their continuity will be linked to the processes taking place within the group sessions. Individual sessions will cease when the patient who receives them can once again function fully within the group analytic context. In practice, the correct moment for this becomes clear to the therapist, the individual patient, and the group-as-a-whole simultaneously, though the full reintegration and the giving up of the individual sessions may be a difficult and lengthy task to complete.

This combined treatment approach, in which the need for individual sessions may at times arise out of the context of the group processes, occurs in heterogeneous as well as homogeneous groups. The levels of narcissistic disturbance and unfulfilled needs must be reached and attended to in groups of predominantly psychoneurotic patients; that is, in the classical heterogeneous groups, as well as in the homogeneous group of the narcissistically badly damaged patients. The following group protocol is taken from such a heterogeneous group.

> In one mature heterogeneous group, a patient went through a phase of intense narcissistic needs to be heard, understood, and placed into the group center in a manner in which he could confirm his unique, misunderstood, unrecognized self. He would miss sessions and deeply resent having in any way to account for his absences. He would reject offers of understanding and similarity of experience. Eventually he told the group that he could not bear the pain of "not being understood." A number of group members reacted to him aggressively, rejecting his isolation and pain as "weak and infantile"; others felt dejected, tired, and hopeless. The group-as-a-whole presented a picture of helpless lethargy into which his aggressive attacks sank and disappeared. The group conductor described the situation in this manner, and suggested that the patient might want to see her in individual sessions. This was accepted by the group with relief. In fact, no reference was made to it in subsequent group sessions other than a request for confirmation that the individual sessions were proceeding. After five such sessions, the group member returned to the group and later brought much of the content of the individual sessions into the group. The ambivalence and envy aroused by the individual sessions remained an important part of the group's work for some time. The experience of a need being recognized and satisfied was the central experience of the patient in question.

Such a handling of the situation would have been difficult had the patient been seen individually by another therapist. In the few instances where this model is followed, nevertheless, it is important for the two therapists to stay in close contact and to share the therapeutic experience, if not necessarily the content, of the therapy sessions. Intense splitting will have to be expected and accepted in such a situation, and it may be considered that this is too high and too unnecessary a price to pay. It would be one's aim at all times to contain the therapeutic action within the setting created, which, as we have seen, includes events taking place on its boundaries.

The countertransference problems which arise in the treatment of narcissistic patients were described by Kohut as an interference with and invasion of the therapist's own narcissistic needs and demands: the therapist is denied the experience of being reacted to as a real person. He is also not perceived as an object in the patient's past. He has to guard against "archaic fears of dissolution through merger" (Kohut, 1971). These countertransference reactions occur in group psychotherapy also, and I have not found that group psychotherapy dilutes negative, or indeed positive and idealizing transference phenomena. However, they occur and are experienced in the network of relationships in the therapy group, the group matrix, which makes possible the multiple experience of the self. This rich network is influenced at the same time by a variety of libidinal and developmental levels of perception and experience, some of them at that moment mature and "whole." The group analyst, unlike the analyst in the dyadic treatment situation, has these multiple reactions and perceptions at his disposal, thus helping him to stay intact and survive the narcissistic distortions of perception and the reactivation of his own archaic responses.

Patients with borderline personality organization are notoriously difficult to treat, be it individually or in groups. Their interpersonal reactions are radically different from those of neurotic patients: it is as if, for them, the outside world is populated by "the others" who are all-aggressive and bent on retaliation and destruction, necessitating an unrelenting and continuous control over one's environment. (One such patient insisted on the group therapist handing over the management of the group to her: "If only you would do this . . . I know I could then give the group back to you"). The patient's own behavior patterns oscillate between feelings of abject misery, rejection, hurt withdrawal, and uncontrollable rages. In this manner, the outside world mirrors an inner world populated by powerful, malevolent part-object representations in continuous conflict with one another. At times there is a sense of temporary success, a lull in the battle as it were, achieved by projections and projective identification mechanisms. However, this leaves the patient with a sense of emptiness, which necessitates frantic activity. Reality testing at such times is almost impossible, and feelings hold sway to the exclusion of all other perceptions. The strength of these feelings is such that it can easily draw the therapist and other group patients into the roles allotted to them. The homing-in on selected and distorted part-objects in the borderline patient's human environment makes it difficult to relate to him as a whole person. The therapeutic process requires that whole objects be returned for part objects (Pines, 1980).

The borderline patient can usually make good use of the analytic group, especially when it is a mature, stable group. The group then represents a sustaining maternal environment which the patient, often for the first time in life, can fully experience and utilize for the maturational processes. At the same time, his presence enhances the affective life of the group by introducing heightened tensions and increased demands into the group. Against this background, part-object relations and primitive fantasies are being experienced, against which neurotic patients are usually well defended. This gives the borderline patient a valued position in the group of which the group members are well aware. The group may be the first setting in which the patient can realistically experience good, reliable, and available objects, which can make up for a real deficit in his early environment. Group therapy is in its very nature the therapy of relationships taking place in a face-to-face stituation. This gives group experiences a convincing immediacy that is difficult to match in the dyad of individual therapy. Group membership affords legitimate gratification: each patient is an indispensable member of the group. Without him, the group would not be what it is. The absence or presence of each member changes the matrix in which all occurrences take place. Individual members offer understanding, genuine feelings (even when they are negative), support, and encouragement. The group can help to negotiate by modification and reality adjustment, violent projections onto one group member, the therapist, or the whole group. Projective identifications can be held, modified, and eventually returned to the projector. Thus, the heterogeneous analytic group provides what Winnicott called "the environment essentials." This is so because it is created to contain the widest possible span of personalities, "a mixed bag of diagnoses and disturbances" (Foulkes and Anthony, 1957, p. 66). It is thus a resilient organism with strong yet permeable boundaries. The group analyst is concerned with the maintenance of the group in its optimal condition, and will, therefore, consider the welfare of the group as well as that of the borderline patient when introducing him into such a group.

In order to avoid isolation, two borderline patients rather than one may be introduced into a slow-open group of six patients in its middle life span, and this may be greatly to the benefit of the group as well as that of the borderline patients. Such an addition of borderline patients tends to intensify the group's contact with early object relations and archaic feelings and fantasies. The borderline patients, on the other hand, benefit from the neurotics' differentiated awareness of relationships and greater tolerance of ambivalent emotions. Inevitable savage scapegoating by the borderline patient is contained by the other patients, who function as the observing ego. The group-as-a-whole affords protection to the attacked member, who does not then need to deny or retaliate. The group analyst also feels supported by the different perceptions of the neurotic group members.

Case Example: Treatment of Borderline Patients in a Heterogeneous Group

Two people with borderline personalities had been introduced into a heterogeneous group in its middle life. This group had been meeting twice weekly for two years, and the newcomers had been in the group for three months. One was a young woman of high intelligence and academic ability. She had grown up in a family of six siblings with a depressed mother and a psychotic father who was a minister of an obscure religious sect. The other patient was an undersized middle-aged man, unmarried, suffering from ill-defined ailments, and despite a good academic position, unable to enjoy his work, love, or play. His father, an army officer, had been accused of gross incompetence, was court-martialed, and dismissed from the Service. He had died when the patient was still a boy. His elder brother had been killed in World War II, and his very old mother was alive and continued to rule from a large house in the country to which our patient returned regularly "for visits."

The group was working on the imminent absence for one session of the group analyst. The absence had been announced well in advance, and the group was in touch with its anger over the desertion, the secret enjoyment the group analyst was fantasized to have away from the group, and at the same time its erotic expectations of "an exciting group session" without the conductor. This absence of the conductor was the first one for the two new group members who, up to that session, had presented a united front of bitter discontent, frequent and unexpected outbursts against individual group members, and admiration and idealized expectations of the group analyst. The group had reacted by trying to pry them apart by splitting the good and helpful from the bad and hindering. They cherished the young woman as "alive, passionate, and brave" and experienced the man as "irritating, ineffectual, and an altogether disappointing group member." He had thus managed to recreate his early infancy experiences in the group: his mother had told him that he had been "too small and sickly to be likely to live." Simultaneous with the group's negative feelings toward this man was another current running through the group which represented care and a wish to "let him live," manifested in the time and space he was given for his endless stories of misunderstandings, harsh treatment, and ill-health.

In the session before the conductor's absence, the old group members addressed one another briskly, exchanging work experiences and displaying interest and animation; it was like being in the presence of late adolescents planning their day's activities. The conductor was and felt temporarily excluded. Then, suddenly, the young woman jumped up, grabbed a high-heeled shoe of the woman next to her and tried to attack her fellow newcomer, aiming her blows at his eyes. Screaming abuse at him, she said she had had as much as she would take, and now he was "not going to see it all anymore." The man jumped out of his chair in great agitation, called her mad and a slut—was this group a brothel where women attacked men and blinded them? Members of the group pulled the two apart, without panic or terrified immobilization, and held them in a manner reminiscent of a strong parent restraining a raging young child. The group analyst was included but not expected to "save the situation." There was a strong feeling of one body experiencing and containing emotions that belonged to it as a whole. Various group members resonated to the theme of the murderous father who must be blinded because he saw with the eye of God and subjugated and usurped the sexual fantasies of the child. The counterpart—the all-powerful, frightening female who, with her sluttish sexuality maims and destroys—was also represented by fantasies of group members and repressed childhood experiences now remembered. The young woman recalled that her father had come to her bedroom and called her "a slut who offends the eye of God." The point here is not the content of the fantasies at this group session, but the active free asssociative participation of all the group members in the psychic state of the two borderline patients, albeit on different libidinal levels, that corresponded to the psychopathology of each. Through the pooling of associations in the group process, the symbolic meanings were understood and worked with. On a conscious level, the isolating "otherness" which the two borderline patients had repeated in the group by pairing was now replaced by an experience of similarity and universality (Yalom, 1975).

Patients with Impaired Selves

These patients can be distinguished from the narcissistically injured and the borderline patients by their high level of functioning in many areas of their lives. They are usually of exceptional intelligence, gifted, and achievers who are often ascending their professional ladders. In spite of the objectively successful and hopeful life situations, they have a history of depression, and many have harbored unspecified death wishes and deep doubts about the value of living since childhood. The syndrome of the mutilated self is nowadays so ubiquitous that it may be erroneous to speak of a patient group; it seems to be present in most patients who present themselves for therapy. The psychoanalyst Alice Miller found that in her 20 years' work experience, there was not one patient whose ability to experience genuine and unique feelings, desires, and needs was not to some degree impaired (Miller, 1979). This may be due to the generations of wartime mothers who had to rear their infants with insufficient inner resources and need fulfillment: the mother's own deficit had to be supplied by her infant, who thus took on mothering functions from birth onwards. The mother was then experienced as intensely demanding, helpless, and fragile. The love given to the infant was experienced as conditional on his ability to supply the vital missing parts of the mother. In the absence of the "helping third," the active father, the tie between the needy mother and her child remained unrelenting. A vital role of the father soon after the birth of the child is to reestablish the primacy of the husband–wife relationship as it was before the arrival of the child. The reclaiming by the father of the mother sets the child free for separation –individuation (Skynner, 1974). Only then can the child begin to own his unique feelings and express them in an age-appropriate way, instead of adapting, mutilating, despising, or denying them.

The small heterogeneous analytic group is the near-optimal setting for the recovering of the lost world of authenticity, and the accepting of the unique self. The therapy group assumes temporarily the holding aspects of a good-enough maternal environment, in which the experience of shame, denigration, ridicule, and inadequacy to supply the vital needs of the parents can emerge and be worked through. The following example illustrates this process:

> In a mature analytic group, angry disapproval of and disappointment with Edward was expressed over a number of sessions. Edward was the oldest member in the group after the departure of an elderly man whom the group had valued highly for his success in life, his gaiety, and his wisdom. Now that he was gone, who would show people how to live? Who would keep the group happy with interesting stories from life? The departed member, Paul, had been a "second conductor" (therapist). Edward, who in age most resembled Paul, had nothing to give, it was said. He was dull and often listless in the sessions. Why did he not live up to his age and life experience? This was what the group members wanted to know; they felt "let down" by Edward. Edward became more and more sullen and silent, and he visibly shrunk into his chair and hung his head. The conductor suggested that the group felt depleted, needy, and fearful, this made then angry and aggressive. Edward must replace Paul, so that

he now could be emulated and admired as a father. Without such a father, they would have only their (female) conductor, who herself might be too depleted by the departure of Paul to remain strong and capable of looking after herself and them.

The ensuing silence was eventually broken by a bitter outburst of anguish from Edward. He was being denigrated by the group because they did not want him as he was; he had to be what Paul had been in order to be allowed "to live in the group." His own feelings were of no value. He then recalled a long-forgotten scene: he was a little boy, sitting on a sleigh, being pulled through the deep snow by a pair of chattering adults, his parents. They were far ahead, he was on a long lead. He was cold and frightened of the snow which threatened to swallow him up. The parents were absorbed in one another, and did not notice that he fell off the sleigh into the snow. When they eventually did notice, they roared with laughter and clearly expected him to laugh also. When he cried, they became angry and ridiculed his behavior. The group listened intently to Edward, and the mood changed into one of awe of the feelings of isolation and humiliation which were now in the group room. A woman began to cry, and she talked about how she rejected and ridiculed her daughter's distress over failure at school and in social situations. She felt inadequate and incomplete in the face of her daughter's temporary failures. A young man then expressed anger with Edward's "insensitive parents—so full of themselves that nothing is left for understanding their son." Another, older man suggested that what Edward's parents had wanted was a tough, brave warrior son; such a son would have made them feel strong and resilient. After this interchange, Edward recalled that his father had been absent from home (he did not know why) before and after the event in the snow. His mother had often cried and hugged him for comfort. The group suggested that this must have been the time of his father's army service, and Edward was greatly relieved by this explanation. The shifting of the focus from the inadequate, humiliated little boy to the needy parents afforded dramatic relief to Edward and changed his stature in the group. It was felt that "his story" had enriched the group-as-a-whole. Much individual work on parents, and on fathers in particular, followed this event. Edward began to bring his mature aspects into the group and into his life outside the group. The group itself had done valuable and valued work.

The therapy group's purpose is the resolution of stifling, limiting neuroses and the furthering of individuation. Its task is the discovery of the meaning of one's behavior and the facilitating of change. The group analytic setting and the group's boundaries make an inclusive yet permeable network of relationships in which to discover the essence of the self. In it there is the possibility of experiencing the functions of feeding, holding, withholding, containing, and discharging; there is a reality experience of "the other" who receives or rejects these functions. There is sensitivity and respect for genuine feelings in the group-as-a-whole, if not always in individual members, because the expression of such feelings is the clearly stated, constantly confirmed, and highly valued task of the group. Shame, ridicule, and denigration are experienced first in a mirror action in other group members and, in time, owned by the individual and worked through. This is often easier to do with the help of the other group members than with the help of the analyst, because the group analyst's interpretations and interventions can be experienced as the "know-all" parent and received with rage or contempt. It may well be that the work on the restoration and acceptance of the self is a precondition for all patients before the classical group analytic work can be undertaken. The retrieving of the genuine, authentic self is at the same time a task to which the patients in the group return in times of crisis and stress all through the group's life. The group analyst must be in tune with the prevailing needs and be prepared to alter the analytic stance when this is required, to return to it time and again, and to resume the analytic function of the therapy group.

Summary/Conclusion

Treatment in analytic groups for the narcissistically impaired, the ego-weak, borderline patients, and those who present a mutilated self, has been proving its usefulness during clinical application in day hospitals and in private practice. The emptiness in relationships, extreme communication difficulties, and excessive demands on the therapist and the group, often make the treatment a succession of traumatic events. However, the carefully constituted analytic group is well suited to meet and contain these demands. The group represents a maternal holding situation in which merging and differentiation can be experienced. The group is what Pines calls a "reservoir of narcissism," which is available for the impaired patient. The heterogeneous group, in particular, is especially suited to provide whole and part-object relations and the perception and resolution of projective identification processes. For the narcissistically most disturbed, a small homogeneous group may be the only social setting in which they can function with safety to themselves and their fellow patients. In both the classical and the special group, it is the group itself, of which the group analyst is an integral part, which is the therapeutic agent. It follows that the constitution and maintenance in optimal condition of the group is a major task of the group analyst. It may become necessary and therapeutically expedient to combine group treatment with individual sessions for one or the other group member. Such treatment is usually best undertaken by the group analyst and not another therapist because it then becomes part of the processes which occur on the boundary of the group life, and the reintegration of the individual treatment into the network of group relationships is facilitated.

The treatment which places the analytic group into the center of the therapeutic process rests on the view that individual emotional disturbances and symptoms can, in the group analytic setting, be transformed into shared, communicable language. An ever-deepening and widening communication is the essence of group analytic treatment. In this manner, optimal socialization is coterminous with optimal individuation.

References

Battegay, R. (1976), The concept of the narcissistic group self. *Group Anal.*, IX/3: 217-220.
Feldberg, T. (1958), Treatment of borderline patients in neurotic groups. *Internat. J. Group Psychother.*, 8:76–84.
Foulkes, S.H. (1948), *Introduction to Group-Analytic Psychotherapy*. London: William Heinemann Medical Books.
――― (1964), *Therapeutic Group Analysis*. London: George Allen & Unwin.
――― (1975), *Group-Analytic Psychotherapy*. London: Gordon and Breach, Science Publishers Ltd.

—— Anthony, E.J. (1957), *Group Psychotherapy: The Psychoanalytic Approach.* Baltimore, MD: Penguin Books, 1965.
Kernberg, O. (1981), *Borderline Condition and Pathological Narcissism.* New York: Jason Aronson.
Koenig, K. (1981), *Angst und Personlichkeit, Das Konzept vom steuernden Objekt und seine Anwendung.* Goettingen (Germany): Verlag für medizinische Psychologie im Verlag Vendenhoeck & Ruprecht.
Kohut, H. (1971), *The Analysis of the Self.* New York: International Universities Press.
Little, M. (1960), Counter-transference. *Brit. J. Med. Psychol.,* 33:29–31.
Miller, A. (1979), *Das Drama des begabten Kindes.* Frankfurt: Surkamp Verlag.
Ogden, T. (1979), Projective identification. *Internat. J. Psycho-Anal.,* IV: 357–373.
Pines, M. (1972), Changes and trends. *Group Analysis: Inter-National Panel and Correspondence* (London), V/2.
—— (1980), What to expect in the psychotherapy of the borderline patient. *Group Anal.,* XIII/3:168–176.
Roth, B. (1979), Understanding the development of the homogeneous identity-impaired group through counter-transference phenomena. *Group,* 3:3–22.
Scheidlinger, S. (1982), *Focus on Group Psychotherapy.* New York: International Universities Press.
Skynner, A. C. R. (1974), School phobia: A reappraisal. *Brit. J. Med. Psychol.,* 47:1.
Winnicott, D. W. (1953), Transitional objects and transitional phenomena. *Internat. J. Psycho-Anal.,* 34:42.
—— (1960), Counter-transference. *Brit. J. Med. Psychol.,* 33:17.
Yalom, I. D. (1975), *The Theory and Practice of Group Psychotherapy.* New York: Basic Books.

Chapter 8

MIRRORING AND GROUP THERAPY

MALCOLM PINES, FRCP., FRC. Psych., D.P.M.

Most of the vast and highly interesting literature on borderline patients and narcissistic personality disorders refers to the patient in individual psychotherapy—either psychoanalysis or a modified form of psychoanalytic psychotherapy. When technique is discussed, the general consensus is that modifications of the standard technique are usually necessary and justified. The reasons given for this include the predominance of narcissistic defenses, which result in interpretation frequently being perceived as an assault, a deprivation, or a threat to omnipotent defensive systems; the development of transference psychosis; the impulsive acting-out nature of the patient; the ubiquity of narcissistic rage; and the mobilization of primitive infantile envy, leading to chronic negative therapeutic reactions. In my experience (Pines, 1975, 1978, 1980), many of these difficult features of the individual psychotherapy of borderline patients appear less frequently and with less intensity if these patients are treated in well-selected and well-established analytic groups, where good results can be achieved. The reasons for this will, I hope, become clear in the course of this chapter. Basically, they refer to the holding, containing (James, 1982), and mirroring (Pines, 1982, 1983; Zinkin, 1983) functions of the group, which can be combined with the analytic and uncovering processes. The group analytic situation can effectively combine the caretaking aspects of the techniques advocated by Winnicott, Balint, and Kohut with more classical psychoanalytic approaches that try to hold to the standard psychoanalytic situation with as few modifications as possible. The caretaking aspects referred to offer containment and tranquil nurture within the alliance, which is real and not only symbolic, and which can help to remedy the effects of defective early object relationships. With the more classical analytic techniques, we try to interest the nonpsychotic, normal part of the personality in the travails of what Grotstein (1980) calls the "psychotic twin part."

The Function of Mirroring in the Development in the Sense of Self

The significance of mirroring came into psychoanalytic theory with Freud's theory of narcissism. The image of Narcissus dying, wasting away in helpless yearning for a mirror image, represents pathological mirroring; the mirror of the water is a dead reflective surface that can give nothing of and by itself. It is indeed the mirror of the narcissistic personality, who only seeks his own reflection. It is a pathological narcissism and a dead mirroring, an attempt to maintain a fragment of life in unchanging form, showing the qualities of aloof grandiosity, arrogance, absence of others, and absence of empathic understanding, which can only come about through a relationship with another person.

Psychoanalytic developmental psychology has moved on to recognize the crucial importance of live mirroring and of healthy narcissism. Mahler (1967), Kohut (1971), Bursten (1977), Winnicott (1971) and Lichtenstein (1977), have all contributed to our understanding of the role of vision in laying down the core of the self, the "primary identity theme" as Lichtenstein terms it, the theme upon which endless variations will be played out through the life cycle. Winnicott says that the first mirror is the mother's face, which shows the child who he is in her eyes. Mahler states that the mother conveys in innumerable ways a kind of "mirroring frame of reference" to which the primitive self of the infant automatically adjusts. Disturbances in mother's mirroring functions leads to disturbances in primitive feelings, to premature and abrupt hatchings from the symbiotic phase. The primary method of identity formation consists of mutual reflections in the symbiotic phase. Lichtenstein suggests that the mother imprints her unconscious image of her child through her selective responses to his activities, which becomes the identity theme. Bursten states that the earliest capacity to sense the self (and boundary) is primarily a maturational and biological phenomenon that arises from within, is exceedingly fragile, and has to be reinforced constantly by empathic mirroring. The empathic mirror, the mother, is an object confirming the existence of the self. Kohut has greatly emphasized the importance of the "self object" in the psychic economy of the narcissistic patient in analysis and relates this to the crucial importance of early mirroring in the secure development of the sense of self. Though Freud did not refer to mirroring as such, he did use the term *self regard* in his discussions of narcissism to emphasize the visual component, which is easily lost when we talk of *self-esteem,* which is an appropriate term for the later stages of development when psychological function has matured.

Bursten (1973) has offered a useful classification that distinguishes three different levels of ability with regard to support of the sense of self. This sense of self rests on a biological substrate but has to be supported by psychological and psychosocial confirmers.

1. It may be maintained with great difficulty and considerable instability so that there are frequent lapses; this is the *borderline* level.

2. It may be maintained with somewhat less difficulty so the confirmers are usually successful in preventing lapses. However, the sense of self is still sufficiently vulnerable that the confirmers play an extremely important role in its maintenance. This is the level of the *narcissistic personality* disorders.

3. It may be so secure that the confirmers are of relatively less importance. This is the level of *normality* and "complementary personalities"; that is, the level of persons who have emerged from childhood with a secure and cohesive sense of self and whose emotional problems therefore occur at the oedipal level. This basically is also the position taken by Kohut.

All these considerations point to the enormous importance of psychological and psychosocial confirmers of the sense of self, factors which arise naturally, constantly, and potentially helpfully in the situation of group psychotherapy in contrast to the situation of individual psychotherapy, where borderline patients can very easily lose the sense of the therapeutic situation and of the therapist as being a confirmer of the sense of self. Massive projections and other primitive defensive operations can quickly transform the therapist into a disconfirmer of the sense of self, a threat to the precarious stability of these types of patients. It is these threats to the sense of self which then can give rise to the vicious cycles of withdrawal or defensive hostility that are so familiar to us. The poet George Herbert said that "The best mirror is a good friend." It is very hard, indeed, for the individual therapist to convey to these patients that he is a good friend, and to do so he may well have to move beyond the position of optimal neutrality which most therapists strive to maintain.

The Psychodynamics of the Borderline and Narcissistic Patient

The broad outlines of the psychodynamics of the borderline patient are now fairly well recognized, and consequently we have a better grasp of the appropriate techniques of psychotherapy. Kernberg (1968), for instance, advocates use of the face-to-face situation with emphasis on the here-and-now and analysis of pathological defenses such as denial, splitting, idealization, and projective identification. In individual therapy, much work has to be directed toward assembling and integrating primitive and fragmented transference manifestations until they become coherent transference patterns; that is, there must be movement from the level of part-object relations to that of whole-object relations. The therapist needs to keep a strategy that will avoid therapeutic stalemates and impasses in which an atmosphere of timelessness overtakes both therapist and patient. Despite advances in the understanding of borderline patients, in treatment they remain difficult and troublesome, particularly to the less experienced therapist. The more severely disturbed patients are often admitted to inpatient units, where their behavior, if not well understood, can lead to vicious cycles of misunderstanding between staff and patients which exacerbate the problems of acting out and of regression.

Persons with narcissistic personality disorders and borderline personality disorders suffer from disorders in the cohesion of the self and from difficulties in object relationships. The narcissistic personality differs from the borderline in the greater ability to make use of object relations to maintain a sense of pseudocohesion. Bennett Roth (1980) uses the term *identity impaired* by which he means "a dynamic organization, existing over time and to varying degrees within persons whose development of a primary identity system, ego and self, and sense of self engenders a constant need for maintenance and repair." Kernberg's differentiation is that, unlike the borderline personality, the narcissistic personality can maintain a sense of identity and avoid the threat of disintegration by the achievement of an integrated but highly pathological grandiose self, which screens off the hungry infantile character, the exaggerated dependency needs, oral rage, and envy.

There is a broad consensus that these patients differ from neurotic patients in their underlying personality structure and that the essence of this is in a failure to develop a secure cohesive and integrated sense of self. There is a structural developmental deficit and psychotherapy had to be directed to facilitating the renewed growth of the personality as well as to dealing with the specific conflicts. The essence of the problem is at the preoedipal rather than the oedipal level. A secure cohesive and integrated sense of self gives to those who have acquired it a background of psychic safety, a sense of containment of one's own thoughts, feelings, and experiences. Lacking this, the borderline patient has not acquired a well-functioning external boundary to the self, a psychic envelope, which will securely and clearly hold the self together and help to differentiate self from other. Borderline pathology is often a form of boundary pathology, and the failure to develop a relatively clear and appropriate boundary to the self leads to many problems in life.

The patient's sense of temporal continuity, spatial integrity, and overall cohesiveness is constantly under threat and is maintained only by massive defensive maneuvers. These will involve other person, who have to be used to hold the self together, much as the small child is incapable of holding itself together in the absence of the mother. There has been an arrest in the process of separation–individuation so that the person, though separate, has not acquired the capacities to be an individual. One of the fixation points in the developmental arrest seems to be at the level of the "rapprochement" phase of the separation–individuation process described by Margaret Mahler (1967). These arrests and fixations leave the patient vulnerable to catastrophic anxiety aroused by the constant threat of disintegration and fragmentation. In contrast to the neurotic patient's sense of anxiety, which is a signal both to and from the intact ego, the borderline patient's anxiety represents an ever-present sense of fragmentation. Object relationships for the borderline patients are at a narcissistic level, where the relationship to the other person is primarily in the service of maintaining self-cohesion. The other person is used narcissistically and is felt to be an extension of the self, not a separate entity. The borderline patient also uses other persons as containers of rejected or projected parts of the self based upon mechanisms of splitting and projective identification. These patients have great power to make other persons feel uncomfortable and to be made to feel how the patient needs them to feel, a process of externalization. Here the unconscious aim may be to make the other person act as if the rejected and unwanted parts of the self actually originated with, and belonged to, the other person, thereby ridding the patient of unbearable inner feelings of guilt, depression, and so on. Another aim may be to make the other person understand through living out the feelings of what the borderline patient himself has to suffer, such as those of uselessness and confusion.

When these underlying processes are not recognized, the patient is easily seen as being manipulative and arouses counterreactions of hostility both in staff and in other patients. When these processes are better understood, staff can be relieved of their sense of confusion and outrage and begin more clearly to see the nature of the patient's problems and to differentiate themselves from them. In this way, more appropriate relationships with the patient can be maintained, which allows patients to begin to contain their own feelings and bear the pain of their own existence.

Loss and Restoration of Self-Cohesion

The painful and frightening threats to the adjustment of the borderline patient can be seen as threats to the pseudo-cohesion, which wards off these fears of disintegration and catastrophic anxiety feelings. The most frequent threats seem to be: (1) Some variation of a situation that the subject experiences as a lack of attention on the part of the person who is vital to the maintenance of that sense of cohesion, a self object. This often manifests itself in individual psychotherapy as the reaction to the weekends, the holiday breaks, and the intervals between sessions. (2) Situations that stimulate guilt, for guilt is often experienced in an intensely persecutory and intolerable form. (3) Emergence of depression, which is as unbearable for the person as is criticism.

Borderline patients adopt emergency restorative measures to counter the threat of loss of cohesion. These activities and psychic compensations can be regarded as attempts at restoration of the boundaries of the self. The most inevitable and immediate is the experience of rage, for it seems that the patient feels that rage strengthens the boundaries of the self and will make him magically invulnerable. Rage produces a pseudo-cohesion and a reinforcement of the external boundaries (Fried, 1970). Other defensive responses, such as gorging with food, the use of stimulant or sedative drugs, masturbation, and sexual activity, can be seen as serving the same end, stimulation of the external boundaries of self. Self-mutilation, cutting, and burning may provide a partial stimulus to the sense of self and an escape from painful feelings of depersonalization. Changes in the threshold of consciousness are used defensively, and states of high tension and maniclike excitement and hyperactivity of thought and fantasy can occur, but so does their opposite, withdrawal into states of isolation, and numbness with denial of perceptions, leading to states of sleepiness and even loss of consciousness. Massive defenses against the experience of mental pain involve the use of primitive defense mechanisms such as denial, splitting, and projective and introjective identification.

In contrast to neurotic patients, borderline patients regularly show cycles and oscillations that represent the loss of cohesion and the attempt to restore it. Typical cycles are as follows:

1. A loss of cohesion, leading to the experience of fragmentation, which is followed by attempts at restoration of cohesion through excitement, leading to overstimulation through the use of drugs, food, and sexuality. The consequences of this are feelings of disgust, shame, and guilt, leading to self-punishment, which, if intensive enough, will restore the sense of cohesion on the basis of a masochistic bargain. The inner experience is that of being very small and of being handled by someone very cruel and powerful, and this restores the sense of a powerful internal relationship and renews the lost sense of safety.

2. States of withdrawal and sensory shutdown can follow a loss of cohesion, this leads to feelings of derealization and depersonalization, emptiness, and blankness. After a period of time, there is a gradual recovery from these states through resort to a great deal of fantasy and magical thinking leading to states of aloof grandiosity which, in turn, restore the lost sense of cohesion.

3. Loss of the narcissistic self-object relationship is followed by an immediate and frantic search for replacement, which leads to promiscuity, the trading of sex for body contact and handling.

Group Psychotherapy with Borderline Patients

It is very striking how these cycles are stimulated by the experiences of individual psychotherapy, but in my experience, are lessened through group psychotherapy. In individual psychotherapy, the patient, being unable to cope with normal vicissitudes of a one-to-one relationship, is unable to accept that separation is inevitable and that it can be coped with by internal psychological mechanisms. In normal psychological development, object loss or the giving up of omnipotence in the relationship to an object can lead to the internalization of qualities of that person and of the relationship, and this leads to the building up of psychological structure (Tolpin, 1971). The constant process of internalization leads to internal differentiation and to the building up of capacities for the higher mental functions, for a psychic apparatus that will eventually enable the person to contain fantasy and affects. When this is not possible, then separation leads to catastrophic anxiety and to the defensive and pseudorestorative cycles that have already been mentioned. Borderline personalities have not securely established the capacities for acceptance of separation, frustration, and loss; that is, the ability to move to the depressive position.

Since the problem is one of structural defects, the aim of therapy must be to remedy that defect. As psychological structure is based upon the internalization of qualities of the relationship by the child with significant others, the defects in the separation–individuation process and in the process of transmuting internalization have led to a pseudoautonomy and a pseudocohesion. The aim of therapy is to create the conditions that will allow for the resumption of internalization of qualities of relationship, which can be used to build up the missing elements of psychic structure. Hence therapy is inevitably long term and involved, close and intense, between the patient and those offering therapy. The essential requirement is the creation of a therapeutic relationship that will be strong enough to contain the inevitable violent swings of affect.

Because there is only a pseudodifferentiation of the self, there is no secure psychic envelope to hold the self together, which means that the therapeutic setting has for a long time to represent this external boundary of the self; it is hoped that this containing function can eventually be internalized and be used to build up the person's own boundary capacities. Whereas the patient will constantly relate to the therapist or to the therapeutic setting on a primitive level, that is, on the level of part-object relationship, it is essential that the person in the setting, particularly the staff, respond to this part-object with more mature whole-object responses. This can become a benign cycle, in contrast to the vicious cycles that the patient is constantly engaged in, so that the patient can then eventually take in these more mature and more differentiated responses, internalize them, metabolize them, and bring them up to new and higher levels of psychic structure. We do this by creating and maintaining dialogue with the patient, even when the patient may be aiming at annihilation of dialogue, and by maintaining the capacity for empathy and understanding of the primitive levels of experience at which the patient operates mentally.

Inpatient Psychotherapy

In considering the case of group psychotherapy with a hospitalized patient, the distinction has to be made between short-term hospitalization necessary because of a regressive swing which arises either from the patient's life situation or, as is so often the case, from the stresses of psychotherapy, and long-term hospitalization with group psychotherapy as the major ingredient. In the past, long-term therapy and hospitalization of nonpsychotic patients were avoided whenever possible. It was feared that long-term regression and dependency would ensue with the institutionalization of the patient and that the therapy would be colluding with the defenses. I was on the staff of one hospital some years ago, where we always reviewed cases that had been in for more than nine months, and the general attitude was that this situation had come about through unresolved transference and countertransference problems. The planned admission of patients for long-term inpatient group psychotherapy did not exist and would not have found favor, as the emphasis was on individual psychotherapy and the group processes were conceptualized as a necessary background to the primacy of individual psychotherapy. In those days, we did not properly recognize the psychopathology and structural defect of the borderline patient and therefore we were tempted to discharge patients who were not ready; as the hospital tried not to readmit patients, there were some patients who did not successfully complete their treatments.

A better understanding of the underlying structural defect has gradually led to the adoption of the viewpoint that the borderline patient is as severely crippled by his illness as is the psychotic patient, and this has lessened the need to see long periods of hospitalization as failures of therapy. Rather, the reverse is beginning to happen and short periods of treatment are seen as failures, for they are likely to lead to further breakdowns and the need for readmission. Therapists are going through the difficult task of coming to accept that helping these patients is indeed a major undertaking and that we have to persuade the wider society that appropriate facilities need to be provided; for example, lengthy periods of admission into units which are conducted on psychodynamic principles. An example of such a regime is at the inpatient psychiatric facility of the University of Leuven, Belgium (see chapter 19) where there are residential psychiatric day and night programs for a population of schizoid personalities, narcissistic personalities, borderline personalities, and not too severely fragmented psychotic personalities. The duration of inpatient treatment is usually between one and two years with a maximum of three years, and the treatment combines large- and small-group activities on different therapeutic levels. The emphasis throughout is on the group interactions, whether in the ward, in the informal setting of living together, cooking, and cleaning, in the interaction of nonverbal psychotherapies such as art and occupational therapy, in the more formal group analytic situation, or in the community meetings that integrate the different parts of the program.

The ward units consist of either 24 or 32 patients and the whole community meets daily. The patients are divided into small groups of eight patients and these small groups have a very active group program. They meet twice a week to look at the problems in living together, they are given the responsibility for cooking and cleaning and the organization of recreational activities, they meet three times weekly for art therapy, once a week for music therapy, and three times a week for what are called psychomotor activities, which include gymnastics, games, and sports. There are two formal group analytic therapy meetings. The progress of each patient is reviewed about once every two months in a meeting with the patient, his small group, a representative of the other small groups, and a representative of the staff. This sort of program requires a large therapeutic team consisting of a senior psychiatrist, psychiatric resident, nursing staff, occupational and art therapists, an activity therapist, and a psychotherapist for the group analytic groups. There is an extensive program of supervision and staff training. Experience in this unit has shown that significant progress with these patients can be made over the period of one to two years, that the necessity for frequent readmissions has thereby been eliminated, and a steady planned form of treatment can be devised.

In another report on inpatient therapy (Macaskill, 1980), the borderline patients initially responded to being brought together as a group with demands for individual sessions. The group situation was devalued, and in many different ways, demands for immediate gratification were evident in the demands for individual sessions, for drugs, and so on. The therapist firmly declined to provide these gratifications and pointed out the common responses of disappointment and anger. The increase in anger which these frustrations produced was evident to the staff. The patients, however, responded with mechanisms of denial, which were interpreted as being motivated by fears of rejection because of the underlying rage and destructiveness which patients felt for the therapist as a transference figure, thereby repeating early patterns of fears of destroying needsatisfying objects through feelings of ruthless rage. This led to a gradual acceptance by the group that they shared common defenses against hostility and to the beginnings of group cohesion. With the lessening of fears of recognizing their hostility and rage, the patients began to be able to tolerate their feelings of envy, which began to appear in the form of attacks upon the superior role and power of the nursing staff.

Over a period of six months considerable progress seemed to be made with this group of patients who were able to become a cohesive group and to raise their level of self-esteem and their capacity to contain and to understand their own affects. There was a move from narcissistic isolation and autism to articulate expression of some of their basic personality problems and they became sufficiently aware of each other as separate entities to begin to work with their feelings of rivalry, envy, and jealousy within the context of the group. As the members of the group became aware of their common patterns of hurt withdrawal and increase of self-interest following hurt, they were able to share more empathically and to give each other increased support. The therapist found himself able to keep to a focal approach and to enable them to understand what they all had in common, which gave the group a sense of predictability, direction, and structure, and allowed for integration of material into the one theme. A group culture began to emerge and the cohesiveness that was originally based upon shared hate and envy shifted to one based on a shared hurt and an understanding of their patterns of coping with loss of self-esteem. The group as an entity began to emerge, giving the patients a sense of security of belonging to a strong body that could help them and in which the capacities for greater reality testing were preserved and fostered.

Though the therapist often felt that he was overwhelmed by the chaos that emanated from the group and which resonated in himself, he was gradually able to differentiate the individual responses in the group and to help patients to see themselves as individuals as well as understanding what they had in common. This group of patients seemed to have in common reactions of narcissistic rage and devaluation as a response to narcissistic injuries; their sense of security based upon a grandiose self-image, was basically very vulnerable. The unstable grandiose narcissistic self-image led to defensive attempts to buttress the self-image with demands for attention and admiration, leading to clinging, demanding, intense dependent relationships with a desperate need to control others. The collapse of these narcissistic defenses leads to distress, shame, and feelings of internal fragmentation.

Thus in inpatient treatment we see two main areas that require the understanding of group dynamics. The first is the impact of the patient upon the staff and fellow patients in day-to-day living. Here the counterreactions and countertransference need to be monitored and metabolized so that empathic understanding can be maintained. The main areas of attention are (1) the way in which the hospital and the ward act as containers for the patient, which reinforces the weak ego boundaries; (2) the distribution of transference patterns between the staff members and patients based upon splitting and projection, which can produce staff conflicts and maintain the patient's externalizations of an unintegrated inner world; and (3) standing up to the negative transference of these patients who have great capacity to make helpers despair and to feel threatened in their professional identities through their chronic negative responses.

Second, we still have the task of working out appropriate forms of inpatient psychotherapy, which can mean the creation of an environment that offers long-term planned regimes based upon group methods. Here group therapy can be the main therapeutic measure or can play a varying part in the program that includes individual psychotherapy.

Outpatient Therapy

Turning to outpatient therapy, the first question we need to consider is the selection of these patients for group psychotherapy and of the composition of the groups. Naturally, there is an interest in working with groups composed mainly of borderline patients in the hope that the common mechanisms might be the focus of the group work in ways that it seems possible to work in the inpatient setting. However, I believe this to be an unrealistic aim and I base my arguments both on theoretical grounds and on the basis of experience. As an inpatient, the borderline patient does not only live as a member of the borderline group. He is a member of the inpatient community composed of all the other patients and staff and is involved in the institutional setting. The setting and the staff group, together with the healthier capacities of the whole inpatient unit, combine to maintain higher levels of psychic functioning in which the borderline patient is defective, such as the capacity for containment, impulse control, self-reflection, and tolerance of frustration without recourse to rage and attacks upon the self when frustrated. Object relations that are not primarily narcissistic are the norm for the other persons. Though often under strain and attack by the borderline group of patients, these capacities survive, and gradually the borderline group is able to accept that these qualities are real and that a real understanding, empathic, and containing world exists. The cycle of projection and externalization, followed by introjection, which maintains the psychopathology, begins to alter as the patient begins to accept the more mature responses of the staff and other patients, an acceptance which can open the way to a new internalization. The borderline group of outpatients, by contrast, does not have these capacities to function at a higher level where containment through reflection and understanding are part of the group process. I will cite some examples.

Kutter (1983), who worked with an outpatient borderline group that eventually disintegrated, suggests that we should envisage a schema of layers of transference reactions in therapy groups. The first is that of social interaction, the next is that of the normal neurotic level, then comes the narcissistic transference involving idealization and grandiosity, followed by the borderline pattern of splitting, and part-object relations. Kutter's (1983) borderline group was from the start very active, chaotic, and fragmented; destructiveness and premature self-revelation were characteristic, cohesion was never long lasting, and was broken up by destructive attacks. Split-off destructive parts projected into each other prevented mutual empathy and understanding. Holidays produced great disturbances, and when patients dropped out it was extremely difficult to introduce new patients into the group. The basic transference paradigm was that of a group with a powerful and dangerous destructive mother, with the therapist as an unhelpful father who failed to protect the children from the devouring mother.

The group members felt like unwanted children, abandoned and never accepted. Retrospectively the therapist saw the patients had regressed to an oral level of drive organization and used primitive methods of projection; therefore, unintegrated, split-off destructive forces were projected into the group. The group conductor did not represent a safe and potent authority figure and therefore there was no protection from mutual attacks and exploitations.

Roth (1980) worked for three years with an outpatient group of borderline and narcissistic personalities and found that at the end of this time the group had moved from a ruthless stage to one in which rudimentary concern for each other was present but that during this time he had been subjected to very intense countertransference pressures. The group cannot meet the reasonable needs of the therapist for (1) a group that is good enough to maintain the therapist's self-esteem as a result of doing good work; or (2) predictable patients who do not make constant affective demands and who are able to accept the "as if" quality of therapeutic relationships.

The group creates great problems for the solo therapist, as members repetitively attempt to externalize inner conflicts in order to maintain the narcissistic structures. These factors strain the therapist's capacity to maintain empathic concern and to allow himself temporary empathic regression to the level at which the group is functioning. The effect on the therapist of a homogenous group of borderline and narcissistic patients is to cause confusion and anxiety at being overwhelmed by the group's collective anger, rage, and neediness, a fear of being driven crazy by the group, a temptation to control or to get rid of part of the group, and a temptation to idealize some of the group's pathological responses as being creative.

From the countertransference point of view, Roth's group went through four stages. First came the nightmare stage, where the therapist experienced very strong affects, initially elated, and later those of depression and hopelessness. Next he noticed the group banding together as subgroups, first dyads and then triads, and then as a whole group against the therapist. At the third stage, in order to cope with rebellion against him, he had to firm up the group rules and to interpret their wish to destroy the group and the therapist's role. This finally led to a fourth stage of slowly developing capacities in patients to care and show concern for one another.

My own experience, in contrast to that of many others who have worked with these patients, is quite encouraging for mixed groups of neurotic and borderline patients. My only preference is to have only one or two borderline patients in a group which consists predominantly of neurotic patients, for here the two levels of development and psychopathology are complementary. Neurotic patients are able to keep the group functioning at a higher psychic level and the borderline patient presents the group members with very considerable challenges to their capacity for empathy, understanding, and containing projected parts of other persons. Inevitably, the borderline patient operates on projection and externalization and develops very intense and persecutory relationships with other members of the group. However, the very fact that this is taking place in the group situation, where other persons are able to observe, intervene, and support attempts to work out these painful confrontations, is of great benefit both to the borderline patient and to the person with whom he or she has become embroiled.

For example, a male member in such a group had viciously attacked all the women in the group, one by one, except for the one who was the most vulnerable. Observing the sameness of his attacks and noting that others had survived them enabled the group members to see that essentially these attacks were motivated by fear and defensiveness. Each of the women who had been involved in the attacks felt that they had gained considerably for themselves in being able to cope with the aggression, and that they had emerged from the situation with a greater sense of internal security. At the same time, the male patient received a lot of support from the male members of the group who, through him, had seen that it was possible to say the things that they never could have said to their mothers. Through identification with this patient, who acted as a spokesman for them, they could see the enormity of the task that needs to be faced when one is sorting out very basic boundary problems between mother and child. In the setting of three-person relationships and whole-object relationships, very important early part-object relationships and dyadic relationships were being gradually worked through and releasing the person from being bound to the primitive, powerful maternal figure. It was very necessary for these split-off and destructive parts of the self, which were indeed murderous in their intensity, to be recognized, verbalized, and accepted, both by the person attacked and by the person doing the attacking, before they could become integrated for the central self.

The working through of these often violent and painful episodes seems to me to be best performed when the person who is the target of the externalization and the projection is able to accept the attack, and to recognize that there is something in him or her which has contributed to the situation; in this way, the person who is doing the attacking is not overwhelmed and overloaded with guilt for loss of control of feared and dangerous parts of the self. Thus, elements of reality testing can enter into a part of the self that would otherwise be dominated by almost entirely fantastic and unrealistic images and projections. This example also shows a powerful advantage of group psychotherapy; because the intense negative transferences are not directed only to one person but are distributed among the members of the group, the impact and intensity as regards any one person is lessened. By contrast, in individual psychotherapy these situations are notoriously difficult to deal with, particularly when the patient operates at a very paranoid level.

Group Psychotherapy with Narcissistic Patients

Our understanding of the structure of the narcissistic patient's psychopathology is that he needs his grandiosity in order to maintain his precarious sense of identity and cohesiveness. In therapy he is unable to give up his defensive structures unless and until a new source of security is available. In individual psychotherapy this is often difficult to achieve without a rather profound level of regression to early symbiotic relationship patterns, appearing as forms of narcissistic transferences, which may be difficult for the therapist to maintain. Because of this, frequent breaks in the new level of narcissistic equilibrium and economy can occur through the therapist's inevitable failures in empathy and responsiveness. By contrast, in group psychotherapy, the necessary conditions for change, for relinquishment of narcissistic defenses, may be achieved not necessarily more quickly but, in my experience, often less painfully. The reasons for this seem to be that there are opportunities for sharing, for identification with each other, for continued empathic responsiveness, for containment and support. The lessening of the transference significance of the therapist also contributes to this effect. The slower rate of change in group psychotherapy seems to allow adequate time for the new internalization, which can lead to the building up of new forms of psychic structure that enable the patient to give up the narcissistic economy.

Case Studies

Some clinical examples will illustrate these points.

Case 1

The following statement was made by Richard, a narcissistic patient in a once-a-week group: "Either I am the successful professional man or I am the very empty, frightened little boy. There is nothing in between. There is nothing that I do that isn't designed to get attention and praise. The only things that give me a real sense of pleasure and achievement are in sport. Hitting a golf ball down the fairway is a much greater pleasure for me than sex."

Addressing Joan, another member of the group, he said: "I understand your husband is a little boy who has to be loved not in spite of the naughty things that he does but because of them." Joan was married to a man who was also in group therapy and who had a highly destructive form of narcissistic personality. Richard had slowly over three years come to recognize and tolerate his sense of inner emptiness and to recognize the defensive nature of his narcissistic grandiosity. When he first joined the group, he had to begin to learn the language of the emotions, which was not his language. During the first few months, he remarked that the other members were talking a foreign language as far as he was concerned. Gradually, he began to relate to, and identify with, other members. Like many such persons with narcissistic personality disorders, he came to therapy when the relationship that had sustained his defensive and adaptive needs (in this case his marriage) was disrupted. He tried to reestablish the narcissistic equilibrium in the group, first by playing his professional role as a lawyer, but gradually he moved beyond this, and the other group members offered him the opportunity for more genuine and empathic emotional exchanges. Poignant and significant discoveries were made by him. First, his previously idealized parents were seen as remote and unempathic. Indeed, his mother had wanted a daughter and had even dressed him as a girl when he was little and allowed him to go to school wearing red hair ribbons, which he had begged her for when he had fallen in love with a little girl there and had wanted to dress just like her. He discovered his sense of outrage at this maternal failure. He recovered a neglected set of memories of a vital mother substitute, a maid who had given him warmth and mothering. He now contributed freely to the group and understood the vital important of discovering and owning his own feelings without wanting to control and punish others with the pain that he might feel at their criticism of him. He was invaluable to Joan, the wife of a very narcissistic man, as he was able to help her to understand the dynamics of her husband's behavior through his identification with him.

For the first two years in the group, Richard often missed sessions and always gave the excuse that he had been delayed at work. Eventually he was able to tell us that on these evenings he used to go to a certain part of the city, have a good meal, a lot to drink, and then go to a strip show. The only times that he felt emotionally alive were when he was engaged in violent primitive arguments with his wife and when excited by surreptitiously drinking, reading pornographic literature, and practicing perverse forms of sexual behavior. This gave us the opportunity to begin to put together the disassociated parts of himself; the successful professional man with empty feelings and the aggressive and desperate small boy who risked destroying the whole of his professional facade. It was then that we began to see more clearly that the professional facade represented a massive identification with his older brother, who was in the same profession and who himself would be disgraced if Richard came to grief. For the first time he could see that behind his identification with his brother and his passive–dependent relationship to him was sibling rivalry. He was able to say that, "I supposed I wanted my parents to pay attention to me and not to him. They never seemed to notice me." Pressed further, he said that what he would have wanted to say to his parents was, "I want you to love me and pay attention to me and give me the love and attention which I see that you are always giving to him." It was only possible for him to make these disclosures in a group where other members themselves were also reaching out to explore areas of narcissistic vulnerability and in this particular session, problems of sibling rivalry. The group explored how if the role of the loved and favored one is already filled, the only role available is that of the destructive one, which tests the capacity of parents and siblings to go on loving despite all the destructiveness.

Joan, a strikingly attractive woman, had a degraded self-image, which she had compensated for by her ability to attract men: "It is as easy as falling off a log." Becoming a mother had enabled her to establish a much healthier and more appropriate form of object relationship to her son, but she still had to contend with the very powerful and seductive psychopathology of her husband, who expected her to condone his constant infidelities and his humiliation of her, and who tried to involve her in perverse sexual practices. The group supported her resistance to this and also sustained her in her need for recognition as a woman who had a heart and head, and was not just a pretty face, an image that she felt that her father had allotted to her when he was disappointed in her failure to meet his academic requirements. It is striking at times how, in a group session, self-disclosures can be made of the narcissistic areas of the personality. They can be made in relative safety in a way which is extremely difficult to achieve in individual therapy. In the group, there can be at times a most remarkable capacity for empathic responsiveness, which reduces the hurt that exploration of narcissistic areas of the personality otherwise evokes.

Case 2

In another group there was an extremely successful, attractive, creative member, Patrick, who also came into therapy because of the breakdown of his marriage; he had assiduously fostered his wife's career, as an extension of his own narcissistic empire. He, too, had to begin to learn the language of the emotions and to begin to understand the significance of his first reported dream. In this dream he was falling 3,000 feet through a hole in a rock after having lost his grip, but in the fall he made a miraculous recovery and escaped without injury. Over a year later, he reported another dream in which he discovered that there was a gap 18 inches wide in the wall of his living room, through which he could see the world outside. He called in a builder and asked him to repair the gap, but was told that the whole structure had to be pulled down. Alarmed by this, he asked if the builder could not somehow fill in the gap by using any old rubble. Ruefully, he himself could see, without any need to interpret to him, the significance of this dream.

One effect of the self-idealization of the narcissistic patient, a manic defense as Grotstein (1980) sees it, is that other members of the group may then unconsciously take over the denied and projected depressed parts. This can sometimes be seen very clearly in the group association, where dynamic links can be made between a narcissistic patient's grandiose statements about himself and subsequent statements that members with low self-esteem make about themselves.

An important clinical differentiation with narcissistic patients is between behavior that arises from narcissistic defenses, and that which follows the exposure and sharing of narcissistic wounds (Fried, 1982). The narcissistic defenses of arrogance, contempt, and devaluation of others cause pain to others, wound them in their own vulnerable areas, arouse reactive hostility, and result in vicious cycles of escalating tension and hostility. By contrast, when a person is able to share with others feelings of hurt and vulnerability, this quickly leads to mutual identification, sharing, caring, and holding.

Case 3

Michael joined a group that had been in existence for several years. He had moved far from his family because he was aware that he was immature and had not properly separated from his family, on whom he was overdependent psychologically and financially. In this group, he quickly became confrontational and hurt the feelings of the other patients. Almost everything that he said seemed to be taken up by the group as being a hostile statement even if he did not consciously intend to hurt other people's feelings. One statement that irritated everyone in the group was his assertion that when he traveled in a train, he would very quickly size up the other passengers and begin to talk with them in terms of the hierarchy of power, influence, and prestige that he felt them to have, so that he would work up conversationally from the weakest to the strongest member of the group. The other group members immediately related this to the therapy situation and to his manipulation. Almost everything that he said after that was seen in the same light. Though on a few occasions he was able to see the effect that he was creating and to make a more direct and sympathetic approach to others, he was mostly tactless and hurtful, particularly to those members who had been in the group for the longest period of time. He was contemptuous of the amount of progress that they had made in the time that they had been there and said that they certainly would have to stay double the time in order to improve. For the other members of the group, he quickly became a representative of hurtful persons with whom they had never gotten along. For one woman in the group, he represented a younger brother, who seemed by all accounts to be impulsive, selfish, and demanding, and who was very much overprotected by the mother, whereas this woman, who was very overcritical of herself, seemed to have a rather negative relationship with her mother. This relationship, which involved sibling rivalry, became a very painful and destructive conflict; eventually, Michael left the group, along with another patient who seemed to share part of the same form of narcissistic psychopathology. Together, they had formed a pairing subgroup.

Narcissistic defense systems are not always hurtful to others. Sometimes the "glass bubble" layer of defense against narcissistic vulnerability may be maintained either by a relative lack of object defenses, so that there is no need to hurt other persons, or else by a sustained form of manic defense. In the latter case, it may take a very long time before these ego-syntonic character traits become sufficiently ego-dystonic so that the person can become self-reflective. First, the person must recognize that he or she has a different range of emotional reactions than do other members of the group. When this happens and the person begins to recognize the defensive nature of greatly valued character traits that have brought the person popularity or a comfortable feeling of always being cheerful, there is often great anxiety and fear of depression. A great deal of support and encouragement is needed from other members of the group during this difficult period of adjustment.

Case 4

One patient, Mary, discovered her vulnerability through finding out how vulnerable she felt whenever a particular male member of the group was not there. Her anxiety and vulnerability when he was not there led another member of the group to say that, to him, it seemed as if she were talking about the sun going out of her life and leaving her in shadows and darkness.

This is exactly what she did feel, and being understood triggered off a breakdown into tears, with a feeling of relief at being understood and of having the opportunity for a very split-off depressed and lost part of herself to begin to come more into the open.

Case 5

Patients whose defenses involve a relative lack of object relatedness will take a very long time before they begin to feel that other members of the group are significant to them and that they, in turn, are a significant other for their fellow group members. One such patient who was a computer expert used to spend all his spare time playing with his home computer or else indulging in grandiose schizoid fantasies about battles in cosmic space. Gradually his fantasies became more down to earth as he became more involved with the other members of the group. Finally, after about three years, when he was the senior member of the group, he became a warm, outgoing, and valuable member of the group, which was in remarkable contrast to his initial presentation.

Case 6

Another example of the responses of the narcissistically damaged patient to empathic mirroring and responsiveness is that of Carole, a militant feminist, divorced, bringing up a child on her own, and studying psychology. She had a brutal, alcoholic father and a rather passive, ineffective mother. She favored wearing heavy mauve-colored boots, easily got angry, offended, and destructive, and resisted showing vulnerability. She neither offered empathic understanding nor experienced it as being often available to her. For some weeks she talked about a new relationship with a man, which evidently reproduced her relationship with her father, in that the present lover was also alcoholic and violent, and the relationship had reached a point where she no longer felt any affection for him and sexuality between them felt like a rape.

In one session, Carole was saying something about the situation between her and her lover, and that it felt like a rape, but the attention of the group did not stay with her and moved to another patient. In response to the therapist making an interpretation that showed an empathic responsiveness to this other patient, Carole said that, if he carried on with any more of his "Psychoanalytic claptrap" she was going to kick him. The therapist's response was not to take up the aggression, the phallic rivalry, or the castration fantasy; he simply said to her, "I think you feel very angry with me because you feel that I did not pay attention to you when you said that you felt that you were being raped." There was an immediate change in the patient, who said that she felt very pleased with what the therapist had said. The level of her anxiety and her aggression immediately dropped and she was able to take a more constructive, realistic part for the remainder of that session. The theme of the session, indeed, was that of being a child who does not know how to get attention and who reacts by either running away or by making sudden moves into adulthood. Carole's version of this was to be angry in order to get attention but also to identify with the violent father. One way of seeing her response to the therapist's empathic mirroring is that he had given her the opportunity to give up the identification with the violent father and to identify with an empathic mirroring person, either a good father or perhaps what she longed for from her mother. In her response, we see the crucial importance between reflection in the group through empathic mirroring, and deflection of attention by a failure to mirror the person's immediate needs. Violence and rage are aroused by deflection when reflection is needed instead. One of the great strengths of the group situation is the multiple mirroring that can occur through the empathic responsiveness of the other group members.

Therapeutic Factors

The Group as a Transitional Object

As Kosseff (1978) has pointed out in his valuable essay, for patients with an underlying schizoid personality structure, the group is a "tangible representation of a relationship between the patient and the therapist," a relationship where some degree of separation from the therapist is evident as, in the group situation, the patient is one among several and is not therefore locked into a dyadic relationship that threatens to represent the locked in, undifferentiated early symbiotic relationship to the mother. Membership in the group offers a combination of support and freedom, the possibility of a new beginning, and the group situation itself structures and preserves the space between patients and therapist, offering an area of freedom that can potentially be filled creatively. Another valuable function that the group performs is to provide a "good enough facilitating environment" in which the patient can give up the symbiotic tie to the mother–therapist at the same time as gaining support of fellow patients whose relationships to him are more active, realistic, and differentiated and who, in contrast to the therapist, need, expect, and are open to reciprocity and exchange.

In the light of the concept of the group as a transitional object, or transitional situation (Macaskill, 1982), the group can help the patient to (1) shift from a set of internalized split self-images to a more unified self-representation through identification with other group members; (2) shift from a part-object level of relationship to a whole-object level aided by the therapist's constant relationship to the group members as whole objects, which is gradually internalized by the patient; (3) gradually give up fears of engulfment by the therapist as the therapist no longer fits the primitive projected imago; his reality, his shortcomings, are a shared perception and discovery for all the group members.

Reciprocity and Exchange

Recent research on very early infantile development has shown how the mother and baby form a responding unit who engage in playful "proto conversation" (Leal, 1983), a mutually understood sequence of acts, "now I do this and now you do this." These represent the earliest form of game and can be conceptualized as the way in which the matrix of self-experience and experience of others begins and through which earliest forms of differentiation of self and other take place. The emerging capacity of the infant to relate to persons leads later to the capacity imaginatively to relate things, to toys, and to sustain this process of self–other differentiation out of which firm selfhood can develop. This seems to be the process through which the healthy form of attachment to mother can occur. It is a prerequisite for the emergence of the true self.

The point has been made that, where these elements, these "proto conversations," have not been responded to sufficiently by the mother, attachment to mother occurs on the basis of a false self and anxious dependency. A one-sided, anxious appeal substitutes for mutual psychological intercourse. This one-sided, anxious, appealing way of relating to the world of others then becomes the basis of existence. "Some anxious dependent adults presenting different types of neurotic symptoms but with an immense unexplicable psychic pain are infants in search of a self who could never form a real and needed attachment" (Leal, 1982).

The group analytic situation sets no task outside the analysis of spontaneous communication; and the task of the therapist is to help establish the matrix of interchange, so that spontaneous initiatives of communication can emerge and gradually a resonating and responding situation can develop. Thus, this situation can be looked at in the light of these earliest mother–child "proto conversations." The group members engage in emotional exchanges and rhythms: "I feel this when you feel that, my response to you is this when you say that." This corresponds to the basic rhythms out of which selfhood emerges, and thus there is a potential in the group analytic situation for recovery from attachments which were not based on an understanding and reciprocation of these basic rhythms of emotional life, from a mode of engagement with the world of others based upon the false self.

References

Bursten, B. (1973), Some narcissistic personality types. *Internat. J. Psycho-Anal.* 54:287–300.
——— (1977), The narcissistic course. In: *The Narcissistic Condition*, ed. M.C. Nelson. New York: Human Sciences Press.
Fried, E. (1970), Individuation through group psychotherapy. *Internat. J. Psycho-Anal.*, 20:450–457.
——— (1982), *The Courage to Change.* New York: Grove Press.
Grotstein, J. (1980), A proposed revision of the psychoanalytic concept of primitive mental states. *Contemp. Psychoanal.*, 16/4:479–546.
James, C. (1982), Transitional phenomena and the matrix in group psy-

chotherapy. In: *The Individual and the Group*, ed., M. Pines & L. Rafaelsen. New York: Plenum Press.
Kernberg, O. (1968), The treatment of patients with borderline personality organization. In: *Borderline Condition and Pathological Narcissism*. New York: Jason Aronson.
Kohut, H. (1971), *The Analysis of the Self*. New York: International Universities Press.
Kosseff, J. (1978), The leader using object relations theory. In: *The Leader in the Group*, ed. Z. Liff. New York: Jason Aronson.
Kutter, P. (1983), Basic aspects of psychoanalytic group therapy. In: *Evolution of Group Analysis*, ed. M. Pines, International Library of Group Psychotherapy and Group Process. London: Routledge & Kegan Paul.
Leal, R. (1982), Resistances and the group analytic process. *Group Anal.*, 15/2:97–110.
——— (1983), Why group analysis works. In: *The Evolution of Group Analysis*, ed. M. Pines, International Library of Group Psychotherapy and Group Process. London: Routledge & Kegan Paul.
Lichtenstein, M. (1977), The dilemma of human identity. In: *Narcissism & Primary Identity*. New York: Jason Aronson.
Macaskill, N. (1980), The narcissistic core as a focus in the group therapy of borderline patients. *Brit. J. Med. Psychol.*, 53:137–143.
——— (1982), The theory of transitional phenomena and its application to the psychotherapy of the borderline patient. *Brit. J. Med. Psychol.*, 55/4:349–360.
Mahler, M. (1967), On human symbiosis and the vicissitudes of individuation. *J. Amer. Psychoanal. Assn.*, 15:740–763.
Pines, M. (1975), Group psychotherapy with difficult patients. In: *Group Psychotherapy 1973*, eds. L. Wolberg & M. Aronson. New York: Stratton Intercontinental Medical Books.
——— (1978), Group analytic psychotherapy of the borderline patient. *Group Anal.*, 11:115–126.
——— (1980), What to expect in the psychotherapy of the borderline patient. *Group Anal.*, 13/3:168–177.
——— (1982), Reflections on mirroring. *Group Anal.*, 15/2:1–26.
——— (1983), On mirroring in group psychotherapy. *Group* 7/2:3–17.
Roth, B. E. (1980), Understanding the development of a homogeneous identity and impaired group countertransference phenomena. *Internat. J. Group Psychother.*, 30:405–426.
Tolpin, M. (1971), On the beginnings of a cohesive self. *Psychoanalytic Study of the Child*, 26:316–352. New York: Quadrangle Books.
Winnicott, D. W. (1971), In: *Playing and Reality*. New York: Basic Books.
Zinkin, L. (1983), Malignant mirroring. *Group Anal.*, 16/2.

Chapter 9

GROUP LEVEL "BOUNDARYING" CONTROL AS AN ISOMORPHIC PROSTHESIS FOR NARCISSISTIC AND BORDERLINE PATIENTS

JAMES E. DURKIN, Ph.D.

The practical problems of the clinical management of narcissistic and borderline cases, the so-called self pathology cases, parallel the theoretical problems of integrating the classical psychoanalytic instinct theories with the newer object relations theories. Most therapists agree that the classical clinical method of the interpretation of transference and resistance is less effective with these preoedipal cases than with the traditional oedipal conflict syndromes. Controversy has arisen, however, as to just what the appropriate alternative clinical management approach should be. Kohut (1977) has proposed that the analysis of transference be limited or even abandoned in favor of a deeply empathic response to the patient. The aim of this response is to incubate a restructuring of ego strength and integration. Only when ego integration is firmly established, it is argued, can the working alliance become established and the classical process of making the unconscious conscious be begun through the analysis of transference and resistance.

Other workers in the field hold that the classical interpretation approach can be adapted to cope with these severe and intractable conditions (Modell, 1968). The issue has been raised, however (Stolorow and Lachman, 1980), as to whether the great clinical differences between the intrapsychic conflict syndrome of the classical oedipal cases and the developmental arrest syndrome of the narcissistic and borderline cases call for two psychoanalyses instead of one. In my view, the self psychology embodied in the object relations approach is better suited to an understanding of the narcissistic and borderline self disorders, while the classical analytic model maps out the territory of oedipal level disorders in a satisfactory fashion. What is the best way, then, of achieving a rapprochement between these two distinct models of psychic functioning and malfunctioning? One possible integration is to *abut* the two models and assign one to the lower level disorders of self, and the other to the higher level disorders which arise in patients whose self structures are more or less secure. The result would be a model with a continuity of ego development levels from primitive to genital. Such a theoretical integration, though parsimonious, actually does not give much practical guidance to the working clinician. The Kohutian prescription of absolute empathy and the Winnicottian prescription of good-enough mothering would then seem to stand unrelated to the classical prescription of making the unconscious conscious through the interpretation of transference and resistance. Such a dichotomous model would suggest handling cases by incubating developmental arrest and interpreting intrapsychic conflict. Over the long run, incubation would go on until ego strength became sufficient to engender a working alliance and then interpretation would take over. That is clearly a rigid and simplistic view of what goes on in the day-to-day management of cases. What is called for is a diagram of the territory of psychic development which offers more flexibility and more concrete guidelines for the working clinician.

General System Theory

A few years ago, the General System Theory Committee of the American Group Psychotherapy Association collaborated on a book entitled *Living Groups: Group Psychotherapy and General System Theory* (Durkin, 1981). In this work, we asserted that General System Theory (GST) offered a new paradigm of scientific understanding that could be applied to clarify the theory and improve the practice of group psychotherapy in such a way as to supplement rather than merely supplant the traditional psychodynamic and other therapeutic models. One of the main features of the GST model we introduced was a fundamental distinction between the *content* mode of human individual and group activity and the *organizational* mode (often called the *structural* mode). The content and organization modes were seen as complementaries rather than contradictories. They were irreconcilable but inseparable, working together in yin/yang fashion. The content mode was largely oriented along an evaluative good/bad continuum where what was designated as good was to be pursued and maximized and what was designated as bad was to be avoided and minimized. The organizational mode was organized around the new operation of *boundarying,* defined as the dialectical interplay of the primitive self-opening/self-closing events, which were axiomatized as fundamental givens within this conceptual schema. The *organization* of any living autonomous system, be it the intrapersonal personality structure of a psychotherapy patient, the pattern of exchange within a psychotherapy group, or the "pattern that connects" (Bateson, 1978) a community or organization, is the way the parts work together to make the whole work. The *boundarying* operation, the way the parts open/close to each other within, and to other living systems and the nonliving environment without, provided the central concept within our GST model to account for how living group psychotherapy systems enable their parts to work together to make their whole work. The organizational mode evaluates not what it is that living groups open/close their boundaries. It is the interplay of opening/closing itself that is the concern of the organizational mode in our GST model.

The inclusion of the new boundarying mode in our GST model of the therapeutic process generates a new map of the territory of psychopathology and its therapy which might be applied usefully to some of the theoretical and clinical problems that have arisen over the "two psychoanalyses" issue discussed above. In effect, the supplementing of the content mode with the organizational mode transforms the diagram or model of psychopathology from a one-dimensional array to a two-dimensional array.

The new two-dimension array is depicted in Figure 9-1.

	CONTENT MODE Diachronic (Historical)	ORGANIZATIONAL (STRUCTURAL) MODE Synchronic (Ahistorical)		
	Psychodynamic Ego Development	GST Boundarying Operation		
		Closing		Opening
GOOD				
Realistic existential dilemmas	Genital	*Thinking/Organization* •self-limitation •delayed gratification •suspicion •personal consolidation •drawing boundary distinctions	↔	*Feeling/Spontaneity* •self-expansion •immediate gratification •trust •personal transformation •withdrawing boundary distinctions
Repetition Compulsion Transference/resistance	Oedipal	*Obsessive compulsive* •paralytic closing off problem •ruminating in fantasy world Resolution: •Take a stand in gender identity •Trade symbols for action	✕	*Hysterical impulsive* •acting out problem •impulse control problems Resolution: •Be one gender but love the other •Trade action for symbols
Ego syntonic character traits	Preoedipal (Preoedipal regressed)	*Anal character* •power and authority struggles •cutting off good feeling •pseudoagression (Bergler) •never get or give anything	✕	*Oral character* •dependency struggles •psychic masochism •I have everything now
Acting out in the transference	Identity disorder (Preoedipal arrested)	*Narcissistic* •idealizing transference •minoring transference •false self, grandiosity •danger of separation •doesn't listen to others	✕	*Borderline* •fragmenting primitive rage •splitting •fear of engulfment •project identification •supersensitive to others
BAD				
Autistic merger	Psychotic	*Depressive* •paranoid schizophrenic	✕	*Manic* •hebephrenic

*Diagonal dialectic: Vertical transformations cannot be caused; horizontal transformations cannot be prevented, but diagonal transformations can be easily facilitated. For example, facilitate borderline into either depressive experience or anal experience.

The *content* dimension is represented in the second column of the figure and the organizational dimension is represented in the two right-hand columns. The continuum of the content dimension is designated as "psychodynamic ego development" level. Its levels in descending order are genital, oedipal, preoedipal, identity disorder, and psychotic. Stolorow and Lachman (1980) would call the third and fourth levels "preoedipal regressed" and "preoedipal arrested" respectively.

Two basic characteristics of the content dimension of ego development in our GST-based model should be noted. First, the continuum upon which the ego development dimension is based is diachronic or historical in nature. A progression of development is assumed from bottom to top so that in the normal course of ego development there will be progress from the psychotic to genital level. Pathological processes can produce a reversal or regression, but this would also be considered diachronic. Second, as with any content-based dimension, there is a value judgment involved. It is considered better to operate at the genital level than the oedipal, and better to operate at the oedipal level than the preoedipal or psychotic. What is designated "bad" and "good" along this content dimension is an arbitrary and local rule. The fact that we cannot see genital level ego functioning as anything but the best is a testament to the locality of our community.

Now let us examine the other dimension of our two-dimensional model, the dimension represented by the two columns labeled "opening" and "closing" and collectively entitled "boundarying." The *boundarying* operation is fundamental to the GST model of group psychotherapy developed in *Living Groups* (Durkin, 1981). Boundarying is dually defined as both the opening *and* closing of an autonomous living system's own boundaries. Boundarying can occur within a system, between living systems at the same level, or between systems at different levels. Boundarying is a dialectical process, which means that normally we transform ourselves back and forth between the opening and closing events. *Opening* and *closing* are considered to be primitive terms in this model and are therefore givens rather than being defined at some deeper level. However, clos-

Figure 9-1. Synthesis of psychodynamic and systemic views of the vicissitudes of ego development

ing can be interpreted in the content mode of experience as the cognitive drawing of distinctions, and opening can be interpreted in the content mode as emotional flow. Within this model, therapeutic change is also seen as a dialectical process. Resistance to change is seen as a closing process involving cognitive defenses, transformation occurs through opening up to feeling flow, and then closing processes reappear to consolidate for future use the transformation that has been made. These characteristics of the boundarying operation are dealt with in more detail in *Living Groups* (Durkin, 1981).

In our two-dimensional diagram, the opening/closing or boundarying operation also has two characteristics. First, the mode is *synchronic* rather than *diachronic*, which means that it cuts across rather than goes along with the grain of time. The boundarying operation coordinates the organization mode of the living system, where organization is the way the parts work together to make the whole work. The parts keep themselves in a synchronic balance as they continually adapt to their environment. Second, the boundarying operation is not oriented in a value hierarchy the way ego development is. Opening is not better than closing; nor is closing better than opening. Boundarying is a dialectical process in which, under normal conditions, opening changes to closing and closing changes to opening without external cause. What must be explained is not how opening closes or closing opens, but rather, why a boundarying system persists in one or the other condition. It is only in this sense that there is an evaluation component of the boundarying operation. It is good to have a fluidity within the living system which enables a smooth alternation back and forth between opening and closing events. It is bad when a configuration develops where the living system gets into a tangle or an endless loop which prevents the living system from moving out of either opening or closing. The synchronic balance with the parts working together in harmony to make the whole work can only be maintained, can only evolve through interaction with its environment, if there is a dialectical yin/yang interplay where opening and closing, feeling and thinking, transforming and consolidating are free to transform into one another.

How do these two dimensions of our GST diagram and the two modes of functioning of living systems represented in this two-dimensional array of psychological functioning fit together? Is diachronic, value-oriented ego development completely independent of synchronic, dialectical boundarying in the same way that length is independent of width in geometrical shapes? Or are the two dimensions opposed in the way in earlier times masculine and feminine were supposed to be, so that the more of one you had, the less you had of the other? Actually the relation between ego development and boundarying, between content and organizational pattern, is neither of these, but involves *complementarity,* which is totally different and generally little understood. Yin/yang complementaries are irreconcilable but inseparable. Though they work under separate principles, one cannot exist without the other. We are wiser now about masculine and feminine and are beginning to experience them as complementaries rather than contradictories, and the same will soon be true for feeling and thinking in our lives. As we have discussed above, opening/closing are complementaries whose synchronic interplay keeps the living system in balance. But the content mode and the organizational mode are also complementaries. Organization, the pattern which connects, cannot exist without manifestation in a concrete historical content form. Content, the particular concrete resolution of an adaptation between a particular living system and a particular environment, would result in blind opportunistic growth without the aesthetic symmetries of boundarying organization.

Our two-dimensional diagram of the territory of psychological functioning treats content and organization as independent dimensions by putting them on the Cartesian coordinates of horizontal and vertical. We must keep in mind that this is a simplified representation of the complementarity idea. A paradoxical surface such as a Möbious strip, Klein bottle, or projective plane would be more adequate, but would not serve the purposes of this presentation. Let us accept that simplification, then, and proceed to explore what conceptual insights and clinical suggestions can be gleaned from this two-dimensional GST-based model for understanding self disorders.

The Ten Boxes of the Diagram of the GST-Based Model

Bearing in mind that the Cartesian projection of our two-dimensional model does not do justice to the complementary relationship between organization and content, let us partition this five-by-two figure in several ways and see what sorts of questions arise in the process. Since the boundarying idea is less familiar than the idea of the stages of ego development, let us discuss how the opening/closing boundarying complementarity operates under normal conditions, that is, at the genital level of ego development.

At the *genital* level, the ego can distinguish fantasy from reality, true object from projection, and mere wish from full-scale action in the world. But even with the accomplishment of this hard-won ego integration in the world, a host of problems, conflicts, paradoxes, and dilemmas remain to do their vexing work. The difference is that these are "world-made" existential dilemmas rather than "person-made" neurotic processes. These inevitable existential dilemmas pose severe adaptive problems to the organization of living systems. Our GST boundarying model, in viewing the living system's responses to these threats to adaptation, looks not at the content of who or what is opened/closed, but at the boundarying action itself. An opening response is a yielding response, a feeling response, an accommodative response in which the subject changes its structure to fit the demands of the external source. A closing response is an asserting response, a cognitive problem-solving response, an assimilative response where the subject maintains its structure in the face of the demands of the external perturbation.

Which is a better adaptive strategy, opening or closing, yielding or asserting, accommodating or assimilating? The answer can only be that it is contingent both on the disposition of the living system and on the environment. What needs to be evaluated is not the choice of opening or closing on a particular contingency, but a pattern of clear perception and resourceful learning from both external and internal experience. Self-knowledge might dictate that a new response is necessary to a situation that had been adapted to adequately for a long time simply because the living system needs a change. The idea that boundarying shifts should sometimes be made for their own sake suggests that *aesthetic* criteria, as opposed to pragmatic criteria, play a large part in keeping harmony within the living organization (Bateson, 1978).

Disharmony in boundarying can occur when the living system persistently misreads a situation that calls for closing as one that calls for opening, or vice versa, when the living system persistently takes action in terms of boundarying that seems to go against the grain of the situation, or when the living system's boundarying solutions result in tangles that make the attempted solution a part of the problem. Psychoanalytic ego development theory can account for such cases. It could be that the boundarying process is operating at the oedipal level of ego functioning and is colored by the issues and dynamics that characterize this level of ego development.

It is characteristic of individuals operating at the *oedipal* level of ego development that they fail to make certain distinctions, for example, between fantasy and reality, between impulse and action, between two-way relationships with others and relationships distorted by projection mechanisms. Let us now examine the oedipal level of ego development and try to describe how these ego integration problems lead to disordered boundarying. Dysfunctional opening behavior occurs at the oedipal level of ego integration when impulse to action is not tempered by insight and thus degenerates into repetitive, unsatisfying, self-destructive acting out. The inability to draw a boundary distinction between symbolic and real goals can set the stage for a symbolically based behavior episode, but what impels behavior into action is the overwhelming pressure of mask feelings, feeling energies that are captured by the symbolic configuration rather than flowing unrestrictedly toward or away from the true object. "I was so angry (hurt, afraid, in love) that I couldn't help myself" explains the oedipal level patient after the dust has settled. Later, the same repetitive cycle will rekindle under the same pressure.

While oedipal-level opening disorders suck us into action, oedipal-level closing disorders paralyze us into ruminative inaction. In this configuration, the typically oedipal confusion between the symbolic inner world and the outer world of action and objects still holds, but if the person is tangled in the closing position, his reality is locked within the inner world of swirling symbols and only gives the appearance of action "out there." The oedipally closed person lives in a world of obsession and compulsion, of fantasy and rumination, a world where life's dramas are enacted from within. External demands for action are given in to grudgingly and carried out perfunctorily; the real excitement is locked within the fantasy world. There can be a real emotional investment within this inner closed system which can make contributions to society. Introspective artists and writers such as Klee, Kafka, and Emily Dickinson seem to have given us glimpses of their inner world without themselves coming out of them.

Moving to the next lower row of our diagram, the one labeled *preoedipal* (preoedipal regressed) we have a lower-level ego integration that is more difficult to manage therapeutically. At this level, we have the so-called character problems and our opening is aligned with oral problems while our closing box is aligned with anal problems. The difficulties posed by entrenched character disorders is that they are ego-syntonic rather than ego-alien as are oedipal-level problems. The pattern of struggle through the oral and anal stages that comes as a natural concomitant of the transition from the maternal symbiosis to a reality orientation has become fused into the grain of the ego. Reality becomes an anal or oral reality for the character enclosed in a preoedipally regressed or fixated ego, and the massive defenses of that ego are recruited to keep that self-definition in place. The lack of boundaries between the ego and its drives, the protection of this situation by various forms of "character armor" employed to ward off underlying anxiety, and the masochistic tendency to control the situation by provoking self-defeating situations make these character disorders very difficult to work with in therapy.

Oral character types are opening pathologies because of their ego identification with the oral drives for magical fusion with the mother. They defend against the anxiety of separation and the loss of magic and express primitive rage when reality frustrates them. Although they fear passivity and helplessness and strive to maintain their omnipotence, they set themselves up in masochistic situations where the feared passivity is the inevitable result. Anal character types are closing pathologies because they are locked in a constant power struggle for independence that can never be won. Hostility in these closed character disorder personalities is often pseudoaggression designed to provoke rejection. These cases can also be cut off from emotional expression. Because these symptoms are egosyntonic, trying to deal with them in a working alliance meets with massive ego resistance.

Finally, in our descent down the path of ego development, we come to the row labeled *identity disorders* (preoedipal arrested) where the self disorders reside. Conceptually, this area of our diagram is the most indistinct and ambiguous. Here the gap between theory and practice is the widest and competing theories add to the confusion. I have drawn dotted lines on the map, both in the boundary between the preoedipal arrested and preoedipal regressed levels and in that between the *narcissistic* and *borderline* categories, to indicate this ambiguity. The distinctions clarified by the boundarying group method aim to alleviate this conceptual vagueness, as well as the corresponding confusion treatment strategies.

Self-disordered personalities exhibit the whole range of preverbal oral and anal drive characteristics from the early years of separation–individuation from the maternal symbiosis. All of the archaic symptoms—splitting, idealization, primitive rage, fragmentation, hopelessness, and so on—are there. The horizontal dotted line speaks to the following problem: while one school of thought accounts for these symptoms as defensive regressions where a struggling but coherent ego identifies with these oral and anal drive processes and makes them part of his or her character structure, the other school of thought considers self disorders to be the result of a developmental arrest in the separation–individuation process which precluded the formation of a coherent ego structure. These two perspectives on the psychodynamics generating these symptoms lead to two quite divergent patterns of therapeutic intervention. The view that this is a defensive regression to these archaic stages prescribes the interpretation of the special kind of "psychotic" and selfobject transferences that arise in the course of treatment. The developmental arrest perspective leads to a prescription of entering empathically into a neosymbiotic self-object relationship so that the arrested development of the ego gets a second chance to develop.

In my view, these two sets of psychodynamics are complementary rather than contradictory and thus the clinical response called for is a gentle yin/yang moving back and forth between the interpretation response and the incubation response.

The conceptual ambiguity of the boundary between intrapsychic conflict and developmental arrest on the horizontal dimension of our diagram has its counterpart in the vertical dotted line drawn between the opening and closing columns. It is not clear, to me at least, whether the diagnostic distinctions between narcissistic and borderline designations are entirely unambiguous or, for that matter, entirely useful in therapeutic management. Although traditional symptomatology is quite distinct, with the borderlines showing a lack of ego boundaries which results in a tendency to fragment into primitive disorganization of psychotic proportions under the slightest pressure; and with narcissistic personalities showing a primitive closing ego boundary pattern that results in a tendency toward grandiosity, an inability to relate to others empathically, and self-absorption; the distinction breaks down when levels of defense are taken into account. Some theorists assert that one category has reached a slightly more advanced stage of separation–integration than the other but, like the dilemma of intrapsychic conflict versus developmental arrest, different perspectives can lead to different observations and explanations of the same phenomenon.

One thing is clear from the perspective of our GST boundarying model. Both of these self-disordered categories have severe boundarying problems, for, from this perspective, it is the ability to articulate both the opening and closing aspects of the boundarying process that marks the development of an autonomous ego organization. As stated above, the boundarying process does not designate opening as higher or lower than closing; nor does it consider the fragile openness of the borderline pattern as higher or lower than the tenuous closing of the narcissistic patient. The model sees these two primitive boundarying configurations as two complementary sides of the same coin and prescribes the therapeutic goal of gaining ego strength through a complementary pair of interventions on the part of the therapist and the group, one opening and empathically supportive, the other helping the patient to develop inner/outer boundaries.

What are some of the practical clinical applications of employing this two-dimensional diagram? In the first place it should indicate to therapists that the territory of psychopathology that the diagram describes is much more richly crossjoined, both "horizontally" and "vertically" than was heretofore supposed. The horizontal or dialectical dimension of this diagram suggests that there is a natural driving force which shifts individual personalities inexorably from one pole to another. This means that the therapist must be prepared for unpredictable swings between opening/closing symptomatology on short notice. He should be on the alert for flashes of hysteria from his most obsessive patients. The conceptual confusion abounding in the identity disorder level, where some theorists see narcissism as more primitive and some see it as less primitive than borderline syndromes, is given a possible explanation. It suggests that the two disorders are dialectically paired and that one swings back and forth to the other. Therapists should not rest too comfortably on their *Diagnostic and Statistical Manual* (DSM-III) diagnoses. Their patients in reality tend to jump all over this diagram and therapists must be prepared to track them and respond appropriately.

Another interesting therapeutic intervention strategy is suggested by the dynamics shown in the diagram. The vector arrows at the interstices of the categories suggest an intervention we will call the "diagonal dialectic." Like all living beings, therapy patients are autonomous. Therapists cannot "cause change" in their clients, for clients only change themselves. The goal in psychotherapy from this perspective is clear: we want to help clients move up the ego-integration ladder as much as we can and as best we can. But if we as therapists think that what we do in sessions causes change in autonomous living systems called patients, we are wrong. According to this diagram, we are wrong in two ways. We cannot unilaterally boost a patient from preoedipal to oedipal, from oedipal to genital, or in general, from any one level to another. We cannot cause it, we can only facilitate the client's own autonomous movement. Ego integration levels are homeostatic, they tend to find their level and stay there. The level at which an ego rests may be dysfunctional in many ways according to *our* value system of what is good (genital) and what is bad (psychotic), but the autonomous individual defines his life on his own terms not on ours. By the same token, a therapist cannot *prevent* the dialectic from moving back and forth in yin/yang fashion between the boundarying poles, no matter what level the patient's ego is on. Patients can get *themselves* in a closed loop in an opening (one piece of acting out embroils them in the next) or closing (paralysis tends to perpetuate itself; depression is a self-exacerbating cycle), but, once again, a therapist cannot pry them loose from such a structural configuration.

What can a therapist *do*, then? The diagonal offers a path: It utilizes the principle of combining vertical intransigency and horizontal fluidity. There is a path of movement that is readily facilitated. It is, in the terms of the diagram, diagonal movement. These are the "creases," the mountain passes, along which egos can readily find a path of transformation. The therapist should find potential pathways of movement wherever they are. In the diagonal dialectic it does not matter, strangely enough, whether you help the patient move in a downward or upward direction. It is facilitating the movement that counts. For example, it is a good diagonal strategy to help a borderline get into his "depression." It is equally felicitous to help the borderline get into his "anal" character configuration. Both the "higher" anal and "lower" depressive configuration represents a movement for the borderline, an unfreezing of the box they are in. We are not talking about a permanent shift to another permanent "box," but a renewal of the natural dynamics of life which normally involves peregrination all over this diagram. Horizontal movement cannot be prevented, so it should be harnessed as an energizer to free movement of an autonomous nature up and down the developmental scale.

The Format of Boundarying Group Therapy

In the book *Living Groups* (Durkin, 1981), I described a boundarying group method of running therapy groups. One of its main features is that the method applies rather abstract ideas about boundarying to the group management procedure in a completely explicit way. If our contention holds that the narcissistic and borderline syndromes are in great measure boundarying pathologies, a therapeutic method that focuses on boundary opening/closing in a very explicit way might make it possible to bring the vexing and perplexing self-disorders out in the open where they can be dealt with more effectively. As we shall see, the boundarying rules can be utilized to give strength and support to such patients' extremely shaky boundarying efforts. They also can provide leaders and other members of groups containing self-disordered patients with the strength and protection they need to learn to trust and relate to these difficult cases.

The boundarying group format utilizes a physical boundary to distinguish the group space from the rest of the world outside that space; however, such a group boundary could be formed of any substance and fabricated into any shape, as long as it distinguishes one space from another. The boundary I have been using is a braided foam rubber ring about 12 feet in diameter and about 4 inches thick. There are two boundary rules to which group members are expected to commit themselves and help each other keep:

1. The group goes on inside the boundary, while the rest of the world goes on outside the boundary.

2. It is *not* of higher value to be inside *or* outside the boundary. It *is* better to make clear for yourself and others just where you stand emotionally with respect to the group by crossing back and forth physically across the boundary to reflect your emotional stand.

Moving inside and moving outside of the group boundary are fundamental events in the organizational dimension. In this case, boundarying goes on between living systems at two different levels, the individual member level and the group level. Because the group boundary is embodied physically, the organizational dimension event of boundary crossing is unambiguously observable. The presence of a physical boundary and the official recognition of boundary crossing events in the group sets up a second language, an organizational mode language, that can operate within the group as a complement to the content mode language. The addition of boundarying language means that there is always a double description of the group process, one in the content mode and one in the organizational mode of the pattern that connects. This, in turn, means that the leaders and members of the group can not only work within each language, but can shift from one language to the other. As indicated above, the content mode and the organizational or boundarying mode of the group process are on two logical levels, as complementaries always are. Sometimes during the group process, boundarying events become the context for the text of content events. At other times, content events become the context for the text of boundarying events. Elsewhere (Durkin, 1987), I have defined paradox as text and context reversing. I would regard an intervention that shifted from content to organization modes as a paradoxical intervention in the most general sense.

The physical boundary and the boundarying rules empower group members to control the rate of their own participation in the group process and control the rate at which the group catalyzes and regulates change in their personal structures. If a member feels at any time that the group is moving too fast, that member can simply cross outside the boundary to slow down the process and everyone else will defend to the death his right to do so. Inside is not better than outside; open is not better than closed; it is better to be able to experience the autonomy of boundary crossing in either direction and in both directions. If anyone gets bored with the lack of progress within the boundary or gets uncomfortable in any way, they are encouraged to exercise their autonomous right to move outside the boundary until things appear safe, interesting, or productive once again. The autonomy of boundary crossing goes a long way to counter the ever-present danger of the group imposing manipulative pressures on its members which, in turn, generate the countermanipulative strategy of saying "yes, sir" on the outside and "no, sir" on the inside.

The living group system achieves its autonomy gradually as the members test and begin to trust their right of boundary crossing. As the group members begin to trust their autonomous ability to engage in boundarying with their group, they will begin to test and trust their autonomous ability to open/close their personal boundaries to each other. The articulation of boundarying within individual living systems is called opening/closing. The articulation of boundarying between living systems at two levels (e.g., between group and member) is called moving inside/moving outside. The articulation of boundarying between living systems at the same level (e.g., between members within a group) is called *systeming/summing*, where systeming is being open to another's openness and summing is being closed to another's closedness. Systeming is experienced in the content mode as emotional flow. Two individuals open their boundaries to each other in the flow of fear, anger, love, or pain and become, for the moment, a unitary system. When they return to their distinctness again, they find their personal structures transformed in the process. Our identities are intermittent despite our cognitive biases, which ascribe and infer self-conservation.

When we engage in summing, our closed boundaries are more often flexible than rigid. Boundaries function to transform actions into messages. In the cognitive exchange of summing, we transmit and receive messages reciprocally, but we operate assimilatively, that is, we translate the other's meaning into our own terms. It is possible to learn through summing by transforming oneself internally in the presence of an external influence. But it must be made clear that the living system, though responsible to external influences, is creating the change on an internal basis. Systeming and summing are complementaries; one is not of higher value than the other, as some writers suggest, for one will always transform dialectically into the other.

The articulation of the systeming/summing relationship between the group leader and the members in the context of the boundary and boundarying rules provides an effective method for resolving one of the primary dilemmas that a group leader has to face—achieving the appropriate balance between professionalism and personalism in running groups. Professional technique is necessary to regulate traffic in the group and to provide a reliable bedrock of understanding and support for patients who come into therapy in a state of confusion and pain. But a cool professionalism, though necessary, is not sufficient. The person of the therapist must also serve as a model for the patient, a model of a real person, not a perfect person, but one who exhibits foibles as well as fortes. The patient has to win a few encounters with the leader within the protection of the group before he can gain the confidence to win them out in the world where he had kept on losing before. And, if the patient is to win, the leader must be willing to yield, to lose, to look bad, and to show that he can grow from the experience. The leader will become a stronger professional by being able legitimately to play such a role in the group on occasion.

The guidelines for boundarying between leader and member, or between members, are different depending upon where they stand with respect to the group boundary. If both L. and M. are outside the boundary, they share the ordinary social world and its guidelines, and the group space, outside of them both, essentially does not exist. The guideline in the outside world is: *Be open to openness and closed to closedness.* Be wary and protect yourself with someone you do not know until there is clear evidence of trust and openness that you can reciprocate and, once a comfortable situation of closeness exists, be open until you pick up something that makes you uncomfortable about the relationship. In terms of boundarying processes, that is the rule of thumb that most people out in the world follow with others.

But when a therapy group member elects to step into that special rehabilitative space defined by the group boundary, his or her role is transformed and the ordinary role expectations of that patient-person are relaxed. While the patient was expected to be "sane" in the outside world, he is expected to get better in the special space of the therapy group by being "crazy." What is the role of the group leader vis-à-vis the behavior of the patient within the group boundary? In the GST boundarying model, the answer is that it depends upon where the leader stands with respect to the group boundary. If the leader is outside the boundary, he is still connected to the outside world, the helping professions, and the particular professional way of working that he has adopted. The leader follows the boundarying guideline for the professional role: *Be open to the patient's closedness and be closed to his openness.* With the patient sequestered behind the boundary and the therapist protected by his professional role as representative of the helping community, the therapist can be genuinely open to all the symptomatology the patient can dish out. To be maximally helpful, the therapist must be nonjudgmental and emotionally open to taking it all in on the patient's terms.

At some level, all but the most deteriorated patients will recognize that the therapist's (outside) attitude of openness is different from the closedness the patient encountered in response to is "craziness" in the outside world. An open reaction to an essentially closed repetitive system, the litany of complaints, the systematic distortion of reality, throws the patient into disequilibrium. Perhaps for the first time in a long time, someone is really listening. The patient's response, insofar as he can muster it, is an opening to openness. This has been called a positive transference, but I feel that it is more genuinely open than that, a special form of a systeming relation. But as this happens, it is the therapist's job to diplomatically invoke the other end of the outside/inside guideline, namely, that the therapist as a professional must remain closed to the patient's openness. The patient brings gifts or wants to meet for lunch outside of the session. The therapist must indicate that the kind of mutuality of good feeling that would emerge if both were outside is not a part of the rules of the game of therapy. But the therapist must also utilize the energy of these good feelings coming from the patient to forge a working alliance so that the arduous task of the therapeutic work can develop a firm basis in trust.

But the professional relationship, in boundarying terms, therapist outside, patient inside, though necessary for the therapeutic process, is not sufficient. Eventually the therapist has to grapple with a patient in a psychological wrestling match for the patient's very soul. This cannot be accomplished merely by the judicious and perceptive application of technique. The therapist, and this is probably the major occupational hazard of being a therapist, has to commit his whole soul into the fray. Opening is what transforms personal structure, and one can only touch openness with an openness of one's own. Eventually, and at a level determined by the situation, the therapist must open his own vulnerability and willingness to make fundamental changes of his own and say "I/thou" to the patient on an equal, personal basis. Sometimes nothing more than a little smile, a little lilt in the tone of voice, can communicate the feeling.

Just as the boundary and the boundarying rules offer the patient protection and control and the opportunity to test and trust the group at his own pace, these same rules give the group leader protection and control in the development of his personal role with the patient. When the leader steps inside the boundary, he separates himself from safe outside connections. The leader stops being an agent of society, of the mental health community, and has only what he has carried inside the boundary (i.e., his own personal strengths and weaknesses and personal commitments). Putting oneself "on the line" like that is a risky venture, even if it is a special space where you are doing it and even if you can always take the option to "split the boundary" and escape back into a cool, protected professionalism. But part of the job of the therapist, within this model, is to take the time to get ready, but eventually get in there inside the boundary with the patient and get into the psychic wrestling match.

There must be boundarying guidelines for this therapist inside, patient inside configuration, too. Inside the boundary, the therapist is primarily responsible for maintaining his autonomy, his own right of opening and closing. Inside the boundary the therapist must serve as a model as well as functioning as an instrument of treatment. The therapist serves as a model of one who is willing to risk change, given a fair amount of trust and control and protection. The boundarying guideline with both therapist and patient inside is: *Be open to openness and closed to closedness.* This is the same guideline as where both are outside the boundary in the normal world, but the difference is that both have elected to enter temporarily into the special world of the group boundary in order to accomplish a special task. Greater risks can be taken because the safety valve of boundary crossing is always available.

What are the special therapeutic benefits of utilizing this inside/inside guideline? Because this is the natural path of pursuing one's own autonomy in the world, pursuing such a policy is a growth experience for the therapist. And because one of the functions of the therapist is to serve as a role model for the patient, it is a good thing for the patient to see this example of autonomy in action. With a clear-cut example of opening/closing before him, the patient can begin to sharpen up his own discrimination about the difference between an open attitude and a closed attitude, about how to articulate these attitudes subtly and diplomatically. The patient learns that opening is inherently neither better nor worse than closing; the two form a complementary pair and each must be trusted and have its due.

But there is an even more powerful function of this inside/inside guideline, an instrumental function. It is assumed in the GST boundarying model that opening/closing is an autonomous function. I cannot cause *your* boundaries to open or close, only my own. Gaining the awareness that despite "allonomous" (nonautonomous, externally imposed) pressures to the contrary, you can open or close to anything or anyone you want is one of the goals of boundarying therapy. Nevertheless, within the trusting relationship of the group boundarying system, there is a strong natural pull to keep boundarying in equilibrium positions, while closed to openness and open to closedness, unless separated by a boundary, are not. If, within the trust of the group, a therapist takes the personal risk of being open to a patient's closedness, natural equilibrating forces (as opposed to manipulative pressures) encourage a responsible reciprocation by risking one's own openness, at least for a while. It is the therapist's personal power—in this case, the power of personal vulnerability—rather than the therapist's professional authority which induces the risk of opening for the patient. This autonomous willingness to take risks on behalf of another is the human core of the boundarying process, slow to achieve, hard to maintain, full of risks and pitfalls, but just as necessary for therapeutic growth as the professional supportive and guiding role.

Patients enter into therapy in a pained and disoriented condition. Nothing has gone well for them and they are at a loss to understand why their attempts at coping with their problems seem to make their problems worse rather than better. Will the task of explaining the GST boundarying guidelines to the pained and disoriented patient in such a way as to begin engendering his trust be too difficult to achieve? In my experience, the "fail safe" nature of the boundarying model makes the way of understanding, trust, and eventual risk a relatively safe and smooth one. First of all, the patient is encouraged to step outside of the boundary without breaking his commitment to the group if he feels uncertain or uncomfortable in any way. Second, the patient has the model of the therapist and the other group members to observe and copy when it seems safe.

Typically, as the group develops, local rules and interpretations of the basic boundarying ground rules are articulated and put into practice. As a leader, I gradually define my own dual professional/personal role both in conceptualization outside the boundary, where I explain what I am trying to do, and inside the boundary, where I do what I am trying to explain. If I have a professional intervention, an intervention based on my authority as a skilled, accredited therapist, I will cross outside the boundary and claim the right to the group's attention. If I have a personal intervention, one based on using my autonomous self and my personal power, I will enter inside the boundary and attempt to inject my energy into the group process. I have no authority to do this because inside the boundary I have left my authority behind. But as the group members gain respect for my humanity, and my willingness to risk my vulnerability and take a chance on losing out to superior personal power in the group, they will begin to accept me as a model and an instrument for the autonomy of boundarying. In my experience, group members, despite their initial pain and confusion, can reactivate their inborn understanding of the boundarying process and begin to utilize the boundarying model. I make it clear by precept and example how my professional and personal roles are complementary, irreconcilable, but inseparable. As group members, they begin to utilize the inside/outside group boundary distinction to carve out two complementary roles for themselves as group members. From an outside position, they develop an attitude much akin to professionalism. They observe themselves or other members of the group and try to formulate conceptualizations about what is going on. They become "observing egos." When they want to get into it, when they are compelled by the impulse to action or to feeling flow, they move inside the boundary and submit themselves more openly, more unconsciously to the process. They can take risks because they can always get out. They can achieve insights because they can always get in and test their ideas in the flux and feeling of action. They can achieve boundarying autonomy because they always know that they will be supported in crossing and recrossing the boundary that distinguishes those two roles for them.

Boundarying Group Therapy with Narcissistic and Borderline Personalities

So far we have argued that the "diagram" of analytically oriented psychotherapy would be made more comprehensible if the traditional ego development dimension were supplemented by an organizational (structural) level dimension of a nonevaluative synchronic nature whose poles consisted of the dialectical complementaries, opening/closing, of the boundarying operation. We have also provided a brief introductory description of a GST-based boundarying therapy method for groups in which the boundarying operation, concretized by the physical boundary and the boundarying rules, plays a central part. Since identity problems characteristic of narcissistic and borderline personalities can be interpreted as boundarying problems of fragmentation and wholeness, the question arises as to whether boundarying therapy might have particular benefits for these self-pathology patients.

In most interaction processes between living systems, therapy groups included, the focus of attention is on the content dimension while the organizational dimension and its associated boundarying processes form the tacit context for the text of content material. The GST-based boundarying method brings the boundarying context of the group process out of the background by means of the physical boundary and the consensually agreed upon boundarying rules. This opens up the way to the process of text and context reversing, the paradoxical process necessary, according to the model, for therapeutic growth. One of the greatest burdens of the therapy group leader, it seems to me, is for him alone to bear the total responsibility for catalyzing and regulating boundarying operations in the group Because these processes are tacit rather than explicit, the leader is vulnerable to manipulation by the members, no matter what their ego developmental level. Making boundarying explicit thus not only reduces this vulnerability to manipulation, but gives the leader, and later the members, a powerful tool of making epistemic or paradoxical shifts between the content and organizational levels. It offers a second path to make productive detours around impasses that develop at the other dimension of the group's reality.

We have presented a model of psychopathology which sees the self disorders, the narcissistic and borderline syndromes, as deep-seated boundarying pathologies. We have presented a method of group therapy in which direct and explicit boundarying interactions supplement the content dimension of the therapeutic work which traditionally has been the exclusive focus of therapy. It was suggested that this boundarying component of the GST-based model was easy for even desperate and disturbed group members to comprehend and learn to utilize; that it provided experiences in developing a fluid articulation back and forth between the opening/closing, inside/outside, systeming/summing complementarities of the boundarying operation, and that it enabled the leader and group members to gain a measure of protection from the provocatively chaotic behavior patterns of the self-disordered personalities which makes doing therapy with them so taxing on leader and member alike. Let's see how group boundarying does it.

When self-disordered patients first enter a therapy group (or, for that matter, any relational situation with other people) there is a tremendous amount of boundarying ambivalence. On the one hand, they want to open completely and merge, instantly recapturing the primary symbiosis. But on the other hand, they are deathly afraid of fragmentation and engulfment, the catastrophic fear that goes hand in glove with the need for merging. The boundarying rules provide a socially supportive way to overcome this initial ambivalence by articulating it in time. The member can stay outside and get his bearings and dip a little toe into the water once in a while by making brief and tentative moves inside. The difference between inside and outside will gradually become apparent, but the major learning will be that of the feeling of being in control of the boundarying situation. Testing and then trusting that boundarying is an autonomous action under no one's control but that of the self. At this initial level, moving inside and outside of the group boundary is the first positive step toward more critical skills in personal boundary control. During this stage of group participation, the group leader can help an entering member distinguish between the proper content mode role appropriate to being inside and outside of the group boundary. With the physical boundary catalyzing clarity, a new group member can begin to discriminate the observing ego role appropriate to the outside position from the involved action of the participating role appropriate to the inside position.

As a new member's participant–observer complementarity is developing, the leader can be establishing his own personal–professional complementarity. The outside vantage point of the professional role is essentially a closing operation where a boundary distinction is drawn between a real situation and a fantasy situation. This would include both the oedipal-level object transferences and the more primitive psychotic and self-object transferences characteristic of self disorders. The inside position, on the other hand, lends itself to empathic incubation à la Kohut (1977). Here the leader can be open to openness and delight in the fellow humanity of his group member and his struggles for ego strength. At first, these moments will be brief and will be few and far between, both parties to the systeming event will probably back off and move quickly out of the boundary after a few seconds of mutual contact. Nevertheless, there is a big difference between a moment of mutual openness, however brief and however quickly covered over by individual or group defenses, and the wish for it. The moment was there as a plainly visible fact, and the retreat reaction was there as well, an equally historical fact. The clarity of the distinction between the opening and the closing facilitates both understanding and later repetition.

As a new group member begins to trust his autonomous right to move inside/outside the group boundary, he will begin to trust the equally autonomous process of opening/closing with the leader or other group members inside the boundary. The new member will be able to observe the leader and other members as models for the opening/closing process. It will gradually dawn upon the self-disordered patient for whom both closing and opening are near-catastrophic experiences that opening can be trusted only if closing is immediately and constantly available to a relationship. The new members observe episodes where the leader or member suddenly moves from opening to closing or from closing to opening for no reason at all, and yet this apparently capricious event is trusted by everyone. These observations will plant the seed that the joy of opening is possible without the catastrophe of abandonment. Gradually, first through the articulation of moving inside/outside of the group boundary and then by tentatively articulating opening/closing within the safety of the group boundary, the self-disordered patient will begin to learn to understand and live the language of boundarying. The tentative first steps taken will be lurching and unsure and will doubtless make the leader and other members uncomfortable and confused. But they are equally protected by the boundarying rules so they can afford to take a risk once in a while to support the new member's faltering steps.

It is absurd to suggest that the supplementing of the content mode of therapeutic theory and practice with the boundarying mode will result in a panacea for working with the self-disordered personality. It must be reemphasized that organization without content, dealing with opening/closing without dealing with who and what is opened/closed to and why, is absolutely sterile. Organizational variables must be embodied in historical and concrete content situations; that kind of working through takes time. But it is equally true within our model that content without organization is haphazard.

Incorporating boundarying action into the therapeutic process does seem to add some features to the process which help self-disordered personalities and their co-members and leaders and does generate some hypotheses that might lead to greater understanding and better clinical management of these problems. The protection of fragile ego structures is there. The possibility of transforming a debilitating and deep-seated ambivalence about merging or being engulfed into a workable complementarity is there. The resolution of the leader's personal–professional role conflicts is transformed into an understandable and workable set of boundarying rules.

One of the hypotheses generated by the group boundarying model concerns the possibility that summing, being closed to closedness, is good for people, especially narcissistic and borderline personalities. As relatively genital personalities, we tend to take our summing for granted. We just impersonally let everyone else bounce right off us. Salespeople, flirts, even our importuning children try to open us up without opening themselves, and we cheerfully but effectively close off to them, politely but clearly. It seems to me that self-disordered personality types are just as desperately in need of reconstitutive closing to closedness experience as they are in need of empathic opening to openness experience, as recommended by the Kohutians. Because of their archaic ambivalence about both opening and closing to another, the safety valve of being able to split the group boundary is always necessary to have around, for a direct, heavy dose of either can be terrifying and fragmenting to the fragile ego. But, given such protection, and given the modeling of opening/closing in articulation by the leader and other members, self-disordered personalities need to develop the capacity to handle closing through firsthand experience. Within the group boundary, the leader is free to be engaged in a personal rather than a professional role. This sets the stage for opening and nurturing out of empathic humanity, but it equally sets the stage for a clear, firm closing process.

Closing down when the sticky, engulfing self-object behavior of a self-disordered person becomes oppressive (perhaps because it activates our own unresolved archaic needs at that level) provides a discriminating experience for the group member, and protection for the leader or helping co-member. It helps make clear what kinds of behavior set off the self-debating cycles with others. The rehabilitative experience through ego incubation must be balanced with the real social experience that other people are not there to give everything all the time, for there are some things that another person just won't take. Learning the boundaries between what others will take and what they won't take is an essential step on the road to antonomy. Boundarying experience, where both opening and closing becomes trusted within the self, provides a path along which, slowly at first, such steps can be taken.

A Case Study

During a two-day weekend boundarying group workshop for professional mental health workers, the group spent the whole first morning session *not* entering the group boundary, which lay all coiled up on a space defined by four full-size mattresses across the room. Because the leader had to embody the rule that being inside was no better *or* worse than being outside the group boundary, he kept a strictly neutral stance on the issue and focused on simply providing information about the method and the theory behind it. By the end of the morning, the group had come to its own autonomous accord that they would all enter the boundary after lunch break. I felt that they were thoroughly ready.

After the lunch break, a new member appeared. I had assumed that he was simply a no-show. He explained that he had wanted for many months to attend this workshop, but on that winter day he had encountered all sorts of storms and other disasters beyond his control that caused his lateness. I was impressed and touched by the somewhat lurid details of his suffering. The grotesque details of his horror story impressed the other group members as well. I was concerned that he had missed being with the group as it autonomously moved through the essential outside trust developing stage of the morning session and considered not letting him participate, but I couldn't bring myself to fault a person for the perversities of nature.

He was eager and supercharged with emotional energy.

Heedlessly he took center stage in the group and began another lurid horror story about how, as a therapist, he kept trying to get therapy groups together while they just as rapidly could not be kept together as groups. Then he went on to *another* horror story about how he and his wife were breaking up. The group members were fascinated but quickly overwhelmed by the chaotic spewing out of this luckless, feckless man's saga. My first response to this innundating flow was to split the boundary. I got up, walked across the boundary, and relaxed outside its circle, cutting off as much as I could. But the man never seemed to run down and the others seemed, outwardly at least, to sit there enthralled. I suddenly began to realize that my splitting the boundary was an inadequate response to a situation in which this chaotic, overwhelming, boundaryless person might very well ruin everything that the group had so carefully built up in the autonomously developing group. His chaotic boundary structure could bring the group down.

    I saw that he was too new as a group member and too far gone as a personality for me as a leader to confront him from inside the boundary in my personal role or to control him from outside the boundary in my professional role. The requisite power or authority for that must be built up slowly and had been with the others. However, I saw that I could work through the boundarying rules, which were givens of the situation immediately applicable as an entrance requirement to the group. I employed the tactic of "tightening the boundary" on him. I told him that it was one of the consequences of the boundarying rules that, when he was in the role of an observing ego, observing the actions and their possible meaning of another group member *or* himself, that he should cross outside the boundary to make that contribution to the group's efforts. On the other hand, when he was participating as a group member and giving of himself and his feelings in a here-and-now relation to other group members or leader, he should cross over inside the group boundary.

    I listened carefully to his stream of woeful experiences and, every time I caught him on the "wrong" side of the boundary, I intervened to ask him to reposition himself. Such directives began to happen so frequently that, rather than moving his body inside and outside, he began to grab the foam rubber ring and sling it back and forth across his head and body so that he would be properly inside or outside. It is important to note that it was not essential that my interpretation of his proper position was

100 percent or even 75 percent correct. The point was that I was imposing boundary control, which was within my commitment and responsibility to the boundarying rules. He was distracted at first, but miraculously soon began to enjoy the process of monitoring his own boundary position vis-à-vis the content of what he was talking about. It was not long before he fully incorporated the inside/outside rule interpretation and began to show introspective curiosity about which side he was on.

His tales of horror and his chaotic emotional innundation began to slow down and he began to show an interest in the others. The rest of the group, who had been both horrified and entranced, began to warm up to him. As I saw it, I had adapted the boundarying rules to effect an "isomorphic prosthesis," which brought this man under enough boundarying control so that the group could begin to trust him. I am not entirely sure that this man could be diagnosed as a self disordered case, but it certainly was clear that his boundary structure was completely chaotic. The term *isomorphic* means that there is an identity of underlying organizational pattern beneath a diversity of content. The developing group boundarying structure was at a different level from this man's own inner boundarying structure, but, through the boundary tightening procedure, I exploited the isomorphism between the two living structures at the two levels. I used boundary control at the group level, which was explicitly visible because of the physical boundary and controllable because of our consensual commitment to the group boundary rules, to gain, at least temporarily, a measure of control of the chaotic inner boundary structures that were threatening to fragment the whole group.

Because the group and the leader sensed that the isomorphic prosthesis had been accomplished, we were better able to trust him and work with him as the workshop went on. We were at one point also able to utilize his archaic functioning for the benefit of the group. Somewhat later, a configuration developed in the group process where three of the men banded together with their arms linked against a single woman in the group who felt strong enough to test her own strength in an eyeball-to-eyeball confrontation, macho against feminist equal. The man of the horror stories was not directly involved, but he had the sensitivity to see that, despite the woman's strong stand against the men, there was an undercurrent of fear. He crawled around the outside of the group boundary, reached in, and held her hand in empathic support. It was the little help she needed, help which the three macho men were too involved or insensitive to see. Trusting him to be under boundary control, and with him trusting himself in a way not possible before, he was able to make his unique group contribution.

Summary

The special problems of psychotherapeutic treatment of the self disorders, the borderline and narcissistic syndromes were discussed. Also presented was Stolorow and Lachman's hypothesis (1980) that empathic incubation of ego strength should be used with these patients rather than the usual procedure of interpreting transference and resistance. A synthesis of the psychodynamic approach and the General Systems Therapy approach (Durkin, 1981) was put forth to address this dilemma of "the two psychotherapies" raised by Stolorow and Lachman. A two-dimensional diagram depicting this attempted synthesis was presented. The diagram's dimension: "Psychodynamic Ego Development," was content oriented and, therefore, value oriented. In the diagram's Organizational Mode Boundarying Operation was not value oriented, but dialectical, with a norm of dialectic flow back and forth between the "opening" and "closing" poles. The "diagonal dialectic" strategy for therapeutic intervention where advantage can be taken of both the vertical and horizontal dimensions of the "diagram" is discussed.

This theoretical model was then applied to group therapy practice. The "Group Boundarying Model" utilizes a physical boundary and two basic boundarying rules: (1) The group goes on inside the boundary and the rest of the world goes on outside the boundary, and (2) it is not better to be either inside the group boundary or outside the group boundary. It is expected that clients will physically move inside the boundary when they become involved with the group and move physically otherwise when uninvolved in the group process. These rules (1) protect the group members from pressures to perform before they are ready; (2) help them clarify experiences of cognitive closing and emotional opening; and (3) enable group leaders to resolve the dilemma of their dual professional and personal roles. The benefits of the group boundarying model for narcissistic and borderline patients were reviewed. It was suggested that an isomorphy, that is, an identity of underlying structure despite differences in surface content, existed between the group boundarying structure set up as a rule for the group and the chaotic boundarying structures that are characteristic of narcissistic and borderline patients. It was hypothesized that the group boundary could serve as an isomorphic prosthesis, that is, a substitute group boundary for the individual boundary tangles of self pathology clients. A case study of the use of an isomorphic prosthesis effect from the group boundary was discussed in which the group, after first being overwhelmed by the confused outpouring of cognition and affect, of separation and fusion, of one of the borderline group members, gained the trust in that patient by his using the group boundary as a prosthesis for his own chaotic personal boundary structure.

References

American Psychiatric Association (1980), *Diagnostic and Statistical Manual* (DSM-III). Washington, DC: American Psychiatric Association.

Bateson, G. (1978), *Mind and Nature*. New York: Bantam Books.

Durkin, J. E. (1981), *Living Groups: Group Psychotherapy and General System Theory*. New York: Brunner/Mazel.

——— (1983), Authority Outside/Power Inside, and the Boundary Lies Between: Two Complementary Roles for the Group Psychotherapist. Unpublished manuscript.

——— (1987), Coevolution in team psychotherapy: Parallel processing on both sides of the window. *J. Strategic System. Ther.* 6:26–38.

Kohut, H. (1977), *The Restoration of the Self*. New York: International Universities Press.

Modell, A. (1968), *Object Love and Reality*. New York: International Universities Press.

Stolorow, R., & Lachman, F. (1980), *Psychoanalysis of Arrested Development*. New York: International Universities Press.

Chapter 10

THE TRANSFERENCE–COUNTERTRANSFERENCE NEUROSIS IN PSYCHOANALYSIS: THE INTERSUBJECTIVE CONTEXT OF DREAM FORMATION

RICHARD B. ULMAN, Ph.D.

Analysts have long debated the role of countertransference in the analytic process. Initially, this debate was between analysts who saw countertransference as detrimental to the success of treatment (and therefore to be excluded from the therapy) and analysts who saw countertransference as integral and vital to the analytic process. The latter group argued that an analyst can gain greater access to the patient's transference through an enhanced understanding of the countertransference.

Although analysts continue to debate this issue, its treatment implications have not yet been fully explored from the perspective of the psychoanalytic psychology of the self. In Kohut's (1971) early work, he discussed how the analyst's countertransference may interfere with the proper analytic stance toward the patient's mirroring and idealizing needs. His clinical data substantiated the claim that patients with narcissistic pathology do not experience others—especially the analyst—as

---

This chapter is an expansion of an article originally published in the *Bulletin of the Menninger Clinic* (1985), 49:37–51. Earlier versions of the chapter were presented at the Inaugural Conference of the Society for the Advancement of Self Psychology in New York (May 1983) and at the Sixth Annual Self Psychology Conference in Los Angeles (October 1983). The author wishes to acknowledge the contributions of Robert D. Stolorow as well as Peter B. Zimmermann and other members of the New York Self Psychology Study Group who suggested several valuable improvements.

separate objects but rather as archaic "selfobjects" incompletely distinguished from the self and serving to maintain the sense of self. The concept of selfobject functions has been extended to describe patients with various degrees of self pathology, but with some notable exceptions (Oremland and Windholz, 1971; Gunther, 1976; Goldberg, 1977; Wolf, 1979), the role of countertransference from the standpoint of psychoanalytic self psychology has been largely bypassed.

In addressing this issue, Stolorow and his collaborators (Stolorow, Atwood, and Ross, 1978; Stolorow, Atwood, and Lachmann, 1981; Stolorow, Brandchaft and Atwood, 1983; Brandchaft and Stolorow, 1984; Atwood and Stolorow, 1984) have brought countertransference to the forefront of analysis by introducing a psychoanalytic theory of intersubjectivity. They maintain that psychoanalysis is neither "a science of the intrapsychic, focused on events presumed to occur within one isolated 'mental apparatus.' Nor is it . . . a social science, investigating the 'behavioral facts' of the therapeutic interaction (Atwood and Stolorow, 1984, p. 41). On the contrary, they (Atwood and Stolorow, 1984) argue that:

> Psychoanalysis is . . . a science of the *intersubjective*, focused on the interplay between the differently organized subjective worlds of the observer and the observed. The observational stance is always one within, rather than outside, the intersubjective field . . . being observed, a fact that guarantees the centrality of introspection and empathy as the methods of observation (p. 41).

Drawing upon earlier work on the psychoanalysis of developmental arrests (Stolorow and Lachmann, 1980), that is, derailments in the structuralization of the subjective world, Stolorow and his co-workers have demonstrated that the analyst's failure to recognize the patient's often unconscious awareness of the analyst's vulnerabilities and archaic needs may interfere with the unfolding, analysis, and working through of the selfobject transference by creating a vicious cycle of misunderstanding.[1] Such failures in understanding are rooted in the unrecognized conjunctions and disjunctions that occur in treatment when the central self and object configurations structuring the subjective worlds of patient and analyst are either too similar or too dissimilar.

In this chapter, I shall clarify how the developmentally arrested psychological structures of both the patient and the analyst interact to codetermine a specific intersubjective field, which I shall refer to as the transference–countertransference neurosis. (I use this term analogously to Freud's concept of transference neurosis as referring, not to a diagnostic category, but the unconscious structuring of the therapeutic relationship by the patient's, and I would add the analyst's, early formative history.)

In the case I present, this intersubjective field was structured on the one hand by the patient's extreme sensitivity and responsiveness to any sign of disturbance in the analyst's feelings of efficacy and grandiosity, and on the other hand by the analyst's need for confirming responses from the patient that would enhance his self-esteem. The case thus illustrates how the analyst may use the patient as a particular type of selfobject and how the patient may feel compelled to fulfill this function. It exemplifies the principle that transference and countertransference continually shape one another in a specific pattern of reciprocal, mutual influence.

My discussion of the case focuses on two interrelated sets of clinical phenomena: (1) a series of dreams of both patient and therapist, and (2) a sequence of the therapist's communications and the patient's reactions to them. The therapeutic communications and productions of both patient and analyst may be understood as indicators of their *immersion* in and experience of the intersubjective field.

A secondary theme that runs through the clinical presentation concerns the intersubjective context of dream formation. Dream images are special instances of the ubiquitous psycho-

---

[1] I use the term *misunderstanding* (rather than the commonly misused concept of "empathic failure") to distinguish the analyst's difficulties in comprehending the central self and object configurations that structure the therapy from the patient's subjective experience of not being understood by the analyst.

logical process that Atwood and Stolorow (1984) refer to as *concretization:* "the encapsulation of structures of experience by concrete, sensorimotor symbols" (p. 85). The concrete perceptual images of dreams symbolically dramatize "the organizing principles and dominant leitmotivs that unconsciously pattern and thematize a person's psychological life" (Atwood and Stolorow, 1984, p. 98). As the case material will demonstrate, in analysis these invariant thematic configurations and corresponding dream symbols crystallize from within the specific intersubjective system constituted by the therapeutic dialogue. Dream analysis, from an intersubjective perspective, enables both participants in the dialogue to gain empathic access to the analytic reality they have both created.

Case Report

When Maureen began treatment, she was 26 years old, single, and shared an apartment with a female roommate. Maureen was studying operatic singing, occasionally appearing onstage. She supported herself by working as an office manager. An attractive woman with long, wavy hair, Maureen normally dressed in casual clothes and wore little makeup. She had spent several years at two universities without obtaining a college degree. All her recent relationships with men had ended unsatisfactorily. She had never been in psychotherapy.

During her first session, Maureen explained that she was seeking treatment at the suggestion of her singing instructor, who had told her that despite her considerable talent and ability, she would never realize her potential unless she overcame some serious "emotional blocks." Maureen admitted that she found attending auditions difficult and that this reticence had seriously interfered with her career. She also said she had been depressed for some time and was finding it increasingly difficult to get out of bed in the morning and go to work. She described herself as socially isolated and alienated from her peers. She hoped therapy could quickly help her to better use what she felt was her unusual intelligence, sensitivity, and perceptiveness.

In the early sessions, Maureen presented a detailed picture of her childhood family experiences. She was born in the Southwest but her family moved several times before they finally settled in Connecticut. Her father was a salesman, her mother a teacher. The fourth of five children, Maureen had two older sisters and one younger and one older brother. Despite her parents' middle-class income, she grew up in an upper-class neighborhood, which made her feel like an outsider.

Maureen recalled that her mother had told her when she was quite young that she was born as a result of an unplanned and unwanted pregnancy, which made her feel throughout childhood as if she were a constant burden on her mother. According to the patient's recollections, her mother was consistently unsupportive and unnurturing, refusing to recognize Maureen's obvious and chronic sadness and unhappiness. Maureen felt compelled to "put on a happy face," suppressing her pain and misery. Even as an adolescent, she believed her mother was unable or unwilling to encourage her; she was convinced that her mother demeaned and belittled her because she felt threatened by Maureen's talents and abilities.

Maureen remembered her father as an alcoholic who verbally abused her mother, which upset all the children. Although she described him as an "emotional wreck," she nevertheless believed he loved her. For example, during the initial phase of treatment, Maureen revealed that some of her earliest memories concerned pleasant scenes of lying in bed with her father as she fell asleep at night or of watching him dress in the morning before he went to work. Despite these positive memories, Maureen noted that her father was never emotionally available to her when she turned to him to offset her mother's unresponsiveness.

Despite her mother's unresponsiveness and her father's unavailability, Maureen said she never relinquished her conviction that she possessed superior intelligence and perceptiveness. In her relationships with her siblings, she paid a high price for maintaining this sense of specialness and uniqueness. Maureen believed that her brothers and sisters resented her talent and ability and that they retaliated by isolating and abandoning her. She spoke with great sadness about feeling profoundly alienated from her family while she was growing up.

Maureen initially saw the therapist twice a week in face-to-face therapy. After approximately eight months, the therapist was sufficiently impressed by the quality of the early sessions to suggest adding a third session each week and using the couch. He intended the suggestion as a sign that he considered Maureen a good candidate for psychoanalysis. Maureen, however, experienced the suggestion as an indication that the therapist thought she was seriously disturbed and "sick." She immediately expressed her dismay and, in a subsequent scene, reported the following dream ("The Seduction"): "I was in a room with an old boyfriend, Thomas, and he suggested that we lie down together on a bed. As we were lying on the bed, he made sexual advances, which I rejected." With little hesitation, Maureen connected the dream imagery with the therapist's suggestion that she consider lying on the couch. This association led the therapist to interpret the dream as an expression of Maureen's fear that he was attempting to seduce her. Although at the time neither the therapist nor Maureen understood the full meaning of the seduction image, in retrospect its meaning can be inferred from the analytic reality that Maureen and the therapist had created. Manifestly, the dream might be interpreted to mean that Maureen thought the therapist was attempting to seduce her. In view of her early memories of lying happily on her father's bed, it is not difficult to understand her association of analyst and couch with father, bed, and sexual fantasies.

On a deeper level, however, Maureen was communicating that she had sensed that the therapist was motivated to use her—motivated not by lust but by self-interest. In fact, at that time he felt pressured to obtain a "control" case to complete his training requirements. In the context of this pressure, the therapeutic relationship became organized around an intersubjective theme—concretized in the dream symbols—that would pervade the entire analysis: the therapist's need for Maureen to function as a selfobject to meet his self-esteem requirements and sustain his narcissistic aspirations, and Maureen's corresponding compulsion to sacrifice herself to fulfill his needs.

Because of Maureen's negative reaction, expressed both directly and in the dream, the therapist temporarily dropped his suggestion of a third weekly session and the use of the couch. As treatment proceeded, Maureen began to feel attached to the therapist. She also continued to display what he thought was a remarkable gift for psychoanalytic work. Several months later, the therapist again introduced the possibility of adding a third session and using the couch, but Maureen again refused, believing that her therapy was proceeding smoothly. She also became angry with the therapist for reintroducing an idea she had recently rejected.

In the session following this exchange, Maureen reported the following dream ("The Race"):

> I was standing in the snow watching people running a race. Then I joined them, although I was not an official contestant. As I was running, I discovered a sled and laid down on it and won the race. Afterwards, I went to my high school gym coach and told him of my victory. He responded enthusiastically. Although I was pleased by his praise, I was upset because he did not notice that I had accidentally cut off my thumb while riding the sled.

In response to a question from the therapist, Maureen quickly connected the race and lying on the sled with the therapy and lying on the couch. In this context, the dream symbols depicted her belief that the therapist needed her to excel in analysis and that she must comply with his wishes and expectations to gain his approval and praise. At the same time, she believed that complying with his narcissistic requirements would entail serious injury through the loss of a vital part of herself, which the therapist would neither notice nor be concerned about. At this juncture in the treatment, Maureen and the therapist replicated a critical pathogenic configuration from her childhood. As a child, Maureen had consistently felt compelled to sacrifice her own treasured qualities and mirroring needs to satisfy the narcissistic requirements of her mother, who seemed oblivious to the loss of self entailed by Maureen's sacrifices.

Once the therapist canceled one of Maureen's two weekly sessions but arranged to see her at another time. When she came to the alternate session, she was dressed in a low-cut blouse—unusually seductive attire. She expressed gratitude for the opportunity of a second session that week but also voiced concern that the day and time of the session inconvenienced the therapist. In exploring these feelings, the therapist learned that Maureen believed she was a burden to him. Already paying a low fee, she had now become a nuisance as well: She worried that he would abandon her by stopping treatment. During this session, Maureen told the therapist about a dream ("The Kiss") she had experienced after he had rescheduled her second weekly session:

> You and I were standing together on a balcony overlooking a beautiful garden. We were talking and gazing romantically into one another's eyes, and you gently kissed me on one cheek. At first I was frightened and taken aback, but we discussed the situation and decided our involvement had been totally innocent and thus was completely compatible with the therapy.

Maureen herself noted this first undisguised appearance of the therapist in one of her dreams. However, at first she was unable to understand the dream's import. The therapist asked whether the dream might be related to her feelings about having a session rescheduled. She replied that although she was concerned about burdening him, she had been "touched" by his offer of another appointment.

As Maureen and the therapist continued to explore the dream's manifestly erotic and romantic imagery, an underlying meaning surfaced. Maureen had perceived in the therapist's offer of a substitute session his narcissistic wish for her to affirm his goodness and desirability. With characteristic responsiveness to his mirroring needs, she accommodated symbolically to this "seduction" through her sexually suggestive attire and an "erotic" dream.

Shortly after this session, the therapist announced his plans for a week's vacation. Although he discussed with Maureen the possible import of his absence on her, he was unprepared for her response. In her first session after he returned, she reported that she had been devastated by his absence. In the preceding months, she had progressed considerably, getting up each morning at a reasonable hour and going to work, spending more time with friends and acquaintances, and feeling less socially isolated. In addition, she was auditioning more and was pursuing her career more actively. With tears streaming down her face, Maureen said the break in therapy sessions had destroyed all this progress; during the previous week she had retreated and withdrawn into herself. She accused the therapist of betraying her trust and confidence, and she decried his lack of commitment to her treatment.

Maureen had experienced the therapist's vacation as the loss of a vital and sustaining selfobject tie to the therapist. Consequently, her sense of self had disintegrated. The therapist had not anticipated this possibility because Maureen's unwavering "progress" in the analysis supplied him with the mirroring experiences that he required.

All efforts to reestablish the ruptured selfobject transference tie failed, the therapy remained derailed, and Maureen's condition continued to deteriorate. At one point during this phase of treatment, Maureen in desperation considered participating in a research project on the effectiveness of a new antidepressant medication. The therapist experienced this possibility as a severe narcissistic wound. Although he tried to conceal the extent to which he was disturbed, his facial expression and tone of voice conveyed his dismay.

In an effort to salvage her therapy, which she sensed was in jeopardy, Maureen suggested that she add the third weekly session and lie on the couch. She said that a third session, on Saturdays, would help combat her sense of social isolation, which was most intense on weekends. Lying on the couch was a gesture of trust to show her willingness to risk her own sense of safety and security to correct the imbalance of the therapy and "plug" herself back into the therapist. An important note here is that Maureen reestablished the selfobject transference bond by *adapting herself* to what she sensed as the *therapist's* narcissistic requirements.

After the third session was added and Maureen began to lie on the couch, her condition steadily improved both within the treatment and in her outside life. She regained her trust in the therapist and felt "reconnected" to him. Her depression began to lift and she felt as if she were "coming back to life." She also reestablished contact with friends and renewed her efforts to pursue a singing career.

Further evidence of the repair of the ruptured selfobject tie was seen in Maureen's response to the therapist's second vacation several months after the first one. In view of the devastation following the first interruption in treatment, Maureen and the therapist spent many sessions exploring the meanings of the second separation. In the first session following the vacation, she reported that she had done well and had not become deflated or collapsed. On the contrary, her personal relationships and her singing career continued to progress. She said she had been able to maintain an image in her mind of lying on the couch and being with the therapist. This image soothed and comforted her and was accompanied by a sensation that reminded her of being held safely and securely in a hammock she had swung in as a child.

After several months of continued improvement, Maureen expressed a gnawing fear that the therapist was experiencing her progress as a burden and a threat. In the context of exploring this feeling, Maureen related the following dream ("The Bad and Good Session"):

> I was late for my therapy appointment, and when I called to tell you I would be delayed, you became angry and yelled, telling me that being late for sessions is cause for immediate termination. I was shocked and expressed dismay and disbelief. You reluctantly changed your mind and permitted me to come to the session, but you warned me that if I was ever late again, you would automatically end the therapy. In the next scene in the dream, I was in a session with you. I was telling you I was certain you were not serious about ending my treatment. You agreed and sat next to me on the couch. I was not wearing any socks or shoes, and you gently stroked one of my bare feet, admiring its beauty.

During several subsequent sessions, Maureen and the therapist explored the various themes in this dream. The imagery of the first dream scene symbolically concretized Maureen's dread that if she did not adhere strictly to the rules of therapy, the therapist would retaliate by abandoning her. An underlying theme, which was not fully understood until later (when the transference–countertransference neurosis became clarified), was that being late for her session represented a willful expression of her independence. Maureen sensed that the therapist needed her as an archaic mirroring selfobject, and she therefore feared he could not tolerate any expression of her autonomy. She believed that if she asserted any autonomy, she would be disregarding his need for unquestioned compliance, which she feared would injure and enrage him. Indeed, the analyst later recognized that he had unconsciously interpreted Maureen's punctuality as a sign of his special significance to her and that it thereby had provided him with a required archaic mirroring experience.

The imagery of the second dream scene symbolically dramatized Maureen's wish to expose valued and treasured parts of herself that she had long kept hidden. Whereas the first dream scene conveyed her dread of enslavement as the price of avoiding abandonment, the second scene depicted a longed-for relationship with the therapist in which he would serve as a mirroring selfobject *for her.*

Before Maureen began using the couch, the therapist had always written his "process notes" after the session. When Maureen went to the couch, however, he took notes during the sessions. Maureen noticed the change and commented that his notetaking made her uncomfortable because it heightened her sense of being the focus of attention, further exacerbating her feeling that she was a burden to the therapist. As if to dramatize her point, Maureen reported to the therapist the following dream ("My Therapist Is Going Crazy"):

> I was in a session with you, and you were furiously and frantically writing down notes. I told you I was upset because you seemed so anxious and burdened. You replied that you were indeed extremely harried and under a great deal of pressure because you had so many patients to see after me. You told me that you really felt overwhelmed. I responded by attempting to soothe and calm you and help you relax.

Maureen quickly associated the dream to her sense that the therapist's notetaking reflected his increased attention to her, which overburdened and overwhelmed him. A genetic interpretation linked this feeling to her early childhood experiences with her mother, who constantly stressed that she was overburdened and overwhelmed by having to care for a fourth child. This dream was linked with the earlier dream of "The Bad and Good Session," and further interpretations were made about Maureen's fear of being abandoned if she indicated any independence or autonomy. The theme of Maureen's need to soothe and calm the therapist was not emphasized, however, and this central aspect of the transference–countertransference neurosis was left unexamined. In retrospect, no dream symbols could have more dramatically conveyed the intersubjective context of the therapy; Maureen and the therapist were reenacting a silent collusion in which Maureen served as the therapist's archaic selfobject, accepting her role as the guardian of his psychological stability.

Following further explorations of "The Good and Bad Session" dream, several enactments (another pathway for the concretization process) signaled a change in Maureen's posture in the transference. First, she wrote a bad check for the monthly fee, which she had never done before. Then, realizing what she had done, she "accidentally" overslept and missed her next session.

In the following session, Maureen and the therapist discussed the bad check. She became extremely upset and berated herself for committing what she regarded as a terrible and unforgivable crime. She thought she had forfeited the therapist's trust and fallen from his good graces, and she anticipated termination as an appropriate punishment. The therapist, on the other hand, saw her behavior as an enactment of the drama depicted in her dream of "The Bad and Good Session." As he and Maureen jointly explored the theme of her failure to serve as his selfobject, they ushered in the next phase of therapy in which, during the third year of treatment, Maureen began to speak of terminating. She said she was handling the "ups and downs" of both her personal life and her singing career with an equanimity that had previously eluded her. More importantly, she noted with dismay that she had become increasingly aware of her "dependence" on the therapist. She felt that such dependence was thwarting the possibility of more independent and autonomous functioning. Having raised the topic of termination, she quickly acknowledged that although it appealed to her, she was terrified of terminating.

Shortly after broaching the topic of termination, Maureen reported two dreams that she related to her feelings about ending treatment. In the first dream ("The Shoplifter"),

> I was shopping in a store and wanted to walk out without paying for the items I had selected. As I walked toward the door, however, I noticed a security guard sitting at the exit, watching for shoplifters. So I hesitated, fearful that he would catch me trying to leave without paying.

Without pausing, Maureen immediately described her second dream ("The Termination"):

> I was walking down the hallway leading to your office. I met you near the office door, where you explained that you could not see me for our scheduled appointment but could speak with me there for a few minutes. You told me we had come a long way in therapy and it was now time to terminate. I agreed and we parted company. As I was standing on the street corner outside your office, I became confused about my directions. I felt confident, however, that I could find my way.

Maureen and the therapist focused on the imagery in her two dreams, agreeing that it reflected her conflicts about terminating. On the one hand, "The Shoplifter," with its image of stealing and theft, symbolically concretized her desire to leave treatment without paying the "cost." In talking about this dream, she described her guilt feelings about terminating. An interpretation linked this dream to a dream she had reported early in therapy, "The Race," in which she sacrificed a vital part of herself to gain the therapist's admiration. But "The Shoplifter" dream indicated that Maureen wished to avoid the cost of losing herself through surrendering to the therapist's archaic selfobject needs.

"The Termination," on the other hand, conveyed Maureen's wish for the therapist to initiate termination, thereby demonstrating that he could allow her to leave. Although she was concerned about her ability to find her way in life, the conclusion of the dream indicated she had acquired some capacity for self-direction. Her underlying need for the therapist to appreciate and mirror her strivings for greater separation was not yet clearly understood.

Despite considerable work on the meaning of these dreams, Maureen continued to express conflicts about terminating. In particular, she worried that ending therapy would gravely injure the therapist. She imagined that he experienced their discussion of termination as a serious affront to his professional dignity and as an assault on his therapeutic pride. Feeling that she was harming him, she feared he would retaliate by abruptly and prematurely stopping treatment.

About this time, the therapist had the following dream ("The Final") which he reported to his supervisor:

> The semester was drawing to an end in my high school math class, and I suddenly realized I had not been paying attention in class and was totally unprepared for the final examination. Much to my dismay, I found out that in addition to the test, a term paper was also due. I was panic-stricken and feared the embarrassment connected with failing, so I found the teacher and tried to explain my predicament.

The therapist and his supervisor related the dream symbols to the therapist's experience of Maureen's expected termination as a humiliating and shameful blow. This countertransference experience, in turn, had been decisive in shaping the patient's current dilemma in the transference.

With his enhanced appreciation of the intersubjective structure of the transference–countertransference neurosis, the therapist explored more openly the meaning of termination as a developmental step for the patient. Maureen asked about reducing the number of her sessions from three to two per week. After much discussion, she and the therapist decided to eliminate her Saturday afternoon session. In the session immediately following what would have been her Saturday session, Maureen reported a dream ("The Crutch") that portrayed her reaction to the elimination of the third session as part of the termination process:

> I was standing at the top of a flight of stairs watching an old woman with a crutch walking down the stairs. The old woman disappeared, leaving the crutch behind. I retrieved the crutch and gave it to Thomas (the former boyfriend who appeared in her first reported dream, "The Seduction"), who needed it because he had hurt his foot. I watched Thomas using the crutch to walk down the stairs and became alarmed because he appeared to be so diseased and sickly. I immediately had an intense desire to care for him.

Then the dream scene changed:

> It was a Saturday afternoon, and Thomas and I were together in a room with other people. Thomas and the others were talking, and I felt like an appendage to him. I asked Thomas about his foot, and he told me his toes were disintegrating. He returned to his previous conversation, and I became worried that he and the others were plotting against me.

Initially, Maureen was quite puzzled about the dream's meaning. When the therapist asked whether it could be related to the elimination of her Saturday afternoon session, Maureen remembered that when she and Thomas broke up, she had feared he would fall apart. Perhaps, she said, she was now worried that the therapist would also fall apart when she terminated treatment.

During this session and many subsequent ones, Maureen and the therapist pursued the theme of the therapist falling apart in response to her terminating. They interpreted the crutch symbol as a self-image and its use, first by the old woman and then by Thomas, as depicting Maureen's belief that she currently served as the therapist's crutch just as she had previously functioned as her mother's crutch. She remembered as a child always having to accompany her mother on shopping trips. She had not wanted to go with her but complied because she hoped her mother would pay more attention to her. Instead, she had been repeatedly disappointed. Even so, she continued to accompany her mother because she feared her mother would retaliate against her if she did not.

By focusing on the close parallels between the thematic

structure of Maureen's dream ("The Crutch") and her recently recovered early childhood memories, Maureen and the therapist were able to work through the transference– countertransference neurosis. Both began to appreciate the enormous strength of Maureen's compulsion to serve as her therapist's archaic selfobject just as she had previously felt required to function as a selfobject for her mother. They gained a keener comprehension of Maureen's acute sensitivity to the slightest hint of the therapist's injured grandiosity which indeed had been his reaction to her wish to terminate (see the therapist's dream "The Final"). Any indication of such disturbance in the therapist confirmed Maureen's long-standing conviction that if she were lost as an appendage to the therapist–mother, the object would decay and disintegrate, and she feared that the therapist would retaliate if she failed to fulfill the required selfobject function.

After three years of treatment, in Maureen's most recent sessions, she described a new vitality derived from having survived intact after pushing herself "to the edge" in several important areas of her personal life. The therapist wondered whether she felt a similar vitality in her relationship to him. She confirmed that she did—that she had tested the limits by bringing up and pursuing the issue of termination. Having done so, she no longer felt enslaved to him and realized that she could now leave him. This realization, she stressed, enabled her to continue exploring the meanings of termination and to further consolidate the expansion of authentic selfhood that termination represented, making it unnecessary for her to actually end treatment.

Summary

I have presented a clinical case from an intersubjective viewpoint that demonstrates how, in all phases of the treatment, both the transference and the countertransference continually shape one another in a specific pattern of reciprocal mutual influence. In the case we described, the transference–countertransference neurosis was structured by the patient's developmentally predetermined compliance with the therapist's need for her to serve as an archaic mirroring selfobject and upholder of his grandiose fantasy. I traced this central intersubjective configuration through a series of therapeutic exchanges, including dreams and other communications of both patient and therapist, from its appearance in the intial stage of analysis to its working through during the period in which the meanings of termination were explored. I believe this consistent focus on the interplay between the patient's and the therapist's developmentally arrested psychological structures was crucial for the unfolding of the therapeutic process. It also exemplified the general principle that dreams and other psychological products cannot be understood psychoanalytically apart from the intersubjective contexts in which they take form.

References

Atwood, G. E., & Stolorow, R. D. (1984), *Structures of Subjectivity: Explorations in Psychoanalytic Phenomenology*. Hillsdale, NJ: The Analytic Press.

Brandchaft, B., & Stolorow, R. D. (1984), The borderline concept: Pathological character or iatrogenic myth? In: *Empathy II*, eds. J. Lichtenberg, M. Bornstein, & D. Silver. Hillsdale, NJ: The Analytic Press, pp. 333–357.

Goldberg, A. (1977), Some countertransference phenomena in the analysis of perversions. *Ann. Psychoanal.*, 5:105–119.

Gunther, M. S. (1976), The endangered self: A contribution to the understanding of narcissistic determinants of countertransference. *Ann. Psychoanal.*, 4:201–224.

Kohut, H. (1971), *The Analysis of the Self*. New York: International Universities Press.

Oremland, J. D., & Windholz, E. (1971), Some specific transference–countertransference and supervisory problems in the analysis of a narcissistic personality. *Internat. J. Psycho-Anal.*, 52:267–275.

Stolorow, R. D., Atwood, G. E., & Lachmann, F. M. (1981), Transference and countertransference in the analysis of developmental arrests. *Bull. Menn. Clin.*, 45:20–28.

―――― ―――― Ross, J. M. (1978), The representational world in psychoanalytic therapy. *Internat. R. Psycho-Anal.*, 5:247–256.

―――― Brandchaft, B., & Atwood, G. E. (1983), Intersubjectivity in psychoanalytic treatment: With special reference to archaic states. *Bull. Menn. Clin.*, 47:117–128.

―――― Lachmann, F. M. (1980), *Psychoanalysis of Developmental Arrests: Theory and Treatment*. New York: International Universities Press.

Wolf, E. S. (1979), Transferences and countertransferences in the analysis of disorders of the self. *Contemp. Psychoanal.*, 15:577–594.

Chapter 11
PROJECTIVE IDENTIFICATION IN THE PSYCHOANALYTIC THERAPY OF A BORDERLINE PATIENT

NONNA SLAVINSKA-HOLY, PH.D.

Borderline personalities are defined as those developmentally arrested at the so-called third level of internalized object relations (Kernberg, 1966). Thus they are said to have a diffuse sense of identity and "ego weakness" (low anxiety and frustration tolerance and defective sublimatory capacity). They rely predominantly on primitive defense mechanisms such as denial, omnipotence, idealization, and early types of projection (Kernberg, 1975). A major ego defense is projective identification.

The hypothesis of this chapter is that projective identification is the most important, fundamental way to gain access to the fragmentary constellation of the borderline *self*.[1] Working through the vicissitudes of projective identification becomes the central means of integrating the split-off aspects of self-representations in the ego and helping the borderline patient achieve an authentic, cohesive identity.

Whether the therapist is aware of it or not, projective identification is the primary object of therapeutic sessions with the borderline patient. Without such therapeutic awareness, treatment sooner or later fails. The awareness itself, however, is not enough. The therapist is still faced with the problem of how this defense can be worked through.

Traditional approaches stress correcting split-off fantasy

---
[1]The terms "self" and "identity" are used loosely and do not refer to advanced intrapsychic structures.

constellations by interpreting to improve "reality testing." The following pages suggest quite a different approach, illustrated by the case of Alice, a young woman diagnosed as a borderline personality with predominantly narcissistic defenses and infantile adaptation. The case discussion covers approximately three years of treatment.

Theoretical Context

We will deal here exclusively with the structural derivatives of object relationships. The work of Melanie Klein (1955) is particularly relevant to this subject, as is that of Fairbairn (1952), Guntrip (1969), and Sutherland (1963) concerning the dynamic interplay of introjection and projection. Also relevant are the formulations of Erikson (1950), Jacobson (1964) and Balint (1968) illuminating the influence of early childhood experiences on the development of ego structures. Perhaps most important, however, are Erikson's ideas about ego identity as the highest level in the organization of internalization processes. The successive development of introjections, identifications, and ego identity in a context of libidinal and aggressive drive derivatives underlying internalized object relationships is skillfully described by Kernberg in "Structural Derivatives of Object Relationships" (1966). I want to emphasize here Kernberg's notion of the self as an outgrowth of self-representations organized into a cohesive structure within the ego. In line with Erikson's conceptualizations, the self is conceived of as an aspect of ego identity that refers to:

> The overall organization of identifications and introjections under the guiding principle of the synthetic function of the ego . . . [implying] continuity of the self, the self being the organization of the self-image components of introjections and identifications to which the child's perception of its functioning in all areas of its life and its progressive sense of mastering the basic adaptational tasks contribute significantly (Kernberg, 1966).

We will observe in the case of Alice how these structural derivatives of object relationships begin to coalesce into a rudimentary sense of self.

Despite seminal contributions on the subject of projective identification by Melanie Klein and her followers, as well as more recent works by Jaffe (1968), Ogden (1979), and others, there has not been a movement to expand these insights into a clearer understanding of the therapeutic relationship. For example, there is as yet no detailed study of how projective identification functions in the *interpersonal* relationship between therapist and patient, though it is precisely in the interpersonal dimension that the success or failure of treatment rests. Ogden (1979), however, has offered a useful outline that takes us some good distance in that direction. According to his thesis, the patient undergoes four stages of evolution in working through projective identification with the therapist.

1. The patient begins with "a fantasy of getting rid of an unwanted 'bad' part of the self by putting it into another person . . . and controlling them (sic) from within" (p. 358). This is a profound blurring of the boundaries between self and object representation. The feeling is of "being at one" with the other.

2. "Pressure exerted by the projector (patient) on the recipient (therapist) for the projector to experience himself and behave in a way congruent with the projective fantasy. This is not imaginary . . . [but a very real] pressure exerted by a multitude of interactions between the projector and the recipient" (p. 359).

3. "A psychological processing of the projection by the recipient (therapist), and the reinternalization of the modified projection by the projector. . . . The recipient is the author of his own feelings, albeit feelings elicited under a very specific kind of pressure from the projector. The elicited feelings are the product of a different personality system with different strengths and weaknesses . . . [so that] the feelings are 'processed,' 'metabolized,' 'contained' and managed differently" (p. 360).

4. "The 'digested' projection is available through the recipient's interactions with the projector for internalization by the projector" (p. 361).

Ogden's analysis implies that the recipient's (therapist's)

maturational level is a crucial element in the working through of projective identification. The patient's maturational level will determine the quality and nature of his reinternalization of the "processed" material—and will therefore range from primitive forms of introjection to more mature identifications. Thus, the relationship between "projector" and "recipient" (patient and therapist) is crucial to the quality of the resulting amalgam of the projected and reintrojected feelings.

One might see the role of the therapist as a "container" and "processor" of projected feelings rather than as a "screen"—the role assigned by traditional approaches. As container and processor, the personality and authenticity of the therapist's affective participation in the interpersonal communication (both verbal *and* nonverbal) represent the central healing influence. The therapist functions to "receive" the terrifying, destructive, negative projections and does not fall into counteraggressive responses. Instead, the therapist tolerates seeing or perceiving them—converting the negative–unbearable into the positive–bearable experience and allowing for intrapsychic digestion of the projected material. Through the therapist's act of engaged perception, the patient reintrojects the positive, ego-structuring elements of the representations. Gradually, repair is made to the narcissistic injury. For example, competitive, fierce, achievement-oriented inclinations give way to authentic self-loving feelings. Authentic intrapsychic growth and transformation permeate the entire being, filling all avenues of ego functions. Positive self-representations coincide with positive object representations and interpersonal behavior as a whole shifts toward the positive. This kind of transformation, arising out of the cognitive–affective engagement of the therapist, can be seen in the case of Alice.

Case History

Alice was 21 years old when she first came for treatment with the presenting problems of "not succeeding at anything" in life, and "being treated like a kid." She was overweight and awkward; her disposition was uneven, vacillating between silent, guarded, and withdrawn, and loud and exhibitionistic. Her complex array of problems unfolded only gradually in the process of treatment in response to our working through the various barriers to communicating in an interpersonal setting. Essentially, her life was characterized by the following split-off behavior constellations: (1) she was socially isolated and quickly withdrew from contact because of assorted grievances of a sadomasochistic nature; (2) in her clerical job, she was an underachiever, constantly fearful of, and angry at, her allegedly authoritarian and conceited superiors; (3) in private, she "played house" with an assortment of nearly 100 puppets.

The clinical picture of Alice suggested that all was not well early in her life in terms of growth-enhancing internalizations. We can hypothesize an insufficiency of internalized good mothering as well as an internalization of destructive maternal attitudes. Recent conceptualizations by psychoanalysts attempting to delineate the area of identity, for example, Erikson (1950), Lichtenstein (1961), the Menakers (1965), and Searles (1965), with their emphasis on reciprocity and mutuality are relevant in this regard. Thus, the mother's conscious and unconscious fantasies in regard to the unfolding of the child's intrapsychic organization and optimal integration of the ego and superego appear to have determined much of Alice's psychopathological adaptation to life.

In our relationship, the patient attempted to induce in me the feeling of her being obnoxious and undesirable, something to be gotten rid of. In my constant alertness to my own emotional reactions and attitudes to patients, understanding the presence of pathological introjects, I began to explore her fantasies and we were able to piece together the picture of constant maternal deprivation. She never ceased to feel ashamed, unwanted, and ridiculed. Alice's mother had been an artist, constantly preoccupied with the development of her own ambitions and satisfactions, and in order to receive care had turned her daughter over to her own mother. Thus, there was a deficiency in Alice's internalization of an empathetic, emotionally nurturing mother, which led to a feeling of not existing herself. Therefore, we see a problem in the development of object constancy related to pathological internalization processes in the symbiotic and separation–individuation phases of development.

When I asked Alice to tell me a little about her mother, she blocked and then reluctantly disclosed that her mother had died in an automobile accident when Alice was 9. The mother had been at the wheel of a vehicle carrying both maternal grandparents, which collided with another car at an intersection. All three were killed in the crash.

"This was an important, tragic time for you," I observed. Beginning to weep, Alice revealed that, on the day of her death, her mother had asked for a kiss when leaving Alice at day camp: "I was angry with her because she dropped me off at camp! I refused to kiss her goodbye." She continued, telling of a recurring dream that she had following the accident: "A little man, a midget, came in and said, 'I killed your mother.' This evil little man invaded my life. He had a bald head, wrinkles, and a very frightening face, not evil but like a goblin, a Halloween trick-or-treat witch costume."

In this dream Alice had created an internalized self-representation—an embodiment of her fantasies of spirits who exerted power and control over individuals, and who could abuse her.

In the process of working through, I heavily utilize free use of fantasy in so-called daydreaming (Colette Muscat, personal correspondence, 1981–1984). On one such occasion, Alice saw a "disgusting creature, all wrinkled up in a forest that was all burned out, all alone, isolated, trying to warm himself over a small fire." She drew the image, seen in Figure 11-1, all in black. At another time, she saw "strange happenings" inside her heart and spoke of some "thing stuck inside" her and made another drawing (see Figure 11-2). This is an interesting depiction of the chaotic, internalized dimensions of an abandoned little girl who sought consolation in the world of fantasy. I asked her to see if she could make things a little more comfortable in her heart. She then immersed herself in fantasy and drew another heart differentiating boundaries of red, orange, and black, this time delineating some tentative shapes (see Figure 11-3). Clearly, sorting out of condensed internalizations was possible. In daydream, we worked through aspects of the false self. I asked her to find "a comfortable place where you could be your *real self*." She immersed herself in a dreamlike state and

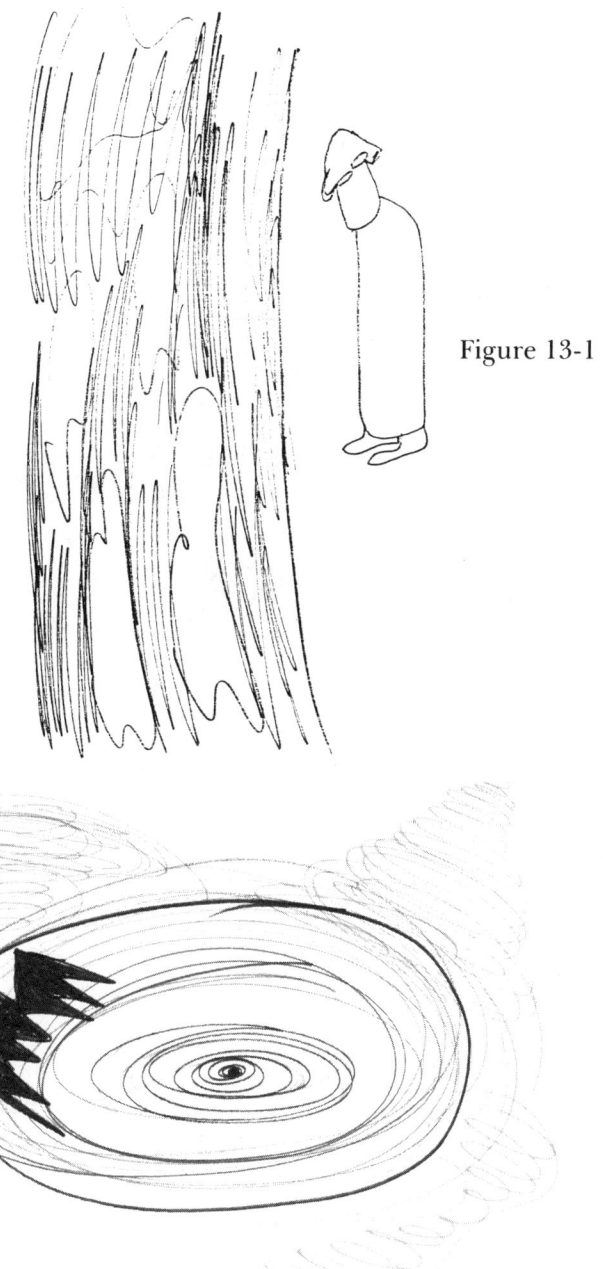

Figure 13-1

Figure 13-2

Figure 13-3

conveyed the following image: "a beautiful meadow, full of flowers, very far away, maybe another planet, maybe a road." When I asked her to follow the road, she found "a pleasant little village." She then recalled an incident when she recently tried to locate someone she knew in early childhood, a neighbor. This was another step toward linking the past with her real self. Increasingly from this time on, her attention focused on being herself and on searching the inner experience within her.

Sometime during the course of the first year of treatment, she came with a large, elephant-shaped bag that clearly concealed all sorts of secrets. She pulled out two puppets: one was distinguished by a small body and extremely large snout, like that of a crocodile or hippopotamus; the other one, smaller, could not be described with ease. It turned out that the smaller one, "Bobby," was a whiny, bothersome "pest," patiently protected by the older one who felt somewhat "secretly resentful" that the little one "gets away with murder." These characters seemed to portray, in my understanding, the relationship between Alice and her younger sister. The older one, "Ollie," corresponded to the representations of her envious, hungry, resigned self. The manner of her characteristic behavior seemed to have been introjected after the mother's death in interplay with her stepmother (the father remarried a few months after the tragedy). She learned to show a smiling, doll-like, charming facade to all the world in the constant terror that her "inner ugliness" would somehow be discovered.

I was thus introduced to an aspect of her inner life that she had thus far kept secret. I learned about her "children," a host of dolls that she manipulated like puppets and conversed with extensively, which remained at home on her shelf while she was "out in life." It quickly became clear that these dolls or puppets represented the split-off aspects of her self, and thus afforded a dramatic opportunity for the development of the interpersonal dimensions of our therapeutic relationship, dimensions so important to the reintrojection process described by Ogden (1979). Her bringing the puppets to me and then relating to me through them was projective identification. I was able to use these projective identifications to foster reintrojection of more appropriate views of her self. As we worked through these projective identifications, I entered freely into her fantasy life with the puppets and through them was able to help her coalesce these identity fragments.

The next puppet she introduced me to was a small rabbit—snow-white, life-sized, and strangely animate: "I'm 'Rascal'—I am one year old." In contrast with all the other puppets which she either created herself or purchased, this one had been given to her as a birthday gift the previous year. Clearly, the "birth" of the "infant" coincided with the onset of the treatment, but she kept it a secret for one year, until she felt safe enough to introduce me to it. Also interesting is that she assigned a masculine gender to the toy, as she did to most others. This is probably linked with her fantasies of her father being preferred by the mother. Alice manipulated the rabbit with remarkable skill, simultaneously emitting pleasurable grunting, chuckling, and cooing sounds, making the rabbit seem full of life and joy, virtually bursting with exuberance. I could hardly restrain myself from reaching out to take the "cutest baby" in my arms. At the end of the session, hearing someone else in the waiting room, Alice hurriedly stuffed the rabbit into a crowded bag, clearly fearful and self-conscious that others might see this very private part of her. She appeared concerned about the "baby's comfort," and looked to me for help. I reassured her that there was room in the bag for the baby.

It seemed clear to me at the time that Alice's visible metamorphosis to the external behavior of an adult was directly linked to her offering me this "adorable" infant self. She evidently trusted me to treat the baby while she took up adult responsibilities.

Alice developed in these puppets a closed system that served the defensive functions of warding off both environmental stresses and her inner terrors. Skillfully constructed enactments, dramatizations where three, four, or more characters interacted, provided her with a multitudinal relief system for her pent-up emotions. In her insulation, one thing she could not obtain, however, was an authentic human relatedness with an adult who would not absorb her into his or her need system. Apparently, the patient had sought treatment before, but the puppets never emerged in the previous therapy; her part objects, self objects, and split-off identifications remained hidden. Alice was terrified of being laughed at for her puppets, her only source of solace and comfort; but I took in this hidden world with the greatest sympathy, respect, and admiration. This helped her to acquaint me with this very special existential system that ran its separate, more authentic course parallel to the one she played out in her detached, formal behavior outside.

As is my frequent practice, I was working with Alice in a group as well as individually. Shortly after my introduction to the rabbit, she brought the puppet to a group session—unbeknownst to the other members, however. When I perceived that she had the rabbit with her and wanted it secretly present, I assented to her intention. I pointed to a small stool under a side table, showing her where the "baby" would be free to observe the group session without being noticed. Alice was delighted and lovingly settled the rabbit on the stool. We both felt concerned for the baby's safety and comfort. I accepted her projective identification of her trusting, exuberant little self so that we could both watch it grow. I felt the rabbit represented intimations of her authentic identity, open to life.

Several months later, I focused on her projection of hopeless rage onto others. We looked at her efforts to protect herself from guilt over her vindictiveness, as well as her need "to keep mother inside" in order not to confront her dependency and her feeling of responsibility for her mother's death. The idealized "inside mother" was her way of continuing her mother's life. As we confronted Alice's competitiveness and rivalry with her mother, her father idealization emerged: "He knows everything!" she would say. We brought the mother into immediate form by having Alice role-play her in interaction with other family members. The relevant internalizations were clearly defined, separated, and sorted out so that Alice could distinguish her authentic self. Thus, Alice seemed to have two mothers with opposite qualities. At times she acted as if she were the natural mother (denying the latter's death), exchanging herself for her mother—then Alice herself was dead.

In one of the sessions during this time, Alice described her phobia about taking journeys. She related terror-stricken feelings and the fantasies that accompanied them. In one fantasy, the train in which she was riding would stop in a tunnel. "My mother's ghost is flying in through the window, persecuting me, terrifying me, wanting something from me. I tell her, 'Leave me alone.' " In the fantasy, Alice's mother wants attention in the same way Alice herself wanted her mother's attention before she died. Her mother had been a music teacher, always preoccupied with other children or with the book she was writing. She had a bad temper and would yell frighteningly at Alice. Nevertheless, Alice "didn't want her to leave me alone." She said she "used to run and chase after" her mother. Alice went on to talk about the robotlike people at work who were her superiors, and the feeling that her boyfriend neglected her and was insensitive to her needs, constantly putting her in the position of demanding time from him. Here, too, her feeling of being "pushed aside" emerged.

I responded to these revelations by observing, "You still want a very strong hold on your mother. You don't want her dead. You seem to live with her inside you." I also drew her attention to the wish to transform her boyfriend into a reliable mother, her exploitation of him, and her insensitivity to *his* needs. Alice accepted this, and with her acceptance of such interpretations, as well as the trust developing in our relationship, a new dimension emerged that allowed for an effective and immediate grappling with projective identifications.

Soon, Alice began to transform herself outwardly into a lovely young woman. A metamorphosis occurred: No longer the giggly, whiny, plump adolescent, she became slender, charming, elegant, and began to display a mature woman's appreciation for her boyfriend, while previously, she had entered only very infrequent, abortive, short-lived relationships with young men, and appeared protected by a massive devaluation and contempt in regard to any young man who showed interest in her. However, her potential to destroy yet another threatening human bond (to protect herself against the terror of abandonment and disintegration) remained a constant focus of our attention. My interpretations helped her enough to allow this relationship to continue, to work through several stormy attempts at breaking it up, until she agreed to spend a vacation with the man. In addition to the fears of the relationship, we began to work on the terror accompanying any sort of travel. I focused on the terror related to anything she cannot control herself, hence cannot depend upon; her own angry, destructive, fantastic, primitive powers were simultaneously projected onto any vehicle. And after two years of therapy, Alice took a vacation with her boyfriend.

During this vacation she acquired a new puppet, "Adele," a glove puppet with huge, expressive eyes and an assertive manner. "She is obnoxious, really—a 9-year-old," Alice noted. "Hi there, I like you," was the doll's greeting to me. Though Alice "hated" Adele, I was delighted with the "resourceful and assertive" character. "She has imagination, she tries to express herself in ways perfectly understandable for her age!" I observed. I added how curious it was that Adele was as old as Alice was when her mother was killed. "But she didn't know me then!" Alice explained. I replied, "It seems to me you had some kind of bond, 'knew' each other in some way, even *before* you met!" They both nodded in quiet understanding.

Adele's presence signaled the reappearance of Alice's deeply repressed identity at age 9. She described herself at that time as "loud-mouthed," "obnoxious," characteristics directly connected with her fantasy that this is what killed her mother; that is, her assertiveness of her own identity in contrast to the mother's unconscious wish for her not to exist. Here we entered the intrapsychic space to repair the damage done at the time of the accident.

I considered it a privilege to have a glimpse into these different stage-specific internalizations. Each character's color, costume, and expression represented metaphors for self-object relationships that expressed themselves only in a very condensed and elusive way in Alice's usual social behavior as split-off ego systems. However, at home, they were "one happy family"—Alice's effort at integration. The way Alice moved the puppets, expressed their different personalities, and handled their frictions and jealousies appeared to be her attempt to create a just, fair, and loving mother for "all her children" or split-off selves.

One day, I received an urgent phone call from Alice who wanted an immediate appointment. She shifted back and forth from whiny and frightened to seductive and assertive tones. "Whose voice is speaking?" I asked. She hesitated: "I'm not sure. I think it's a joint statement. I'll bring them all in; my folks, I mean." This marked the beginning of integration of the split-off parts and Alice's increasing confidence in expressing them to me. It stood in sharp contrast to the secretiveness of previous months, when only intellectualizations and rationalizations had taken place.

A week or so later, as one of my groups was leaving the office, I came upon an amazing scene. Alice was sitting in the waiting room, her puppets on her lap in a confident and loving display. Some of the other patients engaged her in conversation and she interacted through the characters—everybody agreed that the characters were "so cute" and that the puppets were so beautifully made that they could have been used in puppet shows. A few minutes later I entered my office to find Alice with the puppets on her lap, a lively noise going on as she shook the little rabbit. "How adorable," I said. "Rascal," cooing and chuckling, asserted: "I am only one, I laugh and am happy. But Ollie teaches me about life." Alice's voice changed to the sad tones of Ollie, pouting: "I'm hurt. You called Rascal cute."

"You are a nice boy too," I said.

"It's not enough, 'nice'," Ollie sulked.

"I think you are a nice, beautiful, good boy," I said.

"And handsome too," Ollie added.

I inquired about what had happened last October, when Rascal was born. Alice answered, "Nothing special. I was doing a lot of new things." She continued, "Now he (Rascal) no longer soils or needs diapers." Thus she presented a symbolic representation of the growth that had taken place during the year of our collaboration.

Suddenly I asked, "But where's Adele?" Alice lifted herself up and pulled the glove puppet out from under her. She had literally been sitting on the child, dramatizing how forcefully this identity had to be suppressed. In this she demonstrated her obvious need to restrain the assertive, courageous, but somewhat domineering Adele in order to make room for the two younger "children," who were cute, helpless, and in need of affection. This was a fascinating symbolic statement about Alice's need to hide, suppress, and destroy, in every way, the natural self, which was perceived as "obnoxious," and then not permitted to exist as a punishment for "causing" Alice's mother's death. Adele, in fact, symbolized the actual 9-year-old self.

Adele, the "nasty, obnoxious" puppet, immediately addressed me, complaining in an assertive manner about therapy:

"I'd rather go to a zoo, but in the Bronx. The other zoo (Alice's shelf) only has dead and tired animals."

I looked directly at Alice and said: "She is really a very lively and intelligent girl. She knows exactly what she wants. Of course the Bronx Zoo has more space and air. Of course, it's more fun than therapy." I was giving space, acknowledging the validity of the individual needs of these separate identities projected onto the puppets. Her difficulty was seen in integrating all the earlier identities (as symbolized by the different puppets) with the 9-year-old self which symbolically ceased to exist as retribution for the mother's death.

Then some exchanges took place between Adele and me over our relationship. Adele wanted to move in and live with me because it was "much more fun than at home." I made it clear to Adele that, in our relationship, reciprocity was expected and that she had to respect my limitations of time and my other commitments.

It is important to note the successive emergence of these split-off identifications. As she moved from one to another, Alice was totally absorbed in "being" the character at hand. As a "good mother" she talked in a quiet, reassuring manner to all her children. As the characters appeared, the little frictions and jealousies, even some biting and kicking, were not violent or destructive.

In treatment, we needed to accomplish the following tasks: first, the "new" self, Rascal, had to be allowed to grow and pass through the developmental stages and thus to become integrated with the other part-identities symbolized by the other puppets; second, we needed to encourage the 9-year-old, energetic, and creative girl to move past the frozen position precipitated by the mother's death and onto a normal path of unfolding and growth. The split-off part-selves emerged here and there, constituting a condensed, confused, unbearably chaotic intrapsychic situation which dramatically unfolded before me. For a while, we needed the separate identities to "live" through the sessions in their own stage-specific, growth-related manner until they reached the next stage of development. In this way, the previously separated part-self gradually became neutralized and metabolized into a more whole self. Thus we proceeded onto and beyond the 9-year-old Alice and "lived" through her adolescence and reached young adulthood, her authentic stage in life.

For my part, I reacted to these convincing, lifelike puppets as if they were real, live individuals. My reactions were spontaneous and sincere. I did not feel the need for any sort of technique once I had accepted Alice's fantasy. There was a natural flow of interaction that reflected our mutual affection and allowed space for each of our needs. The in vivo emergence of each identity was sometimes breathtaking and always poignant. I was being included in their family life. I treated Alice's projections more appropriately than she did, thus allowing for her to reintroject more reality-oriented attitudes.

It was clear that, as we explored the projections, I was getting to know Alice's family better. Ollie, I learned, was 4 years old, very sweet and helpful but at the same time obviously jealous of Rascal. He adored Adele. This seemed to me to represent the oedipal jealousy and the stage of superego formation. I told Alice that she seemed to put too many burdens on Ollie and to expect too much from him. After all, I said, he's "still a child."

At the end of the dramatic session in which the puppets confessed their relationships, they asked if they could kiss me before they left and affectionately did so. I was almost terrified when I saw Ollie's jaws approaching my head; I could be swallowed up quite easily. I quickly pulled away and exclaimed, "Don't gobble me up." He obliged and made a new, subdued, and apologetic approach. Rascal cuddled into my face and Adele fondly and gently nipped my nose. "She is so gentle," I observed. At this moment, we were all one happy family. I expressed my satisfaction at the large bag in which each family member would have sufficient space to breathe. I felt Alice and I both understood that these were living beings at the same time they were puppets—that they were the extension of Alice's identities.

In group session a couple of months later, I heard Alice speaking to other members of the group in Adele's voice and manner. The Adele–Alice was wildly abandoned in her expression of herself. She began to play "Indians in the Wild West" with one of the other members, who seemed overwhelmed with Adele–Alice's daredevil courage and leadership in some terrifying moments. Others deferred to her: In one exchange, she demanded total obedience as an "important dictator." Later, in an individual session, when I heard again the shy, halting, self-effacing voice of Alice, I inquired where Adele was. "The contrast is so striking," I added. "All that energy and vitality, virtually boundless, and here is this weak and vanishing voice. What happened? How come? Whose is this shy voice?" It turned out to be Ollie, the 4 year old. I wondered what happened to Alice between the ages of 4 and 9.

In her associations, Alice talked about the time when she was 4 and her mother took her to the kindergarten where she taught. "I never wanted to stay. I was following her everywhere. She went off with her guitar and left me behind. Once she took a ribbon and tied me to her waist. Everybody laughed." I interjected that that must have been a very humiliating experience to be laughed at when she was so terrified of losing her mother in a world of strangers.

The process taking place here, it seemed to me, was one in which the separate identities were allowed to express their respective needs and thereby become integrated into one *whole* identity. These transitions were observable, for example, when the line of demarcation between Alice and Adele vanished and Adele became Alice reacting resentfully to her dead mother *before* the fatal accident. As Alice spoke of her "children," the integration was visibly in process: they were all simultaneously, rather than successively, there.

I began to focus on Alice's shifting between sensible and mature aspects of herself and childlike or childish behavior. I helped her to integrate these two sides into coexistence as two aspects of one self. By entering into the projective identification dialogue occurring with her puppets, I was able to tone down her strict, harsh superego demands on herself. Alice began to see the chronology of her assorted identifications and identities and to realize that she was a responsible and intelligent adult who experienced a past in which she had been a frustrated, unloved, abandoned, and angry child.

In later work, we concentrated on how the 4-year-old Ollie and the 9-year-old Adele had become separated. Alice said that the 9 year old had to be alone and had to deny anything that she had felt before. "Since I started therapy with you, I became aware that I needed affection and mothering, and then I saw the separation." "What made you continue the separation?" I inquired. "I can't make them friends," she said, "they hate each other. The strong one is insensitive and rude and gets frustrated with the little and weak one." Thus, delicate and poignant probing of these identities continues.

Discussion

This patient's life was clearly brought to a traumatic psychological halt by the tragic loss of her mother. A complex interplay of rage, terror, and guilt ensued, which culminated in role reversals where, in fantasy, she entered into her mother and she herself ceased to exist. This role reversal became apparent during the second year of treatment, when Alice began to explore more fully the terrifying moments of the dream in which she was traveling through a train tunnel, with the "ghost" of her mother after her. The living mother in her own body was being punished by the angry ghost—the dead self, angry at the mother for abandoning her (the projection of her rage and helpless desire for revenge upon the dead mother).

Her own identity stunted, Alice reenacted in fantasy the past identifications and thus *actively* maintained "family" interactions through the puppets. The dozens of puppets served the purpose of multiple intrafamilial communications. In terms of projective identification, she was acting out the aspects of both the projector and recipient. But, since the recipient was a lifeless object, the projections continued to revolve around themselves in vicious circles.

The sequence in which the puppet characters appeared in living presence is interesting in itself. After the "ugly midget" drawing and daydream working through, these puppet characters were introduced into treatment:

1. "Ollie" and "Bobby," 4- and 2-years-old respectively (in my view corresponding to the two orphaned sisters). These characters tested out the unfamiliar ground of relating to another human being.

2. "Rascal," the rabbit-infant, innocent, adorable, seductive, and determined to be irresistible to the new mother (myself).

3. "Adele," the obnoxious 9-year-old, the criminal who killed the mother. Her appearance was a courageous attempt to test whether the new mother could accept the hated, evil self-representation.

In the future, two more characters would emerge successively. "The Dragon" who was connected with our work on sexual identity and, later "The Philosopher" who was intimately linked with the increasingly clear awareness of a mature, private self.

I witnessed many moving scenes in our sessions in which Alice became a tender, understanding, and patient mother (her ideal object introjections) to the quarrelsome, needy, frightened, helpless puppets (self-representations at various stages of her own development). This aspect of her therapy shifted my differential diagnosis from an impression of pathological narcissism as her predominant personality organization to that of borderline organization with narcissistic overlay. It is my feeling that the latter-type individuals are more capable of warmth in their interpersonal relationships than are narcissistic individuals.

Alice's fascinating, complex arrangement of multiple identities represented an effort both at continuation of life prohibited by guilt and at resolution of severe intrapsychic conflicts centering around issues of oral aggression, envy, and rivalry. Condensed oedipal and preoedipal features came to the fore, together with essentially narcissistic character defenses. While these self and object representations maintained an active family life in her fantasy, her behavior in reality exhibited emotional aloofness, coolness, and ongoing paranoid suspicion of others. She revealed the essential devastation of her inner experience: she saw herself as a tragic, ugly, "monster–creature," not evil but pathetic. Her fantasy life had obviously not succeeded in giving her a sense of living. It only perpetuated a painful inner emptiness.

Beginning therapy became a turning point for Alice. I became the recipient of central projections and the container for all the "family" characters' conflicts. Her acquisition of the baby rabbit, all white and untouched, around the time of commencing therapy was an obvious symbolic projection for her possible new life. An analogous gesture occurred with the acquisition of Adele.

In treatment, a dual but intertwined course unfolded. The first involved my active relationships with the separate "personalities"—the patient herself at different stages of her development. Instead of correcting her illusions for "reality testing," I entered her world of separate identities, and in so doing allowed them, for the first time, to relate to a living human being. This aspect of the interaction represented the corrective emotional experience. My acting as the recipient of the projections and thus digesting or psychologically processing them through my own personality made them available for the patient to reintroject in a different, emotionally enriched way. For example, while Alice hated Adele, I was rather delighted with her resources as a 9 year old. The two pivotal characters, the rabbit and Adele, represented the beginning of Alice's new life in therapy and the end of her former life as she fantasized at the time of her mother's death.

The second course revolved around our relationship as the two individuals we, in fact, were. Here, of course, we needed to work through those aspects of transferential behavior that stood in the way of Alice's authentic self. Unfortunately, a fuller description of its working through is beyond the scope of this chapter.

Alice and I now find ourselves on a path toward resolution of her "false" self (compromising her narcissistic veneer of socially acceptable behavior on the outside and her secret world of fantasy). For the first time in her life, she can maintain an intimate relationship with a boyfriend; in fact, they plan to marry. She experiences herself, she says, "as a woman, a female animal. It's almost frightening. I have never felt so much in my own skin." She has also begun to define herself professionally; instead of working in miscellaneous clerical functions, she has obtained recognition as a budding writer.

References

Balint, M. (1968), *The Basic Fault: Therapeutic Aspects of Regression.* London: Tavistock Publications.
Erikson, E. (1950), *Childhood and Society.* New York: W. W. Norton.

Fairbairn, W. D. (1952), *An Object-Relations Theory of the Personality.* New York: Basic Books.
Guntrip, H. (1969), *Schizoid Phenomena, Object Relations and the Self.* New York: International Universities Press.
Jacobson, E. (1964), *The Self and the Object World.* New York: International Universities Press.
Jaffe, D. (1968), Mechanism of Projection: Its Dual Role in Object Relations. *Internat. J. Psycho-Anal.,* 49:662–677.
Kernberg, O. (1966), Structural derivatives of object relationships. *Internat. J. Psycho-Anal.,* 47:236–253.
——— (1975), *Borderline Conditions and Pathological Narcissism.* New York: Jason Aronson.
Klein, M. (1955), On identification. In: *Envy and Gratitude and Other Works, 1946–63.* New York: Delacorte Press/Seymour Lawrence, 1975.
Lichtenstein, H. (1961), Identity and sexuality: a Study of Their Interrelationship in Man. *J. Amer. Psychoanal. Assn.,* 9:179-260.
Menaker, E., & Menaker, W. (1965), *Ego in Evolution.* New York: Grove Press.
Ogden, T. H. (1979), On projective identification. *Internat. J. Psycho-Anal.,* 60:357–373.
Searles, R. (1965), *Collected Papers on Schizophrenia and Related Subjects.* New York: International Universities Press.
Sutherland, J. D. (1963), Object relations theory and the conceptual model of psychoanalysis. *Brit. J. Med. Psychol.,* 36:109–124.

Chapter 12

THE DIFFICULT PATIENT: AN INTERSUBJECTIVE PERSPECTIVE

BERNARD BRANDCHAFT, M.D.
ROBERT D. STOLOROW, PH.D.

The most compelling motive for reconsidering the problems posed by "difficult" patients is that they mark the limits of existing knowledge. Historically, difficult cases have repeatedly provided evidence that the difficulties are not in the patient alone, but in the patient-therapist system, codetermined by the stance of the therapist in respect to the patient. Hence it is to be hoped that a reexamination of this crucial area will contribute to an altered perspective and thus expand the range of therapeutic efficacy.

In addition, we believe that asynchronies similar to those encountered so floridly with difficult patients are likely also to be found in many or most courses of treatment that are not so stormy, although they appear in a more subtle and covered-over form. Thus, the therapist's ability to deepen his reflective self-awareness when faced with difficult patients can enable him to recognize and decenter from recurrent patterns in himself that, in general, limit his ability to comprehend his patients' experiences of him from within their own subjective frames of reference. This we hold as a cardinal principle that is a prerequisite to understanding the singular meanings that have come to shape each patient's experience and to permit transformation to take place.

This chapter is an expanded and modified version of a paper originally published in *Kohut's Legacy*, edited by P. Stepansky and A. Goldberg (Hillsdale, N.J.: The Analytic Press, 1984).

When despite the therapist's best efforts, an impasse is reached and a patient "refuses" to improve or relentlessly seems to "cling" to a mode of behavior that appears to be self-defeating, the therapist commonly experiences an acute and painful awareness of frustration followed by feelings of helplessness and inadequacy. Therapists tend to experience such impasses in accord with their own archaic organizing principles, which dictate that *someone* must be at fault. Two pathways are open. If the therapist chooses one, then he is to blame, and his own sense of self as a reliable and good therapist can be severely undermined, leading to an experiential cycle of escalating negativity and depression. However, nothing can more immediately and reliably restore a therapist's failing sense of self in such situations than to close down that pathway and open wide the alternative, to diagnose the intractable pathology presumed to reside within the patient, in order to reinforce and reify the perception of how inherently difficult the patient is.

The difficult patients most written about today are those who fall within the category of the so-called borderline. Indeed the single feature of these patients most commonly agreed upon is that therapists find them particularly difficult to treat. Although our observations generally focus on this group of patients, we believe that the principles that we will articulate are relevant not only to the borderline patient, but in some measure to all psychotherapeutic treatments.

Therapists faced with experiences of difficult patients would do well to take heart from the fact that the history of psychoanalysis literally began with "difficult" patients and that it owes every advance it has made to its acknowledgment implicitly or explicitly of the limitations in its efficacy that difficult patients have obstinately exposed. Even before psychoanalysis could be said to exist, Freud had recognized that the difficulty presented by difficult patients did not rest with the patients alone but with how they were understood and consequently how they were treated. As a young neurologist he became dissatisfied with the understanding of aphasia propounded by his teachers, Meynert and others. The essence of his disagreement lay in his belief that various aphasias could not be explained, as they were then being explained, by minute localizing schemes of discrete subcortical lesions. Rather, Freud held, all varieties of aphasia were to be explained by varying degrees of functional derangement radiating from a centrally damaged area (Jones, 1953, pp.214-215). From the onset he recognized that it was imperative to discover new methods for investigating his subject—nervous tissue—and he was exultant when, following a hint by Flechsig, he used a gold chloride stain and found that the picture which emerged was entirely different, "wonderfully clear and precise" (Jones, 1953, p.205).

Freud's discovery that one's perspective determines what one sees, as well as what is obscured, was to be repeated many times in the course of his own development. Many years later he was to declare, "For these ideas are not the basis of science on which everything rests: that, on the contrary, is observation alone" (Freud, 1916, p.34). Almost half a century later, Kohut (1959), attempting to enjoin psychoanalysts to reexamine Freud's suppositions, reaffirmed the principle in his own terms. "The mode of observation," he wrote, "defines the contents and limits of the observed field and thereby also determines the theories of an empirical science" (p.212). It is no less imperative in our day than it was in Freud's that we continually reexamine our theories and their observational base if our science is to expand.

The first syndrome that elicited Freud's psychological interest was hysteria, the quintessential stigma of the late nineteenth century difficult patient. At the time, hysterical women were the target of contempt and indignation on the part of physicians, the best of whom regarded the illness as a matter of simulation (manipulation) or "imagination." In the past, thinking it a peculiar disorder of the womb, they had treated it by extirpation of the clitoris or by valerian, for some believed the smell would cure the disorder.

With the help of Bertha Pappenheim (Anna O.), the first of Freud's difficult patients, he was able to sweep away much of the scientific dogma of that day and to establish hysteria indisputably as a symptom not of neurologic or gynecologic disorganization, but of psychological disorder. The "talking cure," which at first seemed to be curative, proved inadequate. Today we would recognize that the initial benefits to Anna derived from the unusual experience of her having found a physician who was interested in and capable of listening to her own experiences. However, when in the face of the encouragement the novel setting provided, Anna's hopes for herself and concomitantly her attachment to Breuer, Freud's collaborator, grew more intense, Breuer brought the treatment to an unceremonious end. No clearer evidence could be found that the difficulty with difficult patients never arises solely from within the patient but "must be viewed as a difficulty in the more inclusive patient-therapist system" (Stolorow, Brandchaft and Atwood, 1983).

From its beginnings to the present, psychoanalysis has continued to deal with patients who failed to conform to or benefit from existing paradigms arrived at by existing methods of investigation. The development of psychoanalysis has always been nourished by its failures with such difficult patients. It is they who continually challenge our complacency with what is known and who force us to extend the boundaries of our understanding. The scientists of Charcot's day almost uniformly regarded hysterics as impossibly difficult. But despite their nearly universal and authoritative agreement, theirs was still a subjective view. Only an alteration of that view could bring about the scientific revolution known as psychoanalysis. Human interactions took place then as now in a field of reciprocal regulations, and there can be little doubt that when hysterical patients were viewed and responded to as highly abnormal and extremely troublesome, this in itself affected how they experienced themselves, and thereby tended to exacerbate and intensify their symptoms, as it does with today's borderline patients. Freud was able to alter his perspective, as he had previously done with the new stain of nervous tissue, and adopt a new mode of observation from within the hysterical patient's own world of subjective experience. It was a monumental scientific achievement.

Very early, narcissism emerged as a difficult problem for Freud and his followers. Abraham (1919) noted a chronic resistance in certain of his patients to compliance with the fundamental rule. In these patients he detected an "unusual degree of defiance" (p.305). They reported only egosyntonic matters, and were "continually on their guard against suffering and humiliations" (p.305). They were preoccupied with signs of personal interest and wanted to be treated with affection; they reacted intensely to slights and injuries to their self-esteem. These were not the kinds of "nervous disabilities" that analysis at the time had set out to cure, and Abraham noted that his own predetermined treatment plans receded into the background to the extent that "narcissistic interests predominated" (p.306). He concluded that the most fundamental explanation for what he was observing was that his patients wished to thwart him and to grudge him "the role of the father" (p.306).

Abraham's paper, in its time, represented a noteworthy advance. But it is of interest to us primarily for the way it reflects discordant views of the purpose of psychoanalysis on the part of disjunct subjectivities, those of patient and analyst, and a conflict arising not solely from within the patient, but also from the system formed by patient and analyst together. Kohut (1959) was later to define the narcissistic purpose as arising not from any primary need to thwart the therapist, but from an injured and poorly structured psyche "struggling to maintain contact with an archaic object" (p.218) in order thereby to maintain its basic self-regulatory functions. Abraham in his own day was applying the new formulations about drives and defenses as primary organizers of psychic functioning. From that perspective he concluded that the neediness and clinging of his patients demonstrated their fixation at the oral level of psychosexual development and he concluded that his patients' narcissistic preoccupations represented a defense against love for and appreciation of the analyst. When his patients reacted with anger at Abraham's interpretations, and made more urgent efforts to protect themselves against his impact, he believed that they did so solely in consequence of innate, unconscious destructive forces within themselves that were attempting to thwart his efforts to treat them. He proposed that unconscious oedipal rivalry or preoedipal sadism were the basic causes of pathological development and of the difficulties encountered in treatment—an example, we believe, of mistaking effect for cause. From that day to this, those who would treat patients face no more imperative task than to develop the means of distinguishing between derivatives and essentials, between psychological surface and depth.

The term "borderline" first appeared in a paper by Stern (1938). He reported that a large group of patients did not fit into the existing diagnostic categories of neurosis or psychosis. The clinical picture included narcissism, "psychic bleeding," hypersensitivity, rigidity of personality, negative therapeutic reactions, constitutionally rooted feelings of inferiority, and deep organic anxiety. The symptomatology can be recognized today as that of severe self disorders (Kohut and Wolf, 1978). Indeed, Stern himself noted that in the borderline group narcissism formed the basis of the entire clinical picture. He wrote that the disorder seemed to be rooted in very early childhood relations, which had adversely affected the patient's narcissistic development, anticipating Kohut's (1959) conclusion that for such patients "the analyst is not the screen for the projection of internal structures but the direct continuation of an early reality that was too distant, too rejecting, or too unreliable to be transformed into solid psychic structures" (pp.218-219). In at least 75 percent of the histories, the primary caretakers were described as decidedly neurotic or psychotic, and "inflicted injuries on their children by virtue of a deficiency of spontaneous maternal affection" (Stern, 1938, p.469). Just as food deficiencies result in nutritional defects, so these patients, never having acquired "a sense of security by being loved" (p.469), were malnourished, as it were, in their narcissistic development.

Despite these findings, the questions raised by borderline patients continued to revolve mainly around whether they could be treated by psychoanalysis. The more important question—"treated for what?"—receded into the background. Concessions in the form of parameters were made, with the hope that, after an initial period of attention by the analyst to the specific needs of the patient, the patient would then be able to be analyzed "properly"—that is, with the focus on the unconscious intrapsychic structural or drive-related conflicts and defenses that psychoanalysts had come to believe had to be lurking beneath every treatable disorder. So thoroughly has this been ensconced in psychoanalytic dogma that an authoritative view continues to maintain that if these drive-related conflicts are not engaged in the transference in a primary way, it is because of the tenacity of the resistance with which the analyst has likely been colluding (Stein, 1981).

In contemporary times, widely departing from Stern's observations, Kernberg (1975) has come to occupy a preeminent position as theoretician of borderline conditions. His concepts have significantly influenced how clinicians view this disorder. He has attempted to delineate a discrete pathological syndrome, the borderline personality organization, and to distinguish it from the narcissistic personality structure. He maintains that the following are primary characteristics of the borderline disorders: 1. "non-specific ego weaknesses" (lack of anxiety tolerance, impulse control, and sublimating channels); 2. shifts toward primary process thinking; 3. pathognomonic primitive defenses, especially "the intensification and pathological fixation of splitting processes" (p.28) that segregate "good" and "bad" self and object representations. "The major defect in development," Kernberg writes, "lies . . . . in the incapacity to synthesize. . . the aggressively determined and libidinally determined self and object images" (p.28). In direct line with Abraham's formulations of a half century earlier, Kernberg concludes that the primary pathogenic factor is excessive aggression, a condition, in other words, existing solely within the patient.

Patients with borderline organization, Kernberg claims, externalize all-bad, aggressive self and object images, and consequently experience objects as dangerous and retaliatory. They then feel as though they must defend themselves against the "fantasied" harm. The evidence put forth for this set of far-reaching propositions invariably involves instances in which narcissistic and borderline patients experienced their analysts as dangerous and retaliatory, when the analysts did not so perceive themselves.

To insist that when patients feel endangered by a therapist their perceptions of him must be faulty in effect constitutes a "cordon sanitaire" around the therapist. It precludes the unhampered investigation of the patient's subjective reality, so that the persecutory experiences can be understood in greater depth, including the therapist's unwitting contribution to them.

It obstructs the establishment of an intersubjective matrix in which processes of self-healing, self-articulation, and self-consolidation can be resumed and realigned.

Kernberg describes the narcissistic personality disorder as a variant of the underlying borderline organization, in his view the major diagnostic category. He reserves the term narcissistic for patients whose main problem is a disturbance in self-regard, who show an unusual degree of self-reference and an inordinate need to be loved and admired by others. Pathognomonic for this group, according to Kernberg, is an integrated though highly pathological grandiose self reflecting a condensation of real self, ideal self, and ideal object images. He does not regard these features as symptoms of a weakness in the structural foundations underlying the subjective sense of self and its affective valence, with a consequent urgent need for constant and extreme buttressing. Rather, he claims, these narcissistic configurations are used to defend against "real" dependency and the aggression it is presumed to mobilize.

In a recent paper (Brandchaft and Stolorow, 1984) we discussed the borderline concept in some detail. We took issue with the view that borderline refers to a "discrete pathological character structure, rooted in specific pathognomonic instinctual conflicts and primitive defenses" (p. 333). We noted that all such patients seemed to show underlying structural vulnerabilities and propensities for, or rigid defenses against, fragmentation and disorganization. These disturbances in the structural cohesion and temporal stability of the sense of self (Stolorow and Lachmann, 1980) we regarded as pathognomonic of severe primary self disorders.

In that paper (Brandchaft and Stolorow, 1984) we formulated and cited evidence for the following thesis: "The psychological essence of what we call 'borderline' is *not* that it is a pathological condition located solely in the patient. Rather, *it refers to phenomena arising in an intersubjective field—a field consisting of a precarious, vulnerable self and a failing, archaic selfobject*" (p. 342; emphasis in original).

We recognize that borderline symptomatology exists outside the therapeutic situation and precedes it, and that it can arise in any situation in which a bond is experienced as failing in functions needed to sustain a brittle and vulnerable self. We do not overlook or minimize the contribution of the patient's archaic states, needs, and fragmentation-prone self, but stress that in the therapeutic situation the manifest pathology (and its subsequent course) is always *codetermined* by *both* the patient's disorder *and* the therapist's ability to understand it. While we do not claim that borderline *symptomatology* is entirely iatrogenic, we do believe that the *concept* of a borderline personality structure rooted in pathognomonic conflicts and fixed defenses is symptomatic of the difficulty therapists and analysts have in comprehending the archaic intersubjective contexts in which borderline pathology arises.

These markedly different views involve irreconcilable approaches to the treatment of these disorders. Acceptance of the concepts advocated by Kernberg implies a belief that the essential interactions in which the patient is engaged are designed at all costs to avert unconscious dependency conflicts of an instinctually determined, object-related origin. The clinical approach that follows from this belief involves a sustained and systematic attempt to show the patient that his pathological behavior, including especially his rejection of the analyst's perceptions and interpretations of him, derive from these unconscious sources. The alternative view to which we adhere considers the patient's manifest symptomatology to be derived in part from the unintended effect of the analyst upon the patient's basic sense of himself, which lies at the core of the disorder, and from the analyst's consistent misunderstanding of the significance of the patient's experience and consequent rejection of its essential validity.

How are such disparate views to be explained?

The Stance of the Observer

The most essential difference between these contrasting views, and the difference upon which all others rest, is the perspective used to gather and organize the data from which inferences are drawn and by which the various theoretical conclusions are supported. Kohut's (1959) paper, "Introspection, Empathy and Psychoanalysis," set the stage for a reconsideration of the basic methods by which we gather the data that enable us to know what we know about mental life. Where he originally saw "resistances" as arising from internal pressures and endopsychic sources, with his role being that of a neutral observer outside the psychological field, he was able to see, through a profound and crucial shift in focus to his patient's subjective experience of him and his interpretations, that his own specific contributions were intrinsic to the very nature of his patients' reactions. Patients' experiences could be understood only in the context of their perceptions of the analyst, and the subjective validity of those perceptions (Schwaber, 1979).

We have subsequently attempted to spell out the difference between psychoanalysis seen as a science of the intrapsychic, focused on events presumed to occur within an isolated "mental apparatus," the classical analytic stance, and psychoanalysis viewed as a science of the intersubjective focused on the interplay between the differently organized subjective worlds of the observer and the observed (Stolorow, Brandchaft and Atwood, 1983; Atwood and Stolorow, 1984). We are fully in accord with Kohut in stressing the importance of an observational stance that places primary emphasis on understanding the impact of the analyst from within the patient's subjective frame of reference.

This stance is methodologically necessary, we believe, in order to investigate and understand in depth those "difficult" archaic states that involve a loss of self-regulatory function (and its recovery), fragmentation symptomatology, erotization, autoerotization, and narcissistic rage. The loss of self-regulatory functions has been subsumed under the heading of "ego weakness," and consistent with the traditional analytic stance has generally been attributed to the effect upon the ego of repression (Fenichel, 1945), primitive ego defenses such as splitting and projection, and pathologically intensified pregenital sadistic impulses (M. Klein, 1952; Rosenfeld, 1964; Kernberg, 1975). These assumptions were derived from the almost unchallenged doctrine that the patient's psychic reality is secondary to and determined by unconscious defensive measures and primary instinctually determined configurations.

When we view the therapeutic interchange from the vantage point of the patient's subjective perception of the analyst as a fundamental determinant of his ensuing experience, that view yields markedly different data and distinctly different explanatory hypotheses. A similar reorientation in observational stance is now occurring within the field of infant observation, whereby the entire developmental process is increasingly coming to be understood as "the property of an interacting infant-environment system of mutual regulation" (Sander, 1975, p.7). We have elsewhere cited evidence for concluding that psychological development and pathogenesis are best conceptualized in terms of the specific intersubjective contexts that facilitate or obstruct the child's negotiation of critical developmental tasks and that shape the course of the entire developmental process throughout its successive phases (Stolorow and Brandchaft, 1984). Sander has emphasized the different outcome that results from this observational shift, in that the questions asked, the route of discovery, and the understandings available are all different.

It has been claimed (e.g., Kernberg, 1982) that such a stance leads to a "psychology of the conscious." On the contrary, a strict focus on subjective experience not only leads to the discovery of unconscious meanings and purposes, it makes possible as well an unveiling of the forms and patterns that conscious experience repetitively and unconsciously assumes. Access is thereby gained to the underlying structures and organizing principles that unconsciously govern psychological life.

Clinical Illustration

The following is excerpted from the analysis of a patient with a brittle self and borderline symptomatology. It illustrates the extent to which such symptomatology is embedded in an intersubjective context.

> Mr. J., a business executive, entered analysis with a history that betrayed a thoroughly chaotic life. In neither his personal nor professional life could he maintain control. His home life was marked by frequent bouts of violent rage against his wife,

toward whom he would hurl the most extreme insults. At work he was unable to maintain discipline over himself or his employees. His intense need for approval led to his being taken advantage of repeatedly, after which he would lapse into long periods of self-reproach for his "weakness," interspersed with outbursts of resentment. He was predisposed to take offense at the slightest rejection or failure to appreciate or respond to his needs, and would suffer severe disruptive states marked by rage, withdrawal, or urgent restitutive measures to recover his self-esteem or redress his grievances.

Mr. J. was unable to attend to details, was regularly late to appointments, and generally mismanaged his business relationships. In search of relief from the chaotic conditions around him, and from his sense of inner disorganization and recurrent feelings of deadness and meaninglessness, he was driven to behavioral enactments and to preoccupation with sexual fantasies. These were interspersed with excessive alcohol use, occasionally with drugs, which he said made him feel more alive. He was also tormented by recurrent, severe episodes of hypochondriasis, for which he could find relief only by searching out the highest authority in the field of whatever bodily disorder with which he thought himself afflicted.

With the development of an idealizing transference to the analyst, his hypochondriacal symptoms subsided. One Monday, during a phase in the analysis in which his relationship with his father had begun to occupy the focus, he appeared for his session on time, unusual for any day and hitherto unknown on Mondays. He seemed more animated than usual and bore a sheaf of papers that he began to read, after first saying, "I've been working on this all weekend." The papers chronicled an introspective journey into his early relationship with his father, concerning which a number of memories had emerged that fit together to form a pattern of relatedness of which he had previously been unaware. It was beautifully put together and contained a series of highly important, even brilliant insights. The analyst found himself enthralled by the story that unfolded and, eager to make the most of the opportunity, used the patient's report to tie together a series of elements in the patient's symptomatology and behavior that had previously been puzzling and frustrating but now seemed absolutely clear. The patient accepted the explanations and the hour continued. But where originally he had been enthusiastic and bouyant, now he began to sound increasingly dull, repetitive, and uninspired. The analyst noted the change and inquired as to whether the patient was aware of it and whether he could account for it. Thereupon Mr. J. exploded: "You are just like my father—that is exactly what I was writing about. He could never just be pleased with how I was or what I did; he kept showing me and telling me how much better, smarter and ahead of me he was, how much better a son he had been to his mother than I, what great things he could have accomplished if only he had had the glorious opportunities he was providing me with!"

The patient missed the next session, came late for the following one, and reported that he had just spent a night in which he had turned to various drugs in an attempt to counteract feelings of deadness and inner chaos, which feelings had caused him to absent himself from work.

The analyst of course had failed to notice and reflect the patient's pride in the momentous step he felt he had taken in organizing himself in a creative act, modelled after the analyst's ideal of attention to the inner world and presented to the analyst in the hope of evoking his enthusiastic recognition and affirmation. A significant shift in the selfobject transference toward reliance on the analyst's mirror function for self-integration had gone unanswered, resulting in Mr. J.'s fragmented state, rage, and urgent self-restorative efforts.

Mr. J.'s symptomatology, when he began treatment, fit into the "borderline" category that has been described. Included in the array, in addition to his severe hypochondriacal anxieties, were nonspecific "ego-weaknesses," lack of impulse control, and a scarcity of sublimatory channels. He was disposed to magical and primary process thinking, particularly to ideas of reference. For example, he viewed himself as the cause of any misfortune that members of his family might incur. He also believed in omens and in expiatory acts to influence a God whom he experienced as tyrannical and sometimes implacable. His behavior towards others, including the analyst in the transference, could be easily conceptualized as evidence of the "pathognomonic" primitive defenses of splitting and projective identification. His rage when he was thwarted or felt humiliated could not be controlled, sometimes leading to physical attacks, and when in this state, he showed no indication of any awareness of positive aspects of the relationship.

The borderline symptomatology, which had gradually subsided within a responsive analytic milieu, now reappeared when this new but unsteady intersubjective field disintegrated and a traumatic repetition of elements of an original childhood pathogenic field temporarily replaced it.

Such failures, from the perspective of the subjective experience of a patient attempting to revive a developmental process, are common and absolutely inevitable. The unfolding of the particular selfobject need (for recognition and for endorsement of his fitness as a partner and student of great promise), when understood within its developmental context and worked through, would eventually enable Mr. J. to acquire a sustaining confidence in himself and in his ability to understand himself and his object world. It would reduce his dependence upon idealized women, preoccupying fantasies of sexualized exhibitionism, and drugs—his "fixes"—to sustain and recover a positive sense of himself. First, however, it was necessary to focus upon his traumatic disappointment in the analyst and its sequelae, his rage and the other events that had followed. Reactions to disappointments or injuries that repeat chronic traumatic developmental interferences constitute, in our view, the essence of what is often described as the negative transference. The expression of violent anger and other assertions of self will usually be associated with a background of specific meanings and experiences for the patient. Accordingly, the analyst first took up the patient's expectations of the impact of his anger and subsequent absence on the analyst's feelings about himself and toward Mr. J. This inquiry yielded important memories of his early relations with his parents, in which acts of self-demarcation and self-assertion produced hurt and withdrawal on the part of his mother and physical retaliation and threats from his father.

Mr. J.'s expression of hurt and his criticism of the analyst had left him terrified of the analyst's anger and retaliation, providing compelling evidence, in our view, of his urgent need for a more comforting and responsive archaic selfobject. The appearance of this need in a sexualized form repeated regressive retreats of his early childhood in which he sought solace from damaging and humiliating encounters with his father by turning to his mother. In his childhood, this had necessitated a commitment on his part to concentrate his efforts on what would please or delight and not upset her. In his sexualized replaying of this sequence in fantasy, he repeated the compulsion to please at the same time as he preserved the memory of the comforting qualities of his mother in his imagined sexual partner.

The analysis and working through of these reactions clarified the origins of Mr. J.'s chronic rage, his disposition to what some analysts might perceive as an excess of aggression. When the channels for the normal expression of assertiveness and anger at injuries to a child's vulnerable pride and self-esteem are foreclosed, the child has no way of directly repairing the damage and integrating the experience within the context of the total relationship. He retains his vulnerability in the form of a brittleness. He capitulates and preserves the idealization of his objects at the expense of his own development, and he develops various defensive activities to cover over the wounds and the defect. So it was with Mr. J. His mother could never acknowledge that any action of hers might be damaging to him. She insisted, for example, that he be immaculately dressed, inspecting him minutely each day before he left for school. She paid no attention to his complaints that this resulted in his being teased mercilessly by his schoolmates and made him feel awkward and out of step. His father could never say that he was sorry for anything that he did or said to his son, instead always blaming Mr. J. for being "too sensitive" and lacking in "balls."

In the analytic situation just recounted, the analyst's interpretation of Mr. J.'s anxieties following his outburst—in terms of his fear of retaliation by a failing archaic selfobject—had the effect of reducing the severity of his defensive distancing. It was then possible for the analyst to communicate his understanding of Mr. J.'s hurt and anger as reactions to the analyst's faulty responsiveness to his prideful display of the psychological tapestry he had so painstakingly woven. Together analyst and patient were then able to expand the exploration of the many meanings of this experience and the encapsulated and encoded memories it contained and revived. The disruption subsided, the symptomatology disappeared, and the analysis proceeded in greater depth.

We do not doubt, from our previous experiences in such instances (Brandchaft, 1983; Brandchaft and Stolorow, 1984), the consequences that would have followed had the analyst interpreted the situation just described according to concepts that are more familiar. Interpretations might have pointed to a fear of depending upon the analyst or purport to describe a display arising from outmoded, omnipotent, and grandiose needs and an underlying desire to defeat and humble the analyst. In our opinion, these would have been inappropriate and counterproductive. The same might be said about interpreting Mr. J.'s angry response as demonstrating the operation of primitive defenses such as splitting and projection, or as indicative of his inability to synthesize good and bad internal object representations or his lack of appreciation of the analyst's well-intended efforts and interpretive help. Such interpretations, which are often more exculpatory of the analyst than explanatory of and for the patient, both exacerbate the symptomatology and isolate it from its intersubjective context. It is in response to such interpretations that the characteristics that have come to be associated with the borderline personality often become entrenched.

Object Relations

Current perspectives on borderline and narcissistic disorders embody widely divergent views on the nature of the object relations that are engaged. These divergences reflect the contrasting "stains" of each observer, drawn from the analyst's subjective view of transferences that occupy the focus of attention in analytic investigation and provide its observational data. The analyst's conclusions themselves become part of the interacting patient-therapist system and affect subsequent transference configurations. We are in agreement with Rosenfeld's (1964) statement that "as the transference is the main vehicle for any analytic investigation, it seems essential for the understanding of narcissism that the behavior of the narcissist in the analytic situation should be minutely observed" (p. 169). We would add that the intersubjective field within which such behavior takes place should now be equally minutely studied.

Analysts generally regard the nature of object relations as crucial in borderline patients. Frequently emphasized is the incapacity to synthesize good and bad introjections and identifications. All-good and all-bad internal object representations together with all-good and all-bad parts of the self are maintained and repetitively reinforced by splitting, these observers hold, in order to avert painful feelings of dependence upon less than ideal objects. Other factors stressed are a preference for the pleasure principle so as to avoid the pain, humiliation, and rage that the recognition of reality entails, "unneutralized" primitive destructiveness, and unbearable guilt in the mourning process that comes about when the patient is forced to acknowledge that the loved analyst and the hated analyst are one and the same. Most observers maintain that these archaic all-good and all-bad internal object representations or parts of the self—in the form, for example, of a primitive and malignant superego—are constantly projected onto the analyst in the transference, and that this leads to the negative transference and negative therapeutic reactions.

Such concepts, in one or another form, frame and underlie the approach of many analysts treating borderline and narcissistic patients. An absolute precondition for success in treatments that adhere to these concepts is that the patient agree that his own perceptions of the analyst are essentially invalid or of secondary importance. Failure on the part of the patient to do so and thus validate the analyst's perception of himself and of the patient is treated as a "resistance." If the patient persists in expressing his own experience of the analyst, a judgement is generally made that the patient's "reality testing" is impaired, and that the "therapeutic alliance" necessary for the treatment does not exist. The patient is considered to be further over the borderline and to warrant a poor prognosis. Other forms of treatment may then be recommended.

Mahler and those who follow her developmental schema believe that this presumed defensive splitting is responsible for the failure to develop object constancy and that this in turn accounts for the severe anxiety over separation and aloneness. The splitting, Mahler also believes, is maintained because of an excess of unneutralized aggression and serves to avert, delay, or prevent the resolution of painful differentiating and mourning processes (Mahler, Pine, and Bergmann, 1975). In this connection, our observations indicate that when the structural foundations supporting the patient's sense of self crumble, his object representations also may disintegrate. The analyst's consistent focus on the intersubjective contexts underlying these archaic states of disruption and their anxieties serves to reinstate an aborted developmental process and reestablishes the sense of an intact self in an enduring selfobject relationship.

Our understanding of human development, of psychoanalytic transferences, and of the profoundly intersubjective nature of the psychoanalytic situation have all been immeasurably deepened by Kohut's (1971, 1977) concept of selfobject functions and selfobject transferences. The selfobject theory of development is a contemporary theory of object relations. It concerns the most archaic relationships to objects experienced as incompletely differentiated from the self and functionally in its service. These selfobject relationships are necessary in order to maintain the stability and cohesion of the self while the child gradually acquires, bit by bit, the psychological structure it needs to maintain its own self-regulatory capability. The course of selfobject relations reflects the continuity and harmony of the developmental process through its various hierarchically organized stages. In the "omnipotence" that has been described as characteristic of the pathology of archaic object relations (M. Klein, 1952; Rosenfeld, 1964; Kernberg, 1975), we can recognize the persistence of the confident expectation that these selfobject needs will be met (Winnicott, 1965; Mahler, Pine, and Bergmann, 1975). Where archaic selfobject needs persist, the differentiation, integration, and consolidation of self-structures and the developmental line of selfobject relationships have been interrupted. Thus archaic, poorly differentiated and integrated selfobject ties continue to be needed, expected, and used as substitutes for missing psychological structure. When the selfobject unit is intact, the patient experiences himself as "well" and the world as "all right." When the unit is disrupted by physical or psychological absence or prolonged, unrecognized disjunction, symptoms of narcissistic and borderline disorders derived from precariously consolidated and brittle self-structures appear. Such symptoms include fragmentation and depletion phenomena, addiction-like craving for praise or for union with idealized selfobjects (sometimes sexualized), as well as rigid defensive postures, schizoid or paranoid, erected to protect the underlying vulnerability. The predominant anxiety accompanying separations is the terror of disintegration, and the harm that such patients fear in analysis is not, in our view, "fantasied harm," but actual. Psychosis, psychological and physical self-mutilation, and suicide are only extremes of a host of actual dangers to a patient whose vulnerable self-structures are exposed.

The analysis of selfobject transferences indicates that narcissistic and borderline patients defend against or seek to reestablish an arrested, archaic bond with the analyst. If the defenses employed to protect a fragile self are recognized and explained, a selfobject transference will emerge and coalesce around the analyst. The terms "mirror transference" and "idealizing transference" refer to the most intense aspects of the patient's reawakened archaic longings, not to the behavior of the analyst, even if a particular analyst ignores this principle. Countertransference reactions cut through all conceptual frameworks. What is essential in the analysis of selfobject transferences is the provision of a milieu in which the patient's subjective experience, including especially his experience of the analyst, can be sensed, noted, and articulated freely, with the analyst committed to understanding that experience from within the perspective of the patient's subjective world. The archaic needs of the patient are then recognizable as at one time having been those of a normal small child, however intensified and distorted they became in their passage through the particular life experience being investigated and reconstructed.

The analysis of selfobject transferences involves those areas of self-development and self-experience, and consequently of selfobject relations, in which development was derailed or arrested. Through the transference those derailments and arrests and their unconscious determinants can emerge, be demonstrated, and understood. When they are understood, an authentic pattern of development may be resumed, together with a process of gradual differentiation of self from object, which so many analysts hold is being "denied" for defensive reasons. The analysis of those innumerable and inevitable experiences of frustration and disappointment in which the patient perceives the analyst as failing in respect to a particular archaic wish or need is an indispensable part of the treatment. The understanding in depth of the conscious and unconscious meanings of such experiences of selfobject failure restores the disrupted tie and thereby permits the analysis and development to proceed. Such a technique provides an analytic alternative to nonanalytic procedures in which either the patient must renounce his deepest personal narcissistic wishes, or the analyst disregards his own boundaries and supplies parameters. Respect for another's subjective experience, we emphasize, need not imply compliance or enslavement of the analyst.

When the patient feels that the analyst understands, respects, and is concerned with his archaic longings, rooted in a vulnerable and arrested self, the resumption of an interrupted developmental process becomes possible. Then concern and consideration for and gratitude to the analyst can develop naturally and spontaneously, as they seem to do in normal children whose needs, perceptions, vulnerabilities, and assertions have been understood, respected, and responded to by their parents. Feeling valued, they do not exhibit devaluation. If, however, these transferences are engaged, and the patient fails to elicit the analyst's consistent interest in his unique self-experience, the analyst may come to regard the patient's continued attempts to evoke the needed interest as manipulative and the patient's self-experience or its constituents as outmoded, defensive, expressive of a primary hostility toward, or envy of, the analyst. The process of self-delineation then will predictably come to a halt, and all the complications and reactions that have been described in the literature can appear. These include negative therapeutic reactions, interminable analyses, transference psychoses, intractable resistances, borderline symptomatology—all of the characteristics of difficult patients. Perhaps even worse are the cures that come about when the patient is compelled, by his need for the analyst, to substitute the analyst's subjective view of his reality for his own.

Synthesis of "Good" and "Bad" Parts of Self and Object

The experience of objects or the self as "all-good" and "all-bad" has been widely regarded as *prima facie* evidence of defensive splitting and projective identification. The supporting data are derived from transferences in which the analyst is at times the target of intense anger or disparagement, and at other times experienced as ideal, loving and loved. In either case it is believed that the experience is defensive against the countervalent affective configuration. These data are then seen to confirm certain background assumptions regarding the patient's early object relations.

When these interactions are viewed from the perspective of the patient's subjective frame of reference an entirely different ordering of the data emerges. Then it can be seen that idealizations in narcissistic and borderline patients do not most commonly arise as a defense against hostility or disparagement, as "red herrings" designed to throw the analyst off his guard. They arise as a direct continuation of the aborted idealizations of childhood, as a resumption of a tie to an early object that was ruptured by loss or traumatic disappointment. They revive an early developmental phase when only a figure perceived as flawless and godlike can protect against the dangers to existence against which the infant has no other source of protection. The emergence of such an idealization requires no commitment on the part of the analyst to fulfill the patient's archaic expectations, only that the inevitable disappointments be explored nondefensively from the perspective of their current and genetic, conscious and unconscious, subjectively construed contexts.

The violent negative reactions similarly viewed from within the perspective of the patient's subjective experience of the analyst will be seen to indicate specific structural weaknesses and vulnerabilities, rooted in specific developmental interferences. When their expression is freely permitted, we have found that they owe their intensity to the fact that they contain encoded and encapsulated memories of traumatically damaging experiences. This was the case, as was seen, with Mr. J.

Divergences from the focus on the patient's subjective reality and shifts to an assumption that this reality is secondary to more deeply lying pathological defenses or drive derivatives comes about when the patient's experience of the analyst cannot be comfortably assimilated into the structure of the analyst's subjective world. What is, therefore, required of the analyst is the ability to "decenter" from the structures of his own subjectivity in order to be able to understand those of his patient. When we have been able to do this successfully, we have found that the patient's experience of us becomes readily intelligible in the context of specific, discrete elements within the preceding interchange. These elements may have been unnoticed or considered unimportant by us, but can be shown to have enormous significance to the patient. We stress that such disjunctions of experience cannot and should not be reduced to distorting mechanisms on the part of either participant. Instead they must be considered as inevitable consequences of the interaction between differently organized subjectivities. This altered stance on the part of the analyst makes possible the articulation and exploration of their meanings for the patient, and when this is accomplished, a consolidation can occur at a higher level of organization, together with a lessening of vulnerability, a modulation of affect, and a strengthening of the underlying structure.

Aggression

We wish, finally, to touch on the differing view of aggression that accompanies a stance from within the subjective experience of the patient and a focus on the more inclusive patient-therapist system as a field of interacting subjectivities. We emphatically disagree with the claim that "excessive pregenital aggression" is the etiological bedrock of borderline and narcissistic pathology. In the treatment situation, such pervasive aggression is the inevitable, unwitting consequence of a therapeutic approach that insists that certain arrested archaic needs and the archaic states of mind associated with them are in their essence pathological defenses against dependency on or hostility toward the analyst. It is the inevitable consequence of the persistent superimposition of the analyst's subjective reality on that of the patient. When this occurs in the treatment, the patient, attempting to revive a previously aborted or derailed developmental step, comes to experience such interpretations, whatever the intent of the interpreter, as severe breaches of trust and as traumatic narcissistic wounds.

A vulnerable patient in an analytic setting is encouraged to revive and reveal his most personal, nuclear, and vital needs in the relationship to the analyst. If these are misunderstood and misconstrued, and once again the patient is required to see his experiences from another's viewpoint when he so desperately longs for someone to see them from his own, it is not surprising that intense rage, destructiveness, and distrust may follow. It is the therapist's consistent inability to comprehend the developmental meaning of the patient's archaic states and of the archaic bond that the patient needs to establish with him that secondarily produces the pervasive rage that can make such patients seem so difficult. We are convinced that this difficulty does not arise entirely from pathological endopsychic sources within the patient. The frequent occurrence of this difficulty emphasizes for us the necessity for psychoanalysts to follow the courageous lead of the young Freud and to try for themselves a new way of comprehending the data as a function of the more inclusive patient-therapist system.

References

Abraham, K. (1919), A particular form of neurotic resistance to the psychoanalytic method. In: *The Selected Papers of Karl Abraham.* London: Hogarth Press, 1927.

Atwood, G., & Stolorow, R. (1984), *Structures of Subjectivity: Explorations in Psychoanalytic Phenomenology.* Hillsdale, NJ: Analytic Press.

Brandchaft, B. (1983), The negativism of the negative therapeutic reaction and the psychology of the self. In: *The Future of Psychoanalysis,* ed. A. Goldberg. New York: International Universities Press.

——— Stolorow, R. (1984), The borderline concept: Pathological character or iatrogenic myth? In: *Empathy II,* ed. J. Lichtenberg, M. Bornstein & D. Silver. Hillsdale, NJ: Analytic Press.

Fenichel, O. (1945), *The Psychoanalytic Theory of Neurosis*, New York: W.W. Norton.
Jones, E. (1953), *The Life and Work of Sigmund Freud*, Vol. I. New York: Basic Books.
Kernberg, O. (1975), *Borderline Conditions and Pathological Narcissism*. New York: Aronson.
────── (1982), Review of *Advances in Self Psychology*, edited by A. Goldberg. *Amer. J. Psychoanal.*, 139:374–375.
Klein, M., et al. (1952), *Developments in Psychoanalysis*. London: Hogarth Press.
Kohut, H. (1959), Introspection, empathy and psychoanalysis. In: *The Search for the Self*, ed. P. Ornstein. New York: International Universities Press, 1978.
────── (1971), *The Analysis of the Self*. New York: International Universities Press.
────── (1977), *The Restoration of the Self*. New York: International Universities Press.
────── Wolf, E. (1978), The disorders of the self and their treatment: An outline. *Internat. J. Psycho-Anal.*, 59:413–425.
Mahler, M., Pine, F., & Bergman, A. (1975), *The Psychological Birth of the Human Infant*. New York: Basic Books.
Rosenfeld, H. (1964), On the psychopathology of narcissism: A clinical approach. In: *Psychotic States: A Psychoanalytical Approach*. London: Hogarth Press.
Sander, L. (1975), Infant and caretaking environment—Investigation and conceptualization of adaptive behavior in a system of increasing complexity. In: *Explorations in Child Psychiatry*, ed. E. J. Anthony. New York: Plenum.
Schwaber, E. (1979), On the "self" within the matrix of analytic theory. *Internat. J. Psycho-Anal.*, 60:467–479.
Stein, M. (1981), The unobjectionable part of the transference. *J. Amer. Psychoanal. Assn.*, 29:869–893.
Stern, A. (1938), Psychoanalytic investigation of and therapy in the borderline group of neuroses. *Psychoanal. Quart.*, 7:467–489.
Stolorow, R., & Brandchaft, B. (1984), Intersubjectivity: II. Development and pathogenesis. In: *Structures of Subjectivity: Explorations in Psychoanalytic Phenomenology*, ed. G. Atwood & R. Stolorow. Hillsdale, NJ: Analytic Press.
────── ────── Atwood, G. (1983), Intersubjectivity in psychoanalytic treatment: With special reference to archaic states. *Bull. Menn. Clin.*, 47:117–128.
────── Lachmann, F. (1980), *Psychoanalysis of Developmental Arrests*. New York: International Universities Press.
Winnicott, D. (1965), *The Maturational Processes and the Facilitating Environment*. New York: International Universities Press.

Chapter 13
EROTIC COUNTERTRANSFERENCE AND TRANSFORMATION: BORDERLINE AND NARCISSISTIC PATIENTS IN COMBINED TREATMENT

NONNA SLAVINSKA-HOLY, PH.D.

The word *transformation* suggests the transcendence of an old form on the way to becoming a new and different form. Unlike the word *change*, which connotes the substitution, or exchange of one form for another, *transformation* alludes to process and movement and focuses on the moment when the old form is being broken. The prefix *trans* means "across" or "beyond"; thus, during transformation, we can be said to be in a state of being "beyond" a form by going "across" it.

Since, by definition, consciousness operates in a world of "forms," transformation must take place beyond conscious comprehension and intention. This mysterious, even mystical process is the subject of many of the central questions for psychotherapy: What type of force brings about transformation? What sets it in motion? What is the therapist's place in this movement?

It is a physical fact that matter resists change and clings to its form until acted upon by a great enough force. Our patients cling to their maladaptive life-styles with similar intensity. Psychoanalysis has developed elaborate theories for changing these rigid behaviors, but the unwritten premise of them all is that the patient is somehow acted upon by the analyst's presence.

An earlier version of this paper was published in *Group Analysis* (1980), 12/2: 126–134.

In this process, the analyst is presumed to be merely the instrument of the patient's progress, objective and unaffected—an already accomplished model of psychic health after whose image the patient will strive. I contend, however, that, on the contrary, authentic healing can only occur via intense emotional and psychic involvement of both patient and analyst, and that, furthermore, it is within this sharing and involvement that transformation occurs. Transformation, therefore, is not something that *happens to* the patient as object, but is rather a complex, dynamic interaction of energic forces within one joint emotional matrix.

In clinical work, it is the therapist's consistent attention to his or her attitudes, feelings, and reactions to individual patients, as well as to the group as a whole that paves the way to serious introspection, and to extricating whatever neurotic elements may be operating. Such an awareness (and, if necessary, working through with the help of an analyst colleague or supervisor) creates the type of neutralized space that is necessary for the therapeutic work to proceed, rather than founder in the neurotic, subjectively determined matrix of both analyst and patient or group. Thus, countertransference entanglement can evolve into a more appropriate, more open, treatment atmosphere. Furthermore, countertransference (and here I will specifically discuss erotic countertransference) can be understood as a clue to the process of transformation at work.

This chapter will look at borderline and narcissistic patients, whose especially strong relation to erotic behavior underscores aspects of the therapist's participation in the transforming process. It will focus on both individual and group work with these patients, and address the particular pressures placed on the analyst by the group inasmuch as they emphasize the analyst's dilemma in the transforming process.

Reexamining Countertransference

Traditionally transference has been considered the core of all resistances and its negative aspect has been emphasized: a transference is something to be "overcome." However, transference is not just a blind imposition of old images onto new relations, thereby distorting the new; it is more than just displacement. It is, simultaneously, an attempt to forge a new emotional link with another human being. Even the dreaded "negative transference" represents an effort to reach out. Perhaps the failure of many analysts to deal with so-called negative transferential systems might be explained in terms of the analyst's failure to discriminate the salutary aspects of such a system.

There may be a similar confusion involved in our understanding of countertransference. Here I use the term to denote primarily those emotional reactions on the part of the analyst that are not a part of his executive ego, that is, not formally involved in the "official" analysis of transference–resistance. As such, countertransference signals a deepening connection between analyst and patient, a discovery of their intimacy as human beings. This intimacy may be expressed in any number of countertransferential forms—from erotic, loving feelings to rejection and revulsion. Whatever the specific form, the countertransference serves to call the analytic relationship fundamentally into question. Whatever the details, the real issue seems to be the therapist confronted by the fact that the simple definition of "analyst and patient" is inaccurate (or inadequate) to describe what is going on. In other words, the intimacy from which the countertransference emerges involves the therapist's realization that he or she is *not* a perfected instrument unaffected by the patient. Thus countertransference can threaten the analyst's professional and personal identities.

I will not discuss the theoretical and clinical differences in the use of countertransference among practitioners here, or the areas of convergence or divergence of their positions. It is my conviction that the ubiquitous presence of countertransference—as well as transference—in our daily clinical lives, and, in all likelihood, in our lives in general, deserves a central position when we deliberate about what healing is and how it takes place.

No doubt one important ingredient in the responsible use of countertransference is emotional maturity: it is necessary to have the facility for tolerating emotional discomfort and not acting it out. This can be a subtle issue, since we possess infinite resources for rationalizing our own acting-out behavior, even when it takes the form of what we consider to be an apt "interpretation." Thus I have found that, in countertransference matters, silence and rigorous self-examination are my most important therapeutic tools. The calm sharing of an observation, that is, the metaphorical restating of what the patient is conveying, can sometimes be much more useful than any sort of interpretation I might offer. Furthermore, at times my emotional investment in tolerating discomfort instead of acting it out in one disguise or another had paved the way for patients in group to do the same. Thus often they begin the process of differentiation and integration, in short, they gain access to a more advanced approach to living and learning.

Self-observation can allow an immediate retreat into silence when self-defined signals of "neurotic" activation emerge (Slavinska-Holy, 1973). Within this silence, just as a wave in the ocean builds up, strikes, and collapses back into the sea, emotion can build up to an almost unbearable pressure for me to act, to react, and then gradually diminish when I do not give in to it. This is a cycle during which the significance of my reaction often emerges spontaneously to allow for a new and different connection with the patient.

The utility of this cyclical process is illustrated by an interaction with a patient I will call Stuart, with whom I was for a long time aware of intense, erotic countertransferential reactions. One day, in sharp contrast with his usual agreeableness, Stuart began berating me for my insufficient competence, on which he blamed his "still" not having found a suitable partner (i.e., one like myself). His violent reproaches and cruel, angry words felt like actual blows, as if I were being beaten or savagely slashed. When I thought I could not bear it any longer, I opened my mouth to demand that he leave, yet I was able to force myself, with infinite self-denial, to keep quiet. I endured this torturous experience for a very long time, until he finally retreated from his outburst into silence. I noticed how I had gone through a range of successive reactions, always forcing myself to remain silent, because I knew I had not reached my usual calm, attentive equilibrium.

At last I felt humble and quieted; there was nothing for

me to say. Stuart broke the silence between us, with an anxious, yet firm, "*Now* what?" I quietly and honestly responded, "Perhaps you could help now." Now I needed his initiative, the initiative of this passive man, which I had worked toward for so long and which now had come in such an unwelcome manner. Only then did Stuart show us the direction we would follow next by pulling out his notebook and reading a couple of poems he had written just before our session.

Erotic Fantasies in Countertransference

Erotic countertransference, though considered by some to be seriously threatening to the therapeutic alliance, has not been explored very deeply. Erotic fantasies represent a particularly dramatic form of countertransference for a number of reasons:

1. From its beginnings with Freud, psychoanalysis has concerned itself with sexuality. However, the analyst is presumed to have worked through the pathogenic aspects of these feelings in his own therapy, and to have them in perspective. The spontaneous occurrence of sexual feeling toward a patient refutes this presumption directly.

2. Sexuality is the most basic role definition human beings have. Not only is sex typing central to acculturation, but also early infant experience with the mother (which later becomes charged with sexuality) serves to demark the self from the other. But here we find an inherent paradox in erotic behavior: at the same time that it illuminates for us how separate we are, it represents our striving to overcome the separateness and achieve unity. So, erotic countertransference leaves the therapist ambivalent: on the one hand, the eroticism permits a definition of the other as sex object, to replace the suddenly lost definition of the other as "patient" object; on the other hand, the eroticism is an actual expression of the intimacy between doctor and patient, a metaphor for their unity in the forces of life.

3. The human capacity to experience sexual orgasm can be seen as a compromise between love and death. The death here suggested by the erotic countertransference is the death

(albeit momentary) of the definition of the relationship, the death of the analyst's role.

The borderline or narcissistic patient's particular focus on primitive sexuality as a means to avoid intimacy can easily provoke complementary countertransference behavior from the therapist (Slavinska-Holy, 1974). However, as we will discuss, aside from possibly revealing the therapist's pathology, this plunge into erotic countertransference can further express the patient–analyst unity—as if the therapist were learning to understand the patient's language.

Sexualization can serve many different defensive purposes as an individual attempts to retain optimal intrapsychic equilibrium. In addition, it may express a forward thrust, an attempt at emotional connection or contact with another human being, for lack of a more "advanced" way of relating. It is my belief that the analyst's countertransferential and/or empathic reactions constitute the "royal road" to an accurate identification, at each point in the therapeutic process, of the patient's emotional condition, which is so important for assisting the patient in building a mature, cohesive, creative, authentic self.

Countertransference with Borderline and Narcissistic Patients

Borderline and narcissistic patients are characterized by extremely powerful, intense affects and acting out, which require energetic setting of limits; treatment in early phases pulsates with very primitive, oral–aggressive emotions that tend to envelop the therapist with great force. In a diagnostically homogeneous group of borderline and narcissistic patients we observe common pathologically integrated ego and superego, split-off "good" and "bad" introjects, and characteristic defenses of splitting, denial, idealization, and projective identification. This common pathological matrix constitutes the focus and terrain for psychotherapeutic action (Slavinska-Holy, 1984).

There are some differences in the therapy of patients who are truly borderline, in terms of their diffuse identity dimensions, and those who are truly narcissistic, characterized by a pathological organization of the self. The core problem in the former seems to be related to abandonment depression and to events sometime during the later part of the first year of life. In the latter, it appears that the difficulty arose considerably earlier and is primarily related to a deep narcissistic injury. This differentiation is one that is often extremely difficult, if not impossible to make at the outset of treatment, because both of these psychopathologies present clinical features of the other, yet it is a clinically important distinction.

An exploration of countertransferential reaction and application of its insights are particularly useful when dealing with these seriously disturbed individuals, since the sheer intensity of powerful and very primitive affects permeating both individual and group therapeutic sessions makes it virtually impossible for the analyst to maintain a clear therapeutic perspective and stance. Inevitably, the therapist is drowned in counteraggressive acting out or masochistic submission, unless countertransference can be used as a barometer for what is happening in the treatment.

In early stages of such work, in a combined group treatment approach, sadistic thrills predominate, and the patients engage in hostile sadomasochistic behavior. The sexuality is brutal, controlling, and exploitative—the affects are strong and infectious. Verbalizations reflect primitive emotional terrain. Such concreteness protects the group from experiencing uncertainty.

In time, the patients' horizons broaden and subtleties of intellect and emotion begin to emerge. Questions of intimacy are engaged more openly. Against and coincident with these changes, erotic countertransference may appear. I have observed that the therapist's fantasies and ideation seem to correspond to the deep layers of emotional themes and transferential pressures underlying the patients' overt themes. At these times, mechanistic concepts of technique must give way to a considered and concerned self-exploration by the therapist and full, unconditional immersion into the affective interplay with the individual as well as the group. It is particularly important not to dismiss the patients' observations and accusations automatically as pathological transferential projections, but instead heed them, for they often accurately reflect the therapist's unconscious feelings and behavior.

Utilizing Erotic Countertransference as a Therapeutic Tool

The following example of countertransference action takes place within a group of young adult borderline and narcissistic patients of above-average intelligence. I will focus on a countertransferential interaction that occurred between myself and one particular patient, Robert, a homosexual, in an attempt to illustrate how a multiplicity of progressive–regressive phenomena can be contained in one brief moment of compelling force, which came over me as I resonated the group's essential dilemma at that moment, namely, how to deal with longings for closeness and sexuality.

This day in group session I was somehow aware of the physical closeness among group members. Lola seemed withdrawn, so I let her sit in my chair and I took her place on Robert's right. Immediately I became aware of his physical presence—I felt self-conscious, was unable to look at him, and began losing contact with the group as a whole. As I tried to shake off this strong, strange "thing" that had come over me, I felt Robert's intense gaze on me. Next to his big physique, I felt very small and insignificant. I sensed him loosen up and relax, and saw him extend his right arm on the upholstery behind my back, as if ready to embrace me. This felt warm and secure, and I readily enjoyed it. I became aware of the following fantasy: I am lying down next to Robert with our bodies pressed close, as if melting together, filling in each other's curves; I move my warm and tender lips toward his, available and accepting, and he responds with a passionate outburst of uncontrollable kisses, caressing me with a thousand burning and consuming touches.

The group continued, but I was only dimly aware of its process; I attempted with effort to sort out the symbolism of my reactions. After some time I succeeded in recovering my reasoning sensibilities, and then, pressed for the group members to express what they were feeling. One member, Dan, exposed intense jealousy of the suave and articulate Robert, who, as Dan put it, "usurps the group, thinks that the therapist belongs exclusively to him, is his private possession—shows off all his talents to the females, trying to seduce them."

In the emerging, intense group interaction, I intervened as follows to Dan. "It hurts and frightens you to see me so close to Robert. You want to usurp me yourself the way you once tried to possess your mother. You confuse your impressive adult self with the small, inadequate boy you once were. Your allegiance to the past makes you destroy your actuality and adequacy. You are no less desirable than Robert." Although this intervention was worded for Dan, it actually represented an interpretation for the group as a whole. I touched on the "old," unnecessary hang-up of feeling strong only when outdoing someone else, a rival. I emphasized the way people can complement each other's needs (symbolized in my fantasy by "filling in each other's curves") and can open themselves to mutual enjoyment and appreciation (symbolized in my fantasy by "melting together"). In my interpretations, I focused on the simultaneous presence of progressive behavior and the remnants of more primitive, habitual, transferential attitudes, using the terms of my ideation: *consume, burn, burst out,* and so forth. I often find that using words that took shape in my mind while observing my reactions, together with the words used by group members, opens or links intuitive avenues of transformation. My fantasy about Robert that evening was a reflection of powerful erotic and affectionate longings for closeness and togetherness, shared by both child and adult. Symbolically it represented for the alienated Robert, as well as for the group, progress toward intimacy as well as the most primitive desires for symbiosis or merger—I was the instrument resonating these developments.

Sometime toward the end of the first phase of treatment when the therapeutic alliances started to stabilize, the phenomenon of pathological narcissism began to reveal itself through the countertransference. I became aware that I was paying special attention to my appearance, and also that I was feeling rather important and was bearing the attitude of a reigning sovereign toward the group; it felt like my domain, where I could rule as I pleased. After a rather long while, I was able to orient myself in these emotions to some extent; apparently I submitted in a complementary, countertransferential fashion to the group's primitive idealizing transference. This transference can be seen in the following dream related by Robert, who was the group's spokesman: "A male figure in some danger, dark woods, rocks like a gathering storm. I knelt down and screamed to the heavens in a dramatic invocation, raising my arms upward, assuming that with my power I can reach Diana: 'DIANA, DIANA, goddess of the hunt!' A huge tidal wave is coming, and I am the one who is really in peril."

In my intervention I focused on the mixed feelings of wanting help from someone powerful, and fearing and envying the power at the same time. The gathering storm was "the storm of your anger at the gods who are bad; perhaps the maiden goddess stands for a maiden awareness in all of you of some energies within yourselves that you could use for your benefit, without having to bow to any gods."

Then Robert spoke about a female friend who wanted to save him through faith, making a veiled reference to his perception that the analyst demanded his complete devotion and unconditional obedience. He exclaimed defiantly, "but whoring it up is the real me!" thus expressing his terror at "sacrificing" his pathology. However, he continued, "I had a fantasy of performing cunnilingus on women . . . only the genital area," simultaneously confirming his approach–avoidance dilemma. He feared touching the tender, loving, and beautiful aspects of a woman, but Robert was nevertheless now approaching for the first time a woman albeit in a condensed, awkward manner (including both oedipal and preoedipal features) in his fantasy. Interestingly, he also mocked me in group for my role in his individual sessions: "She screws me—a fantastic climax!"

I was clearly conscious of my intense attitude in listening to his material. I was determined to explore in depth his despondency and frustration, and was warmly stirred by the poetic flavor of his associations. Robert clearly thrived in this atmosphere, but needed to verbalize his experience in vulgar, sexual terms. We see here the approach-and-avoidance configurations, represented symbolically in the verbalizations and exclamations about a new type of relating to women by this homosexual male.

The following is an excerpt from my countertransference journal during the second half of treatment progression (the fifth year): "See his sensuous mouth, very magnetic, deep, thoughtful eyes. I sense an impulse to touch him, embrace him, feel his body strength. He tells me he no longer can tolerate the frustrations of my power over him, also somehow wants to protect me from something. Does he sense his 'caressing web of desires' toward me and fear them because he still confuses them with the hostile and angry stirrings?"

Here is the mutually experienced strength of Robert's newly freed erotic feelings toward me, illustrating the group's themes, their terror and guilt over intimacy. In interpretations with the group, I wondered whether they could allow me my own space for dealing with these feelings instead of "protecting" me.

Soon after this session, I saw the group dealing with themes of frustrated pride, parental expectations for submission, masochistic surrender, and an ever-deepening sense of inadequacy. During this period Robert said, "I couldn't sing, I wasn't athletic—there's something wrong with my arms; I can't hit and I can't throw, it's so shameful!" When I inquired for associations about "arms," he came up with the following: ". . . holding, clinging to my teddy bear—he was cute and funny and warm, never talked back, never refused me, was never nasty—mainly, was always mine. Then I got furious one day and tore him apart—tore the stuffing out of arms, legs, pulled the eyes—because he didn't respond! My mother was only tender and caring when I was sick in bed!"

I can still hear something else he said then, ". . . out at night, my heart is about to burst, I know the stars will come, at last I can be enveloped by wet grass, the sense of the flowers, all the sweet night."

A perfectly clear picture of frustrated longings and tender human needs emerged, so my interpretation with the group focused on the need to "be enveloped and soothed, tenderly cared for—the solution is to be a failure: being a failure is the only hope of getting mother's love and attention—you avoided expressing your wants because there was a threat of losing everything!" I also showed how the early childish need to be the passive recipient was linked with the mature need for adult erotic togetherness, and how the destructive rage of early childhood for "unrequited love" led to fear of assertive masculinity and stood in the way of mature erotic and sexual expression. At this moment I chose to touch only briefly on the jealousy and need for exclusive possession related to childhood's insecurity and inadequacy. I did not concentrate on the oedipal rivalry as such, as this was not a barrier to relating at the time.

Discussion

In my view, my compliance, that is, my feeling and behaving in a way that was in total attunement with Robert, in particular, but simultaneously, with the group as well (my "erotic countertransference") cannot be viewed as an expression of reciprocal neuroses. Instead, I see it as the entirely human phenomenon of reciprocal communication on an elusive, unfamiliar, and usually ignored level.

The effect of the interventions prompted by my becoming aware of my erotic countertransference is, as are all cases of therapeutic effect, difficult to judge; but some related transformations seemed to occur in members of the group. Robert, previously isolated, distant, and terrified of contact with me, left therapy "because it's frustrating—there are feelings and longings I can't find expression for!" A few months later he wrote me a postcard from the West, describing his orgasmic sense of the beauty of the Rocky Mountains: "I cried from the sheer beauty of it—hiked alone 12 miles, 9¼ hours in Grand Canyon." The card included a symbolic message to me that he had discovered "a beautiful relationship," an awe for the forces of nature, both outside and within him. It was signed "love." Subsequently, he returned to therapy and began to shy away from his homosexual friends, as well as show interest in those homosexual males who were married and happy with women. He seemed to find himself attracted to females. I saw a strong and tender man as he was confronting his sexuality; male or female, it no longer mattered—it took its natural course.

As I look back on my many pages of notes describing my countertransferential feelings toward Robert, I see that I respond in terms of the other's pressures, the strivings for expression, unable to break through the stone wall of outward control. I have asked myself on many occasions how I can know whether it is the individual patient's or the group's need to which I am responding. It is difficult, if not impossible, to separate us into subject and object.

These examples constitute only small abstracted moments in a long continuum of separation–individuation unifying dimensions that emerged with a zigzag, back and forth movement, centering on the need for a meaningful connection with another human being. They merely suggest an immensely complex event that takes place at many levels at the same time. It is impossible to describe even adequately 10 seconds of this process. The general action, however, involves confrontation with intimacy and how this transforms, that is, how old forms are broken and old roles dropped. The person emerges when roles are left behind. True identity is indefinable, roleless integrity. The individual is lost when pinned down and categorized; when one does not categorize oneself, one is alive, as, in some sense, is the analyst when he or she drops this role.

Conclusion

Analysts and therapists in general, perhaps by the nature of the image of the profession, tend to deny their own emotional barriers to experiencing human intimacy in depth, especially their sexuality, though of course they are quick to spot their patients' problems in this area. Multiple countertransferential phenomena, especially in aggression and sadomasochism, frequently block therapeutic progress and lead to premature termination of treatment. Even more seriously, they sometimes create pseudotherapeutic alliances between analyst and analysand of a prolonged and essentially destructive nature, involving the acting out of unconscious interlocking transference and countertransference bonds.

How can a therapist extricate himself from these bonds? The fact that we convert deep intimacy—which is amorphous, powerful, indefinable, as if one were on the brink of disintegration and nothingness—into sexuality expresses the human tendency to act out or respond, instead of to experience. If the therapist confronts the eroticism without responding to it, denying it, or retreating into compulsive self-analysis, if he or she observes its presence as a sign of connection to the patient, the energy of transformation is set in motion. This is what Kelman has called *"kairos,"* "the auspicious moment" (Kelman, 1969). In the act of this observing, the therapist has given up his definition of the patient–analyst relationship and has opened to intimate feelings toward the patient. These appear as erotic forms but are recognized as metaphors. The therapist's living confrontation of the intimacy irrevocably alters the context for the patient and may also open the way for the patient to shatter old definitions about life.

Kairos, or what Shainberg calls the "transforming moment" (Shainberg, 1973), can be viewed as having special significance in the context of group treatment. The moment when erotic countertransference appears can be seized by the therapist as a response in tune with the group flow. Here all the therapist's knowledge remains in the background; although it provides a matrix for the action, the real impetus is intuitive, not rational. For this reason, it is difficult to offer technical guidelines for "capturing" countertransference and for fostering a creative awareness of its possibilities for growth in both patient and analyst.

Matter remains fixed unless acted upon by a great enough force. The approach we have taken here views Eros as that force that can break up old forms and open the way to transformation. We should keep in mind that sexuality not only has to do with primitive levels of interaction, but operates as a metaphor for our deepest connections to the universe. In myth, for example, Eros expresses the creative forces of nature. We have furthermore tried to suggest that transference and countertransference are not simply symptoms of pathology, but, when observed and confronted, become possibilities for both patients and analyst to go beyond limited referents and definitions, and encounter their intimacy.

References

Kelman, H. (1969), Kairos, the auspicious moment. *Amer. J. Psychoanal.*, 29: 59–83.

Shainberg, D. (1973), *The Transforming Self*. New York: Intercontinental Medical Book Co.

Slavinska-Holy, N. (1973), Countertransference in psychoanalytic group therapy. *Proceedings of the 5th International Congress for Group Psychotherapy*, eds. A. Uchtenhagen, R. Battegay, & A. Friedemann. Bern, Stuttgart, Vienna: Hans Huber, pp. 429–434.

———— (1974), *Reflections on countertransference and sexuality in psychoanalysis*. Paper presented at the Continuing Education Symposium, Postgraduate Center for Mental Health, Puerto Vallarta, Mexico, February 20.

———— (1984), Kernberg's theories: Some clinical applications. *Group*, 8/2: 26–34.

Chapter 14

TREATING CREATIVE DIEGOPHRENICS IN PSYCHOANALYSIS IN GROUPS

ALEXANDER A. WOLF, M.D.
IRWIN L. KUTASH, PH.D.

Psychoanalysis in groups began in 1938 (Wolf, 1949, 1950, 1982; Wolf and Schwartz, 1962; Kutash and Wolf, 1982, 1984) and has been valuable in promoting the creative potentials of diegophrenics (Wolf, 1957, 1980; Wolf and Kutash, 1985).

Diegophrenia develops before the age of 2 under the influence of a controlling and domineering parent; a mother who does not see the infant as an individual, separate and different from herself. Her infant, seeking her approval if not love, and fearful of her disapproval if he does not submit to her will, denies his own perceptions and abides by her judgments. To the extent that he submits to her persistence, he suppresses his own ego and incorporates her views as a negative pseudoego against which he repeatedly and compulsively rebels with an equally protesting pseudoego. Thereafter, the child and later the adult with these two superimposed pseudoegos, separate from his own real self and oppositional to each other, projects on others the original mother or parenting figure. This ambivalence between complying and rebelling leaves little time or energy to allow expression of his own genuine ego, his own perceptions, judgments, appreciation of reality, and own creativity. Eventually the diegophrenic's struggle is not with his parents or their projected surrogates; it is with himself, with his incorporated parents, with their persistence in him with his compulsive submission and rebellion against their incorporation. It is only when he sees the battle as an internal contest that he can be free enough to yield place to the artist in him. It is only when the implanted parental seed dies that his creative ego can bear fruit. In order to be his real self he needs to pass beyond his obsessive pseudoselves. James Agee gave an apt description of a diegophrenic in the character of Ralph in *A Death in the Family*:

> Yes, he was here, for what little good that was, and he was the only son who lived near enough at hand. And he lived so near at hand because he had no courage, no intelligence, no energy, no independence. That was really it: no independence. He always needed to be near. He always needed to feel their support, their company, very near him. He always lived almost from day to day in the hope that by staying near, by always being on hand if he was needed, by always showing how much he loved them, he might at last be sure he had won their approval, their respect. He did not believe, he couldn't remember, one sober breath he had ever drawn, that he had drawn as if in his own right, feeling, I don't care what anybody thinks of me, this is myself and this is how I do it. Everything he did, every tone his voice took, was controlled by his idea of what would make the best impression on others. He was worse a slave to that, to his dread for other people's opinion of him.... And his meanness and recklessness when he was drunk enough, he knew that was no good, no good at all. It wasn't even real. It was just the way he wished he was, and it wasn't even that, for what he wished was not to be reckless, but brave, a very different thing too [1965, pp. 57-58].

And then there is Tully, created by Leonard Gardner in *Fat City:*

> In an uptown bar where Oma was not likely to look for him, he felt her presence still depleting him. Now he thought he should have waited for her. Though he did not want her around, he felt guilty for not taking her with him, and he hated her for this inevitable confusion. He seemed unable to do what he wanted. What he did was either what she wanted or else was spoiled for him because it went against her wishes. Tormented, he longed to be rid of her. If Earl

wants her he can have her, he thought resentfully. Only why would he? [1972, p. 137].

Diegophrenia and Genius

How is it, then, that men and women of genius exhibit both diegophrenic maneuvers and at the same time are able to achieve extraordinary creative production? It was this phenomenon that led to a study of the dual pseudoegos in the lives and works of Shakespeare, Freud, and Einstein (Wolf, 1980). Shakespeare, in fact, 400 years ago, gave us, in Hamlet, the clearest clinical description of diegophrenia up to the present time. Hamlet, in the split between his pseudoegos and between these pseudoegos and his true submerged ego, "fluctuates between sanity and insanity, between submission and rebellion, between inhibition and impulsivity, between depression and aggression, between heterosexuality and homosexuality" (Wolf, 1980, p. 216). Freud alternated between:

> Liberalism and authoritarianism, his wish to "know" women genitally and his wish to return to infantile grandiosity, . . . [he was] a "naive positivist" and an "unscientific idealist," biologist and psychologist, mystic and materialist, revolutionary and reactionary, cosmopolitan and provincial, a believer in the progressive psychodynamic changeability of man and a believer in the immutability of instinct. . . . His preoccupation with the Oedipus complex, profound a discovery as it was, was nevertheless in some degree a displacement of his hostility from the more imposing mother to the less threatening father, a set of circumstances encountered in the creative genius, the homosexual and the diegophrenic [Wolf, 1980, p. 218].

Einstein vacillated between:

> A longing for isolation and a sense of social responsibility . . . being a Jew and a non-Jew, a Zionist and non-Zionist, a German and non-German, a child and an adult, a profound thinker and a gullible boy, decisive and indecisive, stubborn and yielding, impractical idealist and practical realist, political and apolitical, ingenuous and pro-

found, confident and self-doubting, a pacifist who helped to develop the Atomic bomb [Wolf, 1980, p. 220].

Wolf suggested that all diegophrenics have some positive experience with the primary nurturant mother which promotes the development of a substantial ego; later, when the child begins to express its independence and separateness at about 2 years of age, the secondary ego-denying mother emerges. It was assumed, further, that it was this beneficent experience with the primary mother that led to the growth in the infant of a substantial, creative ego, which was only partially and temporarily overwhelmed by the destructive secondary mother, whose emergence led to split pseudoego maneuvers and then to more serious diegophrenia. Let us now explore how genius could be associated with diegophrenia when it appears to develop despite it.

Ego Alien and Ego Syntonic Creativity

Kutash suggested two types of creativity: ego alien and ego syntonic creativity, the first being nihilistic in nature: In trying to rebel or oppose what is, the diegophrenic creates what isn't, something new and creative. "An individual becomes a person only when he can overcome any social and other reality—abolish it—and construct his own reality through a creative act of his own undetermined 'ego' " (Gluzman, 1982, p. 58). According to Gluzman (1982), "it would seem that in extreme conditions of existence, one's calm and inner strength are based on the subconscious knowledge that there is the possibility of an opposite choice—a recognition which now and then does become a conscious awareness" (p. 58). We term this *ego alien or oppositional creativity*.

When the suppressed ego itself is liberated and creativity results, we term this *ego syntonic creativity*. This is what we strive for in psychoanalysis in groups. The former is the product of tortured geniuses, the latter the product of actualized individuals who are able to create and be themselves. Furthermore, the former is limited to creating what is new and opposite; the latter can create what is new, period. The rebellious component of the split pseudoego plays the lesser part in the creative process, because, first, it is simply too obstructively responsive or reactive to the imposing diegophrenigenic parent and surrogate in the incorporated pseudoegos; second, its reactions are too immediate and compulsive to have as much creative quality. When, in the course of treatment, both pseudoegos are disincorporated, and the patient's previously suppressed ego is liberated, the ego is freed to exercise its creative functions more fully. Furthermore, this liberating process enables the ego, formerly in suppression, to dip down more readily into its previously unconscious abode to tap primary-process material and return in the hands of the newly freed ego, to be used and integrated through secondary process along creative channels.

In combining these conjectures, it was concluded that for the diegophrenic to progress from ego alien or oppositional to ego syntonic creativity, he must have had a good primary mother and techniques need to be applied to free the ego submerged by the secondary mother. The creative ego can survive by submission to external necessity, to external pressure, to fate, if you will, but it is inflexibly unyielding to the abandonment of its artistic core. It was not only the association of genius with diegophrenia that led to the work with liberating creativity by means of psychoanalysis in groups but also our clinical finding that among our nongenius patients a similar if less magnificent creative evolution occurred with the liberating of the submerged ego in those with borderline problems. The following quote gives a picture of the premorbid diegophrenic. Some evidence of Flaubert's diegophrenia and suppressed ego, and their relation to genius, is evident in a quotation recorded by Professor Brombert (1967): "Since I did not use existence, existence used me: my dreams wearied me more than great labours. A whole creation, motionless, unrevealed to itself, lived mute below my life. I was a sleeping chaos of a thousand fertile elements which knew not how to manifest themselves nor what to be, still sucking their form and awaiting their mold." We shall attempt in the following pages to illustrate this process by first presenting what creativity is and then how to encourage its emergence in the diegophrenic.

Promoting Creative Potential

Fostering Individuality

First and foremost, it is proposed that individuality needs to be fostered if creative potential is to be promoted (Wolf, 1949; Kutash and Wolf, 1984). The secondary, ego denying mother cannot tolerate individuality in her child. In the first weeks of life, the infant has no reason to rebel. As a consequence, he elicits a wholesome, nurturant support and affirmation from the primary mother. To an extent the infant brings out in the mother latent secondary maternal qualities when he begins to show any autonomous functions. The neurotic primary mother demands of the infant homogeneity with her misperceptions. She is herself symbiotically attached to him; as long as he needs her, she can cling to him; as long as he complies, she is nurturant. When he strives for autonomy, she experiences his struggle for independence as separation from her. Her own dependent needs are threatened. In her fear of losing his symbolic support, she demands homogeneity and conformity from him and thereby becomes the secondary mother. Furthermore, there are forces at work within society which contribute to preventing the development of autonomous egos, which inhibit them and foster a pseudohomogeneity. Examples include crowding out of individual initiative, overmedication, the assembly line with its ability to render people into automatons. For more ample coverage of the link between modern-day stresses and personality, see Kutash and Schlesinger (1980). Individuation is more and more considered an illness by a group-oriented society. These same disturbing tendencies can be found in therapy groups. The authors have observed "automated" groups where group themes limited individual choices, ignoring parental psychopathology as if familial influence could now be neglected. A person submerged in the homogeneity of modern-day society may find himself in a group, expected to shift quickly to "group values" and to follow an externally imposed pace of group process instead of developing his own ego.

It is not surprising, then, that a generation of group therapists raised in such a society should fashion group therapy approaches that can do the same thing (Kutash and Wolf, 1982).

Treatment designed to cure a patient from the wounds of a diegophrenogenic secondary parental figure, a sick family, or sick society, ought not to rely on joint group mood or consensus to help a sick member. The emphasis on group process and group-as-a-whole is an encouragement to collective oppression and reinforces the psychopathology of the diegophrenic. He is further victimized rather than liberated. He becomes an enforced member of a dictatorial collective, a party member, and loses his own creative initiative under group influence as he did with the diegophrenogic parent. Now the group has become the executive bureaucracy. The patient submits to group process and only rebelliously dreams of private fulfillment; even his dreams may be lost and his rebellion expressed in psychosomatic, psychopathic, and masochistic protest. He may be reduced to expressing his personal feelings in private with a pet animal at home, away from the dictation in the group that has scapegoated him.

In contrast to this, psychoanalysis in groups would encourage each member to pursue his own goals. The exploration and working through of the intrapsychic unconscious pathology of each individual member remains the difficult but most valid goal of treatment. The group simply provides a more economical setting where there is the possibility of relationships with peer and authority figures, where both intrapsychic and interpersonal processes occur, and where "brother–sister" as well as "mother–father" transferences develop and can be analyzed.

Group thematic approaches utilizing such techniques as consensual validation can exert strong influences on members toward conformity. The acceptance of group uniformity can only *manifestly* satisfy the needs of those who have always felt different and isolated but frustrates the more basic need for an independent creative ego. The conflict between individuation and the need for a sense of inclusion is engendered by group approaches with group goals as opposed to group approaches that aim to foster individuality and a sense of differentiated identity. In the latter approaches, each person discovers his own goals, which prove mutually beneficial in complementary difference. The primary purpose of psychoanalysis in groups is psychoanalysis of the individual within a group. The group leader needs to protect the members with weaker egos from the danger of incorporation by the group-as-a-whole, which can become the secondary mother.

The Talmud advises "that if someone says you are drunk, you can shrug your shoulders. If two persons say you are drunk, stop and listen. But if three say you are drunk, lie down." These and similar stories have been used to illustrate the powerful influence of the consensual validation process that can occur in a group setting. The authors would see this as an illustration of a danger in the group process. What if these people say the individual is drunk and he is not? The weak ego is further buried. A more valuable experience may occur when a patient correctly tells a group, "you are all mistaken," when the individual is in touch with his internal experience and has the strength to withstand the consensus and even the leader's opinion. The group, rather than suppressing the ego, at times with a short-term behavioral gain, has provided the laboratory for the individual to develop ego strength, to resist the secondary mother, to be himself, and ultimately, to be creative.

A danger for the diegophrenic in group psychotherapy is that he may simply continue to submit and rebel in the face of group pressures and themes, or under the influence of members who are more outspokenly forceful. He may join the aggressor and idealize his bondage and see it as liberating, when it is not. As Dr. Zhivago says (Pasternak, 1958):

> Health is ruined by the system's duplicity, forced on people if you say the opposite of what you feel, if you grovel before what you dislike and rejoice at what brings you nothing but misfortune. Your nervous system isn't a fiction, it's a fact of your physical body and your soul exists in space and is inside you like the teeth in your head. You can't keep isolating it with impunity. I found it painful to listen to you, Nicky, when you told how you were re-educated and grew up in jail. It was like listening to a circus horse describing how it broke itself in.

So, the diegophrenic needs to resist neutralization by a prevailing group and listen to his inward drummer, as the therapist must do with him. The artist–patient treasures in himself this most precious jewel of creative selfhood, because he recognizes in the powers that be an illusion of genuine character and originality. He knows that, with the loss of the privilege of power, they have no independence of thought and genuineness. The group-as-a-whole devalues personal opinion. Everyone must then join the chorus, sing the same tune, or be condemned as a renegade. The so-called deviant is a treasure who prefers to be natural and spontaneous instead of homogenously dull. If he is overpowered by the group-as-a-whole, submits in guilt at his deviance, and renounces his freedom and artistry, he becomes diegophrenically sadomasochistic. The gems must not be lost in the tiara.

Four additional essential ingredients necessary to promote individual (ego-syntonic) creative potential are: freedom, originality and curiosity, realistic problem solving, and the search for the whole in a new synthesis rather than the disordered parts (Wolf and Schwartz, 1964).

Achieving Freedom

To achieve freedom, the availability of choice is necessary, along with the capacity to be selective, to see nature in a new way. The diegophrenic is bound to unfreedom by his ambivalently compulsive pseudoegos. He is limited by his lack of a freed ego which would enable him to choose, to be selective. A liberated ego would help him to examine what he has been told, appraise it, and then create a new perception. He would have the autonomy, the strength, to go beyond the given and propose an independent view.

In the analytic group, he is encouraged to free associate, to fantasy, to dream, to have regard for his own intuition, to be open to his thoughts, feelings, and perceptions, and not to resist saying what is on his mind. He is supported in his right to have access to his suppressed self and to allow himself and the other members a similar privilege. To this end, he is encouraged to take the risk despite his anxiety to explore the unknown in himself and in the other patients and to get ego-promoting confirmation in the process from the group members. They, as a result of their identification, their interaction, and the general encouragement to associate freely, give more and more mutual support to imaginative processes, which, with the help of the therapist as well as their increasing resourcefulness, fosters greater understanding and opens up new possibilities for an emerging self independent of the compulsive ambivalence of the superimposed, split pseudoego.

Group members alternate between free association and conscious appraisal of what they have spontaneously said, just as they tell a dream, free associate to it, and then try to gain insight into its meaning. They are first encouraged to be uninhibited verbally, and then to examine their psychodynamics and psychopathology thoughtfully. Members' anxiety about giving up defenses and exploring unconscious material is relieved by their seeing other patients return safely from primary to secondary process. It is often easier to free associate among one's peers than in the hierarchical vector with the analyst. There are enough egos and superegos available among the group members to pull any one patient back to reality. Dreams and daydreams are associated to multilaterally and then consciously examined in secondary process for insight. The creative ego is given potential to emerge and thrive by dipping into primary process and then examining the material in secondary process. Mutual exposure reduces defenses in multilateral catalysis.

The freedom to be selective is inherent in the presence of eight to ten patients. The multiplicity of persons demands, provokes, and elicits more selective responses. Every member has wider choice to select with whom he will interact and to whom he will or will not respond. He has numerous alternatives. In dyadic analysis, he has less freedom. He can react only to his therapist without the freedom to choose or select an alternative figure. The analyst, too, has more freedom and flexibility in the group to choose with whom to respond and when to provide insight. Everyone in the group has the liberty to shift attention.

The core of unfreedom in diegophrenia is the persistence of ambivalence, a result of the incorporated split pseudoegos. His responses to fellow members are less intense, because they are less the controlling mother figure than is the analyst due to his position in the vertical vector. Comparing each patient's differing perceptions of copatients and the analyst offers a striking study in contrasts and offers all the participants the freedom to choose where and when to resolve any distortions.

The alternate session or leaderless group, which we advocate to alternate with each regular meeting at least weekly, supports the right to be free of the projected parent in the group leader. The absence of the analyst gives all the members that distance from the suppressing parent invested in the leader that liberates them to question his authority as well as the imposing internalized authority of their own split pseudoegos. The group member is free to consider what the therapist offers and yet take room discriminatingly to dismiss it for his own perception or those of his fellow patients. The meetings with and without the analyst help the patient to work through the maternal transference as well as liberating his creative ego from his internalized, maternally derived pseudoegos. The alternate session promotes ego autonomy, independence, and reciprocal interdependence based on reality. The presence of other patients and the alternate sessions displace control from the external and internal authority to the members and to the emerging self, so that each patient directs his own life and encourages every other to do the same in complementary, creative difference.

In promoting the alternate session, the therapist says to his patients, in effect: "I trust and respect you. I have confidence you will not act out in my absence, but rather, will interact with each other reasonably within limits." The analyst's conviction that group members can, independently of him, exercise their creative, resourceful egos, impels them to do so, as does his belief that he can rely on their growing, creative autonomy. Every diegophrenic has had some positive, nurturant experience with the primary, ego-promoting mother. It is the analyst's conviction that this creative treasure can be liberated by the therapist's regard for his unused potential that helps the wholesome ego to blossom. Group members, supported by the analyst's stance, develop increasing regard for themselves and one another.

The diegophrenic needs to hear his internal messages, and so does the therapist. He needs to heed his own imaginings and dreams and we need to listen to him. It is only when his own ego is liberated that he can heed others and then freely choose out of what is offered him the useful, creative, growth-promoting, realistic, and imaginative and reject what is stifling. The freeing of the suppressed ego is experienced by the diegophrenic as a personal and liberating revolution. Whereas before he was carrying a compulsive, private burden, the defensive and useless core of parentally invested pseudoegos, a false self, he can now operate with his genuine self.

Encouraging Originality and Curiosity

Besides individuality and freedom, a third quality characterizes the creative process: originality. To achieve this end, the therapist encourages perceptions that are new and different. Group members, tired of each other's static ambivalence, also appreciate a novel perception, which adds refreshing insight into external and internal reality and unreality. Everyone is stirred by a patient who, previously oppressed by his pseudoegos, manages to go beyond the compulsive given, to achieve a fresh outlook. It is original, creative, imaginative, unique, ego building; it is heedful of intuition and refreshingly perceptive. The analyst's position is that the compulsive search for unconscious psychodynamics and psychopathology is not creative. The creative patient needs to dip into primary process but then reflectively to organize his exploration with secondary process, with ego functions, in the way a dream has to be analyzed to provide insight, a creative process. The patient cannot go beyond his history with his mother and his incorporation of her perceptions unless he examines what has happened to him in the past. He may be just as obsessively limited and overcome with rigidity and uncreativity by a too-exclusive preoccupation with his history. However, if he explores his family history and then goes beyond it, he taps his creative ego.

Psychoanalysis in a group facilitates the emergence of the creative ego of each member. Experience in a heterogeneous group provides a setting of unique individuals so that stereotyping is broken through to a flexible newness. Because the multiple stimuli are so diverse, the analytic group is especially stimulating to the emergence of the creatively new. Group interaction provides new qualities, new responses not previously seen. Fresh material shows itself because of the pressure to interact. The shifting attention from patient to patient is in keeping with the need for alternating periods of activity and relaxation, attention and inattention, so necessary for the creative ego to grow. The analyst, by providing meetings with and without him, is judiciously heedful and judiciously disregardful, which also fosters the emergence of more creative egos.

Realistic Problem Solving

A fourth facet of the creative ego is that it solves problems and reaches a *realistic* goal. The improving patient develops a clearer view of reality that was formerly obscured by illusion. He becomes more engaged in the search for insight with an animating curiosity about himself and the other patients. He joins more avidly in pursuit of an ego-building reality formerly buried by the old split pseudoego. In the analytic group, there are more anchorages in reality, more appeals to reason, more demands on each member to relinquish his inappropriate commitments for more reasonable ones. He is urged to examine his unconsciously provocative role in eliciting the sort of reactions he gets from other patients. He is encouraged to consider the possible reality in their responses. He is confronted by the realities around him: other members' provocation, stimuli, reactions, demands, difficulties, and recommendations for his choosing more legitimate alternatives to his pathology. Awareness of multiple realities grows because the number of patients helps to avoid the persistence of resistive neurotic or psychotic distortions and impels the patient to react more appropriately, because he is less isolated; because anonymity is not neurotically overvalued; because the inner and outer reality are analyzed.

Synthesis of Parts into a Whole

A fifth component of the creative ego is its movement from the detailed parts to a more organized whole, the relinquishing of the more limited view for the more inclusive, better organized, larger view. It is a new perception of the organizing principle which clarifies the relatedness of the parts. It is a larger, abstract conception that explains the interconnection of the parts. The patient's insight into the development of his diegophrenia makes him an eager collaborator with the analyst and other patients in the recovery of his suppressed ego. He becomes creatively involved in obtaining an insight, evaluating it, elaborating it, and developing it. The analyst, in his struggle to replace disorder with order, confusion with clarity, chaos with method, and confusion with analysis, leads the members to pursue a similar course.

Organization is one of the fundamental qualities of the creative ego. In the analytic group, the intrapsychic is integrated with the interpersonal, the authority with the peer, the real with the fantastic, the alternate with the regular meeting, the patient with other group members, treatment with life.

Achieving Ego-Syntonic Creativity with Diegophrenics in Group Analytic Therapy

How then is this creativity achieved in the diegophrenic through psychotherapy, and more specifically, through psychoanalysis in groups?

Since it is necessary in the treatment of the diegophrenic to encourage the emergence and growth of the creative ego, this purpose cannot be achieved by traditional psychoanalysis. This is especially true in the case of the severely ill diegophrenic who functions primarily with his split pseudoego and cannot, therefore, benefit from externally offered attempts to give him insight because he has so little available ego to accept and integrate externally provided understanding. Instead, he continues manifestly to accept insight but, at the same time, to reject it in the submission and rebellion so characteristic of a split pseudoego. The patient who is subject to diegophrenic maneuvers with only moderate suppression of creative ego functions and a more available ego can more readily accept proffers of insight. Nevertheless, it is our clinical experience with both types to withhold offers of understanding until after the patient has passed through the period of unambivalent hostility toward the therapist as the surrogate for the diegophrenogenic parent. This aggressive attitude which does not last long, emerges because the patient feels free at last to protest against a lifetime of sadomasochistic, paranoid, and bisexual submission and rebellion at the hands of a stand-in in the therapist for the diegophrenogenic parent. The patient deeply appreciates the freedom he has gained with the therapeutic help of the analyst and fellow patients, as well as the recovery and growth of his own ego. With his creative ego now available, he can appreciate and constructively utilize offers of insight.

With this clinical experience in mind, it is important not to place the diegophrenic in a therapeutic group before he has gained some accessibility to ego functions, or the prevalence of his split pseudoego functions will lead to repeated and frustrating ambivalence (with an exception to be discussed later). The diegophrenic may sit in silence in the face of a group propelled by the therapist who chooses to emphasize overpowering group process and group themes. This silence is manifestly submissive and latently rebellious and hostile; both the patient and the group must endure it. We need to encourage him again and again to say his piece, no matter what. We need to support his courage, his right to say what is on his mind, to tell his dream, his fantasy, to experiment, to differ with the group, to be original, to be independent, not to be trampled by another's mood or determined insistence.

The severely ill diegophrenic needs to be treated individually until such time that his own ego emerges sufficiently that he can enter a group with less subjection to his compulsive ambivalence. In individual treatment preparatory to group entry, the therapist does not attempt to offer insight or respond to the patient's attempts to manipulate him into taking a stand around which he can continue his ambivalence. Rather, the emphasis needs to be placed on what *the patient* thinks, feels, fantasies, and dreams, on his perceptions, judgments, creative impulses, and ideas, but with only mild or moderate affirmation of them. For, with too empathic or enthusiastic encouragement or signs that the patient is daring to recover his suppressed self, the patient feels the therapist is appropriating him and that the surrogate parent in the therapist is getting too much pleasure out of the treatment process. The patient then becomes too eager to frustrate the stand-in parent, tries to deny him the satisfaction of any accomplishment, and suppresses once more the glimmer of his creative ego function.

A patient's dreams can be the tool to the patient's feeling the accomplishment of progress. They contain the true wishes of the dreamer in a creative format. For this reason, dream analysis is perhaps even more vital with a diegophrenic as a route to the true self, as well as a main part of individual treatment. Dreams are utilized in group to bring out the creative associations of all group members. Here the patient can tune in on his own uncensored self and get to know this self through his own associations.

The first milestone for the diegophrenic comes when he is able to accept the insight that he has spent so much of his life utilizing most of his energy either conforming or rebelling around introjected parental values and has never truly found himself. At this point, the diegophrenic needs psychoanalysis in groups to further discover his complying and rebelling, so he can ultimately resist either side of this coin and be himself. The patient's transference to the therapist can become sufficiently diluted in the group to allow the acceptance of interpretations around his ambivalence within the group.

The exception previously alluded to occurs in the case of severely ill diegophrenic patients. Individual psychoanalysis or psychotherapy proves impossible because the patient has such a strong initial transference to the therapist that he is back with mother or father complying and rebelling, and this cannot be worked through to form a therapeutic alliance. Here group can be utilized to dilute this transference with brothers and sisters or peers, who can help break through to the submerged ego. The alternate session, in fact, carries this process a step further in allowing the diegophrenic to be freer of dyadic parental transference, which can be impossible to deal with early in therapy and can even lead to early termination. Furthermore, in a group patients can take refuge from time to time from the verbal interaction in silent self-examination, in thought, feeling, fantasy, and the structuring of primary process into secondary process.

In general, the patient in individual analysis is under constant scrutiny in his therapeutic hours whereas, in the group, attention shifts from him on occasion, giving him the freedom from such "oppressive" examination, a time to explore his own responses, evaluate what he thinks and feels, be "alone," and be creatively active in secondary rather than primary process. Peers in group free the patient from the parent–analyst, as does the alternate session. There is freedom at times to be silent in group. The individual analyst intrudes if the patient is silent when he says, "What are you thinking or feeling?" This is more accepted from a group peer.

Kutash has been experimenting with a group solely for treating diegophrenics. With the diegophrenic, the group was composed so as not to include overpowering mother, father, or sibling figures and, only at a later date, were less ambivalent potential transferential mothers or fathers added. At this point, their egos were more secure from their previous experience with the leader as a "neutral parent." The analyst in this group places his faith in recovering the integrity of the suppressed ego not only by disincorporating the pseudoegos but by bypassing any dominating group member or process. The patients come to feel respect for their participation and the regard of siblings who were not perceived as overpowering or parental favorites. Initially, all being diegophrenics, they could count on resistance to whatever they interpreted to others, but it soon became apparent to them that all they needed to do was to switch sides to bring out the opposite point of view in their antagonist. This left them feeling safe, not being locked into complying or rebelling against any fixed parental positions. Furthermore, on any issue they found a pro person for every con person, or vice versa, and again felt safe in the evenly divided numbers diegophrenia created. The analyst in the group, and before long the patients as well, observed what was going on in the group and knew that behind this manifest performance something quite different was taking place. This allowed many patients to get past their initial fear of being overpowered by a parent or the therapist and encouraged members safely to let their own submerged egos emerge. This was combined with individual therapy, the one being an adjunct to the other. The goals and results of combined therapy with diegophrenics will now be described in more detail.

Enhancing Ego Functions

Bellak and Fairthorn (1978) list the 12 major ego functions as reality testing; judgment; sense of reality of the world and of the self; regulation and control of drives, affects, and impulses; object (or interpersonal) relationships; thought processes; adaptive regression in the service of the ego; defensive functioning; stimulus barrier; autonomous functioning; synthetic–integrative functioning; and mastery–competence. Since, initially, it is the aim in the treatment of diegophrenia to promote the recovery and growth of the creative ego, it is of interest to examine the way in which each of these ego functions can be enhanced in the therapy of patients with split pseudoego difficulties.

In reality testing, the patient needs to distinguish between inner and outer stimuli. The diegophrenic is relatively unaware of his inner self, his suppressed ego, and operates largely by incorporating and rejecting the views and judgment of every other person, as he formerly did those of the diegophrenogenic parent; he is overly sensitive to outer stimuli. He has little of an available inner self. He is a pseudoself buffeted about, submissive and resistive to every outer stimulus. The outer stimulus is immediately incorporated and expelled by each of his two pseudoegos. His perceptions are inaccurate, because they are too seldom his own. His perceptions are those of everyone else, although he denies the validity of others' perceptions.

He has little psychological-mindedness or awareness of his inner state, because he has too little reflective capacity with which to operate. If he is severely ill, he ambivalates between psychosis and neurosis. If he is only mildly ill, he vacillates between neurosis and normality. In a psychotic episode, he may hallucinate and suffer delusions and be grossly distortive in perceptual functions. If he is less disturbed, he does not hallucinate and is not deluded but has various illusions. From the most serious to the mildest state of diegophrenia, he compulsively projects onto others his introjected oppressive pseudoego, against which he rebels with the other pseudoego. This is the nature of his transference, which he compulsively projects onto everyone with characteristic ambivalence. He is the victim of every outer stimulus, with little of the gratification that comes from the experience of creative ego resources. Not having an available inner self and being the victim of every external attitude, he is confused about his own identity. In the course of treatment, as he begins to recover his own ego, he is better able to distinguish between inner and outer stimuli. He becomes freer of the compulsive necessity to be homogeneous with every other and of his equally compulsive need to deviate. He becomes more able to operate with his own perception and judgment, even to synthesize a new creative perception of reality. He becomes more able to distinguish between his own perceptions and those of others.

He is no longer so needful of approval from others. When formerly he received it, because of his submission, he either could not trust it or believe it. In his paranoidal state, his latent rebellion, his sadomasochism, and his ambivalence, he subverted the acceptance he so desperately sought. Now, better, he no longer compulsively seeks such appreciation. Now he is content in his self-regard and his regard of others. Formerly, he had no sense of belonging. He felt dishonest, undeserving, unloving, and unloved. He felt deeply wounded by any negative appraisal and, feeling derided, he nurtured a private or open, everlasting fantasy of revenge. He gradually becomes more aware of, and has more insight into, his internal reality, and can be equally appreciative of external reality without suppressing his creative ego functions.

The exercise of good judgment is an important aim in promoting the development of the creative ego. The patient with a split pseudoego ultimately, but not too early in treatment, needs to become aware of the appropriateness and possible results of what he intends to say and do. Too early an emphasis on such an aim is liable to inhibit the patient in his free associative hunt for his buried self. To the extent that he lacks judgment, he is liable to serious acting out.

The patient's sense of reality of the outer world and of his own self is a significant ego function. An impaired sense of reality is induced in infancy and childhood by the diegophrenogenic parent who demands from her offspring a homogeneity with parental distortions, so that early on the child loses ego boundaries and suffers consequently from perceptual distortions. The patient with a split pseudoego does not experience his identity from within; it is assigned by outsiders. The patient feels lifeless, empty, unreal, fused with other people. The extent to which he allows himself to be manipulated by external influences and intruded upon and incorporated by his split pseudoego versus a healthier sense that events in large degree can be determined by the exercise of the creative resources of his own ego are measures, respectively, of the extent to which he is ill or improving. If he is developing a personal authentic self, a right to be different from others, self-regard and regard for others, he is on the way to becoming well. The less symbiotically and compulsively attached he is to his incorporated pseudoegos and their projection onto others, the more he permits himself and the others separate and disparate individuality, the closer he is to being well.

Another ego function worth exploring in diegophrenia concerns the capacity to regulate and control drives, affects, and impulses. Involved here is the directness of the expression of impulses, the discriminating exercise of delay, the extent to which the patient can tolerate frustration, and how well he can move from primary to secondary process by thoughtful evaluation, emotional communication, and appropriate behavior. What the diegophrenic tends to act out are split pseudoego functions such as ambivalence, sadomasochism, and paranoidal and bisexual behavior. To the extent that this ego function is less available, he withstands analysis less well, has difficulty understanding or accepting insight, and acts out.

Still another creative ego function is concerned with the nature of the patient's object or interpersonal relations. The diegophrenic tends to alternate between symbiotic attachment and withdrawal, to cling yet be afraid to be close, to want to swallow the other and vomit him up. There is no sense of adult mutuality and reciprocity. He is always in search of the nurturant, good, primary mother in her surrogate, but soon discovers in her the disappointing, demanding, rejecting, bad secondary mother from whom he withdraws in repeated cycles. He is trapped in the fruitless and frustrating archaic views of his childhood instead of pursuing more serviceable and gratifying adult goals. In his symbiotic attachment to the diegophrenogenic parent and her stand-ins, others are used largely for incorporative and disincorporative purposes. He has no adequate ego to see himself and the other as separate and distinct individuals. He cannot sustain an ongoing relationship. He cannot tolerate the actual presence or absence of any other. He longs for and misses the other but finds her on resumption of the relationship too flawed to withstand for long. He suffers from separation anxiety but, shortly after reestablishment of any symbiotic tie, is revolted by the inadequacy of his previously sought after parental substitute. The therapist is at first idealized but shortly thereafter is found to have clay feet. It is only when, in the course of treatment, the patient can relinquish his symbiotic tie, separate, and individuate that he can abandon his ambivalence toward an ongoing, mature relationship.

Thought processing is a significant ego function. Since the seriously ill diegophrenic is subject to alternations of unreality and reality, it is necessary for the analyst not to encourage unlimited free association, but frequently to intervene with suggestions that some thought be given by the patient to what he has just previously said. Nor should the patient immerse himself in dreams or fantasies without thinking about them. Primary-process material must not be allowed to go on for long without pursuit of secondary process. A distinction needs to be made between encouraging primary process and encouraging the development of ego functions.

The therapist needs to observe and value the patient's thought processes, his capacity to pay thoughtful attention to himself, to concentrate, to form his own concepts, to retain his discoveries about himself session after session. Where possible, the therapist can gently affirm the patient's thinking when it is appropriate, reasonable, and sequential rather than pointing out when the patient is irrational, unreasonable, or too loose in his thinking.

Adaptive regression in the service of the ego is useful with mildly or moderately diegophrenic patients, who may be subject only to diegophrenic maneuvers. It is not appropriate to consider such means in the patient with a severely split pseudoego, because of his tendency to unrealistic episodes. Here, again, the therapist needs to distinguish primary process from suppression of ego functions. For, while he cannot encourage primary process early on, he needs as covertly as he can to endorse every creative ego function. When sufficient ego functions begin to emerge, develop, and become more substantial, he can then support the emergence of unconscious processes, free association, fantasy, and dreams, and support the patient's thoughtful examination of his unconscious communication via secondary process. If the patient has developed enough of an ego and expressed his unambivalent hostility toward the analyst, the therapist can now more securely encourage adaptive regression in the service of the ego and safely offer insight.

Defensive components are also aspects of ego function. The infant and child's incorporation of the diegophrenogenic parent's misperceptions and demands are both defensively adaptive and maladaptive. They are adaptive in that they are a way of coping with the harmful parent and in secreting one's creative ego from harm. They are maladaptive in distorting the victim's thought processes and behavior. The diegophrenic tends to misperceive his ambivalence and his other inappropriate responses as being provoked by others rather than as internal problems; his split pseudoego leads to the defense mechanisms of denial and projection.

The stimulus barrier is an ego function. The diegophrenic is overly sensitive to external stimuli, to which he responds by incorporation and disincorporation. This response is both compulsive and disorganizing; he comes close and avoids; he welcomes and withdraws; these are his coping devices. The patient needs to withdraw at first in large degree from external pressure to focus on the recovery of suppressed ego functions rather than on what every other says, does, or requires of him. If his stimulus barrier is low, he is too much distracted by every member of the therapeutic group and often requires the quiet, silent affirmation of the listening and ego supporting therapist.

The development of autonomy is still another ego function. The diegophrenic has little autonomy. He is an angry prisoner in a cell built for him by a parent, who still governs him as a rebellious subject in the cage of his split pseudoego. His freedom and autonomy are impaired; he sees and does not see; he hears but cannot listen; he intends to comply yet will not; he wants to study but cannot; he hopes to remember and forgets; he wants to learn but cannot. He tries to develop athletic and graceful skills but is too awkward; he wants to speak but stutters; he has habits that he breaks, returns to, and breaks yet again, in cycles. He diets, loses weight, and goes off his diet and regains his weight. He makes resolutions which he breaks: He gives up smoking and returns to it; he learns and forgets complex skills; he establishes and breaks his work routines; he tackles problems with resolve and then procrastinates; he is enthused about a new interest or hobby but quickly loses his appetite for it. He is anorexic and overeats at intervals; he eats too much and vomits. In the course of treatment, as he develops autonomous ego functions he increases his own perceptivity and attention to his own thoughts, feelings, and judgment; he gains more capacity thoughtfully to examine his unconscious material; and he obtains a greater facility in recalling the past, he is ready for psychoanalysis in groups.

Synthesis and integration are ego functions. Only a creative ego can reconcile and integrate seemingly discrepant or apparently contradictory attitudes, values, feelings, or conduct and dispel the false for the genuine self. Only a creative ego can energetically integrate intrapsychic process and conduct. Only a creative ego can perceive the relevance of history to the here-and-now, of feeling to thought, of perception to experience. The relative unavailability of this ego function in diegophrenia leads at first to inability to use insight. The analyst cannot here lend his own synthesizing capacity to the patient until he takes over the job on his own. The patient would simply display ambivalence around the therapist's effort to undertake a task the patient needs gradually to assume on his own.

Mastery and competence are also ego functions. These functions are reflected in the patient's ability to interact appropriately and cope effectively with others. They are also reflected in the degree to which he feels adequate and able. These functions are seriously limited in the diegophrenic. It is only when he has recovered his own ego that he has a stable sense of self, a valued image of himself, an independence of what others think of him, an inner identity, and continuity of experience. These, then, are the goals of psychoanalysis and psychoanalysis in groups with diegophrenics.

Summary

The diegophrenic needs the therapeutic process to recover his suppressed ego and free it from the ambivalence of subordination and revolt inherent in his prevailing pseudoegos. The diegophrenic is afraid of success. He might lose the good will of the parent, be unloved, hated, killed. So the diegophrenic maneuver is a defensive maneuver in the service of survival. The secondary mother or father might vengefully destroy him if he takes personal liberties to achieve creative fulfillment. The sadness of the diegophrenic state is that the patient cannot reveal himself; he does not know himself. He believes he is an imposter, a thief as yet uncaught, hiding in a thicket of ambivalence. He is tortured and torturing, self- and other-destructive, self-condemning and intolerant of others. It is the primary task of the analyst to assist the patient in working through the domination of his incorporated split pseudoego toward the liberation of his creative but suppressed ego.

For, with the emergence of his genuine self, he can relax and concentrate, he can rest and then dedicatedly pursue his own perceptions. He can contemplate the traditional and yet come to a new way of dealing with it. He can have the patience to struggle appropriately to produce a novel formulation instead of being mired in vacillation. He can be more inventive autonomously, personally, enthusiastically, industriously. He can use his intellectual functions more creatively than before. Complexities can interest and engage him rather than frustrate him. He comes to feel enriched by his therapeutic experiences. He becomes less defensive, more candid and open to himself and others. He becomes more perceptive and is able temporarily to suspend judgment for intuition. He becomes more flexible, skillful, accurate, and interested in interaction. Instead of the empty-handedness, the prison of his prior submission and rebellion, he now respects tradition but radically changes it for something better.

For the creative powers of the diegophrenic to become available, the suppressed ego needs to be enabled to emerge. It is only then that the patient can permit himself to have his own experience and be guided by it rather than be obsessively governed by his incorporated pseudoegos. As the diegophrenic recovers, he develops through his now available ego functions a clearer understanding of what he wants to do and does it. He can now allow his recollections and his previously suppressed ego to grow and give shape to his creative undertakings. The breaking through of the suppressed ego is itself a creative process.

References

Agee, J. (1965), *A Death in the Family.* New York: Avon Books.
Bellak, L., & Fairthorn, P. (1978), Ego function assessment, Parts I, II, III. *Weekly Psychiatry Update Series,* Vol. 2, Lessons 34, 35, and 36. Princeton, NJ: Biomedia Inc.
Brombert, V. (1967), *The Novels of Flaubert: A Study of Themes and Technique.* Princeton, NJ: Princeton University Press.
Gardner, L. (1972), *Fat City.* New York: Dell Publishing.
Gluzman, S. (1982), Fear of freedom. *Amer. J. Psychiat.,* 139/1:57–61.
Kutash, I. L., & Schlesinger, L. B. (1980), *Handbook on Stress and Anxiety.* San Francisco: Jossey-Bass.
——— Wolf, A. (1982), Recent advances in psychoanalysis in groups. In: *Comprehensive Textbook on Group Psychotherapy,* Vol. II, eds. H. I. Kaplan & B. J. Sadock. Baltimore, MD: Williams & Wilkins.
——— ——— (1984), Psychoanalysis in groups: The primacy of the individual. *Cur. Iss. in Psychoanal. Pract.,* 1/1:29–42.
Pasternak, B. (1958), *Dr. Zhivago.* London: William Collins.
Wolf, A. (1949), The psychoanalysis of groups. *Amer. J. Psychother.,* 3/4:525–558.
——— (1950), The psychoanalysis of groups. *Amer. J. Psychother.,* 4/1:16–50.
——— (1957), Discussion of *Psychic structure and therapy of latent schizophrenia* by Gustave Bydowski. In: *Psychoanalytic Office Practice,* ed. A. H. Rifkin. New York: Grune & Stratton, pp. 135–139.
——— (1980), Diegophrenia and genius. *Amer. J. Psychoanal.,* 40/3:213–226.
——— (1982), Psychoanalysis in groups. In: *Comprehensive Textbook on Group Psychotherapy,* Vol. II, eds. H. I. Kaplan & B. J. Sadock. Baltimore, MD: Williams & Wilkins.
——— Kutash, I. L. (1985), Di-Egophrenia and its treatment through psychoanalysis in groups. *Internat. J. Group Psychother.,* 35/4:519–530.
——— ——— (1982), Book review of *Psychoanalytic group dynamics,* ed. S. Sheidlinger, International Universities Press 1982. *J. Amer. Acad. Psychoanal.,* 10/4:632–635.

―― Schwartz, E. K. (1962), *Psychoanalysis in Groups*. New York: Grune & Stratton.
―― ―― (1964), Psychoanalysis in groups as creative process. *Amer. J. Psychoanal.*, 24/51:46–59.

Chapter 15

LIBERATING THE CREATIVE SELF THROUGH ACTIVE COMBINED PSYCHOTHERAPY

Arnold W. Rachman, Ph.D., F.A.G.P.A.

In introducing the rule of abstinence (Freud, 1915), and later in elaborating the use of activity for the obsessional and phobic neurosis (Freud, 1919 [1918]), Freud began a new era in psychoanalysis and psychotherapy. The rule of abstinence ushered in the use of "activity": "It is the analyst's task to detect these bypaths [... substitutive gratifications] and to require him every time to abandon them, however harmless the performance which leads to satisfaction may be in itself.... In all such situations *activity* on the part of the physician must take the form of energetic opposition to premature substitutive gratifications" (Freud, 1915, p. 377). What is more, he declared that the evolution of psychoanalysis would proceed in the direction of the *active dimension*: "Developments in our therapy, therefore, will no doubt proceed along other lines; first and foremost, along the one which Ferenczi, in his paper 'Technical Difficulties in an Analysis of Hysteria, (1919b), has lately termed 'activity' on the part of the analyst" (Freud, 1919 [1918], p. 157). In this ground-breaking publication, Freud also established Ferenczi as the foremost clinician to follow in the development of psychoanalysis along active lines.

It was Ferenczi's daring, courageous, and innovative experiments in psychoanalysis, to which Freud referred, that initiated one of the most exciting and fertile periods in the history of psychotherapy. There were three contributions which Ferenczi pioneered that are relevant to a contemporary group psychotherapy. First, he established activity as a significant dimension for the analytic process (Ferenczi, 1919a, b; 1920; 1925). Second, he introduced the humanistic role for the therapist in the analytic situation (Ferenczi, 1928; 1930; 1933). Third, in collaboration with Rank, he focused dramatically on the emotional and experiential component in the analytic process (Ferenczi and Rank, 1925).

The contemporary relevance of Ferenczi's work to group psychotherapy has been explored elsewhere, where the author suggests he conducted the first encounter session in the history of psychotherapy (Rachman, 1978).

Since the introduction of the active dimension by Freud and the pioneering efforts by Ferenczi to establish it as a significant part of the analytic process, active intervention has become part of the treatment of phobias as well as other disorders (Stekel, 1950). Gutheil, a student of Stekel, developed active techniques for dream analysis (Gutheil, 1951).

Many other analysts and psychotherapists have introduced and discussed active techniques since the pioneering days of psychoanalysis (Alexander and French, 1949; Masserman, 1955; Rado, 1962; Greenwald, 1967; Wolberg, 1977).

Contemporary developments in psychoanalysis and psychotherapy are also relevant to the evolution of a therapy that incorporates a humanistic analytic group experience. Several such developments are: humanistic considerations in the analytic situation (Greenson, 1967; Lomas, 1978); the broadening of the instinct theory to include object relations (Fairbairn, 1954; Winnicott, 1958; Guntrip, 1961); the advent of an experiential focus in psychoanalysis (May, Angel, and Ellenberger, 1958; Binswanger, 1963; Boss, 1963); and experimentation in the use of confrontation in the psychoanalytic relationship (Garner, 1959; Buie and Adler, 1972; Corwin, 1972).

Active Group Psychotherapy

It must be acknowledged that it was Moreno's innovative work introducing psychodrama, role playing, and sociometry which marked the beginning and development of contemporary action techniques in group psychotherapy (Moreno, 1963).

Active group psychotherapy based upon psychodramatic principles has the inherent characteristics of continuing the evolutionary process of active psychoanalysis. Group therapy encourages a more active interaction for both therapist and member alike, a more dramatic enactment of intrapsychic conflicts, an interpersonal experience, a greater expression of feelings, a greater reliance on noninterpretive forms of intervention, and it provides a laboratory for working through in a psychosocial context.

The appreciation of the use of action in the history of psychotherapy has not been fully synthesized by dynamic psychotherapy because of the unfortunate controversy initiated by some of the major pioneers in the field. A dichotomy has developed between the theory and clinical application of the concepts of action and interpretation. On one hand, the followers of Moreno espoused an action-oriented group psychotherapy based on the use of psychodramas. They employed analytic group psychotherapy as a negative model for comparison (Moreno, 1963). However, the followers of Slavson supported an interpretative mode of intervention in group psychotherapy, citing Moreno's approach as an inappropriate mode of psychotherapy for neurotic individuals (Slavson, 1955).

There have been psychodynamic group psychotherapists who have appreciated the need to broaden the usual process and role of leader (Durkin, 1964; Kadis, 1974; Yalom, 1975; Grotjohn, 1977).

Group psychotherapists with analytic training have recently attempted to integrate the action and interpretive modes (Mintz, 1971; Rachman, 1975a, b, 1979; Yalom, 1975; Knobloch and Knobloch, 1979; Dubska-Papiasvili, Rachman, and Papiasvili, 1982). In addition, several of these analytically trained psychotherapists have also integrated the encounter and intensive group experience into their group therapy program (Rachman, 1969–1970, 1975b, 1979, 1981; Mintz, 1971; Knobloch and Knobloch, 1979).

According to the present orientation, combined psychotherapy, where an individual is seen in both individual and group by the same analyst, is seen as the therapy of choice. When neurosis, character problems, or psychosis occur, they always develop in a psychosocial contest. As the individual matures, he moves beyond the confines of the first group experience of his biological family. Peer group affiliation and peer group influence become the second significant group experience. Personality development, therefore, occurs through emotional communion between significant others in a widening scope of social settings.

The necessary corrective emotional experience for continued psychosocial growth must occur in a psychotherapy group where emotional conflicts that inhibited self-actualization are re-experienced and worked through in the psychosocial context of peers.

The psychotherapy group is a collectivity of individuals where therapy occurs in a democratic social–interpersonal setting of the corrective family experience, fostering peer-to-peer relatedness for the purpose of realizing each individual's full psychosocial potential.

Individual therapy first serves basic functions: the establishment of a humanistic relationship and a therapeutic alliance; the identification of the core personality issues; exploration of the psychodynamics of functioning; and the initial working-through process.

Group therapy is introduced to aid the working-through process by intensifying the emotional experience of the core personality conflicts through the vehicle of action. In this way a continuous vehicle is provided for translating insight into action.

The individual therapy then combines with the group to serve unique and complementary functions. The interpretive function characterizes individual therapy, while the active mode is characteristic of groups.

Oedipus from Brooklyn: A Case History Illustrating the Liberation of the Creative Self through Combined Psychotherapy

"Oedipus from Brooklyn" is the pseudonym used to identify the individual in our study. He was born and spent his formative years in Brooklyn, New York. He has spent his adulthood attempting first to erase, and then to integrate the very special intrapsychic association that Brooklyn has for him. It was the site of "the crimes committed against him" by his mother. As a result of his therapy, he returned to the "Brooklyn in his mind," and worked through the hurt and pain, and began to synthesize some of the positive parts of his origins. So much for the "from Brooklyn" part of his pseudonym.

The "Oedipus" part derives from this individual's fascination with, and absorption in, the study of ancient Greek. It became his hobby for several years. It was one activity that relaxed him and gave him contentment. Then he began to read Sophocles' Oedipus plays. He also became obsessed with traveling to Greece. As a result of his analysis, it became clear that the study of ancient Greek was an attempt to unravel his own oedipal conflict. Traveling to Greece was an unconscious desire, an archetypal wish to return to man's original discovery of the oedipal conflict.

Oedipus from Brooklyn is a white, middle-class Jewish male who was in his mid-twenties when he began analysis. An honors graduate from one of the most prestigious colleges in the United States, he was in a state of social isolation and withdrawal, severe depression, and decompensation at the time of consultation. He was unemployed and living at home with his mother. Days were spent sleeping, smoking, listening to the radio, and masturbating. Paranoid feelings were present. He felt people could see that he had homosexual thoughts.

Prior to entering group, Oedipus spent about eight years in individual analysis. During this period he made some significant changes in his functioning: he became less depressed, anxious, withdrawn, and dysfunctional; he found his own place and moved out of his mother's apartment, he received a master's degree and obtained a high level position in the business world; and he began to socialize with women. In the middle of the individual analysis he found a woman with whom he could share his special world, and they married. His homosexual feelings and thoughts persisted, but they were less of a preoccupation.

The Thwarting of the Creative Self

The story of Oedipus from Brooklyn's early childhood is the key to an understanding of his psychology. At a very early age, perhaps during his first year (even as early as 4–6 months), Oedipus experienced a series of traumas when his emerging creative self was seriously thwarted, and from which he did not begin to recover until recently when the intensive group experiences (IGE) were developed (see p. 321). Therefore, from the age of roughly 6 months to about age 37, Oedipus suffered intense emotional pain because he felt his mother had destroyed his natural desire to create. Instead of being a creative, happy individual, he was forced to work at an uncreative job he hated and a sense of hopelessness, passivity, and resignation to an unfulfilled and unproductive life pervaded his existence.

The development of his psychopathology was inevitable in the family psychodynamics [see Rachman (1981) for a fuller description]. His mother was a controlling, seductive, intrusive woman, who saw herself as a "professional mother," a woman who lived and breathed for her children.

In his dreams, Oedipus depicted her as a "giant mole," an animal-like creature who was boring her way into every cell of his body and mind. A sense of aggression was conveyed to her son by her determined, insistent manner of being the controlling, "all-hovering" mother. Perhaps that is why he would wake up in the middle of the night, as a child, and feel that his parents were "out to kill me."

Oedipus' father was an emotionally distant, self-absorbed man (whose twin sister had been hospitalized most of her adult life for mental illness). In Oedipus' dreams his father was depicted as a "cloud." His conscious thought and feeling was of an uninvolved man who would drift off into his own thoughts when Oedipus tried to make contact. Oedipus longed for fatherliness, and his father's inability or unwillingness to curtail the poisonous effect of his wife's interaction with his son incurred a great deal of anger in Oedipus.

His younger brother was an object of rage. One source of the rage was his usurpation of Oedipus' dominant position with the mother. The other was the rage he could not direct to his parents. The birth of his brother and the subsequent intense sibling rivalry was eventually to become a life-saving device for Oedipus. His brother's presence moved his mother's focus away from him. The intense anger fueled the separation process. By withdrawing, Oedipus allowed a symbioticlike connection to be formed between the brother and mother, which resulted in a homosexual somatic adaptation.

The Building Block Trauma

Although Oedipus' childhood was marked by a continuing controlling, intrusive experience, there was one experience that for him, symbolized the loss of his creative self.

Sometime during the first year of life, probably at about 4–6 months, as he was able to recall and experience it, under analysis, the following event appeared to take place. One day, he was busily engaged in playing with building blocks. He was completely absorbed in building a structure, perhaps a building. He had his back to his mother, completely ignoring her, as he was totally involved in the adventure of creating a structure. His mother, either intentionally or by accident, reached over his shoulder and knocked the blocks over. Oedipus was surprised, but picked the blocks up and proceeded to rebuild the structure. The blocks were knocked down again. This time he was frustrated and angry. He tried to stop the invasion by moving into a corner of his playpen and covering over his building activity. Once again, he returned to his building. This time, when his mother knocked down the blocks, he crawled into a ball and gave up. He did not try to build his structure again. Apparently, the mother, resentful that her son was more interested in his own creation than her, struck out at him and tried to force him to pay attention to her. Oedipus did not experience it as a playful gesture between mother and child, but as a destructive act.

A series of events lend credence to the probability that Oedipus was recalling an experience so early in life. First, he has edetic imagery, the capacity to remember in full detail both intellectual material as well as emotional experiences. For example, he can recall not only the content of a page, but also the sentence in which it occurred. His earliest memory, probably during his first year, which he spontaneously revealed in a session, involved lying in a stroller with the sun filtering through a gauze cover. Finally, in an intensive individual session, where hypnotic age regression was induced, Oedipus was able to recall an experience of maternal seduction during his first two years of life (Rachman, 1985).

The course of Oedipus' treatment will be discussed in the context of the humanistic analytic approach used.

Humanistic Analysis in a Group Setting

In the present frame of reference, humanistic analysis (Rachman, 1981), the process of psychotherapy is divided into three distinct phases: the empathetic phase, the analytic phase, and the action phase.

Empathetic Phase

The empathetic phase characterizes the initial process of psychotherapy, where the relationship is being built on the bedrock of accurate empathetic understanding (Truax and Carkhuff, 1967). It is an essential assumption of humanistic analysis that empathy, conveyed by the analyst to the analysand in a consistent, compassionate, direct, and accurate manner, is what allows the individual to build a sense of basic trust in the therapist (Erikson, 1959); it also encourages a relationship where human rather than "clinical" contact prevails (Ferenczi, 1928; 1933), and a sense of being understood by a "significant other," perhaps for the first time in the individual's life. Both of these elements open the patient up to being helped and activate the growth process (Rogers, 1961, 1980). The profound effect that empathy can have in psychotherapy was originally explicated by Ferenczi (1928), was theoretically expanded and empirically demonstrated by Rogers (1975) and his associates (Truax and Carkhuff, 1967), and was reintroduced in psychoanalysis by Kohut (1971) and his collaborators (Goldberg, 1978).

A genuine sense of empathy means the analyst, as a person, is in a state of "emotional communion" with the individual. This contact is for the purpose of understanding, as fully as possible, the internal frame of reference of the individual, on an experiential and emotional level. It is akin to what Buber (1937) refers to as the "I–thou Relationship" (or dialogue). An individual is deeply moved by such an attempt at understanding, and the analyst by this process comes into profound emotional contact with the analysand. When this experience is felt by both parties, and is maintained over days and months, the second phase of psychotherapy can begin. The establishment of such a meaningful and profound emotional contact depends on the capacity of both parties to be receptive. An individual hampered by intense emotional psychopathology, will need years, not months, to feel a basic sense of empathy. A clinician who insists on emotional detachment and neutrality in the relationship will never achieve this goal. The humanity of the analyst will be the basic ingredient (Ferenczi, 1928; 1933; Fairbairn, 1954; Winnicott, 1958; Guntrip, 1961; Rogers, 1961; 1980; Balint, 1968).

The Empathetic Phase spanned the first five years of Oedipus' treatment. It was characterized by a substantial period during which the analyst responded to him with accurate, empathic understanding. This kind of interaction occurred around any material, conscious or unconscious, that Oedipus presented.

Once it was clear how valuable the role of accurate, empathetic responding (Truax and Carkhuff, 1967) was in relating to this individual, it became a hallmark of the therapy throughout all the rest of the phases. It was the key during the initial phase of individual therapy to Oedipus developing a sense of trust in another human being; in his feeling understood, for the first time in his life; in his sharing the pain of his childhood traumas; in his sharing his private, inner world with another person, thereby moving out of an autisticlike way of being; in the establishment of a working relationship (or therapeutic alliance) where both of us became aware of the psychodynamics and core of personal conflict and developed a mutually agreed-upon direction for change and growth.

Analytic Phase

The analytic phase usually occurs after the first six months to a year, when the therapy focuses on the analysis of dreams, fantasies, early recollections, and the transference aspect of the therapeutic relationship. In addition, any other material, behavior, or feeling state whose unconscious or preconscious message would aid the unfolding process is also analyzed; no single "royal road to the unconscious" is preferred. Each individual is understood in terms of his or her idiosyncratic modes of perceiving and responding in-the-world. An artist, for example, may be best analyzed by a focus on his or her artistic material rather than by a focus on dream analysis. If such an artist is also more cathected to expression through pictures than the spoken word, he or she may be asked to depict feelings, dreams, fantasies, or experiences on paper. These productions can become the focus of the analysis. It is not only artists who are encouraged to depict their inner world in the form of pictures. One individual who was severely emotionally restricted but quite verbal was related to in an analytic fashion through the paintings of his favorite master, De Chirico, who depicted for this individual the deep-seated feelings of depression, anxiety, isolation, and danger he could not spontaneously verbalize.

With Oedipus from Brooklyn, a wide variety of modes and materials were employed in order to analyze the unconscious and latent levels of intrapsychic and interpersonal functioning. We began the analysis with a cognitive understanding of dreams, fantasies, and early recollections, because he was heavily cathected to his intellect, which was a very special area of talent. He was naturally endowed with biological intelligence (special ability to solve puzzles, anagrams, understand puns, teach himself foreign languages, possession of edetic imagery). His intellectual capacity was one of the life-saving devices that had allowed him to survive childhood with some sense of self-esteem, mastery, and positive capacity to function in the light of the overwhelming trauma of seduction and control he experienced with his mother and the emotional abandonment of his father. The most empathetic and significant connection between analyst and patient was the use of his intellect to understand his conflict.

As his ego could tolerate emotional interactions, the integration of feeling with intellect began to predominate. It was through his participation in the intensive group experiences that his emotional life began to emerge (see p. 321).

The analytic phase occurred during the second five-year period of individual therapy and during the initial entry into group therapy. Because Oedipus had such serious problems in trust, rage, and interpersonal relations, he needed an extended period of empathetic analysis. This period was characterized by a focus on the analysis of dreams, fantasies, and early recollections. It was during this phase that hundreds of dreams were reported and analyzed. He would bring in two and three dreams at a time, and we could not proceed until we had analyzed each one. Entire sessions, for months on end, were spent in the sharing of his unconscious world. He did not rest until each and every element in the dreams was associated to and the meaning understood.

The dreams indicated a complete absorption with his childhood feelings about being seduced, intruded upon, and damaged by his mother and the emotional unavailability of his father. Gradually, positive themes developed which indicated the possibility of emotional separation from his mother, the positive qualities of his father, and the desire to change his lifetime adaptation of passivity, resignation, inactivity, and lack of creative fulfillment.

Action Phase

The action phase usually is introduced by combining group psychotherapy with the ongoing process of individual contact. Usually, the group experience comes after several months of individual therapy, when the empathetic relationship has been firmly established and the analytic work has begun. When there is serious resistance to group or when the capacity to relate in a psychosocial situation is impaired, the introduction of group can be delayed. In Oedipus' case, group participation did not occur until five years after the start of individual therapy, due to the difficulty in relating and lack of desire to relate in interpersonal situations [see Rachman (1981) for a fuller discussion of these issues].

Group psychotherapy focuses on the working-through

process by helping the individual translate insights into creative action. The psychosocial context of group encourages spontaneous, emotionally alive, authentic interactions in the here-and-now between members and the leader. Previously introduced and explored transferences, psychodynamics, and unconscious material are amplified and become part of an active mode. An ethos of action encourages members to change personality functioning in the context of their corrective emotional experience with the significant others of the "group family."

The ongoing group experience has been described elsewhere (Rachman, 1981). For the present discussion, the special use of the intensive group experience will be highlighted.

The action phase occurred during Oedipus' final period of therapy which also lasted about five years. During this period, group psychotherapy became the predominant mode, and individual therapy was the adjunctive therapy. As Oedipus put it, "the previous phases just weren't enough. I needed to have different kinds of experiences, I had analyzed all the dreams I could, I had gone over all my history, I had broken down all the factors which caused my problems into their essences. I now needed to act."

Entry into group set in motion a translation of the analytic material into action. Alive, emotional experiences with group members triggered a series of maternal transference reactions, which stimulated the working through of core conflicts.

The introduction of a series of intensive group experiences and intensive individual experiences, in conjunction with group sessions, helped Oedipus reexperience the original traumas. In addition, Oedipus began to translate the insights and corrective emotional experiences into new behavior and personality change.

The Group Analysis

This individual needed a group experience to become more human. However, he was placed in a group with some trepidation because of his severe difficulty with human interaction. His rigid defenses hid an ever-present fear of intrusion, seduction, and abuse by his mother and women he easily perceived as mother. Furthermore, there was a serious lack of cathexis for interpersonal relations or group affiliation. He was hypercritical, demeaning, and often maintained hostile prejudicial feelings toward certain people. Feelings of superiority and elitism were also evident.

A combination of factors lead to the group analysis becoming a successful experience (for a fuller discussion see Rachman, 1981; 1985). They were the extended period of empathetic analysis which built a trust in the analyst, softened his feelings toward others, and allowed the analyst to be a transitional object to further interpersonal reactions; the special techniques for screening the potential group members and assimilating a deviant group member that were used to help Oedipus join and maintain himself in the group; the introduction of action techniques which encouraged projective contact with deep-seated primitive developmental material; the group's positive response to Oedipus' leadership; the analyst's encouragement of peer-to-peer interaction.

The Group

There were eight individuals, four men and four women, who remained together in the group for about four years. All were in their twenties, with occupations including reporter, sales, therapist, art historian, academician, financial analyst. All were in the upper level of intellectual ability, from middle-class urban families. Personality problems included neurotic, passive–aggressive, schizoid, and borderline. Oedipus could be characterized as a severe borderline with paranoid features.

The group was able to work intensively because there were no terminations during the four-year period, and the active experiences developed cohesion, openness, depth, and emotional honesty and directness.

The Intensive Group Experiences

Special group sessions were used in conjunction with Oedipus' ongoing participation in group analysis. An intensive group experience is a time-extended group session, employed as an adjunct to the ongoing group analysis, where several active parameters are introduced to deepen and extend the boundaries of the therapeutic process (Stoller, 1968; Rogers, 1970; Mintz, 1971).

1. The time of the usual group session is extended anywhere from a 3- to a 12-hour period, depending upon the special purpose of the session, and the members' needs.

2. Action is a central focus of group interaction. This can take the form of role playing, psychodrama, encounter techniques, or specially created skits or scenarios suitable for individual or group needs. Physical interaction may also be judiciously employed in either nonverbal encounters, or psychoscenarios where motion and touching are an integral part of the activity.

3. A direct, spontaneous, and honest expression of feelings and thoughts is encouraged.

4. Group members take an active leadership role in the creation, planning, execution, and analysis of the psychodramas or active techniques.

5. Each member is used to help with a specific function in the encounter, based upon his or her ability, willingness to participate, relationship to the main character, and psychological issue he or she wishes to confront.

6. Members use experience to work on similar core issues.

7. About a month before the intensive group experience, the group is prepared for the experience. Positive and negative feelings and fantasies and dreams, and previous experiences about the special session are explored. Distortions are corrected, and anxiety maintained at a therapeutic level. Members are encouraged to select a core conflict on which to focus, and mobilize a desire for risk taking and personal growth.

Group members served a very special function for Oedipus. There was a borrowing of the "group ego" to gain emotional support, strength, and courage to confront the repressed feelings and reexperience the primal trauma with a "community of peers." Corrective family experience was created, as new "parents" and "siblings" supported and confronted individuals around core personality conflicts.

The second subphase of Oedipus' experience in group centered around a series of five intensive group experiences. The first one was introduced after the group had been in existence for two years. A two-year waiting period was somewhat of a deviation from the customary procedure: usually the intensive group experience was introduced during the latter part of the first year of group in order to deepen and extend the uncovering process. Delaying it was a recognition of the special nature of Oedipus' group and his participation in it. Actually, it had been contemplated that an intensive group experience not be scheduled; the therapist was cautious and somewhat anxious about conducting such a session because of Oedipus' severe psychopathology. There was concern that the intense affects released during an intensive session and the heightened sense of intimacy could produce emotional flooding and panic that might overwhelm him and precipitate a breakdown.

His initial and subsequent reaction to the announcement of the special session was used to gauge his readiness for the intensive experience. Several group members had raised the issue of intensive group experience during the first year of the group, having heard about the positive effects of the experience from members in other of the therapist's groups as well as from friends and reports in popular literature and the media. Initially, the author had related positively to the idea, suggesting it would be considered during the second year of the group. When the members returned to a desire for the special session during the next year of group, the opportunity was used to explain the method and goal in conducting an intensive group session.

In explaining the focus on emotional intensity, use of action techniques, and encouragement of sharing and intimacy, I was mindful of Oedipus' reaction. Apparently, the time was ripe for him as well as the group. He was interested in the experience, showed no concern about being overwhelmed by affect, and was looking forward to making a breakthrough in his functioning. His psychic wisdom that he was willing and ready to participate in the intensive group experience was clearly worthy of respect. He had demonstrated, throughout his previous therapy and life experience, a capacity to sense what he could meaningfully relate to and synthesize. If anything, he was conservative and overprotective of his private world of functioning.

Intensive Group Experience 1: "I Want To Cry"

Oedipus expressed a mixture of excitement and despair in anticipation of the first intensive group experience. He was excited because he wanted to change. Much to the group's amazement, he requested that the therapist help him release his emotions during the special session. In particular, he wanted help "to cry." In being able to cry, he would be releasing his pent-up sense of sadness for the traumatic childhood he had suffered.

Although he stated the emotional release "would be good for me," he also sensed that the confrontation with the deep-seated feelings of childhood would also produce despair: "I'll feel weak and vulnerable, which I don't like." The process of this first session was as follows:

1. While the other members were involved in a series of encounters which released anger, Oedipus was told he could directly participate or stay to one side if the emotional experience became overpowering. The group's release of anger was a follow-up to previous analysis and earlier active experiences in group.

2. Observation of Oedipus' nonverbal behavior during the session revealed that he was being reached emotionally, although he verbally denied it.

3. The group turned to Oedipus toward the end of the session, realizing he was the only one who hadn't been the focus of an encounter.

4. The therapist gained his approval to initiate an experience.

5. A "trust encounter" was carried out by having him fall backwards and be caught, first by the therapist, and then by group members. The encounter served to help him let go of control, develop greater trust in the therapist and the group experience spontaneity, and become more comfortable with direct action.

6. Then the group, in a spontaneous gesture of affection, decided to give him "a circle of love." He was surrounded by the group and they all hugged him together. He melted to the floor, and a smile of serenity filled his face, much like a contented infant.

7. After the first intensive session, Oedipus protested the experience, saying he felt controlled and intruded upon during the circle-of-love encounter. The protest was not a renunciation of the intensive group experience as a vehicle for emotional release and change, but a desire to maintain some control over these experiences. The therapist realized that Oedipus was expressing his anxiety regarding the central psychodynamic in his existence, the fear of control and intrusion. From then on, it was decided that all future experiences would be a joint endeavor between patient, therapist, and the group. This became one of the crucial humanistic decisions in the later sessions.

Intensive Group Experience 2: "Exorcism" of the Negative Parental Introject

The major focus of this special group was to help Oedipus work through both his negative maternal transference reaction to the feeling of a group member and to develop a capacity to be more active and less passive to his mother's intrusive and controlling experiences with him. It was Oedipus' idea to have a special experience. The analyst had some misgivings about this, but we devised a psychological scenario as follows:

1. Oedipus dressed up in his hood and fork. These were his symbols of withdrawal and anger as a result of childhood experiences with his mother.
2. The atmosphere of a "Black Mass" or exorcism was created. The room was lit by candle and incense was burned.
3. Group members were all given instruments to hit or shake; drums, tambourines, or noisemakers.
4. Oedipus prepared a list of criticisms of a group member, Laurence, with whom he was involved in an intense negative maternal transference. In this way, he used a group member

as a projective device to begin to confront his negative parental introject.

5. Another group member, Oedipus' "psychological twin," Howard, read the list with disdain and hostility in his voice.
6. After each criticism was read, the group reinforced the criticism by pounding their instruments and noisemakers.
7. Oedipus signaled the beginning and ending of the noise by ringing a bell.
8. The "Symbolic Mother" group member remained silent throughout the encounter.

Much therapeutic work was done in preparation for this session, so that the group member would feel he was "getting something" out of role playing Oedipus' mother. He was able to see the psychodynamic connections between his experience of maternal seduction and control and those of Oedipus, which led the way for the experience. So through "vicarious experience," Laurence began to work through Oedipus' psychodynamics with his mother. He also began to admit that Oedipus' criticism had some validity.

Oedipus felt it was important that he have an opportunity to *get through to this mother and that she be forced to listen*. Oedipus felt that he had gotten through to his symbolic mother, since the group sessions that ensued demonstrated a working through of the negative maternal transference to the group member. Laurence admitted that the criticisms were valid, he heard them, and he decided to change.

Intensive Group Experience 3: "Confronting Mother–Animal"

Oedipus began to build the courage to confront the seductive erotic feelings toward his mother as a result of a hypnotic regression session. [See Intensive Individual Experience (IIE), Hypnotic Regression to the Origins of Maternal Seduction, p. 334.] Another intensive session naturally developed as Oedipus reported the special individual session in group.

Group members urged him to develop a special session to deal with his mother's seductiveness. It proceeded as follows:

1. An earlier active experience, the family album, was reemployed. Oedipus collected early childhood photographs of himself and his parents. They were passed around at a group session and discussed. The members became familiar with his family.

2. In order to recreate a more lifelike experience of confronting his mother, Oedipus tape recorded his mother's voice while she was having dinner with the family.

3. The encounter began when the lights were dimmed; the photographs were passed around while the group listened to his mother's voice on tape. An atmosphere was created whereby his mother came alive. All members who wished brought in photographs of the parent(s) whom they wished to confront. The photographs were placed on the wall for all to see.

4. Various members were chosen to symbolically represent Oedipus' parents. He chose a female member who was direct and free in her sexual expression to wear a red mask, symbolizing his mother's uncontrollable passion and sexuality. A male member wore a blue mask, symbolic of a cloud, sky, and coldness, which represented his father's emotional distance. Other group members wore masks of different colors. He asked the therapist to wear a white mask "because he is the good guy."

5. A life-size geometric figure of Oedipus' mother, created by his wife to his specifications, was mounted on the wall. The distinguishing features were large breasts and a triangularly shaped vagina.

6. As Oedipus lay on the couch, staring at the geometric figure, another group member, who was imitating his mother's voice and speech pattern, read aloud a list of sayings Oedipus and the therapist had compiled, which represented the essence of his mother's seductive and controlling behavior. The father figure, who stood off to the side, sighed from time to time.

7. In response to each statement read by "his mother," he responded by telling her directly how seductive, controlling, and intrusive she was. He also told "his father" he was emo-

tionally absent when he was being seduced. He was angry that his father didn't do anything to help him or protect him from his mother.

The session had a very significant emotional impact. He experienced his mother as being everywhere in the room. Her presence was dominant, much like the experience of childhood, where she "bored her way into every nook and cranny" of his existence. He was pleased, however, that with the group's help he was not overwhelmed by her, and was able to stand up to her and confront her seductiveness.

Intensive Group Experience 4: "Building Blocks Encounter"

The ability to confront his mother's seductiveness freed Oedipus to deal with his creative urges. The analysis became focused on the central issue for his personal growth—the ability to create. Historical material emerged as a result of the special sessions. His inability to be connected to a meaningful career and to be creative was his greatest source of pain. He blamed his mother's intrusive, seductive, controlling behavior as the cause of his incapacity. He began to recall a hazy memory from childhood of being thwarted in an attempt to play or create. As mentioned earlier, there was the hint that his mother had interfered with his attempt to build something one day while he was playing in his playpen (see Building Block Trauma, p. 315).

As a stepping stone to session 4, an unusual session was planned with Oedipus' mother. The exploration of history left him dissatisfied that we had pinpointed the exact factors which caused his creative block. The therapist also felt some need to know more since the analysis had not produced a clarification as to the exact influence of the mother's personality and behavior on the development of her son's psychopathology. As is often the case with an individual who experienced such a troubled childhood, there is the search to know who was responsible for the "craziness." Was Oedipus crazy—or was it his mother? We decided, therefore, that it would be instructive to have the therapist interview his mother, to go over the history and attempt to discern the locus of psychopathology. Two consultation sessions were arranged with Oedipus' mother. The tape recorded material was given to a colleague who was an expert in early mother–infant behavior. After listening to the tapes, her conclusions were that the mother's voice quality, manner of relating, thought processing, exhibition of emotions, and her level of denial suggested a borderline schizophrenic adaptation.

Although these personality characteristics were not as apparent in the face-to-face interview, they were discernible when the therapist also listened to the tapes. What became apparent in trying to reconcile the discrepancy between the independent therapist's assessment and Oedipus' therapist assessment of the mother-functioning, was that being in the mother's presence may have had a "seductive effect" on the therapist. Her vitality, eagerness, and willingness to please and cooperate created the expectation that significant material was going to be forthcoming. She did reveal meaningful historical material. However, she practiced almost total denial when the therapist attempted to link these two significant childhood experiences to Oedipus' adult personality problems.

A detailed inquiry into the possibility of the occurrence of the building block experience at first yielded a total lack of recall. When the issue was pursued more vigorously, she responded that, "it may be possible, I don't remember anything like that," and, "I ask you doctor, do you think I would do something like that to my son? Never!"

Through contact with the same colleague who listened to the "mother" tapes, arrangements were made to view research films of negative mother–infant interactions. The film we viewed was of a diagnosed intrusive mother with an 18-month-old child. Through exploration of the film, Oedipus revealed that he was emotionally touched by the experience and identified strongly with the infant. He thought that this mother was intrusive, but felt *his* mother was still more intrusive. Now he was satisfied that the proper diagnosis had been made about his mother, and he was the victim of her intrusiveness and control. He had been a curious, adventuresome, and potentially creative child, but had been thwarted by her. The fourth session went as follows:

1. After the discussion of the interviews with his mother, we decided to go ahead with an encounter which would attempt to encourage a fuller recall of the trauma which interfered with his creative development, which we hypothesized was a thwarting of an attempt to create through building blocks.
2. The group surrounded Oedipus to form the walls of a symbolic playpen. He sat on the floor, playing with the pillows from the couch. The pillows functioned as symbolic building blocks.
3. A group member role played the intrusive mother. Each time Oedipus built a structure with the pillow blocks, without warning, the member came from behind and knocked it down. This was repeated several times.
4. With each interruption of his attempt to build a structure, Oedipus became more frustrated and withdrawn. Finally, he sat immobilized, unable to continue. The encounter ended.

Oedipus and the group reported that a profoundly moving experience had occurred. He was convinced that he had reexperienced a basic event of his early childhood where his mother had intruded her presence into his physical and emotional space, forcing him to pay attention to her rather than leaving him free to create. The experience involved a basic way of behaving for his mother. In sessions to follow, we were able to discern that he chose to withdraw from her, in frustration, rather than give in to her demands for attention. A protective outer shell developed to fend off her intrusiveness. His withdrawal into a private world of fantasy became the life-saving device. In his private world he was free to create, safe from intrusion. Although the flame of creativity could not burn brightly in a protective shell, the light did not go out, waiting for some event to rekindle it. The group experience began to melt the protective shell and the flame began to burn brighter.

Intensive Group Experience 5: "The Trial"

The analysis produced a growing desire in Oedipus to separate from the infantile feelings of rage toward the mother.

Group members began to confront Oedipus with his responsibility in holding onto his infantile feelings and his unwillingness to separate from his emotional attachment to his mother. At first, he reacted with anger, but the therapist helped him to assimilate the truth of the group's interpretation.

Oedipus became willing to work through a separation and individuation experience, but he felt that he could not give up his rage until his mother was made to face the crimes she had committed against him. He needed some experience that justice would be served. He would not change unless he felt she was punished for the atrocities committed against him.

Some group members had doubts about the necessity of such a ritual. The therapist was also apprehensive about encouraging an "acting out" of rage and murderous thoughts, but he was willing to accept Oedipus' psychic wisdom in sensing what he needed for a profound and enduring change. The group was encouraged not only to help a family member grow but to use the experience to tap their own primitive needs to seek revenge for the emotional damage they had experienced:

1. An encounter experience was developed whereby Oedipus' mother would face a symbolic trial for her emotional crimes against him; a sentence would be delivered, and a fitting punishment would be carried out. Oedipus, in consultation with the therapist, decided to follow through on the theme of ancient Greece.
2. The mother was on trial through an ancient "Greek Court"; Oedipus the King was the prosecutor; a group member was the mother; another assisted the prosecutor to maintain order; other members were used for jurors.
3. The trial began by a member banishing the "unfriendly spirits" from the court by spraying the room. Each member lit a Jewish Memorial Candle to begin the trial, and then they were arranged in the shape of a cross on a table, as a symbolic means of keeping evil spirits away.
4. The therapist brought in the accused, a symbolic representation of the mother, in the form of a large soft sculpture made by a group member.
5. A group member read a passage from a Chinese scroll (which

Oedipus chose) with the significant passage, "Justice outweighs human life," referring to Oedipus' need to have his mother pay for her crimes.

6. Oedipus' arrival in court was heralded by the therapist, who asked the court to rise and pay homage to "Oedipus the King." He was dressed in a white robe and crown.

7. Oedipus recited a passage from *The Iliad*, in ancient Greek, which described a scene before a battle in the Trojan War. One of the Greek warriors said "He would run away from the enemy if it would save his life, but since it would do no good to run away, he has decided to fight as bravely as he can". Oedipus used an identification with a Greek hero, who was able to deal with a life or death struggle by facing his adversary, to gain symbolic strength to face the struggle with his personal enemy, his negative maternal introject.

8. The charges against the mother were read; her voice was played by a group member. The mother responded "guilty" to all charges. The mother was primarily represented by the soft sculpture; however, during this part of the scenario she was represented by a group member.

9. The jury, after deliberation, sentenced her to "death by stabbing."

10. Each member and the therapist took a cardboard dagger and stabbed the symbolic mother, expressing any feeling or verbalization they wished to accompany the act. Oedipus was the last to act. After stabbing the mother, he dismembered a portion of the symbolic mother sculpture. A small portion of this part was given to all members. In turn, they each took the piece and disposed of it, by throwing it down the incinerator.

11. The encounter ended when members took their memorial candles into another room and participated in the burning of another portion of the symbolic mother figure in a ceremonial fire using the candles, overseen by Oedipus.

Before deciding on the candle-burning ceremony, Oedipus had insisted for several weeks that the only meaningful fire ceremony would be a large fire in a fireplace or a fire in a secluded beach area. The therapist convinced Oedipus that the symbolic nature of the fire ceremony was more significant than its size. Reluctantly he agreed.

As has been mentioned, the analyst also had some misgivings in encouraging and sanctioning an activity which released murderous rage in Oedipus as well as the group. He weighed this issue for several weeks, discussed it with colleagues, and searched the literature for some precedent. Select colleagues did encourage it as a daring and somewhat risky move, but in keeping with the clinical experimentation of the writer's therapeutic work to date. The literature on encounter and marathon group therapy lent clinical support for innovation in group interaction. Finally, the therapist called upon two sources for inspiration. He used Ferenczi as a historical role model for clinical experimentation in a psychoanalytic framework. In addition he used his personal experiences in groups with Asya Kadis and Elizabeth Mintz as models of analysts who experimented with technique in order to help individuals.

This session was the final phase of the action sequence of the therapy and was successful in developing a new way of being. After a lifetime of suffering, withdrawal, and passivity, Oedipus was able to take creative action against the source of his misery. Through the clinical experimentation of the intensive group experience, a symbolic, safe outlet for murderous rage was created. What is more, there was a sharing of the most primitive fantasy of revenge against a parent with a community of caring individuals. In order to cope creatively with such feelings, an active means of dealing with frustration, intrusion, control, oppression, and rage was provided. Oedipus was now faced with a very significant emotional crisis: he no longer could hide behind the facade of being a child victim, but would have to own up to being an adult who could act. The intensive group experience had created a new alternative for him. The individual and group sessions to follow would focus on integrating this new way of being into his everyday functioning.

As a result of the intensive group experiences, a number of significant changes in functioning emerged: greater emotionality was available; there was increased recall of early childhood memories and experiences; transference manifestations became vivid; and there was a growing sense that the core emotional issues were being fully understood and resolved.

The effect of the intensive group experience reverberated throughout the therapy, particularly when the emotional and cognitive breakthroughs that occurred were synthesized into the ongoing analytic process. Therefore, not only did the group sessions reflect these changes, but active measures naturally now became part of the individual therapy.

Intensive Individual Experiences: Hypnotic Regression to the Origins of Maternal Seduction

One day, as Oedipus sat in the therapist's office, he was struck by three sensations: the classical music playing on the waiting room radio, filtering through the hallway; the light and sun streaming through the window; the configurations in the primitive wall hanging at eye level, in front of him.

He began the individual session by saying that he could go into a hypnotic state if he continued to stare at the wall hanging. The therapist was excited by this natural occurrence, feeling that it should be used to therapeutic advantage. We planned to have an encounter experience in a time-extended individual session which would incorporate the three sensations. We felt it would help stimulate the reexperiencing of a childhood event of seduction by his mother, which was the emotional material being explored in his therapy as a result of the intensive group experience.

A three-hour intensive individual session was then scheduled.

In anticipation of the time-extended session, he began to develop a feeling that something significant would break loose; "something to do with my mother; an erotic experience." He was apprehensive and excited. We reexplored early childhood material as a preparation for the special session.

Before the intensive individual session, Oedipus borrowed the therapist's tape recorder and recorded his favorite classical music piece.

The mood and scene for the session combined the three elements of music, alteration of light, and primitive configurations in order to produce a hypnotic effect. As the music played in the background, the room was darkened. He stared at the primitive wall hanging. The only light came from a chemical glow tube that Oedipus held in front of his eyes. He gazed at the glowing light and became transfixed after a minute or so. His eyes closed, his head slumped down, and his body went motionless. He appeared to be in a hypnoticlike trance. The therapist sat to his side, remaining "silently present and supportive." As planned, there would be no intervention during the trance period, unless Oedipus requested it, or the therapist became concerned about emotional flooding or serious regression.

After a moment or two of silence, Oedipus began to speak while in the trancelike state. He began to recall an experience of the first year of life when he was being bathed by his mother. He talked about feeling suffocated as he recalled being enveloped by flesh, body smell, and hair.

He felt pressed against his mother's breast in a way that he could not breathe. She was unaware of his growing difficulty in breathing. He pushed against her, tried to bite her, but she was unmoved. After a pause, he revealed a feeling that his mother was pressing him against her vagina. As he spoke, he was offended by the smell of pubic hair and fleshy mass. He then asked me to move closer to him, so he could touch me. Apparently, he became anxious as he reexperienced a primal feeling of seduction, suffocation, and intrusion. He turned to a positive father figure, whom he knew he could trust and who would protect him against the invasion of the bad mother (an experience he had not had as a child with his distant and unavailable father).

Shortly after this sequence, he terminated the encounter. There was a recovery period of several minutes when he reentered from the trance state and the intense emotional experience. The music was stopped, the lights were turned on, and we began to explore what had transpired.

He associated the geometric designs in the primitive wall hanging to his "mother's cunt." The large, dark-brown triangular design in the wall hanging was actually the stimulus for the hypnotic feeling in the individual session, prior to the intensive individual experience.

Significant changes in intrapsychic and interpersonal functioning occurred as a result of these experiences. Oedipus had dreams where there were positive outcomes of serious conflict. Less ominous authority figures appeared in dreams; "good guys" began to surface. He seemed more connected to being able to make an important change in his life. He seemed connected to developing an idea of a creative career choice, and talked about opening an art gallery. We discussed his wife joining a therapy group and he wasn't concerned about feelings of intrusion as long as she went into a different group from his. Intrapsychically, he appeared less preoccupied with his mother as the ultimate source of his destruction. He promised the therapist he would take him to a famous French restaurant for dinner "when he was cured," because he considered dining at an exceptional restaurant the ultimate human experience.

Conclusion: Personal Growth and Creativity Emerge

Oedipus was able to translate the insights of individual therapy and the action of the group experience into meaningful change that led to growth. Several changes occurred, after the analysis of five intensive group experiences, which gave hope of fulfilling the capacities of Freud's definition of a self-actualized individual; the ability to love, to work, and to play.

1. Oedipus lessened his passive adaptation, which had led to a weakened identity as a disabled individual. For the first time in his life, he began to own that he was not constitutionally damaged. Where, in the past, he both abhorred sports and physical activity, he now desired to be physically active. After a series of attempts at some athletic activities suggested by the analyst, he enrolled in a gym and began training to develop body strength and overall physical fitness. "To be strong rather than weak," became his motto. He became devoted to going to the gym and, soon thereafter, convinced his wife to follow his lead.

2. At last, the capacity to be creative was released. An interest

in photography, which was once a faint desire, developed into a full-fledged enterprise. He enrolled in a fine arts college to earn a degree in photography. He shared his creative work with the group. The newly found creativity was assimilated into the therapy by use of an intensive individual experience (see Rachman, 1985). The possibility for a creative work experience became a reality and he contemplated a career as a photographer. After completing his undergraduate studies, he applied to one of the most competitive graduate programs in photography. His portfolio of fifteen photographs was reviewed and he was accepted for study. He is approaching the establishment of an alternate career where his creative self will more fully emerge.

3. As he became freer of his childhood tie to his mother, he began to complain about his relationship with his wife. The relationship came under intense scrutiny, as he realized that it had elements of his relationship with his mother. For the first time, he became aware of the negative elements in this relationship which were contributing to his lack of change and growth. He was willing to own that he had contributed to his wife's stagnation as well as his own. He had created a marriage, whereby he would be taken care of, much the way his mother had catered to him. His wife, because of her emotional problems, used the situation to regress. Oedipus' desire and capacity to individuate now signaled that the relationship needed a change. The therapist encouraged Oedipus to both share his negative reactions to his wife and own his part in the difficulty. He needed to translate the capacity to confront the "bad mother" he had developed in group, into his real life experience with his wife.

He began to encourage her to return to work, to improve her physical appearance, and to develop creative outlets for her natural artistic talents. The issue of homosexual feelings reemerged when he became angry at his wife, as she reminded him of his own mother. Through direct confrontation with her, and continued exploration of his need for fathering, dreams began to appear with positive themes of reaching out to male father figures.

4. After much persuasion and an eleventh-hour threat to end the marriage, his wife agreed to enter couple therapy. This has proven to be a remarkably salutary experience for both

parties. The wife has, for the first time, had a positive therapy experience. In the safety of her relationship with her husband, and with a special attempt at empathetic understanding by the therapist (he translated the awareness of several previously unsuccessful therapy experiences and her own intense fear of change into a corrective emotional experience). She began to develop comfort in exploring her personal issues as well as the ones in the marriage.

She became very concerned one day about her continued inability to perform some of the details of her work as a book restorer. When the analyst inquired about her difficulty in functioning, he assessed her problem to be a perceptual-motor one. A referral to a perceptual retraining professional was arranged. After several months of retraining, her problems subsided and her work improved significantly. Oedipus was impressed with the improvement and felt intuitively that the perceptual exercises tapped a primal level of functioning. He decided to enroll in the perceptual retraining program. Oedipus' participation has not produced the dramatic changes that his wife enjoyed. We are now attempting to integrate the effects of the retraining into the analysis.

References

Alexander, F., & French, T. (1949), *Psychoanalytic Therapy*. New York: Ronald Press.
Balint, M. (1968), *The Basic Fault: Therapeutic Aspects of Regression*. London: Tavistock Publications.
Binswanger, L. (1963), *Being-in-the-World: Selected Papers of Ludwig Binswanger*. New York: Basic Books.
Boss, M. (1963), *Psychoanalysis and Daseinanalysis*. New York: Basic Books.
Buber, M. (1937), *I and Thou*. Edinburgh: R & R Clark.
Buie, D. H., & Adler, G. (1972), The use of confrontation with borderline patients. *Internat. J. Psychoanal., Psychother.*, 1/3:90–108.
Corwin, H. A. (1972), The scope of therapeutic confrontation from routine to heroic. *Internat. J. Psycho-Anal.*, 1:3, 68–89.
Dubska-Papiasvili, E., Rachman, A. W., & Papiasvili, A. (1982), Action techniques in residential therapeutic communities for neurotics. *Internat. J. Therapeut. Commun.*, 2/2:90–100.
Durkin, H. E. (1964), *The Group in Depth*. New York: International Universities Press.
Erikson, E. H. (1959), *Identity and the Life Cycle*. New York: International Universities Press, 1980.

Fairbairn, W. R. D. (1954), *An Object-Relations Theory of Personality*. New York: Basic Books.
Ferenczi, S. (1919a), On the technique of psycho-analysis. In: *Further Contribution to the Theory and Technique of Psycho-Analysis*, ed. J. Ruckman. New York: Basic Books, 1952, pp. 177–189.
────── (1919b), Technical difficulties in the analysis of a case of hysteria. In: *Further Contributions to the Theory and Technique of Psycho-Analysis*, ed. J. Ruckman. New York: Basic Books, 1952, pp. 189–197.
────── (1920), The further development of an active therapy in psycho-analysis. In: *Further Contributions to the Theory and Technique of Psycho-Analysis*, ed. J. Ruckman. New York: Basic Books, 1952, pp. 198–217.
────── (1925), Contra-indications to the 'active' psycho-analytical technique. In: *Further Contributions to the Theory and Technique of Psycho-Analysis*, ed. J. Ruckman. New York: Basic Books, pp. 217–230.
────── (1928), The elasticity of psycho-analytic technique. In: *The Problems and Methods of Psycho-Analysis*, ed. M. Balint. New York: Basic Books, 1955, pp. 87–102.
────── (1930), The principles of relaxation and neocatharsis. In: *The Problems and Methods of Psycho-Analysis*, ed. M. Balint. New York: Basic Books, 1955, pp. 108–126.
────── (1933), Confusion of tongues between adults and the child. In: *The Problems and Methods of Psycho-Analysis*, ed. M. Balint. New York: Basic Books, 1955.
────── Rank, D. (1925), *The Development of Psychoanalysis*. Madison, CT: International Universities Press, 1986.
Freud, S. (1915), Further recommendations in the technique of psycho-analysis. *Collected Papers*, Vol. II. New York: Basic Books, 1959, pp. 377–391.
────── (1919 [1918]), Lines of advance in psychoanalytic therapy. *Standard Edition*, 17:157–168. London: The Hogarth Press, 1955.
Garner, H. H. A. (1959), Confrontation technique used in psychotherapy. *Amer. J. Psychother.*, 13/1:18–34.
Greenson, R. R. (1967), *The Technique and Practice of Psychoanalysis*. New York: International Universities Press.
Greenwald, H., ed. (1967), *Active Psychotherapy*. New York: Atherton Press.
Goldberg, A., ed. (1978), *The Psychology of the Self: A Casebook*. New York: International Universities Press.
Grotjohn, M. (1977), *The Art and Technique of Analytic Group Therapy*. New York: Jason Aronson.
Guntrip, H. J. S. (1961), *Personality Structure and Human Interaction: The Developing Synthesis of Psychodynamic Theory*. New York: International Universities Press.
Gutheil, E. A. (1951), *The Handbook of Dream Analysis*. New York: Liverright.
Kadis, A. L. (1974), *Practicum of Group Psychotherapy*, 2nd ed. Hagerstown, MD: Harper & Row.
Knobloch, F., & Knobloch, J. (1979), *Integrated Psychotherapy*. New York: Aronson.
Kohut, H. (1971), *The Analysis of the Self*. New York: International Universities Press.
Lomas, P. (1978), *True and False Experience: The Human Element in Psychotherapy*. New York: Taplinger.

Masserman, J. (1955), *Dynamic Psychiatry*. Philadelphia: W. B. Saunders.
May, R., Angel, E., & Ellenberger, H. F., eds. (1958), *Existence: A New Dimension in Psychiatry and Psychology*. New York: Basic Books.
Mintz, E. (1971), *Marathon Groups: Reality and Symbol*. New York: Appleton-Century-Crofts.
Moreno, J. L. (1941), Open letter to group psychotherapists. *Sociometry*, 1/1.
—— (1963), Reflections on my method of group psychotherapy and psychodrama. In: *Active Psychotherapy*, ed. H. Greenwald. New York: Atherton Press, 1967.
Rachman, A. W. (1969–1970), Marathon group psychotherapy: Its origin, significance and direction. *J. Group Psychoanal. & Proc.*, 2/2:57–74.
—— (1975a), Humanistic encounter. *Psychother.: Theor., Res., Prac.*, 12/3:249–254.
—— (1975b), Issue of countertransference in encounter and marathon group psychotherapy. In: *Group Therapy. 1975: An Overview*, eds. L. R. Wolberg & M. L. Aronson. New York: Stratton Intercontinental Medical Book.
—— (1978), The first "encounter" session: Ferenczi's case of the female Croatian musician. Paper presented at the American Group Psychotherapy Association Conference, New Orleans, LA.
—— (1979), Active psychoanalysis and the group encounter. In: *Group Therapy 1979: An Overview*, eds. L. R. Wolberg & M. Aronson. New York: Stratton Intercontinental Medical Book.
—— (1981), Humanistic analysis in groups. *Psychother.: Theor., Res., & Prac.*, 18/4:457–477.
—— (1985), *Oedipus from Brooklyn: A Study in Psychological Survival* (Unpublished manuscript).
Rado, S. (1962), *Psychoanalysis of Behavior*. New York: Grune & Stratton.
Rogers, C. R. (1961), *On Becoming a Person*. Boston: Houghton Mifflin.
—— (1970), *On Encounter Groups*. New York: Harper & Row.
—— (1975), Empathetic: An unappreciated way of being. *Counsel. Psychol.*, 5/2:2–9.
—— (1980), *A Way of Being*. Boston: Houghton Mifflin.
Slavson, S. L. (1955), A preliminary note on the relation of psychodrama and group psychotherapy. *Internat. J. Group Psychother.*, 5:361–366.
Stekel, W. (1950), *Conditions of Nervous Anxiety and Their Treatment*. London: Routledge & Kegan Paul.
Stoller, F. H. (1968), Accelerated interaction: A time-limited approach based on the brief, intensive group. *Internat. J. Group Psychother.*, 31/3:319–329.
Truax, C. B., & Carkhuff, R. R. (1967), *Toward Effective Counseling and Psychotherapy: Training and Practice*. Chicago: Aldine.
Winnicott, D. W. (1958), *Through Pediatrics to Psychoanalysis*. London: Tavistock Publications.
Wolberg, L. R. (1977), *The Technique of Psychotherapy*, 3rd ed. New York: Grune & Stratton.
Yalom, I. D. (1975), *The Theory and Practice of Group Psychotherapy*, 2nd ed. New York: Basic Books.

Part II
AUXILIARY TREATMENT MODALITIES AND RESEARCH CONCERNS

Chapter 16

PSYCHODRAMATIC TECHNIQUES IN WORK WITH BORDERLINE PATIENTS

JAMES M. SACKS, PH.D.

Frame of Reference

A conscientious colleague recently informed me that he had "stopped working with borderline patients in group when [he could] . . . no longer entrust them to the 'tender mercies' of a mass of predictably confrontative patients, unrestrained by professional ethics or training." Due, in whatever proportions, to some genuine shift in our culture or merely to a change in the way patient behavior is conceptualized, the borderline diagnosis has become widespread. Clinicians such as my colleague must withhold any potential benefits of group treatment from a considerable proportion of their clients if, indeed, they can even compose borderline-free groups in a limited practice. The case studies and psychodramatic techniques described in this chapter are designed to help extend the applicability of group therapy to these especially vulnerable persons.

For the purpose of this chapter, borderline behavior will be considered behavior that stems from what Laing (1964) characterizes as "ontological insecurity"; that is, behavior that is the consequence of a pervasive uncertainty about one's own existence (p. 140 ff). Following Laing's premise, the exigencies of early life induce some infants or young children to protect themselves from a dangerous or dangerously withholding environment by dissociating themselves from it. To avoid psychological extinction, they erect a "false self" to adapt to external demands and to conduct their behavior while their "true self" backs away into a purely mental world, insulated from the perilous events of material reality.

This safety, however, is illusory because the self-imposed isolation results in a net weakening of security by emotional impoverishment. As the "true self" no longer interacts with real people and objects, it is slowly starved of the gratification which reality alone can provide. It also loses any means of checking on its hopes and fears, which tend to proliferate chaotically. The ordinary events of life come to be seen against the background of exaggerated and terrifying risks to survival even while the "false self" continues, more or less successfully, to go through the motions of living.

So long as the "false self" structure remains intact, and for the most part it is stable throughout life, the borderline status is maintained. Laing sees a reemergence of the "true self," now distorted after a long suppression, as what appears clinically as the horrors of frank psychosis. Yet, in order to help revive the patient as a real person, effective therapy with the borderline must establish contact with the "true self" and nurture it into genuine relationship. High risk is thus entailed and, since group treatment is under less control than individual treatment, the therapist must proceed with special sensitivity and prudence.

"Psychodrama" refers here to the group treatment techniques originated by J. L. Moreno (1964) that consist of improvised dramatizations in which the patients enact roles related to their problems. Psychodrama, like all drama, occupies an intermediate position between the purely mental world of fantasy and the actions of real life (Sacks, 1981). As in life, the players speak aloud and move about but, as in fantasy, the events are contained within a system walled off from its natural consequences. The players "pretend"; the action is not "for real," "doesn't count," or is "only a play."

Role-Playing and the False Self

The parallel between the role-playing system of psychodrama and the "false self" system of the borderline, enables these patients to work within rules analogous to their own. Precisely because he is "only pretending" in the psychodrama scenes, the borderline patient feels safer expressing "true self" feelings than he would in the more real relationships of a conventional group. Though the conventional group is also shielded from many of the consequences of outside life, the borderline patient may feel that too much is at stake, even in that setting.

Artificiality

The artificiality of the "false self" of certain borderline patients is so obvious that the other members of the therapy group either shun them or denounce them mercilessly as "phony." These patients are as unpopular as a clothed man in a nudist colony. For the nudists, still ambivalent about their own exposure, the dressed intruder reminds them that others do *not* necessarily feel safe in their cloistered world. Perhaps, then, it really *is* dangerous to be so visible. If the dressed one is right, the nudists might have to relinquish their special freedom. Also, the dressed man may be the very one who constitutes the danger, staring down at them in judgment from his seat of safety. Perhaps the group's most common reaction is a zealous wish to convert. This group pressure, though essentially aggressive, is disguised as an altruistic attempt to confer freedom.

One such borderline patient walked with a measured, almost military gait, and affected a loud, deep voice. He gave interpretations of the other members' behavior with a contrived authority. The role had somehow been convincing enough to control his subordinates at work but he could gain no respect from the group. At first they confronted him directly about his manner but this set him off into such angry defensiveness that they soon abandoned their attempts to unmask him. Instead they merely ignored or humored him.

A psychodrama scene was used to enhance both the patient's and the group's appreciation of the function of his facade. After a gradual warm-up (Sacks and Weiner, 1969) in which several other group members portrayed themselves as children, the patient was invited to assume the role of himself as a 7-year-old. In this scene he was directed to respond as powerfully as necessary to deter the taunts of the neighborhood bully who had menaced him at that age. He ordered the bully about with angry shouts. He showed an even more exaggerated form of aggressiveness than that which he had exhibited in his natural behavior in the group. Now, however, the group supported his "self-assertion," seen as appropriate within the drama. After some reassurance from the success of his actions and from the group support, he agreed to show us how the "sissy" of their latency-age gang behaved, although he despised the "sissy" as much as the bully. Initially he attempted only to ridicule the "sissy" by stereotyping his behavior, but as the scene continued he was drawn deeper into the role. When he tried to expose the "sissy's" repulsive cowardice, the other players were directed to offer him understanding and consolation. After some time he gratefully accepted the solicitude of the benevolent gym teacher and spoke touchingly about his fear of the other boys. When he returned to the role of himself at 7, he confessed his own fears and admitted his attempt to "put up a front."

After the drama, no direct reference was made to the patient's usual behavior in the group but associations were elicited from the other members about how and when they, too, had felt the need to feign confidence. The group seemed relieved by the relaxation of the patient's chronic bravado and readily admitted similar experiences.

Within the security of the "pretend" nature of the enactment, first in an ego-syntonic, "strong" role, then in the role of the vulnerable other, and, finally, in his own more genuine "weak" self, the patient both experienced and exposed bits of his real attitudes which were otherwise hidden. While facilitating the emergence of these "true self" components was essential to the therapeutic influence of the experience, a negative therapeutic reaction of humiliation was always close at hand. This was reduced by postponing interpretation. The patient was removed from group scrutiny, and the therapist broke in to shift the focus to the empathic vulnerability of the other members. A less fragile patient might have been left to deal with the spontaneous group reactions but his tolerance for feeling "weak" had been exhausted. He was clearly so vigilant and vulnerable at that moment that if an aggressive or insensitive member had used the occasion to draw attention to the soft core beneath his hard authority, the protagonist would surely have been mortified, retreated, and become more impenetrable than ever. Such an experience would have confirmed his fear that "true self" exposure is punished. By joining in the self-exposing process, the group created an atmosphere that highlighted the value of his openness and implicitly credited his courage for leading them in this direction. Similar scenes with different content were directed with this patient on later occasions. Acknowledging his need for artificial strength within the drama helped in the transition toward acknowledging his need for artificial strength within the group and in life. During this transition, I continued to intervene from time to time to inhibit confrontational overdosage or to bring the group's attention back to the patient if they reverted to ignoring him.

Passivity and Inhibition

Another frequent manifestation of borderline patients is exaggerated passivity and inhibition of initiative. Such patients cannot free associate in individual therapy. There, they may remain silent for long periods or engage a therapist who is committed to a passive role, in a contest of wills over who must speak first. They sometimes openly request to be asked questions, which they dutifully answer, but they require repeated prodding with fresh questions in order to continue. They may be unable to change the subject if the therapist introduces any lead. Should the therapist inquire off-handedly about the patient's recovery from his cold at the previous session, the patient may spend the remainder of the hour discussing his health regardless of what else might be preying on his mind. In group, such patients frequently withdraw. The others are usually more interested in their own problems than in drawing out the reticent member. He may project his exclusion onto their lack of concern or masochistically convince himself that their problems are more important than his. The borderline aspect of this form of withdrawal in group is based on the intensity of the striving to conceal personal need in favor of fulfilling the requirements of the environment. The "false self" can be active in compliance but dare not initiate lest it reveal an autonomous will. Inertia and passivity are intrinsic in these borderline characters. Laing (1964) states that this type of person "abhors action" which, as he draws from Hegel, commits the individual to the "objective element" and pins him to reality. Action is contrary to their preference to remain, like Hamlet, "all thought and potentiality," free of any definitive evidence of who they really are, as attested to by what they do (p. 92 ff.). At the same time, the chronic denial of impulse gives rise to an accumulation of longing for self-directed behavior, which Moreno (1964) terms "act hunger" (p. 65). The individual is trapped between dammed up wishes to act as himself versus terror lest he be discovered through his deeds. Because action in the dramatic format is only action *in potentia*, psychodrama can serve as a vehicle for the passive, borderline person to experiment with this very action about which he is so ambivalent. The Walter Mitty character may be able to act in the fictional psychodrama world before being able to tolerate reality testing in life.

For use with markedly act-avoidant patients for whom even the pretend nature of psychodramatic action is insufficient protection, Moreno (1959) described the "mirror" technique. In this process another group member enacts the role of the protagonist while the inhibited patient watches. Later, if the latter so wishes, he may comment on the play about his life which he has just witnessed. For Laing, the "true self" continues to retain the functions of observation and fantasy even after the function of action has been relegated to the "false self." The unembodied "true self" becomes purely an onlooker rather than a participant in all that the body does. The mirror technique, then, is entirely commensurate with the borderline patient's proclivities and induces relatively little anxiety. Even very withdrawn, action-shy patients seem fascinated watching their lives played out by another person, so long as they are not pressed to take part. This freedom to remain passive often reduces the threat of exposure sufficiently so that the latent "act hunger" comes into ascendancy. The observing patient then frequently wishes to correct the actor, who he usually feels is misrepresenting him. He may try to direct the play from the sidelines to improve its accuracy. Under slight guidance by the therapist, the patient may demonstrate how he wishes his role to be played, thus joining in the action by degrees.

Another technique, helpful to the passivity-prone borderline, is a structured go-around procedure in which purely mental, then verbal, and finally action exercises are suggested by the director. Emphasis is placed on the voluntary nature of any participation. The members are urged to "pass" if they feel disinclined to participate for any reason whatever. Thus they are required neither to put themselves forward by volunteering, since participation is by turns, nor to choose their own behavior, which has been prescribed by the structured exercise. Sometimes they may pass for a few rounds until they have seen others participate without disastrous results—the others testing reality for them, as it were. This establishes a field in which the borderline patient may avoid the danger of excessive self-directed action while still providing the opportunity for as much initiative as he can genuinely bear. The chronically silent borderline patient can begin to take part by this indirect route.

Occasionally, in a kind of all-or-none effect, a passive borderline patient may, after a long period of observing, burst forth into a drama of great intensity. He may then regret what he has exposed and retreat more than ever. Still worse, he could decompensate. I know of one (but only one) case in which a heavy-handed psychodrama triggered a psychotic episode. The director not only is responsible for helping to influence group conditions that facilitate the emergence of "true self" elements and autonomous action within the safety of the dramatic format, but he is equally responsible for helping the internally polarized borderline to modulate his activity.

Underachievement

Another way in which action deficiency is manifested in the borderline is by gross underachievement. Certain of these patients were the offspring of high achieving parents with equally high expectations for their children. The children came to feel that nothing they could accomplish would satisfy the parental standards. They tended to make false starts but stopping short of completion which they feared would reveal their inadequacy according to the internalized requirements. They expect that actions are more likely to be judged when they are finished.

Typical of this group was Allen, who was hailed as a child prodigy by his proud father. The father's own ambition had brought him success and power, but this father's attainments could not slake the insatiable narcissistic thirst that required a son befitting such a father. He molded Allen into this idealized role by flattery and tyrannical commands. He dichotomized Allen's future as either "genius" or "bum." To complicate this demand to be a parental extension, the father, paradoxically, was also threatened by Allen's early successes and saw in his son a dangerous rival. He belittled Allen's accomplishments, ostensibly because they were insufficient, but often, actually, because they were excessive. The father betrayed his envy by outdoing his son in Allen's own arenas. The father being politically conservative, Allen joined the left. The father then reconsidered his own position and became a leader in the same left political faction in which Allen had been aspiring for recognition. Allen's mother contributed to the high expectations, hoping her son might help her compensate vicariously for being subordinated to the domineering husband. Until college, Allen was basically successful in his parents' terms, although he experienced little gratification from his A's, plaudits, and popularity. He had chosen and won the perfect girl friend but found himself sexually impotent and uninterested in spending time with her. In college, sensing that "real life" was to begin shortly, Allen shifted from major to major, with steadily declining grades. He entered three different graduate schools, achieved initial success in each, then lost interest and withdrew entirely. Yielding to family pressure, Allen unenthusiastically married the perfect girl friend and soon impregnated her. He made only half-hearted attempts to support his wife and baby. Allen took each bill to his father, who angrily reproved his n'er-do-well son, then paid it to preserve the family image.

Allen's emotional life was uniformly bland. He experienced little conscious guilt about his idleness and only subdued resentment over his wife's nagging. At her urging, he tried several behavioral therapies but soon abandoned these regimens as he had the academic and vocational ones.

In his psychodramas, also, Allen acted in the way he felt was expected of him, which was, usually, to show anger toward his parents. But in the discussions afterward, he confessed that he was lazy and probably deserved their scorn. These guilt feelings, however, were also proclaimed with little conviction. A major advance in Allen's psychodrama work finally occurred in an extended confrontation with himself (played by another group member). Here the focus of his accusation was not his laziness but rather his ambition. He excoriated himself for being so "weak" as to follow a whole life plan whch was not his own. He was irate at the overcompliant Allen who had betrayed him. He berated the alter ego playing the "false self" who had acquiesced and accepted the "genius" model. He hated himself, not for failing or for hating his parents, but for going along with them as much as he had. He was afraid that he had forever lost the ability to want. Since his father had co-opted his achievements, Allen felt that he had sacrificed himself to please his father and it hadn't even worked. Since his mother flaunted his accomplishments as if she had done them herself, even potential achievements came to be feared as providing more fuel for being emotionally exploited. Not only success, but the very act of striving represented selling his soul and receiving nothing in the bargain. The only solution was to make of himself someone who desires nothing and who will become nothing. All ambition represented a loss of selfhood.

After the scene of self-confrontation Allen was more able to apprehend the rationale of his genius–bum complex, the bum being the only role that contained any integrity. The understanding of his own lassitude in this context seemed to engender more tolerance for it and more freedom from it. The group also became able to recognize analogous mechanisms in themselves, where they existed, and reduced their fruitless demands on Allen to get a job.

Grandiosity

Both narcissistic and borderline self-esteem is frequently founded on a superlative but brittle fantasy of passive power.

Passivity functions to insulate the grandiosity from reality testing. But exactly because psychodrama is not reality it can facilitate a return to the action mode. Scenes can be set which temporarily indulge fantastic powers but implicitly underscore their separation from real life. Scenes can also be set which explore fears in a context in which the protagonist can escape by dismissing his demons at will. The queen may say, "Off with her head!" but Alice can reply that her persecutors are only a "pack of cards." The action of the drama is delimited by the edge of the psychodrama stage and by the beginning and ending of scenes. The reality of the group and outside life are represented, but not actually present in the play.

Protected by these reassurances, one passive–aggressive borderline patient created a scene in an Islamic heaven where he lay on a couch waited on by a harem of adoring virgins. This was succeeded at a later date by a scene in which he climbed onto the balcony and delivered godlike pronouncements to his family. Grandiosity, cultivated by extended maternal indulgence in early childhood, had been a habitual regressive refuge when both parents later placed excessive demands for worldly success on him. In his fantasies, made vivid and visible in his dramas, he enjoyed an other-worldly success far above any they could have imagined for him on earth. His supercilious superiority in the balcony scene was another version of the quiet disdain with which he normally regarded the other members of the group. Now, however, he was actively exposing the very arrogance he had previously hidden or rationalized. The value of these self-indulgent scenes lay in the very absurdity of their excess. Later, when he began to insist, for example, that he ought to be in a different group since the others were all "too sick" for him, he spontaneously checked himself and acknowledged that he was "up on the balcony again." Seeing this pattern in himself helped him mitigate his habitual withdrawal into superiority.

Thought Disorder

When borderline behavior manifests itself as a disorder in the thinking process, the effects in the group are usually very alienating for the patient. Typical was a young woman who spoke with obvious sincerity but, because of a subtle incoherence in language, inevitably lost the group's interest. So minimal was the group's response that I often had to rescue her by providing or eliciting reactions to prevent her from counterabandoning the group and reverting to silence. She had the habit of explaining her ideas and feelings in disjunct bits, always shifting away from the central theme before her point had been made. While the group generally liked her, they were unable to follow her meandering narrations or vague abstractions. She never seemed to feel that she belonged since she was, in fact, so rarely understood.

Shifting to a psychodrama format with this patient, the group became involved in taking roles in the scenes, which revived their attention at once. Her reenactments of a traumatic separation from her sister and a homosexual overture by an older cousin, were carried along by the temporal sequence of the action. The protagonist, supported by the group's involvement and by the plot line, engaged in fully directional behavior that was both cognitively cohesive and emotionally intense. Later, the memory of such scenes and their meaning for the other patients forged empathic links which served to integrate her into the group. These patches of coherence from the dramas served as points of reference to help give meaning to her disjunctive comments when she reverted to her former style.

On Being Seen

Laing (1964) describes the borderline patient's dilemma of, on the one hand, wanting to confirm his existence by having other people see and know him, and on the other hand, fearing that being seen will result in annihilation of his frail self by hostile others, armed with new knowledge of his whereabouts and needs. Laing asserts that, to such an individual, "every pair of eyes is in a Medusa's head which he feels has the power actually to kill him" (p. 113). Careful technique is required to negotiate between the intense need to be seen, on the one hand, and the intense terror of being seen on the other (Sacks, 1977).

One taciturn patient commonly sat motionless in the most

inconspicuous corner and observed the group intently. He once reported that it was his habit, whenever he entered a room with strangers, to station himself in a position where he could observe the others in a mirror or some other shiny surface, without himself being seen directly. He had literally availed himself of Perseus' own method of nullifying the Medusa's death-gaze while still retaining his own vigil. Another borderline patient described changing a tire beside a busy highway. Despite soiling his clothes, having mechanical problems with the car jack, and being late for an appointment, his primary concern was making sure that the people in the cars streaking past did not notice any facial expression or body movement that might betray his tension or distress. He strained to keep a poker face and to affect smooth, pseudocalm movements.

Such fears of being seen and understood, especially one's points of vulnerability, are obviously a severe impediment to the patient's communication, even in the haven of individual therapy where bits of "good parent" transference may be carefully cultured. How, then, can such a patient be expected to expose his "true self" in a group of other patients, any of whom could turn the slightest revelation into a weapon against him? And isn't it even more unlikely that such persons would experience being a featured star on a psychodrama stage as gratifying or therapeutic? And yet they do. The extreme shyness of these patients is inevitably matched by a coexisting, equally intense craving to be seen. These borderline patients, usually so avoidant of attention, less consciously but no less ardently hope that by becoming an object in the real world for other people, they can be reassured that they themselves are real. It is this wish that can be harnessed in the service of treatment. The borderline patient can be distinguished from the neurotic exhibitionist by the intensity with which they need, rather than merely crave to be in the awareness of others. For the neurotic attention addict, constant gratification is antitherapeutic, but for those who are existentially terrified, cautious facilitation of their visibility can bring a progressive strengthening of identity. These patients need help, not only in apprehending who they are, but also that they are.

Many months of individual treatment with Joseph, the patient who watched in the mirror, were augmented with treatment in a psychodrama group where progress occurred beyond any that I was able to make with him alone. His treatment in the group proceeded through several phases. The first necessity was to reassure him that his role would be confined to observation for as long as he wished. In order to smooth the way for the group's indulgence of his reticence, I complimented the group for the respect they had accorded to others who had not yet been ready to participate actively. It required three months of silent observation for Joseph to trust that self-exposure was not punished but actually reinforced by the group ethic. He also seemed to become more secure that the dramas were at a safe enough remove from real life.

The potential shock of Joseph's first participation as a protagonist was attenuated by the content of the scene. The wish to hide, was itself the featured element. He was placed on the stage behind a screen with a hole through which he could peek out at the "audience" who were chatting informally. Yet it was he who was on stage. He knew and accepted that he was the real protagonist. After some quiet observing, a "double" joined him in his hiding place to verbalize some of the thoughts and feelings he experienced while watching and listening. The psychodrama "double" sits behind or beside the protagonist and speaks, not in the role of another person but as the protagonist himself (Moreno, 1959). The double helped break the ice by speaking first, so that Joseph had only to confirm or deny the double's contentions. The double avoided referring to any areas of vulnerability or to wishes for attention. Joseph was more accustomed to interacting with himself in inner conversation than to conversing with others and was remarkably able to accept this psychodrama convention. A "soliloquy" took place in which the double generally joined the resistance side in any intrapsychic conflicts while Joseph made increasingly feeling-laden statements (Moreno, 1959).

After several, ever-so-cautious experiences of being protagonist, Joseph quite suddenly burst out of his restraint. Despite the precautions designed to retard emotional inundation, the catharsis was intense and abrupt, driven by a dammed-up passion to be understood. Joseph reenacted a scene following an automobile accident in which he alone was injured, especially on his face. He knew that he would remain scarred for life on that part of his body not covered by clothes, which exhibited his identity to the world, and which most expressed or hid his emotions. According to Joseph's version of what happened, his brother had been driving and had caused the accident. Joseph was named as the driver and blamed. In the hospital, Joseph endured the accusations of his family without defending himself. He then continued, now insistently, to reproduce a series of earlier family scenes in which he was abused both physically and emotionally. His role in each was stoic and silent. He had come to believe that any show of suffering would be seen as whimpering by his father and brother and feed their sadistic rage. He, and most of the group as well, wept throughout. After the drama, he lay exhausted on the floor. It had not been possible to allow this material to come out in a more gradual way without an even more disturbing interruption of his emotional flow. Once begun, he seemed bound to relive it all at once. If Joseph had had the capacity to deliver himself of this burden more slowly, he might have worked it through in measured portions in his individual sessions, but he never touched these traumatic memories (or screen memories) when alone with me. Modeling by the others, the appeal of group attention, the lesser intimacy of group life, and the drama format seemed to have been facilitating conditions for the catharsis.

At the next group meeting we discussed the emotional aftermath of the previous session. The discussion was purposefully kept general in order to take the spotlight off Joseph to allow him to rest from the heavy exposure. Concentrating on the others' reactions helped him gain some needed distance from his traumatic memories. Focusing on his feelings about his feelings (embarrassment upon returning, for example) instead of immediately again on the feelings themselves, also helped him gain some perspective and reduced the overwhelming nature of the memories. This indirect focus also offset the tendency for postcathartic resuppression. (Patients, individually and in groups, sometimes speak in the session immediately following a very painful one, without making any reference to the cathartic content whatever, as if the whole thing had never happened.)

Joseph had fluctuated between elation and depression in the days immediately after the cathartic session. On balance he wished he had never brought it up. Only after several months did his attitude reverse itself after which time he then claimed that it had saved his sanity. In any case, Joseph spoke readily in the group thereafter.

Summary

Psychodrama is useful as a mediating arena for the fragile borderline patient caught between the risks of overexposure in a dangerous reality and slow emotional decomposition in isolation. Special psychodramatic techniques can be used to modulate the degree of action and reality which the borderline personality can tolerate and to prepare the group atmosphere so that tentative attempts of expression are protected.

Several cases were described to illustrate the value of psychodrama in integrating the borderline patient into the psychotherapy group and facilitating his participation. Psychodramatic techniques are designed to provide safety through structure (such as the go-around warm-up and noninterpretive sharing after the drama) and through establishing a benevolent group atmosphere. Before the drama these techniques facilitate self-expression, and after the drama diminish the risk of the humiliation of overexposure. The artificiality inherent in drama offers a natural arena for those patients who feel secure only in "false self" behavior but where they may more toward authenticity. The "mirror" technique allows the action-inhibited, borderline patient to observe others testing reality for him. The dramatic action gives focus to those borderline patients whose speech and thought distortions confuse themselves and the group. The group therapist may use psychodrama cautiously with borderline patients who suffer from extreme fear of exposure. Here the psychodrama director may enlist the patient's opposing wish to confirm his existence by being seen and known. Some borderline underachievers may, in scenes of self-confrontation, gain insight into, and control over, existential guilt for failing to live as their "true self." The disdainful patient, withdrawn into superiority, has an opportunity to fulfill his grandiosity so fully in the setting of the drama, that its exaggerated quality may become apparent, even to himself.

Psychodrama provides a setting in which action, usually excluded from the therapy situation and often from the living patterns of borderline persons, can be sampled in degrees commensurate with the patient's defensive needs and where he can rehearse in the shelter of the artificial microcosm of the stage.

References

Laing, R. D. (1964), *The Divided Self*. New York: Pantheon.
Moreno, J. L. (1959), Psychodrama. In: *American Handbook of Psychiatry*, Vol. 2, ed. S. Arieti. New York: Basic Books, pp. 1375–1396.
——— (1964), *Psychodrama*, Vol. 1. New York: Beacon House.
Sacks, J. M. (1977), The need for subtlety: A critical session with a suicidal child. *Psychother.: Theory, Res. & Prac.*, 14:434–437.
——— (1981), Drama therapy with the acting-outpatient. In: *Drama in Therapy*, Vol. 2, eds. G. Schattner & R. Courtney. New York: Drama Book Specialists, pp. 35–45.
——— Weiner, H. (1969), Warm-up and sum-up. *Group Psychother.*, 22:85–102.

Chapter 17

DUAL ANALYTIC THERAPY WITH SPOUSE COTHERAPISTS: PERSPECTIVES ON THE BORDERLINE MARRIAGE

JOHN P. BRIGGS, M.D.
MURIEL A. BRIGGS, M.A.

In this chapter, we shall describe our conjoint psychoanalytic treatment of couples in a private practice setting. The four-way, two-marriage sessions (patient-couple and therapist-couple) are generally 1½ hours (a double session). In the initial phases of treatment, we meet as often as schedules permit over a period usually averaging one to two years. Subsequently, sessions are held once weekly. Four-way sessions are supplemented, on a "whenever necessary" basis, by dyadic sessions. We do not usually see other family members, but they may be asked in for sessions when the whole family can benefit from what the couple is working through. Ostensibly, our object is treatment of the marital crisis. We consider this modality effective even in cases where we may feel the marriage will not continue, but where its dissolution might be accomplished with less bitterness and acting out between the partners, and greater long-term involvement with the children by both parents.

On a deeper level, our objective is the analysis of old patterns of transference and countertransference as they connect with each spouse's history of responses to their families of origin.

Most couples who seek marital help, and indeed a good many therapists, proceed on the assumption that a marriage is a rather clear-cut psychosocial entity; this assumption is revealed in the mechanistic language one hears about marriage needing to be "repaired," "fixed," or "adjusted." Therapy based on this assumption aims at reexperiencing early childhood disjunctive family systems, resolving separation from parents, fostering behavioral compromises (so that marriage partners can live together), learning new adaptive marital skills, and readjusting earlier marriage "contracts."

Master's and Johnson's landmark work on treatment of the psychopathology of sexual function in marriage unfortunately lent weight to the notion that all of the problems of marriage might be remedied by learning adjustments and behavioral-modifying techniques. If one assumes that a marriage is essentially a partnership governed by psychological and psychosocial contracts, unwritten rules, roles, gender positionings, and power operations, then treatment must address issues. But psychoanalysis has revealed that this view of human relationships as closed systems of rules and roles (necessarily subject to the laws of entropy) is, in fact, a source of relationship problems, not a solution to them.

In dyadic psychoanalytic processes, internal transformations occur in the working through of transference with the therapist: the patient first is piqued by curiosity about areas of thought and behavior outside of awareness, then through the analytic process discovers patterns that are distorting perceptions of reality. The thrust is toward the perception of self and the world.

An analogous psychoanalytic process occurs in the treatment of a married couple. Couples generally seek treatment when there is a "crisis" in the marriage. In Chinese the word *crisis* is composed of two ideograms, "danger" and "opportunity." Marital crises are dangerous, separation-threatening moments, but they also represent an unusual opportunity for the marital partners to begin to explore insights about themselves and their relational systems.

Generally speaking, a marriage crisis occurs when conflict-laden material is pushed to the surface by the changing actualities of the relationship. For example, a husband whose wife is suffering from the "empty-nest" syndrome, and feeling dissatisfied and anxious about her future life without the children, might turn to an extramarital affair to ease his loneliness and pain of feeling neglected or "clutched at." The themes are binding dependency and unsatisfied longing for earlier felt attention to his emotional needs. Old parent–child struggles become reenacted within the marriage. As with individual therapy, psychoanalytic treatment of the marriage involves a focus on these unconscious themes within the partners separately and within the marriage itself.

The Personality of a Marriage

A marriage is more than the sum of its partners. Ackerman (1958) describes it as "a new level of organization that creates new qualities. A marital relationship, like a chemical compound, has unique properties of its own, over and above the characteristics of the elements that merge to form the compound" (p. 42). The marital personality has its own history, beginning with the marriage, its own development of accommodative patterns, and its own creativity. It is, in many ways, like an individual, but an individual wedded inextricably to the two people who join to create it. Whenever the two partners function as "the marriage," this personality is observable. Most have experienced this "marriage personality" in others, some may even have glimpsed it in their own marriage.

Real as it is, however, it is practically impossible to talk about the marriage personality without making it appear to be a static entity. It is no more static than the personality of an individual. What we have is really an interactional process that, for purposes of discussion, we label "husband," "wife," "self," "other," "therapist," "patient," "marriage," as if these were things with identifiably discrete boundaries. So we should bear in mind that the actions described below are not in fact separate from each other but bound in a continuum that we are abstracting into analytical language in order to catch some glimpse of an immensely complex movement.

One of the difficulties of dual analysis of a couple is the presence of the "marriage consciousness" or "marriage personality" and our unfamiliarity in dealing with it. For example, if, as therapists, we want to make contact with the "marriage consciousness," to whom do we address our questions or direct our insights? If Ackerman is correct and marriage is like a new compound, not just the sum of its elements, then simply addressing the spouses together on a conscious level does not help. For one thing, the marriage personality is largely unconscious in the minds of the marriage partners and, strictly speaking, does not reside within either mate, either in whole or in part. It is an unfolding process that takes place between them, a shadowy movement that seems out of the reach of more traditional psychoanalytic techniques.

Other forms of marital therapy (single therapist and unmarried cotherapy teams) can effectively approach major strands of the transference web in a troubled marriage, but we believe that a marriage personality cannot be displaced onto a single individual, or even onto two individuals, so there may be significant dimensions of marriage that can be dealt with only in the presence of another marriage.

As therapists, it is evident to us that working together with patient-couples sometimes involves us in markedly different levels of perception from those we would have if we were working alone. Working together there is a consciousness that occurs when the two of us move as a couple. In the interchange of the sessions we focus, as individuals, on the individual spouses, but the "marriage consciousness" of both marriages also emerges, acts, and reacts. (This will be illustrated in our presentation of clinical material.)

This process is difficult to describe linearly, but it would seem to involve some tacit recognition by both marriage units of the tendency to want terms of old contracts, or new ones, to be fulfilled. Confronting this tendency is the process we call "coliberation."

Cooperative or Coliberative?

Many marriages, even long-standing ones, have drifted into cooperative arrangements. Marital cooperative unions come out of those lessons we learned in childhood about adjusting, pleasing, struggling for recognition and identity, manipulating, finding "common ground." Cooperation, at its best, is strong interest in the other, but largely in proportion to gains toward security for the self. Cooperative relationships are subject to unconscious forces that seek to avoid anxiety, usually by dominating the other, by giving in, by compromise (with resultant repressions of anger), or by flight into a desire to break off the relationship. Sullivan describes cooperative-type alliances as fixed at a "juvenile plateau" (Buber, 1957; Sullivan, 1956). In the marriage context cooperative relationships lead inevitably to conflict or to some psychopathological adjustment to avoid anxiety. Because most couples in trouble tend, consciously or unconsciously, to view marriage as cooperative (like a corporation), they are inclined to believe that their marriage simply needs reorganization, renegotiation of its contracts, or a change in its "personnel" policies.

What we are calling "coliberation," on the other hand, is an ongoing "letting go" of old binds, breaking up of unconscious marriage contracts, repudiation of the implied ownership of the mate, and dissolution of symbiotic systems of "togetherness." Paradoxically, this movement toward individuation becomes a mutual task. So, by the term *coliberation*, we mean to suggest a mutual letting go of each other and of old images of the marriage and a conjoint effort to arrive at a new view of each other.

Coliberation is not a matter of agreeing or disagreeing about aspects of the relationship; it is not indulgence in compromise to avoid anxiety. Rather, there develops a new shared interest and responsibility about seeing what is happening at the moment, relinquishing fantasies about what the moment "should" be. The other is not treated as an object but as an "opener." Coliberation does not involve mate dominance, with a shifting of authority, instead, the partners learn from each other.

Buber (1957) suggests this antinomous relationship when he says: "The chief presupposition for the rise of genuine discourse between two people is that each should *regard his partner as the very one he is*" (emphasis supplied). That is, the partner is both the self and an entirely separate other—not a projection of self, but a reflection of self. This distinction is crucial. Understanding the difference between coliberation and cooperation is one of the central tasks of the two-marriage analytic process.

So a coliberative relationship is a healing one. It moves directly counter to a closed system, is always unfolding in different ways, and is available to new and undiscovered energies. In such a restated marriage, the personality becomes less easily defined, more open, more available to exciting changes.

What Is a Marriage?

Implicit in this discussion is a question, rather simple but more penetrating than most of us who do marital therapy might care to admit: What is a marriage? As we work with the patients, we move to keep this perplexing question open, both with them and with ourselves. Thus, the answer (in the sense that there is one) is not a conclusion for the therapists who set themselves up to teach it to their patients. (Such conclusions would lead us inexorably back to the assumption that marriage is a more or less fixed entity that can be adjusted by learning or unlearning certain adaptive or behavioral skills.) Rather, in the context of the two-marriage therapy, the answer is an experience of the clarity that comes with realizing that marriage (and life) is constantly unfolding.

The objective of two-marriage therapy is not, in our view, to "save" or "counsel" the marriage, but rather, for the partners themselves to discover the nature of their marriage. The therapists, therefore, do not engage in what so often has been described as "role modeling" or creating the "therapeutic marriage." The patient-couple is not coerced or unconsciously encouraged to take the cotherapist-couple as "the model" marriage. We consider it contradictory to think of "modeling" someone toward open-endedness, since a model involves imitation, following a pattern, which is, as we have discussed, a large part of the problem in a troubled marriage. So coliberation, as such, is not a skill, but a state of consciousness that cannot be taught or learned; it is seeing how past designs limit the present.

One might expect that having married cotherapists would indicate to the patient-couple a bias in favor of remaining married, but we have found this bias is effectively discounted when the viability and definition of marriage are not assumed but instead are continuously open to question. The couple then has the choice to discover what their marriage is all about. In a study of our patient-couples over a nine-year period, of the 31 persons who responded to our questionnaire, seven-eighths indicated they had derived significant benefits from the two-marriage therapy, but less than one-third actually had remained married. Over half commented they felt the therapy had enhanced them as individuals. For example, one woman who divorced said: "The therapy has helped me in my new relationships. I feel much less possessive and less manipulative. I feel less concerned about what others think. I do not feel responsible for others' hangups. I still believe in marriage and would like the right marriage, but I no longer need marriage. I have found I am capable and strong and able to live alone."

In other words, the transferential interplay of the two-marriage therapy seems to facilitate the individual's separation from the grip of the marriage personality. Perhaps this is because the marriage personality is actually a kind of metaphor for the way each of the spouses, individually, has responded in the past; it is also a metaphor for the way they each, separately, make and sustain relationships. So seeing this becomes a liberating movement. One of the respondents to the study described the two-marriage therapy as "the business of getting my 'self' in focus and seeing and relating to people directly with present feelings instead of through my projections from the past."

As children, we responded not only to our individual parents, but also to the marital unit. Each mate's responses to the therapists as a marital unit opens up many avenues of unconscious interpretation otherwise unavailable. "The husband-wife team added to the effectiveness. I needed to relearn things in relationship to both my parents and to my role in that basic triangle which affected everything," one spouse said. "I've come to see a great deal of our trouble in marriage was that neither of us was sufficiently separate from our own parents. It was brought out in the sessions that we related to John as a father and Muriel as a mother in many instances. This was a way, I think, we could get at some of the feelings hanging around since childhood. One or both of you commented on this in many sessions—we were relating to each other like siblings instead of marriage partners."

Other transferential relationships also seem to unfold more coherently in a two-marriage setting, such as transference of the wife to the female therapist as mother and of the husband to male therapist as father.

We have found that if a marriage has been built primarily on projections from anamnestic experience, it probably will not continue after two-marriage inquiry since, as those responses are exposed, there is little left of mutual interest to continue the old relationship. If, on the other hand, the marriage contains discoverable elements of creativity, or "coliberative" interest, it may find new impetus for love in all its impacts.

Therapeusis with the Borderline Couple

How does one actually confront the marriage personality which is largely an unconscious phenomenon? Let us say both therapists are exploring an issue with the wife. We ask the husband to work with his own thoughts to apply the mate's predicament to his own past life. Probably unnoticed but implicit in this technique (we ask all our patients to work this way on their own when the therapists are focused on an issue with the spouse) is the sense that the spouses are a reflection of one movement, the marriage movement, or, to use Buber's terms, that the other is "the very one he is." Seeing this, the listening mate may discover coliberative connections. As one of our patients reported: "It actually became possible for me to learn to relate to many people better, for I learned much through observing and listening to the other three of you interact aside from my own involvement."

At times we articulate what we think are the unconscious conflicts of the patient-couple's marriage personality. For instance, John might speak to Muriel in the voice of the husband's unconscious theme of the moment.

> J.: (speaking as if he were the husband) I feel when you "clam up" and refuse to fight back you're reacting exactly like my mother did. She never could stand confrontation and just withdrew every time there was an argument.

M.: (speaking in the wife's unconscious voice) When my father lost control and screamed at me I was terrified and couldn't respond so I feel I've got to bottle up my anger, otherwise I'll be punished or attacked by him.

The couple observes this exchange, which is not an interpretation but, in effect, a portrayal of their marriage personality at work, the hidden plot that lies behind their outward conflicts. We believe their knowledge that the therapists are married gives the dialogue an energy and validity not otherwise possible. It should be said that our use of this technique, and numerous variations of it, is generally spontaneous, occurring in the flow of the therapy when the two of us see what is happening in the marriage consciousness of the couple. In daily life, when the couple engages in the projected forms of this unconscious marriage conflict, they are absorbed in a circular bind. The difference when we are dramatizing the conflict is that our tone is coliberative. Thus, the spouses not only can perceive seriously conflicted feelings in the marriage but also can explore these disjunctive influences without getting inexorably caught up in old patterns of distorted reality.

At other times one therapist will make an observation about one of the patient-spouses which will be supported or challenged by the other. Here we recognize how our own history as a marriage and our coliberative focus enters intimately into our therapeutic work. Often when one therapist has challenged the other, we will go into it explicitly with the couple observing and sorting out through coliberation if and how a distortion out of our own past experience has colored our view of the couple's situation. Obviously, this is possible because we know each other's past working-through. We feel this has a healing effect on the patient-couple's marriage personality by letting the couple observe as participants how it is possible to tease the past out of the present without resorting to criticism.

Couples seeking treatment for a crisis in their marriage frequently present themselves as borderline personality disorders, with either or both partners falling into that diagnostic category. Since these patients often have considerable difficulties developing a therapeutic working alliance with the therapist, these issues are compounded when both of the marital partners present as recognizable character disorders. Couples therapy with a single therapist and two borderline patients is arduous because of the teaming up, collusion, and scapegoating at which these patients are so adept. Subgrouping as a foursome, rather than threesome, facilitates work with a borderline couple by offering more initial hope to the spouses that their individual needs will be met, a hope fostered by the symbolic presence of the two "parents" together in the session with them.

Borderline pathology in one or both spouses presents a special set of transferential problems to therapists who work with couples conjointly. These involve the borderline's tendency to manipulate, seduce, and provoke "side-tracking" behavior in the mate and the therapist similar to what was experienced in the first family. This adds a new dimension to the therapists' countertransference reference points, attacking with particular pointedness the unworked-out areas in the therapists' own lives. Treatment with these couples necessitates constant vigilance concerning these countertransferential traps. A borderline couple is usually quite skillful in the art of avoiding insightful connections and discoveries about their past family marriages as they react with each other in their own marriage. In the service of keeping their inner spaces secretive and their deficits in living out of awareness, the autonomy they say they seek within the marriage is buried in collusive structuring to keep away the sting of sudden insights into their own individual past histories.

In a therapy setting the borderline personality expects the therapist to be essentially compliant, just as he sees himself. Specifically, the therapist is expected to agree, listen, offer encouragement and only "light-handed" confrontation, seldom express any real doubt about the sincerity of the patient's way of talking about himself, and basically acquiesce to the patient. Statements such as "Yes, I see what you mean"; "Somehow what you say confuses me"; "I don't know about that; it doesn't feel right"; or "You say it . . . but I don't feel it" are acceptable to these patients.

Agreement with an interpretation often represents resistance (or, rather, "persistence" of old entrenched views of the self-system). The symbiotic interspaces exert a stranglehold on the significant other person (therapist or mate) and must not give way to any manifest anger, strong disagreement, or aggressivity. This control, the borderline feels, is essential to his system. Borderlines try very hard to think and feel what others want them to feel; they thereby attempt to guarantee that they will be certain of the other's responses. Their psychology hinges on resisting any new views of themselves that would bring up awareness of their overwhelming humiliation and insecurity. Dangerous aggressive impulses and infantile feelings of rage and power remain hidden beneath the thinly veiled exterior self. Although the new views may be cognitively or tacitly recognized by the patient in order not to reveal other feelings, they remain in reality ego alien.

Hidden and more assertive impulses are sublimated, and essentially unneutralized within the unconscious, breaking through as disguised affects; that is, depression, rage, anxiety, restlessness, and feelings of emptiness. Developing autonomy of the self is too risky to the borderline patient, for it implies abandonment and alienation from any sources of nurturance from others. Since there is such a fear of the shattering consequences of feeling dependent and therefore helpless, what develops is a sort of pervasive distrust of the quality of caring of significant others in the patient's life.

To illustrate how these borderline dilemmas are worked through by the dual analytic therapy approach, we offer case material excerpted from a tape recorded session with a couple we will call the Robbins. We frequently tape sessions and ask the couple to listen to the tape, together or separately, before the next session. This encourages the couple to "rehear" the material, our voice interactions, our silences and their meanings, and to discuss their reactions with each other and with us.

Most borderline couples are not really able to talk and listen to each other. The tape affords them the chance to make comments about our participation or interference in their dialogue. The borderline couple needs constant encouragement to develop these new skills in listening and talking. They frequently will avoid listening to the taped sessions outside of the sessions because of their inability to get outside of their own repetitious schizotypal functioning.

Case Material

Alice and Dan Robbins were a childless couple, married for 18 years. Their borderline functioning prior to the marriage continued together in the married state; both avoided facing their enormous unconscious demands. Blaming took the place of self-examination and self-discovery.

The crisis that brought the Robbins to therapy was precipitated by Dan's disclosure of a long-standing intense relationship with another woman.

The Robbins's marriage personality was not unlike their separate personalities, with conflicts ranging between opposing images and impulses. Each partner alternated as child and parent. There was anger at not being taken care of, guilt and humiliation for asking to be taken care of, yet strong demands for separateness. Overall, the marriage personality tried to deny all of these hidden themes and resorted to subtle deceptions and cooperative arrangements to avoid letting these conflicts emerge into the open for analysis.

Alice and Dan were attempting to separate themselves from the old marriage consciousness. In the session excerpted here, their ambivalence is apparent. At the time of this session, Dan was seeing his lover, Joan, frequently and Alice was looking for an apartment, although not happily. In spite of the beginning recognition that their marriage might have to end, they reported they were having some good times together, the first in many years.

Toward the end of a session, the discussion turned to what they would be doing for Thanksgiving. They had accepted an invitation to have dinner with some friends, the Wilsons, in order to avoid the inevitable controversy of Dan spending the holiday with Joan. Neither Dan nor Alice was happy about this solution. Alice openly accused Dan of preferring to be with his mistress. Dan said he had accepted their friends' invitation because he felt guilty about leaving Alice home alone. John observed that Alice's agreeing to this arrangement set her up for later retaliation from Dan. In the ensuing silence, John asked Alice if she could fantasize the therapists asking her to their home for Thanksgiving dinner. John caught Muriel's thoughtful look.

J.: (to M.) What are you puzzling about?

M.: I was just thinking about what caused you to rescue Alice by your suggesting a fantasy.

(J. is responding to her sense that he has acted out of his own history of "rescuing" women.)

J.: All right. Very good. Of course Alice looks very vulnerable, as she frequently does, and finds it hard to say what she is feeling.

Dan: I felt that way, too, like you rescued her. She (meaning Alice) always agrees to my suggestions, then I catch hell after. She sulks and pouts, you know how you do sometimes, two or three days.

(Dan's observation is typical of the mechanism of the borderline marriage personality. He offers to cooperate by going to the Wilsons so he won't have to face her direct hostility, and she agrees so as to delude herself about his intentions but reacts with silent, unconscious fury. Thus the marriage personality shows itself as stubborn, deceitful, and "cooperative" only.)

M.: (to Dan) Did you want John to rescue her? Like good parents to always fall back on.

Dan: I don't know. (He doesn't want to say.)

J.: When Muriel brought it up, I realized that was part of my old reaction to placate the woman. It's an unconscious trap. (To Alice) You don't really need me to feel sorry for you, do you?

Alice: (long silence) I don't think I know what you mean. (She doesn't want to say.)

M.: (to Alice) Maybe you really don't want Dan to dilute your anger about this Joan thing, by dragging you off to the Wilsons when you know he's just doing it to avoid a confrontation with you.

Dan: I said I'd do it because I can't stand thinking about her sitting home alone. I could never stand that feeling I had with my mother, too. It's the same feeling I have.

J.: (to Alice) Can you respond to that?

Alice: That makes me feel horrible. I can't stand being treated like a cripple.

J.: Well, you acted as if you thought it was a good idea. You must have known he'd get back at you for it at some point.

Dan: Because every time I sit with you in your goddam utter silence I want to pay you back. Because there's no freedom between us, no freedom like those few moments we've had since the session Wednesday. Today you're right back in the old shit of 18 years.

J.: (To Alice) Did you feel like I was rescuing you?

Alice: No. I really didn't.

Dan: (to J.) But you did what I did for 18 years. Muriel picked it up and I picked it up.

J.: (to Alice) All right, let's let them sit and listen and work on this. Pretend I'm Dan. Did you really want to go to the Wilsons for Thanksgiving?

(J. takes the role of Dan and assumes a marriage with Alice while M. and Dan are participant observers.)

Alice: No, I really didn't, but I knew it would stop you from seeing Joan.

J.: I don't really want to go either, but I can't take the pain of being alone with you on a holiday. What do you want to do?

Alice: Well, I guess I could go alone, or I could call somebody else, but I couldn't stand for you to go to Joan.

Dan: (to Alice) What would you do if you were already in your own apartment?

Alice: I don't know what I'd do.

Dan: That's just the point. You see, we're worried about you; we're all worried about you.

J.: (ironically) Because you're so helpless?

M.: Why would you be worried about a strong, attractive girl like Alice?

Dan: She doesn't make any attempt to use her strength, to use her attractiveness.

M.: Well, you make sure she doesn't, don't you, by rescuing her ... just as J. did.

J.: (to Dan) See. Muriel put us, you and me, together in that because we rescue Alice; that's our problem, too, not just hers.

Dan: (to Alice) This kind of problem happens every day, every night of our lives. Same thing that happened just now with you and John. He really cares about you, too. When I realized these two people really care, my whole life changed. Because once I began to trust that, my whole therapy began to open. I know I can trust what's happening here.

J.: (picking up on the underlying theme of this statement) Maybe you both want to be rescued. Maybe we ought to have a conjoint session Thanksgiving morning and adjourn for family dinner! That would be really parental, wouldn't it?

In this last exchange the personality of the marriage is underscored. It is not just Alice who wants to be rescued, but Dan as well from his uncertainty and guilt about what she would do if he were not there. The therapists go on to suggest how rescue is a desire to control the other.

The marriage itself is a rescue operation, with roots in the spouses' separate histories. Later, in a discussion of the problems the Wilsons were having, Dan observed that "going to the Wilsons would be a rescue"; that is, it would be the Robbins's marriage personality looking for a mirror in which to see itself and stay in the old patterns. Alice and Dan, in meeting and recognizing their separate problems, came to realize that their marriage had died because it contained no real basis for relating to each other in an autonomous coliberative way. They divorced, and Dan married Joan. Alice started a career, became quite independent, found herself attractive to other men, and cautiously allowed herself to expand her life in many directions.

The Thanksgiving invitation incident, we believe, does illustrate the flexibility inherent in this four-way, marriage-on-marriage treatment modality, exploring issues without regard to stultifying professional stances. With the knowledge we have of each other's past history and self systems, we have found that working coliberatively seems to provide checks and balances on the process and allows a kind of freedom we do not experience working separately. Working this way, we find that our own marriage personality is constantly open for new examination; old patterns and historical reflexes are constantly broken down by the coliberative process.

We believe this vignette also illustrates that real therapeusis does not involve an authoritarian relationship between therapists and patients. In fact, one of the major problems of marriage is the collusion to assign dominant and passive roles and the inevitable conflict that results.

This tendency even appears, covertly, in the initiative of couples to seek therapy, a movement in which their marriage usually makes itself passive, "an object," the couple expecting the therapists to act on it. As long as this pattern persists, unexamined, cooperative relationships will continue to be the focus. The two-marriage arrangement affords the therapists the chance to reduce their authority images because (1) the interaction between the therapists as marriage partners points out that in marriage there is no authority (an insight is an insight, no matter who has it, and each partner has something to offer, something to learn). (2) The forward movement of the therapy is really being accomplished by the coliberative process—not by the "authority" of the therapists. So the patients cease to be objects. They are participants in the act of seeing what is there. As one of our former patients who responded to our questionnaire wrote: "The therapist-couple made comments that seemed more realistic than professional about their own relationship; 'deauthoritizing' the professional without undermining earned respect was important toward our sustaining a better marriage ourselves."

Qualifications for Spouse Cotherapists

The literature of marital therapy by cotherapists has been growing (McGee and Schuman, 1970; Gill and Temperly, 1972, 1974; Schonbar, 1973; Bailis and Adler, 1974; Roman and Meltzer, 1977) but thus far there is scarcely a plethora of work by cotherapists who are marital partners themselves (Belleville et al., 1969). One of the reasons for this is undoubtedly the same as that limiting the number of cotherapists in general, particularly in a private practice setting. Sufficient therapeutic benefits to justify the financial penalties of fielding two therapists for a single conjoint session have not been advanced. Other reasons are perhaps peculiar to the situation of married cotherapists: (1) there are a limited number of married therapists interested in doing this kind of work; (2) married therapists are reluctant to "put their marriage on the line" by confronting the potential power struggles and couples' transference and countertransference possibilities that could ensue from conjoint cotherapeutic work.

We believe, in terms of our own experience, that the most essential training for a husband–wife therapy team is intensive work with their own marriage; having faced the "danger" and "opportunity" together, they know from personal experience what the process entails. Since we feel there are no direct "how-to" methods for treating couples, training does not involve learning techniques or earning specific professional degrees. Coliberation, as we have called it, is not a question of becoming an "expert," but rather, involves allowing oneself to enter into a process where exploration is central with each new couple, much as it is in the dyadic analytic process.

We do recommend, however, that one or both of the therapists have formal psychological and clinical training and be experienced in working with patients on a dyadic basis. This means that at least one of the partners must have considerable familiarity with psychodynamic psychology (or psychiatry), including extensive understanding of the intricacies of transference. Further, both therapists should have undergone thorough individual psychoanalysis with periodic reanalysis.

The key to this modality is transferential interplay between the psychotherapists and patient-couples. The crucial factor for the therapists is the quality of their relationship. Is it coliberative? One study done on cotherapy teams (Rice, Fey, and Kepecs, 1972) indicated a "point of diminishing returns" for cotherapists in their work. They reported that the satisfaction of working together seemed to decrease with increasing caseloads. This has not been our experience over the past 15 years. This may be due to the fact that we work psychoanalytically with our couples and we limit within our own comfort zone the number of couples we see at any one period of time. It may also have something to do with our marriage. We convey to our patients that one of the advantages of this kind of work for us as therapists is that it keeps us focusing on our own autonomy in our marriage personality and constantly activates our curiosity about our lives together. But obviously, working with one's spouse is risky as well as advantageous. It means living together more intensely than in the usual marital situation. If the relationship is not coliberative, it can be damaged by unworked-through neurotic dependency needs.

We believe that coliberative two-marriage therapy stimulates patients, not to model their own marriage after ours, but to examine their own marriage openly, with no expectation of certainty and no real ground rules. We encourage them to pay attention to the substance of their lives, their fantasies, dreams, and fears, and to be curious about the systems under which they have been operating. Learning and feeling coliberation means listening anew and seeing the other in new ways; recognizing the differences as positive forces in the marriage and encouraging them; feeling separate from the problems of the other, yet sharing with the other the painful process of facing those problems; caring and reaching out for help, and giving help to the mate when asked.

References

Ackerman, N. W. (1958), *The Psychodynamics of Family Life*. New York: Basic Books.
Bailis, S., & Adler, G. (1974), Cotherapy issues in a collaborative setting. *Amer. J. Psychother.*, 28/4:599–606.
Bellville, T. P., Raths, O. N., & Bellville, C. J. (1969), Conjoint marriage therapy with a husband and wife team. *Amer. J. Orthopsychiat.*, 39:373–483.
Buber, M. (1957), Elements of the interhuman. William Alanson White Memorial Lectures. *Psychiatry*, 20:650.
Gill, H. S., & Temperly, J. (1972), Treatment of the marital dyad in a foursome: an illustrative case study. *Postgrad. Med.*, 48:555–560.
——— ——— (1974), Time-limited marital treatment in a foursome. *Brit. Med. J. Psychol.*, 47:153–161.
McGee, T., & Schuman, B. (1970), The nature of the cotherapy relationship. *Internat. J. Group Psychother.*, 20:25–38.
Rice, D. G., Fey, W. F., & Kepecs, J. G. (1972), Therapist experience and "style" as factors in cotherapy. *Fam. Process*, 12:1–12.
Roman, M., & Meltzer, B. (1977), Cotherapy: A review of the literature. *J. Sex Marital Ther.*, 3:63–77.
Schonbar, R. (1973), Group cotherapists and sex-role identification. *Amer. J. Psychother.*, 27:539–547.
Sullivan, H. S. (1956), *Clinical Studies in Psychiatry*. New York: W. W. Norton.
——— (1958), *The Interpersonal Theory of Psychiatry*. New York: W. W. Norton.

Chapter 18
THE PHARMACOLOGICAL THERAPEUTIC COMMUNITY

FERNANDO D. ASTIGUETA, M.D.

> *The art of living consists in transforming any negative into a positive emergency.*
> —Jose Ortega y Gasset

This chapter describes the therapeutic work at the Pharmacological Therapeutic Community (PTC), an outpatient unit designed for the care of a severely disabled population characterized by multiproblem, high-risk individuals with psychotic or borderline diagnosis, often with an extensive history of drug or alcohol abuse. A team approach is utilized within a therapeutic community setting (Jones, 1953, 1968; Kroft, 1966). The treatment objectives are to stabilize patients, to facilitate referral to long-term therapies, to provide rehabilitation services, and to allow the eventual return of patients to the working community. Treatment modalities include: Therapeutic Community Medical Meeting (TCMM) (Astigueta, 1980), support groups, and individual psychotherapy. While psychopharmacotherapy, milieu treatment, behavioral modification techniques, and modified group psychoanalytic approaches are utilized, the TCMM is the most important modality because it provides a supportive forum for discussion of dysfunctional manifestations in the cognitive, emotional, and behavioral areas of the individual personality. In the TCMM setting, patients and staff together interact constructively in order to focus on and clarify symptomatology, to discuss openly the impact of prescribed and illicit medication, and to confront problems in object relations as these are manifested within the therapeutic community.

The PTC, an outpatient, therapeutic teaching unit of the Postgraduate Center for Mental Health, was founded and designed by the author in September 1979.

The educational objectives of the PTC consist in learning how to function professionally by means of a cotherapy, interdisciplinary team model. The principle of distributed leadership with full participation of patients in the elaboration of their treatment plans will necessarily alter a rigid adherence to one particular type of treatment intervention. Different theories are considered in terms of their therapeutic validity in a given situation. We mean by this that theory serves the patient rather than the patient being made to fit into the theory. Each patient who comes for treatment is considered as a highly complex system composed of interrelated biological, psychological, and social needs. Therefore, those responsible for treatment have to be well versed in biological, psychological, and sociological approaches.

The unit is staffed by two psychiatrists, one of whom is the program director, two social work supervisors, three social workers (MSW), and three social work trainees.

Prior to the establishment of the PTC, many severely disturbed, acting-out individuals could not be accommodated at the Postgraduate Center; conventional approaches inevitably failed with them. These patients evidenced the revolving door syndrome. They would be referred from one treatment facility, hospital, or private therapist to another, only to drop out or be discharged from treatment. Some returned to mental hospitals for readmission others remained in the community untreated. It was for the latter group that the PTC was created. This population of patients does not fit a single diagnostic category, but it does exhibit pathological characteristics that make it a "type" in its own right.

These patients usually present severe character pathology, such as borderline (Wolberg, 1973, 1977; Kernberg, 1975) or narcissistic personality structures that sometimes reach a psychopathic level. Some are engaged in drug or alcohol programs and have a long history of drug abuse. Others have been in mental hospitals on many occasions (Minkoff, 1978) and, after discharge, have received psychotropic medication on a once-a-month basis during a 10-minute interview (Appleton, 1976). Such counterproductive and brief contact hampers involvement between the psychiatrist and the patient. It also helps generate a significant problem known as the "revolving door" (Talbott, 1980) syndrome leading to a 35% rehospitalization rate within a period of two to six weeks following discharge (Van Putten, 1974).

This group of patients tends to remain in a constant state of emotional instability which makes them live in a permanent state of crisis. Each crisis further increases their embitterment and lowers their self-esteem, bringing on a repeat of the crisis. Each new crisis is similar to the previous one, and the person's repertoire of coping mechanisms for resolving them remains unchanged. Presenting symptoms include: marked impulsivity, multiple suicidal attempts, episodes of unpredictable violence, multiple substance abuse, hostile dependency, recurrent visits to the hospital emergency room, innumerable somatic complaints, and constant blaming of others for their misery.

In addition, they are chronically depressed, demoralized, emotionally vulnerable, and unable to acquire valid and therapeutic insights. To this constellation of symptoms, we can add unfruitful attempts to relate to others, which makes them isolated, distrustful, and eventually antisocial (Newcomb, 1947). Their inadequately balanced ego structure leads them to a frustrating and hostile distortion of their environment. However, this hostility, perceived as coming from the outside world, can also be considered realistic, because the community usually reacts to them with anger and rejection.

We are accustomed to reading about the revolt generated by the presence of ex-mental patients prematurely discharged from mental institutions. (This is known as deinstitutionalization.) What isn't written about is the extraordinary success obtained by the pharmacological revolution. The complex of behavioral traits mentioned above, combined with the resistance of the community to accepting deinstitutionalized patients, not only announces, but also contributes to, impending psychological and psychosocial decompensation. These patients are unable to function in more conventional clinic programs due to their poorly integrated ego and lack of behavioral control (many people consider them to be untreatable). The absence of a supportive social and family network exacerbates the problem to insurmountable proportions. In the rare cases in which such a network is present, it is usually rudimentary and fragmented.

This lack of a positive and supportive (Davidson, Turnbull, and Miller, 1980) social network is supplanted by the treatment milieu generated in the PTC. The unit provides what is known as a "second chance family."

The Therapeutic Setting

The PTC is a therapeutic teaching system which integrates members of the different disciplines of the mental health profession. Because the unit functions both to render services and to serve as a teaching setting, student staff members are also included. Treatment modalities combine individual psychotherapy, group psychotherapy, and pharmacotherapy in a social therapeutic milieu. The staff is organized as a therapeutic team and has basic knowledge about the pathology presented by all patients (presently about 55) forming the community.

Initial interviews are conducted by the whole team in group interview. Together they assess the problems presented by the new patients in their biological, psychological, and social areas of malfunctioning. They also consider personal resources and social skills available within the patient. This detailed evaluation is followed by the delineation of a treatment plan that includes both short- and long-term therapeutic goals. Since the unit is mainly a transitional therapeutic system, patients are not supposed to stay more than two or three years.

However, since the PTC only began in 1979, we are unable to specify an ideal participation time in the program. Once properly evaluated and (in the majority of cases) medicated, the patient is assigned to a therapist (a social worker or a student). Individual sessions, once or twice a week, start immediately after the patient is placed in one or two large groups known as the TCMM. After the patient has been assimilated and engaged in the therapeutic work, he is considered as a candidate for a small group (8 to 10) led by two therapists. Additionally, patients continue individual and large group therapy. The final phase is aimed at facilitating a return to work or at least a referral to the rehabilitation clinic or the psychiatric outpatient clinic for further treatment. In cases of severe decompensation, admission to a hospital is facilitated with close follow-up and return to the unit after discharge. All therapeutic modalities are synchronized and carried out within the atmosphere of the therapeutic community. Here informal encounters between patients and staff occur. The TCMM provides the forum where all patients and staff meet together in order to work for a better understanding of the patients' individual and social identity.

This may seem to be a complicated design. However, it is intrinsically logical and easy to understand if we consider its theoretical foundations. [Therapeutic communities have existed since Maxwell Jones first introduced the concept (1953, 1968)].

The Primary Task

My aim, worked out through the TCMM, is to integrate different therapeutic mentalities that traditionally are regarded as discordant. Thus, psychoanalytically oriented individual therapy, several types of group therapy, and psychopharmacology are all used in the PTC. In addition, the sociological–environmental contribution to mental illness is addressed. In sum, our view is as follows: The psychiatric task consists of perceiving and treating the patient as a holistic unit composed of social and value, genetic, biochemical, and psychologic systems which at some point became disrupted. As a consequence, the therapist is obliged to address each one of these systems in order to obtain maximum therapeutic effectiveness. His aim is to pay attention to all these systems to avoid fragmentation of the afflicted self. If we are only concerned with either the biochemical functioning or the psychodynamics of the individual patient, we run the risk of committing ourselves to the study of clinical cases isolated from the environment. If we believe that society is the sole cause of psychic disabilities without examining the biological and individual psychological components that shape it, we wind up fashioning a cultural structure that requests of its members unconditional adjustment to its basic ideology and norms.

The first approach would lack a substratum, the second would be wanting in interpersonal sensitivity, and the third would deny an experiential reality. All three perspectives are valid, and our present task is their integration. The programmatic working out of the TCMM system has been based on the belief of parity between disciplines. The primary task of the TCMM unit consists of providing low-cost, high-quality, and effective individual, group, milieu, behavioral, and chemotherapy to a vulnerable and transient population generally on the brink of psychosocial decompensation or rehospitalization. Thus far, the rehospitalization rate is only 8.5 percent of active patients; the actual suicidal or homicidal index is nil.

Leadership

Therapeutic communities are based on the principle of shared and functional leadership. The vertical or authority vector (Wolf, 1969) so central in the medical model and individual psychoanalytic psychotherapies is reduced in importance to make room for the horizontal or peer vector characteristic of all forms of group psychotherapy. As Maxwell Jones states it: "This process of one-way communication without interaction is, I think, an inherent part of our culture and in varying degrees permeates the whole field of education, including higher education. But similar trends are discernible in many other fields, including the family, industry, religion, and, despite the talk about democratic countries, in federal administration, too. In all these areas the consumer has relatively little direct control over her relationships with the system or his capacity to change it. Communication is largely one way, from top to bottom in the hierarchy, with the consumer as passive recipient of decisions made for him by the heads of the organization" (1968, p. 133). This shift in emphasis attenuates the overt or covert hostility that all of these patients sense toward authority. They are usually fearful or resentful of anyone in command. As a consequence, they behave either submissively or with passive defiance (e.g., by missing sessions, being late, or misusing or not taking medication as prescribed). They also tend to turn to street drugs, alcohol, or antisocial acting out in the community. Suicidal gestures and/or actual attempts are common and usually performed to mobilize feelings of guilt in the therapists "who do not care enough for their patients." Thus, all therapists, including the unit chief, supervisors, social workers, and students in training must possess, or someday attain, the following characteristics. First, they have to be trained professionals, well versed theoretically and experientially in the principles and practices of psychopharmacotherapy and individual and group dynamics. Training includes personal and group psychoanalysis in which transference and countertransference have been extremely well understood and digested. Second, they will have to have abundant experience with a wide variety of patients, preferably psychotics, borderlines, and narcissistic patients. Third, they must possess a therapeutically adaptive personality capable of dealing in a nontoxic manner with both healthy persons and the very ill. Fourth, they must be free of social and racial prejudices and capable of discerning with sound judgment where authority begins and ends. This requires the strength to tolerate frustration and the flexibility to vary their role from the position of authority to that of underdog, without ever abdicating real leadership. Finally, they must prudently offer their personal feelings as a model of genuine and productive interactions.

The Therapeutic Community Medical Meeting

The TCMM consists of biweekly 75-minute group sessions composed of the entire staff and some ten to seventeen patients. The therapeutic activity combines modified contemporary psychoanalytic group psychotherapy, psychopharmacology, and reinforcement techniques. To promote continuity, meetings begin with the reading of the written summaries describing the highlights of the preceding session. The collected written summaries comprise the "group history."

Patients can relieve their maladaptive functioning through

interactions with members of the therapeutic community. Medication is integrated into the session in different ways. Most importantly, it is used to relieve many of the patient's symptoms, including side effects, through accurate clinical elucidation of their biochemical substratum by the prescription and titration of the indicated drug. This is done on a weekly basis, allowing the psychiatrist to evaluate results with the utmost precision and safety. It also enhances interaction in the group and the ability of patients to discover and understand how others react to the same kind of medication. Additionally, both prescribed and illicit drugs are discussed. The effects on the central nervous system are explained. An attempt is made to thoroughly inform patients about chemical effectiveness, target symptoms, and adverse effects. Warnings are presented by both staff and peers of the consequences of failing to take the prescribed medication and of the dangerous effects of abuse. Minor tranquilizers are not prescribed and are strongly discouraged.

In the TCMM, patients and therapists enter the therapy room together. They sit in a circle in order to have a face-to-face view of one another. If one of the members is late or absent, the discussion moves to this topic in order to establish the norm of punctual attendance. When therapists happen to be late, the patients confront them about it. The most typical way of starting the session is by reading the summary of the prior meeting. This seems to produce a feeling of continuity and a sense of being cared for by the therapists. All staff members call the patients by their first name and invite them to reciprocate. Prescriptions are written out by the psychiatrist during the middle of the session once the interaction is in progress.

The psychiatrist listens attentively and prescribes according to his observations, without interrupting the group process. He has to avoid becoming the center of attention in order to prevent the emergence of the vertical authority vector. Staff is alerted to this possibility and constantly strives to divert centralization by promoting interaction. This is done as much as possible within the framework of the "here and now" or by bringing up the group history. When moments of silence or extreme verbal abuse occur, the theme of medication is referred to, reiterated either didactically or to elucidate symptomatology. In this manner, staff and patients are able to impart and receive information on the course of treatment and the effectiveness, inadequacy, or toxicity of drugs. At the same time, interpersonal and group phenomena including intrapsychic material become discernible, and thus open for discussion.

The Group History

All groups have a history (Astigueta, 1977) based on the events that have occurred since their formation. They may also have a prehistory established by members who are no longer in the group. The written summary of the previous session read by a staff member at the beginning of the TCMM describes the highlights of the preceding session. The collected summaries chronicle the group history. The process of recording, reading, and saving the summaries provides continuity and structure. Each TCMM has its own unique history, which is used as a confrontational screen for different behaviors displayed by the members over the course of its meetings. The summaries crystallize the observations made about group interaction. They focus on verbal and nonverbal communication, seating arrangements, tones of voice, postures, noises, interruptions, and every point that the recorder has detected. While the history is being read, the group members listen with divided attention, at times smiling, grunting, nodding, protesting, or adding comments. However, they seem to be interested and vehemently interrupt the reader when some event has been distorted or ignored. Sometimes they object about the confidentiality of this material, but this is usually promptly forgotten because it never touches "top secrets" and only refers to interactions in the group and the therapeutic community as a whole. All of these reactions are carefully introduced into the narrative as part of the group history.

The group history, as it is presented and has developed, increases the participants' awareness of their own interactions, their repetitive patterns of behavior, their assets, and vulnerabilities. As usually happens within the confines of cohesive groups, all the characterological manifestations of the members come to the surface repeatedly. The group history also serves the important purpose of preventing disclosure of painful material from the personal history of each individual member. It only refers to interpersonal transactions within the PTC setting. Members are afraid that the intrusion into their personal lives would be disruptive to their emotional stability. This material is dealt with quite adequately in the individual or small group sessions. However, excessive secrecy might be used defensively and become antitherapeutic. Drug abuse, suicidal threats, and acting out of a dangerous kind within or outside of the therapeutic community are quite frequent.

Patients are encouraged as part of the therapeutic contract to reveal any incidents occurring among themselves. They have the obligation to bring back to the group everything that concerns their own and other members' safety. There is always a danger that coalitions or subgroups might form without the knowledge of the therapists that could result in serious consequences. The therapists themselves could eventually feel constrained to reveal significant material (e.g., the use of illicit drugs) out of feelings of guilt. Extreme confidentiality must never become a great issue because all therapeutic modalities are geared to investigate and clarify behavior of patients within the therapeutic community.

Particular skill is required to effectively create an atmosphere conducive to dispassionate self-observation and constructive feedback. Instead of utilizing personal history, as is done in traditional psychoanalysis or psychoanalytic group psychotherapy, with exploration and working through of member-to-leader and peer-to-peer transferences, we turn back to the genetic material of the group as a whole and the individual behavior observed since the beginning of membership. Interpersonal distortions are clarified and only relate to manifest behavior of the individual in the entire community. Intimate material is never disclosed, and it is discouraged if presented. Patients are referred to previous analogous events which took place in the group setting.

This technique allows for full participation of all members who, having witnessed past events or listened to the written summaries, signal what is appropriate in terms of group norms and standards. In other words, the group history supplants the individual history and, instead of comparing the childhood of the individual with his present behavior, we use comparisons with the early group sessions as evidence for change. Reconstructions common in individual psychoanalytic psychotherapy become unnecessary because early maladaptive or regressive behavior has been witnessed or charted in the group history. There is no place or time for top secrets and therapy becomes a common task for patients as well as staff.

Clinical Illustration

Seven patients and three staff members were sitting in a circle when the group began with the notes being read. A chronic depressive woman brought up the issue that patients were asked to "rat" about other patients' abuse of drugs. She expressed anger to all staff members for putting such pressure on her, and she feared retaliation from any patient whose identity was revealed.

P., a chronic drug abuser with a history of seizure disorder and criminal behavior, deflected this theme onto the subject of homosexuality and started to become verbally abusive toward F., a borderline homosexual. He added that names of drug abusers should be mentioned and particularly that of T., who had come "high" to the small-group session. The problem, as he expressed it, resided in the presence of all those "fags" coming to the sessions with drugs in their systems. P. became increasingly angry and continued to attack E. in a sadistic manner. Meanwhile, E. was becoming more and more depressed, to the point of crying.

J., a borderline manic depressive young man, addressed P., whom he didn't know, and interpreted his behavior as an escape from group work. P. got up and went toward J., raising his voice in a menacing tone: "Come, and let's settle this in the corner." Two staff members immediately stood up to establish order in the room and prevent physical violence. P. was then commanded by the director of the unit to either sit back in his chair or immediately leave the room; otherwise, he would be expelled from the room, escorted by a security officer. P. returned to his chair more relaxed, with an expression of perplexity on his face. Group members began to provide feedback about his outburst. He seemed to have been totally unaware of it. The group continued to debate about anger, rage, and homosexuality. R., a very depressed and drug-abusing young man, with a strong tendency to rationalize, began a long tirade about the intrinsic badness of social values. Several members tried to bring him back to the "here and now" of the event, but he seemed unable to give up his pseudophilosophical utterances. Finally, the director invited him to give a lecture on this matter at another time.

A young, attractive woman mentioned her own episode of decontrolled behavior during the last weekend. She had been taking cocaine in order to become more a member of the "group." When asked, "what group?", she specified the small group where people talk about drugs. She had never been a substance abuser.

Not all members were attempting to interpret the preceding event as a repetition of old mechanisms of coping with perceived threats. For example, K., an older borderline woman with manic-depressive overtones, said in a moralistic manner, "People should stop taking drugs because they will become shopping bag individuals."

The group then turned its attention to E., the homosexual patient who had been originally attacked by P. He was still slumped in his chair, crying and unable to react. He was told by other members that he allowed P. to continue with his sadistic remarks by not responding vigorously to them. They recalled other situations in this and other groups where something similar had happened. He kept shaking his head in deep sorrow, but with a hint of understanding that at least part of his misery was of his own doing.

This session was closed by the director, who congratulated the group for its capacity to hold the tense incident at a verbal level. The episode was explained to the group as a return to childhood with a loss of the "here and now" reality.

The session was followed by a staff meeting in order to clarify dynamics and techniques. It was assumed that P., with a history of drug abuse, seizure disorder, and possible murderous behavior, went through a micropsychotic episode with consecutive amnesia precipitated by homosexual panic. Many times during the session he affirmed his being straight and denied disliking homosexuals, although referring to them as "fags," "perverts," or "hideous." Thus, when a stranger arrived in the group and asked P. to speak more calmly, he began to use profanity and went on to directly attack him. He was toned down by the immediate intervention of the two staff members.

The above is an illustration of how to proceed when violent behavior is impending. It is, perhaps, one of the few circumstances when the vertical or authority vector has to be forcefully asserted. Another is persistent self-destructive behavior. However, it should be noted that the group can act as a container of extreme maladaptive behavior and attenuate its malignancy by talking it out during the session. They were expressing both individual concerns and concerns about group affiliation and constitution. They wanted to know to which group they belonged, to which culture they should be loyal. Telling who was taking drugs would cast them in the dangerous and disgraceful role of "squealers." If they did not speak up, they would be defying the staff. This would also mean denying a basic therapeutic norm where every event taking place among group members of the PTC has to be brought back to the sessions as material for discussion.

The idea of a "drug group" as anecdotally portrayed here is, in fact, and as Bion saw, one of two "groups" working at cross-purposes. According to Bion, these two groups (or forces) are the "work group" and the "basic assumption group." As used here, "basic assumption group" and "drug group" both refer to a state of mind representing the same unconscious fight-in-flight mechanism while "work group" represents the forces of health.

We can conceive, then, of the group session having two components: (1) latent and (2) manifest. Giving moralistic advice, as K. did, in uttering sociological interpretations, as R. did, in assuming the role of the victim, as E. did, or coming through with machismo bravado, as P. did, are expressions of collective resistance to change. All of these represent irrational and regressive behavior (as pointed out by C.), characteristic of the latent but now manifest basic assumption fight-in-flight group. The therapeutic task consists in returning the group to the working stage of self-observation and constructive feedback with the help of the group history and within the dimension of the "here and now." Events are then examined and put back into logical perspective. More detailed and clarifying work is done in the small groups and the individual sessions.

Measuring Therapeutic Success

Therapists are instructed to keep abreast of all transactions occurring among patients of the PTC in order to clarify distortions and reverse maladaptive patterns of behavior. The ultimate goal is to achieve health with consecutive reintegration into the community or preparatory facilities designed for that effect (rehabilitation clinic and adult clinic). Because the concept of health is difficult to define, we measure success instead by a patient's growth in each of eight value categories taken from Rubinstein and Lasswell (1966), which synthesize what people usually call "wants," "desires," or "needs." These are (1) affection, (2) respect, (3) rectitude, (4) power, (5) enlightenment, (6) skill, (7) wealth, and (8) well-being. The contextual viewpoint implies that all interactions shape and share all values to some extent. By analyzing every specific interaction in terms of all eight value categories, we become aware of ordinarily overlooked value consequences. If we explore the significance of an entire situation for a particular value, we make similar discoveries. This is the importance of the question asked of every detail of hospital life. "Is it therapeutic?" (Does it contribute to the well-being of patients?)

Summary

This chapter describes work at an innovative, on-going program designed to provide holistic treatment services for the deinstitutionalized, severely mentally disabled. Its major contribution consists of integrating, within one free-standing clinic, different therapeutic modalities such as psychopharmacotherapy, contemporary psychoanalytic group psychotherapy, individual casework, behavioral therapy, and milieu therapy. This eclectic approach is unique to the unit.

This therapeutic system provides a pattern for the future because it presents a treatment approach for a population which creates a management problem for more traditional service providers. Patients who attend this unit frequently have a history of multiple mental hospitalizations, yet most are able to live alone and are not yet "burned out." However, the population treated here is in need of psychotropic medication, crisis intervention, and stabilization, which would preclude their acceptance at a conventional analytically oriented clinic, or in a rehabilitation program. These patients are often referred to us by psychiatrists who find them difficult to manage in a private practice model, where there is no backup staff. For those patients who are readmitted to inpatient services, this unit provides on-going liaison work and aftercare.

The program has been able to improve patient's maladaptive behavior by providing multiple social and therapeutic supports in order to achieve stabilization and subsequent improvement. It also serves as a transitional unit able to refer selected patients to other appropriate departments of the therapeutic system.

Program effectiveness is determined by the achievement of treatment goals such as:

1. reducing psychiatric symptoms and maintaining patients in stable remission;
2. elevating self-esteem and assertiveness; improving interpersonal relations and extending the patient's social network; assisting patients with developmental issues which precipitate hospitalization;
3. maintaining contact with other facilities where patients are in conjoint treatment enabling us to coordinate all therapeutic activities entered on each case;
4. preventing rehospitalization; facilitating productive rehospitalization if needed; providing liaison with inpatient units, resuming service upon discharge;
5. providing referral to other community agencies for further

treatment, such as rehabilitation programs and other therapeutic modalities.

Cases

C. M.—35-year-old male

Intake: 4/14/82

Diagnosis: Schizophrenia, Chronic Undifferentiated, Mixed Personality Disorder, Alcohol Abuse history

Symptoms: History of several hospitalizations. Poor general appearance, auditory hallucinations, persecutory delusions, severe immobilizing depression and anxiety with suicidal ideation, episodes of assaultive behavior, low self-esteem, and poor compliance with medication and attendance.

Chemotherapy: Thorazine 800 mg, Endep 300 mg

Treatment: Small group and medical therapeutic community large group meeting twice a week. Patient has been able to work through via feedback his self-denigrating behavior and that many of his sexual difficulties are precipitated by his overall attitude of feeling helpless. Medication has been reduced to Thorazine 400 mg without decompensation.

Outcome (1985): Self-esteem has improved considerably. Relationship with roommates remains stable and now has a girl friend. Attends technical high school. Has stopped drinking and comes regularly to all scheduled therapeutic activities. Psychotic symptoms are in remission and no hospitalizations were necessary. (This is after three years of treatment.)

A. M. 24-year-old female

Intake: 11/80

Diagnosis: Schizoaffective Disorder, Paranoid Personality Disorder

Symptoms: Several hospitalizations. Patient suffers from frequent episodes of depression with suicidal and paranoid ideation. Also very angry and impulsive with poor interpersonal relationships.

Chemotherapy: Mellaril 100 mg QID

Treatment: Individual counseling with biweekly supportive small groups and medical therapeutic community meetings.

Outcome (1985): Although still in the program, she has become strongly motivated for group sessions. She can express her intense emotions in words to other members and receive feedback. She also understands her ability to improve her social skills by comparing her present and past interpersonal behavior in groups. For instance, she does not leave the group abruptly when angry. At most, she leaves but returns; usually she verbalizes her feelings.

O. L. 24-year-old male

Intake: 4/80

Diagnosis: 1. Schizophrenia, Paranoid Type; Bipolar Disorder
2. Narcissistic Personality Disorder

Symptoms: Multiple hospitalizations—Paranoid ideation with delusions of grandeur and manic behavior followed by severe episodes of expression. Tends to become extremely attached and vulnerable to separations. Stops medication at his own will. Smokes marijuana.

Chemotherapy: Prolixin HCl, 5 mg HS, 5mg QID

Treatment: Community medical meeting twice a week. Two small groups a week. Individual counseling. Patient has been able to transfer the need of one-to-one therapy to groups and group members. This is done by constant feedback and understanding his behavior in group via group history.

Outcome (1985): He has become consistent and punctual with his group and individual sessions. He addresses issues of grandiosity and flight from treatment with serenity and insight. He has reduced his rehospitalizations to only one in 1984.

K. D. 28-year-old female

Intake: 10/81

Diagnosis: Borderline Personality Disorder

Symptoms: Heroin addicted, maintained on methadone, and a polysubstance abuser (cocaine). Temper tantrums. Symbiotic relationship with mother, poor observing ego, low self-esteem, sadomasochistic interpersonal relationships.

Treatment: Attended therapeutic community medical meeting twice a week. Small supportive groups twice a week, individual counseling. Received feedback from group members and learned about herself through group history.

Outcome (9/10/84): Patient is currently drug free and no longer in methadone program. She has much better control of her temper tantrums. Her self-esteem has improved and she has been able to separate from a destructive relationship with a boyfriend of many years. She will proceed with her education in a master's program in art education.

D. W. 35-year-old female

Intake: 7/82

Diagnosis: Mixed Personality Disorder with Alcohol Abuse

Symptoms: Obesity, withdrawal from society. Difficulties and deficits in initiating and maintaining interpersonal relationships. Strong reaction to authority, symbiotic merging with family.

Treatment: Exploration with the patient via groups of the process of separation–individuation. Dependency issues are understood through interpersonal relationships with other members of the unit in the present and the past.

Chemotherapy: N/A

Outcome: Completion of bachelor of arts in anthropology. Volunteer job at a museum in his field. Transfer to PGC to start individual and group psychoanalytic psychotherapy.

V. P. 48-year-old male

Intake: 1/81

Diagnosis: Narcissistic Personality Disorder

Symptoms: Patient feels despondent and without direction or purpose then switches to grandiosity, omnipotence, and devaluation of others. He left a managerial position in a bank which he had held for 14 years. Now lives on welfare. Assets: high initiative and articulate—leadership qualities

Treatment: Medical therapeutic community meeting twice weekly, supportive group 3 times per week, individual counseling.

Chemotherapy: No meds

Outcome: Has been able to establish trust in treatment relationships with productive interactions. Discuss his participations in group and changes observed from session to session through group history. Sessions mostly deal with ways of relating to other members and staff. After 3 years he has been able to drop his grandiose façade and to become less defensive. In 1985 he continued treatment in the psychoanalytic program.

S. W. *26-year-old male*

Intake: 12/21/83

Diagnosis: 1. Bipolar Disorder Manic
2. Borderline Personality Disorder

Symptoms: History of multiple hospitalizations. Grandiosity, flight from treatment. Substance abuse, splitting mechanisms, devaluating tendencies. Poor insight. Frequent episodes of manic excitement with loss of contact with reality. Stops taking medication without medical advice thus returning to hospital. Assets. Very articulate, cultivated, violin virtuoso.

Treatment: Twice weekly therapeutic community meeting, weekly small group therapy, activity therapy.

Chemotherapy: Lithium CO_3 #1200 mg daily, Haldol 10 mg PN

Outcome (1985): Patient has learned that his acting-out behavior is an exteriorization of his resistance to treatment. Group members' feedback has proven less threatening than interpretations offered in individual sessions. Also understands that commitment to treatment and medication is not equated with being helped. Has become an example for other patients in taking meds. and giving feedback.

J. B. 25-year-old male

Intake: 1/22/82

Diagnosis: Borderline Personality Disorder

Symptoms: Patient was an institutional child. At present he is constricted and dependent on others for approval and special attention. He is very hard on himself and needs a lot of support and reality testing.

Chemotherapy: Trilafon 12 mg HS

Treatment: Individual counseling two sessions a week; TCMM twice a week. Vocational group and small therapy group twice a week. Has become more assertive in letting others know when he is pleased or displeased. He is working through his high expectations of people and situations and therefore having more realistic attitudes toward things. He is also becoming more tolerant to feelings of rejection and takes risks in making relationships with people.

Outcome: He resides in a supportive living residence with two roommates. Spends a great deal of his time fixing electronic equipment. Has been seeking part-time employment with the help of an agency and independently.

S. I. 28-year-old male

Intake: 7/2/82

Diagnosis: Schizoaffective Disorder

Symptoms: Several hospitalizations, depression, anxiety, difficulties in sustaining a job, low self-esteem. Confusion and hallucinations when not on medication. Overly dependent on mother.

Chemotherapy: Lithium 300 mg BID, Haldol 5 mg BID

Treatment: Individual and group counseling. Clerical work committee. Community meetings, medication.

Outcome (1985): Attendance has become regular. Understands that his behavior in the PTC reflects a long pattern of difficulties with committing himself and accepting responsibility. Changes are due to feedback about his interpersonal relations provided by staff and members in groups and compliance with medications.

References

Appleton, W. (1976), Third psychoactive drug usage guide. *Dis. Nerv. Sys.*, 37/1:39–51.
Astigueta, F. D. (1977), The use of nicknames in delineating character patterns in group psychotherapy. In: *Group Therapy, An Overview*, eds. L. R. Wolberg & M. L. Aronson. New York: Stratton Intercontinental Medical Corp., pp. 103–111.
——— (1980), The integration of psychopharmacology with contemporary psychoanalytic group psychotherapy. Paper read at International Congress Group Psychotherapy Meeting, Abstract Book VII, Copenhagen, Denmark.
Bion, W. (1959), *Experience in Groups and Other Papers*. New York: Basic Books.
Davidson, J., Turnbull, C. D., & Miller, R. D. (1980), A comparison of inpatient with primary unipolar depression and depression secondary of anxiety. *Acta Psychiat. Scand.*, 61:377–386.
Jones, M. (1953), *The Therapeutic Community*. New York: Basic Books.
——— (1968), *Beyond the Therapeutic Community*. New Haven, CT: Yale University Press, pp. 133–136.
Kernberg, O. (1975), *Psychoanalytic Object-Relations Theory, Group Process and Administration: Toward an Integrative Theory of Hospital Treatment*. New York: Aronson, pp. 241–289.
Kroft, A. (1966), The therapeutic community. In: *American Handbook of Psychiatry*, Vol. 3, ed. S. Arieti. New York: Basic Books, p. 542.
Minkoff, K. (1978), A map of chronic mental patients. In: *The Chronic Mental Patient*. ed. J. A. Talbott. Washington, DC.: American Psychiatric Assoc., pp. 11–37.
Newcomb, T. M. (1947), Autistic hostility and social reality. *Human Rel.*, 1:69–86.
Rubinstein, R., & Lasswell, H. D. (1966), *The Sharing of Power in a Psychiatric Hospital*. New Haven, CT: Yale University Press.
Talbott, J. A. (1980), A public policy on the chronic mentally ill patient. *Amer. J. Orthopsychiat.*, 50:53.
Wolberg, A. (1973), *The Borderline Patient*. New York: Stratton Intercontinental Medical Book Corporation.

——— (1977), Group therapy and the dynamics of projective identification. In: *Group Therapy 1977: An Overview*, eds. L. Wolberg, M. Aronson, & A. Wolberg. New York: Stratton Intercontinental Medical Books, pp. 151–180.

Wolf, A. (1969), The psychoanalysis of group. In: *Group Therapy Today*, ed. Ruitenbeeck. Chicago: Aldine-Atherton Press, pp. 92–93.

Van Putten, T. (1974), Why do schizophrenic patients refuse to take their drugs? *Arch. Gen. Psychiat.*, 31:67–72.

Chapter 19

RESIDENTIAL TREATMENT IN A PSYCHOTHERAPEUTIC COMMUNITY

SERGE VERHAEST

For moderately disturbed narcissistic and borderline patients, the treatment of choice is outpatient individual psychotherapy, often in combination with group psychotherapy. The changes in technique required have been described by many authors. However, some severely disturbed narcissistic and borderline patients need long-term psychotherapeutic residential treatment. According to Kernberg (1973) it is indicated for patients with low motivation for treatment, a severe ego weakness (manifested by a lack of anxiety tolerance and impulse control), and extremely weak object relations. Such patients engage in chronic acting-out behavior, are suicidal or promiscuous, have a chaotic life history, and enter into many unsuccessful treatment attempts, including brief hospitalizations for acute psychotic episodes (Hartocollis, 1980).

This chapter describes the therapeutic process in a long-term residential psychotherapeutic community. We call it a psychotherapeutic community because it is an integrated psychotherapeutic system and not just psychotherapy taking place in a residential setting. Within the description of the organizational structure of this community at the University Psychiatric Center St. Jozef, Kortenberg, Belgium, special attention will be given to the relationship between the treatment needs of narcissistic and borderline patients and the way in which the organizational structure has been set up. This is often lacking in the classical literature concerning therapeutic communities. (An exception is Kernberg's (1976) integrative theory of hospital treatment in the psychoanalytic treatment of narcissistic and borderline patients.) I will then discuss the differences between the therapeutic evolution and treatment strategy of narcissistic patients—who have attained a cohesive self and present a stable defensive character organization—and those of borderline patients, who have a more fragmented self and present splitting and projective identification as major defense mechanisms (Kohut, 1971; Kernberg, 1976). Clinical examples of the treatment of narcissistic and borderline patients will illustrate these viewpoints.

Description of the Organizational Structure

The psychotherapeutic community in Kortenberg treats adult patients, most of whom are 25–35 years of age; their diagnosis ranges from severely neurotic to a not too severely fragmented psychotic personality. The purpose of the treatment is an improvement in personality functioning. This is realized to some extent by a reconstruction or a restoration of the personality (Kohut, 1977). The duration of the treatment is usually one to two (maximum three) years. The treatment combines large group, small group, and individual activities on different therapeutic levels that offer support, sociotherapeutic interactions (informal, cooking, cleaning, recreational, and cultural activities); psychoanalytic psychotherapy, psychotherapeutic activity techniques, nonverbal therapies (sports and movement, art); and a community meeting integrating the different parts of the program.

The psychotherapeutic community is part of a larger university psychiatric hospital. It is located on a separate ward with a kitchen, dining room, and living room, a large room for recreational activities, ward, and community meetings, a room for small-group sociotherapeutic meetings, and bedrooms. The community also uses sports facilities, an art therapy room, and group and individual psychotherapy rooms, which are not on the ward.

The whole group of 32 patients and staff have a weekly community meeting (1 hour). There are also daily ward meetings (½ hour) with all patients, the psychiatric resident, and the nurses present.

The whole group is divided into four small groups of approximately eight patients. These small groups are responsible for cleaning, part of the cooking, and the organization of recreational activities, and they share in staff therapeutic decisions and matters of general policy when possible. These sociotherapeutic activities are conducted by elected patients, and the interactions are discussed twice a week in a sociotherapeutic meeting (½ hour) conducted by the psychiatric resident or the nursing staff. Twice a week each small group has psychoanalytic group psychotherapy (1½ hours). An individual psychotherapy session by the same psychotherapist is possible during crises. Each small group has psychotherapeutic activity techniques once a week (1 hour), movement therapy three times a week (1 hour), and art therapy three times a week (1½ hours). The therapeutic progress of a patient is assessed every two months in an assessment meeting with the patient, his small group, a representative of the other groups, and a representative of the staff. A similar assessment is also made, every two months, for the small group as a whole.

The therapeutic staff consists of a supervisor (a psychiatric staff member), a psychiatric resident, the nursing staff, a psychoanalytic group psychotherapist, a psychotherapist for activity techniques, a movement therapist, and an art therapist. The staff meets once a week to assess the therapeutic progress of patients (or group), once a week for a psychodynamic staff group, and every two months for a meeting about general policy matters. The psychodynamic staff group is conducted by an expert who is not a staff member. In addition, every therapeutic discipline has mutual supervision meetings, and a seminar on the literature regarding narcissistic and borderline patients is held every two weeks, and is open to all staff members. Some staff members also carry out research about treatment results and the social atmosphere in the ward.

The positions and activities of the staff members are as follows: the supervisor has the final responsibility for the program and conducts the staff assessment meetings and the meetings about general policy. The psychiatric resident (third year)

TABLE 19-1
Timetable of a Small Group

Monday	Tuesday	Wednesday	Thursday	Friday
Ward meeting 830–900	Ward meeting 830–900	Ward meeting 830–900		Ward meeting 830–900
Psychotherapeutic activity techniques 915–1015	Room cleaning	Cooking	Art therapy 900–1030	Room cleaning 915–1015
	Psychoanalytic group psychotherapy 1030–1200		Community meeting 1030–1130	Preparation of assessment meeting of other groups 1030–1100
Cleaning of the ward 1100–1200				Movement therapy 1115–1200
Lunch 1215–1245	Lunch 1215–1245	Lunch 1215–1245	Lunch 1215–1245	Lunch 1215–1245
Coffee 1315–1345	Coffee 1315–1345	Coffee 1315–1345	Coffee 1315–1345	Coffee 1315–1345

Sociotherapeutic meeting 1400–1430	Movement therapy (swimming) 1430–1515	Free afternoon and evening inside or outside the hospital 1400–2045	Movement therapy 1430–1515	Preparation of recreational activities 1315–1345
Assessment meeting 1500–1600	Art therapy 1530–1700		Analytic group psychotherapy 1545–1715	Art therapy 1400–1530
				Sociotherapeutic meeting 1545–1615
1700–1800 Free inside or outside the hospital	idem		1700–1800 Free inside or outside the hospital	idem
1800: Dinner		Dinner available if desired	1800: Dinner	
1845–2045 (2230) Free (or organized recreational activity) inside or outside the hospital			1845–2045 (2230) Free (or organized recreational activity) inside or outside the hospital	
2230: Bedtime	idem	idem	2230: Bedtime	idem

is responsible for daily management, participates in all staff meetings, and conducts the community and ward meetings and one of the small sociotherapeutic groups. He sees patients individually for supportive psychotherapy, prescribes drugs if necessary, and has a contact with families and outside officials. The nursing staff (a head-nurse and several nurses) is in daily contact with the patients in the ward, conducts one of the small sociotherapeutic groups, and participates in the other small sociotherapeutic group meetings, in the ward meeting, in the community meeting, and in staff meetings. The different therapists conduct their specific therapies and participate in the community and staff meetings.

Table 19-1 shows the weekly timetable for one small group.

Rationale of the Organizational Structure

The organizational structure meets basic needs for a serious long-term psychotherapeutic treatment. All patients in the therapeutic community program participate in the same treatment, in a location that is separate from the rest of the hospital. The slow rate of turnover promotes stability in the group and the presence of so-called culture carriers. Needless to say, the presence of a therapeutic boundary is of paramount importance in the treatment of patients with a pathology of the self.

The patients are all at approximately the same psychic developmental level, so that they can participate in the same program. This facilitates the level of therapeutic interventions and measures that one can use (Slavinska-Holy, 1980). There is enough homogeneity of anxiety level and heterogeneity of problems to promote interactions.

There is contact with the outside world. In the evenings, on Wednesday afternoon, and on weekends patients have free time and can leave the hospital, if their condition permits. There is a structuring of space inside the hospital; some activities take place on the ward, others take place elsewhere. This counteracts the development of regression and destructuralization in those patients with very weak reality testing, difficulties in differentiating inside and outside, and a tendency toward geographical confusions (Meltzer, 1967; Slavinska-Holy, 1975).

The time is clearly structured during the day, with activities of different kinds in a fixed timetable. Breaks are scheduled between the different activities to prevent the formation of a marathon effect.

The overall treatment process is also clearly structured, with assessment meetings every two months providing nodal points in this very long process. This structuring of time is important in preventing regression and destructuralization in these patients who have a very weak evocative memory capacity (Slavinska-Holy, 1975; Adler and Buie, 1979).

Multiple therapeutic approaches are provided on a large-group, small-group, and individual level, on a verbal and nonverbal level, and on a societal, interpersonal, and intrapsychic level. The psychotherapy promotes interpersonal and intrapsychic insight. The participation in psychotherapeutic activities in the first phase of treatment is made less difficult and frustrating through the possibility of an easier participation in all the other activities. The nonverbal approaches of movement therapy and art therapy present less threatening experiences and make it possible to reinvest libidinal psychic functions that have been deinvested. They help patients to sort out the so-called zonal and modal confusions (Meltzer, 1967). The term *zonal* refers to the erogenic zones and *modal* to the unconscious fantasies describing the interaction between the erogenic zone and the libidinal object. Interactions on the ward during cooking, cleaning, organizing recreational activities, leading and participating in different activities, and participating in the therapeutic assessment of their fellow patients, and in the general policy of the treatment program form the basis for the development of sublimatory ego functions (Adler, 1977). Effective reality confrontation and the development of social roles are promoted in a surrounding that is less threatening than the outside world. The nursing staff and the psychiatric resident can give individual support and set limits when needed.

The total treatment is integrated through a community meeting. It is of crucial importance to integrate the different parts of the program, especially with those patients who are narcissistically frustrating or present splitting and projective identification as central defense mechanisms. This prevents the formation of an antitherapeutic culture that results in disturbances in self-esteem, splitting, and fragmentation in the community.

Staff meetings conducted by the supervisor are necessary in order to deal with specific problems on a more intellectual level; for example, the slow progress of the treatment of severely disturbed patients and, on a deeper level, to have some awareness of the countertransference feelings elicited by patients with a pathology of the self. Otherwise these patients will induce problems of self-esteem in the staff, and splitting and fragmentation among staff members. A synthesis is made of the views of the different therapists, followed by some open discussion, which helps to prevent staff splitting (Book, Sadavoy, and Silver, 1978).

The psychodynamic staff group, conducted by a non-staff-member, facilitates analysis of the countertransference attitudes and latent conflicts of the staff, thereby preventing splitting and staff fragmentation induced by the patients. These meetings form the emotional basis for the growth of the therapeutic culture of the staff. Every two months, a staff meeting about general policy matters reviews the structure of the therapeutic program, making changes where necessary.

Mutual supervision, especially for psychotherapists and nurses, where contact with patients is less mediated by technical procedures, is also important in detecting personal countertransference feelings, so that these feelings can be used in an effective way to enable the individual to become more empathic. Theoretical seminars on psychoanalytic concepts regarding narcissistic and borderline personalities are very important because—in combination with the staff assessment meeting where the supervisor can relate theory to practice—they allow the staff members to have greater intellectual satisfaction in their work, and self-esteem is thereby increased. This is often necessary when working with these narcissistically frustrating patients (Salonen, 1975).

In this psychotherapeutic community, we can clearly see a difference in behavior, interpersonal relationships, and therapeutic evolution between narcissistic and borderline personalities. Different treatment strategies are necessary for each category of patient.

The Narcissistic Patient: Therapeutic Evolution and Treatment Strategy

Narcissistic patients present very few major behavioral problems and can follow the structure of the program; that is, take part in the different therapeutic activities. However, they do not establish personal relationships within the group and they cannot define the problems for which they come for treatment. They present themselves as "tourists" or as members of the therapeutic staff, showing in this way a strong denial of their real positions in the structure of the program. They feel superior to the other group members, whom they view as "patients needing treatment."

Narcissistic patients have so little awareness of others as separate human beings that they have difficulty cooperating with them in task-oriented therapies. They have particular difficulty with art therapy. When the narcissistic disturbance is very severe, they often find it impossible to have a creative relationship with materials in art therapy because this would show their limitations and confront them excessively with their problems about hidden feelings of grandiosity and omnipotence. Typical of their coolness is the fact that their rooms are generally without any personal decorative characteristics.

One major problem in treating these patients is to increase the awareness of staff members—not all of whom have training in a particular psychotherapeutic specialty—regarding the weakness behind the patients' façade of "supernormality," in this way preventing narcissistic injuries. In other words, one must handle the countertransference feelings created by these patients' low self-esteem and poor differentiation between self and object. It is useful to differentiate between the narcissistic countertransference of the individual staff members and that of the therapeutic program as a whole (Salonen, 1975).

The fact that a staff member is not seen as an individual person but as an extension of the patient (a selfobject) is often felt as very insulting, with the danger that the provoked anger can disturb the therapeutic relationship. The predominant feeling is that one is denigrated, but here there is also a subtle hidden feeling of idealization. There is a danger that a staff member, defending himself against these feelings, may lose sight of his real importance for the patient. This danger increases if the therapist has chosen his profession because of his own narcissistic weaknesses. The therapy will then have as an essential function the restoration of the staff member's own narcissistic balance. When these countertransference feelings are understood, there is a greater possibility of empathy with patients on this level.

The narcissistic patient very often considers the whole program as a selfobject. The ward is a kind of grandiose extension of the patient. Having the outside world in this way under his control, the patient does not have to be anxious about feeling weak, unappreciated, and rejected. The patient is disappointed when the ward does not satisfy this illusion. He becomes angry and rejects the ward, considering it worthless, bad, and controlling. There is a fantasy that the patient is completely understood or, on the other hand, that the ward is without value for his treatment. It is not possible to arrive at a realistic appreciation. It is important that the staff as a whole interact with this narcissistic transference in a very natural, realistic way. If this does not succeed, there is danger of splitting in the community analogous to splitting in the inner world of the patients, whereby some staff members are idealized, others are driven to rage, and the integrity of the staff as a whole diminishes. The patients very often use latent existing conflicts in the staff for this purpose. The splitting is less extreme than in borderline patients however.

The narcissistic patient can go on denying the reality of his limitations for a long time. The most disturbed patients leave the program when the danger of losing their aloof façade approaches. Others succeed in expressing some feelings of inadequacy and weakness when they are confronted with their real limitations. They can be reached for a while, but they rebuild their façade rapidly, although in a somewhat more human way. In the less severe cases, the narcissistic defenses can be challenged more thoroughly, and the fear of being rejected and abandoned when showing weakness can be worked through to some extent.

The questioning of such a narcissistic transference can only happen very gradually, together with the strengthening of the ego functions. This is very difficult because the staff reacts very quickly with disillusion to recurrent difficulties in the treatment. The staff members tend to judge the patient from their own positions of relative health, without realizing that patients need a long time in an atmosphere where they are not hurried and that, even then, the changes in the patients' psychic structure are very small. The strong tendency toward disillusionment has deeper roots in countertransference feelings, however; these are set in motion when the patient starts feeling disappointed in the treatment and views the ward as worthless. The gradual integration of these partial disappointments leads to an inner strengthening of the ego.

Finally, it is important that the staff has a solid base of enthusiasm deriving from facts and limits. The ability to admire and feel enthusiasm is based on the working through of early narcissistic self object positions. Narcissistic patients, with problems of weak self-esteem, tend to shift from resignation to narcissistic overstimulation. The enthusiasm of the staff should not be based on a sharing of the feelings of the patients, but on a realistic understanding of the personality of these patients and the possibility of influencing them therapeutically.

The Borderline Patient: Therapeutic Evolution and Treatment Strategy

Borderline patients become very restless and disorganized during the first phase of the treatment. They are unable to follow the structure of the program (attend the activities regularly), are agitated, emotionally volatile and variable, have no patience, are inattentive, have impulsive reactions, and have chaotic room arrangements. They can present transient psychotic episodes. Sometimes, they want to leave the program, but they do not have the strength to do this. This behavior lasts several weeks or months, and it can be explained as a severe regression. Anger, rage, and envy are propelled in the quickly developing transference in those patients who have an intense hunger for an object and who fight against their wishes for feeding and "holding" (Winnicott, 1965; Adler, 1980). This results in a breakthrough of the "reizschutz" of the psyche (Pines, 1980a), in a fragmentation of the self with loss of ego boundaries and loss of self object differentiation, and in a loss of the capacity to hold introjects and to have a sufficiently evocative memory (Adler & Buie, 1979).

The main therapeutic problem for the staff in this phase is the "holding" of these patients (Winnicott, 1965). The structure of the program and the interconnected relationships of the different therapists and patients all have a role in this holding. The most active part, however, is played by the nursing staff and the psychiatric resident. They have to follow these patients very closely because of their very short time perspective resulting from a very weak evocative memory capacity (Adler & Buie, 1979). The nurses have to start the formation of a type of transitional object relationship using the more structured activities in the ward (Winnicott, 1965). Nonverbal therapy is also important as a first means of relating, as it is more structured and less threatening than verbal therapy. The psychotherapist will have to decide if he can immediately take the patient in his less structured group, or see him alone during this first period of treatment.

This "holding" is made especially difficult by countertransference feelings associated with the splitting of the internal objects and the mechanism of projective identification that these patients use (Kernberg, 1976). The new patient is difficult, presents acting out, is manipulative. On the other hand, he has a good appearance and seems rather neurotic. He presents his disturbed behavior only with certain persons within the community who are more likely to arouse his desires and disillusions. Very often, the result is that the patient is seen as evil and noncooperative rather than overwhelmed by stress, anxiety, and desperation. This misconception often leads to a premature discharge or dropping out of treatment against medical advice. There is great danger that the staff will feel a desire to punish the patient. This attitude can be seen, on a deeper level, as a result of the mechanism of projective identification. The staff becomes the recipient of the projected bad objects of the patient and starts reacting in this way. More concretely, this means that staff members react in the way the patient induces them to, because these projected bad objects resonate with a similar but more unconscious and less destructive part in themselves. The concrete experience is that the staff member feels manipulated into being punitive. There is great danger that this will interfere with the more mature interactions between staff members and the patient (Adler, 1973).

The mechanisms of splitting associated with this projective identification result in the projection of good objects on some staff members, who are then idealized. They start to react in a very protective, parental manner. Thus, some staff members will consider the patient manipulative and bad and will ask for more structure and punishment, while others will consider him to be in pain or in need and will react with overprotectiveness and oversolicitousness, which only encourage the acting-out behavior. This is a sign of splitting in the staff, which prevents a good "holding" attitude. It leads to conflicts between staff members representing the good object and others representing the bad object, and results in staff fragmentation, which is pathognomonic for the presence of a borderline organization. Hartocollis (1980) described disputes between staff members that escalated to the point of members' destroying each others' professional reputation.

Such a "holding" is often more than presence, empathy, and support. A clear setting of limits is necessary to protect the patient against his acting-out behavior and all the negative consequences resulting from it. Hartocollis (1980) cites as examples, repeated suicidal attempts, self-laceration or burning of the skin, declaration of the patient's intent to leave the hospital, and falling in and out of love. The borderline patient must also frequently be protected against impulsive actions outside the hospital, such as giving up his work or divorcing his spouse on an unrealistic basis. Not setting limits would be a sign of a lack of understanding and "concern" (Winnicott, 1965). In this first phase, the borderline patient needs an outer *reizschutz*, an outer protective barrier against internal and external stimuli, since the inner *reizschutz* is defective. However, this limit-setting very often evokes conflicts within the staff relating to their own aggressivity. This can result in uncaring laxity, which the patient experiences as a new traumatic experience of abandonment, or in controlling sadistic attitudes.

After several months, the borderline patient becomes more relaxed and follows the structure of the program (attends most activities) but feels empty and then helpless, desperate, and alone. The patient has a less fragmented self and reaches a developmental level of cohesion and of self object differentiation analogous to that of narcissistic patients. There is a certain repair of the holding introject failure and of the evocative memory capacity. The resonance in the therapist of the feelings of helplessness, emptiness, and desperation can create major countertransference problems and provoke the therapist to interrupt the treatment in a flight from his own feelings. It is not always easy to differentiate this from the more realistic necessity of stopping treatment and transferring a patient to another facility, when this situation remains unchanged over a long period of time (Sadavoy, Silver, and Book, 1979).

In the successful therapeutic progression of the borderline patient, an idealizing self object transference is set in motion. This results in an improvement of the functioning and a reduction of the symptoms. In contrast to narcissistic patients, the idealizing transference feelings of borderline patients are more directly concerned with the desire for an ideal "holding" relationship that provides support and feeding than they are with self-worth and idealization of the therapist's appearance or intellect (Adler, 1980).

The patient then has to accept his limitations and incompleteness apart from the idealized therapist and work through the abandonment depression and the separation anxiety (Kernberg, 1976). When possible, these transference issues should be related to failures in these functions during early childhood, latency, and even adolescence (Adler, 1980). This is a continuation of the process of introjection and identification resulting in a so-called transmuting internalization (Kohut, 1971). The patient acquires a more differentiated self and more personal identity. The ego functions then become more autonomous and reliable and a mature superego develops (Kernberg, 1976). The patient becomes more active, stronger, listens to what is said, and has more personal opinions; his goals are more realistic. Very often, patients will then be able to choose a more realistic future in the outside world adapted to their fragile realistic possibilities. (Can they live alone? What are their study and work possibilities?) In the final resocializing phase, the patient has to validate (Adler, 1980) these structural achievements in work and in relationships in the outside world.

The various staff problems cited in the section on narcissistic patients, such as the danger of becoming disillusioned, the need for a solid, realistic enthusiasm, as well as the duration of treatment, are of course present in the treatment of the borderline patient. In the narcissistic patient, however, there are fewer problems with the splitting into good and bad internal objects and with the defensive mechanism of projective identification.

Clinical Material

Case 1: A Narcissistic Patient

Charles was a 48-year-old patient who worked as a technician in a garage. He did not appear very disturbed but felt inhibited and guilty about any self-expression. He had always been inhibited, but became especially so after his marriage eight years ago. The relationship with his wife was very unsatisfactory. She functioned on a level of mental deficiency. She could only speak very simply, could not read or write, and never left the closed circle of her family. She had had a total hysterectomy before the marriage. Marital therapy was not successful, and an attempt to divorce did not succeed either. Following these two efforts, he regularly attended encounter groups for three years. In this attempt to break down all his inhibitions, he felt a narcissistic desire for complete freedom and total change, which alienated him from daily realities. Being completely stuck, he went regularly to a psychiatrist who, seeing no solution and fearing a suicide, referred him to the hospital.

Charles described his father as tall, strong, self-admiring, commandeering, and with little affection for mother. Mother was described as rather weak, submissive, and probably depressed. Work was all that counted in the family; there was no interest in human feelings or tenderness. After attending junior high school, Charles worked on the family farm from 14 to 18 years of age and in a garage from 29 to 48 years of age. He was 40 years old when he married.

On the psychological assessment on admission, he had an IQ of 126. The score on the psychopathy scale of the Minnesota Multiphasic Personality Index (MMPI) was pathological. In his self-description, he was careless, off-hand, and complacent. On the Thematic Apperception Test (TAT), the primary ego functions were not undamaged. The perceptions of structured material were good, but the perceptions of unstructured material (Rorschach) were not completely adequate. There were no typical disturbances of thought processes, but his reactions were based on personal conceptions about life and not on facts. The boundary function with the outside world was sometimes absent. There was a general shortage of inhibiting and integrative functions. On a psychodynamic level, the desired relationships were of a narcissistic nature: he "wanted to live a completely free and detached life."

We concluded that we were dealing with a narcissistic personality. We found the vagueness of complaints typical of narcissistic personalities. His choice of a wife who functioned on a level of mental deficiency showed severe insufficiency feelings and a relationship with a nonpartner. The family background showed signs of affective deprivation. We further cited the ego weakness and desire for narcissistic relationships in the psychodiagnostic assessment.

During the first phase of the treatment, Charles attended the therapies initially (followed the structure of the program), with some restlessness (a slight tendency toward fragmentation and borderline level pathology), but this disappeared quickly. He was not integrated in the group and had no relationship with other group members. His room arrangement was very impersonal. He could not cooperate in task-oriented therapies. In movement therapy he was overambitious and had no realistic view of his possibilities. In art therapy, he was not expressive and was busy with the work of other patients. In group psychotherapy, he talked in a very provocative, complicated, sophisticated way. He was an outsider, always on another wavelength from the group, but thought that he was ahead of the group. He wanted to empathize but could not listen to what the others really said. He expressed a wish for complete liberation and searched for warmth and love to be felt in his body (based on his experiences in encounter groups). He blushed and got into trouble when more concrete feelings came to the foreground in the group. He had recurrent dreams of floating above a completely empty landscape, a typical narcissistic dream according to Kohut (1971). When the group members began to know him better and started questioning his attitude, Charles experienced this as an accusation. He was often critical and reproachful of the ward as a whole. In the outside world he had no friends. We would see this as the starting phase of the treatment of a rather typical, moderately disturbed (according to our patient population), narcissistic patient, with the establishment of a defensive narcissistic transference (Giovacchini, 1979).

After five to six months, a minimal change in his behavior appeared. He was calmer, more patient, and started listening to others. He no longer needed to be "special" and showed some feelings but still had difficulties accepting help from others. Meanwhile, he experienced considerable reality-confronting disillusions: he was not successful in organizing the recreational activities; an idealized sexual relationship with the most disturbed female of the ward was a failure. He was still difficult to satisfy, but he was beginning to realize that his isolation during the evenings was due to his extremely unrealistic romantic expectations about these evenings. He was disappointed in group psychotherapy, wherein he behaved more as a cotherapist (giving instructions). This phase lasted about 10 months. We would consider this phase as one where there was a certain questioning regarding his narcissistic transference positions.

Charles then became more confident in himself, and his relationships improved. He realized that he was not as strong verbally as he would like to be. His need for an "ideal" woman to narcissistically compensate for the failures experienced in childhood diminished. He could also question his marital relationship and decided to leave his wife, who did not want a divorce. He became more a member of the group, showed more personal feelings, and was less the cotherapist. He no longer felt narcissistically responsible for all that happened in the group and was less "helping." He became expressive in art therapy. He still felt criticized and rejected when the other group members made remarks about his overambitiousness, and his vanity. He felt guilty about leaving his wife and had difficulty showing his feelings about the separation. He started feeling depressed and alone. Feelings of warmth and concern were still difficult. This period lasted about six months.

We would conceptualize this phase in the following way: The narcissistic defensive transference diminished; there was less discrepancy between ideal self and real self. Charles could allow himself to show some weakness, but depressive complaints related to repressed aggression about feeling rejected and abandoned, came progressively to the foreground.

A psychodiagnostic assessment in this period showed that his MMPI scores had become normal. There was still a weak ego, however. The boundary functions between inside and outside were not yet adequate, but there were more integrative and controlling functions. There was an ambivalent desire for a free and detached life, but also for tender feelings of understanding and support. These desires were at the narcissistic oral level. There were also some paranoid traits.

In the following period of about six months, his depression increased. He felt inadequate and had difficulties in accepting his real limitations. He succeeded in integrating this gradually. He then felt more self-confident, was more satisfied, and prepared himself for leaving the hospital. His interactions in the group were quite good; he was independent and open but not obtrusive. Narcissistic tendencies reappeared when he started thinking about his future and was confronted with real outside problems such as finding a new work at his age; but these tendencies were less pronounced and could be understood and discussed in a much easier way. We would consider that, in this phase, some working through of the separation anxiety, with a transmuting internalization, was achieved.

In the psychological assessment during this period, the ego strength was found to have increased, and the boundary function between self and outside world had improved to the point where one could speak of an adequate boundary function. The patient stressed that he had learned to keep the problems and feelings of others at a distance, whereas before he had been submerged by them. He was more relaxed, had less of a tendency to dominate, was less overambitious, and found it easier to accept his limitations.

He still had difficulties with personal contacts, however. His difficulty in realizing deep affective relationships was due to persisting narcissistic needs. A further assessment would be necessary to tell if this were caused by the confrontation with the future problems in the outside world or if some narcissistic needs still remained.

A decision was then made to stop the treatment. The following months focused on the resocialization and emotional preparation for leaving the hospital. He first looked for a house and went out on weekends to get used to new contacts in the outside world now that he was divorced. He succeeded in making contact with his new neighbors. In the hospital, his interactions remained on the same satisfactory level. He had difficulty expressing his feelings about leaving when the separation grew closer. He started working and came to the hospital at night.

He then left the hospital completely. Work and living were satisfactory. He was looking to establish a new relationship with a woman.

Case 2: A Borderline Patient

Mary, 30 years old, had been working as secretary for a cattle dealer for seven years. She was paid above her real capacities and was satisfied. Her boss picked her up every day at her home to drive her to work. Early on an intimate relationship started, interrupting a relationship with another man, in which money and going to expensive restaurants were major features. Mary interrupted the intimate relationship with her boss after three years to start a relationship with another man. Due to her manipulative conduct, this man stopped the relationship after two years. After breaking off with this man, Mary no longer enjoyed her job. She informed her mother of her prior relationship with the boss and let her mother force her to leave her job a year later. She immediately regretted this decision. She found a new job, but only worked two weeks. She then stayed at home and upset the whole family with her theatrical and manipulative behavior. She said she wanted to go back to her former job, she did not dare to go outside anymore, did not want to go to bed, could not sleep, ate very little, smoked and drank heavily, and repeatedly said that she wanted to be dead. After a year of this regressive behavior, with manipulative suicide threats, a short hospitalization was decided upon. After the hospitalization, outpatient supportive contact was planned. She did not, however, keep the appointments. The family contacted the hospital again four years later because of continuing difficulties at home, lack of work, refusal to consider living elsewhere, and not going outside the house except when drunk. She was finally forced to accept a new hospitalization.

Mary had always gotten what she wanted as a child. She had furious temper tantrums at the smallest frustration. She needed a lot of support in elementary school, was quite punctual, but reacted to stress with stomach aches. When she started a course to become a home economics teacher, she could not stand being away from home for more than three days, went to day school for some time, and finally stopped studying altogether. She finally started working as secretary for the cattle dealer at age 23.

The extreme regressive behavior; the very strong symbiotic ties (not succeeding in leaving home to study); the very superficial relationships (money, glamour); and her spoiled childhood led us to conclude that her psychopathology was more regressive than a hysterical personality disorder. This was confirmed by a psychological diagnostic assessment during the first hospitalization, where Mary was described as a very infantile, naïve person with a dependent and passive relationship to the outside world. She had very little self-confidence and her personality was poorly developed. She wanted total freedom to do and get what she wanted without any thought for the desires of others. She sought support from a man who would take all problems on his shoulders, cherish her, coddle her, and satisfy all her oral needs. Aggression was inhibited.

The treatment started in the following way. She first came for an outpatient consultation but refused to stay. After a week she came back, stayed a week, but left again. She was brought back after a few days. Mary was not motivated for her stay and was even less motivated for her treatment. She continually wanted to leave the clinic. In her contacts with staff and patients she was seemingly easy, superficial, laughed a lot, experienced no problems. After a month, restlessness and fidgeting came more and more to the forefront. She was tense, anxious, missed many therapy sessions, and walked in and out of sessions and could not stay until the end when she did attend them. For a short period, she tended toward bizarre ideation and was somewhat paranoid. In the task-oriented therapies, she was hyperactive and limits had to be set. She had difficulty falling asleep. She was very demanding and clinging toward nurses, fellow-patients, and family. She started a very demanding love affair with a fellow patient who did not respond to her feelings. She spent a lot of money and got into financial difficulties. She ran away to the bus station. She drank when she was away from the clinic in the evenings. The free weekends were a disaster. Very often she was not allowed to go home on weekends or to have an evening free outside the hospital. A light neuroleptic medication was necessary. In the last part of this period of six months, Mary became somewhat more relaxed during the week and the restlessness was only pronounced during weekends. She was a little bit more integrated in the group. She started another amorous relationship. She was dependent and demanding on the nursing staff.

This can be considered as a starting phase, with a certain fragmentation: restlessness, hyperactivity, not keeping appointments. When the activities were structured she succeeded, more or less, in following the program. When the program was less structured (during the evenings), she became more chaotic, with excessive drinking and spending of money. With still less time structure, as on weekends, everything went wrong. The hospital represented a bad object that was threatening and that she had to try to leave. On the other hand, there was the idealizing relationship with one fellow-patient—followed by yet another—which represented the good object. For a short period, there was still more severe fragmentation, with psychotic, bizarre, and paranoid features. Support and limit-setting from nursing staff were often necessary. A neuroleptic medication had to be prescribed.

In the following six months, she became more relaxed, but was viewed as empty. She took less care of herself, ate more, and became fatter. She remained superficial, was still difficult to reach, and had no insight into her situation. It became clear how difficult she found it to cooperate. She still could not sit through the task-oriented therapies. In the group, she was seen as a dominant, arrogant, and denigrating person. A noncomprehending smile was her only reaction to comments about her behavior. She was very isolated in the group. She was sometimes more sensitive and, from time to time, dared to show that she felt hurt by a remark about her attitude. She stayed on the ward more often; talked less about home, but still talked about a departure date. She went to bars less often on weekends, spent less money, but still had difficulty filling her free time. The contact with the outside world was described as somewhat frightening. She had a third relationship with a divorced man outside the clinic.

We would conceptualize this period as one in which a boundary between outside and inside is reached, with the formation of a reizschutz, more evocative memory capacity, self objects, and a more cohesive self. The patient starts longing for an idealized "holding" (Adler, 1980). Splitting and fragmentation are less extreme. The ward becomes a safe, idealized place and the outside world seems more frightening.

In the following five months, Mary became very passive, ate more, and gained even more weight. However, she experienced more feeling—of being alone, helpless, and not understood. From time to time, she was more involved in the group. She sometimes made a correct remark about other patients. She became more concerned with her appearance. We would consider this period more centered around the feelings of abandonment depression (Masterson, 1976) resulting from the repressed desire for an idealized holding, an oral-narcissistic symbiotic relationship.

During the next eight months, a greater involvement with the group and the community (as a whole) developed. She became more accessible, from time to time made good verbal interventions, had more endurance, and stayed with therapies until the end. She took more initiative, and occasionally took on more responsibilities. She expressed more feelings and they were less extreme. In the task-oriented therapies, she was more relaxed and finished what she started. Her room was tidier. Filling her free time was somewhat easier but she still had a tendency to drink. She still talked about leaving but in a more relaxed way. Her plans after leaving were still unrealistic. She had a special relationship with another fellow-patient, who influenced her very much. She had not learned from her previous, unrealistic love affairs. She started telling dreams in group psychotherapy. She presented at some moments a very friendly, dependent attitude, and at others a provocative, condescending, familiar attitude. She filled herself with the problems of the other group members, questioning them in a clinging way as a defense against feelings of loneliness.

At the end of that period (the final two months), she became still more active and involved in the group and the ward. She paid more attention to her appearance in the areas of weight, hygiene, and clothing. The ward had become a home that she did not want to leave. She was more active in task-oriented therapies and carried out her tasks more completely. She started a new love affair with an alcoholic patient outside the ward. Whereas her earlier relationships had been based more on rescue fantasies, in this one sexual contact became more important. The psychotherapist reported signs of a narcissistic fusion with a very idealized sister, idealized parental figures (the staff members), and an idealized ward, but also, a beginning differentiation from them with the expression of open criticism.

We would consider the beginning period of this phase as the start, and the last period of this phase as the full development, of a narcissistic–oral symbiotic or "idealized" holding transference (Adler, 1980).

In a psychological assessment at the end of that period, the patient was described as a dependent oral personality with a desire for admiration and total freedom. There was, however, a greater feeling of being able to do something, which could show more anal positions. She was no longer depressed, and had less antisocial and paranoid tendencies. The aggressivity was directed toward the outside. The ego functions, however, were deficient; norms were not internalized, and the boundary functions between inside and outside and the integration of impulses were deficient, which seemed to point to the fact that her functioning still depended on outside factors. The intellectual functioning that was emotionally decreased at the start of the treatment (IQ: 88) was now increased to an IQ of 110.

This narcissistic transference again showed tendencies toward fragmentation after a change in psychotherapist and a diminution of medication. She had begun to consider leaving the hospital when there was a suicide in the ward, and again became restless and fidgety. She monopolized all the activities in the group, presented all the problems of the group, but got lost in the discussion. She was the barometer of the group. She was extremely concerned about the other group members. This period lasted for five months.

She then began to react more adequately and in a less monopolizing way. She became more sensitive to the remarks of the other group members. She started thinking about her future after leaving the hospital, but her views were very obstinate and rigid. Under pressure from the staff, she finally accepted a job in a sheltered work setting and found rest once she reluctantly accepted this work, which took into account her limited capacities.

We may conceptualize that a certain transmuting internalization (Kohut, 1971) was achieved and that the patient reached a more neurotic adjustment. The psychological assessment during this period showed that she had become more independent and realistic. The impression that she could decide her own future had increased. She perceived the relationship between her actions and the outcomes. The ego functions had improved and the ego strength had increased. She had better control of her impulses. On a psychodynamic level, there was still a tendency to be dependent on supportive and controlling authority figures, although it was less extreme.

During the short period while she had worked in a sheltered setting and returned to the hospital at night, she found an apartment and a job in the town where her family lived. Her lover would come to live with her once his treatment for alcoholism in another hospital was finished. The town where she now planned to live and work was too far away for her to return to the hospital at night. It was agreed that she would leave, although the future of the relationship with her friend was not clear. She was able to talk of her fear of the new environment and her anxiety about losing contact with the group. She said goodbye in a friendly but not very emotional way.

She then started working in the planned administrative job. This was quite satisfactory. She kept house adequately and also kept track of household expenses. Her lover, who still had no job and tended to keep drinking was the source of quite some stress. (The patient was rehospitalized shortly thereafter.)

Summary

Hospitalization cannot be considered as something to be avoided at any price or to be used only for very limited periods with severely disturbed borderline and narcissistic patients, because of their tendency toward severe nontherapeutic regressions. A hospital setting can be an effective psychotherapeutic tool for patients who cannot be treated in any other way.

Such a hospital program must be considered as an integrated psychotherapeutic system. It must have structural characteristics to meet the specific psychopathological needs of patients with a severe pathology of the self (division of space, division of time, verbal and nonverbal approaches, individual, small- and large-group activities on intrapsychic, interpersonal, intergroup, and societal levels). There must be at least a certain amount of theoretical and emotional awareness in the whole staff of the way narcissistic and borderline patients interact and the hidden meaning behind their interactions. Countertransference feelings of the individual staff members and of the staff as a whole must be examined as an ongoing part of the treatment; otherwise there will be a great danger of developing an antitherapeutic culture. Ongoing one-on-one supervision, or supervision conducted at staff meetings is necessary, especially for psychotherapists, nursing staff, and ward psychiatrist. Successful treatment takes between one and two years (maximum three years).

During this period a psychotherapeutic evolution can be seen as analogous to what is described in outpatient expressive psychotherapy with narcissistic and borderline patients (Kohut, 1971, 1977; Kernberg, 1976). Some structural change is achieved but the exact degree is difficult to assess. One can be satisfied if some autonomy is achieved in such severely disturbed patients, even if independence remains shaky (Meltzer, 1967; Horwitz, 1980). Kohut (1977) suggests the term *functional rehabilitation* for the result of the psychotherapeutic processes of recovery of the self. The self objects (and their functions) have been sufficiently transformed into psychological structures so that they can function independently to a certain extent, in conformity with self-generated patterns of initiative (ambitions) and inner guidance (ideals).

I think the indications for such a long-term residential psychotherapeutic treatment are often made on a negative nontherapeutic basis (Hartocollis, 1980); specifically, prolonged heroic attempts at outpatient therapy only make these patients more difficult to treat when they are finally hospitalized as a last resort. More positive indications for residential treatment could and should be made. M. Pines (1980b) reported working with a severe borderline woman over 20 years earlier; she needed to be hospitalized for about two years before she was able to return to a highly disturbed home environment in a state where she could begin to sort out her own problems. He thought this lengthy hospitalization was worthwhile since on follow-up over 20 years later, the former patient was found to have coped reasonably well with a marriage, and to have raised a family. She had not suffered any further breakdowns.

Finally, although it has not been described in this chapter, considerable attention is given to the spouse and/or family of the hospitalized patient. In most cases the interventions are of a supportive type, but more formal marital or family therapy is not excluded when necessary.

References

Adler, G. (1973), Hospital treatment of borderline patients. *Amer. J. Psychiat.*, 130:32–36.
—— (1977), Hospital management of borderline patients and its relation to psychotherapy. In: *Borderline Personality Disorders: The Concept, the Syndrome, the Patient*, ed. P. Hartocollis. New York: International Universities Press, pp. 307–323.
—— (1980), A treatment framework for adult patients with borderline and narcissistic personality disorders. *Bull. Menn. Clin.*, 44:171–180.
—— Buie, D. H. (1979), Aloneness and borderline psychopathology: The possible relevance of child developmental issues. *Internat. J. Psycho-Anal.*, 60:83–96.
Book, H. E., Sadavoy, J., & Silver D. (1978), Staff countertransference to borderline patients on an inpatient unit. *Amer. J. Psychother.*, 32:521–532.
Giovacchini, P. (1979), *Treatment of Primitive Mental States*. New York: Aronson.
Hartocollis, P. (1980), Long-term hospital treatment for adult patients with borderline and narcissistic disorders. *Bull. Menn. Clin.*, 44:212–226.
Horwitz, L. (1980), Group psychotherapy for borderline and narcissistic patients. *Bull. Menn. Clin.*, 44:181–200.
Kernberg, O. (1973), Discussion of G. Adler; Hospital treatment of borderline patients. *Amer. J. Psychiat.*, 130:35–36.
—— (1976), *Object-Relations Theory and Clinical Psychoanalysis*. New York: Jason Aronson.
Kohut, H. (1971), *The Analysis of the Self*. New York: International Universities Press.
—— (1977), *The Restoration of the Self*. New York: International Universities Press.
Masterson, J. F. (1976), *Psychotherapy of the Borderline Adult*. New York: Brunner/Mazel.
Meltzer, D. (1967), *The Psychoanalytic Process*. London: William Heinemann.
Pines, M. (1980a), Group psychotherapy with narcissistic and borderline patients. Paper presented at the University Psychiatric Center St. Jozef, Kortenberg, Belgium, April.
—— (1980b), What to expect in the psychotherapy of the borderline patient. *Group Anal.*, 13:168–177.
Sadavoy, J., Silver, D., & Book, H. E. (1979), Negative responses of the borderline to inpatient treatment. *Amer. J. Psychother.*, 33:404–417.
Salonen, S. (1975), The hospitalized ward from the standpoint of the patients' self esteem. *Psychiat. Fenn.*, 325–331.
Slavinska-Holy, N. (1975), Spatio-temporal consideration in psychoanalytic group psychotherapy of severely disturbed patients. In: *Group Therapy: An Overview*, ed. L. R. Wolberg & M. L. Aronson. New York: Stratton Intercontinental Medical Books, pp. 120–126.

——— (1980), Treatment of the borderline in homogeneous groups and the use of the "body transference technique." In: *Group and Family Therapy,* ed. L. R. Wolberg & M. L. Aronson. New York: Brunner/Mazel, pp. 121–133.
Winnicott, D. W. (1965), *The Maturational Processes and the Facilitating Environment: Studies in the Theory of Emotional Development.* New York: International Universities Press.

Chapter 20
A STUDY OF INTRAPSYCHIC STRUCTURES AND PROCESSES IN THREE GROUPS OF PATIENTS: ONE SCHIZOPHRENIC, ONE BORDERLINE, AND ONE NEUROTIC

Laurice W. Glover, M.S.S.W.

There has long been interest in clinicians' differing experiences with schizophrenic, borderline, and neurotic patient populations. Clinical wisdom flowing from such work has led to certain basic assumptions regarding the contrasts in characterologic structure and functioning in these human beings. A more careful and precise study of such similarities and differences would have implications both for metapsychologic formulations and for clinical interventions.

A small study was initiated in 1980 by the Group Process Department, Bronx Psychiatric Center, in conjunction with the Einstein College of Medicine Psychiatric Residency program at the hospital.[1] There was a review of clinical material from three patient populations: hospitalized patients about to be discharged, hospitalized patients who may never be discharged

---

[1]This project was initiated with the skilled assistance of Joyce Kobayashi, M.D., Chief Resident in Psychiatry, 1980–1981, Albert Einstein College of Medicine, Bronx Psychiatric Center.

In addition, thankful acknowledgment is due to those students in psychoanalytic training who volunteered long hours of work in helping to analyze the verbal communications for this study: from the Postgraduate Center for Mental Health, Karen Dubiner, M.S.W., Pauline Pinto, M.S.W., Margaret Sablove, Ed.D., Stephen Schoenbrot, M.S.W., David Speights, Ph.D., Mari Terzaghi, Ph.D., Joseph Turkel, Ph.D., and Mark Wayne, M.S.W.; from the Training Institute for Mental Health Practitioners, Nancy Auster, M.S.W., Deborah Hirsch, M.S.W., and Israel Rosenweig, M.S.W.

because of severe limitations in functioning, and a community-based population termed *neurotic*. The first group of patients fits the description given by Otto Kernberg (1975) of "borderline character disorders." The second group has been diagnosed as "chronic schizophrenics." The third group includes both "healthy neurotics" and "high functioning borderline character disorders."

The verbal material from three group sessions (see Appendixes 20-1, 20-2, 20-3), one from each population group, was analyzed for the unconscious derivatives of drive elements, ego activity, and self- and object-relational elements. The group therapy setting was deliberately chosen as a means of identifying intrapsychic themes of several patients on any given day, more or less simultaneously. The tabulated results are described, summarized, and tentatively interpreted in the material that follows.

Background and Literature Review

A review of the literature on schizophrenic conditions which has appeared in the past two decades reflects an attention more to behavioral, sensory, and thinking processes than to questions around intrapsychic structures and functioning. One would assume this to be so because of the difficulties inherent in clinically identifying and then measuring the complex emotional operations posed by the psychoanalytic model of the mind. Certain exceptions, however, have provided helpful clinical insights.

Most notable among these is the study by Bellak, Hurvich, and Gediman (1973) on *Ego Functions of Schizophrenics, Neurotics, and Normals*. This research project undertook to review both theoretically and clinically the major ego functions, their interrelationships, assessment, development, and treatment implications. The findings are meant to be used clinically, but were of considerable assistance in identifying and characterizing such phenomena as were of value and interest for the present study.

A study by Arsenian and Semrad (1966) reviewed the use of language in group therapy sessions by acutely ill schizophrenics as contrasted with chronic schizophrenics. Their findings indicated that "the largest part of language disturbance or distortion in chronic schizophrenia is defensive, serving to minimize or insulate the feelings against experiences of pain or anxiety" (p. 449). In contrast, patients striving "toward the restitution of lost objects" were "predominantly ambivalent" in their verbal communication. "Their schizophrenic talk simultaneously discloses and covers up ideas and feelings" (p. 452).

In a paper discussing the clinical implications of the language used by patients undergoing severe ego regression or decompensation, Palombo and Bruch (1964) present the thesis that when human beings are under great emotional stress, "They tend to express their feelings of personal disorder in terms of images which represent a disruption of the normal spatial relationships among their observing selves, their bodies, and the world and people around them" (p. 248). Thus, the expression "I'm falling apart," communicates the subjective experience of ego failure.

Finally, a paper by Silverman, Pettit, and Dunne (1971) dealt with the relationship between self object differentiation and pathology reduction in schizophrenia. Their findings were indicative of a relationship between significant reduction in pathology and the capacity for *diminished* self/object differentiation.

None of these studies was directed at the same phenomena as the study described in this paper, but they were similar in general type and intent. They used trained clinical observers to investigate, identify, and articulate certain aspects of language, symbolization, and intrapsychic structure in the schizophrenic character structure within the framework of psychoanalytic metapsychology.

Method

Three videotapes of psychotherapy group sessions were utilized for this study. Each tape was transcribed, and was then analyzed by this writer assisted by one to five other trained clinicians (one a psychiatry resident, the others advanced students in psychoanalytic training) at any one period. The focus of our analytic work was the identification of the primary unconscious intent of each communication during the group session. We looked for unconscious derivatives of drive elements (both libidinal and aggressive), of ego functions [as explicated by Bellak, Hurvich, and Gediman (1973)], and of self/object representations (as delineated conceptually by Sandler and Rosenblatt, 1962; Jacobson, 1964; Kohut, 1971, 1977; Kernberg, 1975, 1976; Mahler, Pine, and Bergman, 1975; Storolow and Lachmann, 1980, among others). We also made a judgment as to the primary unconscious intrapsychic *function* of each communication: drive, ego, or self/object. If more than one intrapsychic agency was judged to be in operation, notation was made accordingly (see addenda).

The tape of the chronic schizophrenic group was from the eighth session of the group, the tape of the borderline group was from the third session. The tape of the neurotic group was from an on-going group. The chronic group tape had comparatively few responses, presumably as a result of several factors: the paucity of verbal communication in such a group, the necessarily frequent verbalizations of the therapists in comparison to the patients (usually one for one), and the fact that the "therapy discussion" time is quite short, due to low tolerance levels among the patients.

This was not intended to be a formalized research project, but rather a beginning exploration of certain psychological phenomena. It is hoped that this small study might be a precursor of further investigations within the more usual research model.

Presentation of Findings

The findings are grouped below in a manner that reflects the analytic methods employed in the study. They are presented in list form, with the highest percentage of responses first. A brief discussion follows each list with a tentative interpretation or explanation of those intrapsychic processes under scrutiny.

We begin with a breakdown of *all* of the responses in the entire study (I. Total Responses by Population) with basic groupings showing the percentage of responses reflecting drive activity, ego functioning, and self/object representations. A further breakdown of these findings is then given. II. Drive Elements are listed according to psychoanalytic model. III. Ego Functions do not encompass object relations, that is, self/object responses. (This is in the interests of clarity and does not reflect a metapsychological stance.) There follows a further breakdown of the ego functions listing into defenses used and anxieties expressed, as these were felt to be of especial importance to a more explicit understanding of the ego phenomena. Similarly, in the last analyses, IV. Self/object Representations, specific consideration is given to self-responses, father-as-object responses, and mother-as-object responses.

I. Total Responses by Population

    Chronic schizophrenic group—178 responses
        Drive elements, 24.16%
        Ego functions, 47.19%
        Self/object representations, 28.65%

    Borderline group—624 responses
        Drive elements, 42.95%
        Self/object representations, 35.58%
        Ego functions, 21.47%

    Neurotic group—1,017 responses
        Drive elements, 46.9%
        Self/object representations, 31.9%
        Ego functions, 21.14%

Discussion of Total Responses

There is a similarity in the overall responses between the neurotic and borderline populations: The percentage of ego function responses being about 1 in 5, the self/object representation responses about 1 in 3, and the drive element responses close to 1 in 2.

In contrast, the chronic schizophrenic group exhibits ego function responses of almost 1 in 2. One thinks here of Freud's early formulations about the "ego instincts" as closely related to survival of the organism (Freud, 1915, p. 124; 1926). The other responses in the chronic group are almost evenly divided between self/object representation (3 in 10) and drive elements (1 in 4).

II. Drive Elements

Chronic schizophrenic group—43 responses
  Genital (phallic and inner-genital) aggressive, 39.53%
  Anal retentive, 23.26%
  Oral libidinal, 20.93%
  Genital (phallic and inner-genital) narcissistic, 6.98%

Borderline group—268 responses
  Genital (phallic and inner-genital) aggressive, 33.96%
  Genital (phallic and inner-genital) narcissistic, 23.13%
  Oral libidinal, 16.79%
  Oral aggressive, 7.46%
  Genital (phallic and inner-genital) libidinal, 5.97%
  Other: Oedipal, 4.48%; exhibitionistic, 2.24%;
    anal retentive, 2.24%; anal expulsive, 1.87%;
    voyeuristic, 1.12%; urethral, 0.74%

Neurotic group—447 responses
  Genital (phallic and inner-genital) aggressive, 43.40%
  Genital (phallic and inner-genital) libidinal, 28.51%
  Voyeuristic, 10.27%
  Anal retentive, 5.03%
  Other: oral libidinal, 3.50%; anal expulsive, 3.14%;
    exhibitionistic, 2.52%; oedipal, 1.67%; genital
    sadistic, 0.80%; oral aggressive, 0.60%; genital
    narcissistic, 0.40%

Discussion of Drive Elements

The drive elements listed above were understood within the classic psychoanalytic metapsychological model (Freud, 1905, 1915; Abraham, 1916; Sterba, 1968). We looked for unconscious derivatives of libidinal and aggressive impulses, as well as at the developmental level expressed at that moment: oral, anal, preoedipal genital, or oedipal genital.

The word *genital* (i.e., "genital aggressive" and "genital libidinal") was used to encompass any drive element that was both genital and *pre*oedipal genital, including, therefore, both phallic and inner-genital expressions. Some of the criteria for assessing these phenomena were based on earlier work done by this author and Dr. Dale Mendell (Glover and Mendell, 1982).

One approach to assessing the figures above is to compare the total percentages of responses which are primarily libidinal with those which reflect a mixture of libidinal and aggressive impulses. The former include genital libidinal, genital narcissistic, oral libidinal, and exhibitionistic. The latter are comprised of genital aggressive, anal expulsive, anal retentive, oral aggressive, urethral, voyeuristic, and oedipal.

More than half of all drive elements included an aggressive component, within this description. The chronic schizophrenic and neurotic populations included a larger aggression percentage (2 in 3 respectively) than the borderline population (1 in 2). In all groups, the most frequently expressed drive element was that of genital aggressive. Perhaps this is reflective of the group situations: one would not ordinarily expect such striking similarities between the three patient populations.

The second most frequent drive element appearing in the responses is, however, different from population to population. Anal retentive elements are most numerous in the chronic schizophrenic group, genital (both phallic and inner-genital) narcissistic in the borderline group, and genital libidinal in the neurotic group. One would expect, in other words, more concern with the pleasures of withholding in the chronic group, the pleasure of portraying a pleasing appearance and/or performance in the borderline group, and the pleasure of accomplishing, of experiencing genital sexuality, and of creating, in the neurotic group.

The third most frequent element in the neurotic group was the part-instinct voyeurism. Although of a much higher libidinal level than oral receptive impulses, appearing developmentally just before the emergence of the oedipal conflict, voyeurism is, in fact, also concerned with taking in emotionally; that is, with one's eyes. It may also be stimulated in the group therapy situation, as may oral libidinal impulses.

III. Ego Functions (other than object relations)

    Chronic schizophrenic group—84 responses
        Reality testing, 32.14%
            Autonomous functioning (memory, perception, attention, etc.), 23.80%

Defensive functioning, 21.42%
Control and regulation of affects: expression of anxiety, 15.48%
Mastery-competence, 3.57%
Stimulus barrier, 2.38%
Sense of reality, 1.19%

Borderline group—134 responses
Defensive functioning, 29.85%
Control and regulation of affects: expression of anxiety, 29.10%
Reality testing, 26.12%
Mastery-competence, 5.97%
Stimulus barrier, 5.22%
Synthetic-integrative functioning, 2.24%
Sense of reality, 1.49%

Neurotic—215 responses
Defensive functioning, 58.60%
Control and regulation of affects: expression of anxiety, 24.65%
Judgment, 6.98%
Reality testing, 4.19%
Sense of reality, 1.40%
Stimulus barriers, 1.40%
Mastery-competence, 0.93%
Synthetic-integrative functioning, 0.93%
Thought processes: primary process thinking, 0.93%

Discussion of Ego Functions

In identifying the ego functions, we made use of the classification system suggested by Bellak et al. (1973), which suggests 12 major areas of ego functioning. We did *not*, however, subsume object relations under ego functions, as they did. Although we would agree with self/object activity as being under the aegis of the ego, we wished to consider it in the depth and specificity flowing from the more recent metapsychologic models of object relations and self psychology.

Of the remaining ego functions, the differential picture between the borderline and neurotic groups vis-à-vis the chronic schizophrenic group is thought provoking. In the neurotic and borderline groups, defensive functioning and the expression and regulation of anxiety are of primary importance. In the neurotic group, they account for 4 out of 5 ego responses, in the borderline group, 3 out of 5. A further breakdown of the kinds of defenses used and the areas of anxiety expressed will follow below.

Reality testing was frequently seen in the borderline group—about 1 in 4 responses. But in the chronic schizophrenic group, reality testing takes precedence *over all other areas of ego functioning*: 1 in 3 responses. These responses essentially reflect patients' focus on the accuracy of perception and interpretation of external and internal events. The next priority in the chronic schizophrenic group is that of autonomous functioning—1 in 4 responses. These figures suggest the importance of the most primitive and basic of ego functions in the chronic schizophrenic population, functions delineated by Heinz Hartmann (1964) as apparatuses of primary autonomy (attention, concentration, memory, learning, perception, motor function, intention). They did not appear at all in the other two groups in this study, in the sense that automatism is so complete that they function more or less invisibly.

Defensive functioning and the expression and control of anxiety appear in third and fourth place in the chronic schizophrenic group—about 1 in 5 and 1 in 6 responses, respectively. Thus one might speculate that, for purposes of survival, the areas of reality testing and autonomous functioning are the two most necessary ego functions. Defensive functioning and the expression and control of anxiety would achieve prominence only when the organism feels some sense of safety within self and environment.

III A. Defensive Functioning

    Chronic schizophrenic group—18 responses
        Ego regression, 50%
            of thinking processes, 27.78%
            of ego boundaries, 11.11%
            to primary process thinking, 11.11%
        Blocking, 22.22%

Libidinal regression, 11.11%
Other (denial and projection), 16.67%

Borderline group—40 responses
Ego regression, 42.50%
of thinking processes, 15%
of ego boundaries, 15%
to primary process thinking, 7.5%
of stimulus barriers, 5%
Libidinal regression, 12.50%
Denial, 12.50%
Projection, 10%
Other (aggression as a defense, idealization, isolation, displacement, rationalization, reaction formation, flight response), 21.45%

Neurotic group—126 responses
Denial, 25.40%
Libidinal regression, 17.26%
Flight response, 11.11%
Intellectualization, 8.73%
Rationalization, 4.76%
Repression, 3.97%
Other (isolation, idealization, shift to passivity, reaction formation, undoing, identification with the aggressor, turning round on the self, counterphobic, ego inhibition, flight response, displacement, identification, somatization), 21.43%

Discussion of Defensive Functioning

Among the defenses used by each group, there was a striking similarity between the defensive mechanisms most frequently chosen. Both the chronic schizophrenic and borderline populations employed an ego regression extensively—1 out of 2 in the chronic group, and 2 out of 5 in the borderline group. If one includes "blocking," the second most utilized defense in the chronic schizophrenic group, there would be a percentage of almost 3 out of 4 defensive activities where an ego regression was in effect. In the neurotic group, denial was most frequently utilized—about 1 in 4 responses—a defense which is closely related to ego regression in that the ego function of reality testing is disregarded for a moment.

Libidinal regression was the next most frequently selected defense in all groups. It was most used by the neurotic group—although it must be remembered that the neurotic group was functioning on a developmentally later libidinal level more of the time, hence a libidinal regression was more often possible!

The remaining responses indicative of defensive function encompassed denial and projection in the chronic schizophrenic and borderline groups, specific forms of defense which are expected in those populations. As might be anticipated, the neurotic group evidenced "higher level" defenses such as intellectualization, rationalization, and repression. There were, nonetheless, a large number of "fight responses"—which clinically indicated a use of denial cum aggression—and a fair number of projection responses. These responses were perhaps present in such quantity because of the group situation.

III B. Anxieties Expressed

Chronic schizophrenic group—13 responses
Primal anxiety (annihilation anxiety), 38.46%
Separation anxiety (loss of object), 38.46%
Castration and penetration anxieties, 15.38%
Loss of control of impulses (aggressive and/or sexual), 7.69%

Borderline group—39 responses
Separation anxiety (loss of object), 46.15%
Primal anxiety (annihilation anxiety), 23.08%
Loss of self-esteem (genital level narcissism), 15.38%
Loss of control of impulses (aggressive and/or sexual), 12.82%
Castration and penetration anxieties, 2.56%

Neurotic group—55 responses
Castration and penetration anxieties, 49.09%
Loss of control of impulses (aggressive and/or sexual), 32.73%
Loss of love of the object, 7.27%
Breakdown of defenses (i.e., fear of ego regression), 5.45%
Loss of self-esteem (genital level narcissism), 5.45%

Discussion of Anxieties Expressed

In our understanding and identification of the anxieties expressed by the patients, we made use of a modified classical psychoanalytical model. As discussed by Brenner (1976), there is an initial danger to the organism—up to about 1½ years of age—that is experienced as "separation anxiety," "loss of the object," or "primal anxiety." On the premise that it is an earlier phenomenon, we separated out "primal anxiety," also sometimes referred to as "annihilation anxiety," from "separation anxiety." We considered it to be the anxiety response of the infant prior to awareness of the object. "Primal anxiety" might thus emanate from the emotional life of the infant in its first few weeks of life, the developmental moment characterized by Mahler as "normal autism." In contrast, "separation anxiety" would be experienced in the following developmental period, the symbiotic phase (Mahler et al., 1975). Primal anxiety is feelingly experienced as, "I am about to die." Separation anxiety is the feeling, "The *person* I must have to survive is not, and will not be, there."

The next anxiety, at 1 to 2 years of age developmentally, is traditionally specified as "loss of love of the object." It is the feeling, "I am a bad, bad person and *no one* could like me." We added another anxiety related to this developmental moment (the anal libidinal stage) based on clinical experience and patients' communications: "loss of control of impulses." This is the experience of the ego's incapacity to adequately channel and appropriately express aggressive and sexual impulses. The feeling is one of being overwhelmed by the inner world, of the inner emotional contents spewing out in dangerous rapidity and intensity: "I'm coming apart at the seams."

The third developmentally linked anxiety in classic literatures is that of "castration" or other genital injury, at ages 2½ to 4 or 5 years (Freud, 1905). We used the concepts of both "castration" and "penetration" anxieties, reflecting concern regarding bodily damage to the genitalia ("I am going to be psychically hurt and am helpless to prevent it"). We added the anxiety "loss of self-esteem" to reflect narcissistic insults experienced on the genital level (i.e., "I feel so humiliated, embarrassed—such mortification!").

The other anxiety in the classic psychoanalytic model is the "superego anxiety," experienced as "shame on me!" It is understood as the anxiety related to the developmental appearance of oedipal conflict. We did not tabulate the superego responses in this list, but rather in the self/object list. *Had* we analyzed superego responses along with the other anxieties, the results would have shifted only in the neurotic group. But within that patient group, the superego responses would then have totaled a larger number of responses than all other anxiety responses combined.

Given this framework of understanding, we see an almost classic picture of the delineation between the three patient groups. In the chronic schizophrenic group, almost 2 in 5 responses reflected "primal anxiety," and another 2 in 5, "separation anxiety." In the borderline group, these percentages were again very high, but "separation anxiety" was expressed much more frequently than "primal anxiety." The former accounted for almost 1 in 2 responses, the latter for 1 in 4. Might this reflect the greater capacity of the borderline group patients to attain *and* to maintain a symbiotic closeness, in contrast to an autistic regression or developmental lack in the chronic group patients?

In the neurotic group, in marked contrast, the most often communicated anxieties were "castration" and "penetration" (1 in 2), followed by "loss of control impulses" (1 in 3). These would appear to reflect the primacy of genital concerns, with anal interests in secondary position—in comparison to the oral anxieties besetting the other two groups.

IV. Self/Object Structures

Chronic schizophrenic group—51 responses
Self responses, 49.20%
Father-as-object responses, 33.33%
Mother-as-object responses, 15.69%
Superego responses, 1.69%

Borderline group—222 responses
　Self responses, 36.02%
　Father-as-object responses, 34.68%
　Mother-as-object responses, 25.68%
　Superego responses, 3.60%

Neurotic group—325 responses
　Father-as-object responses, 41.54%
　Mother-as-object responses, 26.15%
　Superego responses, 18.46%
　Self responses, 13.85%

Discussion of Self/Object Structures

In this area of our study, we used the notions of object relations and self psychology theories as regards the structuralization of the representational world (Kernberg, 1975, 1976; Stolorow and Lachmann, 1980). We were interested in attempting to delineate the precise aspects of self experiences and the specific attributes of the object representations (of the mother or of the father imagoes) which were awakened by the emotional surround of the moment.

The self phenomena which we examined included: indications of concern regarding maintenance of boundaries (self/object differentiation); self-esteem regulation (both as to homeostasis and as to feelings of adequacy); expectations of self and of object constancy, the pleasurable nature, or fear of, merger experiences, the presence of narcissistic injury or triumph, and the occurrence of autistic responses as reflected in a marked lack of object cathexis.

In our scrutiny of object responses, we focused both on the bad–good qualities of the experienced object (i.e., the presence or lack of splitting phenomena) and also on those particular libidinal and/or aggressive characteristics of the introject to which the patient was cathected at that precise moment. Thus, a patient might be aware of the oral aspects of the introjected mother (e.g., her needs to be given to, to be vituperative, or to be vomitive, etc.) and then shift to a cognizance of her innergenital aspects (e.g., her wish to be nurturing, to be genitally penetrated, to be sexually competitive, etc.). Similarly, the awareness of the father introject might change from a focus on his phallic aspects (his impulses to penetrate, to challenge, etc.) to his anal, oral, or oedipal needs and strivings.

Superego responses were seen as expressed by an experience of conscious or unconscious guilt following an impulse, feeling, action, or thought. They were viewed as introjects of objects which had been assimilated so deeply as to become a part of the core self experience.

In this part of our study, the finding of greatest interest was the difference in the number of self responses vis-à-vis the total self/object responses. Self responses in the chronic schizophrenic group were roughly 1 in 2, in the borderline group, 1 in 3, and in the neurotic group, 1 in 8. These figures support the traditional hypothesis that narcissistic problems are more frequently found in the schizophrenic population.[2]

The superego responses, in contrast, show a preponderance in the other direction, with much greater frequency in the neurotic group. Also of consequence is the very large percentage of father-as-object responses in all of the population groups. This is in spite of the fact that in one group, the borderline group, the therapist was female. Could this somehow reflect the impact of the group situation? In individual therapy, one would expect at least an equal number of mother-as-object responses.

IV A. Self Responses

> Chronic schizophrenic group—25 responses
> > Maintenance of boundaries, self/object differentiation, 32%
> > Impaired self or object constancy (temporal stability), 24%
> > Self/object merger experienced, 16%
> > Regulation of self-esteem, 16% (oral level, i.e., self structure as homeostatic, 8%; genital level, i.e., self structure as worthwhile, 8%)
> > Autistic, with dim perception of object, 12%

---

[2]Narcissism is defined here in the sense of Stolorow and Lachmann (1980): "Mental activity is narcissistic to the degree that its function is to maintain the structural cohesion, temporal stability, and positive affective coloring of the self representation" (p. 10).

Borderline group—80 responses
   Regulation of self-esteem, 48.75% (oral level, 12.50%, genital level, 36.25%)
   Self/object merger experienced, 13.75%
   Maintenance of self object differentiation, 12.50%
   Narcissistic injury experienced, 12.50%
   Failure in regulation of self-esteem, 6.25%
   Self-inflicted narcissistic injuries (genital level), 5%
   Autistic, with dim perception of object, 1.25%

Neurotic group—45 responses
   Regulation of self-esteem, 37.78% (oral level, 8.89%, genital level, 28.89%)
   Narcissistic injury experienced, 31.11%
   Self/object merger experienced, 26.67%
   Narcissistic triumph experienced, 4.44%

Discussion of Self Responses

In our analysis of self responses, we looked for phenomena reflective of the experiences of self as to cohesion, constancy, and positive affective coloring. Differences in self experience *over time* were not measurable in this study, save through indications of anxiety regarding anticipated loss of ego boundaries and/or loss of continuity of self or object experience. We did discover varying experiences of ego boundary phenomena —unpleasant sensations seemed connected with a threatened *loss* of ego boundaries in all of the populations, whereas pleasant affective experience accompanied an indicated *merger* with the object. Might this imply a warding off of merger if the object is experienced as damaging? Or is it the fear of a *further* regression in the direction of imminent self fragmentation?

In the chronic schizophrenic group, 1 in 3 was concerned with the loss of differentiation, 1 in 8 in the borderline group, whereas no responses of this type were evidenced in the neurotic group. Yet, approximately 1 in 4 self responses in the neurotic group concerned the *pleasure* of merger of self and object, contrasted with 1 in 7 (approximately) in both the chronic schizophrenic and borderline groups. It would seem, then, that the stronger the self structure, the more likelihood of a positive experience of merger with the object. The other reflection of instability of self representation is the 1 in 4 response in the chronic schizophrenic group regarding self or object constancy.

In contrast, the theme of regulation of self-esteem appeared most frequently in both the borderline and neurotic populations. When combined with the expression of narcissistic injury, which would reflect the momentary loss of self-esteem due to insult or lack of empathic response, the figures would total about 60% of the borderline responses and almost 70% of the neurotic responses. In both of these population groups, there are about 3 to 1 responses of "genital self-esteem regulation" in comparison to "oral self-esteem regulation"; that is, concern regarding feelings of adequacy in contrast to the search for equilibrium of the self experience.

The other finding of particular moment is that of the regression to autism, with a dim perception of the object: 1 in 8 responses in the chronic schizophrenic group, 1 in 80 in the borderline group, and none at all in the neurotic population. These phenomena might be described as reflecting the experience of the archaic, grandiose self.

IV B. Father-as-Object Responses

Chronic schizophrenic group—17 responses
Father as phallic and as challenged, 58.82%
Father as phallic and as injurious (castrating or harmfully penetrating), 23.52%
Father as phallic identificatory figure, 11.76%
Father as receptive, 5.88%

Borderline group—77 responses
Father as idealized genital father who disappoints, 28.57%
Father as positively phallic-aggressive, 27.27%
Father as object of phallic aggression (Oedipal rivalry), 15.58%
Father as phallic identificatory figure, 14.29%
Father as phallic father who is frighteningly intrusive, 6.49%
Father as idealized phallic father, 5.19%
Father as phallic exhibitionistic father, 2.60%

Neurotic group—135 responses
    Father as phallic identificatory figure, 27.41%
    Father as positively phallic-aggressive, 17.04%
    Father as genitally withholding father, 14.81%
    Father as oedipal choice and responding, 8.89%
    Father as phallic father who is frighteningly intrusive, 8.89%
    Father as idealized genital father who disappoints, 7.41%
    Father as negative oedipal (homosexual) choice who responds, 6.67%
    Father as phallic and as performing (phallic narcissistic), 2.60%

Discussion of Father-as-Object Responses

The father-as-object responses are unexpected in two regards: they are the most frequent self/object response in the neurotic group (41%) and the second most frequent self/object response in each of the other groups (33% and 35%); and, *all* of the father-as-object responses in *all* of the groups focus on the genital aspects of the father. These findings may reflect somehow the group therapy situation, as the mother-as-object responses show a much greater spread of differing aspects of the mother (i.e., aspects of the mother related to the oral needs of the patient and/or herself, the anal needs, and also the genital needs).

Within these limits, however, the father is experienced quite differently from group to group. In the chronic group, the most frequent experience of the father (3 of 5 responses) is as the *object* of phallic aggressivity. Perhaps this is indicative of the greater intensity of the aggressive impulses of the patient (unneutralized aggression), or perhaps reflective of less impulse control (less ego strength vis-à-vis the drives), or perhaps we are seeing the effect of the fragility of the self representation, which must be more aggressively defended to survive, or a combination of these intrapsychic events.

The second most frequent response in the chronic group is of the father as injurious on a genital level (i.e., the phallic father as castrating or harmfully penetrating). The recurring theme of this aspect of the father (1 in 4) may result from the projection of the patient's own aggression. However, a more likely hypothesis is the splitting of a fused mother–father object into "all-bad father" and "all-good mother," since in the chronic group almost 9 out of 10 mother-as-object responses were "all-good object" responses. Perhaps it is necessary to maintain the experience of the parental object as split in order to preserve the wished for nurturing qualities of the mother. As Kernberg (1976) suggested, "Their inability to integrate libidinally determined and aggressively determined self- and object-images is reflected in their maintaining object relations of either a need-gratifying or a threatening nature" (p. 147).

In the borderline group, the experience of the father is still partially narcissistic. The father is used in 3 out of 10 responses as a self/object; that is, as an idealized figure whose presence will provide the patient with the sense of self-cohesion and self-continuity he cannot yet maintain on his own (Kohut, 1971). There is, nonetheless, the start of a movement away from idealization, with the awareness of disappointment. The next response, of the father as aggressive, containing more than 1 in 4 responses, is indicative of perceptual activity without either aggrandizement or identification. In the next group of responses (1 in 6), the father is again the object of aggression, but now within the confines of the Oedipal situation: he is now experienced as a competitor for a specific other human being, not simply as a challenger to the patient's phallic narcissistic needs. And, in the next large group of responses, the father is used as an identificatory figure (1 in 7 responses).

In the neurotic group, by contrast, the most frequent experience of the father is as an identificatory object (more than 1 in 4 responses) and as an object of genital complementarity to the daughter (1 in 10 responses). Aspects of the father as pleasantly aggressive (1 in 6) or disappointingly withholding (1 in 7) are next in frequency. The withholding father is reminiscent of the idealized genital father who disappoints in the borderline group, although the meaning here seemingly indicates a need for the father's presence for the purposes of identification (male patients) or genital complementarity (female patients), not as a self/object.

IV C. Mother-as-Object Responses

Chronic schizophrenic group—8 responses
Mother as orally gratifying, 50%
Mother as genitally receptive, 37.50%
Mother as orally depriving, 12.5%

Borderline group—57 responses
Mother as orally depriving, 29.82%
Mother as orally gratifying, 22.81%
Mother as idealized genital mother who disappoints, 15.79%
Mother as oedipally receptive, 10.53%
Mother as orally destructive (actively harmful: poisoning, etc.), 10.53%
Mother as orally needy, 3.51%
Mother as narcissistically wounded, 3.51%
Mother as idealized genital mother who pleases, 1.75%
Mother as an identificatory figure, 1.75%

Neurotic group—85 responses
Mother as phallic, aggressive, and genitally injurious, 52.94%
Mother as idealized genital mother who disappoints, 10.59%
Mother as oedipally receptive, 9.41%
Mother as anally demanding, 8.25%
Mother as oedipally rejecting to son, 7.06%
Mother as oedipally retaliatory to daughter, 4.71%
Mother as negative oedipal (homosexual) choice who responds, 2.35%
Mother as orally depriving, 2.35%
Mother as orally gratifying, 1.18%

Discussion of Mother-as-Object Responses

The aspects of the mother-as-object responses are also distinctly different from one population group to the next. But all of the group responses include both oral and genital aspects of the mother and of the self as responded to by the mother.

In the chronic group, the mother is seen as an almost completely positive figure: 1 of 2 responses reflect that aspect of the mother which is orally gratifying, 3 of 8 the experience of the mother as genitally receptive. Only 1 response out of 8 indicates a "bad" aspect of the mother: orally depriving. The negative experiences of the mother seem to have been displaced onto the father-as-object imago in this population group.

In the borderline group, there is the picture of the contrasting aspects between "good mother" and "bad mother" as beginning to be tolerated. About 1 in 3 of the responses portray the mother as orally depriving, 1 in 4 as orally gratifying. This apparently indicated a beginning synthesis of the object representations of the nurturing and nonnurturing aspects of the mother (Kernberg, 1975), with a consequent reduction of splitting phenomena. On the genital level, there is a similar configuration: the mother is experienced in 1 of 6 responses as an idealized, disappointing genital figure and in 1 of 9 as gratifyingly receptive on a genital level.

There emerges an interestingly different picture in the neurotic group: 1 out of 2 responses refer to those aspects of the mother that are phallic, aggressive, and genitally injurious in nature. In other words, the aspects of the mother that would interfere with the genital (phallic or inner-genital) adequacy of the self experience. Might this be a castration anxiety response to the group situation, or a displacement onto the mother-as-object imago of some of the potentially damaging aspects of the genital father? Or might it be a defense against regressive oral wishes, or a projection of phallic aggression?

The next groups of responses in the neurotic population were similar to the borderline population: the mother who is oedipally receptive (1 in 10) and the idealized genital mother who disappoints (1 in 9). Other responses refer to a wide spread of experiences of the mother: as anally demanding, as oedipally rejecting, as oedipally retaliatory, and so on. It would seem that the more advanced the intrapsychic representational world of self and of objects, the more specific, varied, and complete is the experience of the other human being.

Summary

In this limited study of characterological phenomena, there appeared some interesting apparent contrasts between the character structure and functioning of the borderline, chronic schizophrenic, and neurotic group patients. In the borderline group responses, there emerged the following phenomena: the verbal responses concerned with drive elements and with self/object structures were each of greater number than those reflecting ego functioning, unlike the schizophrenic group which revealed a focus on ego functioning; of the ego functions displayed, defensive functioning and the expression and control of anxiety took precedence, whereas in the schizophrenic group, reality testing and autonomous functioning were primary. Among the self/object responses, the borderline group gave a lower percentage of self (vis-à-vis object) responses than the schizophrenic group, but a relatively higher number of self responses than the neurotic group.

In the nature of self experience, the borderline group was again closer to the neurotic than the schizophrenic group in its focus on the regulation of self-esteem, whereas the chronic group expressed primary concern with the maintenance of self-object differentiation, that is, the maintenance of self boundaries. In the object responses, there appears less splitting than in the chronic schizophrenic group. But more use of the object as a self/object is evidenced in the borderline group than is true in the neurotic group, where the object is used in the service of identification or complementation, or is experienced as competitive or as genitally satisfying.

In all of these areas, the structure and functioning of the borderline character was quite different from that of the chronic schizophrenic, though somewhat similar to the picture of the neurotic character. In the area of drive functioning, all three groups responded with primacy of phallic aggressive material, a phenomenon that might have been related to the group situation. Differences did occur between the three groups as to the next most frequently expressed drive derivatives: phallic and inner-genital narcissistic in the borderline group, genital (i.e., phallic, inner-genital, and oedipal) libidinal in the neurotic group, and anal retentive in the chronic schizophrenic group.

There were two areas of intrapsychic functioning in the borderline population which seemed to indicate a similarity to the schizophrenic group: the defenses unconsciously chosen, and, the anxieties most frequently experienced. Both groups made particular use of ego regression as a defense, whereas the neurotic group was likely to use denial. Libidinal regression was the second most frequently chosen defense in all of the groups, but the neurotic group evidenced a greater spread of defenses used and also a larger number of higher level defenses. The anxieties expressed were the most markedly different in the neurotic group, which was concerned with castration and penetration fears. Both the borderline and the schizophrenic groups expressed a higher degree of primal (annihilation) anxiety and of separation (loss of the object) anxiety. The percentage of primal anxiety responses were much higher in the chronic schizophrenic than in the borderline, however.

In all groups, the most frequent object responses were of the genital father. Was this because of the group situation? The mother responses were more varied and precise as the representational world became less fragile and less subject to regression or disintegration, that is, in the neurotic group especially.

Whether or not the particular spread of responses discussed above is typical of the three population groups can only be hypothesized, given the small size of our study. But there do appear to be suggested, definitive contrasts between the three groups which might well warrant further study.

Glover-Kobayashi Project
Einstein College of Medicine, 1981

Group Kings Pages 4–9
SESS. 8–81

Appendix 20-1

Typical Working Sheet—Chronic Schizophrenic Group

Person Speaking		Communication	Drive Element	Ego Function	Self/Object Structure (Intrapsychic or interpersonal?)
Melvin	Th1	Did I interrupt, Melvin?			
	(M)6	No.		Defense (denial)	
	Th1	Melvin.			
	Th2	Yea, Melvin, you started to say something.			
Melvin	(M)6	Yes, two pieces less to remember.		Reality testing	
	Th1	Two pieces.			
Melvin	(M)6	There maybe was more than one here that died at the scene.		Affectivity: primal anxiety	Impaired object constancy—merger with object
	Th2	One piece belonged to Linda who is not with us anymore and the other piece is whose, Melvin?			

INTRAPSYCHIC STRUCTURES AND PROCESSES

Speaker	Code	Utterance			
Melvin	(M)6	Excuse me?		Impaired stimulus barrier (anxiety interferes with perception)	
	Th2	Whose is the other piece. One used to belong to Linda.			
Melvin	(M)6	The other one's David's.		Reality testing	
	Th2	What do you think that we should do with it?			
Melvin	(M)6	Take it up and leave it up to the office.	Oral libidinal		Holding wish: M as orally gratifying
	Th1	Take it up to the office?			
June	(F)1	There's one colored girl upstairs.	Oral libidinal	Reality testing	Caretaker mother object (someone is going to take care). M as orally gratifying
	Th1	Huh?			
June	(F)1	There's one colored girl. (Cough Steven 5)	Oral libidinal	Reality testing	
Melvin	(M)6	Is he alive? (cigarette)		Affectivity: primal anxiety	

(continued)

Appendix 20-1 (Continued)

	Th1	Who are you asking about Melvin?	Cig: coping with primal anxiety
Melvin	(M)6	Wondering if Dirk . . .	Reality testing in service of coping with primal anxiety; regulation and control of drive
	Th1	Wondering if Dirk is alive? (6 mumble) Is that what you were wondering? You're wondering if maybe someone leaves the group that means that he's not alive anymore?	
Melvin	(M)6	Yes.	Impaired object constancy—merger with object
	Th1	Maybe Steven knows.	
Melvin	(M)6	Do you know if Dirk's alive anymore?	Reality testing
Steven	(M)5	Dirk is alive.	Reality testing and object constancy

Appendix 20-2

Glover-Kobayashi Project
Einstein College of Medicine, 1981

Group B.P.C. Pages 43–48
SESS. 3–81

Typical Working Sheet—Borderline Group

Person Speaking		Communication	Drive Element	Ego Function	Self/Object Structure (Intrapsychic or interpersonal?)
Dannie	(M)5	"Cut that goddamn radio off, Dannie, 'fore I take the mother fucker and bust it up." That ain't not his radio. My mother bought it. He didn't. He didn't help my mother do nothing in the house.		Defense: regression to oral in response to anxiety re: genital impulses	Response to M's oral needs
John	(M)6	This sound like the dude just like to lay up on women.	Genital oedipal: libidinal and aggressive		Genital narcissistic injury of the object and regulation of self-esteem on genital level
Dannie	(M)5	That's right. That's what he is.	Genital oedipal: libidinal and aggressive		Merger with object as phallic narcissistic mirror
Th		What?			

(continued)

Appendix 20-2 (Continued)

Dannie	(M)5	He just . . . the man just lay up on women's all time.	Genital and oral libidinal	Devaluation of idealized genital F as defense against phallic narcissistic and oral needs
John	(M)6	He sounds like a man that used to like to lay up on women, know . . .	Genital libidinal	Merger with object as phallic narcissistic mirror
Dannie	(M)5 Th	That's what he do. What does it mean? What does that mean?		Mirroring of phallic narcissistic object with devaluation of idealized genital F
Dannie	(M)5	He don't work . . .	Genital libidinal	Devaluation of F on genital level
John	(M)6	Wait a minute. Let me explain it. A person what don't like to work, just like to sit around, eat and start trouble.	Oral libidinal as defense against genital impulses	Defense: libidinal regression to oral
	Th	Uh huh.		
Dannie	(M)5	Right.		Mirroring of phallic narcissistic object

INTRAPSYCHIC STRUCTURES AND PROCESSES 455

John	(M)6	That's th . . . you don't need nobody like that.	Oral libidinal	Defense: projection re: oral needs	Mirroring of phallic narcissistic object
Dannie	(M)5	That's no good, at . . .			
John	(M)6	That sound like just like clowning (?)	Oral libidinal		Narcissistic injury (devaluation) of genital object (F) as defense against oral needs
Dannie	(M)5	Right, uh, he lay up and sleep all the time. I said, I, I'm gonna . . . no. Know, know like my mother . . . and him start fighting. Den, den my mother tell him get his goddamned clothes and get the hell out of the house. She don't, see, I don't, my mother tell me, I say . . . my mother tell him, "See, I don't need your money, I don't need you to help me to do nothing, Claude. I can take care of my own self." And then he said, "I didn't say that." He begging, right?	Phallic-aggression + oral libidinal + oral sadistic	Defense: projection regarding phallic aggression and separation anxiety	Phallic aggressive F and rejecting oral M
Th		Uh hum.			

Appendix 20-3

Glover-Kobayashi Project
Einstein College of Medicine, 1981

Group Neur. Pages 58–62

Typical Working Sheet—Neurotic Group

Person Speaking		Communication	Drive Element	Ego Function	Self/Object Structure (Intrapsychic or interpersonal?)
Stan	(M)1	Did you give me a chance to?	Phallic challenge in service of phallic libidinal		Aggression toward castrating M
Joyce	(F)3	No, we attacked you. No, we were really trying to be helpful.	Genital aggression; OR	Defense against anxiety re: genital libidinal impulse	Re: genital narcissistic injury by F
Bill	(M)5	We did attack you. In fact we even joked about some of your problems.			Super ego response to his own phallic aggression toward oedipal F
Stan	(M)1	No, no.		Defense re: Castrating anxiety	
Bill	(M)5	Do you feel ridiculed in a sense?	Phallic aggression		Toward oedipal F
Stan	(M)1	No, not from here.		Defense: denial re: Castrating anxiety	

INTRAPSYCHIC STRUCTURES AND PROCESSES

Steve	(M)6	Do you have some specific problems you want to talk about?			
Joyce	(F)3	Yes, well I think Stan sometimes you can be provocative toward females.	Genital aggression		Toward frighteningly phallic F
Stan	(M)1	Provocative in which way?	Phallic challenge		Toward castrating M
Judy	(F)4	Yeah, he has been going on all night.	Genital aggression	Defense against penetration anxiety	Re: frighteningly phallic F
Joyce	(F)3	And I think you know I can too.	Phallic challenge		Competitive response with F re: M (negative oedipal)
Stan	(M)1	What do you mean by provocative?	Phallic challenge		Toward castrating M
Joyce	(F)3	Well, maybe this will allay some of your homosexual worries, I don't know. I feel that maybe you can kind of come on and then when you catch it, you don't want it. I think you can sort of be a provocative person toward women, I mean.	Genital aggression; OR	Defense against penetration anxiety +	Genital narcissistic injury by rejecting phallic F

(continued)

Appendix 20-3 (Continued)

Bill	(M)5	Provocative? Antagonistic?	Phallic challenge	
Stan	(M)1	Yeah, that's what I'm trying to get at.	Phallic aggression	
Joyce	(F)3	No, no! Provocative in a sexual sense of trying to elicit a sexual response from them, for example, seductive, that's the word.	Genital aggression + genital libidinal	Defense against penetration anxiety	Response to frighteningly phallic, wished for genital F
Stan	(M)1	Is that supposed to be complimentary?	Phallic gesture	Reality testing in defense of castration anxiety	Re: Ambiguous genital M
Bill	(M)5	I don't get that feeling at all.	Phallic aggression challenge		Toward oedipal F
Stan	(M)1	Well, you're not female.	Phallic aggression challenge		Toward oedipal F
Joyce	(F)3	Right!	Genital libidinal		Re: oedipal F
Bill	(M)5	Well, I'm listening to you describe in your behavior and don't see that at all.	Phallic aggression challenge		Toward oedipal F

References

Abraham, K. (1916), The first pregenital stage of the libido. In: *Selected Papers of Karl Abraham*. New York: Basic Books, 1968.

Arsenian, J., & Semrad, E. (1966), Schizophrenia and language. *Psychiat. Quart.*, 40/3:449–458, 1966.

Bellak, L., Hurvich, M., & Gediman, H. (1973), *Ego Functions in Schizophrenics, Neurotics, and Normals*. New York: John Wiley.

Brenner, C. (1976), *Psychoanalytic Technique and Psychic Conflict*. New York: International Universities Press.

Freud, S. (1905), Three essays on the theory of sexuality. *Standard Edition*, 7:122–243. London: Hogarth Press, 1959.

——— (1915), Instincts and their vicissitudes. *Standard Edition*, 14:117–140. London: Hogarth Press, 1957.

——— (1926), Inhibitions, symptoms, and anxiety. *Standard Edition*, 20:77–178. London: Hogarth Press, 1961.

Glover, L., & Kobayashi, J. (1981), Unpublished study of unconscious derivatives in verbal communications of three groups: One schizophrenic, one borderline, and one neurotic. Einstein College of Medicine, New York.

——— Mendell, D. (1982), A suggested developmental sequence for a preoedipal genital phase. In: *Early Female Development: Current Psychoanalytic Views*, ed. D. Mendell. Englewood Cliffs, NJ: Spectrum Press.

Hartmann, H. (1964), *Essays on Ego Psychology*. New York: International Universities Press.

Jacobson, E. (1964), *The Self and the Object World*. New York: International Universities Press.

Kernberg, O. (1975), *Borderline Conditions and Pathological Narcissism*. New York: Jason Aronson.

——— (1976), *Object Relations Theory and Clinical Psychoanalysis*. New York: Jason Aronson.

Kohut, H. (1971), *The Analysis of the Self*. New York: International Universities Press.

——— (1977), *The Restoration of the Self*. New York: International Universities Press.

Mahler, M., Pine, F., & Bergman, A. (1975), *The Psychological Birth of the Human Infant*. New York: Basic Books.

Palombo, S. R., & Bruch, H. (1964), Falling apart: The verbalization of ego failure. *Psychiatry*, 27/3:248–258.

Sandler, J., & Rosenblatt, B. (1962), The concept of the representational world. In: *The Psychoanalytic Study of the Child*, 17:128–145. New York: International Universities Press.

Silverman, L. H., Pettit, T. F., & Dunne, E. J. (1971), On the relationship between self-object differentiation, symbiotic experiences, and pathology reduction in schizophrenics. *J. Nerv. & Ment. Dis.*, 152/2:118–128.

Sterba, R. F. (1968), *Introduction to the Psychoanalytic Theory of the Libido*. New York: Brunner/Mazel.

Stolorow, R., & Lachmann, F. (1980), *Psychoanalysis of Developmental Arrests*. 4ew York: International Universities Press.

Chapter 21
THE EFFECT OF MATERNAL NARCISSISM ON THE ATTACHMENT RELATIONSHIP

NANCY S. MOLITOR, PH.D.

The critical developmental issue during the first year is the formation of an affective bond or attachment between infant and mother (Ainsworth, 1969; Bowlby, 1969, 1977). This relationship is the "psychological tether" which binds the infant and care giver together (Sroufe, 1979). Ainsworth, Bell, and Stayton (1974) have suggested that the attachment relationship provides the infant with a sense of "felt security" as well as a "secure base" from which to explore the world. Researchers have also shown that the attachment relationship provides the foundation for the infant's later social, cognitive, and affective functioning. Indeed, Freud and other psychoanalytic writers have stressed the importance of this relationship in providing the basis for the infant's development of object relations or characteristic ways in which the infant will come to view both himself as well as others in his environment. These internal representations set the stage for the infant's later intimate relationships (Freud, 1957; Bowlby, 1977; Horner, 1979).

Ainsworth and associates have developed a laboratory procedure to assess the quality of the attachment relationship (Ainsworth et al., 1974; Ainsworth, Blehar, Waters, and Wall, 1978). This procedure, called the strange situation, is a 20-minute structured observation conducted in a laboratory setting. The experimental session consists of eight episodes of separation and reunion of mother and infant. Ainsworth has focused on the reunion behavior of the infant as the key to classifying the attachment relationship as "secure" or adaptive or as "insecure" or maladaptive. Infants classified as secure greet the mother positively and actively attempt to establish proximity and interaction with her. Infants classified as insecure are characterized by one of two differing patterns: (1) avoidant or (2) resistant. Infants classified as resistant mix contact seeking with resistance toward the mother and are difficult to console. These infants frequently show explicit anger in the attachment assessment and are unable to playfully explore the various toys in the experimental room. Sroufe and Fleeson (1985) believe that this behavior is presumedly all based in a history of inconsistent care. Infants classified as avoidant characteristically ignore the mother on reunion. These infants may even prefer the stranger when stressed. Mary Main (1977) and Main, Tomasini, and Tolan (1979) have suggested that these infants have experienced a classic approach avoidance conflict. That is, although their attachment system becomes activated in the strange situation and they seem to desire closeness, they appear to avoid it at the same time, perhaps because closeness has been associated with rejection or intrusion in the past. Main has suggested that these infants displace their fear by denying that they care for the mother and thereby avoiding her.

Researchers are just beginning to follow up these infants, and the preliminary findings confirm what clinicians have long maintained, namely, that the earliest relationship with the mother lays the foundation for the child's later relationships. Children who are secure in their early attachments with their mothers, for example, are more cooperative with their mothers in a tool problem-solving situation at 2 years (Matas, Arend, and Sroufe, 1978; Sroufe and Fleeson, 1985). They are able to tell their mothers when the problem is beyond their own resources and they are able to use their mothers' aid to allow them to solve problems well beyond their own capacity. These children are also more socially competent in preschool (Waters, Wippman, and Sroufe, 1979), more capable of reciprocity, and more empathic (Sroufe and Fleeson, 1985). Resistant infants, at age 2, are easily frustrated in the problem situation and are whiny and negativistic, even when faced with relatively simple problems (Matas et al., 1978; Gove, 1983). These children, in preschool, are socially motivated and oriented, but immature and inept in social interaction. They are chronically dependent on preschool teachers and routinely wait at the edge of a group for the teacher to invite them in (Sroufe and Fleeson, 1985). These kinds of children, if referred for psychotherapy, would most likely present with classic internalizing symptoms such as depression, eating and sleeping disorders, and enuresis. They would be expected to develop highly dependent and ambivalent transference relationships which mirror their earlier attachment relationship. Because their resistance has presumedly been based on a history of inconsistency and coercive tactics on the part of the mother, it is important that the therapist avoid getting into power struggles with the child. It is also necessary that the therapist tolerate the child's extreme dependency needs, but at the same time, avoid infantilizing the child as the mother has done.

Two-year-old avoidant children continue to manifest continuity in their behavior as well. In the same problem-solving situation, these types of children seek little assistance from their mothers and seem to have little affective investment either in problem solving or in interacting with their mothers. These children, in preschool, are hostile or distant with their peers. They frequently victimize or exploit other children, and one study found that a substantial number of these victimizers had been subjected to parental abuse (Egeland and Sroufe, 1981). Their relationships with their preschool teachers are different, however. The avoidant group has strong needs for nurturance, but doubts about the availability of others. Because of these fears, these children manifest their dependency through desperate contact seeking in restricted safe circumstances (Sroufe and Fleeson, 1985). Frequently they do not seek teachers when injured, disappointed, or otherwise stressed. This group of children is the most likely to be referred for psychotherapy. They are likely to present with classic externalizing symptoms such as behavior disorders or school phobia. These children will no doubt find it very difficult to allow any dependence on the therapist. This group is likely to develop pseudomature or controlling transference relationships, again mirroring their earlier attachment history. When treating a child with this type of attachment history, the therapist will need to be consistently available and actively supportive and affirming of the child's attempts to explore his environment. The therapist will need to be able to contain the anger and hostility from the child as well as his own countertransference feelings, which are likely to be negative, and similar in many ways to countertransference aroused when treating a borderline or narcissistic adult.

Investigators have suggested that these two groups of insecurely attached children are at risk, because, by reason of their defensive behavior, they may be in the process of losing the capacity for intimacy or for forming relationships in later adulthood (Bowlby, 1977; Joffe and Vaughn, 1982). Alan Sroufe and his associates are continuing to follow up these children into latency. Further confirmation of these hypotheses must await the outcome of this series of studies. It now seems clear, however, that a child's attachment history will likely affect his psychosexual development during adolescence and his choice of marital partners. Children who have internalized a secure attachment relationship are most likely to choose partners who also experienced a secure attachment relationship. Children with resistant attachment relationships are likely to choose marital partners who foster or encourage their dependency or immaturity. Similarly, children with a history of avoidant attachment may choose marital partners who are equally avoidant.

Many studies have examined and isolated different maternal personality correlates or styles of maternal personality organization thought to be associated with later maladaptive avoidant attachment.

Main (1977) has outlined four characteristics that summarize the behavior of the mothers of these infants: (1) These women appear to be overly rejecting in their interactions with their infants. (2) They manifest aberrant close bodily contact (either overly controlling or abrupt). (3) They appear to have a great deal of submerged anger. (4) They manifest a compulsive rigid perfectionistic adjustment. Main has hypothesized that the relative lack of emotional expression and rigid style in these mothers is attributable to an effort to control their expression of anger. Ainsworth and her associates (1978) have described these women as less aware of their infant's signals and less responsive to them. She suggests that this maternal behavior may be due to a preoccupation with the mother's own psychological needs to the detriment of her infant's needs.

This kind of maternal style, viewed from a psychoanalytic perspective, might be defined as "narcissistic." Narcissistic individuals have a great need to be loved and admired and present a curious contradiction between a very inflated concept of themselves and an inordinate need for tribute from others. They have little capacity for empathy or genuine understanding of others' needs, especially if these needs are different from their own.

The recent psychoanalytic conceptualizations of Heinz Kohut (1978) have revitalized an interest in narcissism and have provided a developmental framework for understanding its origins. Kohut believes that there is a continuum of narcissism ranging from healthy narcissism to narcissistic personality disorders. For Kohut, narcissistic disorders are caused by shortcomings in maternal care which result in a weakened or defective self structure in the infant. Specifically, the mother's own lack of empathy prevents her from providing tasks that are appropriate given the child's level of development. This empathic deficiency results in an asynchrony between what the mother can provide and what is optimal for the infant at a given point in development.

Kohut's interpretation of narcissism as a continuous variable lends itself readily to an investigation of the avoidance phenomena. Similar to narcissism, avoidance is not pathological unless patterned in a particular and extreme manner. Even secure infants can manifest some degree of avoidance in the strange situation. Kohut's approach thus makes it possible to coordinate an analysis of avoidance and narcissism and offers a possible analytic interpretation for the emergence of avoidant attachment relationships. Even though the avoidant infant, like all other children, desires true closeness with his mother, he is prevented from developing a "secure" relationship because of his mother's unempathic and ultimately rejecting narcissistic demands.

This scenario is all the more understandable when examined in the context of the specific developmental tasks thought to occur for both mother and infant at approximately 1 year of age. In many ways, the infant at 1 year makes many more demands on his mother than he did in the previous months of life. Her task becomes more difficult now that her infant is on his way to becoming a separate human being. Although he continues to need her to comfort him when fatigued or stressed, he also needs her to enthusiastically delight in his accomplishments as he actively attempts to master his environment. If a woman has needed the infant to be "hers" and hers alone and has viewed the infant as an extension of herself in an attempt to hide the defects in her own narcissistic personality structure, she will be unable to enthusiastically "mirror" or delight in his accomplishments and her infant's emerging autonomy may anger and threaten her, as well as provoke the infant's defensive anger at being used in such a fashion.

Another important aspect of the mother–infant relationship at this developmental phase is the use which the child makes of this relationship in his struggle to achieve that successful regulation of tensions that leads to a feeling of continuity over time. The mother assists in this tension regulation by helping the child to develop signal anxiety. This leads to the recognition of increased tension and thus to the ability to take measures to regulate the tension. The narcissistic mother may fail to assist her infant in developing this signal anxiety. This may lead to a denial of the anxiety and the subsequent emergence of the defensive displacement behavior known as avoidance.

One study has investigated the relationship between this kind of maternal personality organization and the attachment relationship (Molitor, 1985). An index of maternal narcissism was derived by comparing mother's responses to the Child Rearing Practices Report, a Q-Sort instrument developed by Block (1965) with a criterion Q-Sort developed by four expert clinicians. This index was then used to generate nine clusters of attitudes toward child rearing. One hundred and three mother–child pairs from an upper middle-class population participated in this study. At 1 year of age, greater maternal narcissism was found to be significantly positively correlated with infant avoidance in the strange situation. Mothers who scored higher on the series of narcissism clusters had infants with higher avoidance scores.

These findings suggest several areas for future research. The cluster measures can expand the current psychoanalytic thinking about narcissism by providing an empirical means for differentiating narcissism from other diagnostic entities such as borderline personality, psychosis, or neurosis. By using the cluster measures, it becomes possible, for example, to assess whether infants born to highly narcissistic mothers, later can be classified as narcissistic themselves. This type of investigation could provide a test of Kohut's theory that shortcomings in maternal care lead to narcissistic deficits. It might also be possible to assess whether mothers who score high on these clusters are more likely to have repeat avoidant infants. It might also be interesting to follow up this sample of mothers and infants to the ages of 2 and 3, when issues of autonomy and self-control are more salient. It is quite probable that children of high narcissistic mothers would experience more difficulties with issues of impulse control and obedience at this time. These difficulties might be manifested in one of two different ways. Infants of highly narcissistic mothers might appear as overly dependent on them and fearful of expressing any independent, autonomous behavior, or they might appear overly undercontrolled and resentful of their mother's intrusive demands. By employing this measure of narcissism, it might even be possible to develop a profile of adults likely to have offspring with avoidant attachment relationships. It might also be possible to use the narcissism indices as predictors of other maladaptive outcomes (difficulties in adult interpersonal relationships) or as a general measure of object relations.

References

Ainsworth, M. (1969), *Infancy in Uganda: Infant Care and the Growth of Love.* Baltimore, MD: Johns Hopkins Press.
——— Bell, S., & Stayton, D. (1974), Infant–mother attachment and social development: Socialization as a product of reciprocal responsiveness to signals. In: *The Integration of the Child into a Social World,* ed. M. P. M. Richards. Cambridge, U.K.: Cambridge University Press.
——— Blehar, M. C., Waters, E., & Wall, S. (1978), *Patterns of Attachment.*

Hillsdale, NJ: Lawrence Erlbaum.
Block, J. H. (1965), *The Child Rearing Practices Report*. Berkeley, CA: Institute of Human Development.
Bowlby, J. (1969), *Attachment and Loss*, Vol. 1. New York: Basic Books.
——— (1977), The making and breaking of affectional bonds: Etiology and psychopathology in the light of attachment theory. *Brit. J. Psychiat.*, 130:201–210.
Egeland, B., & Sroufe, L. A. (1981), Developmental sequelae of maltreatment in infancy. In: *Developmental Perspectives in Child Maltreatment*, ed. R. Rizley and D. Cicchetti. San Francisco: Jossey-Bass.
Freud, S. (1914), On narcissism: an introduction. *Standard Edition*, 14:73–102. London: Hogarth Press, 1957.
Gove, F. (1983), *Patterns and Organizations of Behavior and Affective Expression During the Second Year of Life*. Unpublished doctoral dissertation. University of Minnesota, Minneapolis/St. Paul.
Horner, A. (1979), *Object Relations and the Developing Ego in Therapy*. New York: Jason Aronson.
Joffe, L., & Vaughn, B. (1982), Infant–mother attachment theory, assessment and implications for development. In: *Handbook of Developmental Psychology*, ed. B. Wolman. Englewood Cliffs, NJ: Prentice-Hall.
Kohut, H. (1978), *The Search for the Self*. New York: International Universities Press.
——— Wolf, E. (1978), The disorders of the self and their treatment: An outline. *J. Psychoanal.*, 59:413–425.
Main, M. (1977), Analysis of a peculiar form of reunion behavior seen in some day care children: its history and sequelae in children who are home reared. In: *Social Development in Daycare*, ed. A. Webb. Baltimore, MD.
——— Tomasini, L., & Tolan, W. (1979), Differences among mothers of infants judged to differ in security. *Development. Psychol.*, 15:472–473.
Matas, L., Arend, R., & Sroufe, L. A. (1978), Continuity of adaptation in the second year: The relationship between quality of attachment and latter competence. *Child Develop.*, 49:547–556.
Molitor, N. (1985), *The Effect of Maternal Narcissism Upon the Attachment Relationship*. Paper presented at the Society for Research in Child Development, Toronto, April.
Sroufe, L. A. (1979), Socioemotional development. In: *Handbook of Infant Development*, ed. J. Osofsky. New York: John Wiley.
——— (1983), Infant caregiver attachment and patterns of adaptation in preschool: The roots of maladaptation and competence. In: *Minnesota Symposium in Child Psychology*, Vol. 16, ed. M. Permutter. Hillsdale, NJ: Lawrence Erlbaum.
——— Fleeson, J. (1985), *Attachment and the Construction of Relationships*. Unpublished manuscript.
——— Rutter, M. (1984), The domain of developmental psychopathology. *Child Develop.*, 48:1184–1199.
Waters, R., Wippman, J., & Sroufe, L. A. (1979), Attachment, positive affect, and competence in the peer group: Two studies in construct validation. *Child Develop.*, 50:821–829.

Chapter 22

PATTERNS OF SOCIOAFFECTIVE DEVELOPMENT IN DISTURBED MOTHERS' PERCEPTIONS OF, AND INTERACTIONS WITH, THEIR INFANTS

JULIE A. HOFHEIMER, PH.D.
MAURICE APPREY, M.A.C.P.

The fate of the ego in the borderline psychotic woman is a precarious one which has profound implications for her capacity to nurture an infant and provide responsive and facilitative care-giving. Kernberg (1975) referred to the preponderance of primitive defense mechanisms as a pervasive characteristic of ego weakness in borderline personality organization. He also noted other aspects of ego weakness which have serious consequences for psychic equilibrium. These include the mother's inability to tolerate anxiety, to control impulses, and to develop appropriate sublimatory channels. Given the range of difficulties encountered as a result of her compromised functioning, consider the woman suffering from such impairments when she becomes an expectant mother.

This research was sponsored in part by the Division of Mental Health Service Programs of the National Institute of Mental Health Grant #MH-28463 and Contract #278:79-0008 to the Clinical Infant Development Program of Family Services of Prince George's County, Maryland. We are grateful for the leadership and support provided by Serena Wieder, Ph.D., Director of the Regional Center for Infants and Young Children, Rockville, Maryland, and Stanley I. Greenspan, M.D., former Chief of the Clinical Infant and Child Development Research Center, NIMH and DMCH. Their direction of the Clinical Infant Development Program and the diligent efforts of their clinical, research, and support staffs made this work possible. Information concerning this study can be obtained from Dr. Hofheimer: Frank Porter Graham Child Development Center, CB 8180 University of North Carolina, Highway 54 Bypass West 071A, Chapel Hill, NC 27599, (919) 966-7175.

Pregnancy itself is a period of intrapsychic reorganization where the ego undergoes serious developmental and adaptational transitions (Rossi, 1972; Russell, 1974; Sameroff, 1981). In the pregnant borderline woman, a considerable degree of formal regression (i.e., regression from secondary to primary process thinking) is expectable. It becomes important, therefore, to acknowledge the superimposition of the struggle to reorganize as a result of pregnancy over and above an existing regressive condition. This recognition brings us to posit that the transition to motherhood constitutes a dual threat, both to the fate of the mother's psychological well-being, and ultimately, to her child. While this notion of double jeopardy may be more easily observed and therefore more applicable to expectant borderline mothers, it is evident in mothers with other psychological disorders as well. Because of this, it would probably be more useful to refer to mothers who experience functional regressions as simply "disturbed," regardless of the specific ego defect or type of impairment.

Although there is an increasing interest in the influence of maternal psychopathology on infant development, empirical research concerning early interaction has been limited. In general, the risks associated with maternal psychopathology appear to be compounded when the illness is severe and/or chronic, the mother is uneducated, of lower socioeconomic status, has an unstable family and emotional life, and was herself the recipient of poor parenting (Sameroff, Seifer, and Zax, 1982; Walker and Emory, 1983; Belsky, Rovine, and Taylor, 1984; Belsky, 1984). This is due to the disorganization created by poverty, a lack of cognitive competence, and the mother's inability to obtain support and adapt to stressful experiences both intrapsychically and in the outside world (Sameroff, 1981).

In the first prospective longitudinal study of interactions between disturbed women and their infants, Sameroff and his colleagues (1982) found no differences on measures of infant behavior during interaction. Women with personality disorders were less proximal to their infants at 4 months. Mothers who were more severely ill and those who were neurotically depressed were also less proximal, in addition to being less spontaneous, happy, and vocal than healthy controls. Schizophrenic mothers were equally less spontaneous and proximal. More chronically ill mothers were less vocal and more negative.

Boyer (1983) has described more specific difficulties observed during interactions between disturbed mothers and their infants using an illustrative case study of overstimulation by a mother with ego defects. He noted that the dysfunctional maternal characteristics which were predominant included the mother's tendency to treat inner excitations as though they occurred externally; the impaired capacity of the ego's role as mediator; her conflict with reality; the mother's inability to serve as an external ego to her child and to provide protection from traumatic stimuli; and difficulty in modulating physical and interpersonal proximity and distance, or the tendency not to leave their babies alone. The author pointed out that the mother has the upper hand in determining the kinds of behavior she will accept and encourage from her infant. In addition, her attitudes and expectations are communicated during each encounter and are reflected in her behavioral repertoire. We have found this to be observable in every aspect of mothering, from the routine tasks of caregiving, to the most affectionate and intimate social contacts, and in volatile exchanges evoked by anger and frustration.

The attitudes, perceptions, and interactive styles of several disturbed mothers are the focal point of this chapter. Our goals are to describe the intrapsychic and emotional experiences of the women and to suggest possible interpretations of the ways in which these inner experiences influence interactions between the women and their infants. We will first present the experiences conveyed by each mother during the course of unstructured, dynamically oriented interviews from pregnancy through the infant's first year. Following each interview, we will present profiles of several dimensions of the interactive process which were derived from observations of the mothers and their infants during unstructured play sessions. The dyads were participating in the Clinical Infant Development Program (CIDP), an assessment and intervention program which focused on facilitating the development of infants born to disturbed mothers who were also at high risk due to socioenvironmental disadvantages (Greenspan, Wieder, Lieberman, Nover, Lourie, and

Robinson, 1987). Our syntheses of the two sources of information are based directly on these data. Detailed descriptions of the women's clinical profiles, histories, and treatment may be found in Greenspan (1981) and Greenspan et al. (1987) where the anecdotal clinical records of the mothers' psychotherapists and infant specialists who worked with each family are integrated.

In this chapter we will examine the interplay between affect and behavior in the context of the mother's self-perception, her sense of self as a mother, her perception of her infant, her attachment to, and identification with, the infant, and the process of differentiation and psychological separation from the infant. The recent findings of the second author (Apprey, 1985) were, in part, the basis for the present study, and focused on data from the series of interviews with mothers in the CIDP sample whose psychiatric disorders varied and who received different types of treatment. In his forthcoming work, Apprey has described a sequential pattern of affective development observed in disturbed mothers from the third trimester of pregnancy to approximately the third year of the child's life. The phenomenological landmarks which appeared to emerge in women suffering from serious ego defects includes: (1) negativistic and/or destructive attributions which were first delegated to the infant during pregnancy through projective identification; (2) components of projective identification and accompanying primitive mechanisms after the birth; and (3) from 8 to 12 months, when the child had become more mobile and began to initiate brief periods of separation, the mother was assisted in recognizing her infant's individuality, differentiating between herself and her infant, and revising destructive or aggressive attributions.

During the course of the mothers' therapy, they were able to transform their hitherto destructive projections into more adaptive modes of parenting. Adaptive functioning was seen in the mother's increased capacity to support the baby's initiative, respond appropriately to the infant's cues, and engage in reciprocal social and play exchanges involving objects[1] of interest to the baby.

An example of this process can be seen in the associations elicited by the interviews. Consider the following sequence of responses to the Caregiver Perception Profile (CPP) (Liberman, Wieder, and Greenspan, 1977; Lieberman, 1981) which was administered at the birth of the child and through almost 3 years:

> There is nothing in her crib to make me think of crib death. I never thought of abortion. . . . I am not going to give her away. . . . I am tired, but not because of her. . . . But when night comes I feel like I am going to lose her. She doesn't like men too much. She is crazy about women. Maybe I hurt her when I spanked her. . . . spanking her and then hugging her. . . . I am trying to make her different. But I can't change her. She has a bad personality. It's from her father. It's heredity. I have got to change her before she gets too old. . . . Everybody says she is like me. Not too much she does that I don't do. She is going to be wild. She will date at a young[er] age than her sister. . . . Now I deal with her by talking with her.

Three borderline mothers' perceptions of, and interactions with, their infants are presented below. These perceptions are believed to reflect shifts in the emotional world of the mother. Her interactive repertoire can be viewed as the behavioral manifestation of these profound affective changes in combination with her spontaneous responses to her infant's behavior.

The dyads presented here were part of a total sample which consisted of ninety multiparous women from Prince George's County, Maryland, a suburban area of Washington, DC. Each was entered into the program while pregnant with her second or later-born child; eight women had another child while in the study. Mothers were informed of the program through announcements at prenatal clinics, upon referral from agencies or staff at these clinics, or referral by private physicians. The women selected for participation were considered to be at high

---

[1]The term *objects* refers to toys and other inanimate materials—relations involving significant individuals are specified as such. We understand that this may be distasteful to some of our readers, but feel it necessary in discussing infants.

risk for problems in mothering. The initial assessment of risk was decided by consensus among clinicians from a number of disciplines, utilizing information from an extensive clinical interview with the mother and assessments of her other children.

The degree of psychiatric risk was later corroborated by independent ratings of clinical narratives completed by a reliable group of experienced psychologists and psychiatrists. High-risk women were then alternately assigned to either a Community Referral Treatment group (HR/CR) or to a Comprehensive Services Treatment Group, referred to as the Clinical Infant Development Program (HR/CIDP). Low-risk women were assigned to a second Community Referral Group (LR/CR). An exception to sequential assignment was one mother referred directly from a state hospital where she had received treatment for schizophrenia; she was assigned to the CIDP group.[2] The CIDP group received comprehensive services provided by a treatment team consisting of a clinical social worker, an infant specialist, a pediatrician, and a psychologist. The comprehensive intervention included continuous psychotherapeutic services for the mother, parenting assistance, developmental guidance, infant-centered developmental intervention, and provision of any other psychosocial services which were clinically considered to be necessary. Participants in the LR/CR and HR/CR groups received services by a comparable team of specialists who provided consultation and crisis intervention, with extensive use of referral to community agencies.

All women participated in a series of assessments including a multiphasic battery of standardized tests, clinical rating scales, and videotaped sessions of mother–infant interactions during unstructured play episodes. Developmental assessments of the infants, videotaped interaction sessions, and the administration of the Caregiver Perception Profile were conducted at 1, 4, 8, and 12 months, and at 6-month intervals up to 48 months.

The interactions were coded using the Greenspan–Lieberman Observation System (GLOS) which is based on a developmental structuralist theoretical framework (Greenspan

---

[2]Four other schizophrenics were referred to the program, but were assigned to the CIDP group using the alternating method.

and Lieberman, 1981). In this system, 76 distinct behaviors are coded at 15-second intervals. Definitions of the specific behaviors coded may be found in Greenspan and Lieberman (1981). The individual behaviors were selected to reflect not only the separate contributions of mother and infant to the interaction process, but also the fact that the behavior of each partner is both determined by, and is a response to, the behavior of the other. Thirty-two of the behaviors coded describe reciprocal behaviors involving both care giver and infant, while 23 apply to the care giver, and 23 to the infant alone. The interactions are observed in an unstructured play situation, which is described in greater detail below.

In order to summarize the data from the individual behaviors, a clustering system was developed (Hofheimer, Strauss, Lieberman, Poisson, and Greenspan, 1981). These clusters are presumed to reflect several, more global dimensions of individual differences in the mother–infant relationship which may be expected to be present in varying proportions throughout the first year of life. The clusters are presented in Table 22-1, and are measured by adding together the number of 15-second intervals in which each of the behaviors comprising the constructs occur. Several psychometric properties of the GLOS were examined in a multisample investigation of the psychometric properties of the GLOS (Hofheimer et al., 1981), the results of which are available from the first author.

The GLOS measures were derived from observational records of videotapes of mother–infant free play, which were obtained in two ways. The majority of dyads were videotaped in the project's Infant Center. Assessments and tapings took place in the homes of participants who were unable to come to the Center.

Upon collection, tapes were dubbed with audio tones at 15-second intervals of time and randomly assigned to one of seven observers, all of whom were naive to subject characteristics and the study's purpose. Tapes were assigned such that observers rated dyads at only one time point in order to eliminate biases which would have been introduced by the knowledge of earlier behavior.

Observers were trained in the use of the GLOS to a level

TABLE 22-1
Conceptual Clusters of Caregiver and Infant Behaviors

Cluster	Caregiver Behaviors	Infant Behaviors
Consolation/Distress	Attempt to console and soothe Contingent to distress Rhythmic movement	Contingent to soothing
Environmental Exploration	Contingent to exploration Developmental assistance Facilitation of object involvement (verbal and nonverbal) Nonparticipating–available	Exploratory manipulation Exploratory roaming Onlooking behavior Oriented to inanimate environment
Negative Affect/Aversive Stimulation	Abrupt handling Anticontingent behavior Inclusive behavior Direct physical punishment Physical overstimulation	Anticontingent behavior Avoids physical contact Distress Resists physical contact Withdrawal/Fear
Noninvolvement/Detachment	Flat affect Noncontingent responses Nonparticipating–Withdrawn	Aimless movement Flat affect Noncontingent responses Reckless behavior/self-harm
Positive Affect	Physical contacts: Affectionate touch Cuddle Kiss	Affectionate physical behavior Seeks physical contact Seeks proximity
Special Involvement	Contingent to social overtures Engagement in social interaction (verbal and nonverbal) Pleasure Rough and tumble play	Contingent to social overtures Initiates social interaction Pleasure
Reciprocity	Contingent chains—to exploration, pleasure, social overtures	Contingent chains—to exploration, pleasure, social overtures

TABLE 22-1 *(Continued)*

Cluster	Caregiver Behaviors	Infant Behaviors
Routine Activities	Contingent responses—Total Contingent to potential harm Physical contact: neutral Routine caregiving	Contingent responses—Total Contingent to protective commands Eating Sleeping
Vocalizations a. Total	Anticontingent vocal response Contingent vocal response Facilitation of object involvement: vocal	Anticontingent vocal response Contingent vocal response Distress
b. Responsive	Contingent vocal chains Contingent vocal responses	Contingent vocal chains Contingent vocal responses

of agreement of 80% or better, or to the level of agreement of the trainers for the variables for which reliability at this level could not be achieved. They then used the GLOS to code the first 10 minutes (40 segments) of each free-play sequence. Intraclass correlation coefficients were calculated to estimate interobserver reliability on the clusters and ranged from .70–1.0 (Poisson, Hofheimer, Lieberman, and Greenspan, 1983).

Table 22-2 presents the cluster profiles for three dyads at 4, 8, and 12 months of age. These data represent two different approaches to interpretation. The first entry is the percent of intervals in which behaviors comprising the individual clusters were observed. The second entry is the percent of cluster behaviors observed relative to the total types of behaviors and estimates that proportion relative to the range. These profiles and the narratives which follow can best be interpreted by re-

TABLE 22-2

Dyad / Age	Positive Affect		Routine Activities		Social Reciprocity		Consolation/ Distress		Social Involvement	
	M[a]	B	M	B	M	B	M	B	M	B
Anna & Emily										
4 mos.	.06 (.05)	.01 (.01)	.43 (.58)	.11 (.11)	0 (0)	0 (0)	.08 (.10)	.08 (.08)	.07 (.06)	0 (0)
8 mos.	.01 (.01)	0 (0)	.23 (.49)	0 (0)	.03 (.04)	.13 (.07)	.01 (.03)	.03 (.03)	.12 (.18)	0 (0)
12 mos.	.04 (.04)	.04 (.02)	.11 (.18)	0 (0)	.02 (.01)	.02 (.01)	0 (0)	0 (0)	.09 (.09)	.05 (.05)
Lauren & Mikey										
4 mos.	.15 (.16)	.02 (.006)	.15 (.24)	0 (0)	.02 (.01)	.02 (.006)	.14 (.21)	.17 (.14)	.09 (.1)	.02 (.01)
8 mos.	.01 (.008)	.06 (.04)	.03 (.05)	0 (.03)	.02 (.01)	.02 (.01)	.01 (.01)	0 (0)	.17 (.17)	.03 (.04)
12 mos.	.02 (.03)	.02 (.01)	.06 (.13)	0 (0)	.05 (.05)	.17 (.11)	0 (0)	0 (0)	.23 (.30)	.01 (.01)
Liza & Betsy										
8 mos.	.07 (.07)	.1 (.06)	.25 (.36)	0 (0)	.03 (.03)	.12 (.07)	.01 (.01)	0 (0)	.03 (.16)	.03 (.04)
12 mos.	.03 (.02)	.03 (.01)	.03 (.03)	0 (0)	.03 (.01)	.03 (.01)	0 (0)	0 (0)	.08 (.05)	0 (0)

*Percent of intervals in which cluster behaviors occur
(Percent of total number of types of behaviors observed.)
[a] M = Mother, B = Baby

GLOS Cluster Scores At 4, 8, and 12 Months*

Environmental Exploration		Total Vocalization		Responsive Vocalization		Neg. Affect/ Aversive Stimulation		Noninvolvement/ Detachment	
M	B	M	B	M	B	M	B	M	B
.19	.61	.11	.09	.07	.01	0	.08	0	.01
(.13)	(.06)	(.06)	(.04)	(.09)	(.01)	(0)	(.02)	(0)	(.01)
.16	.76	.28	.02	.13	0	.02	.07	0	0
(.18)	(.41)	(.25)	(.01)	(.69)	(0)	(.01)	(.02)	(0)	(0)
.27	.71	.32	.07	.14	.07	.02	.04	0	0
(.22)	(.36)	(.21)	(.04)	(.23)	(.08)	(.01)	(.01)	(0)	(0)
.15	.29	.19	.23	.09	.05	0	.18	0	.05
(.12)	(.12)	(.12)	(.19)	(.15)	(.04)	(0)	(.03)	(0)	(.02)
.21	.80	.33	.04	.21	.04	0	.01	.01	0
(.16)	(.49)	(.20)	(.03)	(.30)	(.05)	(0)	(.003)	(.008)	(0)
.17	.64	.32	.07	.14	.07	0	.04	0	0
(.17)	(.43)	(.26)	(.04)	(.29)	(.09)	(0)	(.01)	(0)	(0)
.17	.68	.21	.01	.07	.01	.02	.04	0	0
(.13)	(.38)	(.12)	(.01)	(.10)	(.01)	(.01)	(.01)	(0)	(0)
.28	.72	.36	.10	.18	.10	.01	.01	0	0
(.13)	(.30)	(.13)	(.04)	(.16)	(.09)	(.003)	(.002)	(0)	(0)

ferring to Table 22-1 where the individual behaviors comprising the clusters are presented.

Case Descriptions

Presented below are three clinical case descriptions of maternal perceptions and dyadic interaction during the infant's first year. When available, we have also included subsequent maternal interviews which serve as epilogues to the early developmental patterns illustrated. In order to interpret these data meaningfully, it is important to keep in mind that the feelings expressed by the women in the interviews are those which they were willing and able to disclose. In addition, their behavior during interaction reflects an awareness and sensitivity to the videotaping situation. In a previous study of the test–retest reliability of the GLOS, warm-up effects associated with the novel setting were found (Hofheimer, Lieberman, Strauss, O'Grady, and Greenspan, 1985). Data for the present study was collected after allowing the dyads to adjust to the situation during earlier assessments. In addition, our observations and those of the clinicians involved in the cases suggest that some mothers' behavior had a contrived or "on-stage" quality and was likely to be atypical of day-to-day style. This may also have been influenced by the modeling behavior of the clinical staff and we have indicated such instances in our interpretations.

Case One: Anna and Emily

During the last trimester of pregnancy, Anna stated that she was "tired of carrying the baby." The baby was in her way, she insisted, and for that reason she did not "want to talk about the baby." Nonetheless, she added some comments which reveal her inner thoughts and expectations of the baby: "I think I am going to have a baby boy . . . a strong baby boy, a bouncing baby boy." He is going to be "mean, because I am." She said she would not like his crying; crying would make her feel negatively about him.

Anna thought she would have a baby boy, but had a girl instead. At 4 months she said, "She is a good baby, she doesn't cry much, she is fun and delightful, she likes people, she likes to talk and play with other people and herself." In addition, "I can see her learning and growing." Seeing her daughter as delightful, she recognized that she felt "different about her now" than she did before, "when you asked me these questions. But now I feel more together about her, and I feel closer to her in a better, very sure, and understanding way." The hostility toward the infant in the prenatal interview had dissipated by this point and reaction formations had been employed to deal with the conflictual feelings: "I don't even get mad if she pees on me or has a bowel movement, even when I have just changed her. It doesn't bother me. I don't know what I told you before, it doesn't matter, but now she is great. I do like her. I'm crazy about her." However, there is a limit to how much defensive mechanisms can compensate for negative feelings about the baby and how effectively they can bring unacceptable thoughts of the mother under control. This mother liked her child because she was good, "pretty, just like me," was "very soft and [had] a soft complexion." But she still wished she had given birth to a boy to fit her original projections and some attributions remained: "She looks like a boy, still." Having a girl forced her to drop most of the original attributions, but brought to light many of her own identity issues. In spite of some of these uncertainties, her sense of self as a mother began to emerge. Asked what made her feel like a mother, she felt responsibilities made her feel like one and continued on to say, "I am hooked on the fact of the word, 'Mommy.' I feel more mature now. I am not pregnant now. The babies are older. I can move around more." Mobility was very important to Anna. In the prenatal interview, the anger and frustration experienced as a result of relative immobility due to the pregnancy was displaced as hostility toward the unborn child. Four months after delivery, her sense of freedom resulting from the restoration of mobility also reflects a certain degree of freedom from her destructive feelings toward the child, and her emergent sense of herself as a competent and caring mother.

As can be seen from the 5-month cluster percentages presented in Table 22-2, over half of Anna's behaviors were those associated with routine activities such as neutral physical contact and routine caregiving. She was involved in a moderate amount of environmental exploration, was somewhat affectionate, and was a verbal and verbally responsive mother. She neither initiated many social exchanges, nor was she behaviorally responsive to her baby during social exchanges. The predominance of the baby's vocal distress, and her involvement with the inanimate environment (i.e., objects and toys) indicated a lack of affection and social involvement with her mother.

In general, while the dyad appears to be "in synch" with respect to the relative amounts of consolation on the mother's part and consolability on the baby's part, there is a worrisome lack of affection, pleasure, and reciprocal social exchanges, in addition to the presence of Emily's overt negativism. The large proportion of maternal warmth accompanied by Emily's detachment is unusual. In light of our previous observations, the inconsistencies in the maternal and dyadic profiles suggest mother's more appropriate affective and social behaviors were contrived for the camera and are not typical of her day-to-day behavior. In sum, the profiles appear to reflect Anna's ambivalence surrounding intimacy, that is, establishing and sustaining an interpersonal connectedness with Emily. This also appears to be related to the anxiety resulting from Anna's acknowledgment of her identification with her daughter.

At 8 months, it looked as if Anna was going to maintain the earlier progress when she was able to recognize Emily's uniqueness and her relative independence, and said that "she's not like the other kids." During pregnancy she had said that she could "see [the expected infant] learning and growing." By 8 months, her attribution to Emily's relative competence and level of understanding was reflected in her interpretation of her baby's ability to play alone as an indication of the baby's empathy for her: "Well, mom, you've got things to do, and I see how busy you are, and I'll be cool and play by myself." In the course of articulating an exchange of her understanding of her baby for her baby's understanding of her as a mother, she began to disorganize and needed to ask, "What did you ask me?" The disorganization continued throughout the interview and was evident in her response to the question, "When do you feel close to your baby?"

> I forget about her sometimes when ... not really forget about her, I know she is mine and I got her and all, but when I am not there, say when I am working or if I am away, you know when I'm so busy or something, I have to keep my mind on what it's on. Even so, I think about my other kids like my oldest daughter and all. With her, I feel closer to her. You know, when I'm right there I can see her and I know she's there in the house.

And to the question, "What makes you feel like a mother?"

> I just have to feel, I mean, you know, I live with it. I am a mother. I beared the pain and, you know, the experience and the time. Everything I do, really. I do things for myself, I sometimes wonder. I question the fact about me being that individual but, you know, not to the extent to where I did before because I can find myself sometimes, but I other than that, I'm mom all the time. I don't know if that is good or not.

The disfluency and disorganization in this otherwise articulate woman is striking. Conflict about the child's growing independence and anxiety about her own instinctual tendencies, that is, her previously warded-off hostility toward the baby, had resurfaced at this point. Their disruption of her psychic equilibrium was thus evident in her verbalizations.

During interaction Anna was again primarily involved in routine caregiving at a rate which is excessive for an 8-month-old infant. There were moderate proportions of affection and social initiatives. As was the case at 5 months, she continued to provide a great deal of developmental support, focused on the inanimate environment, and was quite verbal and verbally responsive. Although reciprocal responses had increased dramatically, Emily still did not take the social initiative and there was a worrisome lack of affection. Her primary interest continued to involve the inanimate environment. Emily's lack of spontaneous and responsive vocalizations were also worrisome. As a dyad, there were equal, but slight increases in reciprocity with again, equivalent proportions of consolability and consolation. These were accompanied by moderately high proportions of negative affect in the absence of both overt aggression and detachment. These profiles are worrisome and confirm earlier indications of difficulties with attachment. The problematic pattern of development in Anna and Emily's relationship also substantiates the earlier hunch that the mother's more appropriate behaviors were contrived for the camera.

By 12 months, Anna had made marked strides in recovering from her regressed state. She recognized that her child was happy and active, that she ate, slept, and played well, in addition to being cute when by herself. She stated that she didn't "feel negative about this baby anymore." Where in the past she had feared that the child's crying would make her feel negative about her, she now interpreted the child's cries as pleas for her help: "She cries for me. . . ." Despite her predominantly realistic and organized perceptions, the disorganization still persisted and was evident toward the end of the interview when she said, "She looks like mom and, um, 'cause she's a small baby she concentrates and studies."

During interaction Anna continued to engage in moderate amounts of routine caregiving, although this was now more in balance with vocalizations, reciprocal responses, and environmental exploration. Both positive and negative affect were observed and responsive vocalizations had decreased at this point. Emily remained primarily interested in the inanimate environment. While she was notably more verbally responsive, she was also significantly less likely to reciprocate socially. The dyadic picture was somewhat more encouraging. There was a slight amount of reciprocity with approximately equivalent social initiatives on the part of the mother and baby, whereas earlier it was Anna who had been the one to initiate all social exchanges. Inanimate involvement was approximately equal, which is usually indicative of mother and baby making a healthy, stage-appropriate, transition together.

What we see in the development of the relationship between Anna and Emily is a consistent lack of warm affective involvement. This is in spite of the baby's accomplishment of several developmental tasks and her increasing social competence during the first year of life. A distressing characteristic is that this dyad is remarkably in synch, but often in a negative sense. When baby is in distress, mother consoles, and when baby is involved with the inanimate environment, mother assists her in pursuing those interests. Although this is highly appropriate, there is no indication of any genuine emotional relatedness and supportiveness on either mother or baby's part. Despite Anna's ability to meet baby's more concrete needs and be vocally responsive, her interpersonal behavior remained primarily task-oriented in general and was often unresponsive to the baby's cues. This is fairly consistent over time, and as such, we got the sense that what we were seeing during the play episode may have been very different from what actually went on in the home most of the time. This explanation appears plausible, for while the mother is often developmentally appropriate, the baby seems to have tuned-out to both her social overtures and any other attempts to engage. In general, we observed a temporal lag between the feelings expressed by the mother about her infant, and her translation of these feelings into actions.

By 18 months there was great improvement in the mother's psychological functioning both as an individual and as a mother. Her articulation of feelings concerning her sense of self as a mother, and the tasks of mothering became more insightful. She saw her child as "very smart," one who plays well by herself, was strong, and whose "legs stretch so far I think she is double-jointed." In addition, the mother felt her toddler to be "very lovable" and likely to be "very intelligent." "I think she is like my brother. . . . I feel like it's this instant attraction when I think of both of them." This improvement continued through 2 years where the mother was once again coherent and articulate: "I feel good about being a mother. I felt there was a big chance with the last baby. I really feel fantastic about it. I grew with them. . . ."

Case Two: Lauren and Mikey

During pregnancy, Lauren employed projective modes extensively to deal with her fears and intolerance of separation from the unborn baby's father. "If I have a boy, I will have a little man, a big boy. If I have a beautiful child, then I am attractive too." It was as if she were saying, if I have a boy, then I can have Mike Sr. If I can keep Mike Sr., hang onto my man, I am whole. Her preconscious attributions centered around the child being beautiful to reverse the ugliness and damage she perceived in herself. There was a great deal of anxiety surrounding aggression: "I'll never kill a baby if I didn't have to." Lauren feared that her hands could bring great harm to and destroy her child. On the other hand, she expressed the hope that her child would make her feel complete. Through this narcissistic wish and through her unborn child—miniature Mike—she believed she could hang onto her man and her sense of self.

The delivery of the child and hence, physical separation, initiated the resolution of ambivalence toward the baby, a reversal in the fear of "killing or losing the child," and of the fear of "being controlled by the baby." At 4 months, Lauren resorted to defensive maneuvers to regain her own psychic balance. Sadistic wishes were transformed into passive experiences as she reportedly "suffered" from the baby's burdensome demands. In addition, her sadistic fears and fantasies were trivialized as jokes. Projection was incorporated to deal with feeling controlled and was heard in her wish "to control her infant." To cope with her anxiety about the small size of the infant she spoke of the baby being big. Rather than verbalizing aggressive wishes, we heard about the child "always asleep." Instead of acknowledging the baby's imperfections, she acclaimed that he was perfect and that he was gorgeous, rather than being less than beautiful.

During interaction Lauren exhibited approximately equivalent amounts of affection, consolation, routine caregiving, environmental exploration, and social initiatives. This pattern is one which tends to facilitate the infant's development and reflects an appropriate attachment to the baby—an encouraging start, given her worrisome perceptions. She vocalized quite frequently and half of these were appropriately responsive. The occurrence of reciprocal responses was low. This, in addition to the absence of negative affect, aggression, and detachment suggested a mother-dominated, "one-way" pattern of interaction which appeared to reflect Lauren's need to be in control. Unfortunately, this tended to be somewhat overwhelming to the infant.

The baby was frequently in distress and primarily involved in being consoled, or focused on inanimate objects and tasks. There were few incidences of affection and social reciprocity and responsive vocalizations, with moderately high proportions of negative affect and detachment. The dyad appeared to be in synch with respect to inanimate involvement, but the mother's attempts at social involvement were not often reciprocated by her baby. This profile suggests that the baby is not engaged affectively or socially with mother and has turned to the inanimate world rather than to her. This is a pattern which can be seen as the baby's way to adapt to his mother's dominance.

No interview data were available at 8 months, but during interaction, there was a striking decrease in Lauren's affection. She was primarily involved in activities of a developmentally supportive nature. This is an often observed, stage-expected pattern. She continued to make social overtures and remained vocal and vocally responsive to her son. There was an isolated instance of detachment which, in the context of other behaviors was not worrisome, though noteworthy. This pattern is more balanced as well as being more stage-appropriate than had been observed earlier.

Mikey was again primarily involved in the inanimate world, but there was an increase in his affectionate behavior at this point. All vocalizations were responsive and he frequently initiated social exchanges. In addition, negative affect had decreased.

This suggests a dramatic shift and indicates the accomplishment of several developmental tasks including the baby's attachment to his mother and concurrent initiatives involving both the animate and inanimate world. The profiles of mother and baby were comparable with respect to social reciprocity. They appeared to be affectively engaged and able to sustain social exchanges where both partners initiate alternately.

By 12 months Lauren had taken back her attributions. We believe this occurred as a function of her ability to accurately perceive and acknowledge the reality of her baby's needs and behavior. In addition, she had become aware of her own drive demands. It appears that the baby's developmental strides had forced her to face his individuality, differentiate between herself and her son, and cope with the feelings of separateness. By this point, the aggression which she had hitherto delegated to her infant son, now was perceived to be more associated with her preschool daughter. The earlier delegation was dismantled when she acknowledged the "similarity between" herself and her daughter. While this acknowledgement provided a very concrete point of reference for Lauren, differentiating between the aggression in her daughter and herself, and between them and her projections to her son was painfully difficult. She reported that she dealt with the resultant disorganization by unconsciously attempting to achieve his submission through harsh discipline and "punishment so that he would not be like his father."

Social exchanges were predominant during the play session at one year. The rate of social reciprocity had increased somewhat and was more in balance with inanimate involvement. In addition, Lauren vocalized frequently and remained responsive. This profile suggests an adaptive adjustment to Mikey's emergent independence and autonomy. The isolated incidence of controlling behavior is common and often necessary in early toddlerhood and is not problematic, given its minimal rate of occurrence relative to the other dimensions.

Mikey continued his environmental explorations while at the same time becoming notably more able to be engaged in and sustain social exchanges. While he was vocally responsive, the absence of spontaneous vocalizations was unusual. The slight amount of negative affect appeared appropriate in that it reflects assertiveness in response to his mother's demands.

As a dyad, the profiles of mother and baby were comparable with respect to affection and on-going social exchanges, which included reciprocal vocalizations. While Mikey continued to be predominately involved in inanimate exploration, interactive competence was gradually emerging, and Lauren was able to be supportive of both initiatives on his part.

It is helpful to look at the pattern which unfolded over the first year. Although this dyad appeared slightly out of synch at 4 months, Lauren apparently persisted in promoting social engagements and Mikey eventually became more responsive. He was slow, however, in taking the initiative to involve his mother in social exchanges. Lauren appeared to be able to support her son's independence once she began to acknowledge their separateness. This is evident in the balance between affection and developmentally facilitating behavior which is supportive of the baby's initiative. In this case, the modulated quality of both mother and baby behavior and the parallels in their profiles suggest that our observations are likely to be representative of their interactive styles.

At 2 years, it was still important to Lauren that her son not be aggressive like his father. In fact, her wish that he not even be a male—a complete reversal from pregnancy—was evident in her dressing him up as a girl, and her preference that he "sit on a pot" for urination. Unable to sustain a constructive separateness from her toddler, she now expressed her wish that "he must be like me: loving, caring, feminine, compassionate." Lauren's disorganization was a result of the bitterness evoked by the child's assertiveness, aggression, and negativism, as well as her attempts to deny these distasteful characteristics. This was evident in her recounting of incidences such as "prying him away from his tractor" and her expectation that he—at 2 years—"be a man of God" frocked as a minister. The price she paid for owning to these attributions was that she fell apart. In the context of a woman struggling to accomplish the developmental tasks of mothering, the period of total disorganization that ensued could be viewed as her defense against a greater catastrophe—a violently destructive rage.

During the 3-year interview, Lauren alternated between themes of sadism and caring, with numerous shifts occurring throughout the single interview. Mikey was now effectively resisting his mother's intrusive projections, but she reported that he resisted "from time to time" by "hanging onto his toys" when she tried to take them and by resisting her repeated attempts to "control him." In reference to these incidences, Lauren referred to his independence and assertive behavior as his "2-year-old attitude," clearly a diminishment of his emerging competence, individuality, and fear-inducing aggression. Her rage at his unwillingness to comply with her unreasonable and intrusive demands was evident when she blamed her son for her daughter's misbehavior. She next stated that she would prefer him to "be a dancer than a pilot." We would suspect that this displacement may again be a reflection of her identification with her daughter which had been observed earlier.

Toward the end of the interview, there was some promise that she could relinquish her hold on him. This was felt to be due, in part, to her recognition of her son's autonomy and competence with guidance from the infant specialist as well as insights acquired in therapy. Her future plans included a decision to "take care of nursery school children" rather than trying to hang onto little Mike as if he were big Mike. By 3 years there were clear indications of an awareness that she would need to let go of her son, that although his "growing away" was inevitable, going away was not.

Case Three: Liza and Betsy

During the third trimester of her pregnancy, Liza reported, "I've never not felt close to my babies" and that she expected to be close to this new baby after the birth. She said she liked infants when they were small and dependent; that when they are dependent, "I feel close to them." This child would, she thought, be born with dark hair and blue eyes. She did not expect to be nervous when the child was born. We did not detect any indication of projection or destructive attribution concerning this expected baby, and were impressed by her insightful acknowledgement of the pleasure she received from her infant's dependency. Liza's emphatic use of double negatives regarding feelings of closeness was of interest, in that they could indicate either a healthy attempt to resolve her ambivalence about intimacy, or be the reflection of conflicted issues which would have serious implications for her relationship with her baby.

The 4-month assessments were not able to be administered, nor was the 8-month interview. Liza did consent to come in for Betsy's 8-month assessments. During the play episode we observed the frequent occurrence of routine tasks and neutral physical contact. This was disproportionate to Liza's moderate amount of "developmental support," a cluster of behaviors which sometimes requires neutral physical contact. Liza made few social overtures and engaged minimally in reciprocal exchanges. These characteristics, in combination with the presence of "negative affect," suggest that she was having difficulty sustaining an interpersonal connectedness and being supportive of her baby while concurrently doing the necessary amount of letting go as she became more mobile. Betsy, on the other hand, evidenced moderate rates of "reciprocity" and was vocally responsive, but did not initiate social exchanges and was primarily involved in inanimate explorations. Neither mother nor baby appeared interested in engaging the other and the rates of social initiatives were low for both. They focused predominately on reciprocal play exchanges involving inanimate objects and exploration. Moderate amounts of affection were observed but in light of the minimal social engagement, Liza's affection appears somewhat contrived given the "negative affect" displayed by both her and her daughter.

At 12 months, Liza reported that she "loved her baby so much." "Except," she continued, "there is only one thing about her that does get on my nerves—in the way she sometimes screams real loud, it's just a piercing scream. . . ." She felt "a little too close" to the child, as the two were hardly ever separated, and said that "she is always in our bedroom." By this point, however, both parents were "beginning to decide if she should not sleep somewhere else." As was the case in the prenatal interview, this mother's use of double negatives, such as those mentioned above and, "I don't usually hardly ever have any negative feelings," are provocative and support the premise that her attachment to her baby is fraught with conflict and ambivalent at best. This was certainly evident in her behavior during early interaction. Despite the ambivalence, the loving feelings toward the baby, rather than negatives, predominate: "I enjoy her lovableness . . . I think I have a real, uh, wonderful personality baby." As was the case prenatally, there were no indications of projection or destructive attributions to the baby.

At 12 months, this mother initiated social exchanges more frequently, was more vocally responsive, and the proportion of developmental initiatives relative to the other types of behaviors had increased. Betsy still did not initiate social involvement, however, and the proportion of reciprocal behaviors had declined, despite an increase in both "responsive" and "total vocalization."

The proportion of intervals in which "inanimate involvement" occurred remained high relative to the rates for other clusters, with the exception of vocalizations. As a dyad, there was an increase in vocalizations which were primarily responsive, with decrements in both "positive" and "negative affect." As was the case at 8 months, there was a strikingly low proportion of social involvement, both in reciprocal exchanges and those reflecting each partner's initiative.

The trend across the first year shows a dramatic decrease in the total number of different behaviors observed. This suggests that the range had become narrower, rather than wider, as would be expected given the more sophisticated behavioral repertoire of the baby. Social reciprocity and initiatives for both partners were markedly low and were accompanied by a worrisome imbalance evident across time. This is suggestive of early attachment difficulties which we were unable to observe, but which were alluded to in Liza's responses to the interview. Betsy was becoming mobile and therefore more autonomous, there also appeared to be difficulty with Liza's acceptance of her independence and the issue of separateness. Without the establishment and maintenance of a strong affective connectedness between mother and baby, it would follow that separation, autonomy, and rapprochement would be extremely difficult in this next phase of development.

The predominance of Liza's reportedly loving feelings toward Betsy continued into the second year. Her toddler's objections, such as " 'no, Mommy, no' when she did not want to eat anymore or wanted to do something else after she is satisfied," were able to be understood and accepted by the mother as appropriate for her daughter in the context of the situation. She also appeared to understand the child's yearnings to be autonomous and was able to disclose her motivation for supporting the baby's individuality: "Since I was a twin, there is a lot of ways I had to be different. I feel I was repressed in a lot of my things that I could have been and I think I am trying in a way to help her . . . and she is also being able to let herself be herself as an individual, what I couldn't do." At this point, possible explanations for Liza's distancing herself from her daughter became quite clear. We had noted that expectable projections and externalizations were absent from her early responses. In this case, unfortunately, resisting the identification with her daughter meant that Liza was unable to establish and sustain a close and loving relationship with Betsy. Her feelings of closeness and attachment, though obviously heartfelt and expressed with sincerity, were unable to be acted on in the reality of her life with her daughter. From the dynamics reflected in the interaction profiles, the relationship between this mother and her infant appears affectively shallow, despite its geniune nature.

Conclusion

The above descriptions have shed light on the socioaffective development of disturbed mothers and their relationships with their infants. The feelings expressed by these women about themselves and their infants have been illuminating to the extent that they were able to share their anxieties and reveal conflicts about becoming a mother and about their children. Themes of hostility, destruction, abandonment, ambivalence, and intrusive wishes were expressed, in addition to those reflecting nurturant, supportive, facilitative, and socializing modes of weaving the child into their own symbolic network. With intervention, mothers such as Lauren traversed from destructive to supportive modes of relating to their babies. Others began with ambivalence and proceeded on to appropriately supportive, but limited relationships, as was the case with Liza and Betsy.

A common thread was seen in the feelings and experiences of the three women: their fragile and vulnerable psyches—once at the mercy of primitive instincts, distorted perceptions, painful conflicts, and an external world that was not in tune with their needs as women and as mothers—were able to be strengthened and each woman's capacity to deal with intrapsychic and extrapsychic infringements increased. Despite serious psychological and functional impairments, the mothers were able to become very capable observers of their own symbolic network and the interplay between symbolism and the reality of their relationships with their infants. This was accomplished by helping the mother take in more accurate information concerning her baby's individuality, thereby short-circuiting the potentially disastrous effects of acting on faulty perceptions during encounters with the baby. It appears that even in a regressed state, the observing ego of the mother can be assisted in joining forces with other integrative functions so that she can establish a rich affective relationship, and, in so doing, facilitate competence and strength in her child.

By and large, these findings suggest that the therapeutic relationship and process enabled these mothers to contain their own intrapsychic pain—rather than to suppress or deny it—in order to pursue more adaptive developmental progressions in the transitions of motherhood. This was observed in the mothers as individuals and in their increased capacity to respond appropriately to their infants. From a dynamic perspective, this adaptation could be viewed as a result of having detoxified the mother's destructive projections during the course of therapy. In so doing, they were able to "reown" the projections, take them back into themselves, and work them through more constructively with the help of the therapist.

Naturally occurring milestones in maternal and infant development are also likely to influence this process. It may be that potentially threatening projections are most poignant when the baby is most dependent (i.e., in utero and early infancy). The actual physical separation at birth and once the baby becomes mobile may make it easier for disturbed women to differentiate their perceptions and feelings from reality. A study of healthy dyads (Hofheimer et al., 1985) has suggested that the transitions through symbiosis, the acknowledgment of separateness, and individuation can be difficult for most women, regardless of the integrity of their psyches. The process of the mother's emotional "letting go" of her infant and renegotiating the parameters of their relationship was seen in the predominance of behaviors reflecting affection and social reciprocity at 4 months. At 8 months, these healthy mothers became intrusive as their infants were more involved in exploration and less socially engaging. By 12 months, however, the mothers were appropriately less proximal, but once again emotionally available and supportive of their infants' independence and initiative.

The stage-expected transitions by the women in the present study were characterized by more extreme changes, more destructive behavior, and by frequent regressions throughout the course of their constructive conflict resolution. Similarly adaptive changes were also seen in the untreated comparison group, but the changes were less systematic in the sense that they were inconsistent or unsustained. Exceptions to this were the few mothers in the comparison group who were insightful and psychologically minded enough to elicit information and guidance. Some of these women were able to use both the assessments and the feedback sessions in a therapeutic manner.

The characteristics of the three infants reflect central themes which were present in each of their affective environments. In addition, patterns in the development of their interactive repertoires were revealed. In Anna's and Emily's cases, we see task-oriented mothers whose affection appears contrived, and infants who had tuned them out by the age of 5 months, preferring to pursue experiences involving inanimate objects. This pattern continued throughout the eighth month, and while Emily became more socially responsive, she did not initiate social exchanges and remained unaffectionate. This preference for inanimate involvement was also observed in both Mikey and Betsy, and their patterns have been prevalent in many of our other CIDP infants. The result of early difficulties with attachment—especially with respect to the lack of spontaneous affection and responsivity on the part of the mother—is that the infant often appears to acquire an emotional aloofness. Without intervention, affective and behavioral problems predominate the outcomes for these infants. Infants who received intervention, however, were still found to be delayed in language and social development. As might be expected, they were extremely competent on cognitive tasks involving inanimate objects and those reflecting psychomotor abilities.

Considerably more in-depth research with large samples is needed to more precisely determine the course of developmental disturbances in relationships between mothers and their infants. The present study does illustrate the means by which mother and infant impact on each other, and the affective and interactive patterns which develop from pregnancy through toddlerhood. Intervention provided to these women included individual and group therapies, home visits, infant assessments, and feedback sessions, and consult–liaison services with pediatric health care, and social service agencies. Because of the comprehensive nature of this program, it was also possible to examine the ways in which the treatment process influenced the mother's ability to care for her infant and ameliorated potentially problematic outcomes for these vulnerable families.

References

Belsky, J. (1984), The determinants of parenting: A process model. *Child Develop.*, 55: 83–96.
────── Rovine, M., & Taylor, D. G. (1984), The Pennsylvania infant and family development project, III: The origins of individual differences in infant–mother attachment: Maternal and infant contributions. *Child Develop.*, 55:718–728.
Boyer, L. (1983), *The Regressed Patient*. New York: Jason Aronson.
Greenspan, S. I. (1981), Psychopathology and Adaptation in Infancy and Early Childhood: Principles of Clinical Diagnosis and Preventive Intervention. *Clinical Infant Reports*, No. 1. New York: International Universities Press.
────── Lieberman, A. F. (1981), Infants, mothers, and their interaction: A quantitative clinical approach to developmental assessment. In: *The Course of Life: Infancy and Early Childhood*, ed. S. Greenspan & G. Pollack. Washington, DC: National Institute of Mental Health, Monograph, pp. 271–312.
────── Wieder, S., Lieberman, A., Nover, R., Lourie, R., & Robinson, M. eds. (1987), *Infants in Multirisk Families: Case Studies of Preventive Intervention*. New York: International Universities Press.
Hofheimer, J. A., Lieberman, A. F., Strauss, M. E., O'Grady, K. E., & Greenspan, S. I. (1985), An Assessment of Stability and Videotaping Effects in Observations of Mother–Infant Interaction. Unpublished manuscript.
────── Strauss, M. E., Lieberman, A. F., Poisson, S. S., & Greenspan, S. I. (1981), *The Reliability, Validity, and Generalizability of Assessments of Transaction Between Infants and Their Caregivers*, NIMH Technical report. Washington, DC: National Institute of Mental Health.
Kernberg, O. F. (1975), *Borderline Conditions and Pathological Narcissism*. New York: Jason Aronson.
Lieberman, A. F., Wieder, S., & Greenspan, S. I. (1977), *Caregiver Perception Profile*. NIMH Technical Report. Washington, DC: National Institute of Mental Health.
Poisson, S. S., Hofheimer, J. A., Lieberman, A. F., & Greenspan, S. I. (1983), The Assessment of Interobserver Reliability and Agreement in Observations of Mother–Infant Interaction. NIMH unpublished manuscript.
Rossi, A. (1972), Family development in a changing world. *Amer. J. Psychiat.*, 128/9: 1057–1066.
Russell, C. S. (1974), Transition to parenthood: Problems and gratifications. *J. Marr. & the Fam.*, 36:294–301.
Sameroff, A. (1981), The psychological needs of the mother in early

mother–infant interactions. In: *Neonatology*, ed. G. B. Avery. Philadelphia: J. B. Lippincott, pp. 303–321.
——— Chandler, J. J. (1975), Reproductive risk and the continuum of caretaking casualty. In: *Review of Child Development Research*, Vol. 4, eds. F. Horowitz, M. Heatherington, S. Scarr-Salapatek, & G. Siegle. Chicago: University of Chicago Press.
——— Seifer, R., & Zax, M. (1982), Early development of children at risk for emotional disorder. *Monographs of the Society for Research in Child Development*, 47:Serial No. 199. Chicago: University of Chicago Press.
Walker, E., & Emory, E. (1983), Infants at risk for psychopathology: Offspring of schizophrenic parents. *Child Develop.*, 54:1269–1285.

Appendix 22-1

Caretaker Perception Profile (CPP)

I. Before Delivery

A. Free Association
   Mothers usually have ideas about their babies even before they are born. What are your ideas or feelings about this baby?
B. Structured Questions
   1. All women when they're pregnant wonder how they will feel about their babies. Will you feel close to the baby, or will you often feel that you don't understand him/her?
   2. What about the baby will make you feel close to him/her?
   3. What about the baby will make you feel not so close
   4. What will make you feel that this baby is really yours?
   5. When do you think this will happen? (that you will feel the baby is really yours?)
   6. What about your baby will you enjoy the most?
   7. Sometimes mothers feel negative about their babies, for example, because they cry a lot or are spoiled. What will make you feel negative about your baby?
   8. How would you describe the kind of baby you'll have? Then add, as appropriate: Physically? In terms of personality?

II. Birth–12 months

A. Free Association
   I have been asking you many questions about the delivery and the way things have been for you and your baby. Please tell me now as much as you can about your baby. What is he/she like?
B. Structured Questions
   1. All mothers have different kinds of feelings about their babies.

Do you feel close to the baby, or do you feel you don't understand him/her?
2. When do you feel close to your baby?
3. When do you feel not close to your baby?
4. What makes you feel that this is really your baby?
5. What do you enjoy most about your baby?
6. Sometimes mothers feel negative about their babies, for example, because they cry a lot or are spoiled. What makes you feel negative about your baby?
7. How would you describe the kind of baby you have? Then add, as appropriate: Physically? In terms of personality?
8. What makes you really feel like a mother?

III. 12–36 months

NOTE: The parents' initial response when asked to just talk about their baby is the most critical one for the CPP. If they do not say much, first try to encourage them further to tell you a little more before proceeding with the questions. If a parent spontaneously answers one of the specific questions before being asked it is not necessary to ask it again.

A. Free Association

Babies grow a lot during their first years and mothers feel different things as their children grow older and change. Please tell me as much as you can about your baby, what is he/she like? And what are your experiences or feelings about being a mother now?

B. Structured Questions

I would also like to ask you a few questions about the baby. Some of these you have heard already and some of these are new.

1. How would you describe your baby now? What is your baby like physically? What about your baby's personality?
2. How is it different for you being the mother of a toddler compared to being the mother of a little infant?
3. All mothers (fathers) have different kinds of feelings about their babies. What feelings do you have? Sometimes they feel closer or warmer, sometimes angry or distant. When do you have such feelings?
4. What do you enjoy most about your baby now? Enjoy least?
5. How is your baby like you? How is your baby different than you? Is your baby like anyone else?
6. All babies at times get very angry or very loving. When does your baby get this way and how do you deal with it?

7. All babies at times feel like they want everything done for them and are very passive, while at other times they take charge and want to control everything. When does your baby get this way and how do you deal with it?
8. What do you think your baby will be like when he/she grows up? What will make him/her that way?
9. There are different ways in which women (men) really feel like mothers (fathers). When do you really feel most like a mother (father)?

Chapter 23
IMPLICATIONS OF OBJECT RELATIONS THEORY FOR RESEARCH ON GROUP PSYCHOTHERAPY OF BORDERLINE PATIENTS

Les R. Greene, Ph.D.

One of the few points upon which reviewers of group psychotherapy research can agree is that the quality of those scientific efforts designed to evaluate the effectiveness of this treatment modality has been generally disappointing. Methodologically flawed and conceptually impoverished, the experimental literature to date has been of only minimal value for its several prospective audiences. For the empirical investigator, the extant data base is intractable and resistant to attempts at integration; findings from each discrete study tend to lack generalizability and remain in isolation. As a consequence, research efforts seem fixated at the most global level of inquiry, namely, asking whether group therapy "works." Even the more ambitious undertakings, such as the well-known outcome study of interpretative, group-as-a-whole therapy for neurotic patients by Malan, Balfour, Hood, and Shooter (1976), fail to achieve appreciably more experimental rigor and sophistication. A similarly dismal picture besets the group therapist who turns to the research literature for technical guidance. The accumulated findings seem trivial, irrelevant, or worse; they offer little consolation for, or clarification of, the complex technical questions which the practitioner must continuously face. And, finally, the theorist finds little in the extensive research endeavors to aid in the construction of new formulations, either in terms of comprehensive group psychological theories or, more narrowly, in models of group therapeutic techniques.

The reasons for this state of affairs are numerous, ranging from the very real, pragmatic difficulties in establishing laboratorylike precision and controls in clinical contexts to the atheoretical, experiential foundations of much of group psychotherapy. The aim of the present chapter is neither to belabor this point further nor to explicate its causes; incisive critiques, unfortunately unheeded for the most part, have been written by others (Bednar and Kaul, 1978; Hartman, 1979). Rather, this chapter will discuss recent advances in object relations theory that, as applied both to primitive character psychopathology and to group psychology, provide a new conceptual backdrop for informing group therapy research. We posit that these new formulations can serve to guide more technically and theoretically sophisticated lines of research, precisely because they contain core constructs regarding the reciprocal influence between intrapsychic organization and social relationships. Thus, we focus specifically upon the patient diagnosed as borderline personality disorder and look toward these new theoretical developments for generating testable hypotheses of interest to the group therapy researcher, practitioner, and theorist.

Object Relations Theory, Borderline Psychopathology, and Group Psychology

Those recent clinical offerings based on object relations theory seem to represent not so much new insights as a burgeoning acknowledgement and appreciation within American psychoanalytic circles of earlier contributions by those within the British school, most notably Melanie Klein (Sutherland, 1983). This increasing acceptance of British object relations thinking is due, in large measure, to efforts by Kernberg and others at integrating this work into more established theoretical traditions. To date, object relations theorizing, as it appears in the American literature, consists of an amalgam of "middle-level" constructs, more abstract than clinical formulations but not on the conceptual scale of metapsychology, a synthesis of

British ideas with ego psychological and developmental perspectives (Slavinska-Holy, 1984).

The key structural concept within this framework, and the one most responsible for the gradual shift in psychoanalytic thinking away from an instinctually rooted, one-person psychology to a social, interactional perspective, is that of representation. Representations of self and others refer both to the capacity to internalize, retain, and organize interpersonal experience and to the nature of those intrapsychic schemata of self-in-the-world. Normal development implies an evolution in these internal mappings along several dimensions. The earliest images are formed at a time when the infant has only rudimentary capacities for perceptual discrimination and memory. As a result, the most salient characteristic of these archaic introjects is their lack of structural definition. The boundaries separating an image of self from that of the earliest maternal representation, if they exist at all, are vague and volatile; that is, contents of self are basically indistinguishable from those of others, thereby limiting object relations to fusion dynamics (Smith, 1983). These contents, moreover, are unstructured, consisting of only the most global affective experiences of satiation and deprivation. In addition, the distinction between the actual object and its internal representation cannot yet be drawn; the earliest representations have neither permanence nor constancy. In essence, the initial cognitive limitations in discriminating self from other, inside from out, and external object from intrapsychic symbol give rise to object representations and internalized relations which are extremely transitory and amorphous, fantastically distorted by, and exclusively expressive of, the infant's somatically based cravings.

As cognitive and perceptual functions mature during later phases of preoedipal development, a number of differentiations in these object representations are normally achieved. Gradually, the prototypical internalization of an all-good, fused self–other unit is supplanted by multiple, discrete self and object representations, each image essentially defined by one concrete or functional attribute. Self–other relations, while still based exclusively on need gratification, expand as affective bonds become somewhat variegated and delineated. In essence, the representational world begins to acquire some degree of permanence and differentiation from both instinctually derived fantasies and from the actual objects in the social field.

During the unfolding and resolution of the oedipal crisis, further differentiations in these representations and, for the first time, their integration occur. Heretofore disparate, partial images of self, both libidinally and aggressively invested, are now brought together; a sense of self emerges as whole, complex, and continuous in time and space. In similar fashion, part objects are synthesized and an object world that more realistically depicts the actual social field is gradually constructed. The good versus bad, powerful versus impotent crude categorizations of part objects are replaced by multifaceted and three-dimensional whole objects. Further, need gratification is reduced to only one portion of an ever-widening range of object tie, which includes for the first time an appreciation of work–role relatedness. Also appearing for the first time is an acknowledgement of the reality of objects relating to other objects, independent of any connection to self; relations expand from dyadic and vertically stratified units of self and maternal authority to oedipal paradigm, triadic associations, and eventually, peer ties.

Concomitant with these developments in object representations are parallel progressions in other ego functions, including defense mechanisms. Contributions from object relations theory have been particularly helpful in elucidating early, archaic defense strategies. While not fully understood, the earliest defensive-coping operations seem to involve efforts in regulating the sense of differentiation of self from the symbiotic mother. Although the literature discusses vicissitudes in self boundaries, primarily from developmental–maturational perspectives, there is some recognition of a motivational component. In normal development, fantasies of fusion adaptively allow the infant to rely totally upon the mother to modulate and organize the bombardment of internal and external stimuli. The infant, however, seems capable of prolonging or restoring fusion imagery beyond its phase-specific time; and, as Silverman (1979) postulates, this capacity can serve several defensive needs. In the same way, the developmental lines toward separation and differentiation also seem to have a dynamic, motivated aspect; increasingly sophisticated observations of mother–infant interactions suggest that the infant actively regulates degree of separateness and disengagement, via imagery and nonverbal behaviors, and that such operations are part of the earliest repertoire of defensive maneuvers (Beebe and Stern, 1977).

The emergence of splitting and related intermediate-level defenses of projective identification, idealization, and devaluation co-occur with and reciprocally reinforce the maturation of perceptual functions, especially discrimination. The principal aim of these operations is to preserve all too fragile good self and object representations from destruction by aggressively imbued images. These defenses work primarily through the polarization of affective experience. Pleasant and unpleasant sensations and corresponding good and bad objects are kept actively apart by emphasizing and exaggerating the differences between them. To experience ambivalence risks the obliteration of libidinally invested representations and is thus avoided, at the cost of impaired reality testing. As ego functions, especially synthetic capacities, develop further, and as a sense of goodness is gradually fortified, the adaptive value of, and need for, splitting mechanisms diminishes, and other defenses, chiefly repression, are thought to gain ascendance.

An object relations framework views psychopathology as the result of developmental arrest, with each pathological condition identifiable in terms of specific and unique organizational levels of object representation and defense mechanism. There is general conceptual agreement about the phase-specific fixation in borderline disorders, namely the rapprochement subphase of Mahler's (1975) postulated sequence of separation–individuation. Whether due to constitutionally determined excessive aggression or to early severe frustration around strivings for autonomy, the toddler develops inordinate anxiety over the annihilation of good self and object representations by persecutory or abandoning objects, and consequently, never risks their synthesis, the normal culmination of this stage of development. Instead, splitting and related defenses are called into service to actively keep apart good from bad.

The internal template of good and bad part objects that are forcefully segregated from each other totally determines the borderline's stance toward social reality. Any social field is scrutinized only in terms of its providing suitable containers for these externalized representations. Because the projective processes are so massive and forceful and because the externalized contents are not readily recoverable, the borderline is basically unable to distinguish transference from reality, internal object from external figure; confabulatory responses, involving affectively inappropriate and excessive reactions, predominate. Perception of the external world, as with the representational world, is oversimplistic and emotionally dichotomous. And, unlike the neurotic, whose capacities for integration and for mature identifications facilitate the modification of the internal world in response to new interpersonal relationships, the individual functioning at the borderline level can only repeat the experiences of fragmented, split-off relations in every new social setting. All of the manifest symptoms of borderline patients—the "push–pull," volatile relations; the severely curtailed capacity to contain, neutralize, or sublimate instinctual, especially aggressive, expression; the pervasive sense of emptiness and identity diffusion—can be reasonably accounted for by an object relations view of developmental arrest at the level of part object representation and splitting defenses.

These very same symptoms of borderline disorders have long been noted to arise in groups, including groups of psychologically higher functioning individuals, especially as the social settings become less overtly structured. Applications of object relations notions to group psychology have primarily focused upon the nature of these regressive, group-induced phenomena and their vicissitudes over time and in relation to more mature and rational psychosocial structures and processes. As with the case of individual psychopathology, much of the theorizing about groups is not new. Over two decades ago, Bion (1959) shared his insights into the all-good (as implied in his "dependency" and "pairing" basic assumptions) and all-bad (reflected in the "fight–flight" assumptions) fantasied social relations in groups. At the same time, Ezriel (1952), Sutherland (1952), and Whitaker and Lieberman (1964), in their analyses of small therapy groups, and Jaques (1955), in his formulations of organizations, described the psychodynamics of participants' pooling their more primitive, internal objects and collectively externalizing them onto commonly identified actual objects in the social field. The more recent theoretical contributions largely seem to emphasize the borderline-specific quality of primitive group dynamics and serve to integrate a number of somewhat terminologically diverse observations and ideas.

While it is beyond the scope of this chapter to review in detail an object relations perspective of group psychology, we do agree with Kernberg's (1975, 1976) argument that such an understanding is invaluable to the group therapist, regardless of specific therapeutic orientation and focus. All groups are seen as having the potential for reactivating intermediate-level object representations and defensive operations. Why this is so can be explained primarily in economic terms. Immersion in any sort of work group can arouse intense existential anxieties stemming from the rationally dictated requirement to develop object ties rather quickly to a number of unknown others. Each participant is faced with a number of real dilemmas around inclusion and power, which arise most saliently during the formative stages of the group but also recur throughout the life of the group in response to changes in task, structure, or content.

Typical questions that confront each group member are: How much personal identity and uniqueness are to be renounced in the interest of group cohesion and collaboration? How much power and authority are to be exercised over and delegated to others? Such real concerns resonate with corresponding residual anxieties over object loss and control of aggression, which originate in the primordial relation to the symbiotic mother. Group-wide regression is the typical reaction to these anxieties because it serves all the members' defensive needs relatively efficiently while simultaneously preserving a sense of group cohesion. The enactment of primitive psychological structures and processes vastly simplifies the complex work of forming relationships in new and unknown situations. Immediately and magically, the group can be transformed into rigidly compartmentalized and all too familiar good and bad part objects. The rational and difficult task of evaluating self and others in the group is reduced to a set of unrealistic, but totally unambiguous, expectations and assessments of each member: from a completely egocentric viewpoint, others are seen and related to exclusively in terms of their capacities for nurturance or destructiveness. Precisely because the qualities and characteristics ascribed to objects in the social field become so broad and encompassing and because interpersonal relations are reduced to considerations of archaic, basic needs of self-preservation, group members can easily act in concert, reinforcing each other's creation of fantasied social structures. While much remains to be understood about these covert structures, it is important to underscore their defensive nature. Just as splitting, at an intrapsychic level, ontogenetically serves to allay anxieties over the loss of a fragile sense of goodness as the toddler experiments with separation from the preoedipal mother, so similar processes, at a group-wide level, operate to ensure the viability of the group as a whole and of each individual as an interacting participant.

Group Psychotherapy for Borderlines

Theory posits the ultimate aim of expressive psychotherapy to be the examination, working through, and resolution of the defensive need to split the representational world—exchanging part objects for whole objects, as Pines (1980) aptly phrased it. As reflected in the burgeoning literature on treating the borderline, however, translating theory into clinical practice is far from a clear-cut task. In particular, the consideration of group psychotherapy for borderline patients raises a host of unresolved technical issues concerning the therapist's role as manager of the several levels of psychosocial boundaries which define the therapeutic enterprise. Included here are questions of group composition: Should membership be homogeneous or heterogeneous (Slavinska-Holy, 1980; Wong, 1980)? How many therapists should conduct the group (Greenblum and Pinney, 1982; Greene, 1983)? And what of the relationship of the group to the external environment, especially to other treatment modalities? Is the group to be considered as complementary to, ancillary to, or exclusive of, other forms of treatment (Slavinska-Holy, 1983; Goren and Kretsch, 1984)? Once such questions regarding the external boundary of the group are tackled, the therapist faces ongoing management decisions about the nature of social processes to be promoted and the focus of interventions. Considerations about valued kinds of social interaction and group culture, including such dimensions as degree of structuring, limit setting, transference gratification, therapist transparency, and confrontation, must be theoretically thought through (Kernberg, 1980, 1984; Campbell, 1982). With respect to focus, the therapist needs to decide whether the group is to concern itself with the internal processes and historic material of individual patients, with here-and-now dyadic interactions, with group-as-a-whole dynamics, or even with intergroup events.

To date, the group therapist can find little in the literature—clinical, theoretical, or research—which helps to sort out these technical and management dilemmas. Only a few generalizations can be drawn thus far. Perhaps the most general conclusion, accompanied by two caveats, is that group psychotherapy seems to be a useful treatment for this population. One qualification to this rather insipid statement is that, for those patients near the psychotic end of the borderline spectrum, this modality is contraindicated (Kernberg, 1976; Horwitz, 1980). A second cautionary note is that the success of group treatment hinges on especially careful attention to the referral and intake processes, since these patients are particularly resistant to the idea of a therapy group. The notion of "dyadic primacy" (Morrison, 1981) is relevant here. These patients characteristically prefer to enact in their current interpersonal relationships their internalized conceptions of an exclusive, idealized self–other dyad. To the extent that a small group of peers can interfere with this externalization, and consequently, give rise to reactions of envy and abandonment depression, the borderline patient is likely to devalue and avoid this modality.

Beyond such bits of clinical wisdom drawn largely from impressionistic and anecdotal evidence, a few attempts are now appearing in the literature to conceptually elucidate the rationale of group psychotherapy for this population. We have found the idea of "projective fit" to be particularly compelling (Greene, 1983). A group context, and specifically a group led by two or more therapists, can be viewed as more isomorphic with the borderline's internalized social schemata of multiple good and bad part objects than is a dyadic setting. We have proposed that this structural correspondence facilitates the emergence of both positive and negative transference relations *at the same time*. Specifically, in a co-led group, the two therapists, who realistically hold greater authority in their roles than do the patients, can readily serve as repositories for contradictory experiences of preoedipal maternal authority. The opportunity to observe splitting dynamics that occur spatially (i.e., across different real figures in the here-and-now), as compared to temporally, may more forcefully serve to confront the borderline with the reality-distorting, confabulatory aspects of this defensive operation. This rationale and others, such as the likelihood for better modulation of countertransferential reactions in co-led groups, are providing the beginnings of a conceptual framework for the judicious planning of this treatment modality for borderline pathology.

Prospects for Research

Research activities designed to assess any of the theoretical assumptions regarding borderline psychopathology have, to date, focused on the validity of the nosological category itself. Two primary methodological strategies have been implemented to evaluate whether this diagnosis can be reliably operationalized and differentiated from others. A descriptive-level approach has involved both the development of ad hoc inventories of pathognomonic signs and symptoms and the search for unique response configurations in standardized objective tests. The most extensively researched of the newly devised diagnosis-specific instruments is the Diagnostic Interview for Borderlines (Gunderson, Kolb, and Austin, 1981), a semistructured interview protocol, also applicable to clinical records (Armelius, Kullgren, and Renberg, 1985); several clinician-report and patient-report questionnaires, somewhat more expedient to administer but tapping essentially the same symptomatology, have also appeared in recent years (Conte, Plutchik, Karasu, and Jerrett, 1980; Sheehy, Goldsmith, and Charles, 1980). In this same methodological realm, such standardized tests as the Minnesota Multiphasic Personality Index (MMPI) have been investigated with the aim of discovering unique and discriminating patterns of responses (Evans, Ruff, Braff, and Ainsworth, 1984). The early empirical work with these procedures has generally supported the view of borderline pathology as an identifiable, although not necessarily monolithic, disease entity which can be assessed at least as reliably as other diagnostic categories.

Psychologically deeper than these various indices of symptomatology are a number of more theoretically rooted methodologies, based primarily on projective test data, that are designed to assess the individual's attained organizational levels of object representation and defensive operation. Pioneering in this work are Mayman and his colleagues at the University of Michigan and Blatt and collaborators at Yale who have constructed developmental continua to capture, respectively, the predominant thematic and structural aspects of internalized object relationships (Blatt and H. Lerner, 1983a). Early empirical returns with these and similar measures are offering preliminary validation of such formulations as the centrality of malevolence in the representational world of the borderline and specific boundary disturbances signifying the failure to differentiate inside from out (Blatt and H. Lerner, 1983b; H. Lerner and St. Peter, 1984; Spear and Sugarman, 1984; H. Lerner, Sugarman, and Barbour, 1985).

With respect to operational definitions of primitive defense mechanisms, H. Lerner and P. Lerner (1982) have constructed a Rorschach-based scoring system for the borderline-level defenses of splitting, projective identification, idealization, devaluation, and denial. Their system rather straightforwardly translates object relations notions by examining and categorizing the affective associations to, and fantasy distortions of, human figure percepts. Construct validation of these measures, assessed through comparison of different diagnostic groups that presumably rely upon different defensive operations, has been promising. Using a similar conceptual rationale, we have developed an index of splitting which is applicable to group therapy contexts (Greene, Rosenkrantz, and Muth, 1985). As suggested earlier, the defensive tendency to projectively endow real figures as all-good or all-bad should be manifested most clearly in co-led groups by participants' differential reactions to the two leaders. Our working assumption, in other words, is that splitting operations in co-led groups should be most apparent in attempts to portray the leaders as polar opposites (Cooper, 1976; Greenblum and Pinney, 1982; Greene et al., 1985). With this idea in mind, we have employed a semantic differential methodology, elaborated below, to tap perceptions of group cotherapists and have taken the divergence in these perceptions as evidence of splitting. As with the scales by Lerner and Lerner, our initial work has tended to validate this operationalization.

In addition to these instruments, which explicitly address borderline defenses, we think earlier empirical work can be recast into an object relations framework and considered applicable to the study of primitive defenses in groups. In particular, we want to cite the studies of group dynamics by Stock and Thelin (1958) and by Mann, Gibbard, and Hartman (1967). The former collection of research projects contains operationalizations of Bion's constructs of basic assumptions. If we view those covert, irrational social structures identified by Bion as the likely, although not inevitable, outcomes of splitting and externalization processes on a group-wide basis (Kernberg, 1976), then Stock and Thelin's (1958) instruments, as applied to the individual group member, could be used to assess a participant's reliance upon primitive defensive operations. While most of their work focused on group-level phenomena rather than personality, they did suggest that a measure of therapeutic progress in groups could be the change in an individual's collusion in group basic assumption activity. The elaborate scoring system by Mann et al. (1967) also has implications for the assessment of primitive defense mechanisms in group settings. A major part of their system codifies the nature and intensity of the affective bond of each group member to the leader. It would seem that such a categorization could readily be adapted to assess tendencies toward idealization and devaluation. While such group process scoring systems as these seem to have lost favor among researchers, largely, we suspect, because of their complexity, it would seem that their conceptual linkages to object relations notions of primitive defenses might fruitfully stimulate a renewed interest in them.

Taken together, then, these methodologically diverse instruments for tapping developmental levels of object representations and defensive organization are intrinsically related to a theory of borderline psychopathology and its treatment. As such, these kinds of measures represent a significant departure from the types of dependent variables that have heretofore been employed in group psychotherapy research. Up until now, the most frequently used assessment tools have been selected not on the basis of theoretical relevance, but for such reasons as expedience and popularity. Such assorted measures as those borrowed in wholesale fashion from personality theory (e.g., locus of control) or those adapted from descriptive psychiatry (e.g., MMPI) or from sociological theory (e.g., measures of group cohesion) may yield interesting, but conceptually isolated findings. And as Bednar and Kaul (1978) state: "Evidence of a fact in isolation is important to scientific progress. But even if all the individual facts are undeniable, without an integrating conceptual framework, they carry no more thematic power than a telephone directory" (p. 810).

While far from being a panacea for the difficulties in conducting group therapy research, the choice of variables, both independent and dependent, that derive from an object relations theoretical perspective may well facilitate the synthesis of the empirical findings, and equally important, stir the development of a systematic, progressive line of inquiry. Returning for a moment to reconsider the Malan et al. (1976) study cited at the outset of this chapter, it doesn't seem unreasonable to believe that its atheoretical context was a primary factor in the limitations of its heuristic value and scientific impact. Instead of promoting additional, empirically testable questions, the study seems to have invited the simplistic and premature conclusion that the group-as-a-whole approach to group psychotherapy "doesn't work." A conceptual framework, and, as we are arguing, an object relations perspective in particular, might have stimulated a number of subsequent investigators to better understand the apparently negative findings. One readily obvious follow-up, for example, would be a comparative study which examines the effectiveness of this modality for patients at differing levels of defensive organization; a hypothesis of differential therapeutic outcome in favor of those patients relying primarily on borderline-level, as compared to higher level defenses, can be directly derived from an object relations point of view. If support were garnered for such a hypothesis, one could, at the least, imagine a sorely needed momentum in group therapy research consisting of increasingly sophisticated and theoretically derived questions addressed by technically meaningful measurement instruments.

Splitting Dynamics and Self Representations: Some Early Empirical Findings

To illustrate this kind of investigative approach, we offer a preliminary report on a series of group therapy process and outcome studies currently in progress (Greene et al., 1985). This specific study is being conducted in the clinical context of a specially designed, long-term day treatment program for character disordered adults. The core psychotherapeutic modules consist of thrice weekly community meetings for the approximately twenty patients and multidisciplinary staff (Greene, 1983), immediately followed by small, co-led psychotherapy groups. This investigation originated from the theoretical notion, backed by our clinical observations, that borderline-specific transference manifestations in these small groups consisted primarily of efforts, both intrapsychic and interpersonal, to "divide and conquer" the cotherapists, projectively creating one as the all-good maternal entity and rendering the other as the evil persecutor. We attempted, first, to develop a clinically feasible means of capturing this phenomenon and then to assess its correlates, in terms of theoretically suggested personality variables, group psychological constructs, and descriptive indices of borderline symptomatology. This initial report focuses upon some relationships between splitting processes enacted vis-à-vis the group therapists and patients' conceptions of self.

Procedurally, all patients are informed of the evaluation aspects of the treatment program during their intake screenings. Approximately one to two weeks after admission, they are administered a battery of psychological tests which includes a four-part semantic differential. On nine bipolar continua that tap Osgood's basic factors of evaluation, potency, and activity, patients are asked to rate their current perceptions of themselves, each of their group therapists, and the therapy group as an entity. Similar to the rationale underlying the use of the interpersonal repertory grid technique (Watson, 1970), in which inferences about interpersonal dynamics are made on the basis of differential attributes of social objects, we have derived three measures of splitting by calculating absolute differences between ratings of the two cotherapists along each semantic dimension. Eventually, we hope to study changes over time in these indices to assess their validity as measures of therapeutic change; for now, however, we concentrate on intake data only and examine relationships between these indices and self representations, as assessed from the semantic differential and from the recently published self-report inventory of subjective experiences held by borderlines (Conte et al., 1980).

The correlational analyses presented here are based on data obtained from a sample of twenty-six patients and, more importantly, across five psychotherapy groups, each with a unique cotherapy constellation. This point is stressed to address the frequently raised criticism that most of group therapy research follows an "$N = 1$" design; that is, all too often, research findings are based on only one group and statistical significance is then erroneously equated with generalizability. It is important to remember, however, that generalizability of significant results from one group to others can be assumed only if those other groups are identical in all respects to the group under investigation, an essentially impossible condition. By aggregating data across several groups we hoped to cancel, or at least reduce, those unrecognized and uncontrolled sources of variance emanating from any specific grouping of individuals, and thereby increase the generalizability of the present findings.

We turn first to the data based on the 52 item self-report borderline inventory by Conte et al. (1980). Based on the pre-

TABLE 23-1
Correlates of Splitting

Measure	Splitting Dimension		
	Evaluation	Potency	Activity
Self-report Borderline Scale	.43**	.30	.22
Semantic Differential Scales			
Self-evaluation	−.56‡	−.42†	−.22
Self-potency	.03	.15	.36*
Self-activity	.37*	.57‡	.44**
Absolute Difference Scores			
Self-evaluation Minus Self-potency	.29	.37*	.19
Self-evaluation Minus Self-activity	.65‡	.63‡	.35
Self Minus Group	.39**	.23	.12

*$p < .10$
**$p < .05$
†$p < .02$
‡$p < .01$

liminary norms provided by those researchers, the obtained mean of 31 endorsed items for our sample would seem to provide empirical support for the diagnosis of borderline personality disorder. As displayed in Table 23-1, correlations of this measure with the three indices of splitting were all in the positive direction, with one reaching statistical significance. The more items endorsed on the self-report inventory, the more the patient perceived his or her group therapists as polar opposites on the evaluation (i.e., "good" versus "bad") dimension. Similarly, the more the individual patient characterized his or her experiential world in borderlinelike ways, the greater the tendencies to dichotomize the group cotherapists as powerful versus weak and as active versus passive.

Further validational support for our measure of splitting is derived from the semantic differential data on perceptions of the self. Six of the nine correlations reached at least marginal significance, although, surprisingly to us, these relationships were not all in the same direction. We had generally assumed inverse relationships; that is, we had hypothesized that reliance upon splitting operations, while ultimately preserving a sense of self, would exact the cost of impoverishment and depletion.

Two of the significant correlations supported this hypothesis. The more the individual patient disparaged and devalued a sense of personal worth, the stronger the tendencies to split the cotherapists on the evaluation and potency dimensions. Unexpectedly, on the so-called "dynamic" dimensions of self-potency and self-activity, direct relationships obtained. In these instances, the more the self-concept was ascribed as active, the more likely the splitting of the therapists on all three semantic dimensions; and the stronger the sense of self as potent, the greater the tendency to polarize the therapists on the activity dimension. While a number of interpretations can be offered regarding this complex pattern of correlations, the data fit our view that reliance upon splitting operations in this clinical population diminishes a sense of self-esteem and personal goodness, but, more importantly from the perspective of the borderline patient, ensures a sense of viability and invincibility.

Object relations theory enabled us to develop additional measures from the semantic differential data on self-perceptions and examine their relationships to splitting dynamics. Masterson's (1981) work, in particular, emphasizes the fragmented, unintegrated aspects of self-representations in borderline patients. He posits two predominant conceptions of self held by these individuals: the loved, but clinging and compliant self; and the unloved, abandoned, but autonomous self. We attempted to operationalize these postulated tendencies to perceive self in these "either–or" ways by calculating absolute differences between ratings of self-evaluation and self-potency and between ratings of self-evaluation and self-activity. Correlations between these partial self-representations and the use of splitting dynamics are also reported in Table 23-1. Three of the six correlations reached at least marginal significance, all in the expected, positive direction. Particularly impressive were the associations between views of self as either "good but passive" or "active but bad" and tendencies to split the cotherapists. Again, these data would seem to provide validation for our operationalization of splitting manifestations.

Finally, in this preliminary report, we can briefly comment upon some additional indices we are developing that examine the patient's sense of self in relation to the group as a whole.

These relationships seemed important to explore because the theoretical literature emphasizes how readily the group entity, in addition to its leaders or individual members, can become projectively imbued, particularly with aspects of early maternal representations. The one measure discussed here is an index of the overall psychological disparity between self and the group, calculated as the absolute difference in ratings of the self and the group on the semantic differential. Several theoretical notions would seem to converge on the prediction of a positive relationship between this index of self-group divergence and reliance upon splitting. The most compelling of these is Morrison's (1981) idea of "dyadic primacy," cited earlier. This construct suggests how a social context composed of authority figures and peers can inherently threaten a borderline patient by potentially interfering with the defensive need to enact an exclusive, all-good dyadic relationship. Borderline individuals can protect against this threat by creating psychological distance, via projective processes, between themselves and the group. Thus, the very same intrapsychic need to preserve an all-good dyad which is typically manifested through crude categorizations and polarizations of real objects (i.e., interpersonal splitting) also leads to efforts to avoid potentially competitive, need-thwarting social settings.

A second line of reasoning, offered by Grotstein (1980), is that both splitting dynamics and psychological differentiation of self from the group require the same cognitive functions of perceptual discrimination, exaggeration of boundaries, and sharpening of differences. Finally, Masterson (1981) postulates that the more severe the borderline pathology and, by implication, the greater the reliance on splitting, the stronger is the residual, archaic fear of loss of self through engulfment, a fear frequently potentiated in unstructured groups. For all these reasons, then, we anticipated positive associations between our index of self–group distance and splitting. The data in Table 23-1 provide partial empirical support for this hypothesis. All three correlations were in the anticipated direction, one reaching statistical significance. The more the sense of self was perceived as different from the group identity, the stronger the tendency to compartmentalize the two therapists into "good" and "bad" categories.

As a whole, then, the findings from this preliminary study seem quite encouraging. The data not only provide initial validation of our measures of splitting, but also offer empirical support for postulated relationships between the self concepts of borderline patients and their enactment of splitting operations in small groups. Beyond this, the results reported here seem to lend credence to our argument about the fruitfulness of theory-based group therapy research. A simple methodology, but one tied to a depth theory of the individual-in-the-group, yielded a greater number of significant findings than typically appears in the group therapy research literature. Clearly much more work is needed; we concur with Stone and Gustafson (1982) that we are far from a model of group psychotherapy for borderline patients which reaches the levels of sophistication and comprehensiveness of current models of individual psychotherapy for this clinical population. But at the risk of sounding overly optimistic, particularly in light of the "track record" of group therapy research, we are now hopeful that systematic, quantitative research efforts, of the kind advocated in this chapter, can facilitate this development.

References

Armelius, B., Kullgren, G., & Renberg, E. (1985), Borderline diagnosis from hospital records: Reliability and validity of Gunderson's Diagnostic Interview for Borderlines. *J. Nerv. Men. Dis.*, 173:32–34.

Bednar, R., & Kaul, T. (1978), Experiential group research: Current perspectives. In: *Handbook of Psychotherapy and Behavior Change: An Empirical Analysis*, eds. S. Garfield & A. Bergin. New York: John Wiley, pp. 769–815.

Beebe, B., & Stern, D. (1977), Engagement–disengagement and early object experiences. In: *Communicative Structures and Psychic Structures*, eds. N. Freedman & S. Grand. New York: Plenum, pp. 35–55.

Bion, W. (1959), *Experiences in Groups*. New York: Basic Books.

Blatt, S., & Lerner, H. (1983a), Investigations in the psychoanalytic theory of object relations and object representations. In: *Empirical Studies of Psychoanalytical Theories*, Vol. 1, ed. J. Masling. Hillsdale, NJ: Lawrence Erlbaum, pp. 189–249.

——— ——— (1983b), The psychological assessment of object representation. *J. Pers. Assess.*, 47:7–28.

Campbell, K. (1982), The psychotherapy relationship with borderline personality disorders. *Psychother.*, 19:166–193.
Conte, H., Plutchik, R., Karasu, T., & Jerrett, I. (1980), A self-report borderline scale: Discriminative validity and preliminary norms. *J. Nerv. Men. Dis.*, 168:428–435.
Cooper, L. (1976), Co-therapy relationships in groups. *Small Group Behav.*, 7:473–498.
Evans, R., Ruff, R., Braff, D., & Ainsworth, T. (1984), MMPI characteristics of borderline personality inpatients. *J. Nerv. Ment. Dis.*, 172:742–748.
Ezriel, H. (1952), Notes on psychoanalytic group therapy: Interpretation and research. *Psychiat.*, 15:119–126.
Goren, Y., & Kretsch, R. (1984), The borderline patient in individual and group psychotherapy. *Group Anal.*, 17:227–231.
Greenblum, D., & Pinney, E. (1982), Some comments on the role of co-therapists in group psychotherapy with borderline patients. *Group*, 6:41–47.
Greene, L. R. (1983), The patient–staff community meeting as therapeutic agent for borderline personality disorders. In: *Group and Family Therapy 1982*, eds. L. R. Wolberg & M. L. Aronson. New York: Brunner/Mazel, pp. 78–92.
────── Rosenkrantz, J., & Muth, D. (1985), Splitting dynamics, self representations and boundary phenomena in the group psychotherapy of borderline personality disorders. *Psychiat.*, 48:234–245.
Grotstein, J. (1980), *Splitting and Projective Identification*. New York: Jason Aronson.
Gunderson, J., Kolb, J., & Austin, V. (1981), The diagnostic interview for borderline patients. *Amer. J. Psychiat.*, 138:896–903.
Hartman, J. (1979), Small group methods of personal change. *Ann. Rev. Psychol.*, 30:453–476.
Horwitz, L. (1980), Group psychotherapy for borderline and narcissistic patients. *Bull. Menn. Clin.*, 44:181–200.
Jaques, E. (1955), Social systems as a defense against persecutory and depressive anxiety. In: *New Directions in Psychoanalysis*, eds. M. Klein, P. Heimann, & R. E. Money-Kyrle. London: Tavistock, pp. 478–498.
Kernberg, O. (1975), A systems approach to priority setting of interventions in groups. *Internat. J. Group Psychother.*, 25:251–271.
────── (1976), *Object Relations Theory and Clinical Psychoanalysis*. New York: Jason Aronson.
────── (1980), *Internal World and External Reality*. New York: Jason Aronson.
────── (1984), *Severe Personality Disorders*. New Haven, CT: Yale University Press.
Lerner, H., & Lerner, P. (1982), A comparative study of defensive structure in neurotic, borderline and schizophrenic patients. *Psychoanal. & Contemp. Thought*, 5:77–115.
────── St. Peter, S. (1984), Patterns of object relations in neurotic, borderline and schizophrenic patients. *Psychiat.*, 47:77–92.
────── Sugarman, A., & Barbour, C. (1985), Patterns of ego boundary disturbance in neurotic, borderline, and schizophrenic patients. *Psychoanal. Psychol.*, 2:47–66.

Mahler, M. (1975), *Psychological Birth of the Human Infant.* New York: Basic Books.
Malan, D., Balfour, F., Hood, V., & Shooter, A. (1976), Group psychotherapy: A long-term follow-up study. *Arch. Gen. Psychiat.*, 33:1303–1315.
Mann, R. D., Gibbard, G. S., & Hartman, J. J. (1967), *Interpersonal Styles and Group Development.* New York: John Wiley.
Masterson, J. (1981), *The Narcissistic and Borderline Disorders.* New York: Brunner/Mazel.
Morrison, A. (1981), Peer theory, dyadic primacy, and destruction of the group: The borderline patient and group interaction. *Group*, 5:33–42.
Pines, M. (1980), What to expect in the psychotherapy of the borderline patient. *Group Anal.*, 13:168–177.
Sheehy, M., Goldsmith, L., & Charles, E. (1980), A comparative study of borderline patients in a psychiatric outpatient clinic. *Amer. J. Psychiat.*, 137:1374–1379.
Silverman, L. (1979), Two unconscious fantasies as mediators of successful psychotherapy. *Psychother.*, 16:215–230.
Slavinska-Holy, N. (1980), Treatment of the borderline in homogeneous groups and the use of the "body transference technique." In: *Group and Family Therapy 1980*, eds. L. R. Wolberg & M. L. Aronson. New York: Brunner/Mazel, pp. 121–132.
———— (1983), Combining individual and homogeneous group psychotherapies for borderline conditions. *Internat. J. Group Psychother.*, 33:297–312.
———— (1984), Kernberg's theories: Some clinical applications. *Group*, 8:26–34.
Smith, K. (1983), Object-relations concepts applied to the psychotic range of ego functioning: With special reference to the Rorschach test. *Bull. Menn. Clin.*, 47:417–439.
Spear, W., & Sugarman, A. (1984), Dimensions of internalized object relations in borderline and schizophrenic patients. *Psychoanal. Psychol.*, 1:113–129.
Stock, D., & Thelin, H. (1958), *Emotional Dynamics and Group Culture.* New York: New York University Press.
Stone, W., & Gustafson, J. (1982), Technique in group psychotherapy of narcissistic and borderline patients. *Internat. J. Group Psychother.*, 32:29–48.
Sutherland, J. D. (1952), Notes on psychoanalytic group therapy: Therapy and training. *Psychiat.*, 15:111–117.
———— (1983), The self and object relations: A challenge to psychoanalysis. *Bull. Menn. Clin.*, 47:525–541.
Watson, J. P. (1970), A repertory grid method of studying groups. *Brit. J. Psychiat.*, 117:309–318.
Whitaker, D., & Lieberman, M. (1964), *Psychotherapy Through the Group Process.* New York: Atherton.
Wong, N. (1980), Focal issues in group psychotherapy of borderline and narcissistic patients. In: *Group and Family Therapy 1980*, ed. L. R. Wolberg & M. L. Aronson. New York: Brunner/Mazel, pp. 134–147.

NAME INDEX

Abraham, K., 246, 247, 265, 432, 459
Ackerman, N. W., 361, 376
Adler, G., 11, 12, 15, 33, 44, 310, 338, 374, 376, 405, 410, 411, 412, 413, 420, 421, 424
Agee, J., 284, 307
Aichhorn, A., 105, 121
Ainsworth, M., 461, 464, 467
Ainsworth, T., 509, 518
Akhtar, S., 6, 15
Akiskal, H. S., 7, 15
Alexander, F., 310, 338
Angel, E., 310, 340
Anthony, E. J., 135, 142
Appleton, W., 379, 397
Apprey, M., 472, 495
Arend, R., 462, 468
Armelius, B., 508, 517
Aronson, M. L., 28, 44
Arsenian, J., 428, 459
Astigueta, F. D., 377, 385, 397
Atwood, G., 51, 58, 204, 206, 219, 246, 252, 265, 266
Austin, V., 508, 518
Azima, F. J., 11, 15

Bailis, S., 374, 376
Balfour, F., 39, 44, 499, 511, 519
Balint, M., 143, 222, 240, 317, 338
Barbour, C., 509, 518
Bateson, G., 173, 179, 202
Battegay, R., 124, 141
Bednar, R., 500, 511, 517
Beebe, B., 503, 517
Bell, S., 466, 467
Bellak, L., 300, 307, 428, 430, 434, 459

Bellville, C. J., 374, 376
Bellville, T. P., 374, 376
Belsky, J., 470, 495
Benedetti, G., 95, 121
Beran, M., 27, 30, 31, 44
Bergman, A., 33, 44, 260, 266, 430, 438, 459
Berkowitz, D., 80, 92, 93
Binswanger, L., 310, 338
Bion, W. R., 79, 93, 109, 110, 121, 389, 397, 504, 517
Blatt, S., 509, 517
Blehar, M. C., 461, 464, 467
Block, J. H., 466, 468
Blos, P., 79, 93
Book, H. E., 406, 412, 424
Boss, M., 310, 338
Bowlby, J., 461, 464, 468
Boyer, L., 471, 495
Braff, D., 509, 518
Brandchaft, B., 73, 74, 204, 219, 243, 246, 250, 252, 253, 258, 265, 266
Brenner, C., 438, 459
Brombert, V., 287, 307
Bruch, H., 429, 459
Buber, M., 317, 338, 363, 376
Buie, D. H., 33, 44, 310, 338, 405, 410, 424
Bursten, B., 144, 145, 169

Campbell, K., 507, 518
Carkhuff, R. R., 316, 317, 340
Chandler, J. J., 496
Charles, E., 509, 519
Conte, H., 509, 513, 518
Cooper, L., 510, 518

NAME INDEX

Corwin, H. A., 310, 338

Davidson, J., 380, 397
Deutsch, H., 117, 121
Dubska-Papiasvili, E., 311, 338
Dunne, E. J., 429, 459
Durkin, H. E., 27, 44, 311, 338
Durkin, J. E., 171, 172, 175, 185, 186, 201, 202

Egeland, B., 463, 468
Ellenberger, H. F., 310, 340
Emery, E., 470, 496
Endicott, J., 95, 122
Erikson, E., 222, 225, 240, 316, 338
Evans, R., 509, 518
Ezriel, H., 504, 518

Fairbairn, W. D., 222, 241, 310, 317, 339
Fairthorn, 300, 307
Feldberg, T., 123, 141
Fenichel, O., 252, 266
Ferenczi, S., 309, 310, 316, 317, 333, 339
Fey, W. F., 375, 376
Fleeson, J., 462, 463, 468
Foulkes, S. H., 124, 125, 128, 129, 130, 131, 135, 141
Frances, A., 7, 15
Freedman, M. B., 13, 15
French, T., 310, 338
Freud, S., 144, 145, 205, 244, 245, 285, 309, 310, 339, 431, 432, 438, 459, 461, 468
Fried, E., 27, 44, 149, 164, 169
Friedman, H. J., 12, 15

Gardner, L., 284, 307
Garner, H. H. A., 310, 339
Gediman, H., 428, 430, 434, 459
Gibbard, G. S., 510, 519
Gibbon, M., 95, 122
Gill, H. S., 374, 376
Giovacchini, P., 415, 424
Glover, L., 432, 450, 453, 456, 459
Gluzman, S., 286, 307
Goldberg, A., 204, 219, 243, 316, 339
Goldsmith, L., 509, 519

Goren, Y., 507, 518
Gove, F., 462, 468
Green, J., 27, 30, 44
Greenblum, D., 506, 510, 518
Greene, L. R., 506, 508, 510, 512, 518
Greenson, R. R., 310, 339
Greenspan, S. I., 471, 472, 473, 474, 475, 477, 480, 493, 495
Greenwald, H., 310, 339
Grinker, R. R., Sr., 95, 121
Grotjohn, M., 311, 339
Grotstein, J., 163, 169, 516, 518
Gunderson, J. G., 4, 7, 11, 15, 71, 95, 121, 508, 518
Gunther, M. S., 204, 219
Guntrip, H. J. S., 222, 241, 310, 317, 339
Gustafson, J., 517, 519
Gutheil, E. A., 310, 339

Hamm, D., 77
Hartman, J. J., 500, 510, 518, 519
Hartmann, H., 435, 459
Hartocollis, P., 399, 411, 423, 424
Hearst, L. E., 123
Hofheimer, J. A., 475, 477, 480, 493, 495
Hood, V., 39, 44, 499, 511, 519
Horner, A. J., 10, 15, 22, 44, 462, 468
Horwitz, L., 13, 15, 39, 44, 423, 424, 507, 518
Hulse, W. C., 28, 44
Hurvich, M., 428, 430, 434, 459

Jacobson, E., 222, 241, 430, 459
Jaffe, D., 223, 241
James, C., 143, 169
James, D. C., 13, 15
Jaques, E., 505, 518
Jerrett, I., 509, 513, 518
Joffe, L., 464, 468
Jones, E., 245, 266
Jones, M., 377, 381, 382, 397

Kadis, A., 311, 333, 339
Karasu, T., 509, 513, 518
Kaul, T., 500, 511, 517
Kelman, H., 280, 281
Kepecs, J. G., 375, 376
Kernberg, O. F., 3, 4, 5, 6, 7, 8, 9, 12, 15,

NAME INDEX

33, 43, 44, 62, 75, 79, 93, 95, 102, 121, 124, 142, 146, 147, 170, 221, 222, 241, 249, 250, 251, 252, 253, 260, 266, 378, 397, 399, 400, 410, 411, 412, 423, 424, 428, 430, 440, 445, 447, 459, 469, 495, 505, 507, 510, 518
Kibel, H. D., 3, 8, 15
Klein, D. F., 11, 15, 96, 121
Klein, M., 222, 223, 241, 252, 260, 266
Knobloch, F., 311, 339
Knobloch, J., 311, 339
Kobayashi, J., 432, 450, 453, 456, 459
Koenig, K., 129, 142
Koenisgsberg, H. W., 11, 16
Kohut, H., 3, 4, 5, 6, 8, 9, 16, 33, 34, 39, 43, 44, 48, 49, 50, 58, 59, 60, 63, 75, 133, 142, 143, 144, 170, 171, 195, 202, 203, 219, 247, 248, 251, 252, 260, 266, 316, 339, 400, 412, 415, 421, 423, 424, 430, 445, 459, 465, 468
Kolb, J. E., 78, 80, 93, 95, 121, 508, 518
Kosseff, J. W., 13, 16, 167, 170
Kretsch, R., 507, 518
Kroft, A., 377, 397
Kullgren, G., 508, 517
Kutash, I. L., 283, 288, 299, 307
Kutter, P., 157, 170

Lachmann, F., 47, 48, 49, 50, 55, 58, 171, 201, 202, 204, 219, 250, 266, 430, 440, 441, 459
Laing, R. D., 343, 348, 353, 358
Laplanche, J., 77, 93
Lasswell, H. D., 390, 397
Leal, R., 168, 169, 170
Lerner, H., 509, 517, 518
Lerner, P., 509, 518
Lichtenstein, H., 225, 241
Lichtenstein, M., 144, 170
Lieberman, A. F., 471, 472, 473, 474, 475, 477, 480, 493, 495
Lieberman, M., 504, 519
Little, M., 128, 142
Lomas, P., 310, 339
Lowrie, R., 471, 472, 495

Macaskill, N., 154, 168, 170
Magid, B., 59

Mahler, M. S., 33, 45, 144, 170, 259, 260, 266, 430, 438, 459, 503, 519
Main, M., 462, 464, 468
Malan, D. H., 39, 44, 499, 511, 519
Mann, R. D., 510, 519
Masserman, J., 310, 340
Masterson, J. F., 33, 44, 420, 424, 513, 516, 519
Matas, L., 462, 468
May, R., 310, 340
McGee, T., 374, 376
Meltzer, B., 374, 376
Meltzer, D., 404, 405, 423, 424
Menaker, E., 225, 241
Menaker, W., 225, 241
Mendell, D., 432, 459
Milich, R., 47, 49, 50, 53, 55, 58
Miller, A., 137, 142
Miller, R. D., 380, 397
Minkoff, K., 379, 397
Mintz, E., 311, 322, 333, 340
Modell, A. H., 33, 45, 50, 58, 77, 79, 93, 171, 202
Molitor, N., 466, 468
Moreno, J. L., 310, 311, 340, 344, 348, 355, 358
Morrison, A., 507, 516, 519
Muscat, C., 226
Muth, D., 510, 512, 518

Newcomb, T. M., 379, 397
Nover, R., 471, 472, 495

Ogden, T. H., 126, 142, 223, 229, 241
O'Grady, K. E., 480, 493, 495
Oremland, J. D., 204, 219
Ormont, L. R., 114, 121
Ornstein, P. H., 34, 45

Palombo, S. R., 429, 459
Papanek, H., 26, 28, 45
Papiasvili, A., 311, 338
Pasternak, B., 290, 307
Pettit, T. F., 429, 459
Pine, F., 33, 44, 260, 266, 430, 438, 459
Pines, M., 123, 130, 141, 142, 143, 170, 423, 424, 506, 519
Pinney, E., 506, 510, 518

NAME INDEX

Plutchik, R., 509, 513, 518
Poisson, S. S., 475, 477, 495
Pontalis, D., 77, 93
Porter, K., 26, 30, 45
Pulver, S. E., 4, 16

Rachman, A. W., 309, 310, 311, 314, 316, 319, 320, 321, 337, 338, 340
Racker, H., 20, 45
Rado, S., 310, 340
Rank, D., 310, 339
Raths, O. N., 374, 376
Renberg, E., 508, 517
Rice, A. K., 109
Rice, D. G., 375, 376
Rinsley, D. B., 11, 16, 33, 44
Robinson, M., 471, 472, 495
Rogers, C. R., 316, 317, 322, 340
Roman, M., 374, 376
Rosenblatt, B., 430, 459
Rosenfield, H. A., 115, 121, 252, 258, 260, 266
Rosenkrantz, J., 510, 512, 518
Ross, J. M., 204, 219
Rossi, A., 470, 495
Roth, B. E., 24, 25, 45, 113, 114, 115, 121, 123, 142, 147, 157, 158, 170
Rovine, M., 470, 495
Rubinstein, R., 390, 397
Ruff, R., 509, 518
Russell, C. S., 470, 495
Rutter, M., 468

Sacks, J. M., 344, 345, 353, 358
Sadavoy, J., 406, 412, 424
Sager, C., 26, 45
St. Peter, S., 509, 518
Salonen, S., 406, 407, 424
Salvson, S. L., 340
Sameroff, A., 470, 495, 496
Sander, L., 253, 266
Sandler, J., 430, 459
Schecter, 26, 27, 45
Scheidlinger, S., 26, 30, 45, 123, 142
Schlesinger, L. B., 288, 307
Schmideberg, M., 105, 122
Schonbar, R., 374, 376
Schuman, B., 374, 376
Schwaber, E., 252, 266

Schwartz, E. K., 283, 291, 308
Searles, R., 225, 241
Seifer, R., 470, 496
Semrad, E., 428, 459
Shainberg, D., 61, 75, 280, 281
Shapiro, E. R., 77, 78, 79, 80, 84, 92, 93
Shapiro, R., 80, 92, 93
Sheehy, M., 509, 519
Shooter, A., 39, 44, 499, 511, 519
Silver, D., 406, 412, 424
Silverman, L. H., 47, 49, 50, 53, 55, 58, 429, 459, 502, 519
Singer, M. T., 4, 7, 11, 15, 95, 121
Skynner, A. C. R., 138, 142
Slavinska-Holy, N., 25, 45, 95, 221, 267, 270, 272, 281, 404, 405, 424, 501, 506, 507, 519
Slavson, S. R., 10, 13, 16, 311, 340
Smith, K., 501, 519
Spear, W., 509, 519
Spitzer, 95, 122
Spotnitz, H., 21, 45
Sroufe, L. A., 461, 462, 463, 468, 468
Stayton, D., 461, 467
Stein, A., 10, 11, 13, 16
Stein, M., 249, 266
Stekel, W., 310, 340
Stepansky, P., 243
Sterba, R. F., 432, 459
Stern, A., 248, 266
Stern, D., 503, 517
Stock, D., 510, 519
Stoller, F. H., 322, 340
Stolorow, R., 47, 48, 49, 50, 51, 55, 58, 73, 74, 171, 201, 202, 204, 206, 219, 243, 246, 250, 252, 253, 258, 265, 266, 430, 440, 441, 459
Stone, M. H., 8, 14, 16, 95, 96, 121, 122
Stone, W. N., 36, 45, 517, 519
Strauss, M. E., 475, 480, 493, 495
Sugar, M., 13, 16
Sugarman, A., 509, 519
Sullivan, H. S., 45, 363, 376
Sutherland, J. D., 222, 241, 500, 504, 519
Sweet, 13, 15
Szalita, A., 119

Tabachnick, N., 27, 45
Talbott, J. A., 379, 397
Taylor, D. G., 470, 475

NAME INDEX

Temperly, J., 374, 376
Thelin, H., 510, 519
Thomson, J. A., 6, 15
Tolan, W., 462, 468
Tolpin, M., 151, 170
Tomasini, L., 462, 468
Truax, C. B., 316, 317, 340
Turnbull, C. D., 380, 397

Ulman, R. B., 203

Van Putten, T., 379, 398
Vaughn, B., 464, 468
Volkan, V. D., 7, 16

Waelder, R., 49, 58
Walker, E., 470, 496
Wall, S., 461, 464, 467
Waters, E., 461, 464, 467
Waters, R., 462, 468
Watson, J. P., 513, 519
Weiner, H., 345, 358
Weissman, R., 95
Werble, B., 95, 121

Whitaker, D., 504, 519
Whitman, R. M., 36, 45
Wieder, S., 471, 472, 495
Wilder, J., 27, 45
Windholz, E., 204, 219
Winnicott, D. W., 50, 58, 77, 79, 94, 113, 122, 124, 127, 135, 142, 143, 144, 170, 260, 266, 310, 317, 340, 410, 411, 425
Wippman, J., 462, 468
Wolberg, A., 26, 45, 377, 397
Wolberg, L. R., 310, 340
Wolf, A. A., 28, 45, 283, 285, 286, 288, 291, 307, 308, 382, 398
Wolf, E. S., 204, 219, 248, 266, 468
Wong, N., 6, 11, 16, 17, 120, 122, 506, 519

Yalom, I. D., 10, 16, 22, 23, 39, 45, 137, 142, 311, 340

Zax, M., 470, 496
Zetzel, E. R., 11, 16
Zinkin, L., 143, 170
Zinner, J., 80, 92, 94

SUBJECT INDEX

Abstinence, creative self and rule of, 309
Act-avoidant patient, 348
Acting out in combined therapy, 18
Active psychotherapy
  liberating creative self through, 309-340
  group and; creative self in, 310-312; psychodrama in, 310; role playing in, 310; sociometry in, 310
Activity, psychotherapy and, 309, 310
Adaptive functioning
  disturbed mothers and, 472
  neurotic versus psychotic and, 95-96
Adaptive level
  expressive group therapy and, 102
  homogeneity of, 102
Adaptive regression, 303
Adolescent, 77-94
  case material and, 81-91
  containment and, 80
  family therapy with individual treatment and, 91
  separation-individuation and, 79
  theory of working-through process in, 79-81
  treatment of, 84-91
Affect
  control of, 434; diegophrenia and, 302
  regulation of, 434
  self-perception and, 472
  strong; release of, 74; self psychology and interpretation of 61-65
Affective bond in group psychotherapy, 510
Affective borderline subtype, 96
Affective development, disturbed mothers and, 472

Affective instability, 12
Affirmation, developmental advances and, 57
Aggression
  as defense, 436
  and difficult patient, 264-265
  and identification, 436
Ambivalence
  diegophrenia and compulsive, 297
  disturbed mother and, 482, 489
Ambulatory borderline patient in expressive group therapy, 100
Anal expulsive drive, 432-433
Anal retentive drive, 432-433
Analytic stance, 39
Anger and narcissistic injury, 74
Anxiety
  expression of, 434
  intrapsychic structures and processes and, 437-439
  tranquilizers and, 64
Approach-avoidance conflict
  avoidant child and, 462
  erotic countertransference and, 276
  resistant child and, 462
Art therapy, narcissistic patient and, 407
Artificiality, borderline patient and, 345-347
As-if mechanism, 117
Attachment relationship
  avoidant child and, 462-468
  maternal narcissism and, 461-468
  resistant child and, 462-468
Authenticity, heterogenous group and, 138
Autistic self response, 441, 442
Autonomous ego, development of, 288

SUBJECT INDEX

Autonomy, diegophrenia and, 304
Auxiliary ego, 62, 79
Auxiliary treatment modalities, 341-519
　dual analytic therapy with spouse cotherapists and, 359-376; *see also* Two-marriage therapy
　intrapsychic structures and processes in 427-460; *see also* Intrapsychic structures and processes
　maternal narcissism and attachment relationship in, 461-468
　object relations theory and, 499-519; *see also* Object relations theory
　pharmacological therapeutic community in, 377-398; *see also* Pharmacological therapeutic community
　psychodrama in, 343-358; *see also* Psychodrama
　residential treatment and, 399-425; *see also* Residential psychotherapeutic community
　socioaffective development and disturbed mothers and, 469-498; case descriptions in, 480-492
Avoidant child
　approach avoidance conflict and, 462
　characteristics of mother and, 464
　countertransference and, 464
　maternal narcissism and attachment and, 462-468
　parental abuse and, 463

Bantering humor, expressive group therapy and, 111
Basic assumption group, 389
Behavior
　DSM-III and, 6
　self-perception and, 472
Being seen, need for, 353-357
Blocking, 435
Borderline, term discussed, 3, 95-96, 248
Borderline adolescent, 77-94
Borderline group
　expressive group therapy and evolution of, 116-119
　intrapsychic structures and processes working sheet for 453-455
　psychotherapy and, 150-152, 506-508
Borderline marriage, spouse cotherapists and, 359-376; *see also* Two-marriage therapy

Borderline patient; *see also* Borderline personality disorder
　adolescent, 77-94
　affective subtype, 96
　ambulatory, 100
　analytic group and part-object relations and, 134
　artificiality and, 345-347
　auxiliary treatment modalities and; *see* Auxiliary treatment modalities
　bantering humor with, 111
　being seen and, 353-357
　boundarying and, 171-202; *see also* Boundarying
　case study of heterogenous group and, 135-137
　clinical perspectives and; *see* Clinical perspectives
　cohesion and, 150
　composition of expressive group and, 100
　concordant identification and, 20
　confrontation and, 110
　countertransference and, 18, 116, 272-274, 410-411
　defense mechanism and, 18
　denial and, 18
　denigration and, 20
　diagnostic interview for borderlines and, 508
　difficult patient and, 244
　difficulty in treating, 133
　disorganization and, 250
　drive elements and, 430-433
　DSM-III diagnosis and group psychotherapy and, 3-15
　dyadic primacy and, 516
　ego and, 469
　ego functions and, 430-431, 433-439
　erotic countertransference and transformation in, 267-281
　expressive group therapy and, 95-122
　false self and, 344
　family and adolescent, 77-94
　features for diagnosing, 7-8
　fragmentation and, 250
　grandiosity and, 351-352
　group level boundarying and, 171-202
　group psychotherapy and, 150-152, 506-508
　holding and, 410-411

SUBJECT INDEX 529

idealizing self-object transference and, 412
indications for expressive group therapy and, 97-100
inhibition and, 347-349
intrapsychic structures and processes and, 427-460; *see also* Intrapsychic structures and processes
last-name policy and, 113-114
loss of self and splitting in, 516
neurotic-countertransference and, 115
object relations and, 259, 500-506
object relations theory and, 499-519; *see also* Object relations theory
objectivity in group therapy and, 116
omnipotence and, 19
ontological insecurity and, 343-344
outpatient therapy and, 156-160
passivity and, 347
personality organization and, 4, 469
pregnancy and female, 470
primitive defense mechanism and, 469
primitive idealization and, 20
projective identification and, 18, 19, 134, 221-241
projective processes and, 504
psychodramatic technique and, 343-358
psychodynamics and, 146-149
rage and, 149-150
reizschutz and, 410-411
residential psychotherapeutic community and, 409-413
schizotypal subtypes of, 96
self psychology and, 59-75
self-cohesion and, 149-150
self-imposed isolation and, 343-344
self-object representations and, 430-431, 439-447
sense of self and, 145, 250
social insensitivity and, 98
splitting and, 18
thought disorder and, 352-353
true self and, 344
underachievement and, 349-351
withdrawal and, 150
Borderline personality disorder; *see also* Borderline patient
diagnostic interview for borderlines and, 508
DSM-III and, 7-8, 95
Friedman and, 12

group psychotherapy and, 13-14, 500-506
Kornberg and, 12
Minnesota Multiphasic Personality Index and, 509
object relations theory and, 500-506
projective test data in, 509
research and, 508-512
term discussed, 4, 95
treatment implications for, 11-14
Borderline symptoms
differing views and, 251
difficult patient and, 262
object relations theory of developmental arrest and, 504
Boundarying, 171-202
case study in, 198-201
classical interpretation approach and, 171
definition of, 173, 175
empathic response and, 171
general system theory and, 172-177; model of, 178-185
group therapy in; application of, 193-201; format of, 185-193; fragmentation in, 193
language and, 186
maintenance of, 441, 442
opening/closing and, 175, 185
operation of, 194-196
outside/inside guideline and, 189
yin/yang complementaries and, 177
British object relations theory, 500
Brother-sister transference, diegophrenia and, 289

Care-giver and infant behaviors
disturbed mother and, 488
table of, 476-477
Caregiver or caretaker perception profile
disturbed mother and, 473, 474
socioaffective development and disturbed mothers and, 473, 496-498
Castration anxiety, 437
Changing faces of narcissistic patient, 41-42
Character defense, 14
Character structure, 14
Child Rearing Practices Report, 466
Childhood, intensive group experience and recall of, 333

Chronic schizophrenic group, working sheet and, 450-452
Chronic schizophrenic patient, 427-460; *see also* Intrapsychic structures and processes
  drive elements and, 430-433
  ego functions and, 430-431, 433-439
  self-object representations and, 430-431, 439-447
CIDP, *see* Clinical Infant Development Program
Classical analytical model, 172
Classical interpretation approach, boundarying and, 171
Clinical Infant Development Program, 471
Clinical perspectives, 1-340
  adolescent and, 77-94; *see also* Adolescent
  combined individual and group treatment in, 17-46, 309-340; *see also* Combined therapy
  creative diegophrenics in psychoanalysis and, 283-308; *see also* Diegophrenia
  difficult patient in, 243-266; *see also* Difficult patient
  DSM-III diagnosis and group psychotherapy in, 3-15; *see also Diagnostic and Statistical Manual* diagnosis
  erotic countertransference and transformation in, 267-281; *see also* Erotic countertransference
  expressive group therapy in, 95-122; *see also* Expressive group therapy
  group level boundarying control in, 171-202; *see also* Boundarying
  mirroring and, 143-170; *see also* Mirroring
  projective identification and, 221-241; *see also* Projective identification
  psychoanalytic therapy of developmental arrests in, 47-58; *see also* Developmental arrest
  restoration of impaired self in, 123-142; *see also* Impaired self
  self psychology contributions in, 59-75; *see also* Self psychology
  transference–countertransference neurosis and, 203-219; case report in, 206-219

Closed group, combined treatment and, 25-26
Closing, boundarying and, 175
Closing down, 197
Cohesion, 150
Coliberation
  cotherapy team and, 375
  versus cooperation, 362-364
Combined therapy, 17-46
  acting out and, 18
  active group psychotherapy and, 310-312
  case history and, 312-338
  changing faces of narcissistic patient in, 39-42
  closed or open-ended groups in, 25-26
  conjoint versus combined treatment in, 17-19
  creative self and, 311
  definition of, 17
  denial and, 18
  emergence of creativity in, 336-338
  group as transitional object in, 42
  group analysis in, 320-321
  group-as-a-whole versus individual-in-the-group approach in, 38-39
  heterogeneous group and, 43
  homogeneous group and, 43
  homogeneous versus heterogeneous group and, 24-25
  humanistic analysis in group setting and, 316-320
  hypnotic regression and, 334-336
  identification and internalization in, 21-22
  intensive group experiences and, 321-334
  intensive individual experiences and, 334-336
  liberation of creative self through, 312-318
  narcissistic patient and, 130-135
  nature of group in, 24-25
  objectives of, 29-32
  object-relations approach and, 33
  passive-narcissistic patient and, 27-28
  personal growth and, 336-338
  potential for intensive and reconstructive therapy in, 22-24
  projective identification and, 18
  reconstructive therapy and, 22-24

SUBJECT INDEX

special advantages of, 19-20
splitting and, 18
therapist as stabilizer and, 22
timing of introduction of, 26-29
transference in, 20-21; management of, 33-38
treatment issues in, 32-33
use of therapist as stabilizer in, 22
versus conjoint treatment, 17-19
Competence, diegophrenia and, 305
Complementary personality, sense of self and, 145
Composite approach, 39
Compulsive ambivalence, diegophrenia and, 297
Conceptual clusters of care-giver and infant behaviors, 476-477
Concordant identification, 20
Concretization, 206
Condenser phenomenon, impaired self and, 124
Conflict-laden object relationship, 33
Confrontation, 110
Conjoint therapy; see also Two-marriage therapy
  definition of, 17
  versus combined treatment, 17-19
Consensual validation, diegophrenia and, 289
Consolation, disturbed mother and, 482, 486
Contact, disturbed mother and neutral physical, 489
Containment
  adolescent and, 80
  definition of, 79
  group therapy and, 143
  inpatient psychotherapy and, 155
  outpatient therapy and, 157
  working through and, 77
Content dimension of ego development, 175
Content mode, 173, 174
  language and, 186
Cooperation versus coliberation, 362-364
Correlates of splitting, table, 514
Cotherapist
  countertransference and, 113
  expressive group therapy and, 107
  transference and, 108
  two-marriage therapy and spouse, 359-376; see also Two-marriage therapy
Cotherapy team, coliberation and, 375
Counterphobic response, 436
Countertransference, 35, 268-271
  avoidant child and, 464
  borderline patient and, 18, 116, 272-274, 410-411
  combined treatment for transformation and erotic, 267-281
  cotherapist and, 113
  denial and, 272
  erotic fantasies and, 271-272
  expressive group therapy and, 112-116
  idealization and, 272
  intersubjectivity and, 204
  narcissistic patient and, 133, 272-274
  outpatient therapy and, 158
  projective identification and, 272
  residential psychotherapeutic community and, 406
  self-object and, 204
  separation and, 113
  splitting and, 18, 272
  two-marriage therapy and, 368
  use of first names and, 113
CPP, see Caregiver or Caretaker Perception Profile
Creative diegophrenic, see Diegophrenia
Creative self
  active combined psychotherapy and, 309-340; case history in, 312-338; group psychotherapy and, 310-312
  edetic imagery and, 315
  group therapy and, 320-321
  humanistic analysis in group setting and, 316-320
  intensive group experience and, 321-334
  I-thou relationship and, 317
  rule of abstinence and, 309
  time-extended group session and, 321-334
Culture carrier, 404
Curiosity, diegophrenia and, 294-295

Dead mirroring, 144
Deepening identification, case study and, 77-94
Defense mechanisms, 434-437
  borderline personality and, 18
  breakdown of, 437

SUBJECT INDEX

diegophrenia and, 304
object relations theory and, 502
representation and, 502
Defensive functioning, 434-437
Defensive meaning, family assumptions and, 81
Denial, 436
  borderline patient and, 18
  combined therapy and, 18
  countertransference and, 272
Denigration, 20
Descriptive diagnosis, DSM-III and, 5-8
Devaluation
  perceptual functions and, 503
  splitting dynamics and, 515
Developmental advance
  affirmation and, 57
  therapeutic acknowledgment and, 55-57
Developmental arrest, 47-58
  borderline symptoms and, 504
  definition of, 47
  merger fantasies in self-object transference in, 50-55
  psychopathology and, 503
  therapeutic acknowledgment of developmental advance in, 55-57
Developmental initiative, disturbed mother and, 484, 490
Developmental support, disturbed mother and, 481, 486
Diagnostic and Statistical Manual diagnosis, 3-15, 24
  behavior and, 6
  borderline personality disorder and, 7-8, 11-14
  descriptive, 5-8
  narcissistic personality disorder and, 6-7, 9-11, 39
  personality disorder and, 5
  symptoms and, 6
  treatment implications of, 9-14
Diegophrenia, 283-308
  achieving freedom and, 291-294
  adaptive regression and, 303
  autonomy and, 304
  brother-sister transference and, 289
  competence and, 305
  compulsive ambivalence and, 297
  consensual validation and, 289
  control of drives, affects and impulses in, 302
  creative potential and, 288-296
  defensive components and, 304
  dreams and, 292, 298
  dyadic analysis and, 292
  dyadic parental transference and, 298
  ego alien and, 286-288
  ego-syntonic creativity and, 286-288; group therapy and, 296-300
  enhancing ego functions in, 300-306
  external reality and, 301
  fostering individuality and, 288-291
  genius and, 285-286
  group psychoanalysis and creative, 283-308
  group therapy and, 289
  group-as-a-whole and, 289
  hostility and, 296
  individuality and, 288-291
  inner self and, 300
  integration and, 305
  internal reality and, 301
  interpersonal relations and, 302
  judgment and, 301
  leader as neutral parent and, 299
  leaderless group and, 293
  mastery and, 305
  mother and, 287
  mother-father transference and, 289
  object relations and, 302
  oppositional creativity and, 286-288
  originality and curiosity in, 294-295
  primary process and, 292
  problem solving and, 295
  pseudoego and, 283
  reality testing and, 300
  secondary process and, 292
  sense of reality and, 301
  split pseudoego and, 302
  stimulus barrier and, 304
  synthesis of parts into whole and, 295-296, 305
  thought processing and, 303
Differentiation, 151
Difficult patient, 243-266
  aggression and, 264-265
  borderline category and, 244
  borderline symptomatology and, 262
  clinical illustration and, 253-255
  interminable analyses and, 262
  intersubjective perspective and, 243-266

SUBJECT INDEX 533

intractable resistance and, 262
narcissism and, 246
negative therapeutic reactions and, 262
object relations and, 258-263
patient-therapist system and, 246
psychoanalysis and, 246
self-integration and, 255
self-object transference and, 255
stance of observer in, 251-253
synthesis of good and bad parts of self and object and, 263-264
transference psychoses and, 262
Disorganization, borderline concept and, 250
Displacement, 436
Disturbed mother
 adaptive functioning and, 472
 affective development and, 472
 ambivalence and, 482, 489
 Caregiver Perception Profile and, 473, 474
 caring and, 488
 Clinical Infant Development Program and, 471
 consolation and, 482, 486
 developmental initiative and, 484, 490
 developmental support and, 481, 486
 double negatives and, 489, 490
 Greenspan-Lieberman Observation System and, 474, 475
 identification and, 491
 inanimate involvement and, 486, 490
 intimacy and, 482
 intrusive projection and, 488
 negative affect and, 483, 486, 487, 490
 neutral physical contact and, 489
 noninvolvement and, 486
 overstimulation and, 471
 primitive mechanism and, 472
 projection and, 472, 485
 reciprocal response and, 483, 484
 responsive vocalization and, 490
 sadism and, 488
 sadistic wishes and, 485
 social initiative and, 486
 social reciprocity and, 491
 socioaffective development and, 469-498
 spontaneous vocalization and, 487
 sustenance and, 481, 483, 484, 486
 total vocalization and, 490
 vocalization and, 483, 484
Doctor's assistant personality, 39-40
Double negatives, disturbed mother and, 489, 490
Dream analysis, 206
Dream formation, 203-219
 case report and, 206-219
 diegophrenia and, 292, 298
Drive elements
 anal expulsive, 432-433
 anal retentive, 432-433
 borderline patient and, 430-433
 chronic schizophrenic patient and, 430-433
 diegophrenia and, 302
 exhibitionistic, 432-433
 genital aggressive, 432-433
 genital narcissistic, 432-433
 genital sadistic, 432-433
 intrapsychic structures and processes and, 430-433
 neurotic patient and, 430-433
 oedipal, 432-433
 oral aggressive, 432-433
 oral libidinal, 432-433
 urethral, 432-433
 voyeuristic, 432-433
Drug group, 389
DSM-III diagnosis; *see Diagnostic and Statistical Manual* diagnosis
Dual analytic therapy, *see* Two-marriage therapy
Dyadic analysis
 diegophrenia and, 292
 internal transformation and, 360
Dyadic parental transference, diegophrenia and, 298
Dyadic primacy
 borderline patient and, 516
 group psychotherapy and, 507

Early childhood, intensive group experience and recall of, 333
Edetic imagery, 315
Ego; *see also* Ego function
 autonomous, 288
 auxiliary, 52, 79
 borderline personality organization and, 469
 development of, 174, 175
 genital level, 178-179

identity disorders and, 181
inhibition and, 436
integration and, 81
object relationship and, 222
oedipal level, 179-180
oral character type, 180
preoedipal arrested, 181
preoedipal regressed, 180
regression and, 435, 436
strength of, working through and, 77
tripartite model and, 59
Ego alien
diegophrenia and, 286-288
ego syntonic creativity and, 286-288
Ego function; *see also* Ego
borderline patient and, 430-431, 433-439
chronic schizophrenic patient and, 430-431, 433-439
intrapsychic structures and processes and, 430-431, 433-434
neurotic patient and, 430-431, 433-439
Ego psychology, 5
Ego-syntonic creativity
diegophrenia and, 286-288, 296-300
ego alien and, 286-288
Embryonic experience enhancement, 60
Emergent self, 74
Emotional life, infant development and, 470
Empathic acknowledgment, 60-61, 74
Empathic failure, fragmentation and early, 59
Empathic identification, 81
Empathic mirroring, 145
Empathic response, 49, 57, 171
Environment essentials, heterogenous group and, 135
Eros, definition of, 280
Erotic countertransference
approach-avoidance dilemma and, 276
combined treatment, transformation and, 264-265
erotic fantasies in, 271-272
kairos and, 280
oedipal features and, 276
preoedipal features and, 276
reexamining countertransference and, 268-271
as therapeutic tool, 274-278
transformation defined and, 267

Erotic fantasies, 271-272
Exchange, group psychotherapy with narcissistic patients and, 168-169
Exhibitionistic drive, 432-433
Explorative approach, narcissism and, 9
Expressive group
borderline patient and composition of, 100
Expressive group therapy, 95-122
borderline patient and, 95-122; ambulatory, 100; bantering humor in, 111; indications in, 97-100; neurotic population versus, 108; objectivity and, 116
composition of groups and, 100-104
cotherapist and, 106-112
countertransference and, 112-116
evolution of group and, 116-119
fight and, 116
flight and, 116
homogeneity of adaptive level and, 102
hypomanic patient and, 97
indications for, 97-100
inpatient and, 102-104
limitations of, 104-106
narcissistic traits and, 105
pairing and, 116, 118
paranoid traits and, 105
peer pressure and, 97
projective identification and, 115
psychoanalytic level and, 108
A. K. Rice techniques and, 109
separation and, 118
therapeutic considerations in, 106-112
ultimate aim of, 506
unworkable patient and, 106
External reality, diegophrenia and, 301
Extra-group individual sessions, 131

False self
borderline patient and, 344
role playing and, 344-345
Family
adolescent and, 77-94; interactions of, 81; studies of, 80
infant development and, 470
Family therapy for adolescent, 91
Father, self-object and, 49
Father-as-object response, 443-446
Fight, expressive group therapy and, 116
Figure and ground, transferences and, 48

SUBJECT INDEX

First names, countertransference and, 113
Flight, expressive group therapy and, 116
Flight response, 436
Fragmentation
 borderline concept and, 250
 boundarying group therapy and, 193
 early empathic failure and, 59
Freedom, diegophrenia and, 291-294
Freud study of aphasia, 244-245
Friedman approach to therapy, 12
Functional rehabilitation, residential community and, 423

General System Theory
 boundarying and, 172-177
 content mode and, 173, 174, 186
 model of, 178-185
 organizational mode and, 173, 174
Genital aggressive drive, 432-433
Genital narcissistic drive, 432-433
Genital sadistic drive, 432-433
Genius, diegophrenia and, 285-286
GLOS. see Greenspan-Lieberman Observation System
Grandiosity
 borderline patient and, 351-352
 narcissism and, 10
Greenspan-Lieberman Observation System
 cluster scores of, 478-479
 disturbed mother and, 474, 475
Group
 boundarying and; see Boundarying
 as isomorphic prosthesis, 171-202; see also Group psychotherapy
 protocol in heterogenous narcissistic group and, 132
 as transitional object in combined treatment, 42
Group psychology, 500-506
Group psychotherapy
 affective bond and, 510
 borderline patient and, 13-14, 150-152, 506-508; object relations theory and, 499-519; projective fit and, 507; psychotic, 507
 containing and, 143
 creative self and, 320-321
 diegophrenia and, 289
 DSM-III diagnosis and, 3-15
 dyadic primacy and, 507

 ego-syntonic creativity in diegophrenia and, 296-300
 group-as-a-whole approach and, 511
 holding and, 143
 humanistic analysis and creative self in, 316-320
 mirror function and, 125
 mirroring and, 143-170
 narcissistic personality and, 10-11, 160-167; case studies in 161-167; group as transitional object in, 167-168; reciprocity and exchange in, 168-169; therapeutic factors in, 167-169; transference in, 160
 narcissistic traits and, 10
 objectives in combined treatment and, 30-32
 personality type and, 96
 referral and intake processes and, 507
 restoration of impaired self and, 123-142
Group-as-a-whole approach
 diegophrenia and, 289
 group psychotherapy and, 511
 versus individual-in-the-group approach in combined treatment, 38-39
Group-centered approach, 39

Heterogeneous group
 authenticity and, 138
 case study of, 135-137
 combined treatment and, 43
 environment essentials and, 135
 impaired self and, 124-130
 narcissistic patient in, 130; protocol and, 132
 unique self and, 138
 versus homogeneous group in combined treatment, 24-25
Holding, 79
 borderline patient and, 410-411
 group therapy and, 143
 homogeneous group and, 124
 working through and, 77
Homogeneity of adaptive level, expressive group therapy and, 102
Homogeneous group
 adaptive level and, 102
 combined treatment and, 43
 holding functions and, 124

SUBJECT INDEX

impaired self and, 124-130
versus heterogeneous in combined treatment, 24-25
narcissistic, case study and, 125-129
Hostility, diegophrenia and, 296
Humanistic analysis
action phase of, 319-320
analytic phase of, 317-319
creative self and, 316-320
group setting and, 316-320
Humor, expressive group and, 111
Hypnotic regression, 334-336
Hypomanic patient, 97
Hysteria, 245

Id, tripartite model and, 59
Idealization, 263, 436
countertransference and, 272
perceptual functions and, 503
Idealizing transference, 35, 412
Identification, 436
with aggressor, 436
case study and deepening, 77-94
concordant, 20
disturbed mother and, 491
and internalization in combined treatment, 21-22
object relationships and, 222
Identity disorder, 147, 181; *see also* Impaired self
Identity formation
ego development and, 181
mutual reflections in symbiotic phase, 144
Impaired self, 123-142
combined treatment approach in, 130-135
condenser phenomenon and, 124
distinguishing patient with, 137-140
exceptional achievement and, 123
group psychoanalytic treatment and restoration of, 123-142
high level of functioning and, 137
heterogeneous group treatment and, 135-137
homogeneous versus heterogenous group and, 124-130
object constancy and, 441, 442
socialization and, 124
socioeconomic stratification and, 123
Important other, 117

Impulse control
diegophrenia and, 302
loss of, 437
Impulsive family interactions, 81
Inanimate involvement, disturbed mother and, 486, 490
Incubation response, 181
Individual therapy
adolescent in, 91
objectives for, in combined treatment, 29-30
Individual-in-the-group versus group-as-a-whole approach, 38-39
Individuality, creative potential and, 288-291
Individuation, group-oriented society and, 288
Infant
avoidant, 462
development of, 470
maternal narcissism and, 466-467
resistant, 462
Inhibition, 347-349
Inner self, diegophrenia and, 300
Inpatient therapy, 152-156
borderline patient and, 152-156
containment and, 155
expressive group and, 102-104
transference and, 155
Integration, diegophrenia and, 305
Intellectualization, 436
Intensive group experience
creative self and, 321-334
parameters and, 322
recall of early childhood and, 333
transference manifestation and, 333
trust encounter and, 324
Intensive individual experience, hypnotic regression and, 334-336
Interminable analyses, difficult patient and, 262
Internal differentiation, 151
Internal reality
diegophrenia and, 301
Internal transformation, dyadic process and, 360
Internalization, 151
and identification, combined treatment and, 21-22
working through and, 77
Interpersonal relations

SUBJECT INDEX 537

diegophrenia and, 302
instability and, 12
Interpretation response, 181
Intersubjectivity
   countertransference and, 204
   difficult patient and, 243-266
   dream formation and, 203-219; case report of, 206-219
   self-object and, 205
Intimacy, disturbed mother and, 482
Intractable resistance, 262
Intrapsychic matters, 29
Intrapsychic reorganization, pregnancy and, 470
Intrapsychic structures and processes, 427-460
   anxieties expressed and, 437-439
   background and literature review and, 428-429
   defensive functioning and, 435-437
   drive elements and, 430-433
   ego functions and, 430-434
   father-as-object response and, 443-446
   method in study of, 429-430
   mother-as-object response and, 446-447
   presentation of findings in, 430-431
   self responses and, 439, 441-443
   self-object representations and, 430-431
   self-object structures and, 439-441
   working sheet for patient, 450-458
Intrapsychic symbol, 501
Introjection, 222
Intrusive projection, disturbed mother and, 488
Isolation, 436
I-thou relationship, creative self and, 317

Judgment, 301, 434

Kairos, 280
Kernberg's psychostructural formulation, 4
Kohut's interpretation of narcissism, 465
Kornberg
   borderline personality disorder and, 12
   narcissistic personality disorder and, 6-7

Last-name policy, 113-114
Leaderless group, 293
Leadership, pharmacological therapeutic community and, 382
Level of adaptive function, neurotic versus psychotic, 95-96
Libidinal regression, 436
Live mirroring, 144
Loss of self, 516
Love of object, loss of, 437

Marital therapy, transference web and, 362; *see also* Two-marriage therapy
Marriage
   cooperative versus coliberative, 362-364
   personality of, 361-362
   therapy and; *see* Two-marriage therapy
Mastery, 305, 434
Maternal narcissism
   attachment relationship and, 461-468
   avoidant child and, 462-468
   Child Rearing Practices Report and, 466
   index of, 466
   infant at 1 year and, 466-467
   resistant child and, 462-468
   signal anxiety development and, 466
Maternal psychopathology, infant development and, 470
Merger fantasies, 47, 50-55
Metapsychological concepts, 59
Microtransference, 61
Minnesota Multiphasic Personality Index, 509
Mirror function, group therapy and, 125
Mirror technique, act-avoidant patient and, 348
Mirroring, 143-170
   borderline patients and, 150-160; group psychotherapy in, 150-152; inpatient psychotherapy in, 152-156; outpatient therapy in, 156-160
   dead, 144
   developing sense of self and, 144-146
   empathic, 145
   group as transitional object in, 167-168
   live, 144
   mother and, 144
   narcissistic patients and, 160-167
   psychodynamics and, 146-149
   reciprocity and exchange in, 168-169
   self-cohesion and, 149-150
   therapeutic factors and, 167-169
MMPI. *see* Minnesota Multiphasic Person-

ality Index
Modal confusions, 405
Monopolizer personality, 39-40
Mother
 as auxiliary ego, 79
 avoidant child and, 464
 diegophrenia and, 287
 mirroring and, 144
 resistant child and, 464
 self-object and, 49
 separation or reunion with infant and, 461
Mother-as-object response, 446-447
Mother-father transference, 289
Mutual supervision, residential community and, 406

Narcissism; *see also* Narcissistic patient; Narcissistic personality disorder
 dead mirroring and pathological, 144
 difficult patient and, 246
 healthy, 144
 Kohut's interpretation of, 465
 object relations approach and, 172
Narcissistic, definition of, 3
Narcissistic defense system, 165
Narcissistic group, heterogeneous, 132
Narcissistic injury, 74, 442
Narcissistic patient; *see also* Narcissism; Narcissistic personality disorder
 art therapy and, 407
 auxiliary treatment modalities and *see* Auxiliary treatment modalities
 changing faces of; case example of, 41-42; combined treatment and, 39-42
 clinical perspectives and; *see* Clinical perspectives
 combined treatment and, 130-135; changing faces and, 39-42
 countertransference and, 133, 272-274
 difficult patient and, 244
 disorganization and, 250
 DSM-III criteria of, 39; group psychotherapy and, 3-15
 empathic mirroring and, 145
 erotic countertransference and transformation in, 267-281; *see also* Erotic countertransference
 expressive group therapy and, 105
 extra-group individual sessions and, 131

 fragmentation and, 250
 grandiose self-importance and, 10
 group level boundarying and, 171-202; *see also* Boundarying
 group psychotherapy and, 10-11
 heterogeneous group and, 130
 homogeneous group and, 125-129
 intrapsychic structures and processes and, 427-460; *see also* Intrapsychic structures and processes
 psychodynamics of, 146-149
 residential psychotherapeutic community and, 407-409
 self-object and, 145, 150, 407-408
 sense of self and, 145, 250
 sharing of narcissistic wounds and, 164
 task-oriented therapy and, 407
Narcissistic personality disorder, 250; *see also* Narcissism; Narcissistic patient
 definition of, 4
 DSM-III and, 6-7
 explorative approach and, 9
 Kornberg's description of, 6-7
 treatment implications for, 9-11
Narcissistic self-object relationship, 145, 150, 407-408
Narcissistic traits, group therapy and, 10, 105
Narcissistic triumph, 442
Negative affect, disturbed mother and, 483, 486, 487, 490
Negative therapeutic reactions, difficult patient and, 262
Negative transference, 34, 62
Neurotic group, intrapsychic structures and processes working sheet for, 456-458
Neurotic patient
 countertransference and, 115
 drive elements and, 430-433
 ego functions and, 430-431, 433-439
 expressive group therapy and, 108
 level of adaptive function and, 95-96
 self-object representations and, 430-431, 439-447
 working sheet for, 456-458
Neurotic-countertransference feelings, 115
Neutral physical contact, disturbed mother and, 489
Noninvolvement, disturbed mother and, 486

SUBJECT INDEX 539

Normality, sense of self and, 145

Object constancy, 441, 442
Object relations approach, 172
  combined treatment and, 33
Object relations theory, 499-519; *see also* Object relationship
  borderline psychopathology and, 259, 500-506
  British school of, 500
  defense mechanism and, 502
  diegophrenia and, 302
  difficult patient and, 258-263
  group psychology and, 500-506
  group psychotherapy and, 499-519
  primitive defenses in groups and, 510
  representation and, 501
  self representation in, 512-517
  research prospects in, 508-512
  splitting dynamics in, 512-517
Object relationship, 48; *see also* Object relations theory
  ego identity and, 222
  identification and, 222
  introjection and projection interplay and, 222
  sense of self and structural derivatives of, 222-241; *see also* Projective identification
Objectivity, expressive group therapy and, 116
Oedipal complex, 60
Oedipal crisis, representation and, 502
Oedipal drive elements, 432-433
Oedipal features, erotic countertransference and, 276
Oedipal phase, 60
Oedipal transference, 29
Omnipotence, 19
Ontological insecurity, 343-344
Open-ended group, combined treatment and, 25-26
Opening, boundarying and, 175
Opening/closing, definition of, 187
Oppositional creativity, 286-288
Oral aggressive drives, 432-433
Oral libidinal drives, 432-433
Organizational mode, 173, 174, 186
Originality, 294-295
Outpatient therapy, 156-160
  containment and, 157
  countertransference and, 158
  transference and, 157
Outside/inside guideline, boundarying and, 189
Overstimulation, disturbed mother and, 471

Pairing, expressive group therapy and, 116, 118
Paranoid traits, expressive group therapy and, 105
Parental abuse, avoidant child and, 463
Parental functioning, therapeutic tasks and, 77
Part-object relations, analytic group and, 134
Passive-narcissistic patient, combined treatment and, 27-28
Passivity, 436
  borderline patient and, 347
  combined treatment and, 27-28
  shift to, 436
Pathognomonic transference, 34
Pathological narcissism, dead mirroring and, 144
Peer group, 312
Peer pressure, 97
Penetration anxiety, 437
Perceptual functions, 503
Personality disorders, DSM-III and, 5
Personality type, group therapy and, 96
Pharmacological therapeutic community, 377-398
  basic assumption group and, 389
  cases in, 392-396
  clinical illustration of, 387-390
  drug group and, 389
  educational objectives of, 378
  group history in, 385-387
  latent and manifest components of, 389
  leadership and, 382-383
  measuring therapeutic success and, 390
  medical meeting of, 383-385
  primary task of, 381-382
  severely disturbed patient and, 378
  therapeutic setting and, 380-381
  therapeutic success in, 390
  treatment modalities and, 380
  violent behavior and, 387-389
  work group and, 389
Physical contact, disturbed mother and

neutral, 489
Positive transference, 34
Pregnancy, 470
Preoedipal development, representation and, 501
Preoedipal features
  erotic countertransference and, 276
  transference and, 29
Primal anxiety, 437
Primary identity theme, 144
Primary process, diegophrenia and, 292
Primary process thinking, 434
Primitive defense mechanism, 469
  disturbed mothers and, 472
  object relations theory and, 510
  scoring system for, 509
Primitive idealization, 20
Problem solving, diegophrenia and, 295
Projection, 436
  disturbed mother and, 485
  object relationships and, 222
Projective fit, group psychotherapy and, 507
Projective identification, 80, 81, 126, 221-241, 263
  borderline patient and, 18, 19, 134
  case history and, 224-240; discussion of, 238-240
  combined therapy and, 18
  countertransference and, 272
  disturbed mothers and, 472
  expressive group therapy and, 115
  perceptual functions and, 503
  stages of evolution and, 223
  theoretical context in, 222-224
Projective processes, 504
Projective test data, research and, 509
Pseudodifferentiation of self, 151
Pseudoego, 283
Pseudohomogeneity, 288
Psychoanalysis
  developmental arrests and, 47-58; see also Developmental arrest
  difficult patient and, 246
  expressive group therapy and, 108
  sexuality and, 271
Psychodrama, 343-358
  active group psychotherapy and, 310
  artificiality in, 345-347
  definition of, 344
  frame of reference in, 343-344

grandiosity in, 351-352
inhibition in, 347-349
need to be seen and, 353-357
passivity and, 347-349
role playing and false self in, 344-345
terror of being seen and, 353-357
thought disorder and, 352-353
underachievement and, 349-351
Psychodynamics
  of borderline and narcissistic patient, 146-149
  ego development and, 174
Psychopathology
  developmental arrest and, 503
  object relations theory and, 503
Psychotherapeutic community, 399-425; see also Residential psychotherapeutic community
Psychotherapy
  activity and, 309-310
  group; see Group psychotherapy
  individual; adolescent, 91; combined therapy and, 29-30
Psychotic patient
  level of adaptive function and, 95-96
  group psychotherapy and, 507
  schizophrenic patient; chronic, 427-460; self psychology and 59-75; see also Intrapsychic structures and processes; Self psychology
PTC. see Pharmacological therapeutic community

Rage, 149-150
Rapprochement phase, separation-individuation and, 148
Rationalization, 436
Reaction formation, 436
Reality testing, 60, 433-434
  diegophrenia and, 300
  working through and, 77
Recall of early childhood, group experience and, 333
Reciprocal response, disturbed mother and, 483, 484
Reciprocity, group psychotherapy and, 168-169
Reconstructive therapy, combined treatment and, 22-24
Referral and intake processes, 507
Reischutz, 410-411

SUBJECT INDEX

Release of strong affects, 74
Representation
  defense mechanism and, 502
  intrapsychic symbol and, 501
  object relations theory and, 501
  oedipal crisis and, 502
  preoedipal development and, 501
Repression, 436
Research concerns, 341-519; see also Auxiliary treatment modalities
Residential psychotherapeutic community, 399-425
  borderline patient and, 409-413; case study of, 417-422; idealizing self-object transference in, 412
  clinical material in, 413-422
  countertransference and, 406
  culture carrier and, 404
  functional rehabilitation and, 423
  indications for, 399, 423
  modal confusions and, 405
  mutual supervision and, 406
  narcissistic patient and, 407-409
  narcissistic patient case and, 413-417
  organizational structure and, 400-404; rationale of, 404-407
  purpose of, 400
  sublimatory ego functions and, 405
  theoretical seminar and, 406
  therapeutic boundary and, 404
  therapeutic evolution and treatment strategy in, 407-413
  timetable of small group and, 402-403
  zonal confusions and, 405
Resistant child
  approach avoidance conflict and, 462
  characteristics of mother and, 464
  maternal narcissism and attachment relationship and, 462-468
Responsive vocalization, disturbed mother and, 490
Restoration of impaired self, group therapy and, 123-142; see also Group psychotherapy
Reunion, mother and infant, 461
Rice, A. K. techniques, 109
Role playing
  active group psychotherapy and, 310
  false self and, 344-345
Rule of abstinence, 309

Sadism, disturbed mother and, 485, 488
Schizophrenic patient
  chronic, 427-460; see also Intrapsychic structures and processes
  self psychology and, 59-75; see also Self psychology
Schizotypal borderline patient, 96
Secondary process, diegophrenia and, 292
Self cohesion, 60-62
Self pathology, 48
Self psychology
  borderline and schizophrenic patients and, 59-75
  case examples in, 65-74
  empathic acknowledgment in, 60-61
  interpretation of affects and, 61-65
  metapsychological concepts and, 59
  self cohesion and, 60-61
  splitting and, 67
  treatment principles in, 60-61
Self representations
  self-report borderline inventory and, 513
  splitting dynamics and, 512-517
Self responses, intrapsychic structures and processes and, 439, 441-443
Self-cohesion, 149-150
Self-consolidation, 47
Self-disordered personality, 181
Self-esteem
  loss of, 437, 438, 439
  regulation of, 441, 442
Self-imposed isolation, 343-344
Self-integration, difficult patient and, 255
Self-object, 260; see also Self-object representations
  countertransference and, 204
  differentiation and, 441, 442
  father and, 49
  intersubjective field and, 205
  merger and, 441, 442
  mother and, 49
  narcissistic patient and, 145, 407-408
Self-object representations
  borderline patient and, 430-431, 439-447
  chronic schizophrenic patient and, 430-431, 439-447
  intrapsychic structures and processes and, 430-431
  neurotic patient and, 430-431, 439-447

Self-object structures, intrapsychic structures and processes and, 439-447
Self-object transference, 261
  difficult patient and, 255
  merger fantasies and, 47, 50-55
Self-observation, 270
Self-perception, 472
  splitting dynamics and, 515
Self-report borderline inventory, 513
Self–self-object bond, 48
Sense of reality, 434
  diegophrenia and, 301
Sense of self
  borderline concept and, 250
  borderline patient and, 145
  mirroring and, 144-146
  narcissistic patient and, 145
  normality and complementary personalities and, 145
  structural derivatives of object relationships and, 222-241; *see also* Projective identification
Sensory shutdown, 150
Separation, 151; *see also* Separation-individuation
  countertransference and, 113
  expressive group therapy and, 118
  mother and infant and, 437, 461
Separation anxiety, 437
Separation-individuation; *see also* Separation
  adolescence and, 79
  rapprochement phase and, 148
  working through and, 77
Sexuality, psychoanalysis and, 271
Signal anxiety development, 466
Silent member personality, 39-40
Social initiative, 486
Social insensitivity, 98
Social reciprocity, 491
Socioaffective development, 469-498
  caregiver or caretaker perception profile and, 473, 496-498
  case descriptions in, 480-492
  Clinical Infant Development Program and, 471
  conceptual clusters of care-giver and infant behaviors in, 476-477
  Greenspan-Lieberman Observation System in, 474-480
  impaired self and, 124

Socioeconomic status
  impaired self and, 123
  infant development and, 470
Sociometry, 310
Somatization, 436
Split pseudoego, diegophrenia and, 302
Splitting, 263
  borderline personality and, 18
  combined therapy and, 18
  correlates of, 514
  countertransference and, 18, 272
  dynamics of; *see* Splitting dynamics
  loss of self and, 516
  perceptual functions and, 503
  self psychology and, 67
Splitting dynamics
  devaluation and, 515
  self representations and, 512-517
  self-perceptions and, 515
  self-report borderline inventory and, 513
Spontaneous vocalization, 487
Spouse cotherapists, *see* Two-marriage therapy
Stabilizer, therapist as, 22
Stimulus barrier, 434
  diegophrenia and, 304
Strong affects
  release of, 74
  self psychology and interpretation of, 61-65
Structural conflict, 48
Sublimatory ego functions, residential community and, 405
Summing, 187, 197
Superego, 59
Sustenance, disturbed mother and, 481, 483, 484, 486
Symptoms, DSM-III and, 6; *see also specific disorder*
Synthesis
  diegophrenia and, 295-296, 305
  difficult patient and, 263-264
  of parts into whole, 295-296
Synthetic-integrative functioning, 434
Systeming, definition of, 187

Task-oriented therapy, 407
Tavistock model, 39
TCMM; *see* Therapeutic Community Medical Meeting

SUBJECT INDEX

Theoretical seminar, residential community and, 406
Therapeusis, borderline couple and, 366-369
Therapeutic acknowledgment, developmental advance and, 55-57
Therapeutic boundary, residential community and, 404; *see also* Boundarying
Therapeutic Community Medical Meeting, 377, 383-385
  group history and, 385-387
  primary task of, 381-382
Therapeutic tasks, parental functioning and, 77
Therapist as stabilizer, 22
Thorazine, 69
Thought disorder, 352-353
Thought processes
  diegophrenia and, 303
  primary, 434
Time-extended group session, 321-334
Total vocalization, 490
Tranquilizers, anxiety and, 64, 69; *see also* Pharmacological therapeutic community
Transference, 30, 48
  cotherapist and, 108
  in combined treatment, 20-21; and case example, 36-38; and management, 33-38
  difficult patient and, 262
  figure and ground and, 48
  group psychotherapy with narcissistic patients and, 160
  idealizing, 35
  inpatient psychotherapy and, 155
  intensive group experience and, 333
  negative, 34
  oedipal, 29
  outpatient therapy and, 157
  pathognomonic, 34
  positive, 34
  preoedipal, 29
  psychoses and, 262
Transference web, marital therapy and, 362
Transference-countertransference neurosis, 203-219
  case report and, 206-219
Transferential interplay, two-marriage therapy and, 365, 375
Transformation
  erotic countertransference and, 267-281; *see also* Erotic countertransference
  definition of, 267
  dyadic psychoanalytic process and internal, 360
Transitional object, combined treatment and group as, 42
Treatment modalities, auxiliary; *see* Auxiliary treatment modalities
Trilafon, 64
Tripartite model, 59
True self, 344
Trust encounter, 324
Turning round on self, 436
Two-marriage therapy, 359-376
  borderline marriage and, 359-376; therapeusis in, 366-369
  case study and, 370-373
  cooperative versus coliberative marriage and, 362-364
  countertransference and, 368
  dual analytic therapy and, 359-376
  marriage defined in, 364-366
  objective of, 364
  personality of marriage and, 361-362
  spouse cotherapists in, 359-376; qualifications of, 374-376
  transferential interplay and, 365, 375

Underachievement, 349-351
Undoing, 436
Uneducated mother, 470
Unique self, heterogenous group and, 138
Unworkable patient, expressive group therapy and, 106
Urethral drive elements, 432-433

Validation, consensual, 289
Violent behavior, pharmacological therapeutic community and 387-389
Vocalization, disturbed mother and, 483, 484
Voyeuristic drives, 432-433

Withdrawal, patient, 150
Work group, pharmacological therapeutic community and, 389

Working-through process
  adolescent and; *see* Adolescent
  case material in, 81-91
  containment and, 77
  deepening identification and, 77-94
  ego strength and, 77
  holding and, 77
  internalization and, 77
  parental functioning and, 77
  reality testing and, 77
  separation-individuation and, 77
  term of, 77
  theory of, 79-81
  therapeutic tasks and, 77

Yin/yang complementaries, 177

Zonal confusions, 405